EIGHTH EDITION

Computers:
Tools for an Information Age

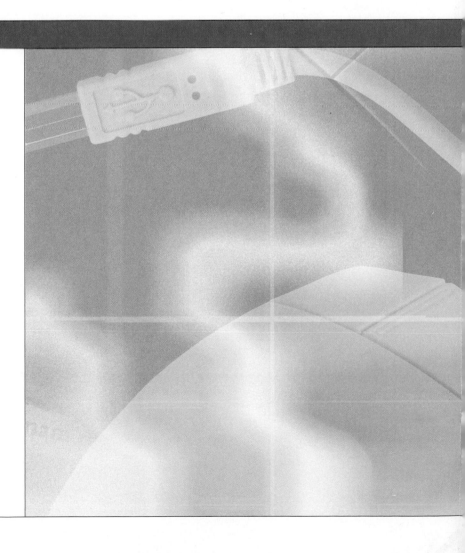

Computers:
Tools for an Information Age
Eighth Edition

H. L. Capron

J. A. Johnson

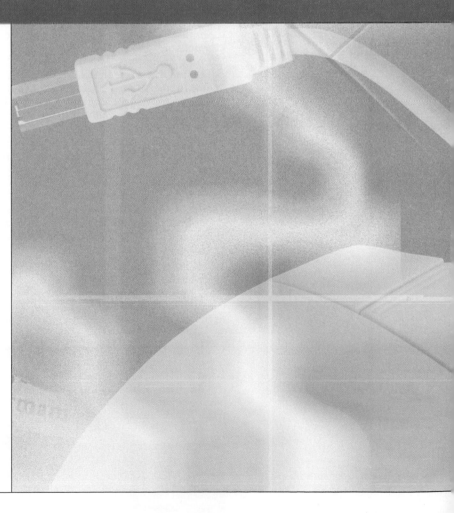

PEARSON

Prentice
Hall

Prentice Hall
Upper Saddle River
New Jersey, 07458

Library of Congress Cataloging-in-Publication Data

Capron, H. L.
    Computers: tools for an information age / H. L. Capron, J. A. Johnson—8th ed.
        p. cm.
    Includes index.
    ISBN 0-13-140564-0
    1. Computers. 2. Microcomputers. I. Capron, H. L. II. Johnson, J. A.

QA76 .5 .C6167 2003
004-dc21

2003009628

Executive Acquistions Editor: Jodi McPherson
VP/Publisher: Natalie E. Anderson
Editorial Assistants: Jodi Bolognese and Jasmine Slowik
Development Editor: Mark Cierzniak
Senior Project Manager: Eileen Clark
Senior Media Project Manager: Cathleen Profitko
Marketing Manager: Emily Williams Knight
Marketing Assistant: Danielle Torio
Associate Director, Manufacturing: Vincent Scelta
Manager, Production: Gail Steier deAcevedo
Permissions Supervisor: Suzanne Grappi
Design Manager: Patricia Smythe
Interior Design: Debbie Iverson
Illustrations (interior): Precision Graphics
Cover Design and Illustration: Marjory Dressler
Manager, Print Production: Christy Mahon
Composition: Pre-Press Company, Inc.
Printer/Binder: Von Hoffmann
Cover Printer: Phoenix Color

Credits and acknowledgments borrowed from other sources and reproduced, with permission, in this textbook appear on pages 563–564.

10 9 8 7 6 5 4 3
ISBN 0-13-140564-0

Janet E. Johnson

BRIEF CONTENTS

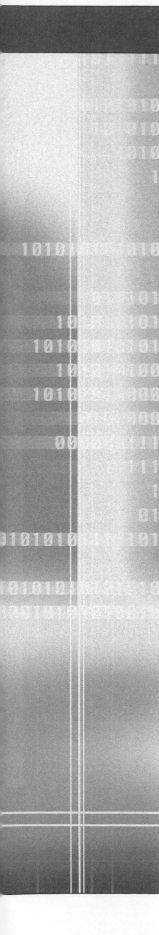

CONTENTS

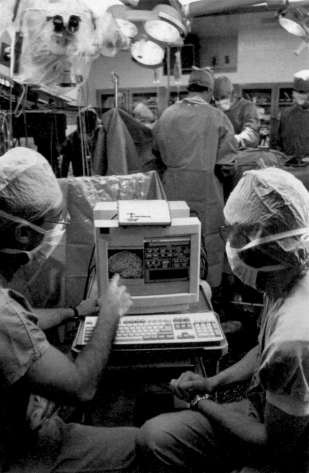

Chapter 9
Social and Ethical Issues in
Computing: Doing the Right
Thing   257

Chapter 10
Security and Privacy: Computers and
the Internet   287

PREFACE

J. A. Johnson and H. L. Capron have again teamed up to provide students with the most comprehensive, up-to-date introduction to computers in the eighth edition of *Computers: Tools for an Information Age*. This edition has new coverage on the latest in microcomputer operating systems, hardware, and e-commerce, and new material on ethics and the societal impacts of information technology, to ensure that students have the most current information as they learn about today's technology.

Connectivity is paramount in today's society. In this edition, the connectivity theme is integrated into several aspects of the book. Exploring the Internet is also simplified with a basic introduction in Chapter 1, a more detailed discussion in Chapter 8, and in the Planet Internet features at the end of every chapter. In addition, Prentice Hall's Explore Generation IT Labs are included, free of charge, to give an interactive component to the course material.

CONTENT CHANGES: FOCUS ON THE INTERNET/EMERGING TECHNOLOGIES/ETHICS

CHAPTER 1. Jump-start the text with an introduction to the Internet in Chapter 1. Learn basic information about the Web, browsers, servers, and Internet protocols at the beginning and be able to use it throughout the course.

CHAPTER 8. "The Internet: At Home and in the Workplace" explains the important aspects of Internet technology from URLs to links to search engines and focuses on various aspects of business use of the Internet, particularly electronic commerce.

PLANET INTERNET. The Planet Internet feature offers a nontechnical look at various aspects of the World Wide Web in a two-page spread at the end of each chapter. Topics include places to start, global aspects of the Internet, FAQs, business, shopping, careers, privacy, multimedia, entertainment, resources, and Internet relay chat. Each Planet Internet suggests hands-on Internet exercises.

- *Additional Internet Topics.* Chapter 9 addresses ethical and social issues involved with the Internet and Chapter 10 discusses the security and privacy implications of the widespread use of the Internet.

- *Multimedia.* Whether on CD-ROM, DVD or the Internet, multimedia continues to be a major newsmaker in the computer industry. Underlying CD-ROM and DVD technology and multimedia applications are described in Chapter 6.

Features

GETTING PRACTICAL. Various topics of practical interest to students, such as using the computer as a digital darkroom to produce semiprofessional pictures, caring for diskettes and CDs, and choosing an Internet service provider, are covered in the Getting Practical boxes in each chapter.

MAKING CONNECTIONS. Links people to computers. Topics include personalizing your desktop screen, using your computer as a video telephone, updating software online, and Bluetooth communications.

MARGIN NOTES. To further engage the student, margin notes are placed throughout the text. The margin notes extend the text material by highlighting interesting computer applications. Topics include chips that see, the networked home, cyberwarfare, and the wired campus.

BUYER'S GUIDE. Students and their families are making important economic decisions about the purchase of a computer for educational, personal, and business needs. This concise guide offers information to aid in hardware and software purchases.

MAKING MICROCHIPS GALLERY. The gallery text, supplemented by color photos, describes how microprocessors are made.

DAY IN THE LIFE. This feature details the life of an IT professional within a certain area that applies to the chapter material. Students see how the concepts they are learning in the text apply to the working world.

In-Text Learning Aids

Each chapter includes the following pedagogical support:

- *Learning Objectives* at the beginning of each chapter provide key concepts for students.

- *Key terms* appear in bold throughout the text.

- A *Chapter Review* offers a summary of core concepts and key terms.

- *Critical Thinking Questions* encourage students to discuss more thoroughly the information presented in each chapter.

- The *Student Study Guide* offers objective questions that test comprehension of essential concepts.

- A *Glossary* and a comprehensive *Index* are included at the end of the text.

STUDENT LEARNING SUPPLEMENTS

Prentice Hall's Explore Generation IT Labs

The Explore IT labs offer students an interactive look at computer concepts. The labs are delivered on the Web and on CD-ROM, allowing access in the classroom, the dorm, at home, and wherever computer and/or the Internet access are available.

These 16 labs have three key sections that encourage participation from students:

- *Introduction:* A multimedia exploration of the topic engages students and helps them fully understand the material presented in an interactive environment.

- *Explore:* Through further interaction and exploration of the material, students get a better understanding of the concepts in the lab.

- *Quiz:* Each lab includes a ten-question quiz that requires students to demonstrate an understanding of the concepts and material.

EXPLORE IT LABS cover the following hot topics:

Computer fundamentals
Mouse and keyboard
Directories, folders, and files
Troubleshooting
Computer systems
Hardware
Operating systems
Buying a computer
Computer applications
Application software
Multimedia
Databases
Internet and networking
Internet and the World Wide Web
Building a Web page
E-commerce
Building a network
Programming
Introduction to programming
Binary representation
Logic

Train and Assess Generation IT!

In addition to the traditional methods of teaching Computer Concepts, Prentice Hall proudly gives you COMPUTER CONCEPTS training modules in its wildly popular Internet-based training and testing software, *Train and Assess Generation IT!* This program offers interactive exploration in computer concepts topics such as

- Using e-mail

- Internet I: Overview

- Internet II: Finding what you need on the Internet

- Internet III: Connecting to the Internet from home

- File management

- Exploring the Windows interface

- Inside the box

- PC troubleshooting basics

- Working with graphics

- Buying a PC

- Installing and uninstalling software
- Security and privacy

INSTRUCTOR TEACHING SUPPLEMENTS

Instructor's Resource CD-ROM

The Instructor's Resource CD-ROM that is available with *Computers: Tools for an Information Age, 8e* contains:

- Instructor's Manual in Word and PDF
- Solutions to all questions and exercises from the book and Web site
- A Windows-based test manager and the associated test bank in Word format with over 1500 new questions
- PowerPoint lectures with Present IT:

  The software is a user friendly, browser-based interface, organized by chapter with search and sort functions, prebuilt PowerPoint slides and the ability to build a presentation from scratch incorporating any of the expanded content on the CD, Browse and Preview functions along with PowerPoint. You will find the following content resources in this software:

  - Multiple, customizable PowerPoint slide presentations for each chapter
  - Image library of all of the figures from the text
  - Videos with case notes
  - Animations for each chapter with audio

Tools for Online Learning

www.prenhall.com/capron

This text is accompanied by a companion Web site at www.prenhall.com/capron. This Website is designed to bring you and your students a richer, more interactive Web experience. The Website contains the following content and features:

- An interactive study guide
- Computer concepts learning games
- Internet exercises
- On-line end-of-chapter material

- Technology updates
- PC buying guide
- WWW links
- Careers in IT

ONLINE COURSEWARE FOR BLACKBOARD, WEBCT, AND COURSECOMPASS

Now you have the freedom to personalize your own online course materials! Prentice Hall provides the content and support you need to create and manage your own online course in WebCT, Blackboard, or Prentice Hall's own CourseCompass. Content includes lecture material, interactive exercises, additional testing questions, and projects.

CourseCompass (www.coursecompass.com)

CourseCompass is a dynamic, interactive online course-management tool powered exclusively for Pearson Education by Blackboard. This exciting product enables you to teach market-leading Pearson Education content in an easy-to-use, customizable format.

Blackboard (www.prenhall.com/blackboard)

Prentice Hall's abundant online content, combined with Blackboard's popular tools and interface, result in robust Web-based courses that are easy to implement, manage, and use—taking your courses to new heights in student interaction and learning.

WebCT (www.prenhall.com/webct)

Course-management tools within WebCT include page tracking, progress tracking, class and student management, grade book, communication, calendar, reporting tools, and more. Gold Level customer support, available exclusively to adopters of Prentice Hall courses, is provided free of charge upon adoption and provides you with priority assistance, training discounts, and dedicated technical support.

ACKNOWLEDGMENTS

Many people contributed to the success of this project. Although a single sentence hardly suffices, we would like to thank several of the key people. Thomas Park, Senior Project Manager, was instrumental in planning the changes and updates for this edition and shepherding the manuscript through several revisions. Mark Cierzniak, the Development Editor, provided invaluable assistance in turning the manuscript into a polished product. Others at Prentice Hall who made significant contributions to the project include Jodi McPherson, Executive Editor; Eileen Clark, Senior Project Manager, Editorial; Jodi Bolognese, Editorial Assistant; and Lynne Breitfeller, Project Manager, Production. Julie Tesser, photo researcher, spent many hours locating appropriate photographs to illustrate the text. Without all these people, and many more, there would be no book.

We would also like to thank the following reviewers for their valuable input. Without them, our work would have been much more difficult.

Brenda Britt, Fayetteville Technical Community College

Kevan Croteau, Francis Marion University

Rory DeSimone, University of Florida

Allen Dooley, Pasadena City College

David Evans, Pasadena City College

Nancy Goettel, Coastal Carolina University

Warren Jones, University of Alabama at Birmingham

Cherylee Kushida, Santa Ana College

Lynn Lazar, Lander University

Jean Upson, Lorain County Community College

Linda Vandiver, Paris Junior College

Vahid Zardoost, Pasadena City College

Computers:
Tools for an Information Age

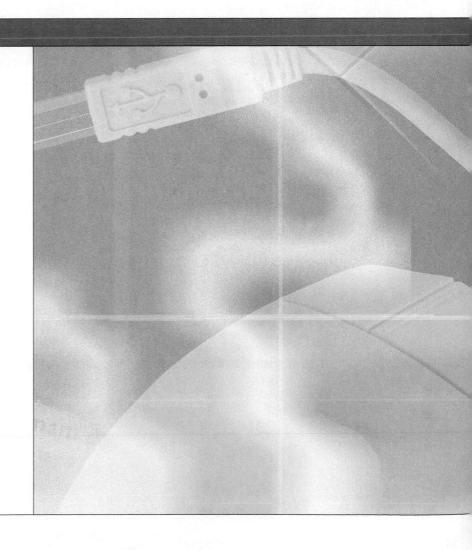

Computers:
Tools for an Information Age

CHAPTER 1

For years Mike McDowell refused to buy a personal computer. The 38-year-old McDowell, owner of a 1,200-acre farm in Wisconsin, told his disappointed children that they would just have to use the computers at school. The family simply could not justify the expense of a computer in the home. "If I buy a new tractor," he noted, "I can make the farm more profitable. But a computer? I just can't see it."

He can now. Mr. McDowell took a look at the new price tags. As personal computer prices ducked below $1,000, they attracted a whole new audience of home users. In fact, more than half of new computers are purchased by first-time buyers. In addition, computers are continuing their winning ways: Almost 80 percent of computer buyers are "satisfied" or "very satisfied" with their computers.

Mr. McDowell ticks off the uses his family has found for the computer. He took a class at his local community college and learned to use spreadsheets, a kind of rows-and-columns report, to plan his crop planting and rotations. He uses the computer to send for weather and crop reports from agencies of the federal government. His wife favors e-mail, which lets her use the computer to send messages back and forth to her sisters in Duluth and Sioux Falls. His teenage daughter, who wrote her high school reports using a word processor, saved her summer job earnings to buy a laptop computer to take with her to college. Mr. McDowell now counts himself in the "very satisfied" category.

◀▶ STEPPING OUT

Your first steps toward joining the Information Age include understanding how we got to where we are today. Perhaps you recall from history books how the Industrial Age took its place in our world. In just a few decades, society accepted the dizzying introduction of electricity, telephones, radio, automobiles, and airplanes. The Information Age is evolving even more rapidly. It is likely to continue to evolve well into the twenty-first century.

Forging a Computer-Based Society

Traditional economics courses define the cornerstones of an economy as land, labor, and capital. Today we can add a fourth key economic element: information. As we evolve from an industrial to an information society, our jobs are changing from physical to mental labor. Just as people moved physically from farms to factories in the Industrial Age, so today people are shifting from muscle power to brainpower in a new, computer-based society.

You are making your move, too, taking your first steps by signing up for this computer class and reading this book. But should you go further and get your own computer? We look next at some of the reasons why you might.

A Computer in Your Future

Computers have moved into every nook and cranny of our daily lives. Whether or not you personally know anything about it, you use computers when you make a bank withdrawal, when you buy groceries at the supermarket, and even when you drive your car. But should you have a computer at your personal disposal? The answer today is "probably." Although only a little more than half of Americans have personal computers in their homes, a much higher percentage use computers on the job. Almost any career in your future will involve a computer in some way.

In their homes, people use computer technology for writing papers and memos, for keeping track of bank accounts, for communicating with friends and associates,

Computers have moved into every nook and cranny of our daily lives.

People use their home computers to compose letters and memos, play games, and keep track of their finances.

for accessing knowledge, for purchasing goods, for entertainment, and for so much more.

Computer Literacy for All

Why are you studying about computers? In addition to curiosity (and perhaps a course requirement), you probably recognize that it will not be easy to get through the rest of your life without knowing about computers. We offer a three-pronged definition of **computer literacy:**

- **Awareness.** As you study about computers, you will become aware of their importance, their versatility, and their pervasiveness in our society.

- **Knowledge.** You will learn what computers are and how they work. This requires learning some technical jargon, but do not worry—no one expects you to become a computer expert.

- **Interaction.** There is no better way to understand computers than through interacting with one. So being computer literate also means being able to use a computer for some simple applications.

Note that no part of this definition suggests that you must be able to create the instructions that tell a computer what to do. That would be akin to saying that anyone who plans to drive a car must first become an automotive engineer. Someone else can write the instructions for the computer; you simply use the instructions to get your work done. For example, an accountant might use a computer to prepare a report, a teenager to play a video game, or a construction worker to record data from the field.

Computers are characterized by speed, reliability, and storage capability.

◢ THE NATURE OF COMPUTERS

Every computer has three fundamental characteristics that make it useful. Each characteristic has by-products that are just as important. The three fundamental characteristics are:

- **Speed.** Computers provide the processing speed essential to our fast-paced society. The quick service that we have come to expect—for bank withdrawals, stock quotes, telephone calls, and travel reservations, to name just a few—is made possible by computers. Businesses depend on the speedy processing that computers provide for everything from balancing ledgers to designing products.

- **Reliability.** Computers are extremely reliable. Of course, you might not think this from some of the stories you may have seen in the press about "computer errors." However, most errors supposedly made by computers are really human errors.

- **Storage Capability.** Computer systems can store tremendous amounts of data, which can be located and retrieved efficiently. The capability to store volumes of data is especially important in an information age.

These three characteristics—speed, reliability, and storage capability—have the following by-products:

- **Productivity.** When computers move into business offices, managers expect increased productivity as workers learn to use computers to do their jobs better and faster. Furthermore, jobs such as punching holes in metal or monitoring water levels can be more efficiently controlled by computers.

- **Decision making.** To make decisions, managers need to take into account financial, geographical, and logistical factors. The computer helps decision makers sort things out and make better choices.

- **Cost reduction.** Finally, because it improves productivity and aids decision-making, the computer helps us hold down the costs of labor, energy, and paperwork. As a result, computers help reduce the costs of goods and services in our economy.

Next we look at some of the ways in which we use computers to make the workday more productive and our personal lives more rewarding.

► WHERE COMPUTERS ARE USED

Computers can do just about anything imaginable, but they really excel in certain areas. This section lists some of the principal areas of computer use.

● **Education.** Most schools in the United States have computers available for use in the classroom, and some colleges require entering freshmen to bring their own. Many educators prefer learning by doing—an approach uniquely suited to the computer.

Most schools in the United States have computers in the classroom because many educators prefer the learn-by-doing method.

● **Graphics.** Business people make bar graphs and pie charts to convey information with more impact than numbers alone convey. Architects use computer-generated graphics to experiment with possible exteriors and to give clients a visual walk-through of proposed buildings. Finally, a new kind of artist has emerged, one who uses computers to express his or her creativity.

● **Retailing.** Products from meats to magazines are packaged with bar codes that can be read by computer scanners at supermarket checkout stands to determine prices and help to manage inventory. Computers operate behind the scenes too; for example, this book was tracked from printer to warehouse to bookstore with the help of computers and the bar code on the back cover.

● **Energy.** Energy companies use computers to locate oil, coal, natural gas, and uranium. Electric companies use computers to monitor vast power networks. In addition, meter readers use handheld computers to record the amount of energy used each month in homes and businesses.

● **Law enforcement.** Recent innovations in computerized law enforcement include national fingerprint files, a national file on the mode of operation of serial killers, and the computer modeling of DNA, which can be used to match traces of hair, blood, or other evidence found at a crime scene to a suspect.

● **Transportation.** Computers are used in cars to monitor fluid levels, temperatures, and electrical systems. Computers also are used to help run rapid transit systems, load container ships, and track railroad cars across the country. The workers in an airport tower rely on computers to help monitor air traffic.

● **Money.** Computers speed up record keeping and allow banks to offer same-day services and even do-it-yourself banking over the phone and Internet. Computers have helped to fuel the cashless economy, enabling the widespread use of credit cards and instantaneous credit checks by banks and retailers.

Recent innovations in computerized law enforcement include national fingerprint files and computer modeling of DNA.

Airport control tower personnel use computers to monitor and direct air traffic.

- **Agriculture.** Farmers use small computers to help with billing, crop information, cost per acre, feed combinations, and market price checks. Cattle ranchers can use computers for information about livestock breeding and performance.

- **Government.** Among other tasks, the federal government uses computers to forecast weather, manage parks, process immigrants, produce Social Security benefit checks, and collect taxes. State and local governments also use computers routinely.

Cattle ranchers use computers for information about livestock breeding and performance.

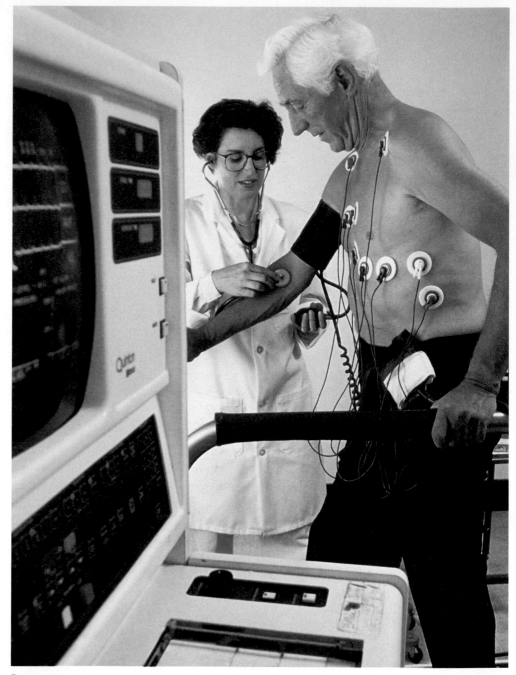

Doctors use computers to monitor the health of their patients and to make diagnoses.

- **Home.** People have computers in their homes, often justifying them as educational tools for their children. But that is only the beginning. Personal computers are being used at home to keep records, write letters, prepare budgets, draw pictures, publish newsletters, and connect with others.

- **Health and medicine.** Computers help to monitor the seriously ill in intensive care units and provide cross-sectional views of the body. Physicians can also use computers to assist in diagnoses; in fact, computers have been shown to correctly diagnose heart attacks more frequently than physicians do. If you are one of the thousands who suffer one miserable cold after another, you will be happy to know that computers have been able to map, in exquisite atomic detail, the structure of the human cold virus—the first step toward a cure for the common cold.

These factory robots weld a new car under computer control.

- **Robotics.** Computers have paved the way for robots to take over many of the jobs that are too unpleasant or too dangerous for humans, such as opening packages that are believed to contain bombs. Robots are best known for their work in factories, but they can do many other things, not the least of which is finding their way through the bloodstream.

Athletes can use computers to assess and improve their physical performance.

- **The human connection.** Are computers cold and impersonal? The disabled do not think so; children, in particular, consider the computer their main educational tool. Can the disabled walk again? Some can, with the help of computers. Can dancers and athletes improve their performance? Maybe they can, by using computers to monitor their movements. Can we learn more about our ethnic backgrounds and our cultural history with the aid of computers? Indeed we can.

- **The sciences.** Scientific researchers have long benefited from the high-speed capabilities of computers. Computers can simulate environments, emulate physical characteristics, and allow scientists to provide proofs in a cost-effective manner. Also, many mice—and other animals—have been spared since computer models have taken over their roles in research.

- **Connectivity.** One of the most popular uses of computers today is communicating with other people who have computers, whether for business or personal reasons. In addition, computers can give people the option of working at their homes instead of commuting to offices.

- **Training.** It is much cheaper to teach aspiring pilots to fly in computerized training simulators than in real airplanes. Novice railroad engineers can experience running a train with the help of a computerized device. Training simulations are relatively inexpensive and are always available on a one-to-one basis, making for a personal learning experience.

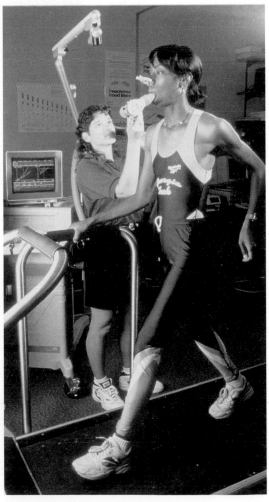

Have It Your Way

Have it your way exactly. The name of the new movement is mass customization, and the computer makes it possible.

Companies with millions of customers are starting to build products designed just for you. The woman in the photo is being measured for a pair of Levi jeans, which will be cut to fit her body. But clothes are just the beginning. You can buy a Dell computer made to your exact specifications. You can also buy eyeglasses molded to fit your face, CDs with music tracks you select, cosmetics mixed to match your skin tone, or a specially designed Barbie doll. Although these are mass-marketed goods, they can be uniquely tailored to the customers who buy them.

● **Paperwork.** In some ways the computer contributes to paper use by adding to the amount of junk mail you find in your mailbox. However, in many ways it cuts down on paper handling. Using a computer, for example, you might type several drafts of a term paper before printing anything. Computerized record keeping and ordering have also made paperwork more efficient.

Computers are all around us. You have been exposed to computer hype, computer advertisements, and computer headlines. You have interacted with computers in your everyday life—at the grocery store, your school, the library, and more. You know more about computers than you think you do. The beginnings of computer literacy are already apparent.

▶ THE BIG PICTURE

A computer system has three main components: hardware, software, and people. The equipment associated with a computer system is called **hardware.** A set of instructions called **software** tells the hardware what to do. People, however, are the most important component of a computer system. They use the power of the computer for some purpose.

Software is also referred to as programs. To be more specific, a **program** is a set of step-by-step instructions that directs the computer to do the required tasks and produce the desired results. A **computer programmer** is a person who writes programs. Users are people who purchase and use computer software. In business, **users** are often called **end-users** because they are at the end of the "computer line," actually making use of the computer's capabilities.

This chapter examines hardware and looks at the big picture; therefore many of the terms introduced in this chapter are discussed only briefly. Subsequent chapters define the various parts of a computer system in much greater detail.

▶ HARDWARE: THE BASIC COMPONENTS OF A COMPUTER

What is a computer? A 6-year-old called a computer "radio, movies, and television combined!" A 10-year-old described a computer as "a television set you can talk to." The 10-year-old's definition is closer but still does not recognize the computer as a machine that has the power to make changes. A **computer** is a machine that can be programmed to accept **data** (*input*), process it into useful **information** (*output*), and store it (in a *secondary storage* device) for safekeeping or reuse. The processing of input to output is directed by the software but performed by the hardware, the subject of this chapter.

To function, a computer system requires four main aspects of data handling: input, processing, output, and storage (Figure 1-1). The hardware responsible for these four areas is as follows:

Input devices accept data or commands in a form that the computer can use; they send the data or commands to the processing unit.

The *processor*, more formally known as the central processing unit (CPU), has electronic circuitry that manipulates input data into the information people want. The central processing unit actually executes computer instructions.

Output devices show people the processed data—information—in understandable and usable form.

Storage usually means *secondary storage*, which consists of secondary storage devices such as a disk—hard disk or diskettes or some other kind of disk—that can

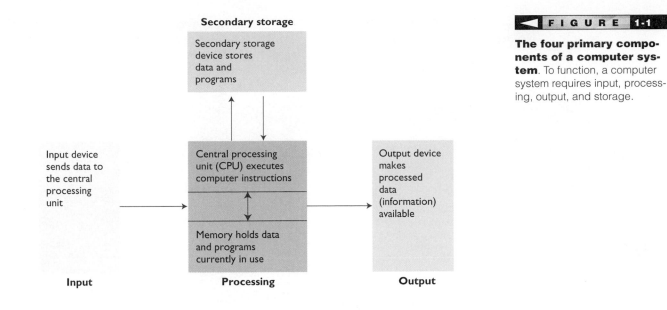

The four primary components of a computer system. To function, a computer system requires input, processing, output, and storage.

store data and programs outside of the computer itself. These devices supplement *memory* or *primary storage*, which data and programs only temporarily.

Before looking at each of these hardware aspects, consider them in terms of what you would find on a personal computer.

► YOUR PERSONAL COMPUTER HARDWARE

Let us look at the hardware of a personal computer. Suppose you want to do word processing on a personal computer using the hardware shown in Figure 1-2. Word-processing software enables you to input data such as an essay, save it, revise and resave it, and print it whenever you wish. The *input* device, in this case, is a keyboard, which you use to key in (type) the original essay and any subsequent changes to it. You will also probably use the mouse as an input device. All computers, large and small, must have a *central processing unit*, so yours does too—it is within the personal computer housing. The central processing unit uses the word-processing software to accept the data you input through the keyboard. Processed data from your personal computer is usually *output* in two forms: on a screen and by a printer. As you type the essay on the keyboard, it appears on the screen in front of you. After you have examined the essay on the screen, made changes, and determined that you are satisfied with the result, you can print the essay on the printer. Your *secondary storage device*, as shown in Figure 1-2, which stores the essay until it is needed again, will probably be a hard disk or removable diskette. For reasons of convenience and speed, you are more likely to store your data—the essay—on a hard disk than on a diskette. (However, if you are using someone else's computer, such as a school computer, you will probably keep your own files on your own diskette.)

Next is a general tour of the hardware needed for input, processing, output, and storage. These same components make up all computer systems, whether small, medium, or large.

Input: What Goes In

Input is the data that you put into the computer system for processing. Here are some common ways of feeding input data into the system:

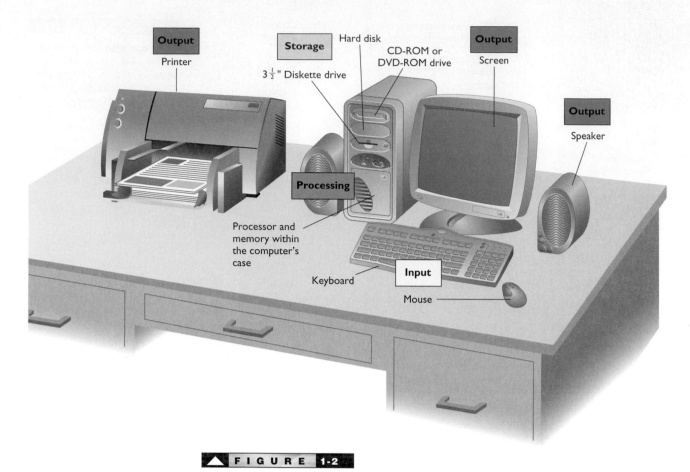

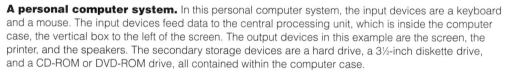

A personal computer system. In this personal computer system, the input devices are a keyboard and a mouse. The input devices feed data to the central processing unit, which is inside the computer case, the vertical box to the left of the screen. The output devices in this example are the screen, the printer, and the speakers. The secondary storage devices are a hard drive, a 3½-inch diskette drive, and a CD-ROM or DVD-ROM drive, all contained within the computer case.

Typing on a **keyboard** (Figure 1-3a). Thekeys on a computer keyboard are arranged in much the same way as those on a typewriter. The computer responds to what you enter; that is, it "echoes" what you type by displaying it on the screen in front of you.

Pointing with a **mouse** (Figure 1-3a). A mouse is a device that you move over a flat surface. The mouse movement causes corresponding movement of a pointer on the computer screen. Pressing buttons on the mouse lets you select commands.

Scanning with a **wand reader, bar code reader, flatbed scanner,** or **sheet-fed scanner.** Wand and bar code readers, which you have seen used by clerks in retail stores, use laser beams to read special letters, numbers, or symbols, such as the black-and-white bar codes found on many products (Figure 1-3b). Flatbed or sheet-fed scanners are used to scan pictures or printed documents into your computer.

An input device may be part of a terminal. The simplest **terminal** includes a keyboard as the input device, a screen display for output, and some method of connection to a computer. For example, operators taking orders over the phone for a mail-order house would probably use terminals to input orders and send them to be processed by a large computer. You can input data into a computer in many other interesting ways, including by writing, speaking, pointing, or even just looking at the data.

MAKING CONNECTIONS ◄ The Wired Campus

Campuses are "wired" in more ways than one. At most schools, each incoming student is automatically assigned an e-mail address and given access to Internet services. Some schools require incoming freshmen to possess a computer. Others include the cost of a new computer in their tuition. Students can often count on high-speed network connections for their computers right in their dorm rooms. Standard services offered by computer are registration for classes—no more lines!—applications for financial aid, and access to grades and transcripts. Coursework can often be submitted to a professor via computer, and many classes are supported by chat rooms and message boards. Wireless networks, which allow students access to the school's network through their laptops from anywhere on campus, are the latest trend among leading-edge colleges and universities.

The Processor and Memory: Data Manipulation

In a computer the processor is the center of activity. The **processor,** as has already been noted, is also called the **central processing unit** (**CPU**). The CPU consists of electronic circuits that interpret and execute program instructions and communicate with the input, output, and storage devices.

It is the CPU that actually transforms data into information. **Data** is the raw material, such as grades in a class, touchdowns scored, or light and dark areas in a photograph, to be processed by a computer. Processed data becomes **information**—data that is organized, meaningful, and useful. In school, for instance, an instructor could enter various students' scores (data), which could be processed to produce final grades and perhaps a class average (information). Note that the instructor's final grade information could, in turn, become the data for the school's student records system, which would produce grade reports and GPAs as its information. Data that is perhaps uninteresting on its own may become very interesting once it is converted to information. The raw facts (data) about your finances, such as a paycheck or a donation to

(a)

(b)

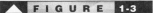

▲ **FIGURE** 1-3

Input devices. (a) The keyboard is the most widely used input device, though almost all systems also have a mouse. Movement of the mouse on a flat surface causes corresponding movement of a pointer on the screen. (b) The information contained in the bar code on this package of green beans is scanned into the computer.

Curling Up with a Good Computer

It looks like a book, sort of, but it holds 50,000 pages. It weighs less than three pounds. It is, in fact, a computer book, and it has a beautiful screen. It can hold reference books and several of your favorite novels.

In addition to the familiar comforts, this book knows a few tricks. You can still dog-ear a page by pressing a corner of the touch-sensitive screen, and you can use a stylus-type pen to write notes or underline. You can also enlarge the typeface or touch a word to look it up in the dictionary.

Computer books are not cheap—yet. And, of course, you have to pay for the books you want to read on them too. New books can be purchased on the Internet and downloaded directly to the computer book.

charity or a medical bill, may not be captivating individually, but together these and other items can be processed to produce the refund or amount you owe on your income tax return (information).

Computer memory, also known as **primary storage,** is closely related to the CPU but separate and distinct from it. Memory holds the data after it is input into the system and before it is processed; also, memory holds the data after it has been processed but before it has been released to the output device. In addition, memory holds the programs (computer instructions) needed by the CPU. Memory can hold data only temporarily because memory requires a continuous flow of electric current; if the current is interrupted, the data is lost.

Output: What Comes Out

Output—the result produced by the CPU—is a computer's whole reason for being. Output is usable information—that is, raw input data that has been processed by the computer into information. Common forms of output are text, numbers, graphics, and even sounds. Text output, for example, might be made up of the letters and memos prepared by office workers using word-processing software. Other workers may be more interested in numbers, such as those found in formulas, schedules, and budgets. In many cases numbers can be understood more easily when output is in the form of graphics.

The most common output devices are computer screens and printers. A **screen,** or **monitor,** can vary in its form of display, producing text, numbers, symbols, art, photographs, and even video, in full color (Figure 1-4a). **Printers** produce printed reports as instructed by a computer program (Figure 1-4b). Many printers, particularly those associated with personal computers, can print in color.

You can also produce output from a computer in other ways, including film, voice, and music.

Secondary Storage

Secondary storage provides additional storage separate from memory. Recall that memory holds data and programs only temporarily; therefore there is a need for secondary storage. The most common secondary storage media for personal computers are magnetic disks. A **magnetic disk** can be a floppy disk (diskette) or a hard disk. A floppy **disk** usually consists of a flexible magnetic disk 3½ inches in diameter, enclosed in a plastic case (Figure 1-5a). **Hard disks** have more storage capacity than diskettes and also offer much faster access to the data they hold. On large computer systems, hard disks are often contained in disk packs. Disk data is read by **disk drives.** Most personal computers have a built-in hard disk and a drive that reads diskettes. **Optical disk drives,** such as **CD-ROM**s and **DVD-ROM**s, use a laser beam to read large volumes of data relatively inexpensively (Figure 1-5b).

Magnetic tape is a storage medium that is used primarily with large computer systems, although some personal computers also use this form of secondary storage. This tape usually comes on a cartridge and is similar to tape you play on a tape recorder. Magnetic tape cartridges are inserted in a **tape drive** when the data on them needs to be read by the computer system or when new data is to be written on the tape. Magnetic tape is usually used for backup purposes—for "data insurance "—because tape is inexpensive. The chapter on storage presents more detailed information about storage media, notably alternative types of disk storage.

The Complete Hardware System

The hardware devices that are attached to the computer are called peripheral equipment. **Peripheral equipment** includes all input, output, and secondary storage devices. In most personal computers, the CPU and disk drives are all contained in the same housing, a metal case; the keyboard, mouse, and monitor are separate.

◄ **F I G U R E** **1-4**

Output devices. Monitors and printers are two common types of output devices. (a) This monitor can display text and the colorful graphics shown here. (b) This ink-jet printer produces high-quality text and graphics output.

(b)

(a)

In larger computer systems, however, the input, processing, output, and storage functions may be in separate rooms, separate buildings, or even separate countries. For example, data may be input on terminals at a branch bank and then transmitted to the CPU at the bank's headquarters. The information produced by the CPU may then be transmitted to the international offices, where it is printed out. Meanwhile, disks with stored data may be kept at the bank headquarters, and duplicate data may be kept on disk or tape in a warehouse across town for safekeeping.

Although the equipment may vary widely from the simplest computer to the most powerful, by and large, the four elements of a computer system remain the same: input, processing, output, and storage. These basic components are supplemented by hardware that can make computers much more useful, giving them the ability to connect to one another.

(a)

(b)

▲ **F I G U R E** **1-5**

Secondary storage devices. (a) A 3½-inch diskette is being inserted into a disk drive. (b) Optical disks can hold enormous amounts of data: text, music, graphics. even video and movies.

Like people who have boats or cameras, computer owners are tempted to buy the latest gadget. There are many from which to choose, some new, neat, and nifty, and some more useful than others.

For greater flexibility, check out a wireless keyboard or mouse, which can minimize the cable clutter on your desk. For everyday computer comfort, consider gel-based wrist rests for your keyboard and mouse pad. To reduce neck strain, get a document holder that attaches to the side of your monitor. While you are at it, you

can reduce eyestrain by attaching a magnifier to the screen itself.

If you prefer to say what you think instead of writing it, you can purchase a microphone and accompanying software to accept your voice input. Road warriors can buy practical laptop cases, with lots of padding and pockets for accessories. Webcams enable you to send video images across the Internet. If music and gaming are a big part of your computer life, you could invest in the very best: surround-sound speakers with a separate subwoofer.

NETWORKING

Many organizations find that their needs are best served by a **network,** a system that uses communications equipment to connect computers and their resources. Resources include printers, hard disks, and even software and data. In one type of network, a **local area network (LAN),** personal computers in an office are connected together so that users can communicate with one another. Users can operate their personal computers independently or in cooperation with other computers to exchange data and share resources. The networking process can be much more complex; we describe how large computers can be involved in networks in the chapter on networking.

Individual users in homes or offices have joined the trend to connectivity by hooking up their personal computers, often via telephone lines, to other computers. Users who connect their computers to other computers via the phone lines must use a hardware device called a **modem** as a go-between to reconcile the inherent differences between computers and the phone system. From their own homes, users can connect to all sorts of computer-based services, performing such tasks as getting stock quotes, making airline reservations, and shopping for videotapes. An important service for individuals is **electronic mail,** or **e-mail,** which lets people send and receive messages via computer.

Whether the user is operating in a business capacity or simply exploring the options, a popular conduit for connectivity is the Internet.

Being the Computer Training Manager in a furniture production company requires a lot more than just being able to teach. Besides actually teaching the training sessions herself (from one-on-one tutoring to classroom labs with a dozen people at once), Maria is also responsible for evaluating each group's training needs and recommending training based on those needs. She then has to create and plan the training herself, book the location, and finally teach it.

Take her most recent project. The Accounts Receivable group was about to upgrade from Microsoft Office 97 to Office

XP. Maria's job was to consult with the group to find out in what ways they use Excel most often. She then had to investigate how those procedures might have changed in Excel 2002, and especially see if there were ways in which the software could improve on the procedures. That finished, she prepared a refresher training session on how to carry out these procedures in the new software, and proceeded to train all six AR staff in one-on-one training sessions.

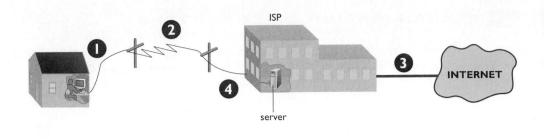

◄ FIGURE 1-6

The Internet. (1) At his or her own computer, a user accesses the ISP's server computer, probably over the (2) phone line. (3) The server computer communicates with the Internet, perhaps passing on e-mail messages or requests for Web pages and picking up responses. (4) Incoming e-mail or requested Internet information is returned to the original requesting computer. This back-and-forth communication goes on as long as the user remains connected to the Internet.

▶ THE INTERNET

The **Internet,** sometimes called simply "the Net," is the largest and most far-flung network system of them all, connecting users worldwide. Surprisingly, the Internet is not really a single network but a loosely organized collection of thousands of networks. Many people are astonished to discover that no one owns the Internet. It has no central headquarters, no centrally offered services, and no comprehensive index to tell you what information is available.

Originally developed by the U.S. government, the Internet connects libraries, college campuses, research labs, government organizations, businesses, and any other organization or individual who has the capacity to hook up.

Getting Connected

How are all kinds of different computers able to communicate with one another? To access the Internet, a user's computer must connect to a type of computer called a server. Each server uses the same special software called **TCP/IP** (for **Transmission Control Protocol/Internet Protocol**); it is this standard that allows different types of computers to communicate with each other (Figure 1-6). The supplier of the server computer, often called an **Internet service provider** (**ISP**), charges a fee, usually monthly, that either covers unlimited access or is based on the amount of service provided. Once a user has chosen a service provider, he or she is furnished with the information needed to connect to the server and, from there, to the Internet.

Getting Around

Because the Internet did not begin as a commercial customer-pleasing package, it did not initially offer attractive options for finding information. Most of the information was text-only, and only a hardy and determined few mastered the arcane commands needed to find it. Furthermore, the vast sea of information, including news and trivia, can seem an overwhelming challenge to navigate. As both the Internet user population and the types and amount of available information grew, new ways were developed to tour the Internet.

The most common method used to move around the Internet is called *browsing*. Using a program called a **browser,** you can use a mouse to point and click on screen text or pictures to explore the Internet, particularly the **World Wide Web** (**WWW** or the **Web**), an Internet subset of text, images, and sounds linked together to allow users to peruse related topics. Each different location on the Web is called a **Web site** or, more commonly, just a **site.** You may have heard the term **home page;** this is just the main page of a Web site.

The Internet is an important and complex topic. Although it is easy to use once you know how, there is much to learn about its use and its place in the world of computers. This opening chapter merely scratches the surface. More detailed information can be found in the chapter devoted to the Internet. In addition, this book has a two-page spread, called "Planet Internet," at the end of each chapter, giving examples of some aspect of the Internet. The more generic topic of connectivity is discussed in the feature "Making Connections," offered in each chapter of the book.

Move Over, Kid

Computers in business? Of course. Computers for youngsters? Certainly. But senior citizens are the fastest-growing group of computer users. Furthermore, the average senior spends about twice as much time per month at a personal computer as the average teenage user spends. This is partly because many seniors have more discretionary income and more time on their hands than teenagers do.

The majority of seniors say that they were drawn to computers because they did not want to be left behind. They flock to classes, both private and public. Many senior students use their new word-processing skills to write memoirs for their grandchildren. Others monitor their investments,

▶ CLASSIFICATION OF COMPUTERS

Computers come in sizes from tiny to monstrous, in both appearance and power. The size of a computer that a person or an organization needs depends on the computing requirements. Clearly, the National Weather Service, keeping watch on the weather fronts of many continents, has requirements that are different from those of a car dealer's service department that is trying to keep track of its parts inventory. And the requirements of both of them are different from the needs of a salesperson using a small notebook computer to record client orders or those of a student writing a paper. Although we will describe categories of computers here, keep in mind that computers do not fall too readily into groups of distinct islands; the boundaries between the categories are not clearly defined and are changing all the time.

Personal Computers

Most often called **personal computers,** or **PCs,** desktop computers are also known as **microcomputers.** Personal computers now fall into categories; most are low-end functional computers (sometimes ungallantly referred to as "cheap PCs") or else fully powered personal computers. A third category, consisting of upper-end PCs called **workstations,** is used by specialized workers such as engineers, financial traders, and graphic designers. Workstations are small enough to fit on a desktop but approach the power of a mainframe.

Most users choose between personal computers in the first two categories: less expensive or more expensive. For many years, PCs were offered only in the fully powered state-of-the-art category and cost upwards of $2,000, enough to make some home buyers hesitate. But now, for a few hundred dollars, anyone can own a personal computer. At the low end, a cheap PC has less of everything: a slower and less powerful microprocessor, less memory, a smaller and less crisp screen, less hard drive space, and fewer software choices. Nevertheless, cheap PCs perform primary functions more than adequately. Customers who want a computer mainly for basic applications such as word processing, personal finance, record keeping, simple games, and access to the Internet are usually happy with computers at the low end.

There are, of course, people who should buy the more expensive, cutting-edge computers. You will want all the computer you can get if you plan to spend a lot of time on graphic images, heavy-duty calculations, programming, and—above all—action-oriented arcade games.

A variation on the personal computer is the **network computer,** a limited piece of hardware with a CPU and minimal memory, designed to be connected to a network. In the office, this is also called a **thin client** and relies on the processing and storage capabilities of the company's network servers. In the home, people can use a network computer to connect to the Internet, with a television set as the com-

---

puter screen and a keyboard as an optional add-on. (The best-known consumer network computer is the WebTV®.) Most network computers have no disk storage at all. The original idea behind this un-PC was simplicity and low price. However, network computers have faltered in the marketplace, mainly because cheap PCs have cut into their territory.

Notebook Computers

Notebook computers are lightweight (often under six pounds) and portable. Travelers use them to work while on the move in trains and airplanes; consultants load their analytical software on them to take to client locations, and salespeople use them as presentation tools (Figure 1-7). Somewhat larger and heavier versions of these computers are known as laptops and can be used as desktop replacements for those with occasional portability requirements.

The memory and storage capacity of notebook computers today can compete with those of desktop computers. Notebooks have a hard disk drive and most accept diskettes, so it is easy to move data from one computer to another. Many offer a CD-ROM or DVD-ROM drive. Furthermore, notebooks can run most available software. Notebooks are not as inexpensive as their size might suggest; they carry a price tag greater than that of a full-size personal computer with the same features. However, like other technology, notebook computers are getting faster, lighter, and more feature-rich.

research their family genealogy, create greeting cards, or even begin post-retirement businesses.

One 72-year-old took her laptop on an eight-month journey by boat, bus, and bicycle around the world. She sent back periodic reports that were published in her local newspaper. Now, she says, she answers her grandchildren's questions about the world—and about computers.

◄ **FIGURE 1-7**

Notebook computer. This woman can use her notebook computer to make productive use of otherwise wasted time.

Your Notebook Is a Sissy

Your notebook computer has probably never had to defend itself from life's knocks. Compare your notebook to notebooks that have been ruggedized to withstand shock, falls, vibration, dust, and water. Who needs all this hardiness? The military, construction engineers, oil rig managers, and anyone else whose center of operations is based on sand, water, or ice.

Smaller Still: Handheld Computers

A handheld computer called a **personal digital assistant (PDA)** can be used to keep track of appointments and other business information, such as customer names and orders. PDAs are also called pen-based computers because, with the use of a pen-like stylus, they can accept handwritten input directly on a touch-sensitive screen. Many PDAs offer multiple functions, including wireless e-mail and fax capabilities (Figure 1-8). The **Pocket PC** is a handheld computer with slightly more power than a PDA. In addition to the functions performed by a PDA, the Pocket PC can also run stripped-down versions of PC productivity software, such as word processing and spreadsheets. Some models of both PDAs and PocketPCs come with integrated cell phones, allowing connection to the Internet.

Users of handhelds are often clipboard-carrying workers, such as parcel delivery drivers and meter readers. Other potential users are workers who cannot easily use a notebook computer because they are on their feet all day: nurses, sales representatives, real estate agents, and insurance adjusters. But the biggest group of users is found right in the office; these users like the fact that this convenient device can keep their lives organized.

Midrange Computers

Midrange computers (formerly referred to as **minicomputers**) are multi-user computers designed to serve the needs of medium-sized organizations. Hundreds, or sometimes even thousands, of users can be connected to a midrange computer via terminals or networked PCs to access company-wide applications, such as order-entry and inventory control. Larger midrange computers are often difficult to distinguish from smaller members of the next classification, mainframes.

Mainframes

In the jargon of the computer trade, large computers are called **mainframes.** Mainframes are capable of processing data at very high speeds—billions of instructions per second—and have access to trillions of characters of data. The price of these large systems can vary from several hundred thousand to many millions of dollars. With that kind of price tag, you will not buy a mainframe for just any purpose. Their principal use is for processing vast amounts of data quickly, so some of the obvious customers are banks, insurance companies, and manufacturers. But this list is not

► FIGURE 1-8

PDAs Personal digital assistants can be used to keep track of appointments and other business information, such as names and orders.

all-inclusive; other types of customers are large mail-order houses, airlines with sophisticated reservation systems, government accounting services, aerospace companies doing complex aircraft design, and the like. As you can tell from these examples of mainframe applications, a key characteristic of large computers is that they are designed for multiple users. For example, many reservations clerks could be accessing the same computer at the same time to make reservations for waiting customers.

As computer users have marched inexorably toward personal computers and networking, pundits have erroneously predicted the demise of mainframes. But "big iron," the affectionate nickname for these computers, is proving to be hardy and versatile. More recent uses include helping large businesses carry out critical applications, such as running automated teller machines and delivering e-mail. Thus, the mainframe has taken on the coloration of a server and is often referred to as a server. On the Internet, where computers of all stripes can coexist and even work in concert, vast data stores are being kept on large servers. The large server—the mainframe—is still the most reliable way to manage vast amounts of data. As an example, national retailer L.L. Bean is using an IBM mainframe system to offer its entire catalog of merchandise on the Internet.

Typically, the machine's innards are housed in a titanium alloy case, about 20 times as strong as the plastic that is generally used in conventional notebooks. The keyboard is sealed to prevent liquid from seeping into the internal circuitry, and all external connections are dust-resistant. The disk drives are mounted in a shock-absorbing gel compound.

Supercomputers

The mightiest computers—and, of course, the most expensive—are known as **supercomputers.** Supercomputers are also the fastest: They can process trillions of instructions per second. Supercomputers can be found in mainstream activities as varied as stock analysis, automobile design, special effects for movies, and even sophisticated artwork. However, for many years supercomputer customers were an exclusive group: agencies of the federal government. The federal government uses supercomputers for tasks that require mammoth data manipulation, such as worldwide weather forecasting and weapons research (Figure 1-9).

This chapter has taken a rather expansive look at computer hardware. However, hardware by itself is only an empty shell. Software is the ingredient that gives value to the computer.

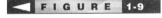

◄ F I G U R E 1-9

Supercomputer. The Blue Horizon supercomputer, built by IBM, is housed at the San Diego Supercomputer Center and used for academic research.

CHAPTER REVIEW

► Summary and Key Terms

- **Computer literacy** has three components: an awareness of the importance, versatility, and pervasiveness of computers in society; knowledge of what computers are and how they work; and the capability of interacting with a computer to use simple applications.

- Every computer has three fundamental characteristics: speed, reliability, and a large storage capability. Through these characteristics computers increase productivity, aid in decision making, and reduce costs.

- The equipment associated with a computer system is called **hardware.** The **programs,** or step-by-step instructions that run the machines, are called **software. Computer programmers** write programs for **users,** or **end-users**—people who purchase and use computer software.

- A **computer** is a machine that can be programmed to process **data** (input) into useful **information** (output). A computer system comprises four main aspects of data handling: input, processing, output, and storage.

- **Input** is data to be accepted into the computer. Common input devices are the **keyboard;** a **mouse,** which translates movements of a ball on a flat surface to actions on the screen; a **wand reader** or **bar code reader,** which uses laser beams to read special letters, numbers, or symbols, such as the zebra-striped bar codes on products: and a **flatbed** or **sheet-fed scanner,** used to scan photos or documents into the computer.

- A **terminal** includes an input device, such as a keyboard or wand reader; an output device, usually a television-like screen; and a connection to the main computer.

- The **processor,** or **central processing unit (CPU)**, processes raw **data** into meaningful, useful **information.** The CPU interprets and executes program instructions and communicates with the input, output, and storage devices. **Memory,** or **primary storage,** is related to the CPU but is separate and distinct from it. Memory holds the input data before processing and also holds the processed data after processing until the data is released to the output device.

- **Output,** which is raw data processed into usable information, is usually in the form of words, numbers, and graphics. Users can see output displayed on a **screen,** or **monitor,** and use **printers** to display output on paper.

- **Secondary storage** provides additional storage space separate from memory. The most common secondary storage devices are **magnetic disks.** Magnetic disks are **floppy disks (diskettes)**, usually 3.5 inches in diameter, or **hard disks.** Hard disks on large systems are contained in a disk pack. Hard disks hold more data and offer faster access than diskettes do. Disk data isread and written by **disk drives. Optical disk drives,** such as **CD-ROM**s and **DVD-ROM**s, use a laser beam to read large volumes of data. **Magnetic tape** comes on reels or in cartridges and is primarily used for backup purposes. Magnetic tape is mounted on a **tape drive.**

- **Peripheral equipment** includes all the input, output, and secondary storage devices that are attached to a computer. Some peripheral equipment may be built into one physical unit, as in many personal computers, or contained in separate units, as in many large computer systems. Often organizations use a **network** of personal computers, which enables users to operate independently or in cooperation with other computers, exchanging data and sharing resources. Such a setup is called a **local area network (LAN)**.

- Users who connect their computers via the phone lines must use a hardware device called a **modem** to reconcile the inherent differences between computers and the phone system. Individuals use networking for a variety of purposes, especially **electronic mail,** or **e-mail.**

- The **Internet,** sometimes called simply the Net, connects users worldwide. To access the Internet, a user's computer must connect to a type of computer called a server, which has special software called **TCP/IP** (for **Transmission Control Protocol/Internet Protocol**) that enables different types of computers to communicate with one another. The supplier of the server computer, often called an **Internet service provider** (**ISP**), charges a fee that either covers unlimited access or is based on the amount of service provided.

- With software called a **browser,** a user can manipulate a mouse to point and click on screen text or pictures to explore the Internet, particularly the **World Wide Web** (**WWW** or the **Web**), an Internet subset of text, images, and sounds linked together to enable users to view related topics. Each different location on the Web is called a **Web site** or, more commonly, a **site.** A **home page** is the main page of a Web site.

- Desktop computers are called **personal computers** (**PCs**), or **microcomputers. Workstations** combine the compactness of a desktop computer with power approaching that of a mainframe. Lower-priced PCs are sometimes called "cheap PCs." A **network computer** is a limited machine that has had difficulty competing with cheap PCs. In an office environment, a network computer is often referred to as a **thin client. Notebook** computers are small portable computers; somewhat larger, heavier versions are called **laptop** computers.

- **Personal digital assistants** (**PDAs**), also called pen-based computers, are handheld computers that enable users to keep track of appointments and other information. **Pocket PCs** add the capability of running stripped-down versions of some desktop software.

- **Midrange** computers (formerly referred to as **minicomputers**) are multi-user computers designed to serve the needs of medium-sized organizations.

- Large computers called **mainframes** are used by businesses such as banks, airlines, and manufacturers to process large amounts of data quickly. The most powerful and expensive computers are called **supercomputers.**

► Critical Thinking Questions

1. Try to think of two or three career fields in which computer literacy is not necessary. Share your list with another student and see if you both can come up with ways in which computer knowledge could be useful in those fields.

2. This chapter contains the statement, "most errors supposedly made by computers are really human errors." Think of some mistakes you have heard of that were blamed on a computer and discuss how those errors might have been caused instead by a human.

3. Do you think that computers make most peoples' jobs easier or more difficult? Explain your answer.

4. Are you considering a particular career? Discuss how computers are used, or could be used, in that field.

▶ STUDENT STUDY GUIDE

Multiple Choice

1. The central processing unit is an example of
   a. software
   b. hardware
   c. a program
   d. an output unit

2. Additional data and programs not being used by the processor are stored in
   a. secondary storage
   b. output units
   c. input units
   d. the CPU

3. Step-by-step instructions that run the computer are
   a. hardware
   b. CPUs
   c. documents
   d. software

4. Which of the following is not necessary to be considered computer literate?
   a. knowledge of what computers are and how they work
   b. the ability to write the instructions that direct a computer
   c. an awareness of the computer's importance, versatility, and pervasiveness in society
   d. the ability to interact with computers using simple applications

5. Desktop and personal computers are also known as
   a. microcomputers
   b. mainframes
   c. supercomputers
   d. peripheral equipment

6. The raw material to be processed by a computer is called
   a. a program
   b. software
   c. data
   d. information

7. A home page is part of a
   a. terminal
   b. Web site
   c. NC
   d. LAN

8. A bar code reader is an example of a(n)
   a. processing device
   b. input device
   c. storage device
   d. output device

9. The computer to which a user's computer connects to access the Internet is called a
   a. server
   b. supercomputer
   c. notebook
   d. PDA

10. Printers and screens are common forms of
    a. input units
    b. storage units
    c. output units
    d. processing units

11. The unit that transforms data into information is the
    a. CPU
    b. disk drive
    c. bar code reader
    d. wand reader

12. The device that reconciles the differences between computers and phones is the
    a. TCP/IP
    b. LAN
    c. wand reader
    d. modem

13. PDA stands for
    a. protocol disk administrator
    b. primary digital assistant
    c. processor digital add-on
    d. personal digital assistant

14. An example of peripheral equipment is the
    a. CPU
    b. printer
    c. spreadsheet
    d. microcomputer

15. A stripped-down computer that accesses resources on a network is called a
    a. desktop computer
    b. thin client
    c. supercomputer
    d. PDA

16. Software used to access the World Wide Web is called
    a. a browser
    b. Web
    c. a server
    d. e-mail

17. Which of the following is not one of the three fundamental characteristics of a computer?
    a. high cost
    c. reliability
    b. speed
    d. storage capability

18. Another name for memory is
    a. secondary storage
    b. primary storage
    c. disk storage
    d. tape storage

19. Which is not a computer classification?
    a. maxicomputer
    b. microcomputer
    c. notebook computer
    d. mainframe

20. A Web site may be found on the
    a. PDA
    b. WWW
    c. TCP/IP
    d. CPU

21. Which of the following is an input device that, when moved by the user on a flat surface, causes a pointer on the screen to move accordingly?
    a. wand reader
    b. bar code reader
    c. keyboard
    d. mouse

22. Computer users who are not computer professionals are sometimes called
    a. librarians
    b. information officers
    c. peripheral users
    d. end-users

23. The most powerful computers are
    a. super PCs
    b. supermainframes
    c. supercomputers
    d. workstations

24. Raw data is processed by the computer into
    a. number sheets
    b. paragraphs
    c. updates
    d. information

25. Laser beam technology is used for
    a. terminals
    b. keyboards
    c. optical disks
    d. magnetic tape

True/False

T F   1. The processor is also called the central processing unit, or CPU.

T F   2. Secondary storage units contain the instructions and data to be used immediately by the processor.

T F   3. A home page is the main page of a Web site.

T F   4. Two secondary storage media are magnetic disks and magnetic tape.

T F   5. A diskette holds more data than a hard disk does.

T F   6. Many PDAs accept handwritten data on a screen.

T F   7. The most powerful personal computers are known as supercomputers.

T F   8. An Internet service provider provides Internet connections to its customers.

T F   9. Processed data is called information.

T F 10. The Internet is a subset of the World Wide Web.

T F 11. A modem is the hardware device that is the go-between for computers and telephones.

T F 12. Secondary storage is another name for memory.

T F 13. The most powerful personal computer is the workstation.

T F 14. TCP/IP is hardware that connects to the Internet.

T F 15. These computers are arranged from least powerful to most powerful: microcomputer, midrange computer, mainframe, supercomputer.

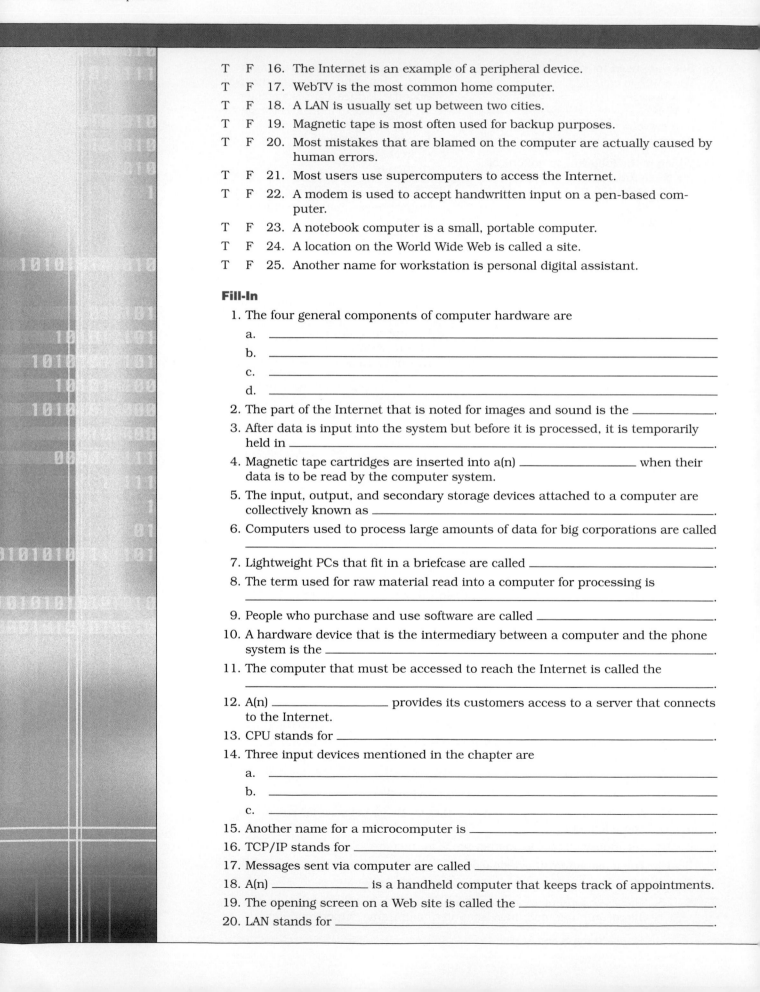

T F 16. The Internet is an example of a peripheral device.

T F 17. WebTV is the most common home computer.

T F 18. A LAN is usually set up between two cities.

T F 19. Magnetic tape is most often used for backup purposes.

T F 20. Most mistakes that are blamed on the computer are actually caused by human errors.

T F 21. Most users use supercomputers to access the Internet.

T F 22. A modem is used to accept handwritten input on a pen-based computer.

T F 23. A notebook computer is a small, portable computer.

T F 24. A location on the World Wide Web is called a site.

T F 25. Another name for workstation is personal digital assistant.

Fill-In

1. The four general components of computer hardware are

   a. _____

   b. _____

   c. _____

   d. _____

2. The part of the Internet that is noted for images and sound is the _____.

3. After data is input into the system but before it is processed, it is temporarily held in _____.

4. Magnetic tape cartridges are inserted into a(n) _____ when their data is to be read by the computer system.

5. The input, output, and secondary storage devices attached to a computer are collectively known as _____.

6. Computers used to process large amounts of data for big corporations are called _____

7. Lightweight PCs that fit in a briefcase are called _____.

8. The term used for raw material read into a computer for processing is _____

9. People who purchase and use software are called _____.

10. A hardware device that is the intermediary between a computer and the phone system is the _____.

11. The computer that must be accessed to reach the Internet is called the _____

12. A(n) _____ provides its customers access to a server that connects to the Internet.

13. CPU stands for _____.

14. Three input devices mentioned in the chapter are

    a. _____

    b. _____

    c. _____

15. Another name for a microcomputer is _____.

16. TCP/IP stands for _____.

17. Messages sent via computer are called _____.

18. A(n) _____ is a handheld computer that keeps track of appointments.

19. The opening screen on a Web site is called the _____.

20. LAN stands for _____.

◀ ANSWERS

Multiple Choice

1. b	8. b	15. b	22. d
2. a	9. a	16. a	23. c
3. d	10. c	17. a	24. d
4. b	11. a	18. b	25. c
5. a	12. d	19. a	
6. c	13. d	20. b	
7. b	14. b	21. d	

True/False

1. T	8. T	15. T	22. F
2. F	9. T	16. F	23. T
3. T	10. F	17. F	24. T
4. T	11. T	18. F	25. F
5. F	12. F	19. T	
6. T	13. T	20. T	
7. F	14. F	21. F	

Fill-In

1. a. input units
   b. processor
   c. output units
   d. storage units
2. World Wide Web (or just the Web)
3. memory (or primary storage)
4. tape drive
5. peripheral equipment
6. mainframes
7. notebook computers
8. data
9. users, or end-users
10. modem
11. server
12. Internet service provider, or ISP
13. central processing unit
14. keyboard, mouse, wand reader, or bar code reader
15. personal computer (or home computer)
16. Transmission Control Protocol/Internet Protocol
17. electronic mail (or e-mail)
18. personal digital assistant, or PDA
19. home page
20. local area network

Planet Internet

What Is It All About?

First, just what is the Internet?

The Internet is a huge network made up from a loosely organized global collection of other networks. It's millions of computers. It's technology, protocols, software, servers, routers, and human organizations. This text explains a lot of that. But that's not how most citizens of Planet Internet view the Internet most of the time.

For anyone with a computer and appropriate software today, the "Net" represents a source of news, images, conversation, shopping, music, video, entertainment, and controversy. When you connect your personal computer to another computer—a "server"—across the Internet, you're part of the largest and least-regulated information exchange on the planet.

Why is the Internet so important?

The Internet is powerful, it's pervasive, and it's still evolving.

You can reach more information from your computer desktop than is contained in most libraries. Increasingly, the Internet is like television—it's everywhere and it's always on. And, like TV, the ready access to the Internet afforded by personal computers, Internet appliances, shopping mall kiosks, palm-tops, and mobile phones is already changing our lives and our lifestyles.

Maybe the most exciting thing about the Internet is that it is always changing. Of course, the technology we use to get to the Net improves at an amazing pace, but perhaps more dramatic is the incidence of new cultural, legal, and ethical issues posed by the quick, cheap, and unchecked exchange of ideas across traditional boundaries. Issues of intellectual property, free speech, individual rights, contracts, liability, morality, and taste abound on the Net.

When you use the Net; you enjoy; you learn; and you confront new, technology-driven variants of age-old problems. What could be more exciting than that?

Why should I use the Internet?

The one answer that applies to everyone is that you don't dare risk being left behind. Futurists predict that networking of some kind will be as necessary to work and to living as technologies such as the telephone or computers. After that, the answer to this question depends on you. Are you curious? Would you like to connect with people around the world? Would you like an amazing library at your finger-

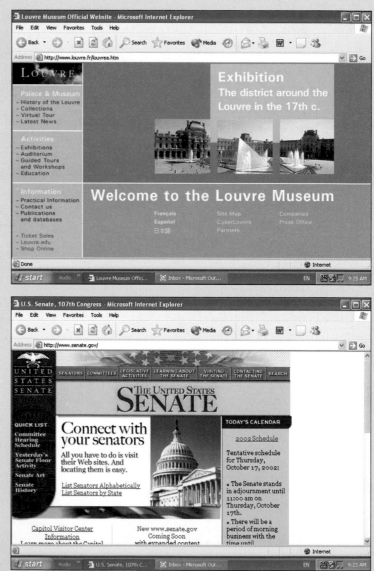

tips? Would you like the convenience of finding out about almost anything current—political events, the weather, the score of your favorite team's game, the verdict of a court case—by typing at the keyboard? Do you plan to travel abroad in the near future? The Internet offers informative sites describing tourist attractions, such as the Louvre site shown here. Need some information on what your U.S. senators are up to? The Senate site shown here is a good place to begin.

Is this going to cost money?

Maybe. Free Internet access is common in schools and libraries and other government organizations. Your employer may offer free access. If you want to hook up from your own personal computer, the required software is probably free, but you will have to pay some sort of monthly charge to the company providing the physical connection.

Ok, how can I be an informed consumer of the Internet?

You can learn, you can experiment, and you can think critically.

This text is one way of learning about the Internet. The Planet Internet features that follow this one each address a specific aspect of the Internet. You can learn about e-shopping, on-line chats, security and hackers, computer games and entertainment, Web programming languages, privacy, and other topics in these features.

There's nothing that helps you learn better than trying things out yourself. Use the links provided in this section and in many other places in the text to explore the Web. If you want an easy start, try the structured activities at the end of each Planet Internet. If you're feeling more adventurous, use the free-form activities. If you already know your way around portions of the Net, you may enjoy the challenge of the advanced activities.

Finally, you can apply what you already know, what you learn here, and your own culture and beliefs to critically examine what goes on in Planet Internet. Sure, the Internet is about technology, but it's also about people and ideas. As you learn more about how things are on the Net, ask yourself, "Is this how things should be?" Some of the Focus on Ethics features in each chapter can help highlight the implications of the Net for your beliefs and your ideals.

Welcome to Planet Internet. Enjoy.

Internet Exercises:
At the end of the Planet Internets, three exercises are suggested. The first exercise is structured since it's based on using links provided at the publisher's Web site. Use the URL supplied here to get started. If you are feeling a little daring, try the free-form exercise, where we make suggestions but no guarantees. If you are fairly familiar with the Web, try the advanced exercise.

1. **Structured exercise.** Begin by browsing to the Web site for this text at http://www.prenhall.com/capron. What information and assistance are offered on these pages? Examine the materials on the Web site for at least two chapters. First, find a chapter topic with which you are reasonably familiar. Then look at the study materials available for a chapter addressing a topic that is mostly new to you. Try to list two features or links you think you will find useful and why.

2. **Free-form exercise.** What on-line assistance is available to you from your school, your lab, or your instructor? Does your institution provide Internet access as part of your student fees? If so, what type of access and support does your school provide? Does your instructor have a Web site? If so, what resources are available (e.g., syllabus, class notes, FAQs, links to other sites)? Do you have access to a lab where you can use the types of software discussed in your text? Be sure to ask your instructor if you have difficulty finding the answers to these questions.

3. **Advanced exercise.** Investigate and speculate on the future of Internet access. What Internet-capable devices are available now? What new devices are being planned for the future? Which devices would be most relevant to a typical student at your school? Why? You may find it helpful to begin with http://www.prenhall.com/capron and follow the links to TechTV and on-line technology publications such as Salon, Wired, Slashdot, and Forbes to begin your research.

Applications Software:
Getting the Work Done

CHAPTER 2

LEARNING OBJECTIVES

Distinguish between operating systems and applications software

List the various methods by which individuals and businesses acquire software

List and briefly describe various types of task-oriented software

Identify the kinds of software that are available for both large and small businesses

Discuss ethical issues associated with software

Describe the functions of various computer professionals

After her first year in college, Joan Alexander got a summer job in the resort town of Friday Harbor. She waited tables for both the noon and evening shifts at a small family-owned restaurant. Her wages were supplemented by generous tips from tourists. An accounting major, Joan would have preferred a job in a business office, but at least her summer income would make a significant dent in her upcoming tuition.

As it turned out, Joan's summer was more valuable than she expected. When the owners learned that Joan had taken introductory computer and accounting classes during her first two semesters, they asked her whether she would be willing to help them out in the office for a few hours several mornings a week. She readily agreed, figuring not only that the extra money would come in handy, but also that the experience would look good on her résumé.

Her first project was to design a "Specials of the Day" menu insert. By studying the software manuals and Help files, she learned how to add graphics, color, and attractive typefaces (fonts) to the basic typed information, resulting in an eye-catching insert design. The owners were able to easily enter the current specials each morning and print the inserts for lunch and dinner on their ink-jet printer.

Joan completed several other office projects that summer, but the one of which she was proudest was a detailed analysis of the cost to produce each of the restaurant's entrées. She used spreadsheet software to list the cost and amount of the basic ingredients in each entrée, along with its preparation time. She used the built-in charting feature to develop a chart that visually compared each menu item's cost with its price. The owners could easily see which dishes were most profitable and adjust prices as necessary. What's more, as ingredient costs changed, simple numeric entries on the spreadsheet automatically updated the charts, allowing the owners to decide quickly if price changes were necessary.

▶ APPLICATIONS SOFTWARE: GETTING THE WORK DONE

When people think about computers, they usually think about machines. The tapping on the keyboard, the rumble of whirling disk drives, the changing flashes of color on a computer screen—these are the attention getters. However, it is really the software—the planned, step-by-step set of instructions required to turn data into information—that makes a computer useful.

Generally speaking, software can be categorized as systems software or applications software. Chapter 3, "Operating Systems: Software in the Background," deals with systems software. This chapter covers **applications software**, software that users apply to real-world tasks. It can be used to solve a particular problem or to perform a specific task: to keep track of store inventory, design a car engine, draft the minutes of the PTA meeting, or play a game of solitaire. We will discuss software that individuals use to accomplish personal tasks and use to run businesses.

Applications Software

Applications software may be either custom or packaged. Many large organizations pay **computer programmers**—people who design, write, test, and implement software—to write **custom software** that is specifically tailored to the organization's needs. Custom software for the tasks of a large organization may be extremely complex and take a lot of time—possibly years—to write.

The average person is most likely to deal with software for personal computers, called packaged software or commercial software. This software is packaged in a container of some sort, usually a box or folder, and is sold in stores or through catalogs or Web sites. Some commercial software is available for downloading (for a fee, of course) on the Internet. Packaged software for personal computers often comes in a box that is as colorful as that of a board game. Inside the box you will find one or more CDs or DVDs holding the software and, usually, an instruction manual, also referred to as **documentation** (Figure 2-1). Note, however, that some packaged software has little written documentation; the information about the software is mostly stored on CD or DVD with the software for handy future reference. Documentation for software downloaded on the Internet is usually contained in an accompanying file.

Large organizations also purchase and use an assortment of commercial software. They may buy some of the same software that you might buy, although they probably buy it from a distributor or directly from the publisher. They also are likely to consider purchasing software for major applications, such as payroll and personnel management. This software is purchased directly from the software publisher for tens, or even hundreds, of thousands of dollars. The factors that determine whether an organization buys or custom-makes its software are discussed in Chapter 14, "Systems Analysis and Design: The Big Picture."

Although it is not possible to tell you how to use a specific software package, in general you begin by installing the software on your computer. This usually involves inserting the CD-ROM or DVD-ROM into the drive, then following the instructions that appear on your screen. Complex packages, such as a full-featured database

◀ **F I G U R E 2-1**

Packaged software. Each of the colorful software packages shown here includes one or more disks containing the software and at least a minimal instruction manual, or documentation, describing how to install and use the software.

system or word processor, often provide numerous installation options for advanced users. Luckily, there is almost always a standard installation that the beginner can choose. During installation the setup process copies some or all of the new software to the hard disk drive. Some software may require the CD-ROM to be in the drive whenever the software is used. After the software is installed, you can click its icon (its picture image) on the screen, select it from a menu, or type an instruction (command) to get the program started.

A great assortment of software is available to help you with a variety of tasks, such as writing papers, preparing budgets, storing and retrieving information, drawing graphs, playing games, and much more. This wonderful array of software is what makes computers so useful.

Most personal computer software is designed to be user-friendly. The term "user-friendly" has become a cliché, but it still conveys meaning. It usually means that the software is supposed to be easy—perhaps even intuitive—for a beginner to use, or that the software can be used with a minimum of training and documentation.

But What Would I Use It For?

New computer owners soon discover a little secret: The box is only the beginning. Although they may have agonized for months over their hardware choice, they are often uncertain as to how to proceed when purchasing software. The most common pattern for a new user is to start out with some standard software packages, such as word processing and other basic applications that are preinstalled by the computer manufacturer. Later, the user may add applications after becoming aware of what software is available. The needs of different people will be met with different software. Here are two real-life scenarios.

Lisa Macon is a private detective who, using a computer, runs her business from her home. Her computer came with word-processing software plus some CD-ROMs holding an encyclopedia, a "family doctor" reference program, and several games. Lisa's primary interest in the software was focused on business information and certain public files on the Internet. She selected an Internet service provider and used software supplied by the provider. She also prepared her income taxes using a question-and-answer tax preparation program (Figure 2-2).

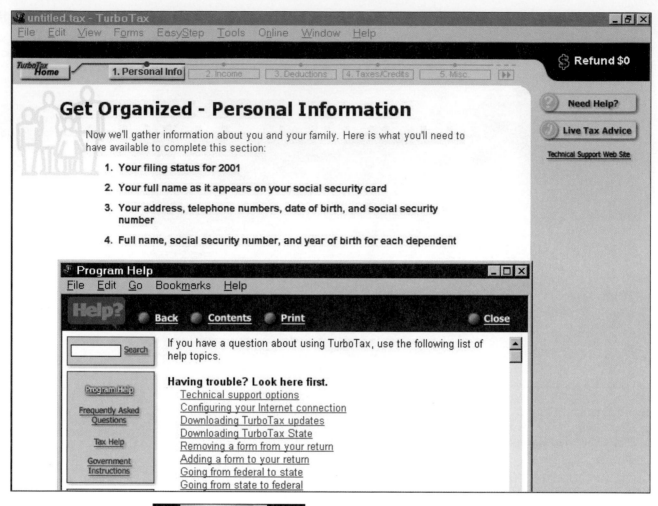

FIGURE 2-2

Tax preparation software. This software simplifies the complex process of preparing income tax returns.

Over the next year, Lisa purchased other software that was unrelated to business applications: software to help her plan and record her aerobic workouts, a program to help her daughter learn to play the guitar, and a combination game/book called Happy and Max for her six-year-old.

As a second example, consider Andrew Eisler, whose first job as an apprentice carpenter did not involve computers. But Andrew made a computer one of his first acquisitions. He subsequently purchased various software: software containing an atlas and quotations; an on-screen version of The Far Side calendar; and an all-in-one package that included software for a personal phone book, home budget planning, and home repair. But he eventually focused on the large National Geographic map images available on CD-ROM (Figure 2-3).

The point of these stories is that different people want different software applications. You have only to stroll through a few aisles of software racks to appreciate the variety of software available. Whether you want to learn to type, tour a museum, build a deck, or perhaps try such crazy-but-real titles as Internet for Cats or the sci-fi thriller called I Have No Mouth, and I Must Scream, someone offers the software.

Acquiring Software

Sometimes software is free. Software is called **freeware** if its author chooses to provide it free to all. However, freeware is copyrighted: that is, the author retains legal

▲ **F I G U R E 2-3**

Images from CD-ROM software. These images are from a National Geographic CD-ROM of maps that have been featured in the magazine.

ownership and may place restrictions on its use. Software that is not copyrighted is called **public domain software** and may be used, or even altered, without restriction. Software developed by universities and research institutions using government grants is usually in the public domain.

Open-source software is a variation of freeware. A freeware program is normally distributed in a machine-readable format that is unreadable by humans. You can use it, but even if you know how to write programs, you can't make changes to it. The developers of open-source software, however, make the source code available, which means that programmers can understand how it works and modify it. When many programmers can examine the source code, bugs are found quickly and improvements made. More and more commercial-quality software is being made available under the open-source concept, especially software designed to run under the Linux operating system.

Shareware is a category of software that is often confused with freeware. Like freeware, it is freely distributed, but only for a trial period. The understanding is that if you like it enough to continue using it, you will pay a nominal fee to register it with the author. Many authors add incentives such as free documentation, support, and/or updates to encourage people to register.

The software that people use most often is packaged software, sometimes called *commercial software,* such as word-processing or spreadsheet software. This type of software is usually copyrighted and costs more than shareware. You must not copy commercial software without permission from the manufacturer. In fact, software manufacturers often complain of **software piracy**, the making of illegal copies of commercial software. Microsoft and other manufacturers pursue violators to the full extent of the law.

What is the best way to purchase commercial software? The small retail software store has all but disappeared because the price of software has declined too much to provide an acceptable profit margin. So software has moved to the warehouse stores and mail-order houses, each with thousands of software titles. College students have another option: their college bookstore. To encourage students to become familiar with their products, many software publishers make their most popular products available through college bookstores at deep discounts.

An organization, in contrast to individual users, must take a different approach in acquiring software. Most organizations—such as businesses, governments, and non-profit agencies—have computers, and their users need software. Although software publishers' policies vary, several options are usually available. If an organization is going to install the software on individual computers, it might be able to arrange a volume discount for the required number of packages. Alternatively, the organization

---

FOCUS ON ETHICS   Any Guarantees?

Most software packages are covered by "shrink-wrap licenses." The license information is visible through the shrink-wrap packaging and the purchaser is supposed to read it before opening. The act of opening the package signifies the user's acceptance of the terms of the license. Although many packages display the license agreement during installation and require the user to check a box to signify acceptance, by that time it's too late to change your mind. Most vendors will not accept returns of opened software. These licenses contain language shielding the vendor from all claims other than those arising from physical defects in the CD. Recently, Congress and the courts have moved to make these licenses more enforceable and to allow software

manufacturers the right to change the terms of the license after purchase.

Read the shrink-wrap license that came with some software that you or your school purchased. What remedies does the license give you if the product doesn't work or if it damages your computer? Now read the warranty from an inexpensive electronic device, say a VCR, CD player, or TV. What similarities and differences do you see?

Software corporations argue that they need the protective terms of the shrink-wrap licenses to shield them from frivolous lawsuits. Consumer advocates assert that consumers need recourse if the product doesn't work as advertised. How would you balance these competing claims?

could purchase a **site license**, which allows the software to be installed either on all its computers or on a specific number of computers, depending on the license terms. The customer agrees to keep track of who uses the software and takes responsibility for copying and distributing the software and manuals to its own personnel. Incidentally, if you work for a large corporation, check with your employer before you buy a copy of the expensive software you use at the office. Under some license agreements, employees are allowed to use the same software at home.

Organizations with local area networks (LANs) often install a network version of widely used software, such as word processing, on the network's server computer. Thus the software is available to users connected to the network without the necessity of installing the software on each user's computer. In this case, the license fee may be based on the total number of users on the network or may provide for a maximum number of concurrent users.

Another software movement is gaining in popularity: **electronic software distribution**. Never mind the trip to the store. You can get freeware, shareware, and even commercial software from the Internet. One common scenario is to download copyrighted software free from the manufacturer for a trial period. When you use the software, you are encouraged to go back online and register (pay with a credit card); unregistered software often disables itself automatically after a given time period, such as 21 days. In the not-so-distant future, users will not need to purchase software, but will be able to download it temporarily from a vendor via the Internet for a per-use rental fee.

Application service providers provide an alternative method of delivering applications to businesses via the Internet. An **application service provider (ASP)** is a company that sets up and maintains application software on its own systems and makes the software available to its customers over the Internet. By using an ASP for its complex applications, a business can avoid the expenses of installing and maintaining those applications on its own system. According to some estimates, the cost of renting a major enterprise-wide application, such as a human resources package, can be as much as 30 percent less than the cost of buying, deploying, and supporting it in-house.

► SOME TASK-ORIENTED SOFTWARE

Most users, whether at home or in business, are drawn to task-oriented software, sometimes called productivity software, that can make their work faster and their lives easier. The major categories of task-oriented software are word processing (including desktop publishing), spreadsheets, database management, graphics, and communications. Office suites and integrated packages offer some combination of these categories in a single package. A brief description of each category follows. Later chapters discuss each category in detail.

Word Processing/Desktop Publishing

Word processing is the most widely used personal computer software. Business people use word processing for memos, reports, correspondence, minutes of meetings, and anything else that someone can think of to type. Users in a home environment type term papers, letters, journals, movie logs, and much more. Word processing software lets you create, edit, format, store, and print text and graphics in one document. Because you can store the memo or document you typed on disk, you can retrieve it another time, change it, reprint it, or do whatever you like with it. Unchanged parts of the stored document do not need to be retyped; the whole revised document can be reprinted as though new.

As the number of features in word-processing packages has grown, word processing has crossed the border into desktop publishing territory. **Desktop publishing** packages are usually better than word-processing packages at meeting high-level

Disney Magic

New users sometimes worry that a computer will be used mostly for games. Surveys show that about 70 percent of personal computer users happily admit that they play games—at least a little—almost daily. In fact, entertainment is a perfectly valid use of a personal computer in the home. But the entertainment need not be limited to games. There are many types of entertainment packages.

Here is an example: Disney's Magic Artist Studio software lets young children have fun coloring Disney images and learn at the same time. For instance, children can use a mouse to select images and apply different tools, such as pen, paintbrush, chalk, and spray paint, to color the image. They can also resize, flip, and rotate images. They can combine images with backgrounds and even, if they wish, add music.

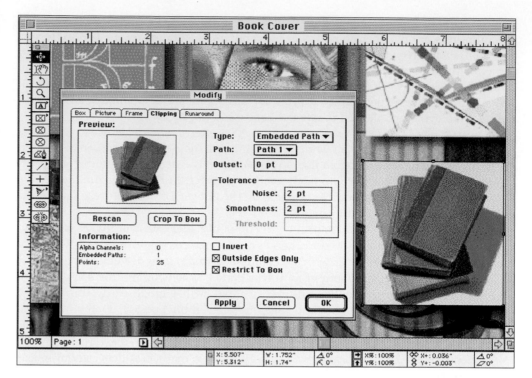

The Killer App

In computing, the term "killer app," short for "killer application," refers to an application that is so compelling that everyone must have the underlying technology so that they can use the application. The first electronic spreadsheet program, named VisiCalc, was the first killer app for the microcomputer. Almost immediately, what had been viewed as a toy was now a must-have for everyone whose job required manipulating numbers. By one estimate in 1981, over one half of all Apple IIs sold between 1979 and 1981 were purchased solely to run VisiCalc.

One other example of a killer app is the combination of the browser with the World Wide Web. Until these appeared in the early 1990s, Internet use was mostly limited to scientists, researchers, and computer geeks using text-based communications. Almost everyone is familiar with what has happened with the Internet since then.

publishing needs, especially when it comes to page layout and color reproduction. Many magazines and newspapers today rely heavily on desktop publishing software (Figure 2-4). Businesses use it to produce professional-looking newsletters, reports, and brochures—both to improve internal communication and to make a better impression on the outside world.

Electronic Spreadsheets

Spreadsheets, made up of columns and rows of numbers, have been used as business tools for centuries (Figure 2-5). A manual spreadsheet can be tedious to prepare, and when there are changes, many calculations may need to be redone. An **electronic spreadsheet** is still a spreadsheet, but the computer does the work. In particular, spreadsheet software automatically recalculates the results when a number is changed. For example, if a spreadsheet calculates the distance based on rate and time, a change in the rate triggers a new calculation so that the distance changes too. This capability lets business people try different combinations of numbers and obtain the results quickly. The ability to ask, "**What if . . . ?**" and then immediately see the results on the computer before actually committing resources helps business people make better, faster decisions.

What about spreadsheet software for the user at home? The ability to enter combinations of numbers in a meaningful way, such as different combinations of down payments and interest rates for the purchase of a home, gives users a financial view that they could not readily produce on their own. Users at home employ spreadsheets for everything from preparing budgets to deciding whether to take a new job to tracking their progress at the gym.

Database Management

Software used for **database management**—the management of a collection of interrelated facts—handles data in several ways. The software can store data, update it, manipulate it, retrieve it, report it in a variety of views, and print it in many forms. By the time the data is in the reporting stage (given to a user in a useful form) it has

EXPENSES	JANUARY	FEBRUARY	MARCH	APRIL	TOTAL
RENT	425.00	425.00	425.00	425.00	1700.00
PHONE	22.50	31.25	17.00	35.75	106.50
CLOTHES	110.00	135.00	156.00	91.00	492.00
FOOD	280.00	250.00	250.00	300.00	1080.00
HEAT	80.00	50.00	24.00	95.00	249.00
ELECTRICITY	35.75	40.50	45.00	36.50	157.75
WATER	10.00	11.00	11.00	10.50	42.50
CAR INSURANCE	75.00	75.00	75.00	75.00	300.00
ENTERTAINMENT	150.00	125.00	140.00	175.00	590.00
TOTAL	1188.25	1142.75	1143.00	1243.75	4717.75

(a)

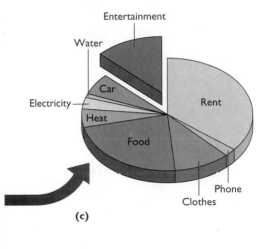

(b)

(c)

▲ FIGURE 2-5

A simple expense spreadsheet. (a) This paper-and-pencil expense sheet is a typical spreadsheet of rows and columns. You have to do the calculations to fill in the totals. (b) This screen shows the same information on a computer spreadsheet program, which does the calculations for you. (c) The spreadsheet program can also present the expenses graphically in the form of a pie chart.

become information. A concert promoter, for example, can store and change data about upcoming concert dates, seating, ticket prices, and sales. After this is done, the promoter can use the software to retrieve information, such as the number of tickets sold in each price range or the percentage of tickets sold on the day of the concert.

Database software can be useful for anyone who must keep track of a large number of related facts. Consider crime detection, which involves a process of elimination, a tedious task. Tedious work, however, is often the kind the computer does best. Once data is entered into a database, searching by computer is possible. Consider these examples: Which criminals use a particular mode of operation? Which criminals are associates of this suspect? Does license plate number AXB221 refer to a stolen car? One particularly successful crime detection database application is a fingerprint-matching system, which can match crime-scene fingerprints with computer-stored fingerprints (Figure 2-6).

Home users can apply database software to any situation in which they want to retrieve stored data in a variety of ways. For example, one hobbyist stores data about

► FIGURE 2-6

Crime detection.
Fingerprint-matching systems can match crime-scene fingerprints with fingerprints stored in a computerized database.

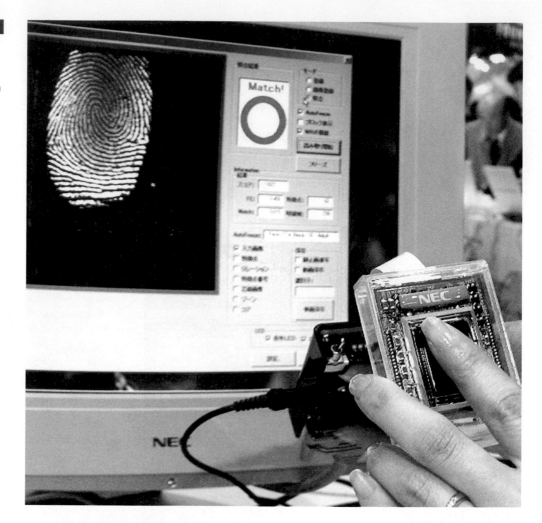

► FIGURE 2-7

Presentations. Presentation graphics packages enable business people to develop professional-looking "slide show" presentations containing high-quality graphics, audio, and video.

her coin collection. She can retrieve information from the coin database by country, date, value, or size. Another user, an amateur genealogist, stores data on the lives and relationships of hundreds of ancestors. He can easily retrieve biographical data by branch of the family tree, country of birth, or any other criterion.

Graphics

It might seem unnecessary to show **graphics** to business people when standard computer printouts of numbers are readily available. However, graphs, maps, and charts can help people compare data, spot trends more easily, and make decisions more quickly. In addition, visual information is usually more compelling than a page of numbers. **Presentation graphics** packages enable business people to develop professional-looking "slide show" presentations containing high-quality graphics, audio, and video (Figure 2-7). A salesperson attempting to sell a new piece of machinery to a factory manager might list the features of the product using text displays, show cost/benefit projections on charts, include a video clip of the product in operation, and present audio/video testimonials from satisfied customers.

The most pleasing use of graphics software is the work produced by **graphic artists**, people who have both artistic ability and the skills to use sophisticated graphics software to express their ideas. Artists use software as a tool of their craft to produce stunning computer art.

Communications

From the viewpoint of an individual with a personal computer at home, **communications** means—in simple terms—that he or she can hook the computer up to a phone line or cable and communicate with the computer at the office, access data stored in another computer in another location, or send a message to a friend or family member. The most likely way for such a user to connect to others is via the Internet. A user needs software called a **browser** to access Web sites and other parts of the Internet (Figure 2-8). A browser may be a stand-alone software package or it may be

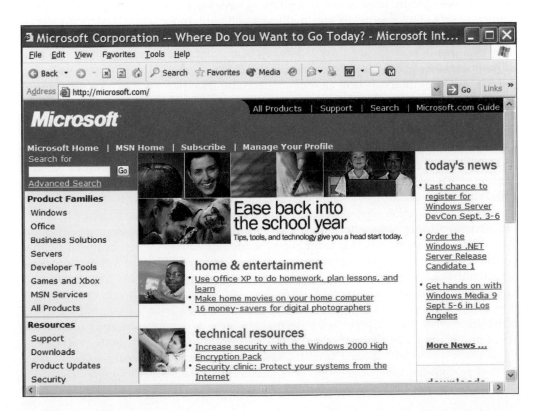

◄ **F I G U R E 2-8**

An Internet browser. This screen shows Microsoft's home page using Microsoft's Internet Explorer browser.

included as part of other software offerings. Internet access is described in more detail in later chapters.

Although the Internet is heavily used by both individuals and businesses, organizations—mostly business, government, and academic organizations—were major users of communications software long before the Internet was in the mainstream. Consider weather forecasting. Some businesses, such as agriculture, amusement parks, and ski areas, are so dependent on the weather that they need constantly updated information. Various services offer analysis of live weather data, including air pressure, fog, rain, and wind direction and speed.

For a totally different type of communications application, consider the stock exchange. Stock portfolios can be managed by software that takes quotations over communication lines directly from established market monitors, such as Dow Jones. The software keeps records and offers quick and accurate investment advice. And, of course, the stock exchange itself is a veritable beehive of computers, all communicating with one another and with remote computers that can provide current information.

Personal Information Managers

Personal Information Managers (**PIM**s) are programs that provide the functions necessary for you to keep track of all the activities in your busy life. Features vary according to the specific product, but typically include an appointment calendar, address book, task manager, notepad, and calculator. These features are all integrated; you can get a display of your daily, weekly, or monthly calendar showing all meetings and the contact information for attendees, a list of tasks with due dates and notes you've made about those tasks, or even have your system notify you with an audible alarm shortly before scheduled meetings.

Most handheld computers include many of the same PIM functions and can be synchronized with your PC software so that both contain the same information.

Office Suites

Because most people need to use the kinds of task-oriented software just described, some choose to buy a **suite**—a group of basic software applications designed to work together. The phrase "work together" is the key. If you buy word-processing software from one manufacturer and a spreadsheet package from another, you may run into difficulties transferring data from one to the other. Using suite software, however, means that you can easily build a spreadsheet and then move it into a report you are preparing using word processing. Another advantage of suites is that the various applications have the same "look and feel"—the same buttons, menus, and overall appearance. Once you learn one application, the rest are easy. Finally, the cost of a suite is much less than the combined costs of the individual packages.

Many inexpensive personal computers come with an **integrated application** that combines basic word-processing, spreadsheet, and graphics capabilities in a single program. Microsoft Works is the best-known example of this type of software. An integrated program is easier to learn and use than a suite, but even moderately sophisticated users may quickly outgrow its limitations. The next step up, whether you are a professional working from home, a small business owner, or just a hobbyist, includes suites containing more sophisticated versions of these applications and additional software types, such as database management and Web page design. In fact, one of the most common office applications of suites is mail merge, in which certain names and addresses from a database are used on letters prepared by using word processing. Two or three software makers have dominated the suite market for years and continue to offer software upgrades—newer, presumably better versions.

Software makers have long tried to outdo one another by offering software with myriad seldom-used features—a process often referred to as feature creep. However, they have recently begun to take a different approach. Vendors now focus on ease of use and on throwing in nifty programs, such as personal time organizers, to-do list makers, e-mail programs, and—best of all—access to the Internet.

The do-everything programs, of course, need significant amounts of memory and also require a lot of disk space; so be sure that the requirements listed on the software box fit your hardware. The good news, however, is that competition continues to heat up the price wars, causing the prices of these packages to fall.

▶ BUSINESS SOFTWARE

We have already mentioned that many large organizations often hire their own programmers to write custom software. The Boeing Company, for example, will not find software to plan the electrical wiring of an airplane among off-the-rack packages. However, not all a company's software need be custom-made. Many companies use standard packages for standard tasks, such as payroll and accounts receivable. Furthermore, some software vendors specialize in a certain "vertical" slice of the business community, serving similar customers, such as plumbers or accountants.

Vertical Market Software

Software that is written especially for a particular type of business, such as a dentist's office or a drugstore, is called **vertical market software**. This user-oriented software usually presents options with a series of easy-to-follow screens that minimize the training needed. Often, the vendor includes the software as part of a complete package that also includes hardware, installation, training, and support. This all-in-one approach appeals to business owners who often have limited computer expertise.

An auto-repair shop is a good example of a business that can make use of vertical market software. Designed in conjunction with people who understand the auto-repair business, the comprehensive software for an auto-repair shop can prepare work orders, process sales transactions, produce invoices, evaluate sales and profits, track parts inventories, print reorder reports, and update the customer mailing list.

GETTING PRACTICAL | Computer User Groups

You have started your own business and even have a computer to keep track of things. The knowledge you have from your computer classes sustains you, but you wish you had some ongoing source for help and even enrichment. Unfortunately, the very people who could be helped the most—new users—often don't know that user groups exist. User groups are run by volunteers with minimum funds and thus have little money to advertise.

There are hundreds of user groups; some focus on a particular type of computer, such as the Apple Macintosh, or a particular software package, such as Microsoft Excel, and some cover all aspects of computing. Typically, a group meets once a month to share ideas and knowledge and also publishes a newsletter. In addition, many general computing groups have subgroups called special interest groups (SIGs) that focus on a single topic, such as graphics or a particular software package.

Some people have the impression that user groups are for the die-hard techie, but anyone is welcome to join. Just show up at a meeting, pay your (nominal) dues, and you belong. Interested? You can probably find out about local user groups at local computer stores or the library, or you can check the Web. The Association of Personal Computers User Groups (APCUG) maintains a directory of worldwide user groups on its Web site: http://www.apcug.org

Software for Workgroups

If you work on a project with a group of people, it is likely that you use software especially made for that scenario. **Groupware**, also called **collaborative software**, can be defined generally as any kind of software that lets a group of people share information or track information together. Using that general definition, some people might say that e-mail is a form of groupware. But simply sending data back and forth by e-mail has inherent limitations for collaboration, the most obvious being confusion if there are more than two group members. To work together effectively on a project, the data being used must be in a central place that can be accessed and changed by anyone working on the project. That central place is a database, or databases, on disk. Having the data in one place eliminates the old problem of having separate and possibly different versions of the same project.

A popular groupware package called Notes combines e-mail, networking, scheduling, and database technology (Figure 2-9). Using such groupware, business people can work with one another and share knowledge or expertise unbounded by factors such as distance or time zone differences. Notes can be installed on all computers on the network.

Groupware is most often used by a team for a specific project. A classic example is a bid prepared by Price Waterhouse, an accounting firm, for a consulting contract. They had just a few days to put together a complex proposal, and the four people who needed to write it were in three different states. They were able to work together using their computers and Notes which permitted a four-way dialog on-screen. They also extracted key components of the proposal from existing company databases, including the résumés of company experts, and borrowed passages from similar successful proposals.

Getting Software Help at Work: The Help Desk

More often than not, a worker in an office has a computer on his or her desk. It is just a matter of time until that user needs help. If personal computer users compared notes, they would probably find that their experiences are similar. The experience of

► F I G U R E 2-9

Notes. These screens are from a groupware package called Notes. Groupware lets workers use the computer to collaborate on a project.

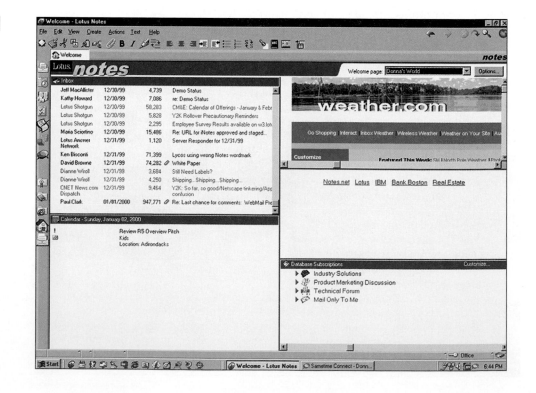

budget analyst Bonnie Campassi is typical. She was given her own personal computer, so that she could analyze financial data. She learned to use a popular spreadsheet program. She soon thought about branching out with other software products. She wanted a statistics software package, but was not sure which one was appropriate or how to get it. She saw that a colleague was using a database management program, but had no idea how to use it herself. Most of all, Bonnie believed that her productivity would increase significantly if she knew how to use the software to access certain data in the corporate data files.

The company information center, often called simply the **help desk**, is one solution to these kinds of needs. Although no two centers are alike, all information centers are devoted to giving users service. Help desk staff usually offer assistance with software selection, software training, and, if appropriate, access to corporate computer systems. They might also perform software and hardware installation and updating, as well as troubleshooting services when problems arise.

Software for a Small Business

Suppose that, as a fledgling entrepreneur with some computer savvy, your ambition is to be as competitive as one personal computer will let you be. You are not alone. Two interesting statistics are that more than half of U.S. workers would like to own their own businesses and that the number of home-office workers is increasing by 5 percent a year. Savvy entrepreneurs realize that a computer is a major asset in running the business, even at the start. The software industry has responded to this need with various packages that come under the generic heading of **small office/ home office**, or **SOHO** for short (Figure 2-10).

You know that you cannot afford expensive software, but you also know that there is an abundance of moderately priced software that can enhance all aspects of your business. A look through any store display of software packages reveals many that are aimed at small businesses, from marketing-strategy software to software for handling mailing lists.

The following basic list is presented according to business functions—things that you will want to be able to do. The computer can help.

Accounting. Totaling the bottom line must be the number one priority for any business. If you are truly on your own or have just one or two employees, you may be able to get by with simple spreadsheet software to work up a ledger and balance sheet and generate basic invoices and payroll worksheets. Larger operations can consider a complete accounting package, which produces profit-and-loss statements, balance sheets, cash flow reports, and tax summaries. Most packages also write and print checks, and some have payroll capability.

Writing and advertising. Word processing is an obvious choice because you will need to write memos and the like. Desktop publishing can be a real boon to a small business, letting you design and produce advertisements, flyers, and even your own letterhead stationery, business forms, and business cards. A big advantage of publishing your own advertisements or flyers is that you can print small quantities and start anew as your business evolves. Finally, you may think it worthwhile to publish your own newsletter for customers.

Customer service. Customer service is a byword throughout the business world, but the personal touch is especially important in a small business. Database software can be useful here. Suppose, for example, that you run a pet-grooming service. You surely want to keep track of each customer by address and so forth for billing and advertising purposes. But this is just the beginning. Why not store data about each pet too? Think how impressed the customer on the phone will be when you recall that Sadie is a standard poodle, seven years old, and that it is time for her to have her booster shots.

The Virtual Help Desk

IBM has come up with a solution to the problem of the perennially understaffed computer help desks experienced by many major corporations. Their solution is a software package called Virtual Help Desk, which runs on the company's network and responds to help requests entered by puzzled users. The software analyzes the request and if necessary, can examine the user's computer for clues to the source of the problem. In some cases, it can make a repair over the network. In other situations, it can suggest steps the user can take to solve the problem. If none of this works, a technician is scheduled for a visit.

Don't plan on using this software at home, though. The Virtual Help Desk software sells for several hundreds of thousands of dollars and is aimed at networks of 10,000 or more users.

▶ **FIGURE** **2-10**

Working at home. The number of home-office workers is increasing by 5 percent a year. The software industry has responded with various packages that come under the generic heading of small office/home office, or SOHO for short.

Keeping and making contacts. Even if you have only one computer, you can still be networked to the outside world. Business connections are available in many forms from dozens of sites on the Internet.

Making sales pitches. If your business depends on pitching your product or service in some formal way, presentation software can help you create colorful demonstrations that are the equivalent of an electronic slide show. Presentation software is designed for regular people, not artists, so putting together a slick sequence of text and graphics is remarkably simple (Figure 2-11).

Finally, consider an all-in-one software package that is specifically designed to help you get your home office organized. This is a variation on the suites described earlier but is geared specifically to the small business. If you are on your own, you need the organizational skills of a secretary, the research skills of a librarian, the accounting skills of a bookkeeper, and the experience of someone who has done it before. Comprehensive SOHO packages address all these needs, providing a searchable library of resources, a legal guide, and a tax guide. The packages also include collections of business documents for every situation, from asset depreciation to press releases. Such packages also typically offer links to useful business and government sites on the Internet.

▶ **ETHICS AND APPLICATION SOFTWARE**

The most sizzling ethics issue related to software is the acquisition and use of illegal software copies, the software piracy that we mentioned earlier. Lamentations by both business and the computer industry are so persistent and so loud that we are devoting a separate section to this issue.

Have you ever copied a friend's music CD or tape onto your own blank tape? Many people do so without much thought. It is also possible to photocopy a book. Both acts are clearly illegal, but there is much more fuss over illegal software copying than over

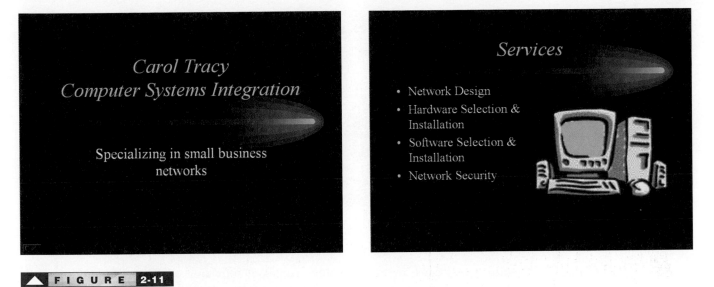

▲ **FIGURE** **2-11**

A computer-produced presentation. Shown here are just two of the screens that Carol Tracy uses when making a presentation about her business. She was able to prepare them quickly using graphics software (Microsoft PowerPoint). She can show the screens directly on a projector connected to a computer or have them converted to conventional slides or transparencies.

copying music or books. Why is this? Well, to begin with, few of us are likely to undertake the laborious task of reproducing a Stephen King novel on a copy machine. The other part of the issue is money. A pirated copy of a top 20 CD sets the recording company—and the artist—back just a few dollars. But pirated software might be valued at hundreds of dollars. The problem of stolen software has grown right along with the personal computer industry.

Software publishers have traditionally turned a blind eye toward individual pirating, because prosecution would be time-consuming and expensive, and most of those making illegal copies wouldn't have purchased the software anyway. However, a number of recent cases have involved pirating within small and medium-sized businesses, often with the knowledge and participation of management. In the typical scenario, a company might buy two or three legitimate copies of a software package, then make and distribute copies to dozens, or even hundreds, of employees. This type of piracy costs the software industry significant amounts of money. Counterfeiting is another type of piracy that results in large financial losses. Large numbers of CD-ROMs or DVD-ROMs are copied and packaged to resemble the real thing and then sold in flea markets or small stores for much less than the regular price. While much of this type of piracy occurs overseas, some copies find their way into U.S. and European markets. Two software industry organizations, the Business Software Alliance and the Software & Information Industry Association, actively pursue and prosecute software pirates worldwide.

OK If I Copy That Software?

Consider this incident. Bill Huston got his computer education at a local community college. One of his courses taught him how to use software on personal computers. He had access to a variety of copyrighted software in the college computer lab. After graduating, he got a job at a local museum, where he used database software on a personal computer to catalog museum wares. He also had his own computer at home.

One day Bill stopped back at the college and ran into a former instructor. After greetings were exchanged, she asked him why he had happened to drop by. "Oh," he

MAKING CONNECTIONS ◄ We Mean Really Remote

Need to send immediate reports from the Alaska hinterlands? No problem. As you can see, this troubleshooter carries a laptop computer to check out glitches along the Alaska pipeline. He can connect his computer's modem to a conventional phone hookup or to a cellular or satellite phone.

But what if a far-flung user needs to access files that are located else-where? Again, no problem. Remote control software lets a user, whether in a snow bank in Alaska or a home office in Albuquerque, access a network, transfer files, or even run a program. We hasten to add that not just anyone can pop into a network; proper authorization is required, even at long distance.

said, "I just came by to make some copies of software." He wasn't kidding. Neither was the instructor, who, after she caught her breath, replied, "You can't do that. It's illegal." Bill was miffed, saying, "But I can't afford it!" The instructor immediately alerted the computer lab. As a result of this encounter, the staff strengthened policies on software use and increased the vigilance of lab personnel. In effect, schools must protect themselves from people who lack ethics or are unaware of the law.

There are many people like Bill. He did not think in terms of stealing anything; he just wanted to make copies for himself. But as the software industry is quick to point out, unauthorized copying is stealing, because the software makers do not get the revenues to which they are entitled. If Bill had used illegally copied software at his place of work, his employer could have been at risk for litigation.

Why Those Extra Copies?

Copying software is not always a dirty trick. There are legitimate reasons for copying. To begin with, after paying several hundred dollars for a piece of software, you will definitely want to make a backup copy in case of disk failure or accident. You probably want to copy the program onto a hard disk and use it, more conveniently, from there. Software publishers have no trouble with these types of copying. But thousands of computer users copy software for another reason: to get the program without paying for it. This is clearly unethical and illegal.

► COMPUTERS AND PEOPLE

These first few chapters describe hardware, software, and data, but the most important element in a computer system is people. Anyone who is nervous about a takeover by computers will be relieved to know that computers will never amount to much without people—the people who help make the system work and the people for whom the work is done.

Computers and You, the User

As we noted earlier, computer users have come to be called just users, a nickname that has persisted for years. Whereas once computer users were an elite breed—highly educated scientists, research-and-development engineers, and government planners—today the population of users has broadened considerably. This expansion is due partly to user-friendly software for both work and personal use and partly to the availability of small, low-cost personal computers. It's likely that all of us will be computer users, even if our levels of sophistication vary.

Computer People

Many organizations have a department called **Management Information Systems (MIS)** or **Computer Information Systems (CIS), Computing Services, Information Services**, or **Information Technology (IT).** Whatever it is called, this department is made up of the people who are responsible for the organization's computer resources. Large organizations, such as universities, government agencies, and corporations, keep much of the institution's data in computer files: research data, engineering drawings, marketing strategy, student records, accounts receivable, accounts payable, sales figures, manufacturing specifications, transportation plans, and so forth. The people who maintain the data are the same people who provide service to the users: the computer professionals. Let us touch on the essential personnel required to run large computer systems.

Data entry operators prepare data for processing, usually by keying it in a machine-readable format. **Computer operators** monitor the computer systems, review procedures, keep peripheral equipment running, and make backup copies of data. **Librarians** catalog the processed disks and tapes and keep them secure.

Computer programmers, as we noted earlier, design, write, test, implement, and maintain the programs that process data on the computer system; they also maintain and update the programs. **Systems analysts** are knowledgeable in the programming area but have broader responsibilities. They plan and design entire computer systems, not just individual programs. Systems analysts maintain a working relationship with both programmers and the users in the organization. The analysts work closely with the users to plan new systems that meet the users' needs. A professional called a **network manager** implements and maintains the organization's network(s). The department manager, often called the **chief information officer (CIO)**, must understand more than just computer technology. This person must understand the goals and operations of the entire organization and be able to make strategic decisions.

These are some standard jobs and standard titles. There are many others, most notably those associated with creation and maintenance of Internet sites; these will be discussed in detail in the Internet chapter.

▲

This chapter discussed the type of software that enables users to get their work done. The next chapter covers the more technical area of operating systems.

D A Y   I N   T H E   L I F E | **Geoff Kehler, IT Assistant**

As Geoff can tell you, an IT assistant's work is never done. In addition to his many other duties, Geoff is responsible for making sure that all his company's workstations, old or new, have consistent operating systems and applications.

To do this, he has to make a "standard desktop install" workstation for each department in the organization. After all, different people require access to different applications to get their jobs done. For example, a computer for a member of the sales group would first have Windows 2000 installed. Next, links to key shared resources on the company's local network are added. Finally, after installing all the applications that are needed by the sales group, he creates a disk image (an exact duplicate of everything on the computer's hard drive). With this disk image, he can quickly and reliably set up more workstations in the amount of time it takes to connect the hardware and copy the image to the computer's hard drive. Each department gets its own disk image for its standard workstation, as each requires a slightly different setup.

Finally, he actually has to visit the department's location and connect the computers. Needless to say, everyone loves receiving new equipment, so Geoff is always greeted with a smile.

CHAPTER REVIEW

▶ Summary and Key Terms

- Software is the planned, step-by-step set of instructions required to turn data into information. **Applications software** can be used to solve a particular problem or to perform a particular task. Applications software might be either custom-designed or packaged.

- **Computer programmers** are people who design, write, test, and implement software. Organizations might pay computer programmers to write **custom software**, software that is specifically tailored to their needs.

- **Packaged software**, also called **commercial software**, is packaged in a container of some sort, usually a box or folder, and is sold in stores or catalogs. Inside the box one or more disks contain the software. An instruction manual, also referred to as **documentation,** is sometimes included.

- The term **user-friendly** means that the software is supposed to be easy for a beginner to use or that the software can be used with a minimum of training.

- **Freeware** is software for which there is no fee. **Public domain** software is not copyrighted and therefore may be used or altered without restriction.

- **Open-source software** is freely distributed in a format that enables programmers to make changes to it.

- **Shareware** is freely distributed; the user is expected to register and pay a nominal fee to use it past a free trial period.

- Commercial software is copyrighted, costs money, and must not be copied without permission from the manufacturer. Making illegal copies of commercial software is called **software piracy** and is punishable under the law.

- A **site license** permits an organization, for a fee, to distribute copies of a software product to its employees. **Electronic software distribution** means that a user can pay to download the software—move it from another computer to the user's computer.

- **An application service provider (ASP)** is a company that sets up and maintains applications software on its own systems and makes the software available for its customers to use over the Internet.

- **Word-processing** software lets you create, edit, format, store, and print text and graphics in one document. It is those three words in the middle—edit, format, and store—that reveal the difference between word processing and plain typing. **Desktop publishing** packages meet high-level publishing needs to produce professional-looking newsletters, reports, and brochures.

- An **electronic spreadsheet**, made up of columns and rows of numbers, automatically recalculates the results when a number is changed. This capability lets business people try different combinations of "**what if . . .?**" numbers and obtain the results quickly.

- **Database management** software manages a collection of interrelated facts. The software can store data, update it, manipulate it, retrieve it, report it in a variety of views, and print it in as many forms.

- **Graphics** software enables users to manipulate images. **Presentation graphics** software can produce graphs, maps, and charts and can help people compare data, spot trends more easily, and make decisions more quickly. **Graphic artists** use graphics software to express their ideas visually.

- **Communications software** enables computers to communicate with each other via phone lines or other means. A **browser** is software that is used to access the Internet.

- **Personal Information Managers** (**PIM**s) are programs that typically include an appointment calendar, address book, task manager, notepad, and calculator.

- A **suite** is a group of basic software applicaitons designed to work together. A typical suite application is mail merge, in which certain names and addresses from a database are applied to letters prepared using word processing. An **integrated application** combines basic word processing, spreadsheet, and graphics capabilities in a single program.

- Software that is written especially for a particular type of business is called **vertical market software.**

- **Groupware,** also called **collaborative software,** is any kind of software that lets a group of people share information or track information together.

- The company information center, or **help desk**, is devoted to giving users help with software selection, software training, problem resolution and, if appropriate, access to corporate computer systems.

- Software designed for small businesses is termed **SOHO**, for **small office/home office**.

- Many organizations have a department called **Management Information Systems (MIS)**, **Computer Information Systems (CIS)**, **Computing Services, Information Services,** or **Information Technology (IT)**. This department is made up of the people who are responsible for the organization's computer resources.

- **Data entry operators** prepare data for processing, usually by keying it in a machine-readable format. **Computer operators** monitor the computer systems, review procedures, and keep peripheral equipment running. **Librarians** catalog the processed disks and tapes and keep them secure. **Computer programmers** design, write, test, and implement the programs that process data on the computer system; they also maintain and update the programs.

- **Systems analysts** are knowledgeable in the programming area but have broader responsibilities; they plan and design not just individual programs but entire computer systems. A professional called a **network manager** implements and maintains the organization's network(s). The department manager, often called the **chief information officer (CIO)**, must understand computer technology as well as the goals and operations of the entire organization.

► Critical Thinking Questions

1. Consider these firms. What uses would each have for computer software? Mention as many possibilities as you can.
   a. Security Southwestern Bank, a major regional bank with several branches
   b. Azure Design, a small graphic design company that produces posters, covers, and other artwork
   c. Checkerboard Taxi Service, whose central office manages a fleet of 160 cabs that operate in an urban area
   d. Gillick College, a private college that has automated all student services, including registration, financial aid, and testing

2. If you have, or will have, a computer of your own, how will you get software for it?

3. How does software piracy affect individual users? How does it affect businesses?

4. Several common office applications are often integrated together and sold as a "suite" of products. Based on your major, or intended major, explain how you would professionally use each of the following software applications:
   a. word processing
   b. spreadsheet
   c. database
   d. Presentation
   e. PIM

5. Although they are not as popular as the task-oriented software typically found in office suites, there are many career-specific applications that are routinely used by professionals. Identify and describe how you would use a software application that is specific to your major or intended major. To find this information you may wish to visit a department computer lab, talk to an instructor who teaches courses in the major, or look at the literature related to the major.

6. Discuss the advantages and disadvantages of open-source software compared to standard commercial software. You can easily find more information on this topic by entering "open source software" into an Internet search engine, such as Google (http://www.google.com).

7. Business and institutions frequently purchase site licenses for their software applications. What are the advantages and disadvantages of using this method to purchase software? Does your school use licensed software and is student home use of software applications included in the agreement? (It is on some campuses.)

8. Go to your institution's computing services and interview some of the computer personnel. Describe their title, duties, and educational/professional preparation.

9. Explain why some software companies allow you to download their software from the Internet, install it on your computer, and run it for an initial trial period without having to pay for it. As a consumer, what do you think about this method of distributing and selling software?

10. Do any of your instructors use presentation software in their classroom lectures or demonstrations? If they do, then explain why you like or dislike their use of this software.

▶ STUDENT STUDY GUIDE

Multiple Choice

1. A computer professional who writes and tests software is called a(n)
   a. programmer
   b. systems analyst
   c. librarian
   d. operator

2. Step-by-step instructions that run the computer are called
   a. hardware
   b. CPUs
   c. documents
   d. programs

3. CIS stands for
   a. Computer Internet System
   b. Commercial Internet System
   c. Collaborative Information Systems
   d. Computer Information Systems

4. Which of the following terms is not a description of a type of software?
   a. custom
   b. freeware
   c. download
   d. collaborative

5. The department within an organization that is designed to help users with software is the
   a. browser
   b. SOHO
   c. help desk
   d. network

6. Software that is written especially for a single type of business is called
   a. freeware
   b. word processing
   c. shareware
   d. vertical market software

7. Making illegal copies of copyrighted software is called
   a. software piracy
   b. browsing
   c. collaboration
   d. electronic distribution

8. Software that allows the production of professional newsletters and reports is called
   a. database management
   b. groupware
   c. spreadsheet
   d. desktop publishing

9. The type of software that can store, update, manipulate, and retrieve data is called
   a. desktop publishing
   b. spreadsheet
   c. database management
   d. graphics

10. Another name for commercial software is
    a. secondary software
    b. packaged software
    c. systems software
    d. peripheral software

11. CIO stands for
    a. Channeled Input Output
    b. Chief Information Officer
    c. Computer Integrated Operation
    d. Complete Interactive Object

12. Pie charts are typically created by using which of the following?
    a. word-processing software
    b. browser software
    c. database software
    d. spreadsheet software

13. Which of the following would you use to keep track of your daily schedule?
    a. word-processing software
    b. PIM software
    c. database software
    d. presentation software

14. Information about a coin collection is best kept by using which of the following?
    a. word-processing software
    b. spreadsheet software
    c. database software
    d. presentation software

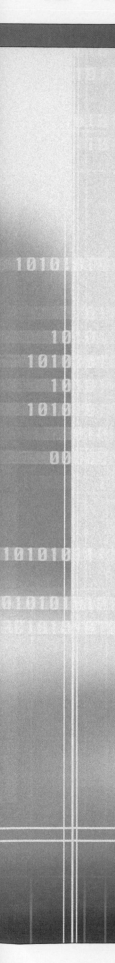

15. What type of software is used for collaborative efforts?
    a. vertical-market software
    b. user-friendly software
    c. groupware
    d. electronic distribution software

16. Where can you find documentation for software applications?
    a. on CD-ROM or DVD-ROM
    b. on the Internet
    c. printed in hard copy form
    d. all of the above

17. E-mail means
    a. electronic mail
    b. enhanced mail
    c. effortless mail
    d. easy mail

18. Which of the following is a tax-preparation program an example of?
    a. groupware software
    b. communications software
    c. desktop publishing software
    d. none of the above

19. Which of the following would *not* be considered to be SOHO software?
    a. groupware
    b. presentation software
    c. accounting software
    d. desktop publishing

20. Which application is not typically included in an office suite?
    a. word processor
    b. spreadsheet
    c. antivirus
    d. database

True/False

T   F   1. A browser is software that is used to access the Internet.

T   F   2. Making illegal copies of copyrighted software is called software piracy.

T   F   3. Users must purchase a license to use open-source software.

T   F   4. Workers using groupware must be physically in the same office.

T   F   5. Software documentation might be printed or might be included as part of the software.

T   F   6. The operating system is an example of applications software.

T   F   7. The term "user-friendly" refers to a special kind of computer.

T   F   8. Custom software is specially tailored to user needs.

T   F   9. Word processing is a type of task-oriented software.

T   F   10. Desktop publishing software is used to manage numbers in columns and rows.

T   F   11. The network manager is the person who plans new systems.

T   F   12. Another name for groupware is SOHO.

T   F   13. Copyrighted software is in the public domain.

T   F   14. An advantage of groupware is the ability to collaborate with others.

T   F   15. A site license entitles an individual to use freeware.

T   F   16. As long as you paid for a software application, you are allowed to give copies of it to others.

T   F   17. A systems analyst designs and maintains computer networks.

T   F   18. A help desk is a place where you can call for assistance with hardware and software problems.

T   F   19. You are legally required to pay for shareware after a trial period.

T   F   20. The price of an applications suite is less than the combined prices of the included applications.

Fill-In

1. A group of software applications designed to work together is called a(n) _____.

2. _____ software works with numbers organized in columns and rows.

3. SOHO stands for _____.

4. Another term for collaborative software is _____.

5. The general name for software that can be used to solve a problem or perform a task is _____.

6. Software that is written for a particular type of business is called _____.

7. _____ software is freely distributed in source code form and can be altered by the programmer.

8. The department within an organization that is dedicated to giving software help is known as the _____.

9. A(n) _____ is a company that sets up and maintains application software on its own systems and makes the software available to its customers over the Internet.

10. A(n) _____ is a single program that has word-processing, spreadsheet, and graphics capabilities.

11. In a computer center, _____ are the people who catalog the processed disks and tapes and keep them secure.

12. _____ are the people who prepare data for processing, usually by keying it in a machine-readable format.

13. _____ software is uncopyrighted software that can be used and altered without restriction.

14. People who design, write, test, and implement software are called _____.

15. Spreadsheets are helpful because of their ability to answer _____ questions.

16. An instruction manual for using the software is also referred to as _____.

17. The title of _____ is often given to the person who manages a company's information technology department.

18. _____ software can keep track of appointments, contacts, and tasks.

19. A(n) _____ is software that is used to access the Internet.

20. _____ is used most often by a group of people who need to share information or track information together.

► ANSWERS

Multiple Choice

1. a	6. d	11. b	16. d
2. d	7. a	12. d	17. a
3. d	8. d	13. b	18. d
4. c	9. c	14. c	19. a
5. c	10. b	15. c	20. c

True/False

1. T	6. F	11. F	16. F
2. T	7. F	12. F	17. F
3. F	8. T	13. F	18. T
4. F	9. T	14. T	19. T
5. T	10. F	15. F	20. T

Fill-In

1. suite
2. spreadsheet
3. small office/home office
4. groupware
5. applications software
6. vertical market software
7. open-source
8. information center or help desk
9. application service provider (ASP)
10. integrated program
11. librarians
12. Data entry operators
13. Public domain
14. computer programmers
15. "what if"
16. documentation
17. CIO or Chief Information Officer
18. PIM or Personal Information Manager
19. browser
20. Groupware

Planet Internet

Jumping-off Points

How Do I Start?

Briefly, to get started, you need a URL for the Web. Translation: You need a starting address ("URL" stands for "Uniform Resource Locator") to find a site on the subset of the Internet called the World Wide Web, also called WWW or just the Web. You can read more detailed information about URLs and the Web, and most important, links, in Chapter 8.

Where Do I Find a URL?

A URL is often pretty messy—a long string of letters and symbols. No one likes to type URLs, and, what's more, there is a good chance of making an error. Fortunately, you rarely have to type a URL because, once started, you can click your mouse on links—icons or highlighted text—to move from site to site on the Internet.

The publisher of this book has set up this URL for our readers: http://www.prenhall.com/capron.

Once you use this URL to reach the publisher's site, you will find links—colored and/or underlined text—to all other sites mentioned in this and other chapters. Simply click the desired link. Almost everything on the Internet (including URLs) is subject to change. For these exercises, we supply here the publisher's URL, which will not change.

What Other Starting Points Are There?

Keep in mind that, unlike a commercial product, the Internet is not owned or managed by anyone. One consequence of this is that there is no master table of contents or index for the Internet. However, several organizations have produced ordered lists that can be used as a helpful starting place. Users often favor one or more of these as comprehensive starting places: Yahoo!, Netscape, or MSN.

Each of these sites has a set of major categories, and each major category has links of its own, as do the topics at the next level, and so on. Major cate-

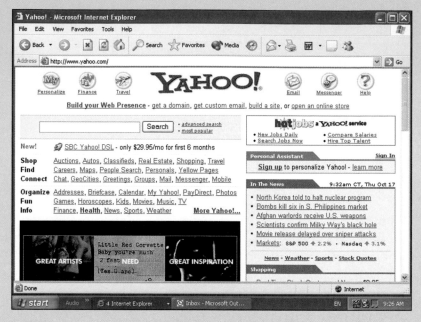

gories typically include careers, computers, business, politics, education, society, kids, shopping, travel, magazines, recreation, government, events, science, sports, health, reference, and family. Most major starting sites also include special lists of new and "hot" sites. You could literally hang around for days, burrowing deeper and deeper, just from a starting point such as Yahoo!

Favorites.

Many sites make no attempt to be comprehensive but instead list their own favorites, sites they consider to be of high quality. The Lycos Top 50 site lists the hot search topics for the past week. Examples of other sites that offer special lists are the Yahoo! Picks and Netscape. The Cool Site of the Day Web site offers the Cool Site of the Day, and of the Month, as well as an archive of every Cool Site of the Day since 1994. Remember that the links for all of these sites can be found at the publisher's site. Just point and click and go to any of the listed sites. Another good starting point for the technologically-inclined is SlashDot, which bills itself as "News for Nerds."

But I Need to Get to the Web First.

Yes. To use the Web, you need a browser, special software devoted to navigating the Web and displaying all the content that can be found there. You can get general information about browsers in Chapter 8, but you will need to ask your instructor, lab personnel, or a designated employee how to use the Web browser at your location. If you are using a browser that you acquired for your personal computer or have access to the Internet via some online service, then these suppliers will provide instructions.

Internet Exercises:

At the end of most Planet Internet features, three exercises are suggested. The first exercise is structured, since it's based on using links provided on the publisher's Web Site. Use the URL supplied here to get started. If you are feeling a little adventurous, try the free-form exercise, in which we make suggestions but not guarantees. If you are fairly familiar with the Web, try the advanced exercise.

1. **Structured exercise.** Go to the URL http://www.prenhall.com/capron. Link to the Yahoo! site, and then link to the list of new sites. From there, choose two places to link to. Write a brief evaluation of the sites to share with classmates, friends, or family, using such criteria as overall ease of use, quantity and quality of information, availability of information about the privacy policy, contact person, and key features of the site.

2. **Free-form exercise.** Using the same URL, choose a site that lists favorites. Then go to several sites they recommend. (Choose a site.)

   Write a brief evaluation of the site to share with classmates, friends, or family, using such criteria as overall ease of use, quantity and quality of information, availability of information about the privacy policy, contact person, and key features of the site.

3. **Advanced exercise.** Find a page for a hobby or recreational interest of your own that serves as the jumping-off point to many other pages, including shopping information, FAQs, chat rooms, and so on. Follow two or three links from this page and total up the number of links from there. Write a brief report to share with classmates, friends, or family on the features of this Web site. For example, the Knitting page in About—The Human Internet's Hobbies section, includes basic information about knitting, free patterns, information about charity projects, discussion groups, and a host of other topics.

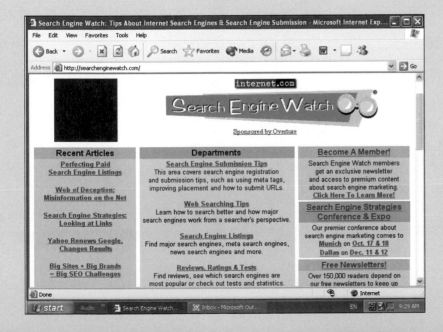

Planet Internet

Operating Systems:
Software in the Background

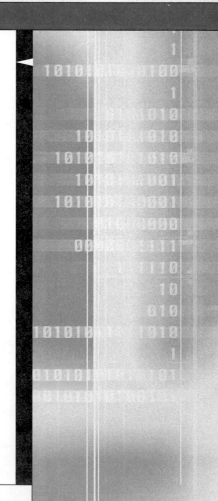

CHAPTER 3

LEARNING OBJECTIVES

Describe the functions of an operating system

Explain the basics of a personal computer operating system

Describe the advantages of a graphical operating system

Differentiate among different versions of Microsoft Windows

Explain the need for network operating systems

Describe the methods of resource allocation on large computers

Describe the differences among multiprocessing, multiprogramming, and time-sharing

Explain the principles of memory management

List several functions that are typically performed by utility programs

When Linda Ronquillo was taking a night class in applications software at a community college years ago, she did not have to worry much about the operating system, the necessary software in the background that runs the computer. The college personal computers were on a network that managed all the computers. As Linda sat down to begin work, the computer screen showed a menu of numbered choices reflecting the software packages available: WordPerfect, Microsoft Word, Microsoft Excel, and so forth. At the bottom of the screen, Linda was instructed to type the number of her chosen selection; if she typed 1, for example, the system put her into WordPerfect. Linda did have to learn operating system commands to prepare her own diskettes and save data on them so that she could take her work with her, but she had little other contact with the operating system.

On her first job as a supervisor for a small airport freight company, Linda needed to use word processing, spreadsheets, and database software packages on her personal computer. But no one had set up a menu shortcut there; with a little advice from colleagues, she learned what she needed to know about the operating system MS-DOS. She learned, among other things, to execute the software she needed to use and to take care of her data files, copying files from one disk to another and sometimes renaming or deleting them. She eventually felt fairly comfortable with her operating system knowledge.

Two months later, the company personal computer manager informed Linda that the company's three personal computers were going to be updated to Microsoft Windows 95, an operating system that included a user-friendly interface. Despite assurances that the new system would be colorful and easy to use, Linda was less than thrilled to be making another change. But she didn't say so. She knew that being a computer user meant being willing to adjust to change. So Linda learned to use a mouse and mastered icons, overlapping windows, pull-down menus, and other mysteries.

A few years later, Linda took a job at another, larger airline freight company. Part of the reason she was hired was her response to the revelation that the new company had just installed Windows XP, which she knew was yet another operating system. Linda said, "Oh, I have already learned several systems. It shouldn't be any problem learning another." She was right, of course. In fact, she had little trouble switching to the new operating system.

▶ OPERATING SYSTEMS: HIDDEN SOFTWARE

When a brand-new computer comes off the factory assembly line, it can do nothing. The hardware needs software to make it work. Part of the story is the application's software, such as word processing or spreadsheet software that enables users to perform useful work. This type of software was discussed in Chapter 2. But applications software cannot communicate directly with the hardware, so the operating system software serves as an intermediary between the applications software and the hardware. An **operating system** is a set of programs that lies between applications software and the hardware; it is the fundamental software that controls access to all other hardware and software resources. Figure 3-1 illustrates this concept. Incidentally, the term **systems software** is often used interchangeably with operating system, but systems software means all programs related to coordinating computer operations. Systems software includes the operating system but also includes other elements, such as programming language translators and a variety of utility programs.

Note that we said that an operating system is a set of programs. The most important program in the operating system is the **kernel,** which manages the operating system. It remains in memory and is therefore referred to as resident. The kernel controls the entire operating system and loads into memory other operating system programs (called nonresident) from disk storage only as needed (Figure 3-2).

No matter which operating system is being used, when the computer is turned on, the kernel is loaded from the hard drive into the computer's memory, making it

▶ FIGURE 3-1

A conceptual diagram of an operating system.
Closest to the user are applications programs, software that helps a user compute a payroll, play a game, or write a report. The operating system is the set of programs between the applications programs and the hardware.

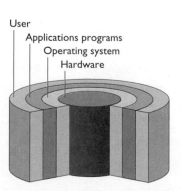

User
Applications programs
Operating system
Hardware

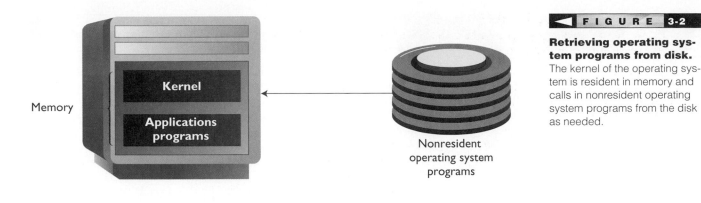

◄ **FIGURE** **3-2**

Retrieving operating system programs from disk.
The kernel of the operating system is resident in memory and calls in nonresident operating system programs from the disk as needed.

Memory

Nonresident operating system programs

available for use. This process of loading the operating system into memory is called *bootstrapping*, or **booting,** the system. The word "booting" is used because, figuratively speaking, the operating system pulls itself up by its own bootstraps. When the computer is turned on, a small program stored in a ROM chip performs some internal hardware component tests then loads the kernel from the hard disk.

An operating system has three main functions: (1) managing the computer's resources, such as the central processing unit, memory, disk drives, and printers; (2) establishing a user interface; and (3) executing and providing services for applications software. Keep in mind, however, that much of the work of an operating system is hidden from the user; many necessary tasks are performed behind the scenes. In particular, the first listed function—managing the computer's resources—is taken care of without the user being aware of the details. Furthermore, all input and output operations, although initiated by an application program, are actually carried out by the operating system.

Although many of its functions are hidden from view, you will have to communicate directly with the operating system to begin using an applications software package and to perform various housekeeping tasks. This communication occurs through the operating system's **user interface,** which determines how the user interacts with the operating system. The two basic forms of user interfaces are the command-line interface and the graphical user interface (GUI). The command-line interface is text-based and requires you to type in complete operating system commands. MS-DOS, Unix, Linux, and many large-computer operating systems use a command-line interface, as you will see in the following pages. GUIs use visual images and menus to enable users to enter commands. Windows and Mac OS use GUIs. Many installations of Linux and Unix are set up to offer a GUI.

Operating systems for large computers must keep track of several programs from several users, all running in the same time frame. You will examine the inherent complexities of such systems later in the chapter. For now, the focus is on the interaction between a single user and a personal computer operating system.

► OPERATING SYSTEMS FOR PERSONAL COMPUTERS

If you browse the software offerings at a retail store, you will generally find the software grouped according to the platform on which the software can run. The term **platform** refers to a combination of computer hardware and operating system software. The most common microcomputer platform today consists of some version of Microsoft Windows running on an Intel-based PC, often referred to as *Wintel* for short. Generally, applications software—word processing, spreadsheets, games, and so on—can run on only one platform. Just as you cannot place a Honda engine in a Ford truck and expect it to run, you cannot take a version of WordPerfect that was designed to run on a computer using the Wintel platform and run it on an Apple

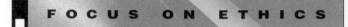

F O C U S   O N   E T H I C S   **Bugs and Back Doors: Who Is Responsible?**

Operating systems, like all software, are far from perfect. In fact, because of their complexity and demanding performance requirements, they probably have more defects than common application programs do. Suppose you are a programmer and you discover a serious software bug in a widely used operating system. Imagine further that this bug could allow an attacker to read or alter sensitive files on many computers. Weigh the following possible actions and decide which one you think is most practical and ethically sound.

1. Keep quiet about the bug. Maybe it will get fixed in a new release, and at least you aren't helping potential hackers by publicizing it.

2. Contact the manufacturer and describe the bug. Ask them to fix the bug in the next release but realize that they may give it a low priority.

3. Contact a popular computer magazine and describe the nature of the bug, hoping that publication of the problem will pressure the manufacturer to fix it immediately but knowing that publicity about it might help potential exploiters of the bug.

Macintosh using the Mac OS operating system. Software makers must decide for which platform to write an applications software package, although some make versions of their software for more than one platform.

Most users do not set out to buy an operating system; they want computers and the applications software to make them useful. However, because the operating system determines which software is available for a given computer, users must be aware of their own computer's operating system.

Although operating systems differ, many of their basic functions are similar. The following sections examine some of the basic functions of operating systems by examining MS-DOS.

► A BRIEF LOOK AT MS-DOS

The MS-DOS operating system was introduced in the early 1980s. It employs a command-line user interface. When a computer using MS-DOS (often called DOS, rhyming with "boss") is booted, the screen is blank except for the characters C:\> appearing in the upper-left corner. The C:\ refers to the disk drive; the > is a **prompt,** a signal that the system is expecting you to do something. At this point, you must give some instruction, or command, to the operating system. Although the prompt is the only visible result of booting the system, DOS also provides the basic software that coordinates the computer's hardware components and a set of programs that lets you perform the many computer tasks you need to do. To execute a given DOS program, you must type a **command,** a name that invokes a specific DOS program. Some typical tasks that you can perform with DOS commands are listing the files on a disk, copying files from one disk to another, and erasing files from a

► **FIGURE 3-3**

MS-DOS commands.

Sample MS-DOS Commands

C:\>**FORMAT A:** Prepares an unformatted diskette on drive A: for use.

C:\>**DIR A:** Lists the files on the diskette in drive A: (DIR stands for directory)

C:\>**COPY MRKTDATA.SUM A:** Copies file MRKTDATA.SUM on drive C to Drive A.

C:\>**DEL A:SALESRPT.TXT** Deletes file SALESRPT.TXT from drive A:

C:\>**RENAME MRKTDATA.SUM SSDATA.CHT** Renames the file MRKTDATA.SUM on drive C: to SSDATA.CHT

disk. Figure 3-3 gives some examples of MS-DOS commands. As you can see, these are not the easiest commands to remember. Command-line interfaces have the reputation of not being very user-unfriendly and have been largely replaced by GUIs. However, you can still execute DOS commands from within Windows, Microsoft's GUI operating system.

▶ MICROSOFT WINDOWS

Today there is another—most say better—way to interact with the computer's operating system. **Microsoft Windows**—Windows for short—uses a colorful graphics interface that, among other things, eases access to the operating system. Microsoft Windows defines the operating environment standard for computers with Intel processors. Most new personal computers come with Windows already installed. The following sections describe Windows for the individual desktop or notebook system; versions designed to control network operations are covered later in this chapter.

A Windows Overview

Windows started out as an **operating environment** for MS-DOS, another layer added to separate the operating system from the user and thus make it easier to use. This layer is often called a **shell** because it forms a "coating," with icons and menus, over the operating system. Earlier versions of Windows, culminating in Windows 3.1, were shells for MS-DOS. With **Windows 95,** Windows became a self-contained operating system and therefore requires no preinstalled DOS. However, DOS commands are still available. The following discussion covers features common to all versions since Windows 95.

The feature that makes Windows so easy to use is a **graphical user interface** (**GUI,** pronounced "goo-ee"), in which users work with onscreen pictures called **icons** and with **menus** rather than keyed-in commands (see Figure 3-4). Clicking the icons or menu items activates a command or function. The menus in Figure 3-5 are called

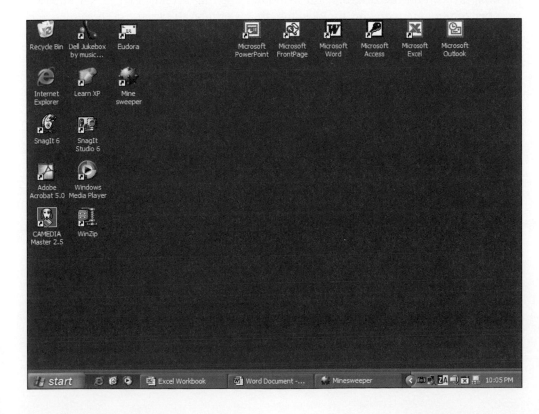

◀ FIGURE 3-4

A typical Windows desktop display. The icons represent programs, which can be run by double-clicking the corresponding icon. The taskbar across the bottom of the screen contains the Start button on the left, which you can click to display a pop-up menu with various options, including shutting down. Next are three clickable icons (left to right) that launch Internet Explorer, return you to the desktop, and launch Windows Media Player. Next are the buttons representing active application programs; here Microsoft Excel, Microsoft Word, and Minesweeper (a game) are shown. The notification area on the right side typically displays the time and icons representing task status, such as a new e-mail arrival or printer activity.

Windows menus. This screen from Microsoft Word illustrates Windows menus. Here, the user has clicked the Insert choice on the menu bar to get a drop-down menu. Note the little triangular arrowhead to the right of the Picture option; this indicates that a submenu will be displayed if this option is highlighted. The submenu shown presents a series of locations from which a picture may be inserted into a Word document.

pull-down menus because they appear to pull down like a window shade from the original selection on the menu bar. Some menus, called **pop-up menus,** originate from a selection at the bottom of the screen or when the user right-clicks the mouse. Icons and menus enable pointing and clicking with a mouse, an approach that can make computer use fast, easy, and intuitive.

Windows features a Start button in the lower-left corner (refer to Figure 3-4). From this button you can find a program or a file. You can also invoke programs by double-clicking an icon on the desktop, the Windows opening screen. Figure 3-4 shows a number of program icons on the desktop area. Perhaps the greatest convenience is the taskbar along the bottom of the screen, which contains an array of buttons for the programs that are currently in use. You can click from program to program as easily as you change channels on your TV. Windows allows longer file names of up to 255 characters. MS-DOS and Windows 3.1, the shell version of Windows, permitted only eight.

Anyone who has added a new component, perhaps a modem or a sound card, to an existing computer knows that it must be configured into the system, a process that involves some software and perhaps even hardware manipulations. Windows supports **Plug and Play**, a concept that lets the computer configure itself when a new component is added. For Plug and Play to work, hardware components must also support the Plug and Play standard. When a peripheral is built to the Plug and Play standard, a user can install it by simply plugging it in and turning on the computer. Windows recognizes that the new device has been added and proceeds to configure it.

A Windows technology called **object linking and embedding** (**OLE**—pronounced "oh-lay") lets you embed or link one document to another. For instance, you can embed a spreadsheet within a report created in a word processing program that supports OLE. When you click the spreadsheet to modify it, you are taken to the program that you used to create the spreadsheet.

Windows has been a family of operating systems, with three branches serving different users. The branch that has served the home/consumer market is often referred to as Windows 9x and consists of a series of versions called Windows 95, Windows 98, and Windows Millennium Edition (Me). For the corporate market the

◄ **FIGURE** 3-6

Wizards. Wizards are easy-to-use, step-by-step software tools that make tasks more user-friendly. This wizard helps configure Windows for users with special needs.

two most recent versions are Windows NT and Windows 2000. In 2001, Microsoft introduced the newest member of the Windows family, Windows XP. Windows XP replaces Windows 9x and Windows 2000, serving both the consumer and corporate desktop markets with a single product. Finally, Windows CE has been introduced for pocket computers and Internet appliances. All of these are discussed next.

Windows 98 and Me

Windows 98 and **Windows Millennium Edition** (**Me**) are improvements on Windows 95 and have much the same screen look.

Features added by **Windows 98** include the following:

- **Internet/intranet browsing capabilities.** Microsoft's browser, Internet Explorer, is included with Windows and Windows itself has been made to look more like a browser.

- **Support for state-of-the-art hardware** including digital video disk (DVD) and the latest multimedia components. DVD and multimedia are described in the chapter on storage.

- **Support for multigigabyte disk drives.**

- **TV viewer and broadcast ability.** A broadcast-enabled computer blends television with new forms of information and entertainment. It enables the reception of broadcast Web pages and other live data feeds, such as across-the-screen news headlines and stock quotes.

- **Wizards.** Windows lets users accomplish various tasks by using wizards, step-by-step software tools that make tasks more user-friendly (Figure 3-6).

The major features added in **Windows Me** include the following:

- **Multimedia support.** Windows Media Player 7 includes a jukebox and music database controls, and enables you to record music CDs as digital files. Windows

Movie Maker provides basic video editing capabilities on your PC. Windows Image Acquisition provides additional support for manipulating scanner and digital camera images.

- **Reliability features.** If any system files are accidentally deleted or overwritten with out-of-date versions, the System File Protection feature automatically restores them the next time you boot the system. An AutoUpdate function automatically checks appropriate sites on the Internet for updates to installed system and application software. A system restore feature lets you return to an earlier system configuration if the addition of hardware or software disrupts your system's settings. Finally, a Help Center contains a variety of problem-solving tools to help users troubleshoot their systems.

- **Home network support.** As the number of homes with multiple PCs increases, the demand for home networking grows. Windows Me includes the Home Networking Wizard to guide the user through the often confusing process of interconnecting multiple computers and peripherals.

Windows NT

The operating system called **Windows NT** (NT stands for "new technology") is meant mostly for corporate, networked environments. Version 4.0, the last with the NT designation, looks exactly like Windows 98 and runs most of the same software that runs under Windows 98. But beneath the surface, Windows NT is far more robust. It was engineered for stability and, as befits a networked environment, has much stronger security features. Because Windows NT lacks support for older Windows and MS-DOS software and hardware, is more complex to learn and use, and requires more memory and processor power than the Windows 9x family, it is seldom used on PCs that are not a part of a network.

Windows 2000

Windows 2000 is the final generation in the Windows NT series. As such, it maintains the stability and security features that are NT's hallmark and incorporates Windows 98's ease of setup and hardware awareness. As with Windows NT, there are two versions: Windows 2000 for network servers (discussed later) and Windows 2000 Professional for individual users. Microsoft originally intended that Windows 2000 would be the convergence of the 9x and NT series, providing a single operating system for both home and corporate users. However, Windows 2000's complexity and heavy demand for computer resources convinced Microsoft to update the Windows 9x home user series with a newer version (Windows Me, discussed previously) and delay convergence for another software generation.

The most noticeable new feature of Windows 2000 is that it knows who you are. One computer can serve many people. Once you identify yourself, it immediately reconfigures to your preferences. It personalizes the Start menu so that the programs you use most frequently are visible and others are hidden. A particularly attractive feature is the self-healing applications software: If you accidentally delete a necessary component, Windows 2000 automatically restores it. Other improvements over Windows NT include support for the Windows 98 file structure, Plug and Play features, and much better support for laptops.

Windows XP

Windows XP, the latest generation of Windows, brings Microsoft's consumer and corporate operating systems together into a single product. It incorporates and extends the consumer-oriented features of Windows Me into the stable, dependable Windows

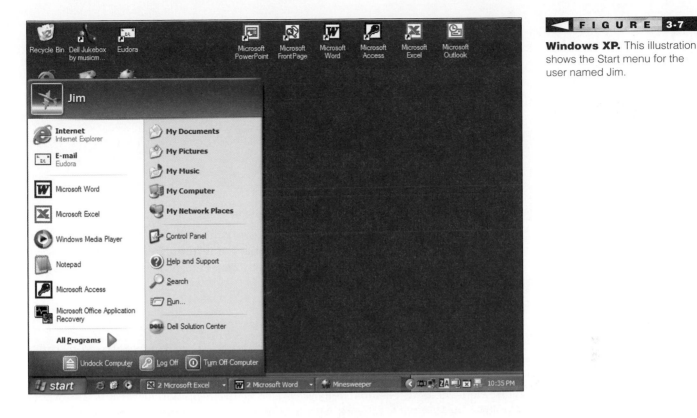

◄ **FIGURE 3-7**

Windows XP. This illustration shows the Start menu for the user named Jim.

2000 environment. Windows XP comes in two versions designed for desktop computers. The Professional Edition is aimed toward business users connected to corporate networks. It contains all the features described in the following list and adds features for file encryption, remote desktop access, and dual processor support. New features in the consumer-oriented Home Edition include the following:

- **Improved user interface.** The desktop appears clean and uncluttered (see Figure 3-7). Most icons have been replaced with entries in a redesigned Start menu. The Desktop Cleanup Wizard places any desktop shortcuts that you haven't used recently into a separate folder.

- **Improved multimedia support.** Support for digital media, such as MP3 music and digital still and video cameras, has been integrated into the operating system. Much plug-in software is no longer required.

- **More extensive personalization.** A feature called Visual Styles enables the user to customize the appearance of many Windows components. What's more, applications written to the new standards automatically take on the same appearance.

- **Multiple user support.** Because many home computers have more than one user, Windows XP allows multiple users to be logged on at the same time. One user can walk away leaving applications running, come back later and resume work with all applications still active. During that time, other users can log on and leave their own applications running. A child can be assigned a limited use configuration that restricts what can be done on the computer.

- **Internet support features.** The Internet Connection Feature allows multiple computers on a home network to share a single Internet connection and the Internet Connection Firewall provides protection from Internet attacks.

A specialized version, Windows XP Media Center Edition, adds the ability to play DVDs and receive and record television programs. It is designed to allow your

▶ **FIGURE 3-8**

Windows CE on the Pocket PC. Windows CE includes an interactive scheduling calendar, an address book for contacts, electronic mail, and Web browsing.

personal computer to act as the center of your home entertainment system and is only available prepackaged with new systems containing the required hardware extras: a TV tuner card, a remote control, an infrared receiver, lots of storage capacity, and a high-powered processor.

Windows CE

Windows CE (CE stands for "consumer electronics") is a Windows-based modular operating system designed for the embedded system and Internet appliance market. Its most noticeable use is as the operating system for the Pocket PCs being produced by Hewlett-Packard, Toshiba, and others (see Figure 3-8). Windows CE is a subset of Windows, scaled back to work with less memory on smaller screens and without much, if any, file storage. **Embedded systems** are computing devices that are integrated into other products. Embedded systems powered by Windows CE are currently being used in such diverse products as industrial controllers, robots, office equipment, digital cameras, telephones, home entertainment devices, and automobile navigation systems. In addition to giving all these devices a familiar Windows-like interface, Windows CE provides one other important feature: Internet connectivity. The latest version, Windows CE .NET, supports Microsoft's .NET platform for Web services, described under operating systems for networks.

▶ MAC OS

Apple's Macintosh operating system (**Mac OS**) was introduced along with the Macintosh microcomputer in 1984. It had the first commercially successful GUI and quickly gained a reputation for user friendliness. Based on concepts developed at Xerox's PARC research center in Palo Alto, California, the Mac OS GUI has served as a model for most of the graphical interfaces that have been developed since then. Still considered by many to be easier to use than Windows, Mac OS X (X is the Roman numeral for 10) contains enhancements in multimedia support and multitasking—the ability to do several things at once. It also enables you share files with Windows-based systems. See Figure 3-9 for an illustration of the Mac OS X desktop.

▶ UNIX

Unix, a multiuser time-sharing operating system, was developed in 1971 by Ken Thompson and Dennis Ritchie at AT&T's Bell Laboratories for use on its DEC minicomputers. In the late 1970s Bell gave Unix away to many colleges and universities, and students became accustomed to using it. Consequently, when many of these school's graduates entered the work force, they began agitating for the

GETTING PRACTICAL | Accessibility Options

Long hours staring at the computer screen can be hard on the eyes. As shown in the menu and toolbar here, Windows offers the option of enlarged letters and high-contrast colors.

Improved visibility is only part of the story. The Accessibility Options icon, found in the Control Panel, offers aids for seeing, hearing, and touching. For example, a hearing-impaired individual can elect to have any computer sound show up as a visual indicator on the screen. Furthermore, spoken words can be seen as screen captions.

An option called Sticky Keys permits keys that normally must be

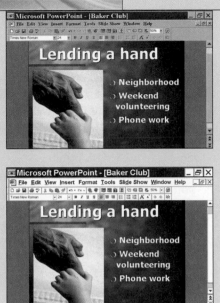

pressed at the same time to invoke a command, such as Ctrl-Alt-Del, to be pressed separately but still achieve the same effect. Another option, handy for anyone who has a habit of inadvertently pressing the Caps Lock key, is to sound a beep whenever the Caps Lock, Num Lock, or Scroll Lock key is pressed. Mouse movements can also be replaced by using the arrow keys on the numeric keypad.

acceptance of Unix in industry, thus producing what is known as the "Unix graduate" phenomenon.

At its basic level, Unix is a character-based system with a command-line user interface, although several GUI interfaces are available. In contrast to the operating systems we have discussed up to this point, Unix is not tied to any specific family of processors. It runs on just about every type of computer available, from microcomputers to mainframes, from any manufacturer. No one company controls Unix, and several versions are available. These versions are similar enough that an experienced Unix user would be comfortable with any of them, but there are some software

◄ **FIGURE** **3-9**

Mac OS X. The Mac OS interface has served as a model for most of the graphical interfaces available today. Still considered by many to be easier to use than Windows, Mac OS X contains enhancements in multi–media support and multitasking.

compatibility problems. The main reason that you need to be aware of Unix is that it is commonly used on Internet servers today.

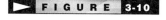 LINUX

In 1991 Linus Torvalds, a student at the University of Helsinki in Finland, created the kernel of a Unix-like operating system named **Linux** (pronounced LYNN-uks). He made the source code available to the public free of charge, under a concept known as **open-source** software. Users can download Linux for free, make any changes they wish, and freely distribute copies. The only restriction is that any changes they make must be freely available to the public.

Currently, most PC systems come with Windows preinstalled; if you would like to use Linux, you must install it yourself. Although the Linux code can be downloaded for free from the Internet, installing it is a complex task suitable only for the most advanced users. Several companies have packaged the Linux code with an installation program, documentation, customer support, and a number of utilities and application packages. These packages, known as distributions, make it easier for a typical user to install and use Linux and are relatively inexpensive (less than $50). Because Linux uses a command-line interface, most distributions also provide a GUI that the user can install (Figure 3-10). Many users install Linux in a **dual-boot** configuration with Windows; that is, when you boot the system, you choose which operating system to load.

Linux has several advantages over Windows. Windows users accustomed to the occasional system crash will be happy to learn that Linux is extremely stable—it rarely ever crashes. Also, Linux users form a close-knit community. If you have a problem or question, posting it on the Internet almost always results in a quick, accurate answer from Linux experts who are happy to share their knowledge. Finally, if the operating system should somehow become corrupted, reinstallation of Linux is a much simpler task than reinstalling Windows.

The biggest disadvantage of Linux is the relative scarcity of applications. Although a number of applications have become available, many under the same open-source concept as Linux itself, the numbers are still far fewer than for Windows. As Linux gains acceptance, this disparity may disappear.

► FIGURE 3-10

Linux. Linux is the fastest-growing operating system for Intel-based computers. Linux includes all the respected features of Unix and it's free.

OPERATING SYSTEMS FOR NETWORKS

A **network operating system (NOS)** is designed to let computers on a network share resources such as hard disks and printers. A NOS resides on a network server and handles network functions. In addition to resource sharing, a NOS supports data security (determining whether a user has the right to that data), troubleshooting (computer XYZ on the network failed to receive a message intended for it), and administrative control (track the online hours and track the number of messages to and from each computer).

One of the network operating system's main tasks is to make the resources appear as though they are running from the client's computer. Whether issuing commands, running applications software, or sending jobs to a printer, the role of a NOS is to make the desired services appear to be local to that client computer. The whole point of a client/server system is to provide expanded services to individual users at their networked computers; the network operating system is the software that makes it possible.

In a client/server relationship, parts of the NOS (mostly file access and management programs) run on the server computer, while other NOS components, such as software that permits requests to the server and messages to other computers, run on the client (user) computers. The client components can be integrated into the desktop operating system or be in a separate program.

The Windows network operating systems are designed to interact with the client components that are included in the Windows desktop operating systems discussed previously. The first generation was **Windows NT Server.** The **Windows 2000 Server** family is an upgrade to Windows NT, and includes three versions: Windows 2000 Server for typical business networks, Windows 2000 Server Advanced for e-commerce applications, and Windows 2000 Datacenter Server for enterprise-wide, large-scale networks. In addition to supporting Windows desktop systems, Windows 2000 Server also supports clients running Mac OS X, Unix and Linux.

Windows Server 2003, an upgrade to Windows 2000 Server, is Microsoft's current NOS. It has four different versions, designed for different levels of network complexity. In addition to providing all the functionality of Windows 2000 Server, it also supports **Microsoft's .NET platform,** designed to allow easy development and deployment of Web-based software services accessible by any Web-enabled device.

Novell's **Netware** is another popular NOS designed for the client/server environment. It supports clients running most operating systems. Its client components are installed in addition to the native operating system of the desktop or notebook client.

Both Unix and Linux were designed as multiuser operating systems and can support networks without installing any additional components.

OPERATING SYSTEMS FOR LARGE COMPUTERS

Large computers—mainframes—have been around about twice as long as personal computers. Those big computers are usually owned by businesses and universities, which make them available to many users. So, unlike the scenario with which you may be familiar—one person per personal computer at a time—many people use a large computer at one time. This presents special problems, which must be addressed by the operating system.

Computer users often have questions when they first realize that their program is "in there" with all those other programs. At any given moment, which program gets the CPU? If several programs are in memory at the same time, what keeps the programs from getting mixed up with one another? How is storage handled when several programs want to get data from disk or send processed data to disk at the same

Computers in Cars
Microsoft may dominate the desktop and laptop software markets, but it is trying to come from behind in the race to control the automobile dashboard. Sun Microsystems has had agreements with Ford and General Motors to power onboard automobile computers with its Java technology, but Microsoft recently announced deals with BMW, Volvo (a unit of Ford Motor Co.), Subaru, Mitsubishi, and Citroën to use Windows CE as the embedded OS on their auto computers.

In a concept referred to as telematics, these computers are paired with GPS satellite navigation systems and cellular telephone technology to provide navigation aid and trouble reporting service to drivers. In the future, drivers will be able to access the Internet and connect to home and office networks while on the road.

time? Why doesn't printer output from several programs get all jumbled up? The operating system anticipates these problems and takes care of them behind the scenes so that users can share the computer's resources without worrying about how it is done.

► RESOURCE ALLOCATION

Notice that the preceding questions all address sharing problems, that is, multiple users sharing the CPU, memory, storage, and the printer. Shared resources are allocated. **Resource allocation** is the process of assigning computer resources to certain programs for their use. Those same resources are deallocated—released—when the program using them is finished, and then they are reallocated elsewhere.

Sharing the Central Processing Unit

Because most computers have a single CPU, all programs running on the computer must share it. The sharing process is controlled by the operating system. Two approaches to sharing the CPU are multiprogramming and time-sharing. A similar-sounding (but very different in meaning) term, **multiprocessing,** refers to the use of a powerful computer with multiple CPUs so that multiple instructions can be executed simultaneously, each on a separate processor.

MULTIPROGRAMMING   If there is only one central processing unit (the usual case), it is not physically possible for more than one program to use it at the same time. **Multiprogramming** means that two or more programs are being executed in the same time frame, that is, **concurrently,** on a computer. What this really means is that the programs are taking turns; one program runs for a while, and then another one runs. The key word here is *concurrently* as opposed to *simultaneously.* One program could be using the CPU while another does something else, such as sending output to the printer or waiting for data to be read from the disk drive. Concurrent processing means that two or more programs are using the CPU in the same time frame—during the same minute, for instance—but not exactly at the same instant. In other words, concurrent processing allows one program to use one resource while another program uses another resource; this gives the illusion of simultaneous processing. As a result, there is less idle time for the computer system's resources. Concurrent processing is effective because CPU speeds are many times faster than input/output speeds. During the time it takes a disk drive to perform a read instruction for one program, for example, the CPU can execute thousands or even tens of thousands of calculation instructions for another program.

Multiprogramming is **event-driven.** This means that programs share resources based on events that take place in the programs. Normally, a program is allowed to complete a certain activity (event), such as a calculation, before relinquishing the resource (the CPU, in this example) to another program that is waiting for it.

The operating system implements multiprogramming through a system of interrupts. An **interrupt** is a signal that causes normal program processing to be suspended temporarily. Suppose, for example, that several programs are running on a large computer: two of them being a payroll program and an inventory-management program. When the payroll program needs to read the next employee record, that program is interrupted, or, in a sense, interrupts itself, while the operating system takes over to do the actual reading. Once the read operation has begun and the payroll program is waiting for the results, the operating system may allocate the CPU to the inventory program to do some calculations. When the read operation is completed, another interrupt is generated. The operating system suspends the inventory program, determines the reason for the interrupt—completion of the payroll program's read operation in this case—and then determines which program gets to

► MAKING CONNECTIONS ◄   **Personalizing Your Windows Desktop**

Many users quickly become bored with the standard plain blue Windows desktop. Windows does provide a few simple alternatives, such as clouds and red blocks, but many more creative options are available for free on the Internet. Windows uses the term "wallpaper" to refer to an image used for the desktop background. An Internet search on the term "Windows wallpaper" will turn up thousands of sites providing free (or minimal cost) images in many categories, including scenery, celebrities, sports, commercial products, abstract art, and just about anything else you can imagine.

resume using the CPU. That determination may be based on priorities—the program with the highest priority goes next—or on which has been waiting the longest.

The point of this discussion is not to clarify which program does what when. Rather, it is to show that shared resources are being managed by the operating system in the background. Although it may appear to the user that a program is running continuously from start to finish, in fact it is constantly being interrupted. This process is not without cost; the operating system does use some of the CPU resources itself. However, the overall effect is much more efficient use of the CPU.

In large computer systems, programs that run in an event-driven multiprogramming environment are usually batch programs that don't require user input. Typical examples are programs for payroll, accounts receivable, and sales and marketing analysis. If any interactive programs are running, they can be given the highest priority so that the users won't have to wait.

TIME-SHARING   A special case of multiprogramming, **time-sharing** is usually **time-driven** rather than event-driven. A common approach is to give each user a **time slice**—a fraction of a second—during which the computer works on a single user's tasks. However, the operating system does not wait for completion of an event; at the end of the time slice—that is, when time is up, the resources are taken away from that user and given to someone else. This is hardly noticeable to the user. When you are sitting before a terminal in a time-sharing system, the computer's response time will be quite short—fractions of a second—and it may seem as if you have the computer to yourself.

Response time is the time between your typed computer request and the computer's reply. Even if you are working on a calculation and the operating system interrupts it, sending you to the end of the line until other users have had their turns, you may not notice that you have been deprived of service. Not all computer systems give ideal service all the time, however; if a computer system is trying to serve too many users at the same time, response time may slow down noticeably.

Typical time-sharing applications are those with many users, each of whom has a series of brief, randomly occurring actions; examples include credit checking, point-of-sale systems, and airline reservation systems. Each of these systems has many users, perhaps hundreds, who need to share the system resources.

Sharing Memory

What if you have a very large program for which it might be difficult to find space in memory? Or what if several programs are competing for space in memory? These questions are related to memory management. **Memory management** is the process of allocating memory to programs and of keeping the programs in memory separate from one another.

There are many methods of memory management. Some systems simply divide memory into separate areas, each of which can hold a program. The problem is how to know how big the areas, sometimes called partitions or regions, should be; at least one of them should be large enough to hold the largest anticipated program. Some systems use memory areas that are not of a fixed size; that is, the sizes can change to meet the needs of the current assortment of programs. In either case, whether the areas are of a fixed or variable size, there is a problem with unused memory between programs. When these memory spaces are too small to be used, space is wasted.

FOREGROUND AND BACKGROUND   Large all-purpose computers often divide their memory into foreground and background areas. The **foreground** is generally for programs that have higher priority and therefore receive more CPU time. A typical foreground program is in a time-sharing environment, with the user at a terminal awaiting response. That is, a foreground program is interactive, with the CPU often unused while the user is entering the next request. Thus there is CPU time available for the waiting background programs. The **background,** as the name implies, is for programs with less pressing schedules and therefore lower priorities and less CPU time. Typical background programs are batch programs in a multiprogramming environment. Foreground programs are given privileged status—more turns for the CPU and other resources—and background programs take whatever they need that is not currently in use by another program. Lists of programs waiting to run are kept in **queues** suitable to their job class.

VIRTUAL STORAGE   Many computer systems manage memory by using a technique called **virtual storage** (also called **virtual memory**). The virtual storage concept means that the programs currently being executed are stored on disk and portions of these programs are brought into memory as needed. Because only one part of a program can be executing at any given time, the parts that are not currently needed are left on the disk. Because only part of the program is in memory at any given time, the amount of memory needed is minimized. Memory, in this case, is considered to be **real storage;** whereas the secondary storage (hard disk, most likely) holding the rest of the program is considered virtual storage.

Virtual storage can be implemented in a variety of ways. Consider the paging method, for example. Suppose you have a very large program, which means that there will be difficulty in finding space for it in the computer's shared memory. If your program is divided into small pieces, it will be easier to find places to put those pieces. This is essentially what paging does. **Paging** is the process of dividing a program into equal-size pieces called **pages** and storing them in equal-size memory spaces called **page frames.** All pages and page frames are the same fixed size, typically 2 kilobytes (KB) or 4 KB. The pages are stored in memory in noncontiguous locations—locations that are not necessarily next to each other (Figure 3-11).

Even though the pages are not right next to each other in memory, the operating system is able to keep track of them. It does this by using a **page table,** which, like an index, lists each page that is part of the program and the corresponding beginning

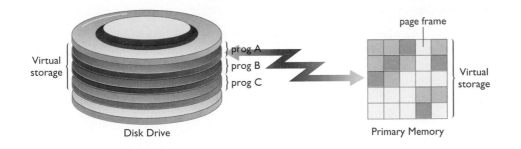

◄ **F I G U R E** 3-11

Virtual Storage. In this illustration, three programs (A, B, and C) are currently running. All three programs in virtual storage are divided into standard-sized segments called pages. Primary memory, referred to as real storage, is divided into the same sized segments called page frames. As pages of each program are needed for execution, they are copied from virtual storage into available page frames. If all the page frames are in full, the system will copy the contents of the least recently used page frame back into virtual memory to make room for the new page.

memory address where it has been placed. The operating system does require CPU time to control paging. If too large a portion of available CPU time is spent performing this paging, very little is left over to actually execute user programs. This situation, called **thrashing,** can be eliminated by running fewer programs concurrently or by adding additional memory.

MEMORY PROTECTION   In a multiprogramming or time-sharing environment it is theoretically possible for the computer, while executing one program, to destroy or modify another program by transferring to the wrong memory locations. That is, without protection, one program might accidentally hop into the middle of another, causing destruction of data and general chaos. This, of course, is not permitted. To avoid this problem, the operating system confines each program to certain defined limits in memory. If a program inadvertently attempts to enter some memory area outside its limits, the operating system terminates the execution of that program. This process of keeping one program from straying into another is called **memory protection.**

Sharing Storage Resources

The operating system keeps track of which file is where and responds to commands to manipulate files. But the situation is complicated by the possibility that more than one user may want to read or write a record from the same disk pack at the same time. Again, it is the operating system that keeps track of the input and output requests and processes them, usually in the order in which they were received. Any program instruction to read or write a record is routed to the operating system, which processes the request and then returns control to the program.

Sharing Printing Resources

Suppose half a dozen programs are active but the computer has only one printer. If all programs took turns printing out their output a line or two at a time, interspersed with the output of other programs, the resulting printed report would be worthless. To get around this problem, a process called spooling is used: Each program writes onto a disk each line that is to be printed. Or, to be more accurate, the program "thinks" that it is writing the line to the printer, but the operating system intercepts the line and sends it instead to a disk file. When the program finishes printing, the disk file is placed into a queue to be printed when the printer becomes available.

Spooling also addresses the problem of relatively slow printer speeds. Writing a record to disk is much faster than writing that same record to a printer. A program therefore completes execution more quickly if records to be printed are written temporarily to disk. The actual printing can be done at a later time when the program has completed execution. Some large installations use a separate (usually smaller) computer dedicated exclusively to the printing of spooled files; some print lengthy reports during off-hours or overnight so that smaller, more immediate jobs can use the printer during the day.

Utility Programs

Most of the resource allocation tasks just described are performed by the operating system without user involvement. For example activities such as paging and spooling go on without explicit commands from users. But the operating system can also perform explicit services at the request of the user.

Why reinvent the wheel? Duplication of effort is what **utility programs,** or just **utilities,** are supposed to avoid. Such programs perform many secondary chores, such as backing up and restoring files, compressing files and entire hard disks, locating files, and ferreting out computer viruses. Strictly speaking, these utilities are considered part of the system software but not part of the operating system. Some utilities are packaged with operating systems; others can be purchased separately. A few typical utilities are described in the following sections.

FILE MANAGER   Most storage devices can store large numbers of files. Imagine how difficult it would be to locate a single file among thousands of files on your hard drive. The **file manager** utility enables you to store your files in a hierarchical directory structure that is organized in a way that makes sense to you. A **directory** is a named area in storage that can contain files and other directories. For example, you might have a directory called Word Processing, in which you plan to store the files that you create with your word processor. You could then create a subdirectory named School within the Word Processing directory for all your schoolwork. Within the School directory you might create individual subdirectories for each of your classes. Incidentally, the newer versions of Windows refer to directories as folders.

In addition to enabling you to create this directory structure, the file manager also provides the capability to display lists of files in directories; to copy, move, rename, and delete files; and to format and copy diskettes. Figure 3-12 shows a display from Windows Explorer, the file manager that comes with the Windows operating system.

BACKUP AND RESTORE   Backing up files involves making duplicate copies and storing them in a safe place, in case anything happens to the originals. **Backup and**

▶ **FIGURE 3.12**

Windows Explorer.
Windows Explorer is the file manager utility that is part of the Windows operating system. The left screen pane shows the systems device and folder structure; the right pane shows the contents of the selected device or folder.

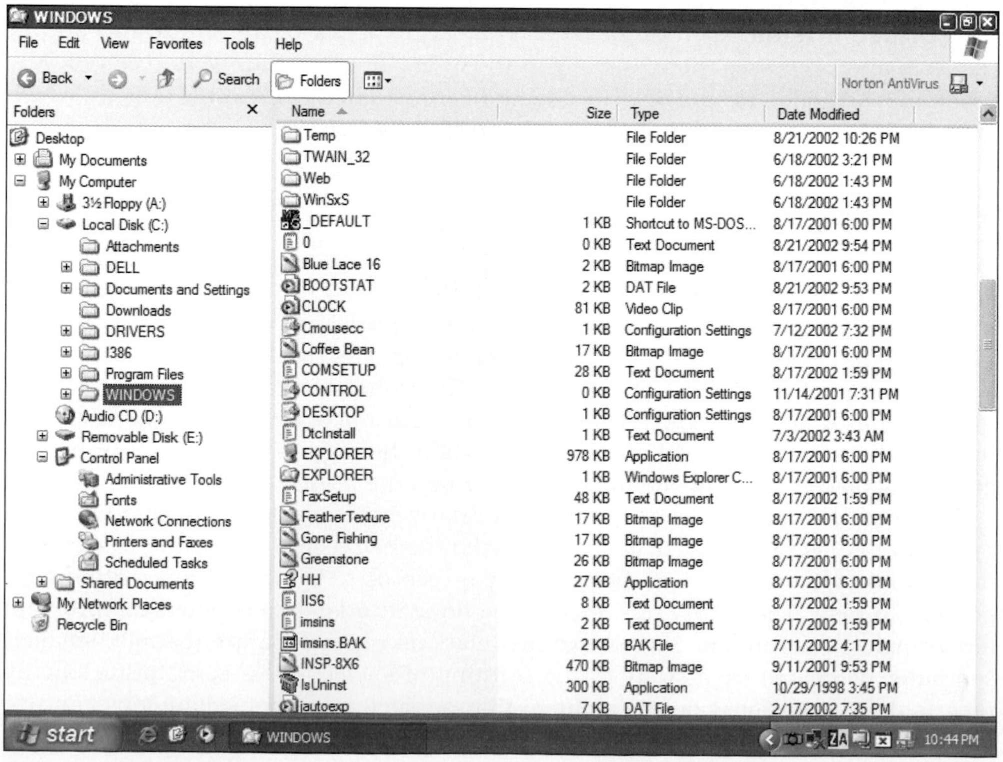

restore utilities enable you to make backups of entire hard drives or of selected directories. These backups could be made to diskettes but are normally stored on high-capacity media such as CD or tape (see Chapter 6, "Storage and Multimedia: The Facts and More," for more detail on these devices). Because the utility creates the backup files in a specialized format to minimize space requirements, the copies must be processed by the restore routine before you can use them. Rudimentary backup and restore utilities accompany most operating systems, but more capable utilities are provided with tape and CD devices or can be purchased separately.

FILE COMPRESSION A file compression utility reduces the amount of space required by a file. Compressed files take up less space on disk and also take less time to transmit across communication lines. Many files available for downloading from the Internet are in compressed format and must be decompressed into their original form before they can be used. PKZIP and WinZip® are two popular file compression utilities (Figure 3-13).

► **FIGURE** **3-13**

WinZip®. WinZip® is one of the best-known file compression utilities.

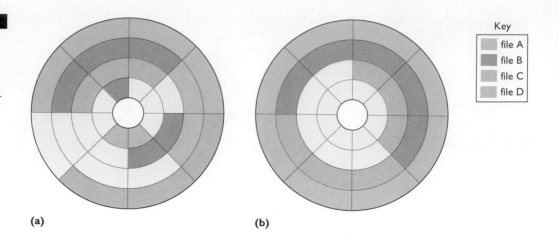

► **FIGURE** 3-14

Disk defragmentation.
(a) Before defragmentation, portions of files are scattered over the disk surface, slowing access. (b) After defragmentation, each file is stored in a group of contiguous sectors.

Key
file A
file B
file C
file D

(a)   (b)

DEFRAGMENTER   When the operating system is looking for space in which to store a file, it cannot always find enough space in one place on the disk. It often has to store portions of a file in noncontiguous, or separated, disk locations. When this happens, the file is fragmented. Although this process makes efficient use of disk space, it slows down access to the file. If a lot of files are fragmented, the effect on system performance can be very noticeable. A **disk defragmenter** utility reorganizes the files on the disk so that all files are stored in contiguous locations (Figure 3-14). Windows' defragmenter utility is called, not surprisingly, Disk Defragmenter.

DEVICE DRIVERS   The commands necessary to print a line on one manufacturer's laser printer are much different from the commands necessary to print the same line on another manufacturer's ink-jet printer. An operating system cannot possibly know the proper commands for every model of every type of peripheral device on the market. This problem is handled by small utilities called **device drivers.** A device driver accepts standard commands from the operating system and converts them into the proper format for the device it supports. Manufacturers provide device drivers for each of their products. Installing the product includes copying the appropriate driver(s) to your hard drive. Manufacturers often improve the performance of their products after they have been put on the market by rewriting the device drivers. They then make the improved drivers available on their Web site for purchasers of the product to download and install.

▲

This chapter discussed the software used to control the hardware and enable you and the application programs to interact with the computer. In the next chapter, you begin looking at the hardware parts of the computer system, starting with the CPU and memory.

CHAPTER REVIEW

► Summary and Key Terms

- An **operating system** is a set of programs that lies between applications software and the computer hardware. **Systems software** means all programs related to coordinating computer operations, including the operating system, programming language translators, and service programs.

- The **kernel,** most of which remains in memory, is called resident. The kernel controls the entire operating system and loads into memory nonresident operating system programs from disk storage as needed.

- Loading the operating system into memory is called **booting** the system.

- An operating system has three main functions: (1) managing the computer's resources, such as the central processing unit, memory, disk drives, and printers, (2) establishing a user interface; and (3) executing and providing services for applications software.

- The user communicates with the operating system through the **user interface.**

- A **platform** is a combination of computer hardware and operating system software that determines which applications users can run on their systems.

- The > in "C:\>" is a **prompt,** a signal that the system is waiting for you to give an instruction to the computer. To execute a given DOS program, a user must type a **command,** a name that invokes a specific DOS program.

- A **major operating system for PCs** is **Microsoft Windows,** software with a colorful **graphical user interface** (**GUI**). Windows offers onscreen pictures called **icons** and lists called **menus;** both encourage pointing and clicking with a mouse, an approach that can make computer use faster and easier. **Pull-down menus** pull down like a window shade from a selection on the menu bar. **Pop-up menus** originate from a selection at the bottom of the screen or when the right mouse button is clicked. Early versions of Windows were merely a layer of software over the operating system, called an **operating environment** or **shell.**

- **Microsoft Windows 95** is a true operating system, not a shell. A key feature is **Plug and Play,** a concept that lets the computer configure itself when a new component is added. A Windows technology called **object linking and embedding** (**OLE**) lets you embed or link one document with another. **Windows 98** is built on the same code base as Windows 95 and has a similar look and user interaction. In particular, Windows 98 incorporates Internet Explorer, a Web browser, into the operating system. **Windows Me** is the last in the Windows 9x series.

- **Windows NT** (for "new technology") is meant mostly for corporate, networked environments. It looks exactly like Windows 95 but has been engineered for stability and has much stronger security features. **Windows 2000** is the final generation in the NT series.

- **Windows XP** replaces both Windows 9x and Windows 2000, serving both the consumer and corporate desktop markets with a single product.

- **Windows CE** (for "consumer electronics") is a Windows-based modular operating system for **embedded systems** (systems built into other products) and other new digital appliances.

- The **Mac OS,** introduced with Apple's Macintosh computer in 1984, had the first generally available GUI. Its latest version, Mac OS X, is still considered to be the easiest to use for beginners.

- **Unix** is a multiuser, timesharing operating system that runs on all types of computers. It is a common operating system used on Internet servers today.

- **Linux** is a Unix-like operating system available under the **open-source** concept, which means that it is freely available and not under control of any one company. Many users install Linux in a **dual-boot** system, enabling them to choose between Windows and Linux each time they boot their PCs.

- A **network operating system** (**NOS**) is designed to let computers on a network share resources such as hard disks and printers. A NOS supports resource sharing, data security, troubleshooting, and administrative control. Parts of the NOS run on the server computer; whereas other NOS components run on the client computers.

- The Windows family of NOSs started with Windows NT Server and upgraded to Windows 2000 Server. **Windows Server 2003** is an upgrade to Windows 2000 Server that supports **Microsoft's .NET platform,** designed to allow easy development and deployment of Web-based software services accessible by any Web-enabled device.

- Novell's **Netware** is another popular NOS designed for the client/server environment.

- **Resource allocation** is the process of assigning computer resources to certain programs for their use.

- **Multiprocessing** means that a computer with more than one CPU can run multiple programs simultaneously, each using its own processor.

- **Multiprogramming** is running two or more programs in the same time frame, **concurrently,** on the same computer. Multiprogramming is **event-driven,** meaning that one program is allowed to use a particular resource (such as the CPU) to complete a certain activity (event) before relinquishing the resource to another program. In multiprogramming, the operating system uses **interrupts,** which are signals that temporarily suspend the execution of individual programs.

- **Time-sharing** is a special case of multiprogramming in which several people use one computer at the same time. Time-sharing is **time-driven;** each user is given a **time slice** in which the computer works on that user's tasks before moving on to another user's tasks. **Response time** is the time between the user's typed computer request and the computer's reply.

- **Memory management** is the process of allocating memory to programs and of keeping the programs in memory separate from each other. Some systems simply divide memory into separate areas, sometimes called **partitions** or **regions**, each of which can hold a program. Large all-purpose computers often divide memory into a **foreground** area for programs with higher priority and a **background** area for programs with lower priority. Programs waiting to be run are kept on the disk in **queues.**

- In the **virtual storage** (or **virtual memory**) technique of memory management, part of the application program is stored on disk and is brought into memory only when needed for execution. Memory is considered **real storage;** the secondary storage holding the rest of the program is considered virtual storage.

- Virtual storage can be implemented in several ways, one of which is paging. **Paging** divides a program into equal-size pieces (**pages**) that fit exactly into corresponding noncontiguous memory spaces (**page frames**). The operating system keeps track of page locations using an index-like **page table. Thrashing** occurs when the CPU spends all its time swapping pages in and out of real memory.

- In multiprogramming, **memory protection** is an operating system process that defines the limits of each program in memory, thus preventing programs from accidentally destroying or modifying one another.

- **Spooling** writes each file to be printed temporarily onto a disk instead of printing it immediately. When this spooling process is complete, all the appropriate files from a particular program can be printed intact.

- **Utility programs** (**utilities**) are programs that perform many common tasks for users. Examples include **file managers** to organize and manage disk files in a directory structure, **backup and restore** utilities to facilitate making file backups, **file compression** utilities to reduce the amount of space required by files, **disk defragmenters** to relocate disk files into contiguous locations, and **device drivers** to allow the operating system to communicate with peripherals.

▶ Critical Thinking Questions

1. How would the use of computers be affected if there were no GUIs and all operating systems still used a command-driven interface?

2. Even though the Mac OS is generally considered to be easier to use than Microsoft Windows, Windows dominates the market. Why do you think this is and what might Apple do to increase its market share?

3. One feature of Windows XP is that it can access Microsoft's Web site over the Internet and find and download updates. You can configure your system to do this automatically, without telling you, or you can require it to ask your permission first. What advantages and disadvantages do you see for each approach?

4. Which of these kinds of operating systems might you expect to use in your career: Personal computer operating system? Large computer operating system? Network operating system? All of these? Will it depend on the type of job you have?

5. Even though the operating system Linux is available at no cost and is generally considered to be well-written and robust software, many businesses are reluctant to adopt it. Why do think this is? What do you think would have to happen before more businesses would be willing to install Linux on their computers?

▶ STUDENT STUDY GUIDE

Multiple Choice

1. What does an operating system consist of?
   a. A sct of users
   b. A set of programs
   c. A form of time-sharing
   d. A kernel program

2. In multiprogramming, how can two or more programs be executed?
   a. By optimizing compilers
   b. Simultaneously
   c. With two computers
   d. Concurrently

3. Time-sharing of resources by users is usually
   a. based on time slices
   b. event-driven
   c. based on input
   d. operated by spooling

4. What is the main program in an operating system called?
   a. Kernel
   b. File manager
   c. Directory
   d. NOS

5. What is the process of allocating main memory to programs and keeping the programs in memory separate from one another called?
   a. Memory adjustment
   b. Virtual storage
   c. Memory management
   d. Real storage

6. What is the Windows version that is the convergence of the consumer and business desktop operating systems called?
   a. DOS
   b. 3.1
   c. XP
   d. 2000

7. What is the technique in shared systems that avoids mixing printout from several programs called?
   a. Paging
   b. Slicing
   c. Queuing
   d. Spooling

8. What is the technique whereby part of the program is stored on disk and is brought into memory-for execution as needed called?
   a. Memory allocation
   b. Virtual storage
   c. Interrupts
   d. Prioritized memory

9. Part of a NOS runs on client computers with Where does the other part run?
   a. Page frame
   b. Page table
   c. Server
   d. Host

10. What is another name for an operating environment?
    a. Page
    b. Shell
    c. Layer
    d. Supervisor

11. What is loading the operating system into a personal computer called?
    a. Booting
    b. Interrupting
    c. Prompting
    d. Paging

12. Which one of the following uses graphical icons?
    a. Command-line interface
    b. Utility program
    c. Page
    d. GUI

13. In multiprogramming, what is the process of confining each program to certain defined limits in memory called?
    a. Spooling
    b. Program scheduling
    c. Time-sharing
    d. Memory protection

14. What are the corresponding memory spaces for pages called?
    a. Page utilities
    b. Page blocks
    c. Page frames
    d. Page modules

15. What is the time between the user's request and the computer's reply called?
    a. Concurrent time
    b. Allocation time
    c. Response time
    d. Event time

16. What is an onscreen picture that represents an object, such as a program or file, called?
    a. Page
    b. Icon
    c. NOS
    d. Spool

17. What is running programs with more than one CPU called?
    a. Interrupting
    b. Multiprocessing
    c. Embedding
    d. Multiprogramming

18. What is the memory area for programs with highest priority called?
    a. Frame
    b. Page table
    c. Foreground
    d. Background

19. What are lists of programs waiting to be run called?
    a. Page frames
    b. Shells
    c. The background
    d. Queues

20. What are system programs that handle common user tasks called?
    a. Pull-down menus
    b. Supervisors
    c. Pages
    d. Utilities

21. What is the signal that the computer is awaiting a command from the user called?
    a. Prompt
    b. Event
    c. Time slice
    d. Interrupt

22. What does the acronym NOS refer to?
    a. Memory management techniques
    b. Virtual storage
    c. The booting process
    d. An operating system for a network

23. What is the combination of hardware and operating system for which an application program is written called?
    a. Shell
    b. Interrupt
    c. Platform
    d. Operating environment

24. Which of the following operating systems contained the first commercially successful GUI?
    a. Mac OS
    b. Windows
    c. Unix
    d. Linux

25. Which of the following is an operating system designed for embedded systems?
    a. Windows XP
    b. Mac OS X
    c. MS-DOS
    d. Windows CE

True/False

T F 1. A DOS program is invoked by typing a command.

T F 2. The central program in an operating system is called the kernel.

T F 3. Multiprogramming means that two or more programs can run simultaneously.

T F 4. Time-sharing is effective because input/output speeds are much faster than CPU speeds.

T F 5. Resource allocation means that a given program has exclusive use of computer resources.

T F 6. Background programs are usually batch programs.

T F 7. Virtual storage is a technique of memory management that appears to provide users with more memory space than is actually the case.

T F 8. Windows employs a graphical user interface.

T F 9. Windows CE is designed to run on network servers.

T F 10. Shell is another name for page.

T F 11. An operating system includes system software, programming language translators, and service programs.

T F 12. Utility programs avoid duplication of effort.

T F 13. In a given memory system, all page frames are the same size.

T F 14. Virtual memory is another name for virtual storage.

T F 15. Loading the operating system into memory is called booting.

T F 16. An interrupt causes a program to stop temporarily.

T F 17. Portions of a NOS reside on both client and server computers.

T F 18. Paging divides a program into pieces of various sizes to fit in the available memory spaces.

T F 19. Response time is the elapsed time for program execution.

T F 20. Device drivers allow the operating system to control I/O devices.

T F 21. Multiprocessing is concurrent processing of several programs by a single CPU.

T F 22. The shared resources that the operating system manages include the CPU, memory, storage devices, and the printer.

T F 23. Multiprogramming is one approach to sharing the CPU.

T F 24. All operating system programs must be in memory during the time an application program is running.

T F 25. A knowledgeable user can interact directly with the hardware without invoking the operating system.

T F 26. A typical time-sharing application is processing payroll checks.

T F 27. Open-source software is freely available but may not be modified by the user.

T F 28. A prompt is used in a command-line interface and indicates that the operating system is waiting for the user to enter an instruction.

T F 29. Unix is a multiuser time-sharing operating system that is available for most computers.

T F 30. Interactive programs would most likely be assigned to background memory.

Fill-In

1. NOS stands for _____.

2. The operating system program that remains resident in memory is the _____.

3. The term used for the time between a user's request at the terminal and the computer's reply is _____.

4. The type of system that lets two or more programs execute concurrently is _____.

5. What are the program pieces called in the virtual storage technique of paging? What are the corresponding memory spaces called?
   a. _____
   b. _____

6. Simultaneous processing of more than one program using more than one processor is called _____.

7. Another name for partition is _____.

8. High-priority programs usually operate in this part of memory: _____.

9. The process of assigning computer resources to certain programs for their use is called _____.

10. The operating system keeps track of page locations by using a(n) _____.

11. The process that an operating system uses to avoid interspersing the printout from several programs is called _____.

12. A program that overlays the operating system to provide a more user-friendly environment is the _____.

13. In time-sharing, each user is given a unit of time called a(n) _____.

14. _____ is a Windows technology that enables you to link to or embed one object within another.

15. A utility that reorganizes disk files into contiguous storage locations is the _____.

16. Loading the operating system into memory is called _____.

17. Time-sharing is time driven but multiprogramming is _____ driven.

18. The situation that occurs when the CPU spends all its time swapping pages into and out of real memory is _____.

19. A utility that translates operating system commands into instructions that operate a peripheral is a(n) _____.

20. GUI stands for _____.

21. In multiprogramming, a(n) _____ is a condition that temporarily suspends program execution.

22. Keeping programs in memory from interfering with each other is called _____.

23. A utility that reduces the amount of space required to store a file is a(n) _____.

24. A Unix-like operating system that is available under the open-source concept is _____.

25. A Windows feature that automatically configures new hardware is known as _____.

► ANSWERS

Multiple Choice

1. b	6. c	11. a	16. b	21. a
2. d	7. d	12. d	17. b	22. d
3. a	8. b	13. d	18. c	23. c
4. a	9. c	14. c	19. d	24. a
5. c	10. b	15. c	20. d	25. d

True/False

1. T	7. T	13. T	19. F	25. F
2. T	8. T	14. T	20. T	26. F
3. F	9. F	15. T	21. F	27. F
4. F	10. F	16. T	22. T	28. T
5. F	11. F	17. T	23. T	29. T
6. T	12. T	18. F	24. F	30. F

Fill-In

1. network operating system
2. kernel
3. response time
4. multiprogramming
5. a. pages
   b. page frames
6. multiprocessing
7. region
8. foreground
9. resource allocation
10. page table
11. spooling
12. operating environment (or shell)
13. time slice
14. object linking and embedding (or OLE)
15. disk defragmenter
16. booting
17. event
18. thrashing
19. device driver
20. graphical user interface
21. interrupt
22. memory protection
23. file compression program
24. Linux
25. Plug and Play

Planet Internet

Web Games

"While it is nice to win a game, losing is a part of life. All squadron members should have a firm grasp of this reality." (From a game clan's "Squadron Code of Conduct".)

You know the stereotype of the computer gamer: a lone, pasty-complexioned, geeky guy, locked in his dimly lit room, obsessively blasting away at imaginary enemies, or wrapped up in a medieval fantasy world of dragons, elves, and aliens. Enter the Internet. He's still pasty, he's still obsessive, and, yes, he's still likely a guy, but he's no longer alone, and he's definitely not confined to his room anymore.

Ever since Doom opened up the LAN network to the First Person Shooter, interactive play with and against other players has become a permanent part of the gaming landscape. Doom's boom has passed, but its wildly successful successors like Half-Life still offer the opportunity to pit your trigger-happy self, via the Internet, against the talents of thousands of other players scattered around the world.

Most console video games aren't online yet, but manufacturers such as Sony and Sega are building high-speed Internet connectivity into the current generation of their gaming machines, ensuring that the Internet doesn't solely belong to computer gamers.

What drives gamers (and game developers) onto the Net? One thing is competition. For all the highly touted artificial intelligence that is carefully programmed into gameplay engines, nothing yet beats a real human for skillful competition and challenging game play.

Despite their highly competitive (and sometimes downright gory) nature, online games can also foster cooperation and socializing. Many gamers organize into clans, and some games—most notably Tribes 2—have been specifically designed to support team play.

To join a clan, players might have to pass an audition of sorts in which they demonstrate proficient game play.

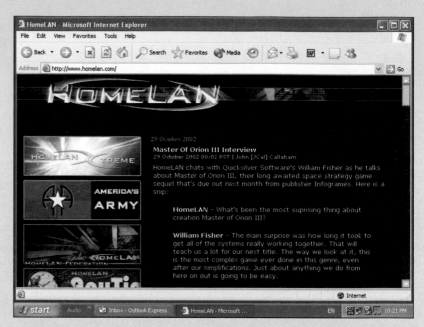

Clans have their own membership, bylaws, customs, jargon and leadership; in many ways they mirror (or parody) teams in the real world.

The real-time communication abilities that are built into the latest online games allow textual and spoken dialog among team members, and some games even feature voice-over narration "shoutcasts" to provide blow-by-blow coverage and color commentary. Gamers can personalize their players with "skins" that replace the default appearance of their character with a picture of themselves, or another person, real or imaginary. (In election years players clad in the skins of candidates are not unheard of.)

Although online gamers can be widely separated (Tribes is hosted on servers in the United States, the United Kingdom, Asia, and Russia), the urge to actually meet the members of your own and others' clans has spawned a new trend: the LAN party. For a LAN party all you need is a local area network—preferably a very fast one—a lot of computers, and some dedicated gamers. Everyone sits in the same building at his or her PC, playing against opponents only a few feet, instead of a world, away. One Quake-based LAN party recently drew over a thousand participants, and featured video projection screens and gigabit Internet connections.

The Massively Multiplayer Online Role-Playing Game is another recent gaming experience made possible by the Internet. MMORPGs, as they are called, are basically a virtual world where gamers can log in and create a character, to role-play and interact with other gamers in the game's context and story. Ultima Online was one of the first games of this type to achieve massive popularity, but many others are now in place and have many devoted players, like Everquest or Star Wars Galaxies.

Unlike a regular computer game, where you pay once to buy the software and then use it as much or as little as you like, MMORPGs will often give away the software for free. Once the game is installed and running, players then pay a monthly or yearly subscription fee to play the game.

Similar to a paper-and-dice role-playing game, in the MMORPG, a player can direct his/her character on quests, interact with others players, and in general play out the role of their persona in the game's world. In addition to gaining skills, treasure, and experience, role-playing activities also include things like finding food, ensuring a place to sleep, and buying and selling clothes and other items for their character.

Even if you're not drawn to computer gaming, you should be aware that computer entertainment, and games in particular, are one of the driving forces behind computer hardware innovation. After all, you don't think all those folks bought 3.0-gigahertz machines with those 3D graphics cards and Ethernet network connections exclusively for spreadsheets, did you?

Internet Exercises:

1. **Structured exercise.** Starting with www.prenhall.com/capron, browse some of the online gaming links provided. Find out what computer hardware and software are required to run one of the games you find described there.

2. **Free-form exercise.** Watch someone playing an online game or try to play one yourself. How does this experience compare to playing a game alone on a PC, or at an arcade?

3. **Advanced exercise.** Visit the Web page of one or more game clans. Report on what you find there as if you were an anthropologist. What customs, rules, and jargon did you find? How would you describe the culture of this online gaming community?

The Central Processing Unit:
What Goes on Inside the Computer

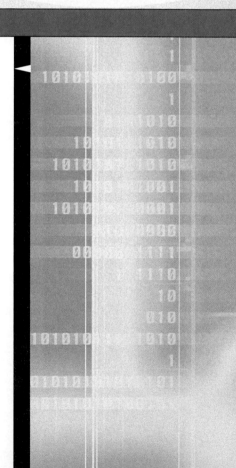

C H A P T E R 4

LEARNING OBJECTIVES

Identify the components of the central processing unit and explain how they work together and interact with memory

Describe how program instructions are executed by the computer

Explain how data is represented in the computer

Describe how the computer finds instructions and data

Describe the components of a microcomputer system unit's motherboard

List the measures of computer processing speed and explain the approaches that increase speed

Mark Ong, who hoped to be a scriptwriter, planned a double major in creative writing and drama. During the summer before he entered college, he took a job as an intern editorial assistant, where he first used word processing. He decided that it would be helpful to have a personal computer of his own when he went to college in the fall, but he felt unsure of how to make a purchase. In fact, he felt that he did not even know what questions to ask. He discussed this with an office colleague, who casually noted that any computer setup comes with the standard stuff—processor, keyboard, mouse, screen, disk drives—and that all Mark had to do was go to a computer store and pick one that fit his price range. Mark was not satisfied with this approach, especially in light of the advertisements he had seen in the local newspaper and in computer magazines.

Most advertisements displayed photos of personal computers, accompanied by cryptic descriptions of the total hardware package. A typical ad was worded this way: Pentium 4, 3.0GHz, 256MB RAM, 512KB cache, 1.44MB diskette drive, 16x DVD-ROM, 80GB hard drive. The price for this particular machine was pretty hefty, more than $1,800. Mark noticed that the ads for machines with lower numbers, such as 2.4GHz, also had lower price tags. Similarly, higher numbers meant higher price tags. Although he did recognize the disk drives, he had no idea what the other items were or why the numbers mattered. Clearly, there was more to a purchasing decision than selecting a system with the standard stuff.

Mark tore out some of the ads and went to a nearby computer store. After asking a lot of questions, he learned that Pentium 4 is a microprocessor type; that GHz stands for gigahertz and is a measurement of the microprocessor's speed; that RAM is the computer's memory; that cache is a handy storage place for frequently used data and software instructions; and that GB is an abbreviation for gigabytes, a measurement of storage size for the hard disk. Most importantly, Mark learned that the number variations matter because they are factors in determining a computer's capacity and speed.

Many buyers select their personal computer system merely on the basis of a sales pitch and price range. Those people could argue, with some justification, that they do not need to know all the computer buzzwords any more than they need to know the technical details of their television sets or sound systems. They know that they do not have to understand a computer's innards to put it to work.

But there are rewards for those who want to dig a little deeper and learn a little more. Although this chapter is not designed to help you purchase a computer, it does provide some background information and gives you the foundation on which future computer knowledge can be built.

▶ THE CENTRAL PROCESSING UNIT

The computer does its primary work in a part of the machine we cannot see: a control center that converts data input to information output. This control center, called the **central processing unit (CPU)**, is a highly complex, extensive set of electronic circuitry that executes stored program instructions. All computers, large and small, must have at least one CPU. As Figure 4-1 shows, the CPU consists of two parts: the *control unit* and the *arithmetic/logic unit*. Each part has a specific function.

Before examining the control unit and the arithmetic/logic unit in detail, consider data storage and its relationship to the CPU. Computers use two major types of storage: primary storage and secondary storage. The CPU interacts closely with primary storage, or memory, referring to it for both instructions and data. For this reason this chapter discusses memory in the context of the central processing unit. Technically, however, memory is not part of the CPU.

Memory holds data only temporarily, while a program is working directly with it. Secondary storage holds permanent or semi-permanent data on some external medium, such as a disk, until it is needed for processing by the computer. Because the physical attributes of secondary storage devices determine how data is organized on them, secondary storage and data organization are discussed together in the chapter on storage.

Now let us consider the components of the CPU.

The Control Unit

The **control unit** contains circuitry that uses electrical signals to direct the entire computer system to carry out, or execute, stored program instructions. Like an orchestra leader, the control unit does not execute program instructions; rather, it directs other parts of the system to do so. The control unit must communicate with both the arithmetic/logic unit and memory.

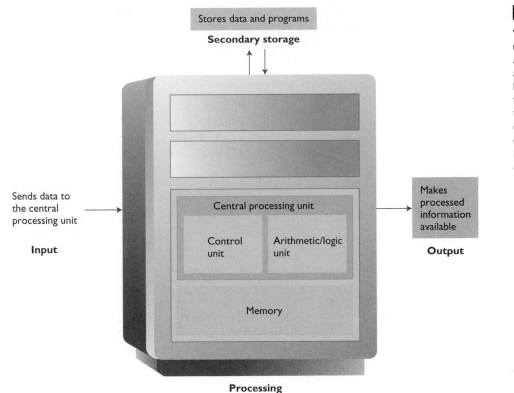

Stores data and programs
Secondary storage

Sends data to
the central
processing unit

Input

Central processing unit

Control
unit

Arithmetic/logic
unit

Memory

Makes
processed
information
available

Output

Processing

◄ **F I G U R E** 4-1

**The central processing
unit.** The two parts of the CPU
are the control unit and the
arithmetic/logic unit. Memory
holds data and instructions
temporarily while the program
they are part of is being executed. The CPU interacts
closely with memory, referring to it for both instructions
and data.

The Arithmetic/Logic Unit

The **arithmetic/logic unit (ALU)** contains the electronic circuitry that executes all arithmetic and logical operations.

The ALU performs four kinds of arithmetic operations, or mathematical calcula-tions: addition, subtraction, multiplication, and division. As its name implies, the ALU also performs **logical operations,** or comparisons. The unit can compare numbers, letters, or special characters to test the conditions described below. The computer then takes action based on whether the test produces a true or false result. This is a very important capability. Through comparison, a computer can tell, for instance, whether there are unfilled seats on airplanes, whether charge card customers have exceeded their credit limits, or whether one candidate for Congress has more votes than another.

Logical operations can test for three conditions:

- **Equal-to condition.** In a test for the **equal-to condition**, the ALU compares two values to determine if they are equal. For example, if the number of tickets sold equals the number of seats in the auditorium, then the concert is declared sold out.

- **Less-than condition.** To test for the **less-than condition,** the ALU compares two values to determine if the first is less than the second. For example, if the number of speeding tickets on a driver's record is fewer than three, then the insurance rate is $425; otherwise, the rate is $500.

- **Greater-than condition.** In testing for the **greater-than condition,** the ALU de-termines if the first value is greater than the second. For example, if the number of hours a person worked this week is greater than 40, then the program multiplies every extra hour by 11, twice the usual hourly wage, to compute overtime pay.

In addition to these three basic conditions, the computer can test for combinations of conditions: less-than-or-equal-to, greater-than-or-equal-to, and less-than-or-greater-than conditions. Note that less-than-or-greater-than is the same as **not-equal-to.**

Chips That See

No, chips won't be inserted into your eyes anytime soon. It's the other way around: the power to see is being given to chips. These chips are called imaging chips because they can see, and respond to, images that are put in front of them. An example on the market today is a machine at the checkout stand that is like the one that scans your groceries, but is for your fingertips. In just seconds, a computer with an imaging chip can compare your fingerprint with thousands on file and send a yes or no decision. This technology has been used to eliminate check fraud.

What might an imaging chip watch over? Technical futurists see several possibilities. Chips on airplanes could watch to ensure that the landing gear descends properly. Imaging chips in cars could detect the size of a passenger and adjust the force of the air bag accordingly. Surgeons could plant tiny chips in a patient's chest to watch over their handiwork in the critical hours following an operation.

The symbols that programmers use to tell the computer which type of comparison to perform are called **relational operators.** The most common relational operators are the equal sign (=), the less-than symbol (<), and the greater-than symbol (>).

Registers: Temporary Storage Areas

Registers are special-purpose, high-speed, temporary storage areas for instructions or data. They are not a part of memory; rather, they are special additional storage locations located within the CPU itself that offer the advantage of speed. Registers work under the direction of the control unit to accept, hold, and transfer instructions or data and perform arithmetic or logical comparisons at high speed. The control unit uses a register the way a store owner uses a cash register—as a temporary, convenient place to store what is used in transactions.

Special-purpose registers have specific tasks, such as holding the instruction that is currently being executed or keeping track of where the next instruction to be executed is stored in memory. (Each storage location in memory is identified by an address, just as each house on a street has an address.) Some CPU designs include general-purpose registers, which the control unit can use for different tasks as required.

Consider registers in the context of all the means of storage discussed so far. Registers hold data that is immediately related to the operation being executed. Memory stores data that will be used in the near future. Secondary storage holds data that may be needed later in the same program execution or perhaps at some time in the future.

This section examines how a payroll program, for example, uses all three types of storage. Suppose the program is about to calculate an employee's gross pay by multiplying the hours worked by the rate of pay. The control unit has placed a copy of the data representing the hours worked and the data for the rate of pay in their respective registers. Other data related to that employee's salary calculation, such as overtime hours, bonuses, and deductions, is waiting nearby in memory. The data for other employees is available in secondary storage. As the computer finishes calculations for one employee, the data for the next employee is brought from secondary storage into memory and eventually into the registers.

► MEMORY

Memory is also known as **primary storage, primary memory, main storage, internal storage,** and **main memory;** people in computer circles use these terms interchangeably. Manufacturers often use the term **RAM,** which stands for random-access memory. Memory is the part of the computer that holds data and instructions for processing. Although closely associated with the CPU, memory is separate from it. Memory stores program instructions or data only as long as the program they pertain to is in operation. Keeping these items in memory when the program is not running is not feasible for these reasons:

● Most types of memory used in computers today store items only while the computer is turned on; data is lost when the machine is turned off.

● If more than one program is running at the same time (usually the case on large computers and sometimes on small computers), a single program cannot lay exclusive claim to memory. There may not be room in memory to hold all the processed data.

● Secondary storage is more cost-effective than memory for storing large amounts of data.

The CPU cannot process data directly from an input device or disk; the data must first be available in memory. How do data and instructions get from an input or storage device into memory? The control unit sends them. Likewise, when the time is right, the control unit sends these items from memory to the ALU, where an arithmetic operation or logical operation is performed. After being processed, the result is sent to memory, where it is held until it is ready to be released, or sent, to an output or storage device.

The chief characteristic of memory is that it enables very fast access to instructions and data, no matter where the items are within it. A discussion of the physical components of memory, memory chips, appears later in this chapter.

► HOW THE CPU EXECUTES PROGRAM INSTRUCTIONS

This section examines the way the CPU, in association with memory, executes one instruction in a computer program. Many personal computers can execute an instruction in less than one millionth of a second; whereas the speed demons known as supercomputers can execute an instruction in less than one trillionth of a second.

Before an instruction can be executed, program instructions and data must be placed into memory from an input device or a secondary storage device. As Figure 4-2 shows, once the necessary data and instruction are in memory, the central processing unit performs the following four steps for each instruction:

1. The control unit fetches (gets) the instruction from memory and puts it into a register.

2. The control unit decodes the instruction (decides what it means) and determines the memory location of the data required. These first two steps together are called instruction time, or **I-time.**

3. The control unit moves the data from memory to registers in the arithmetic/logic unit. The ALU executes the arithmetic or logical instruction. That is, the ALU is given control and performs the actual operation on the data.

4. The control unit stores the result of this operation in memory or in a register. Steps 3 and 4 together are called execution time, or **E-time.**

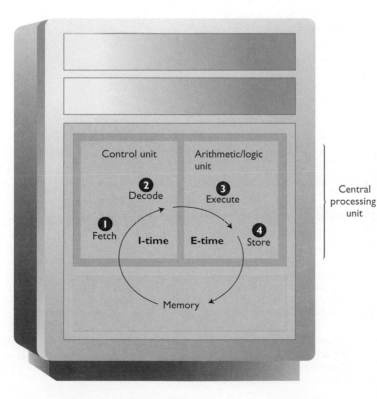

◄ **FIGURE 4-2**

The machine cycle.
Program instructions and data are brought into memory from an external source, either an input device or secondary storage medium. The machine cycle executes instructions one at a time, as described in the text.

The control unit eventually directs memory to send the result to an output device or a secondary storage device. The combination of I-time and E-time is called the **machine cycle.** Figure 4-3 shows an instruction going through the machine cycle.

Each CPU has an internal **system clock** that produces pulses at a fixed rate to synchronize all computer operations. Note that this is not the clock that the computer uses to keep track of the date and time; that's a separate chip. A single program instruction may be made up of a substantial number of sub-instructions, each of which takes at least one machine cycle. Each type of central processing unit is designed to understand a specific group of instructions, such as ADD or MOVE, called the **instruction set.** Just as there are many different languages that people understand, there are many different instruction sets that different types of CPUs understand.

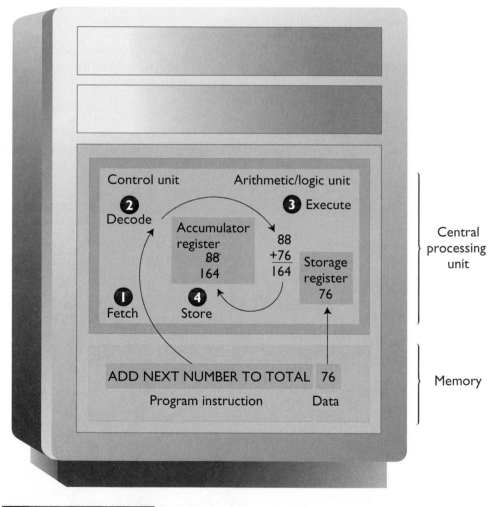

▲ **F I G U R E 4-3**

The machine cycle in action. Suppose a program must find the average of five test scores. To do this, it must total the five scores, and then divide the result by five. The program begins by setting the total to 0. It then adds each of the five numbers, one at a time, to the total. Suppose the scores are 88, 76, 91, 83, and 87. In this figure, the total has been set to 0, and then 88, the first test score, has been added to it. Now examine the machine cycle as it adds the next score, 76, to the total. Follow the four steps of the machine cycle. (1) Fetch: the control unit fetches the ADD instruction from memory. (2) Decode: the control unit decodes the ADD instruction. It determines that addition must take place and gives instructions for the next number, 76, to be placed in a register for this purpose. The current total, 88, is already in the accumulator register. (3) Execute: the next number, 76, is placed in the register. The ALU does the addition, increasing the total to 164. (4) Store: in this case, the ALU stores the result in the accumulator instead of in memory because more numbers still need to be added to it. The new total of 164 replaces the previous total, 88.

▶ STORAGE LOCATIONS AND ADDRESSES: HOW THE CONTROL UNIT FINDS INSTRUCTIONS AND DATA

It is one thing to have instructions and data somewhere in memory and quite another for the control unit to be able to find them. How does it do this?

The location in memory for each instruction and each piece of data is identified by an address. Each location has an address number, like the mailboxes in front of an apartment house. And, like the mailboxes, the address numbers of the locations remain the same, but the contents (instructions and data) of the locations may change. New instructions or new data may be placed in the locations when the old contents no longer need to be stored in memory. Unlike a mailbox, however, a memory location can hold only one instruction or piece of data at a time. When a new instruction or piece of data is placed in a memory location, that location's prior contents are destroyed.

Figure 4-4 shows how a program manipulates data in memory. A payroll program, for example, may give instructions to put the rate of pay in location 3 and the number of hours worked in location 6. To compute the employee's salary, instructions tell the computer to multiply the data in location 3 by the data in location 6 and move the result to location 8. The choice of locations is arbitrary—any locations that are not already spoken for can be used. Programmers using programming languages, however, do not have to worry about the actual address numbers, because each data address can be given a meaningful name. The name is called a **symbolic address.** In this example, the symbolic address names are Rate, Hours, and Salary.

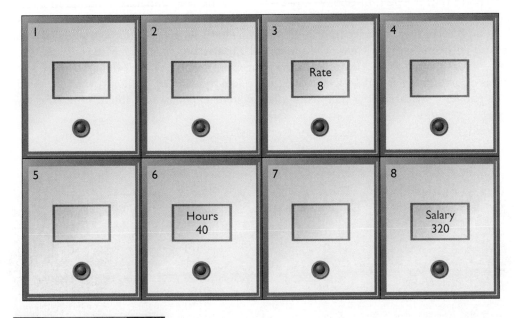

▲ FIGURE 4-4

Addresses are like mailboxes. The addresses of memory locations are like the identifying numbers of apartment house mailboxes. Suppose you want to compute someone's salary as the number of hours worked multiplied by the rate of pay. Rate ($8) might go in memory location 3, hours (40) in location 6, and the computed salary ($8 x 40 hours, or $320) in location 8. Therefore, the addresses are 3, 6, and 8, but the contents are $8, 40, and $320, respectively. Note that the program instructions are to multiply the contents of location 3 by the contents of location 6 and store the result in location 8. Computer languages enable the programmer to use symbolic names, such as Rate or Pay-Rate, rather than location numbers. The data items are the actual contents—the value stored in each location.

►🔲 DATA REPRESENTATION: ON/OFF

We are accustomed to thinking of computers as complex mechanisms, but the fact is that these machines basically know only two things: on and off. This two-state on/off system is called a **binary system.** Using the two states, which can be represented by electricity turned on or off, the computer can construct sophisticated ways of representing data.

For example, look at one way in which the two states can represent data. Whereas the decimal number system has a base of 10 (with the ten digits 0, 1, 2, 3, 4, 5, 6, 7, 8, and 9), the binary system has a base of 2. This means it contains only two digits, 0 and 1, which correspond to the two states, off and on. Combinations of 0s and 1s represent larger numbers (Figure 4-5).

Bits, Bytes, and Words

Each 0 or 1 in the binary system is called a **bit** (for binary digit). The bit is the basic unit for storing data in computer memory: 0 means off, 1 means on. Notice that because a bit is always either on or off, a bit in computer memory is always storing some kind of data; it can never be empty.

Because single bits by themselves cannot store all the numbers, letters, and special characters (such as $ and ?) that a computer must process, the bits are put together in a group called a **byte** (pronounced "bite"). Most computers today are designed to use eight-bit bytes. For text data, each byte usually stores one character of data: a letter, digit, or special character.

Computer manufacturers express the capacity of memory and storage in terms of the number of bytes each contains. The number of bytes can be expressed as **kilobytes.** Kilo represents 2^{10}, or 1024. Kilobyte is abbreviated **KB,** or simply **K.** A kilobyte is 1024 bytes. In an older computer, a memory of 640K means that the computer can store 640×1024, or 655,360, bytes. Today, memory capacity is stated in terms of **megabytes.** One megabyte, abbreviated **MB,** means roughly one million bytes. Personal computer memory may be 256MB or more. With secondary storage devices, manufacturers express capacity in terms of **gigabytes** (abbreviated **GB**), billions of bytes. Mainframe memories are also measured in gigabytes. Secondary storage systems on mainframes and networks often have **terabytes** (**TB**), trillions of bytes of storage capacity. With rapidly increasing disk system capacities, it might only be a few

► **FIGURE 4-5**

Decimal and binary equivalents. Seeing numbers from different systems side-by-side clarifies the patterns of progression. The two numbers in each row represent the same value; they are simply expressed differently in different number systems.

BINARY EQUIVALENT OF DECIMAL NUMBERS 0–15	
Decimal	Binary
0	0000
1	0001
2	0010
3	0011
4	0100
5	0101
6	0110
7	0111
8	1000
9	1001
10	1010
11	1011
12	1100
13	1101
14	1110
15	1111

Term	Abbreviation	Approximate Number of Bytes
Kilobyte	K (or KB)	one thousand
Megabyte	MB	one million
Gigabyte	GB	one billion
Terabyte	TB	one trillion
Petabyte	PB	one quadrillion

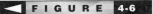

FIGURE 4-6

Storage sizes. This table gives the terminology used to specify primary memory and secondary storage capacities.

years until sizes are measured in **petabytes (PB)**, quadrillions of bytes! Figure 4-6 summarizes the terms used to specify memory and storage sizes.

A computer **word** is defined as the number of bits that the CPU processes as a unit. The length of a word varies by CPU, but is almost always a whole number of bytes. Generally, the larger the word, the more powerful the computer. There was a time when word size alone could classify a computer. Word lengths have varied from 8 bits for very early personal computers to 32 or 64 bits for most personal computers today.

Coding Schemes

As noted, a byte, which is a collection of bits, can represent a character of data. But just what particular set of bits is equivalent to which character? In theory, we could each make up our own definitions, declaring that certain bit patterns represent certain characters. Needless to say, this would be about as practical as each person speaking his or her own special language. Because we need to communicate with the computer and with each other, it is appropriate that we use a common scheme for data representation. That is, there must be agreement on which groups of bits represent which characters.

Because each byte contains eight bits, each of which can hold a 1 or 0, there are 2^8 (256) possible combinations of 1s and 0s in a byte. A **coding scheme** (or **code**) assigns each one of those combinations to a specific character. The **ASCII** (pronounced "as-kee") code, which stands for American Standard Code for Information Interchange, is the most widely used code. ASCII is used on virtually all personal computers and on many larger systems. An earlier version of ASCII used a seven-bit byte and could represent only 128 characters. Another code, Extended Binary Coded Decimal Interchange Code (**EBCDIC**, pronounced "ebb-see-dik"), is used primarily on IBM and IBM-compatible mainframes. Figure 4-7 shows the ASCII and EBCDIC codes for a selected set of characters.

Character	ASCII	EBCDIC
0	0011 0000	1111 0000
1	0011 0001	1111 0001
2	0011 0010	1111 0010
3	0011 0011	1111 0011
4	0011 0100	1111 0100
5	0011 0101	1111 0101
6	0011 0110	1111 0110
7	0011 0111	1111 0111
8	0011 1000	1111 1000
9	0011 1001	1111 1001
A	0100 0001	1100 0001
B	0100 0010	1100 0010
C	0100 0011	1100 0011
D	0100 0100	1100 0100
E	0100 0101	1100 0101
F	0100 0110	1100 0110
G	0100 0111	1100 0111
a	0110 0001	1000 0001
b	0110 0010	1000 0010
c	0110 0011	1000 0011
d	0110 0100	1000 0100
e	0110 0101	1000 0101
f	0110 0110	1000 0110
g	0110 0111	1000 0111
!	0010 0001	0101 1010
#	0010 0011	0111 1011
$	0010 0100	0101 1011
+	0010 1011	0100 1110

FIGURE 4-7

The ASCII and EBCDIC codes. ASCII and EBCDIC binary representations for selected characters are shown. This is not the complete code; many characters are missing. The binary representations are split into groups of four bits each to improve readability.

The 256-character capability of ASCII and EBCDIC is sufficient for English and Western European languages, but is much too small to handle the many alphabets used throughout the rest of the world. The **Unicode** coding scheme is designed to solve this problem. Unicode uses two bytes (16 bits) to represent one character. This gives it the capability of representing 2^{16} (65,536) different characters, more than enough for all the world's languages. The obvious disadvantage is that text data takes up twice as much space in Unicode as it does in ASCII or EBCDIC. Unicode is downward-compatible with ASCII, meaning that Unicode recognizes ASCII characters. Most new operating systems and software packages include support for Unicode.

► THE SYSTEM UNIT

The **system unit** is the case that houses the electronic components of the computer system. The **motherboard,** the flat circuit board within the personal computer housing that holds the computer circuitry (Figure 4-8), is the main system unit component. The motherboard, also called the main circuit board, is a mass of chips and connections that organize the computer's activities. The central processing unit, the microprocessor, is the most important component of the motherboard. Most microcomputer system units also contain one or more storage devices, such as a hard drive, a floppy drive, and a CD-ROM or DVD-ROM drive. Some Apple Macintosh models include the system unit within the monitor housing.

► **FIGURE 4-8**

The motherboard. The motherboard is a flat circuit board that holds the computer circuitry, a mass of chips and connections that organize the computer's activities.

Microprocessors

A miniaturized central processing unit can be etched on a chip, a tiny square of silicon. A central processing unit, or processor, on a chip is called a **microprocessor** (Figure 4-9). A microprocessor may be called a **logic chip** when it is used to control specialized devices (such as the fuel system of a car). Microprocessors contain tiny **transistors,** electronic switches that may or may not allow current to pass through. If current passes through, the switch is on, representing a 1 bit. If current does not pass through, the switch is off, representing a 0 bit. Thus combinations of transistors can stand for combinations of bits, which, as we noted earlier, represent digits, letters, and special characters.

The transistor is the basic building block of the microprocessor. Today's microprocessors contain tens of millions of transistors. Microprocessors usually include these key components: a control unit and an arithmetic/logic unit, which together are the central processing unit; registers; and the system clock. Notably missing is memory, which usually comes on its own chips.

How much smaller can a processor be? How much cheaper? How much faster? Three decades of extraordinary advances in technology have packed increasingly greater power onto increasingly smaller chips. Engineers can now imprint as much circuitry on a single chip as filled room-size computers in the early days of computing. But are engineers approaching the limits of smallness? Current development efforts focus on a three-dimensional chip that is built in layers. Chip capacities in the future do seem almost limitless.

In addition to factors such as increased speed, microprocessors have historically increased their power by swallowing up functions that were previously accomplished by other hardware. For example, in the 1980s, chipmaker Intel incorporated a math coprocessor, a separate chip favored by engineers, into its microprocessor. Currently, Intel's **Pentium®4** chip includes multimedia instructions that boost a computer's ability to produce graphics, video, and sound. The more functions that are combined on a microprocessor, the faster the computer runs, the cheaper it is to make, and the more reliable it is.

Intel's Pentium® 4 microprocessor is currently the workhorse in the PC marketplace. Intel also produces the Celeron® microprocessor for lower-cost PCs and the Xeon™ and Itanium® microprocessors for high-end workstations and network servers. Several companies, notably Cyrix and AMD, make Intel-compatible microprocessors. In the past, these companies have tended to follow Intel, but lately they have been pushing the technology envelope, sometimes beating Intel to market with faster speeds and more advanced capabilities.

There are two other microprocessors of note in the non-Intel world. The **PowerPC** family of chips was designed through the cooperative efforts of Apple, IBM, and

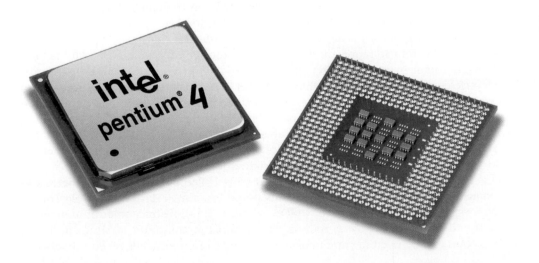

◄ **FIGURE 4-9**

A microprocessor. A CPU, or processor, on a single chip is called a microprocessor. Microprocessors contain millions of tiny transistors, electronic switches that may or may not allow current to pass through.

MAKING CONNECTIONS

Let Your Idle Computer Earn You Money

The Search for Extraterrestrial Intelligence (SETI) project uses the Arecibo Radio Telescope in Puerto Rico to scan the universe for radio signals generated by intelligent aliens. The project gathers huge amounts of digital data, far more than the project's computers were able to handle. In 1995, project leaders came up with an idea to both gain significant processing power and generate interest in SETI among the public. Their idea was to harness the idle CPU cycles of personal computers by distributing packets of their gathered data and letting individual PCs process that data during idle time. They developed client software that PC users could download from the Internet and install like a screensaver. When the PC is idle, that software downloads digital radio data and processes it, sending the results back to SETI. The organizers released the software in mid-1999,

hoping to get 100,000 people to participate. In the first week, more than 200,000 signed up, and the number exceeded 2,000,000 within a year, giving SETI the computing power of a supercomputer operating at more than 12 trillion instructions per second!

How, you might ask, does this enable you to make money from your idle computer? After all, the SETI project is done on a strictly voluntary basis. Well, it didn't take long for entrepreneurs to realize the moneymaking potential of all this unused computing power. By mid-2000, several companies had begun registering users with the promise of payment for any work done on the users' computers. In turn, that computing power is sold to businesses on an as-needed basis. If you are the altruistic sort, they allow you to donate some or all of your computer's work efforts to nonprofit agencies. Unfortunately, you don't get a tax deduction.

Motorola and is currently manufactured by both IBM and Motorola. The PowerPC's primary use is in the Apple Macintosh family of personal computers, but it is also used in servers and embedded systems. The **Alpha** microprocessor, produced by Compaq (now part of Hewlett Packard), is used in high-end servers and workstations.

Memory Components

The first part of this chapter described the CPU and how it works with memory. The next section examines the memory components. Memory components have evolved from primitive vacuum tubes to today's modern semiconductors.

SEMICONDUCTOR MEMORY   Most modern computers use **semiconductor memory** because it has several advantages: reliability, compactness, low cost, and lower power usage. Because semiconductor memory can be mass-produced economically, the cost of memory has been considerably reduced. On the basis of a variety of economic and political factors, chip prices have fallen and risen and fallen again, but they remain a bargain. Semiconductor memory is **volatile;** that is, it requires continuous electric current to represent data. If the current is interrupted, the data is lost.

Semiconductor memory is made up of thousands of very small circuits—pathways for electric currents—on a silicon chip. A chip is described as **monolithic** because all the circuits on a single chip together constitute an inseparable unit of storage. Each circuit etched on a chip can be in one of two states: either conducting an electric current or not; that is, on or off. The two states can be used to represent the binary digits 1 and 0. As we noted earlier, these digits can be combined to represent characters, making the memory chip a storage bin for data and instructions.

One important type of semiconductor design is called **complementary metal oxide semiconductor** (**CMOS**). This design is noted for using relatively little electricity. In personal computers, one use for CMOS is CMOS RAM, a small amount of memory that, thanks to battery power, retains data when the computer is shut off. Thus, CMOS RAM can be used to store information your computer needs when it boots up, such as time, date, and hardware configuration data. When the computer is running, CMOS RAM can be updated, and the new contents remain until changed.

RAM AND ROM   Memory keeps the instructions and data for whatever programs you happen to be using at the moment. Memory is referred to as **RAM—random-access memory**—in this discussion, both to emphasize its random function and to distinguish it from ROM. No matter where it is, data in memory can be accessed randomly in an easy and speedy manner. RAM is usually volatile, as we noted above. This means that its contents are lost once the power is shut off. RAM can be erased or written over at will by the computer software.

RAM can be of two types: static RAM (**SRAM,** pronounced "ess-ram") and dynamic RAM (**DRAM,** pronounced "dee-ram"). DRAM must be constantly refreshed (recharged) by the central processing unit or it will lose its contents, hence the name dynamic. Static RAM retains its contents without intervention from the CPU as long as power is maintained. Although SRAM is much faster, DRAM is used for most personal computer memory because of its size and cost advantages (Figure 4-10). Synchronous DRAM (**SDRAM,** pronounced "ess-dee-ram") is a faster type of DRAM used in most PCs today. An even newer technology, Rambus DRAM (**RDRAM,** pronounced "are-dee-ram"), is faster than SDRAM and will undoubtedly become popular after the cost decreases. SRAM is used for special purposes that are described later in this chapter.

In recent years the amount of RAM storage in a personal computer has increased dramatically. An early personal computer, for example, was advertised with a full 4K of RAM. Now 256MB of RAM, or even more, is common. More memory has become a necessity because sophisticated personal computer software requires significant amounts of memory. Also, many users have several programs active at the same time, each using its own portion of memory. You can augment your personal computer's RAM by buying extra memory modules to plug into your computer's motherboard. Memory is usually packaged on circuit boards called single in-line memory modules (**SIMMs**) or dual in-line memory modules (**DIMMs**). The connecting pins on the SIMM board form a single set of contacts, while the DIMM boards have two sets of contacts, allowing for a wider data path and faster data transfer. The motherboard design determines the maximum amount of memory that you can install in your computer.

Read-only memory (**ROM**) contains programs and data that are permanently recorded into this type of memory at the factory; they can be read and used, but they cannot be changed by the user. For example, the boot routine that is activated when you turn your computer on is stored in ROM. ROM is **nonvolatile**—its contents do not disappear when the power is turned off.

Using specialized tools called ROM burners, you can change the instructions within some ROM chips. These chips are known as **PROM** chips, or programmable read-only memory chips. There are other variations on ROM chips, depending on the

◄ **F I G U R E   4-10**

DRAM. Dynamic RAM (DRAM) must be constantly refreshed (recharged) by the CPU or it will lose its contents. DRAM is used for most computer memory because of its size and cost advantages.

methods used to alter them. Programming and altering ROM chips are the province of the computer engineer.

FLASH MEMORY   We have stated that memory is volatile; it disappears when the power is turned off, hence the need for secondary storage to keep data on a more permanent basis. A long-standing speed problem has been the slow rate at which data is accessed from a secondary storage device such as a disk, a rate that is significantly slower than internal computer speeds. It seemed unimaginable that data might someday be stored on nonvolatile memory chips (nonvolatile RAM) close at hand. A breakthrough has emerged in the form of nonvolatile **flash memory.** Flash chips are used in cellular phones, digital cameras, and digital music recorders, and they are replacing disks in some handheld computers.

Flash memory chips are produced in credit-card-like packages, which are smaller than a disk drive and require much less power. For these reasons, they are used in notebook computers and handheld personal digital assistants and as removable storage on digital cameras and music players. Product names include the CompactFlash card and the SmartMedia card.

The System Bus

The computer term "bus" is borrowed from its common meaning: a mode of transportation. A **bus line** (or **bus**) is a set of parallel electrical paths that transport electrical signals. The **system bus,** usually copper tracing on the surface of the motherboard, transports data between the CPU and memory. The number of bits of data that can be carried at one time is called the *bus width*, which indicates the number of electrical paths. The greater the width, the more data can be carried at a time. Just as a four-lane expressway can move traffic faster than a two-lane road, wider buses enable faster data transmission. The system bus width is dependent on the CPU design and normally is the same as the CPU's word size. A larger bus size means that:

● The CPU can transfer more data at a time, making the computer faster.

● The CPU can reference larger memory address numbers, allowing more memory.

● The CPU can support a greater number and variety of instructions.

In general, the larger the word size or bus width, the more powerful the computer. Bus speed is another factor that affects system performance. As with processor speed, bus speed is measured in megahertz (MHz). The faster the bus speed, the

◄ **F I G U R E 4-11**

An interface card. By plugging expansion boards (also called interface cards or adapter cards) into expansion slots on the computer's motherboard, you can connect various peripheral devices to your computer.

faster data travels through the system. Current microcomputers generally have bus speeds of 400 or 533 MHz.

Expansion Buses

In addition to the system bus, the motherboard also contains several expansion buses. Some of these buses connect to **expansion slots** on the motherboard. **Expansion boards** (also called **interface cards** or **adapter cards**) are plugged into these slots. A connector on the end of the board is accessible through an opening on the back of the system unit. You can attach various peripheral devices to your computer using these connectors (Figure 4-11). Other buses provide external connectors, called **ports,** for you to plug in peripherals such as a printer, a mouse, and a keyboard. Ports come in two basic types: serial and parallel. **Serial ports** transmit data one bit at a time, similar to cars on a one-lane road, and are typically used for slow-speed devices such as the mouse and keyboard. **Parallel ports** transmit groups of bits together, similar to a group of cars traveling side-by-side down a multilane highway, and are used for faster devices such as printers and scanners (Figure 4-12).

The following buses and ports are commonly found on personal computers:

- **Industry Standard Architecture (ISA) bus.** The oldest expansion bus still in common use, the **Industry Standard Architecture (ISA)** bus is used for slow-speed devices such as the mouse and modem.

- **Peripheral Component Interconnect (PCI) bus.** The **Peripheral Component Interconnect (PCI)** bus is a high-speed bus used to connect devices such as hard disks and network cards.

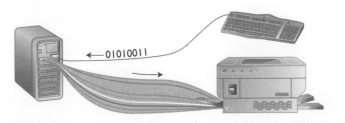

01010011

◄ **F I G U R E 4-12**

Serial and parallel transmission. Serial ports, used for slower devices such as the keyboard, transmit bits one at a time. Parallel ports are used for higher-speed devices such as printers and transmit entire bytes at a time.

- **Accelerated Graphics Port (AGP).** The **Accelerated Graphics Port (AGP)** is a bus that is designed to provide a dedicated connection between memory and an AGP graphics card. The direct connection provides much faster video performance without interfering with other peripherals.

- **Universal Serial Bus (USB).** Access to the **Universal Serial Bus (USB)** is provided through a port on the back of the system unit. Devices with USB connectors can be daisy-chained (connected in a series) to each other and plugged into the USB port, eliminating the need for multiple expansion cards. USB devices are hot-swappable, meaning that you can connect and disconnect them without turning off the power to your computer. Low-powered devices can also draw power through the USB connection, eliminating the need for a separate power supply. The newer USB 2.0 standard allows for much higher data rates, up to 480Mbps.

- **IEEE 1394 bus.** Also referred to as **FireWire,** the **IEEE 1394** bus is a high-speed (up to 400 Mbps) serial bus that is normally used to connect video equipment to your computer. It is also accessed through a port on the back of the system unit and allows daisy-chaining and hot-swapping.

- **PC Card bus.** Access to the **PC Card bus** is provided through a slot or slots in the computer case. The slot accepts credit-card-sized PC Card (formerly referred to as PCMCIA Card) devices and is normally found on laptops. PC Cards can contain solid-state memory, modems, network adapters, and even miniature hard drives.

► SPEED AND POWER

The characteristic of speed is universally associated with computers. Power is a derivative of speed as well as of other factors such as memory size. What makes a computer fast? Or, more to the point, what makes one computer faster than another? Several factors are involved, including microprocessor speed, bus line size, and the availability of cache. A user who is concerned about speed will want to address all of these. More sophisticated approaches to speed include RISC computers and parallel processing. A discussion of each of these factors follows.

Computer Processing Speeds

Although all computers are fast, there is a wide diversity of computer speeds. The execution of an instruction on a very slow computer may be measured in less than a **millisecond,** which is one thousandth of a second, or perhaps in **microseconds,** each of which is one millionth of a second. Modern computers have reached the **nanosecond** (one billionth of a second) range. Still to be broken is the **picosecond** (one trillionth of a second) barrier (Figure 4-13).

Term	Abbreviation	Fraction of a Second
millisecond	ms	1/1,000 second
microsecond	μs	1/1,000,000 second
nanosecond	ns	1/1,000,000,000 second
picosecond	ps	1/1,000,000,000,000 second

▲ **FIGURE 4-13**

Fractions of a second. Note that each fraction is 1/1,000th of the fraction above it in the table.

Building your own computer may seem like a fanciful idea indeed, especially if you have not even decided to buy a computer that comes prepackaged. However, the option of building a computer, once the territory of hardcore techies, is now a possibility for mainstream consumers. Some people like the idea of the adventure. They also like getting exactly the components they want rather than what a PC manufacturer has decided to include.

What skills do you need? And what equipment? Surprisingly, very little of either. You do not need to do anything as dramatic as soldering. In truth, your task is really to acquire and then assemble the various components, screwing and snapping them into place, rather like an electronic LEGO set.

Begin with the shopping list. You will need a motherboard, microprocessor, RAM, case with a power supply, diskette drive, hard drive, video card, monitor, keyboard, and mouse. You may also want a modem, a CD-ROM or DVD-ROM drive, a sound card, and speakers. Now the question becomes which ones. A visit to your local electronics store can be a high-tech reconnaissance mission in which you can gather information from both salespeople and fellow customers. Be sure to check the store's return policy; you should be able to return any component unconditionally within a certain time

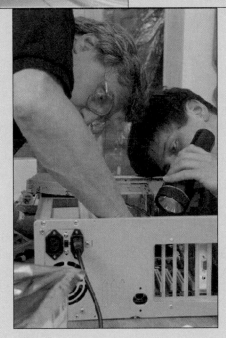

frame. If reduced personal service is an acceptable trade-off for lower costs, you may prefer to buy from a mail-order house or an Internet site. Check the advertising section of any major computer magazine. Buy the major components from the same company to cut down on compatibility problems.

We do not have the space here to describe the components in detail, much less the assembly process. Detailed instructions, which you should read carefully, accompany each hardware item. You can get further advice from magazines, a local computer club, and the Internet.

Don't expect to save a lot of money. Profit margins are slim in the PC marketplace, and the PC manufacturers can buy components a lot cheaper than you can, so the total component cost will not be significantly less than what you would pay for a fully assembled computer. The real savings come in the future when you are able to upgrade your computer on your own—adding more memory, a new microprocessor, a new hard drive, or whatever you want—rather than buying a new computer.

Building a computer can be a satisfying experience, but it is not for everyone. Generally speaking, if you have any doubts, don't do it.

One way of comparing the performance of personal computers is by comparing their microprocessor speeds. Microprocessor speeds are determined by their clock speed and are usually expressed in **gigahertz (GHz)**, billions of machine cycles per second. A personal computer that is listed at 2.2 GHz has a processor capable of handling 2.2 billion machine cycles per second. A top-speed personal computer can be much faster, with newer ones exceeding 3.0 GHz. Direct comparison of clock speeds is meaningful only between identical microprocessors. Thus, while it is accurate to say that a Pentium 4 running at 2.4 GHz is approximately one-third faster than a Pentium 4 running at 1.8 MHz, it is not correct to say that a 1.6 GHz Pentium 4 is faster than a 1.0 GHz PowerPC. This is because of the internal designs of the microprocessors; each accomplishes a different amount of work during each of its clock ticks.

Another measure of computer speed is **MIPS,** which stands for one million instructions per second. For example, a computer with speed of 100 MIPS can execute 100 million instructions per second. High-speed personal computers can perform at 500 MIPS and faster. MIPS is often a more accurate measure than clock speed because some computers can use each tick of the clock more efficiently than others. A third measure of speed is the **megaflop**, which stands for one million floating-point operations per second. It measures the ability of the computer to perform complex mathematical operations.

Cache

In computer terminology **cache** (pronounced "cash") is a temporary storage area designed to speed up data transfer within the computer. In this section we will discuss memory cache. Disk cache is covered in Chapter 6. **Memory cache** is a relatively small block of very fast memory designed for the specific purpose of speeding up the internal transfer of data and software instructions (Figure 4-14). Think of cache as a selective memory. The data and instructions stored in cache are those that are most recently or most frequently used. When the processor first requests data or instructions, they must be retrieved from main memory, which delivers at a pace that is relatively slow in comparison with the speed of the microprocessor. As they are retrieved, those same data or instructions are stored in cache. The next time the microprocessor needs data or instructions, it looks first in cache; if the needed items can be found there, they can be transferred at a rate that far exceeds a trip from main memory. Of course, cache is not big enough to hold everything, so the needed data or instructions might not be there, but there is a good chance that frequently used items will be. Because the most frequently used data and instructions are kept in a handy place, the net result is an improvement in processing speed.

Caching is such a vital technique that microprocessors offer **internal cache** built right into the processor. This is referred to as **Level 1 (L1)** cache, which is the fastest type of cache because it is right there for the microprocessor to access. However, cache memory takes up precious space and increases the cost of the microprocessor, so a processor would probably have no more than 128KB of L1 cache. Older computers also included **external,** or **Level 2 (L2)**, cache on separate chips, usually 256KB or 512KB. L2 cache uses SRAM technology and is cheaper and slower than L1 cache but still much faster (and more expensive) than memory. On current microprocessors, L2 cache has been incorporated into the processor chip for even faster access, where it is referred to as advanced transfer cache. Systems using this type of cache can include a third level of cache (**L3**) on a separate (external) chip.

RISC Technology: Less Is More

It flies in the face of computer tradition: instead of reaching for more variety, more power, more everything-for-everyone, proponents of **reduced instruction set computing (RISC)** suggest that we could get by with a little less. In fact, RISC-based microprocessors offer only a small subset of instructions; the absence of bells and whistles increases speed. So there is a back-to-basics movement in computer design.

RISC supporters say that in conventional microprocessors, which are based on **complex instruction set computing (CISC)**, many of the most complex instructions in the instruction set are rarely used. Those underused instructions, they note, are an impediment to speedy performance, often taking several clock cycles to execute. RISC computers, with their stripped-down instruction sets, zip through programs like racing cars—at speeds 4 to 10 times faster than those of CISC computers. They do slow down, however, when they run into program operations that are normally handled by the complex instructions that were deleted from their instruction set.

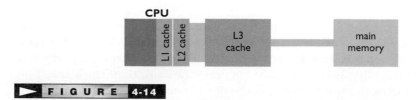

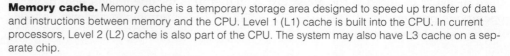

Memory cache. Memory cache is a temporary storage area designed to speed up transfer of data and instructions between memory and the CPU. Level 1 (L1) cache is built into the CPU. In current processors, Level 2 (L2) cache is also part of the CPU. The system may also have L3 cache on a separate chip.

Musicians pay a lot of money to record in a professional studio, so they expect everything to work smoothly. Quinlan's job is to ensure that the computer side of the studio runs perfectly and is more than up to the task of meeting each client's demands. After all, these days a computer in a music studio is used for many different things: It records the audio of the musicians playing their songs; it arranges and mixes all the audio data exactly as the producer wishes it; it applies special effects to the recordings, like distortion or reverb; it controls electronic instruments like drum machines, and so on.

Quinlan is also responsible for maintenance of all the computers. Recently, the management invested in upgrad-

ing their computers and Quinlan was responsible for replacing the CPUs in all six studio machines. The new, more powerful CPUs mean that the studio computers can process more audio tracks at a time, or apply more effects to a track at one time. The job involved not only removing the old processors and replacing them with the new ones, but also individually testing each computer with the studio's audio software, to ensure that everything was working properly with the new Pentium 4 CPU. That finished, Quinlan can finally take a well-deserved break and enjoy a nice cup of freshly brewed tea.

These operations have to be broken down into smaller steps and handled by a sequence of simple instructions, slowing execution speed. For programs with few operations requiring complex instructions, such as those in graphics and engineering areas, RISC computers have a significant performance advantage. Of the processors discussed earlier, the PowerPCs and Alphas use RISC designs, while Intel's Pentium family follows the CISC approach.

◄ **F I G U R E   4-15**

Pipelining. Pipelining is a processing technique that feeds a new instruction into the CPU at every step of the processing cycle so that four or more instructions are worked on simulta-

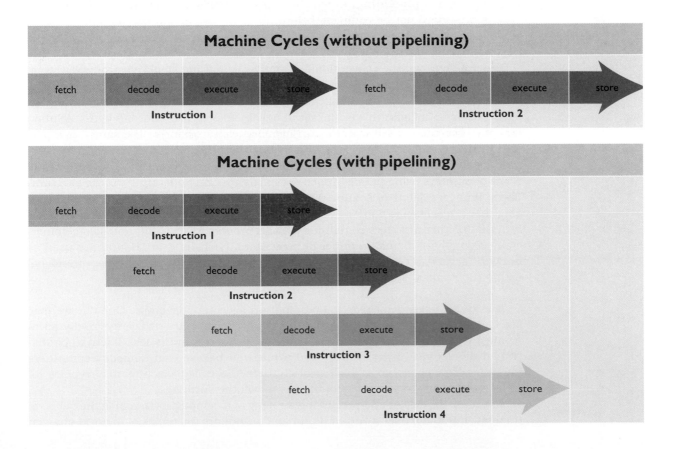

Machine Cycles (without pipelining)

fetch | decode | execute | store | fetch | decode | execute | store
Instruction 1 | Instruction 2

Machine Cycles (with pipelining)

fetch | decode | execute | store
Instruction 1

fetch | decode | execute | store
Instruction 2

fetch | decode | execute | store
Instruction 3

fetch | decode | execute | store
Instruction 4

► **F I G U R E** **4-16**

Parallel processing. In parallel processing, a control processor breaks a problem into pieces, then passes each piece into a separate processor for computation.

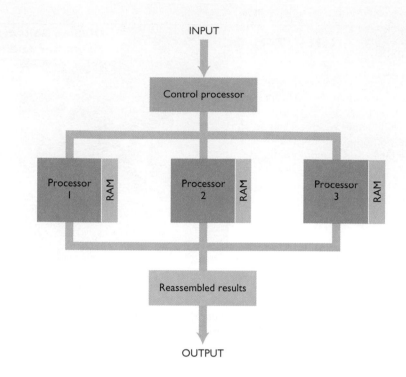

Pipelining and Parallel Processing

The ultimate speed solution is **parallel processing,** a method of using multiple processors at the same time. Consider the description of computer processing you have seen so far in this chapter: the processor gets an instruction from memory, acts on it, returns processed data to memory, and then repeats the process. This is conventional serial processing, the execution of one instruction at a time. A variation on this approach is **pipelining,** in which an instruction's actions—fetch, decode, execute, store—need not be complete before the next instruction begins. For example, when fetch is complete for an instruction and it moves to decode, fetch begins for the next instruction (Figure 4-15).

The problem with the conventional computer is that the single electronic pathway, the bus line, acts like a bottleneck. The computer is restricted to handling one piece of data at a time. For many applications, such as simulating the airflow around an entire airplane in flight, this is an exceedingly inefficient procedure. A better solution is many processors, each with its own memory unit, working at the same time: parallel processing. A control processor analyzes the problem and divides it into parts that are sent to multiple processors, then assembles the results (see Figure 4-16). Some computers using parallel processors are capable of operating in terms of **teraflops,** that is, trillions of floating-point instructions per second. Recall, for comparison, that a megaflop is a mere one million floating-point operations per second.

A number of computers containing parallel processors are built and sold commercially. Some have a small number of processors, typically 4 to 16, and are used as network servers. Others use hundreds or even thousands of processors and fall within the realm of supercomputing.

▲

The future holds some exciting possibilities for computer chips. One day we may see computers that operate by using light (photonics) rather than electricity (electronics) to control their operation. Light travels faster and is less likely to be disrupted by electrical interference. And would you believe that someday computers might actually be grown as biological cultures? So-called biochips may replace today's silicon chip. As research continues, so will the surprises.

Whatever the design and processing strategy of a computer, its goal is the same: to turn raw input into useful output. Input and output are the topics of the next chapter.

CHAPTER REVIEW

► **Summary and Key Terms**

- The **central processing unit** (**CPU**) is a complex set of electronic circuitry that executes program instructions; it consists of a control unit and an arithmetic/logic unit.

- The central processing unit interacts closely with primary storage, or memory. Memory provides temporary storage of data while the computer is executing the program. Secondary storage holds the permanent or semipermanent data.

- The **control unit** of the CPU coordinates execution of the program instructions by communicating with the arithmetic/logic unit and memory—the parts of the system that actually execute the program.

- The **arithmetic/logic unit** (**ALU**) contains circuitry that executes the arithmetic and logical operations. The unit can perform four **arithmetic operations:** addition, subtraction, multiplication, and division. Its **logical operations** usually involve making comparisons that test for three conditions: the **equal-to condition,** the **less-than condition,** and the **greater-than condition.** The computer can test for more than one condition at once, so it can discern three other conditions: less-than-or-equal-to, greater-than-or-equal-to, and less-than-or-greater-than (**not-equal-to**).

- Symbols called **relational operators** (=, >, <) define the comparison to perform.

- **Registers** are special-purpose, high-speed areas for temporary data storage.

- **Memory** is the part of the computer that temporarily holds data and instructions before and after they are processed by the ALU. Memory is also known as **primary storage, primary memory, main storage, internal storage,** and **main memory.** Manufacturers often use the term **RAM,** which stands for random-access memory.

- The CPU follows four main steps when executing an instruction: it (1) fetches (gets) the instruction from memory, (2) decodes the instruction and determines the memory location of the data required, (3) moves the data from memory to ALU registers and directs the ALU to perform the actual operation on the data, and (4) directs the ALU to store the result of the operation in memory or a register. The first two steps are called **I-time** (instruction time), and the last two steps are called **E-time** (execution time).

- A **machine cycle** is the combination of I-time and E-time. The internal **system clock** of the central processing unit produces pulses at a fixed rate to synchronize computer operations. Each CPU has a set of commands that it can understand called the **instruction set.**

- The location in memory for each instruction and each piece of data is identified by an address. Address numbers remain the same, but the contents of the locations change. A meaningful name given to a memory address is called a **symbolic address.**

- Because a computer can recognize only whether electricity is on or off, data is represented by an on/off **binary system,** represented by the digits 1 and 0.

- Each 0 or 1 in the binary system is called a **bit** (binary digit). A group of bits (usually eight bits) is called a **byte,** which usually represents one character of text data, such as a letter, digit, or special character. Memory capacity was once expressed in **kilobytes** (**KB** or **K**). One kilobyte equals 1024 bytes. A **megabyte** (**MB**), about one million bytes, is used today to express memory size. A **gigabyte** (**GB**) equals about one billion bytes. A **terabyte** (**TB**) is about one trillion bytes. A **petabyte** (**PB**) is about one quadrillion bytes.

- A computer **word** is the number of bits that make up a unit of data, as defined by the CPU design.

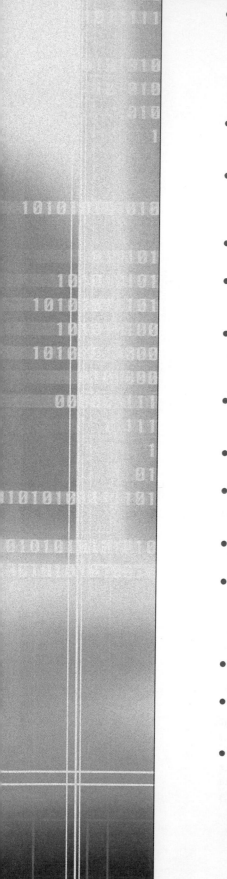

- A **coding scheme** (or **code**) assigns each possible combination of 1s and 0s in a byte to a specific character. Two common coding schemes for representing characters in an 8-bit byte are **ASCII** (American Standard Code for Information Interchange), used on most personal computers, and **EBCDIC** (Extended Binary Coded Decimal Interchange Code). Each of these can represent 256 different characters. The **Unicode** coding scheme uses two bytes (16 bits) to represent a character and can represent 65,536 different characters.

- The **system unit** is the case that contains the **motherboard,** the flat board within the personal computer housing that holds the chips and circuitry that organize the computer's activities. The system unit may also house various storage devices.

- A CPU, or processor, on a chip is a **microprocessor.** A microprocessor may be called a **logic chip** when it is used to control specialized devices. Microprocessors contain tiny **transistors,** electronic switches that may or may not allow current to pass through, representing a 1 or 0 bit, respectively.

- The more functions that are combined on a microprocessor, the faster the computer runs, the cheaper it is to make, and the more reliable it is.

- Common personal computer microprocessors are the Intel **Pentium 4,** used in IBM-compatible PCs; the **PowerPC,** used in the Apple Macintosh; and the **Alpha,** used in high-end workstations and servers.

- **Semiconductor memory,** thousands of very small circuits on a silicon chip, is **volatile;** that is, it requires continuous electrical current to maintain its contents. A chip is described as **monolithic** because the circuits on a single chip constitute an inseparable unit of storage.

- An important type of semiconductor design is called **complementary metal oxide semiconductor (CMOS);** it is noted for using little electricity, making it especially useful for computers requiring low power consumption, such as portable computers.

- **Random-access memory (RAM)** keeps the instructions and data for whatever programs you are using at the moment.

- RAM is divided into two types: static RAM (**SRAM**), which is faster, and dynamic RAM (**DRAM**), which is slower and much less expensive. **SDRAM** and **RDRAM** are faster and more expensive types of DRAM.

- RAM is normally mounted on single in-line memory modules (**SIMMs**) or dual in-line memory modules (**DIMMs**), boards that plug into the motherboard.

- **Read-only memory (ROM)** contains programs and data that are permanently recorded into this type of memory at the factory; they can be read and used but cannot be changed by the user. ROM is **nonvolatile.** The instructions within some ROM chips can be changed by using ROM burners; these chips are known as **PROM** chips, or programmable read-only memory chips.

- **Flash memory** is nonvolatile and is used to store programming and data in devices such as cellular phones and data in digital cameras and digital music recorders.

- The motherboard contains several **bus lines,** or **buses,** sets of parallel electrical paths that transport electrical signals. The **system bus** transfers data between the CPU and memory. Bus width and speed affect system performance.

- Some expansion buses connect to **expansion slots** on the motherboard and can receive **expansion boards** (also called **interface cards** or **adapter cards**) that enable you to connect various peripheral devices to the computer. Other expansion buses provide external connectors, called **ports.** A **serial port** enables data to be transmitted one bit at a time, while a **parallel port** transmits a group of bits at a time. Some ports and buses found on a typical personal computer are the **Industry Standard Architecture (ISA)** bus, the **Peripheral Component Interconnect (PCI)** bus, the **Accelerated Graphics Port (AGP),** the **Universal Serial Bus (USB),** the **IEEE 1394 (FireWire)** bus, and the **PC Card** bus.

- Computer instruction speeds fall into various ranges, from a **millisecond,** which is one thousandth of a second; to a **microsecond,** one millionth of a second (for older computers); to a **nanosecond**, one billionth of a second. Still to be achieved is the **picosecond** range—one trillionth of a second.

- Microprocessor speeds are usually expressed in **gigahertz (GHz)**, billions of cycles per second. Another measure of computer speed is **MIPS,** which stands for one million instructions per second. A third measure is the **megaflop,** which stands for one million floating-point operations per second.

- A **cache** is a relatively small amount of very fast memory that stores data and instructions that are used frequently, resulting in an improved processing speed. **Internal,** or **Level 1 (L1)**, cache, the fastest kind, refers to cache built right into the processor's design. Older computers also included **external,** or **Level 2 (L2)**, cache on separate chips. L2 cache is incorporated into current processors, which may have an additional level of cache (**L3**) on an external chip.

- **Reduced instruction set computing (RISC)** microprocessors are fast because they use only a small subset of instructions. Conventional microprocessors using **complex instruction set computing (CISC)** include many instructions that are rarely used.

- Conventional serial processing uses a single processor and can handle just one instruction at a time. **Pipelining** means that an instruction's actions—fetch, decode, execute, store—need not be complete before the next instruction is begun. **Parallel processing** uses multiple processors in the same computer at the same time. Some parallel processors are capable of operating in terms of **teraflops,** that is, trillions of floating-point instructions per second.

► Critical Thinking Questions

1. Why is writing instructions for a computer more difficult than writing instructions for a person?

2. Do you think there is a continuing need to increase computer speed? Can you think of examples in which more speed would be desirable?

3. It may soon be possible to have microchips implanted in our bodies to monitor or improve our physical conditions. Do you think this is a good idea or a bad idea?

4. A common misconception is that the prefix mega means one million. Actually, if someone has one megabyte of memory, instead of having 1,000,000 bytes of memory they really have 1,048,576 bytes. Explain why it appears that there are an extra 48,576 bytes of memory.

5. There are two fundamental types of computer memory: RAM and ROM. Define what these letters represent, and explain the functional differences between these two types of memory.

6. Although processor speeds are frequently specified in hertz (machine cycles per second), explain why a 3.0GHZ processor may not be twice as fast as a 1.5GHz processor.

7. The most popular method of transferring images from a digital camera to your computer is through a cable connection. Explain which type of computer port you would want to connect your digital camera to and why.

8. Besides being able to purchase a fully assembled computer, consumers have the option of building their own computer. List advantages and disadvantages of building a computer system. Would you build your own computer? Why or why not?

9. Original computer systems were byte-oriented and used the ASCII and EBCDIC schemes for coding data. The preferred scheme is now Unicode. Explain why this coding scheme is superior to the other two.

10. Explain the differences between RISC and CISC computers.

► STUDENT STUDY GUIDE

Multiple Choice

1. The electrical circuitry that executes program instructions is the
   a. register
   b. operator
   c. central processing unit
   d. bus line

2. The entire computer system is coordinated by
   a. the ALU
   b. the control unit
   c. registers
   d. arithmetic operators

3. A bus line consists of
   a. registers
   b. parallel data paths
   c. megabytes
   d. machine cycles

4. Equal-to, less-than, and greater-than conditions are tested for in
   a. logical operations
   b. subtraction
   c. locations
   d. arithmetic operations

5. The primary storage unit is also known as
   a. a register
   b. mass storage
   c. secondary storage
   d. memory

6. Data and instructions are put into primary storage by
   a. memory
   b. secondary storage
   c. the control unit
   d. the ALU

7. During E-time the ALU
   a. examines the instruction
   b. executes the instruction
   c. enters the instruction
   d. elicits the instruction

8. Computer operations are synchronized by
   a. the CPU clock
   b. the binary system
   c. megabytes
   d. E-time

9. Which is not a type of memory?
   a. SRAM
   b. ROM
   c. DRAM
   d. QRAM

10. Another name for a logic chip is
    a. PROM
    b. microprocessor
    c. memory
    d. ROM

11. Data is represented on a computer by a two-state, on/off system called
    a. a word
    b. a byte
    c. the binary system
    d. RAM

12. A letter, digit, or special character is represented by a code in a
    a. bit
    b. byte
    c. kilobyte
    d. megabyte

13. Memory capacity may be expressed in
    a. microseconds
    b. MHz
    c. megabytes
    d. cycles

14. _____ cache is built into the CPU chip.
    a. internal
    b. L3
    c. external
    d. disk

15. A design technique that enables the CPU to begin processing one instruction before the previous instruction is finished is called
    a. pipelining
    b. RISC
    c. parallel processing
    d. serial processing

16. The main circuit board in a personal computer is called the
    a. fatherboard
    b. motherboard
    c. ram/bus board
    d. ASCII board

17. The Intel processor that is used on IBM-compatible computers is the
    a. Alpha
    b. Pentium 4
    c. PowerPC
    d. none of the above

18. The FireWire bus is also known as the
    a. IEEE 1394 bus
    b. IEEE 2294 bus
    c. Universal serial bus
    d. PC card bus

19. The processor speed for top-end personal computers is measured in
    a. kilohertz (KHz)
    b. megahertz (MHz)
    c. gigahertz (GHz)
    d. terahertz (THz)

20. Which of the following is/are not part of the CPU?
    a. Control unit
    b. ALU
    c. Registers
    d. Primary storage

True/False

T F 1. The control unit consists of the CPU and the ALU.

T F 2. Secondary storage holds data only temporarily.

T F 3. The control unit directs the entire computer system.

T F 4. MIPS is an abbreviation for megaflop.

T F 5. The electronic circuitry that controls all arithmetic and logical operations is contained in the ALU.

T F 6. The three basic logical operations may be combined to form a total of nine commonly used operations.

T F 7. Memory allows fast access to instructions in secondary storage.

T F 8. Registers are temporary storage areas located in memory.

T F 9. Memory in most computers is volatile.

T F 10. RISC computers have a smaller instruction set than traditional computers.

T F 11. All computers except personal computers can execute more than one instruction at a time.

T F 12. The machine cycle consists of four steps, from the first step of fetching the instruction to the last step of storing the result in memory.

T F 13. The internal clock of the CPU produces pulses at a fixed rate to synchronize processor operations.

T F 14. A cache is a small amount of secondary storage.

T F 15. Computers represent data using the two-state binary system.

T F 16. A bit is commonly made up of 8 bytes.

T F 17. A kilobyte (KB) is 1024 bytes.

T F 18. Unicode is a coding scheme that uses two bytes to represent 65,536 different characters.

T F 19. The Pentium 4 is the microprocessor used on most Apple Macintosh computers.

T F 20. SIMMs and DIMMs are boards containing memory chips that are plugged into the motherboard.

Fill-In

1. A millionth of a second is called a(n) _____.

2. The _____ consists of both the control unit and the arithmetic/logic unit.

3. Processing instructions one at a time is called _____.

4. When the control unit decodes an instruction, the machine cycle is in I-time or E-time? _____

5. MHz is an abbreviation for _____.

6. _____ is nonvolatile memory used in cellular phones and digital cameras.

7. The combination of I-time and E-time is called a(n) _____.

8. The symbols =, <, and > are called _____.

9. Each memory location is identified by a(n) _____.

10. A 0 or 1 in the binary system is called a(n) _____.

11. MIPS stands for _____.

12. _____ is a high-speed temporary storage location for data moving between memory and the CPU.

13. The _____ consists of all the commands a CPU is capable of executing.

14. The _____ is the main circuit board found inside the system unit.

15. A(n) _____ is a connector on the back of the system unit that allows you to connect slow-speed devices that transmit data one bit at a time.

16. Special-purpose, high-speed areas within the CPU for the temporary storage of data are called _____.

17. _____uses multiple processors in the same computer at the same time.

18. The four steps in a machine cycle are _____, _____, _____, and _____.

19. The ability of a computer to overlap the steps in a machine cycle is known as _____.

20. The primary storage unit is a bit. Bit is an acronym and it means _____.

21. The _____ transfers data between the CPU and memory.

► **ANSWERS**

Multiple Choice

1. c	6. c	11. c	16. b
2. b	7. b	12. b	17. b
3. b	8. a	13. c	18. a
4. a	9. d	14. a	19. c
5. d	10. b	15. a	20. d

True/False

1. F	6. F	11. F	16. F
2. F	7. F	12. T	17. T
3. T	8. F	13. T	18. T
4. F	9. T	14. F	19. F
5. T	10. T	15. T	20. T

Fill-In

1. microsecond
2. central processing unit or CPU
3. serial processing
4. I-time
5. megahertz
6. flash memory
7. machine cycle
8. relational operators
9. address
10. bit
11. million instructions per second
12. cache
13. instruction set
14. motherboard
15. serial port
16. registers
17. parallel processing
18. fetch, decode, execute, and store
19. pipelining
20. BInary digiT or Binary digIT
21. system bus

Computers Helping Computers

What better place to get help for your PC problems than on the Web?

Of course if there's no light on the monitor or your PC won't boot, you might have to use a friend's computer to surf the Web for help. But if your computer is running but not performing up to its full potential, or if you could really use that upgrade or replacement, there are Web sites designed to help.

WaterWheel.com's Building a PC site has a step-by-step guide to building your own PC, with easy-to-understand instructions. Beginning with the case, it has step-by-step instructions for preparing and connecting each part of the computer. Hardware Masters, by contrast, is aimed at more experienced computer users. It provides reviews of new products, articles, current computer news, links to related information, and other features on its site.

PC Mechanic features step-by-step guides to building a PC and upgrading your computer and reviews of and editorials on new products and companies. You can buy e-book versions of some of their publications, including one on how to set up a network. The site also has general troubleshooting tips to try before "trading your screwdriver for a sledge-

hammer," such as "What has changed since it last worked?" and most importantly: "Don't panic. Chances are the problem is really simple."

For example, suppose you use a modem to reach the Internet. There was a nasty storm last night, with thunder and lightning galore, and you can't surf today. Everything worked fine before the storm. It might be the modem, or it might be the phone line. You had your computer plugged into a surge protector outlet, but it turns out that doesn't protect your modem (higher-end models do provide that protection).

Thinking logically and examining all simple possibilities first leads to step-by-step processes such as the following:

1. If your modem has its own diagnostic software, run that. However, be aware that it won't necessarily detect that your modem won't talk to the phone line anymore.

2. Plug a phone into the line; if that works, the line is OK. If the line is OK, it's probably time to take the computer in to be checked out by a professional, and possibly have the modem replaced if it was indeed damaged by a power surge during the storm.

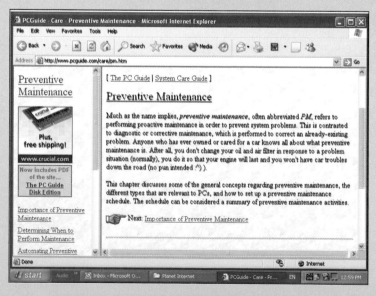

The PC Guide page includes recommendations for preventative maintenance for your PC and a schedule for preventive maintenance which will keep your PC in good working order and virus resistant. Finally, don't forget to check TechTV's *Call for Help* show notes to see whether they have answered your question.

Internet Exercises:

1. **Structured exercise.** Begin with the URL http://www.prenhall.com/capron and link to the Computer Care Association page. Read the information about preventive maintenance for your computer. Answer the following questions if you own a computer, or interview someone you know who does own a computer.

   • Do you do everything on the list about as often as recommended? If not, why not?

   • Have you ever experienced a problem with your computer that could have been avoided if you had followed their preventive maintenance recommendations? What should you have done?

   • In your opinion, what are the three most important items on the list?

2. **Free-form exercise.** Write down the features you would need in a computer, including the applications you want, your budget, and so on. Consider how you plan to use the In-

ternet. Then go to a Web site that helps you build and design your computer. If you already have a computer, do this exercise for a friend or family member who is thinking about buying a computer.

3. **Advanced exercise.** Practice troubleshooting a PC problem. Pick a question from the PC Mechanic site or a question that you have heard from someone else. Using an approach similar to that recommended on the PC Mechanic site, explain your troubleshooting process, step by step. Double-check your approach by seeing the answer on the Web page, by having a knowledgeable friend critique your approach, or by implementing your approach to solve a problem.

Making Microchips

Computer power in the hands of the people–we take it for granted now, but not so long ago computers existed only in enormous rooms behind locked doors. The revolution that changed all that was ignited by chips of silicon smaller than your fingernail: microchips. Silicon is one of the most common elements on Earth, but there is nothing commonplace about designing, manufacturing, testing, and packaging the microprocessors that are made from silicon. In this gallery we will explore the key elements in the process by which those marvels of miniaturization–microchips–are made.

The Idea Behind the Microchip

Microchips form the lightning-quick "brain" of a computer. These devices, though complex, work on a very simple principle: They "know" when electric current is on and when it is off. They can process information because it is coded as a series of on-off electric signals. Before the invention of microchips, these signals were controlled by thousands of separate devices laboriously wired together to form a single circuit. However, *millions* of circuits can be embedded on a single microchip; a microchip is often called an integrated circuit.

Silicon is a semiconductor—it conducts electricity only 'semi' well. This does not sound like such an admirable trait, but the beauty of silicon is that it can be doped, or treated, with different materials to make it conduct electricity well or not at all. By doping various areas of a silicon chip differently, designers can set up pathways for electricity to follow. The pathways consist of grooves etched into layers placed over a silicon substrate. The silicon is doped so that the pathways conduct electricity. The surrounding areas do not conduct electricity at all.

1. This simplified illustration shows the layers and grooves within a transistor, one of thousands of circuit components on a single chip. Pathway C controls the flow of electricity through the circuit. (a) When no electric charge is added to pathway C, electricity cannot flow along the circuit pathway from area A to area B. Thus the transistor is "off." (b) A charge added to pathway C temporarily allows electricity to travel from area A to area B. Now the transistor is "on," and electricity can continue to other components in the circuit. The control of electricity here and elsewhere in the chip makes it possible for the computer to process information coded as "on-off" electric signals.

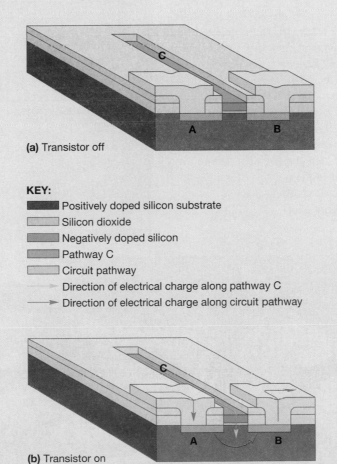

(a) Transistor off

KEY:
- ▬ Positively doped silicon substrate
- ▭ Silicon dioxide
- ▬ Negatively doped silicon
- ▬ Pathway C
- ▭ Circuit pathway
- → Direction of electrical charge along pathway C
- → Direction of electrical charge along circuit pathway

(b) Transistor on

1. How a transistor conducts electricity.

2. Microchip designers execute their plans using the computer.

Preparing the Design

Each microprocessor is constructed like a multistory building, with multiple layers of material combining to create a single complex unit. Try to imagine figuring out a way to place thousands of circuit components next to one another so that electricity flows through the whole integrated circuit the way it is supposed to. That is the job of chip designers. Essentially, they are trying to put together a gigantic multilayered jigsaw puzzle. The circuit design of a typical chip requires over a year's work by a team of designers. Computers assist in the complex task of mapping out the most efficient pathways for each circuit layer.

3. Close-up of what a chip designer sees on the screen.

2. A designer can arrange and modify circuit patterns and display them on a screen. Superimposing the color-coded circuit layers allows the designer to evaluate the relationships between them. The computer allows the designer to electronically store and retrieve previously designed circuit patterns.

3. Here the designer has used computer graphics software to display a screen image of the circuit design.

4. The computer system can also provide a printed version of any or all parts of the design. This large-scale printout allows the design team to discuss and modify the entire chip design.

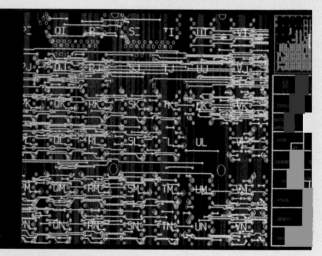

4. A chip designer team works with an enlarged printout of the design.

Manufacturing the Chip

The silicon used to make computer chips is extracted from common rocks and sand. It is melted down into a form that is 99.9 percent pure silicon, and then doped with chemicals to make it either electrically positive or electrically negative.

6. A silicon wafer.

5. A cylinder of silicon that will be sliced into wafers.

5. The molten silicon is then "grown" into cylindrical ingots in a process similar to candle dipping.

6. A diamond saw slices each ingot into circular wafers four or six or eight inches in diameter and four-thousandths of an inch thick. The wafers are sterilized and polished to a perfectly smooth, mirror-like finish. Each wafer will eventually contain hundreds of identical chips. One silicon wafer can produce more than 100 microprocessors.

Since a single speck of dust can ruin a chip, chips are manufactured in special laboratories called clean rooms. The air in clean rooms is filtered, and workers dress in "bunny suits" to lessen the chance of chip contamination. A chip-manufacturing lab is 100 times cleaner than a hospital operating room.

7. Chip-manufacturing processes vary, but one step is common: electrically positive silicon wafers are placed in an open glass tube and inserted into a 1,200° Celsius oxidation furnace.

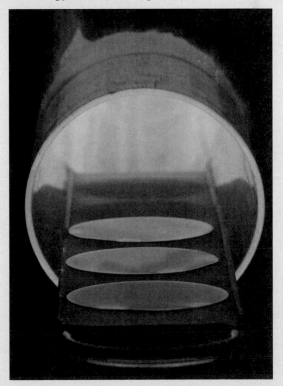

7. Analogy of silicon being cooked.

Oxygen reacts with the silicon, covering each wafer with a thin layer of silicone dioxide, which does not conduct electricity well. Each wafer is then coated with a gelatin-like substance called photoresist, which hardens. The final design of each circuit layer must be reduced to the size of the chip. A stencil called a mask, representing the schematic design of the circuit, is placed over the wafer. Ultraviolet light is shined through the mask, softening the exposed—non-masked—photoresist on the wafer.

8. The wafer is then taken to a washing station in a specifically lit "yellow room," where the wafer is washed in solvent to remove the soft photoresist. This leaves ridges of material—hardened photoresist in the pattern of the mask—on the wafer. Next the silicon dioxide revealed by the washing is etched away by hot gases. The silicon underneath, which forms the circuit pathway, is then doped to make it electrically negative. In this way, the circuit pathway is distinguishable from the rest of the silicon. In the final step, aluminum is deposited to connect the circuit components and form the bonding pads to which wires will later be connected.

9. The result: one wafer with many chips.

10. Computerized coloration enhances this close-up view of a wafer with chips.

11. This image shows circuit paths on a microprocessor chip magnified 3,000 times.

8. Wafer washing room.

9. Close-up of chips on a wafer.

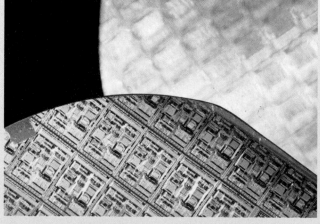

10. Chips still on the wafer.

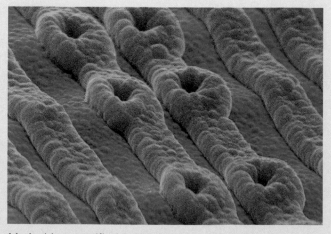

11. A chip magnified 3,000 times.

126

Testing the Chip

Microprocessor manufacturers devote extraordinary efforts to testing their chips. The chips are tested all along the way, from design to manufacturing to packaging. A microprocessor is so complex that it is impossible to literally check every possible state it could be in; the number of elements—millions of transistors—and the number of different combinations is simply too great. However, months of continuous, specialized, and extremely expensive testing will yield a working, reliable product. Even after a chip reaches production, testing continues. Each new chip is tested while still on the wafer and after it is packaged.

Although chips on a particular wafer may look identical, they do not perform identically.

12. A probe machine must perform millions of tests on each chip, to determine whether it conducts electricity in the precise way it was designed to. The needle-like probes contact the bonding pads, apply electricity, measure the results, and mark ink spots on defective chips.

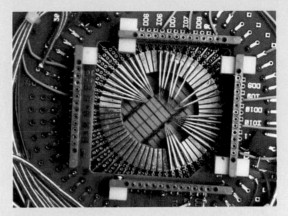

12. Needle-like probes test each chip.

13. A defect review performed by a computer finds and classifies defects in order to eliminate them from the wafer.

14. After initial testing, a diamond saw cuts each chip from the wafer, and defective chips are discarded.

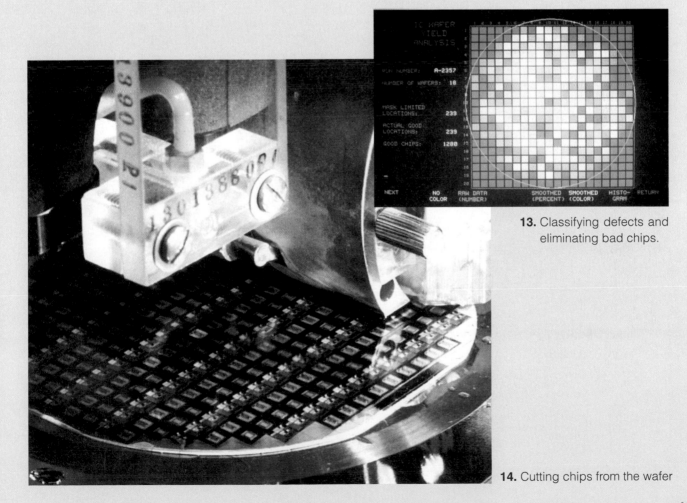

13. Classifying defects and eliminating bad chips.

14. Cutting chips from the wafer

Packaging the Chip

Each acceptable chip is mounted on a protective package.

15. An automated wire-bonding device wires the bonding pads of the chip to the electrical leads on the package, using aluminum or gold wire thinner than a human hair. A variety of packages are in use today.

16. Dual in-line packages have two rows of legs that are inserted into holes in a circuit board.

17. Square pin-grid array packages, which are used for chips requiring many electrical leads, look like a bed of nails. The pins are inserted into the holes in a circuit board. In this photo the protective cap has been cut away, revealing the ultrafine wires connecting the chip to the package.

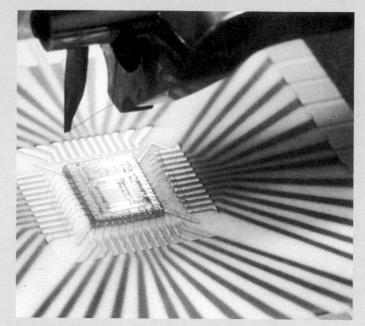

15. Wiring the chip

16. Chip mounted on surface so that legs can be inserted into holes on the circuit board

17. Square pin-grid chip package

From Chip to Computer

At a factory that manufactures circuit boards, **18.** a robot makes a circuit board and **19.** another robot inserts a pin-grid package into holes in a circuit board. Several surface mount packages have already been placed on the board.

20. Dual in-line packages of various sizes have been attached to this circuit board.

21. This circuit board is being installed in a Compaq computer.

18. A factory robot makes a circuit board.

19. A factory robot lines up the pins on the chip package with holes on the receiving circuit board.

21. Installing the circuit board.

20. A finished circuit board.

129

Input and Output:
The User Connection

CHAPTER 5

LEARNING OBJECTIVES

Describe the user relationship with computer input and output

Explain how data is input into a computer system and differentiate among various input equipment

Describe how a monitor works and the characteristics that determine quality

List and describe the different methods of computer output

Differentiate among different kinds of printers

Explain the function of a computer terminal and describe the types of terminals

Describe the ethical considerations involved in handling computer data

McKenna University long ago abandoned the practice of having students stand in line to register for classes. Now almost everything is handled through the computer. Because these procedures save time and trouble, they suit Elizabeth Montes just fine. Elizabeth did begin with a manual procedure when she first applied to the university. She prepared her application, the source document, which was scanned into the university's computer and examined by various college personnel. Elizabeth was accepted and, from that point forward, she has communicated directly with the computer.

Elizabeth can phone the computer and supply it with her data, using her Touch-Tone phone as a sort of miniature keyboard. When the computer responds to the number she dials, she enters her Social Security number, followed by the unique personal identification number (PIN) assigned to her by the university. She then follows the procedure to register for classes, entering class item numbers from the college's class schedule. Various options, such as taking a class for credit or audit, can be selected by entering a number from her telephone keypad. The computer delivers voice output, telling her she has—or has not—been accepted in a class. After she has entered all her classes, Elizabeth can push other buttons for other options, such as hearing her class schedule, dropping a class, hearing the tuition amount owed, and paying by credit card.

Once Elizabeth is registered, the computer prints her student identification card, complete with bar code, which she can pick up in the library. The

ID card is used for checking books out of the library and for making use of computer and science labs. The computer produces a lot of other outputs, such as class rosters for instructors and registration summaries, that are only indirectly related to Elizabeth.

Elizabeth is not particularly familiar with computer-related input and output terms such as source document, scan, keyboard, voice output, and bar code, nor does she need to be to register. But understanding these terms, and other terms related to input and output, helps users navigate all sorts of computer systems.

▶ HOW USERS SEE INPUT AND OUTPUT

The central processing unit (CPU) is the unseen part of a computer system; users are only dimly aware of it. But users are very much aware of the input and output associated with the computer. They submit input data to the computer to get processed information, the output.

Sometimes the output is an instant reaction to the input. Consider these examples:

- Zebra-striped bar codes on supermarket items provide input that enables instant retrieval of outputs, price and item name, right at the checkout counter.

- A forklift operator speaks directly to a computer through a microphone. Words such as left, right, and lift are the actual input data. The output is the computer's instant response, which causes the forklift to operate as requested.

- A sales representative uses an instrument that looks like a pen to enter an order on a special pad. The handwritten characters are displayed as typed text and are stored in the pad, which is actually a small computer.

- Factory workers input data by punching in on a time clock as they go from task to task. The time clock is connected to a computer. The outputs are their weekly paychecks and reports for management that summarize hours per project on a quarterly basis.

Input and output may be separated by time, distance, or both. Here are some examples:

- Data on checks is used as input to the bank computer, which eventually processes the data to prepare a bank statement once a month.

- Charge-card transactions in a retail store provide input data that is processed monthly to produce customer bills.

- Water sample data is collected at lake and river sites, keyed in at the environmental agency office, and used to produce reports that show patterns of water quality.

The examples in this section show the diversity of computer applications, but in all cases the process is the same: input–processing–output. This chapter examines input and output methods in detail.

▶ INPUT: GETTING DATA FROM THE USER TO THE COMPUTER

Some input data can go directly to the computer for processing. Input in this category includes bar codes, speech that enters the computer through a microphone, and data entered by means of a device that converts motions to on-screen action. Some

► MAKING CONNECTIONS ◄ **Face to Face**

Perhaps you can send e-mail, and you may even have learned how to include a photograph, but can you talk face-to-face with someone using a computer connection? You can if you buy one of the video kits that have made the process easy and affordable. A typical kit includes a camera and software, both of which are easy to install. Shown here is Intel's Create & Share Camera Pack; note the camera atop the monitor. Of course, this works only if the party at the other end of your communication has a video setup, too.

The technology for video telephones has been around for a long time, but it never caught on with the general public. Perhaps people didn't want to be seen with their hair in curlers or in their bathrobes. But computer video telephony is attractive, partly because it is inexpensive even over long distances and partly because it is still sufficiently novel that it is planned in advance—no curlers.

input data, however, goes through a good deal of intermediate handling, such as when it is copied from a **source document** (the original written data) and translated to a medium that a machine can read, such as a magnetic disk. In either case, the task is to gather data to be processed by the computer, sometimes called raw data, and convert it into an electronic form that the computer can understand. Conventional input devices include the keyboard, mouse, trackball, touch pad, and joystick. These are described in the following sections.

Keyboard

A **keyboard,** which usually is similar to a typewriter keyboard, may be part of a personal computer or part of a terminal that is connected to a computer somewhere else (Figure 5-1a). Not all keyboards are traditional, however. A fast-food franchise such as McDonald's, for example, uses keyboards with keys that represent items such as large fries or a Big Mac (Figure 5-1b). Portable folding keyboards have been developed for use with handheld computers (Figure 5-1c).

Many users who spend a lot of time keying data on standard keyboards experience repetitive strain injury (RSI) of their wrists. **Ergonomic keyboards** attempt to reduce or eliminate this problem with designs that provide users with more natural, comfortable hand, wrist, and arm positions (Figure 5-1d). The field of **ergonomics** is concerned with designing equipment so that people interact with the equipment in a healthy, comfortable, and efficient manner. In keyboard design, this may involve setting the keys at an angle, either fixed or adjustable, and/or providing padded wrist

(a)　　　　　(b)　　　　　(c)　　　　　(d)

▲ FIGURE 5-1

Keyboards. Keyboards allow the user to input data into the computer by typing. (a) This is a standard keyboard found on the majority of personal computers. (b) This specialized keyboard allows the user to enter the price of an item by pressing a single key. (c) This folding keyboard makes it easier for the user to enter data into a PDA. (d) This ergonomic keyboard is designed to minimize repetitive stress injuries.

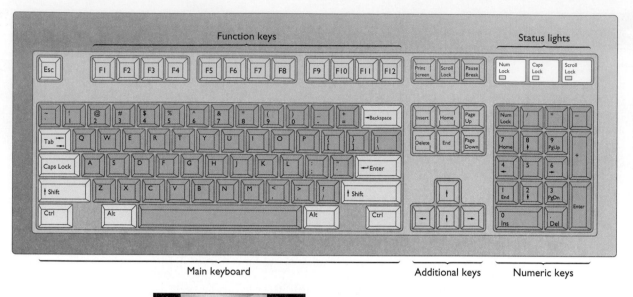

▲ **FIGURE** **5-2**

Finding your way around a keyboard. Most personal computer keyboards have at least three main parts: function keys, the main keyboard in the center, and the numeric keys and status lights. Extended keyboards, such as the one shown here, have additional keys between the main keyboard and the numeric keys. **Function keys:** The function keys (highlighted in tan on the diagram) are an easy way to give certain commands to the computer. What each function key does is defined by the particular software you are using. Some keyboards have the function keys on the left instead of across the top. **Main keyboard:** The main keyboard includes the familiar keys found on a typewriter key-board (dark blue), as well as some special command keys (light blue). The command keys have differ-ent uses that depend on the software being used. **Numeric keys:** The numeric keys (purple) serve one of two purposes, depending on the status of the Num Lock light. When the Num Lock light is on, these keys can be used to enter numeric data and mathematical symbols. When the Num Lock light is off, the numeric keys are used to move the cursor and perform other functions, as shown on the bottom of each key cap. The Num Lock key is used to toggle the Num Lock light on and off. **Additional keys:** Extended keyboards include additional keys (green) that duplicate the cursor movement func-tions of the numeric keys. Users who enter a lot of numeric data can leave their keyboards in the Num Lock mode and use these keys to control the cursor.

rests. Many other features of a computer work area also contribute to worker well-be-ing, including fully adjustable chairs and monitors that tilt and swivel.

Most keyboards have a cable that connects to a port on the back of the system unit. **Cordless keyboards** contain a battery-operated transmitter that communi-cates via infrared or radio waves with a receiver plugged into the port. This reduces cable clutter and provides the user more flexibility in positioning the keyboard.

Figure 5-2 shows the complete layout of a traditional keyboard.

Pointing Devices

You use a **pointing device** to position a **pointer** on the screen. The pointer can have a number of shapes but is most often an arrow. A pointing device usually has one or more buttons or other mechanisms to indicate the action to take once the pointer has been positioned in the desired location. To modify text in an application such as word processing, you move the pointer to the desired place in the screen text, and then click the button to set the insertion point, or cursor. (The insertion point can also be moved by pressing various keyboard keys.) The next text that is typed begins at the insertion point. In graphics-based applications, you use the pointing device to control various drawing tools, such as a paintbrush, pen, or eraser.

You can also use the pointing device to communicate commands to the operating system or an application program by clicking a button. In particular, a button is often used to click an **icon**, a pictorial symbol on a screen. The icon represents a computer activity, a command to the computer, so clicking the icon invokes the command. The command may be to launch an application, such as word processing or a game, or to activate a feature within an application, such as underlining.

A number of different pointing devices are available for use on a computer. Your choice of device depends on personal preference and on the types of applications you use. Some of the most common pointing devices are described in the following sections.

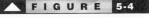

Mouse. As the mouse is moved over a smooth surface, the pointer on the computer screen makes corresponding movements. An optical mouse is shown here.

MOUSE The mouse is by far the most common pointing device for personal computers. A **mouse** is a palm-sized device that is moved around on a flat surface to cause a corresponding movement of the pointer on the screen. A **mechanical mouse** has a small ball on its underside that rolls as the mouse is moved. Sensors inside the mouse determine the direction and distance of movement and signal the computer to move the pointer on the screen accordingly. An **optical mouse** uses a light beam to monitor mouse movement. Most mice connect via cable to a port on the computer, but a **cordless mouse** (either mechanical or optical) uses either infrared or radio waves to communicate with a receiver connected to the PC. As mice have evolved, new features and new buttons have been added. Mice such as Microsoft's IntelliMouse offer an extra wheel, positioned between the two mouse buttons, that can be clicked like a button or rolled to affect the cursor (Figure 5-3). With software designed to be used with this mouse, you can move through a document line-by-line or page-by-page, zoom in on a special spreadsheet cell, or flip backwards through Web pages you have already seen. Some mice have as many as five programmable buttons.

TRACKBALL The **trackball** is a variation on the mechanical mouse. You may have used a trackball to play a video game. The trackball is like an upside-down mechanical mouse—you roll the ball directly with your hand. Buttons are mounted alongside or below the ball. The popularity of the trackball surged with the advent of laptop computers, when traveling users found themselves without a flat surface on which to roll the traditional mouse. Miniature trackballs are designed to be used with portable computers, while larger ones can be used as separate input devices with any computer (Figure 5-4).

TOUCHPAD A **touchpad** is a rectangular pressure-sensitive pad. Slide your finger across the touchpad's surface and corresponding pointer movements are made on the screen. Buttons at the bottom of the unit serve the same functions as mouse buttons, but most touchpads also recognize a finger tap as a click. Stand-alone touchpads are available to use with any computer, but most are built into laptops (Figure 5-5).

POINTING STICK A **pointing stick** is a small pressure-sensitive post mounted in the center of the keyboard between the G and H keys (Figure 5-6). Pushing the post in one direction causes the pointer to move in that direction. The pointer stops moving when pressure is released. Buttons are located below the keyboard.

Trackball. This trackball can be used with a desktop system.

Touchpad. This notebook computer uses a touchpad (located below the spacebar) as a pointing device.

▲ FIGURE 5-6

Pointing stick. This keyboard contains a pointing stick embedded in its center to move the pointer on the screen.

► FIGURE 5-7

Joystick. The joystick is most commonly used for playing action games.

JOYSTICK A **joystick** is a short lever with a handgrip that resembles the floor-mounted gearshift in a sports car (Figure 5-7). The distance and speed of movement control the screen pointer's position. Pressing *triggers*, buttons on the lever, causes various actions to take place, depending on the software in use. Although the joystick is most often used with games, such as flight simulators, it can be used as a mouse replacement.

GRAPHICS TABLET A **graphics tablet,** also called a **digitizing tablet,** is a rectangular board that contains an invisible grid of electronic dots (Figure 5-8). As the user moves a pen-like **stylus** or a mouse-like **puck** with crosshairs around the board, the dot locations that are passed over are sent to the computer. Architects and engineers use these tablets to trace or create precise drawings.

► FIGURE 5-8

Graphics tablet. Architects and engineers often use graphics tablets to enter and make changes to technical drawings.

TOUCH SCREENS One way of getting input directly from the source is to have a human simply point to a selection. The edges of some **touch screens** emit horizontal and vertical beams of light that crisscross the screen. When a finger touches the screen, the interrupted light beams can pinpoint the location selected on the screen. Another type of touch screen senses finger pressure to determine the location. A variation of this concept has the user use a **light pen** for pointing. Light pens enable a greater level of precision in pinpointing screen locations. Some light pens require a special monitor; others work with any monitor.

Kiosks, self-contained self-help stations often found in public places such as malls

► FIGURE 5-9

A kiosk. Kiosks use touch screens to provide information and services to the public. Kiosks are found in public places, such as malls, supermarkets, and banks.

and supermarkets, offer a variety of services. A kiosk's touch screen is so easy to use that it attracts patrons (Figure 5-9). 7-Eleven convenience stores have installed kiosks in many of their locations that not only act as ATMs, but also enable you to purchase concert, movie, and theater tickets, check news, weather, and traffic, get driving directions, and even apply for a loan! The most widespread use of kiosks is in government offices. They are becoming sufficiently commonplace that people are no longer startled when a pleasant female voice from the kiosk screen says, "If you want to file for divorce, touch here." In fact, kiosks in California, Arizona, and Utah handle uncontested divorces, probates, evictions, small claims, and other legal matters.

PEN-BASED COMPUTING   Small handheld computing devices often use an electronic pen, or stylus, to input data. The pen can be used as a pointer on the device's screen or to input data in handwritten form. Software translates the handwriting into characters that the computer can work with (Figure 5-10).

Electronic pen. Small hand-held computers often use an electronic pen, or stylus, to input data. The pen can be used as a pointer on the device's screen or to input data in handwritten form.

Source Data Automation: Collecting Data Where It Starts

Efficient data input means reducing the number of intermediate steps required between the origination of data and its processing. This is best accomplished by **source data automation,** the use of special equipment to collect data at its source as a byproduct of the activity that generates the data, and then send it directly to the computer. Recall, for example, the supermarket bar code, which can be used to send data about a product directly to the computer. Source data automation eliminates keying, thereby reducing costs and opportunities for human-introduced mistakes. Because data about a transaction is collected when and where the transaction takes place, source data automation also improves the speed of the input operation and is much less expensive than other methods.

For convenience, this discussion is divided into the primary areas related to source data automation: magnetic-ink character recognition, scanners and other optical recognition devices, and even your own voice, finger, or eye.

Magnetic-Ink Character Recognition

Magnetic-ink character recognition (MICR, pronounced "mike-er") involves using a machine to read characters made of magnetized particles. The banking industry is the predominant user of MICR equipment. Banks use the numbers encoded across the bottom of your personal check to route your check from the bank cashing the check to the bank where you have your account. Figure 5-11 shows what some of these numbers and symbols represent.

Most magnetic-ink characters are preprinted on your check. If you compare a check that you wrote that has been cashed and cleared by the bank with one that is still unused in your checkbook, you will note that the amount of the cashed check has been reproduced in magnetic characters in the lower-right corner. These characters were added by a person at the bank where the check was deposited by using a **MICR inscriber.**

Virtual Ads

If you've ever watched a baseball game on television, chances are you've seen a virtual ad—an ad that doesn't exist at the ballpark.

Prior to the event, an operator selects which advertisements to insert and chooses where in the stadium they will appear. During the broadcast, the system automatically inserts the advertisement into position, correctly adjusted for the position of the television camera. The inserted images appear as if they actually exist in the stadium, even to the extent that players pass in front of, and obscure, the inserted image.

Unlike the usual 30-second television commercial, this ad may loom in front of a viewer for much of the game. Furthermore, advertisers can target local audiences, showing an ad for hot soup in Juneau while, in the same spot, showing an ad for cold soda in San Diego.

Scanner

There was a time when the only way to transfer an existing document into the computer was to retype it. Now, however, an **optical scanner,** usually referred to as a **scanner,** can convert text or even a drawing or picture into computer-recognizable data by using a form of optical recognition. **Optical recognition** systems use a light beam to scan input data and convert it into electrical signals, which are sent to the computer for processing. Optical recognition is by far the most common type of source input; just think of all those supermarket scanners.

Now consider all those drawers filled with receipts, warranties, and old checks. If you let the computer take care of them, you can save space and, even better, find an item when you want it. Large businesses often use a process called **document imaging,** in which a scanner converts all incoming paper documents, such as invoices and order forms, to electronic versions, which can then be stored on disk, routed to the proper people, and retrieved when needed. This eliminates the need for moving large volumes of paperwork around within the company, improving the speed and efficiency of operations. Most consumers use a scanner to turn snapshots into images that can be printed, incorporated into a craft project, e-mailed, or posted on their Web site. Another popular use is converting printed documents, perhaps a letter or magazine article, into text that can be edited (changed or revised) by word-processing software.

Business people also find imaging useful because they can view an exact computer-produced replica of the original document at any time. Processed by related software, the words and numbers of the document can be manipulated by word-processing and other software. The Internal Revenue Service uses imaging to process 17,000 tax returns per hour, a significant improvement over hand processing.

Optical scanners fall into three categories. A **flatbed scanner** typically scans one sheet at a time, though some offer an attachment for scanning multiple sheets. Flatbed scanners are space hogs, taking up about as much room as a tabletop copy machine (Figure 5-12a). The advantage of a flatbed scanner is that it can scan bound documents, such as pages from books and other bulky items. In a **sheetfed scanner,** motorized rollers feed the sheet across the scanning head. A key attraction of sheetfed scanners is that they are usually designed to fit neatly between the keyboard and the monitor (Figure 5-12b). However, sheetfed scanners are less versatile and more prone to errors than flatbed scanners. A **handheld scanner,** the least expensive and least accurate of the three, is a handy portable option. It is often difficult to get a good scan with a handheld scanner because the user must move the scanner

(a)   (b)

◄ **F I G U R E** 5-12

Scanners. After an image has been scanned into the computer, it can be stored and used again, perhaps in a document that combines text with photos. (a) With a flatbed scanner, the image to be scanned is laid face down on the scanner, which looks something like a small copy machine. (b) Paper can be fed to the motorized rollers of a sheetfed scanner, which has the added advantage of fitting nicely between the keyboard and monitor.

in a straight line at a fixed rate. If the document being scanned is wider than the scanner, several passes must be made, and software must stitch the images together, a tedious and error-prone process.

Many users like scanners because they can use them to scan photographs directly into the computer. However, if you want to scan text and then be able to edit it using word-processing software, another step is involved. Because the result of a scan is simply a picture of the document being scanned, special software—usually called **OCR software,** for **optical character recognition**—must analyze the picture and convert it into characters. Most scanners come with OCR software.

More Optical Recognition Methods

In addition to text and images, optical recognition can process data in a variety of forms: optical marks, optical characters, bar codes, and even handwritten characters.

OPTICAL MARK RECOGNITION **Optical mark recognition (OMR)** is sometimes called **mark sensing** because a machine senses marks on a piece of paper. As a student, you may immediately recognize this approach as the technique used to score certain tests. Using a pencil, you make a mark in a specified box, circle, or space that corresponds to what you think is the answer. The answer sheet is then graded by an optical device that recognizes the locations of the marks and converts them to computer-recognizable electrical signals.

OPTICAL CHARACTER RECOGNITION **Optical character recognition (OCR) devices** also use a light source to read special characters and convert them into electrical signals to be sent to the central processing unit. The characters—letters, numbers, and special symbols—can be read by both humans and machines. They are often found on sales tags on store merchandise. A standard typeface for optical characters, called **OCR-A,** has been established by the American National Standards Institute (Figure 5-13).The handheld **wand reader** is a popular input device for reading OCR-A. Wands are being used more and more in libraries, hospitals, and factories, as well as in retail stores.

BAR CODES Each product on the supermarket shelf has its own unique number, which is part of the **Universal Product Code (UPC)**. This code number is represented on the product label by a pattern of vertical marks, or bars, called **bar codes.** (UPC, by the way, is an agreed-on standard within the supermarket industry; many other kinds of bar codes exist. You need only look as far as the back cover of this book to see an example of another kind of bar code.) These stripes can be sensed and read by a **bar code reader,** a photoelectric device that reads the code by means of reflected light. When you buy, say, a can of corn at the supermarket, the cashier moves it past the bar code reader (Figure 5-14a). The bar code merely identifies the product to the store's computer; the code does not contain the price, which may vary. The price is

```
A B C D E F G
H I J K L M N
O P Q R S T U
V W X Y Z ⌐ ·
$ / * Ñ 1 2 3
4 5 6 7 8 9 0
```

▲ **F I G U R E** 5-13

The OCR-A typeface. This is a common typeface for optical character recognition.

► FIGURE 5-14

Bar codes. (a) This laser bar code scanner, often seen at supermarket checkout counters, reads the product's zebra-striped bar code. The bar code identifies the product for the store's computer, which retrieves price and description information. The price is then automatically rung up on the point-of-sale terminal. (b) FedEx uses a bar code system to identify and track packages in transit.

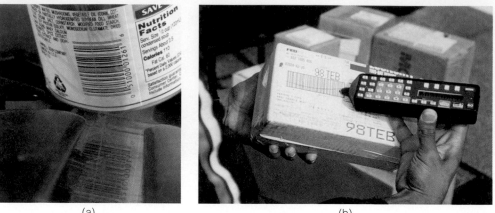

(a)   (b)

stored in a file that can be accessed by the computer. (Obviously, it is easier to change the price in the computer than it is to restamp the price on each can of corn.) The computer returns the price and then a printer prints the item description and price on a paper tape for the customer. Some supermarkets are moving to do-it-yourself scanning, putting the bar code reader, as well as the bagging, in the customer's hands.

Although bar codes were once found primarily in supermarkets, there are a variety of other interesting applications. Bar coding has been described as an inexpensive and remarkably reliable way to get data into a computer. It is no wonder that virtually every industry has found a niche for bar codes. Federal Express, for example, attributes a large part of the corporation's success to the bar-coding system it uses to track packages (Figure 5-14b). Each package is uniquely identified by a 10-digit bar code, which is input to the computer at each point as the package travels through the system. An employee can use a computer terminal to query the location of a given shipment at any time; the sender can request a status report on a package or track the package on the FedEx Web site.

HANDWRITTEN CHARACTERS   Machines that can read handwritten characters are yet another means of reducing the number of intermediate steps between capturing data and processing it. In many instances it is preferable to write the data and immediately have it usable for processing rather than having data entry operators key it in later. However, not just any scrawl will do; the rules governing the size, completeness, and legibility of the handwriting are fairly rigid (Figure 5-15).

Voice Input

Speaking to a computer, known as **voice input** or **speech recognition,** is another form of source input. **Speech recognition devices** accept the spoken word through a microphone and convert it into binary code (0s and 1s) that can be understood by the

► FIGURE 5-15

Handwritten characters. Legibility is important in making handwritten characters readable by optical recognition systems.

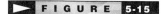

	Good	Bad
1. Make your letters big	EWING	EWING
2. Use simple shapes	57320	57320
3. Use block printing	KENT	Kent
4. Connect lines	5BE4	5BE4
5. Close loops	9068	9068
6. Do not link characters	LOOP	LOOP

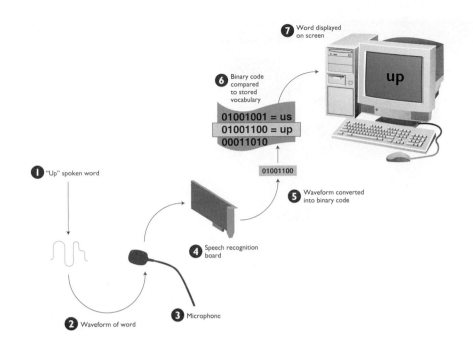

◄ FIGURE 5-16

How voice input works.
The user speaks into a microphone or telephone. A chip on a board inside the computer analyzes the waveform of the word and changes it to binary numbers that the computer can understand. These digits are compared with the numbers in a stored vocabulary list; if a match is found, the corresponding word is displayed on the screen.

computer (Figure 5-16). There are two basic uses for voice input. One use is to direct the computer to perform tasks by speaking the commands, such as starting a particular application program, opening a file, or moving to a specific location in a file. A second use is to enter large volumes of text, as in dictating a letter or creating a report. Typical users are the disabled, those with busy hands or hands too dirty for the keyboard, and those with no access to a keyboard (Figure 5-17).

Some speech recognition systems are speaker-dependent; that is, they must be separately trained for each user. The speech recognition system learns the voice of the user, who speaks isolated words repeatedly. The voiced words the system knows are then recognizable in the future. Speaker-independent speech recognition systems are designed to recognize anyone's voice, but have a much more limited vocabulary.

Speech recognition systems that are limited to isolated words are called **discrete word systems,** and users must pause between words. These systems are very accurate and are often used to enable users to issue brief commands to the computer. However, they are very tedious and awkward to use for inputting large amounts of text, as in dictation. The technology for **continuous word systems,** which can interpret sustained speech so that users can speak almost normally, has improved dramatically in the last few years. A key advantage of delivering input to a computer in a normal speaking pattern is ease of use. It is faster and easier for most people to dictate a letter than to key it in. However, voice recognition software is not perfect, currently claiming about 95 percent accuracy. That translates to 15 or more errors per dictated page, so you'd better proofread that report carefully!

Speech recognition is built into many current application programs. The Microsoft Office XP suite enables you to use spoken commands to operate the software and to dictate text into the application if your system is equipped with a microphone.

Although speech recognition has made great strides, the computer still has extreme difficulty understanding the meaning of the words that are recognized. Teaching the computer to understand normal human speech is one of the major challenges facing computer scientists.

Digital Cameras

Point, shoot, edit, print; the steps for taking a picture that are noticeably missing are loading film and, later, trips to the photo-processing lab. With a **digital camera** you take a photo that is stored internally on a chip; there is no film (Figure 5-18). You can see the result immediately on the LCD window, delete it if you don't like it, and take the

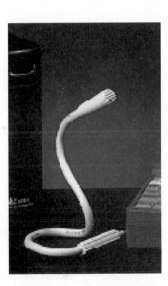

▲ FIGURE 5-17

Microphone. This twistable, and inexpensive, microphone is an input device for speech recognition.

▲ FIGURE 5-18

Digital camera. Digital cameras do not use film. They store images internally and then send them via cable or disk to your computer.

GETTING PRACTICAL · Digital Darkroom

Never mind the traditional darkroom, where a photo buff squints in dim red light while sloshing photos through smelly development chemicals. And, frankly, the results of all that sloshing, especially enlargements, probably would not be confused with professional work. Now that has changed. With the right computer equipment, you can be a professional, or close enough. You can make prints and enlargements that could not be differentiated from professional work without the aid of a magnifying glass.

First, consider the source of your pictures. How does one get the photos into the computer in the first place? There are several possibilities. A straightforward approach is to use a digital camera, storing the pictures in some computer-readable form, such as a chip, card, or disk, and then transferring the images directly to the computer. If your photos were recorded on the camera's embedded chip, they can be transferred by means of a cable hooked up to your computer's serial port or USB port, a plug-like input in the back. Another choice is to scan photos into the computer; a good-quality scanner maintains the quality of the photos.

Another possible photo source is the Internet, which offers free images, some as part of clip-art collections. Keep in mind, however, that professional photos on Internet sites are probably fee-based. If your interest goes beyond casual snapshots, you can pay for and download images from professional services on the Internet. Whatever method you choose to input photos, the net result is that you then can edit and reproduce those photos.

After you have the photos in digital form, you may want to use some photo-imaging software to manipulate them. Such software is an option rather than a necessity, but many people find that they like to improve or change their pictures in some way. However, despite a bit of photo manipulation by software, the printed photo image you hope for can be only as good as the image the program is given to work with.

Processing photographs at home is a trend in progress. People love to take pictures. People also love enlargements. Yet, mostly because of the high cost, only a tiny percentage of photos are enlarged. Home computer photography systems offer a new level of flexibility and creativity, enabling users to make professional-looking prints, reprints, and enlargements of photos that can be incorporated into personalized greeting cards, calendars, and postcards.

photo again if desired. Photos can easily be transferred to your computer, where you can use photo-editing software to crop, enlarge, or add special effects to them. You can store photos permanently on CDs or DVDs, e-mail them to friends and relatives, print them, or post them on the Web for all to see. A number of Web merchants will accept your images over the Internet and print them on mugs, T-shirts, and even posters.

Digital photographs are composed of many tiny dots, or **pixels,** of color. The number of these dots determines the clarity, or **resolution,** of the image. Inexpensive digital cameras use as many as one million pixels (referred to as one **megapixel**) for an image, more than adequate resolution for posting on a Web site or viewing on a computer screen. For printing high-quality photos as large as 5 inches by 7 inches, a two-megapixel camera would provide more satisfactory results. For larger, higher quality prints, three-, four-, and five-megapixel cameras are available to consumers. Professional photographers use even higher-resolution digital cameras, often at a cost of $10,000 or more.

As each picture is taken, it is stored internally in the camera using one of several different storage technologies. Most digital cameras use some form of removable memory card, such as the CompactFlash or SmartMedia cards mentioned in the previous chapter. These cards come in various capacities, from 8MB up to 1GB. The number of photos that can be stored on a card depends not only on the capacity of the card, but also the resolution of the pictures. With most cameras, you can select the resolution for each picture, up to the limit of the camera. Using a 16MB memory card, a three-megapixel camera can store only one image at its highest resolution, but more than 150 images at its lowest.

After the photos have been taken, you have to **download,** or transfer a copy of, them to your computer. This is most commonly accomplished using a cable to con-

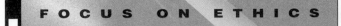

nect the camera to a serial or USB port on your computer. If you frequently download large numbers of images, you can purchase special reader devices that connect directly to the computer and accept your camera's media. Using these devices, the downloads occur much more quickly and you don't have to be constantly connecting and disconnecting cables. After the images are transferred to your computer, you can erase them from the camera's storage, enabling you to start all over again.

Digital cameras have many other features that make them more useful and easier to use. Most consumer-oriented cameras have point-and-shoot features such as automatic focusing, exposure control, and electronic flash that enable almost anyone to take good pictures. More expensive versions allow experienced photographers to override the automatic settings and some cameras have interchangeable lenses. Some digital cameras have the capability to record short video clips, possibly even with sound. Many digital cameras have both optical and digital zoom for getting closer to the subject. Finally, because digital cameras, especially the higher-resolution ones, use a lot of power, you might want to invest in a set of rechargeable batteries and a charger.

Digital Video

Digital video consists of a series of still images, called **frames,** that are displayed rapidly enough to give the illusion of motion. There are several methods available for capturing video input. The least expensive method uses a small, low-resolution video camera, often called a **Web cam.** Although the video can be recorded, these cameras are typically used to transmit images over the Internet. Depending on the rate of frame transmission, these images may appear as still images that change frequently, or as jerky, discontinuous video.

To capture video from traditional analog sources, such as TV and analog video cameras, you need to install a **video capture card** in your computer. This card converts the analog input signals into digital signals that you can store on a hard drive or CD and manipulate with video software. Many of the newer video cameras use digital technology and can transfer digital signals directly to a computer via cable.

► OUTPUT: INFORMATION FOR THE USER

As we noted earlier, computer output usually takes the form of screen or printer output. Other forms of output include voice, sound, and various forms of graphics output. Devices have even been designed to produce odors as computer output.

A computer system may be designed to produce several kinds of output. An example is a travel agency's computer system. If a customer asks about airline connections to, say, Toronto, Calgary, and Vancouver, the travel agent probably makes a few queries to the system and receives on-screen output indicating availability and pricing for the various flights. After the reservations have been confirmed, the agent can ask for printed output that includes the tickets, the traveler's itinerary, and the invoice. In addition, the agency's management may periodically receive printed reports and charts, such as monthly summaries of sales figures or pie charts of regional costs.

Computer Screen Technology

A user's first interaction with a computer screen may be to view the screen response to that user's input. When data is entered, it appears on the screen. The computer response to that data, the output, also appears on the screen. The screen is part of the computer's **monitor,** which also includes the housing for its electrical components. Monitors usually include a stand that can be tilted or swiveled to enable the monitor to be easily adjusted to suit the user.

Screen output is known in the computer industry as **soft copy** because it is intangible and temporary, unlike **hard copy,** which is produced on paper by a printer and is tangible and can be permanent.

Computer monitors come in many varieties (Figure 5-19), but the most common kind is the **cathode ray tube (CRT).** CRT monitors that display text and graphics are in common use today. Although most CRTs are color, some are **monochrome,** meaning that only one color, usually green or amber, appears on a contrasting background. Monochrome screens, which are less expensive than those with color, are used in business applications such as customer inquiry or order entry, which have no need for color.

Most CRT screens use a technology called **raster scanning,** a process of sweeping electron beams across the back of the screen. The backing of the screen display has a phosphorous coating that glows whenever it is hit by a beam of electrons. But the phosphorus does not glow for very long, so the image must be **refreshed** often. If the screen is not refreshed often enough, the fading screen image appears to flicker. A **scan rate**—the number of times the electron beam refreshes the screen—of 75 or more times per second is usually found on quality monitors. This is essentially the same process used to produce television images.

A computer display screen that can be used for graphics is divided into dots that are called **addressable** because they can be addressed individually by the graphics software. Each dot can be illuminated individually to a desired color and brightness on the screen. Each dot is referred to as a picture element, or **pixel.** The **resolution** of the screen, its clarity, is directly related to the number of pixels on the screen: the more pixels, the higher the resolution. Another factor of importance is **dot pitch,** the

► **FIGURE 5-19**

Computer monitors.
(a) This CRT monitor is inexpensive and produces high-quality color output. (b) LCD monitors are found on notebook computers, due to their light weight and low power requirements, but are becoming increasingly common on desktop systems.

(a)   (b)

amount of space between the dots. The smaller the dot pitch, the sharper the screen image. High-quality monitors have a dot pitch of .28 mm or less.

The electrical output signals that the control unit sends to the monitor have to be converted into the signals that control the monitor. This can be accomplished by chips permanently affixed to the motherboard, but most computers have a **graphics card,** or **graphics adapter board,** plugged into an expansion slot. This approach enables the user to upgrade the graphics capability if desired. The graphics card and the monitor must be compatible to produce a high-quality image.

Graphic standards were established in the early years of the personal computer. The intention of standards is to agree on resolutions, colors, and so forth to make it easier for the manufacturers of personal computers, monitors, graphics boards, and software to ensure that their products work together.

The standard in most common use today is **Super Video Graphics Adapter (SVGA).** There are several varieties of SVGA, each providing a different resolution: 800 (horizontal) x 600 (vertical) pixels, 1024 x 768 (XGA), 1280 x 1024 (SXGA), and 1600 x 1200 (UXGA). All SVGA standards support a palette of 16 million colors, but the number of colors that can be displayed simultaneously is limited by the amount of video memory on the video card. **Video memory** is a high-speed form of RAM installed on the graphics card, separate from main memory. The image to be displayed on the screen is first placed in video memory by the software. Displaying 16 million colors at a resolution of 1024 x 768 requires 4MB of video memory.

Is bigger really better? Screen sizes are measured diagonally. However, unlike television screens, computer screen size is not regulated. CRT screens usually have a **viewable image size (vis)** an inch or more less than the stated screen size. For instance, an advertisement for a 17-inch monitor might specify a 15.9-inch vis. When making comparisons, a user would do well to bring a ruler. A typical office worker who handles word processing and spreadsheet duties will probably find a 15- or 17-inch screen adequate. A user who is involved with high-powered graphics will probably want a 19-inch screen or larger. At the high end, screens that are as large as television sets, 24 inches and up, can be purchased.

To answer the question, yes, bigger is usually better, but it is also more expensive and takes up much more space on your desk. For your own personal computer, after you try a larger screen, you will not want to go back. In addition to the reduced strain

on the eyes, larger screens are particularly useful for Web pages, page layout, graphics, and large photos and illustrations.

Flat-Panel Screens

Another type of screen technology is the **liquid crystal display (LCD)**, a **flat-panel display** often seen on cell phones and PDAs. LCD screens are commonly used on laptop computers, but flat-panel screens are getting bigger and are making their way to desktop computers (Figure 5-19). Although traditional CRT monitors get deeper as they get wider, flat-panel monitors maintain their depth, a super-skinny few inches, regardless of screen size. LCD monitors can use one of two basic technologies: **active-matrix,** based on **TFT** (thin-film transistor technology), and passive-matrix. **Passive-matrix** technology uses fewer transistors and therefore is cheaper and uses less power, but TFT displays produce a brighter image and can be viewed from wider angles.

LCD screens provide sharper text images than CRTs, but CRTs are considered superior for color graphics display. LCD screens are also easier on the eyes; they do not flicker but just brightly shine on. The full dimension of a flat-panel screen is usable, so a 15-inch flat-panel monitor has a viewing area nearly as large as that of a 17-inch CRT monitor. Although prices of flat-panel screens are coming down, they are still quite a bit higher than prices for equivalently sized CRT monitors.

A newer form of flat-panel display uses **gas plasma** technology, in which each pixel consists of a tiny amount of gas that can be activated by an electrical current, similar to a tiny neon light. These displays come in sizes up to 60 inches and have a brilliant color display, viewable at much wider angles than LCD monitors. They maintain the same slim profile and are often wall-mounted. This is the same technology that is used in the latest home theater systems and is many times more expensive than LCD monitors.

Smart Displays

A new class of displays is based on flat panel technology. These portable touch-screen **smart displays** contain their own processor and a wireless transmitter-receiver that enable the user to control a desktop system from anywhere in the house. The initial versions run the Windows CE operating system and connect with computers using Windows XP Professional, but versions for Mac OS and Linux shouldn't be too far behind.

Printers

A **printer** is a device that produces information on paper output. Some older printers produce only letters and numbers, but most printers used with personal computers today can also produce information in graphic form. Most printers have two orientation settings: portrait and landscape. The default setting is **portrait mode,** in which output, such as a memo, is printed in a vertical alignment, that is, with the longest dimension up and down. **Landscape mode** prints output sideways, or horizontally, with the longest dimension across the width of the paper; this is especially useful for spreadsheets that have a lot of data across the sheet. Graphics images may be more suited for printing in one mode over another.

There are two ways of printing an image on paper: the impact method and the nonimpact method. An **impact printer** uses some sort of physical contact with the paper to produce an image, physically striking paper, ribbon, and print hammer together. Mainframe users who are more concerned about high volume than high quality usually use **line printers,** impact printers that print an entire line at a time. These users are likely to print lengthy reports, perhaps relating to payroll or costs, for internal use. Impact printers are needed when multiple copies of a report are printed; the impact carries the output through to the lower copies. Personal computer users

◄ **FIGURE** 5-20

Dot matrix printing. The print head on a dot matrix printer contains columns of tiny pins that strike the ribbon against the paper leaving a pattern of tiny dots that form characters and images.

who need to print multipart forms can use **dot-matrix printers,** which have a print head consisting of one or more columns of pins. These pins form characters and images as a pattern of dots produced by the pins striking the ribbon against the paper as the print head moves back and forth across the paper (Figure 5-20). Dot-matrix printers used to be the primary type of printer found on microcomputer systems, but they have largely been replaced by ink-jet and laser printers.

A **nonimpact printer** places an image on a page without physically touching the page. The major technologies competing in the nonimpact market are laser and ink-jet, the two kinds of printers that you find in your local computer store. **Laser printers** use a light beam to transfer images to paper (Figure 5-21). Today's laser printers print 600 or 1,200 dots per inch (dpi), producing extremely high-quality results. Laser printers print a page at a time at impressive speeds, using technology similar to that of a photocopier. Printing speeds of personal laser printers are generally around 8 to 10 pages per minute (ppm), while network laser printers are capable of between 35 and 50 ppm. Large organizations such as banks and insurance companies use expensive, high-volume laser printers that can produce reports at up to 1,000 ppm. Low-end black-and-white laser printers for use with personal computers can be purchased for a few hundred dollars. Color laser printers are much more expensive.

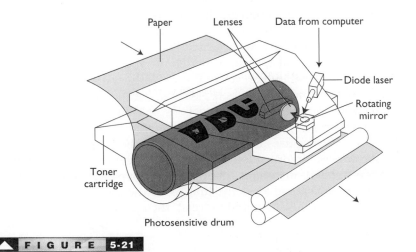

▲ **FIGURE** 5-21

Laser printers. A laser printer works like a photocopy machine. Using patterns of small dots, a laser beam conveys information from the computer to a positively charged drum inside the laser printer. Wherever an image is to be printed, the laser beam is turned on, causing the drum to become neutralized. As the drum passes by a toner cartridge, toner sticks to the neutral spots on the drum. The toner is then transferred from the drum to a piece of paper. In the final printing step, heat and pressure fuse the toner to the paper. The drum is then cleaned for the next pass.

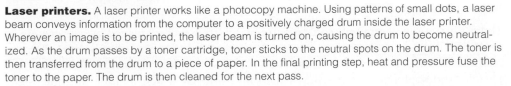

FIGURE 5-22

Ink-jet printers. A color ink-jet printer is an affordable and popular addition to many home computer systems.

Ink-jet printers, which spray dots of ink from multiple jet nozzles, can print in black and white as well as several different colors of ink to produce excellent graphics (Figure 5-22). However, the print quality of an ink-jet printer, though more than adequate, usually does not match that of a laser printer, nor is the printing as speedy. Furthermore, ink-jet printers need a fairly high quality of paper so that the ink does not smear or bleed. Nevertheless, low-end ink-jet printers, which cost a little more than a hundred dollars, are a bargain for users who want high-quality color output capability. Home users involved with digital photography can buy ink-jet printers optimized for photo quality output. Using special coated paper and high-quality ink, these printers can produce output matching the quality of lab-developed photographs. Some printers even have slots to accept the removable storage media used in digital cameras, enabling users to print photos without using the computer.

If you choose a color printer, whether ink-jet or laser, you will find that its colors are not perfect. The color you see on your computer screen is not necessarily the exact color you see on the printed output. Nor is it likely to be the color you would see on a professional four-color offset printing press.

Choosing between a laser printer and an ink-jet printer comes down to a few factors. If printing speed is important to you or if the quality of the printed text is a top priority, you probably want a black-and-white laser printer. If you cannot resist the prospect of color and are not overly concerned about text quality or speed, an ink-jet printer may be your best choice. If you want it all, color laser printers are available, but in a higher price range.

Voice Output

We have already examined voice input in some detail. As you will see in this section, computers are like some people in the sense that they find it easier to talk than to listen. **Speech synthesis,** the process of enabling machines to talk to people, is much easier than speech recognition. "The key is in the ignition," your car says to you as you open the car door to get out. Machine voices are the product of **voice synthesizers** (also called **voice-output devices** or **audio-response units**), which convert data in main storage to vocalized sounds understandable to humans.

There are two basic approaches to getting a computer to talk. The first is **synthesis by analysis,** in which the device analyzes the input of an actual human voice speaking words, records the spoken sounds, and replays them as needed. This produces a voice that sounds natural, although the pace is a little awkward. However, this approach is limited by the number of words recorded. The second approach to synthesizing speech is **synthesis by rule,** in which the device applies a complex set of linguistic rules to create artificial speech. Although the speech is understandable, no one would mistake it for a real human voice.

Voice output has become common in such places as airline and bus terminals, banks, brokerage houses, and even some automobiles. It is typically used when an inquiry is followed by a short reply, such as a bank balance or flight time. Many businesses have found other creative uses for voice output over the telephone. Automatic telephone voices take surveys, inform customers that catalog orders are ready to be picked up, and perhaps remind consumers that they have not paid their bills. For the personal computer user, software is available that reads the information contained on the screen, enabling the visually impaired to "read" their e-mail, surf the Web, and use many application programs.

Music Output and Other Sounds

Today's personal computers can be equipped with speakers placed on either side of the computer or, in some cases, mounted on the sides of the monitor or buried in the computer housing. Users want good-quality sound from certain kinds of software, especially the sophisticated offerings called multimedia, which include multiple sight

The Eyes Have It

The computer can be a godsend for many people who have physical limitations. Various input devices have been developed to assist people with varying degrees of limitations. But what about the totally paralyzed, who lack the ability to do almost anything other than move their eyes? A system called the Eye Science Gaze Tracker enables users to perform mouse functions with their eyes. Two low-powered infrared LEDs

continued

and sound effects. Even the zap-and-crash sounds of action games deserve to be heard. To enhance the listening experience further, manufacturers are now producing sound cards containing sophisticated audio chips that, by varying the frequencies and timing of the sound waves as they reach the human ear, can fool the brain into thinking that it is hearing three-dimensional sound from two speakers. Couple that with a separate sub-woofer, a speaker specially designed to produce room-vibrating, low-frequency sounds, and you have a system that will satisfy a serious audiophile.

Musical Instrument Digital Interface (**MIDI**), pronounced "mid-ee") is a set of rules designed for connecting musical instruments, synthesizers, and computers. Devices that conform to the MIDI standard can communicate with each other and with a computer containing a MIDI interface. In much the same way that two computers communicate via modems, two musical devices can communicate via MIDI. The information exchanged between two MIDI devices is musical in nature, concerning data about the start of a note, its pitch, length, volume, and musical attributes, such as vibrato. Music can be recorded in MIDI format from instruments such as guitars, drums, and keyboards; modified using a synthesizer; and then played back under computer control, possibly in combination with live performers. A number of software programs are available for composing and editing music that conforms to the MIDI standard. They offer a variety of functions. For instance, when you play a tune on a keyboard connected to a computer, a music program can translate what you play into a written score. MIDI is supported by many makes of personal computer sound cards.

Using relatively inexpensive MIDI equipment, musicians can set up home studios that rival the capabilities of professional recording studios.

Microform

Computer Output Microform (**COM**) refers to the output of photographically reduced images on microfilm or microfiche. With **microfilm,** the images are stored on a continuous roll of film, similar to that used in cameras. **Microfiche** (pronounced "micro-feesh") stores the images in rows and columns on a card, up to 1,000 page images on a single four-inch by six-inch card. A COM recorder produces the output at speeds much faster than printing on paper. COM is used extensively in libraries to store back issues of periodicals and by businesses that are required to keep large volumes of historical records, such as banks and insurance companies. The biggest disadvantage of COM is the necessity of using a special reading device.

▶ TERMINALS: COMBINING INPUT AND OUTPUT

A **terminal** is a device (or combination of devices) that combines both input and output capabilities. The simplest type of terminal, known as a **dumb terminal** because it has no processing capability, consists of a keyboard for input and a monitor for output and connects directly to a host computer. Everything that is typed into the keyboard is sent to the host for processing, which sends results back to the terminal screen to be displayed. An **intelligent terminal** combines a keyboard and monitor with memory and a processor, giving it the ability to perform limited processing functions. For example, an intelligent terminal could display an input form on the screen, accept user input through the keyboard, perform editing and error-checking functions on the data (requesting reentry if necessary) and then send the entire set of data to the host computer for processing. When the results are sent back, the terminal could format and display those results on the screen.

A **point-of-sale (POS) terminal** is a combination of input and output devices designed to capture retail sales data at the point where the transaction takes place. The most familiar POS terminal is the supermarket checkout station. The primary input device is the bar code reader built into the counter. For items with no bar code, such

mounted on the monitor illuminate the user's eye. The reflections from the eye are detected by a digital camera, which is also mounted on the monitor. By analyzing the image from the camera, software can determine where on the screen the user is looking and move the screen pointer accordingly. Mouse clicks can be simulated by slow eye blinks or by allowing the gaze to linger for a time on one location. No hardware has to be attached to the user, a big advantage over previous systems that required affixing electrodes to the eye muscles. The Gaze Tracker even works with eyeglasses. Jason Becker, the former lead guitarist in David Lee Roth's band, is one person who is grateful for the capabilities provided by the Gaze Tracker. Becker suffers from amyotrophic lateral sclerosis, also called Lou Gehrig's disease, a degenerative neurological disease that has robbed him of almost all muscle control. The Gaze Tracker enables him to continue writing music.

POS terminal. This sales clerk is using a retail POS terminal to process a sale.

as loose produce, the cashier can use a keyboard to enter the data. Checkout stations may also include a digital scale to weigh items sold by weight and a magnetic stripe reader to read credit card information. For output, the station includes both a small screen display and a printer that prints the customer receipt. Another common POS terminal in retail stores uses a wand reader to read the merchandise code from the product tag and transmit it to the computer, which retrieves a description (and possibly the price, if it is not on the tag) of the item. A small printer produces a customer receipt that shows the item description and price. The computer calculates the subtotal, the sales tax (if any), and the total. This information is displayed on the screen and printed on the receipt (Figure 5-23).

The raw purchase data captured by the POS terminal becomes valuable information when it is summarized by the computer system. This information can be used by the accounting department to keep track of how much money is taken in each day, by buyers to determine what merchandise should be reordered, and by the marketing department to analyze the effectiveness of its ad campaigns.

▶ COMPUTER GRAPHICS

Now for everyone's favorite: computer graphics. You have probably seen the lines and charts of business graphics (Figure 5-24). Just about everyone has seen TV commercials or movies that use computer-produced animated graphics. Computer graphics can also be useful in education, science, sports, computer art, and other areas, but their most prevalent use today is still in business.

Business Graphics

Graphics can be a powerful way to impart information. Colorful graphics, maps, and charts can help managers compare data more easily, spot trends, and make deci-

Business graphics. These charts were made with powerful but easy-to-use graphics software.

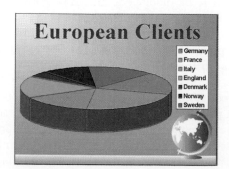

sions more quickly. Also, the use of color helps people get the picture—literally. Although color graphs and charts have been used in business for years, usually to make presentations to upper management or outside clients, the computer enables them to be rendered quickly, before information becomes outdated. As the underlying data changes, the graphs and charts can be updated instantaneously. One user refers to business graphics as "computer-assisted insight." Business graphics are discussed in more detail in Chapter12, Spreadsheets and Business Graphics.

Video Graphics

Video graphics can be as creative as an animated cartoon. Although they operate on the same principle as a moving picture or cartoon, one frame at a time in quick succession, video graphics are produced by computers. Video graphics have made their biggest splash on television, but many people do not realize that they are watching a computer at work. The next time you watch television, skip the trip to the kitchen and pay special attention to the commercials. If there is no live human in the advertisement (and perhaps even if there is), the moving objects you see, such as floating cars and bobbing electric razors, are doubtlessly computer output. Another fertile ground for video graphics is a television network's logo and theme. Accompanied by music and swooshing sounds, the network symbol spins and cavorts and turns itself inside out, all with the finesse that only a computer could supply.

Video graphics are well known to people who like to play arcade games; their input device is the joystick, which allows fingertip control of figures on the screen.

Computer-Aided Design/Computer-Aided Manufacturing

Computer graphics have become part and parcel of a field known by the abbreviation **CAD/CAM,** short for **computer-aided design/computer-aided manufacturing.** On the CAD side, computer software is used to create two- and three-dimensional designs of everything from hand tools to tractors to highway designs. When the design is complete, additional software can perform various engineering tests, such as stress tests and performance analyses. The design data can then be passed to CAM systems, which use computers to control production equipment (Figure 5-25).

CAD/CAM provides a bridge between design (planning what a product will be) and manufacturing (actually making the planned product). As a manager at DaimlerChrysler said, "Many companies have design data and manufacturing data, and the two are never the same. At Chrysler, we have only one set of data that

◀ FIGURE 5-25

CAD/CAM. This designer is using CAD software to design components. This design can then be passed to a CAM system that will control manufacturing.

everyone dips into." Keeping data in one place, of course, makes changes easier and encourages consistency.

Computer-integrated manufacturing (CIM) integrates CAD/CAM and the entire manufacturing process. Production planning, scheduling, materials management, and production control are automated under computer control, providing a balanced, efficient production process.

◀▶ ETHICS AND DATA

Few people pause to ponder the relationship between ethics and data, but it is an important one. After the data is in the computer, there are many ways it can be used, sold, or even altered. Data can also be input and stored in a great variety of ways. Consider these data ethics issues, all of which are at least debatable and most of which could be defensible in some situations:

● Is it ethically acceptable to use a computer to alter photographs? Is it ethical to substitute one person for another in a photograph? Should we be able to change pictures of ourselves? Of group photos from school or work? Is it ethical to use a computer to add a celebrity to a photo? Does it matter whether the celebrity is alive or dead?

● Suppose you perceive that the contents of certain e-mail messages may be of interest to a plaintiff who is suing your company. Is it ethical to erase the messages?

● A friend who has worked on a political campaign has a disk file of donors. Is it ethical to use that same list to solicit for your candidate?

Note that not all of these scenarios inherently require a computer, but the computer makes them that much easier.

▲

New forms of computer input and output are announced regularly, often with promises of multiple benefits and new ease of use. Part of the excitement of the computer world is that these promises are usually kept, and users reap the benefits directly. Input and output just keep getting better.

CHAPTER REVIEW

► Summary and Key Terms

- A **source document** is the original written data to be input into the computer.

- A **keyboard** is a common input device that may be part of a personal computer or a terminal connected to a remote computer. **Cordless keyboards** communicate with the system unit via infrared or radio waves.

- The field of **ergonomics** is concerned with designing equipment so that people interact with the equipment in a healthy, comfortable, and efficient manner. **Ergonomic keyboards** are designed to provide users with more natural, comfortable hand, wrist, and arm positions.

- A **pointing device** is used to position a **pointer** on the screen. The pointer can have a number of shapes but is most often an arrow. You move the pointer and then click the button to place the **insertion point,** or **cursor,** at the pointer location. An **icon,** a pictorial symbol on a screen, can be clicked to invoke a command to the computer.

- A **mouse** is an input device whose movement on a flat surface causes a corresponding movement of the pointer on the screen. A **mechanical mouse** has a ball on its underside that rolls as the mouse is moved. An **optical mouse** uses a light beam to monitor mouse movement. A **cordless** mouse uses infrared or radio waves rather than a cord to send signals to the computer. A **trackball** is like an upside-down mechanical mouse; the ball is rolled with the hand. A **touch pad** uses finger movement on its surface to control the pointer. A **pointing stick** is a small pressure-sensitive post mounted in the center of the keyboard that uses pressure to indicate the direction of pointer movement. A **joystick** is a short lever with a handgrip that is moved in one direction or another to move the pointer.

- A **graphics tablet,** also called a **digitizing tablet,** is a rectangular board that contains an invisible grid of electronic dots. As the user moves a pen-like **stylus** or a mouse-like **puck** with crosshairs around the board, the dot locations it passes over are sent to the computer.

- **Touch screens** enable the user to input information by pointing to locations on the screen with a finger. Some screens use a **light pen** as the input device, enabling more precise pointing.

- **Source data automation** involves the use of special equipment to collect data at its origin and send it directly to the computer.

- **Magnetic-ink character recognition (MICR)** enables a machine to read characters made of magnetized particles, such as the preprinted characters on a personal check. Some characters are preprinted, but others, such as the amount of a check, are added by a person using a **MICR inscriber.**

- An **optical scanner,** or just **scanner,** can convert text or even a drawing or photograph into computer-recognizable form by using **optical recognition,** a system that uses a light beam to scan input data and convert it into electrical signals that are sent to the computer for processing. In a process called **document imaging,** a scanner converts those papers to an electronic version, which can then be stored on disk and retrieved when needed.

- A **flatbed scanner,** a tabletop machine, typically scans one sheet at a time, although some offer an attachment for scanning multiple sheets. A **sheetfed scanner,** usually designed to fit neatly between the keyboard and the monitor, uses motorized rollers to feed the sheet across the scanning head. A **handheld scanner,** the least expensive and least reliable of the three, is handy for portability. **Optical character recognition (OCR) software** can convert the digital picture produced by the scanner into text for processing.

- **Optical mark recognition (OMR,** also called **mark sensing)** devices recognize marks on paper. **Optical character recognition (OCR) devices** read special characters, such as those on price tags. These characters are often in a standard typeface called **OCR-A.** A commonly used OCR device is the handheld **wand reader.** A **bar code reader** is a photoelectric scanner used to input **bar codes,** patterns of vertical marks. One standard code is the **Universal Product Code (UPC)** that identifies a supermarket product. Some optical scanners can read precise handwritten characters.

- **Voice input,** or **speech recognition,** is the process of presenting input data to the computer through the spoken word. **Speech recognition devices** convert spoken words into a digital code that a computer can understand. The two main types of devices are **discrete word systems,** which require speakers to pause between words, and **continuous word systems,** which allow a normal rate of speaking. The two primary uses for voice input are entering commands and dictating large amounts of text.

- A **digital camera** takes photos that are stored internally on a chip or card, and then sent directly to your computer, where they can be edited and printed. Digital images are composed of **pixels.** The number of pixels determines the **resolution,** or clarity, of the image. Digital camera resolution is normally expressed in terms of **megapixels,** or millions of pixels. Images must be **downloaded,** or transferred, from the camera to a computer.

- Digital video consists of a series of still images, called **frames,** that are displayed rapidly enough to give the illusion of motion. **Web cams** are inexpensive video cameras that capture images typically transmitted on the Internet. A **video capture card** accepts an analog signal from a video source such as a TV or video camera and converts it into a digital signal for processing by a computer.

- The **monitor** features the computer's screen, includes the housing for its electrical components, and often sits on a stand that tilts and swivels. Screen output is known in the computer industry as **soft copy** because it is intangible and temporary, unlike **hard copy,** produced by a printer on paper, which is tangible and can be permanent.

- The most common kind of computer monitor is the **cathode ray tube (CRT).** Some computer screens are **monochrome**—the characters appear in one color, usually green or amber, on a contrasting background. Most CRT screens use a technology called **raster scanning,** in which the backing of the screen display has a phosphorous coating, which glows whenever it is hit by a beam of electrons. The screen image must be **refreshed** often to avoid flicker. The **scan rate** is the number of times the screen is refreshed per second.

- A computer display screen that can be used for graphics is divided into dots that are called **addressable** because they can be addressed individually by the graphics software. Each screen dot is called a **pixel.** The more pixels, the higher the screen **resolution,** or clarity. **Dot pitch** is the amount of space between the dots on a screen. If a computer does not come with built-in graphics capability, you need to add a **graphics card** or **graphics adapter board** to convert the electrical signals from the control unit into the signals that control the monitor.

- The most common graphics standard today is **SVGA (Super VGA),** providing various levels of resolution and potentially supporting a palette of 16 million colors. **Video memory** is a high-speed form of RAM installed on the graphics card.

- Screen sizes are measured diagonally. CRT screens have a **viewable image size (vis)** smaller than the stated screen measurement.

- A **liquid crystal display (LCD)** is a type of **flat-panel screen** found on laptop computers and on some desktop computers. **Active-matrix** displays, also known as **TFT** displays, produce a better image but use more power and are more expensive than **passive-matrix** displays. These screens are noted for their slimness and bright, flicker-free images, but they are more expensive than CRTs. A newer form of flat-panel display uses **gas plasma** technology, which produces a brighter image and comes in larger sizes than LCD displays.

- Smart displays contain their own processor and a wireless transmitter-receiver and are used to remotely control a desktop computer.

- **Printers** produce printed paper output. The default printer orientation setting is **portrait mode,** in which output is printed with the longest dimension up and down; **landscape mode** prints output sideways on the paper. Printers can be classified as either **impact printers,** which form characters by physically striking the paper, or **nonimpact printers,** which use a noncontact printing method. **Line printers** are impact printers used on mainframe systems that print an entire line at a time. **Dot-matrix** printers use a print head containing one or more columns of pins to produce images as a pattern of dots. **Laser printers** and **ink-jet printers** are nonimpact printers. Today's laser printers print 600 or 1,200 dots per inch (dpi), producing extremely high-quality results. Laser printers print an entire page at a time, and their speed is rated in pages per minute (ppm).

- Computer **speech synthesis** has been accomplished through **voice synthesizers** (also called **voice-output devices** or **audio-response units**). One approach to speech synthesis is **synthesis by analysis,** in which the computer records spoken sounds and replays them as needed. In the other approach, called **synthesis by rule,** the computer applies linguistic rules to create artificial speech.

- **Musical Instrument Digital Interface** (**MIDI**) is a set of rules designed for recording and playing back music on digital synthesizers.

- A **terminal** is a device (or combination of devices) that combines both input and output capabilities. A **dumb terminal** consists of a screen and keyboard and has no processing power of its own. An **intelligent terminal** combines a keyboard and monitor with memory and a processor, giving it the ability to perform limited processing functions.

- A **point-of-sale** (**POS**) **terminal** is a combination of input and output devices designed to capture retail sales data at the point where the transaction takes place.

- **Video graphics** are a series of computer-produced pictures that, when displayed in rapid succession, appear to be in motion. Video-graphic arcade games are played with a joystick, which allows fingertip control of figures on the screen.

- In **computer-aided design/computer-aided manufacturing** (**CAD/CAM**), computers are used to design and manufacture products. **Computer-integrated manufacturing** (**CIM**) integrates CAD/CAM and the entire manufacturing process.

► Critical Thinking Questions

1. For this question, use your knowledge from reading or experience or imagine the possibilities. What kind of input device might be convenient for these types of jobs or situations?
   a. A supermarket stock clerk who takes inventory by surveying items that are currently on the shelf
   b. A medical assistant who must input existing printed documents to the computer
   c. An airport automated luggage-tracking system
   d. A telephone worker who takes orders over the phone
   e. A restaurant in which customers place their own orders from the table
   f. An inspector at the U.S. Bureau of Engraving who monitors and gives a go/no-go response on printed money passing by on an assembly line
   g. A retailer who wants to move customers quickly through the checkout lines
   h. A psychologist who wants to give a new client a standard test
   i. An environmental engineer who hikes through woods and streams to inspect and report on the effects of pollutants
   j. A small-business owner who wants to keep track of employee work hours

2. Most people use a mouse as their pointing device. Discuss the reasons why someone might prefer to use one of the other pointing devices described in the text.

3. Some cities have contracted with private companies to set up cameras at intersections to take pictures of cars running red lights. Tickets are sent to the registered owners of the vehicles. Discuss your views of the ethics involved. Does it make any difference that, in many cases, the companies are paid a percentage of the fines collected?

4. Do you think that voice input is practical for your own use? Explain your answer.

5. If price were not a consideration, what kind of printers would you buy for your home or business personal computers?

► STUDENT STUDY GUIDE

Multiple Choice

1. The distance between the pixels on a screen is called
   a. OCR
   b. LCD
   c. dot pitch
   d. refresh rate

2. A pictorial screen symbol that represents a computer activity is called a(n)
   a. pointer
   b. icon
   c. touch screen
   d. MICR

3. Using computers to design and manufacture products is called
   a. inscribing
   b. CAD/CAM
   c. detailing
   d. imaging

4. Soft copy refers to
   a. printed output
   b. music sounds
   c. screen output
   d. digitizing

5. The type of scanner that fits between the keyboard and the monitor is the
   a. sheetfed scanner
   b. handheld scanner
   c. flatbed scanner
   d. video scanner

6. An ink-jet printer is an example of a(n)
   a. laser printer
   b. impact printer
   c. LCD printer
   d. nonimpact printer

7. Entering data as a by-product of the activity that generates the data is known as
   a. source data automation
   b. a discrete word system
   c. CAD/CAM
   d. MICR entry

8. The rate of screen refreshment is called
   a. pixel speed
   b. bit-map speed
   c. raster rate
   d. scan rate

9. Magnetic characters representing the check amount are entered onto your bank checks by
   a. bar code readers
   b. mice
   c. MICR inscribers
   d. OCR

10. Mark sensing is another term for
    a. MICR
    b. POS
    c. OMR
    d. XGA

11. Which of the following is a device that is used for optical character recognition?
    a. wand reader
    b. cursor
    c. stylus
    d. MICR reader

12. OCR-A is a
    a. portrait
    b. standard typeface
    c. wand reader
    d. bar code

13. Some POS terminals are similar to
    a. calculators
    b. Touch-Tone telephones
    c. UPCs
    d. cash registers

14. Which of the following monitors shows single-color characters on a contrasting background?
    a. monochrome
    b. blank
    c. addressable
    d. liquid crystal display

15. Voice input devices convert voice input to
    a. digital codes
    b. bar codes
    c. OCR-A
    d. optical marks

16. Document imaging uses which device to input data?
    a. scanner
    b. bar code reader
    c. icon
    d. tablet

17. The pointer can be positioned on the screen by moving which device on a flat surface?
    a. UPC
    b. mouse
    c. wand reader
    d. interactive tablet

18. Which input device is often attached to laptop computers?
    a. trackball
    b. joystick
    c. inscriber
    d. wand reader

19. Which of the following displays has a screen that is lighter and slimmer than a CRT?
    a. OCR
    b. graphics card
    c. flat-panel
    d. terminal

20. Computer animation is a form of
    a. LCD
    b. CAD/CAM
    c. video graphics
    d. color printer output

True/False

T   F   1. The greater the number of pixels, the poorer the screen clarity.

T   F   2. Printers produce hard copy.

T   F   3. Discrete word systems enable a normal rate of speaking.

T   F   4. Data is scanned into the computer by using a mouse.

T   F   5. Voice recognition software is very good at understanding the meaning of spoken words.

T   F   6. Optical recognition technology is based on magnetized data.

T   F   7. OMR senses marks on paper.

T   F   8. A wand reader can read OCR characters.

T   F   9. A sideways printer orientation is called portrait mode.

T   F   10. LCD is a type of flat screen found on laptop computers.

T   F   11. A gas plasma monitor is an inexpensive type of flat-panel display.

T   F   12. A mouse can be clicked to execute a command.

T   F   13. The MICR process is used primarily in retail stores.

T   F   14. The cursor indicates the location of the next interaction on the screen.

T   F   15. Dot pitch refers to the number of pixels on a screen.

T   F   16. The best way to scan a page from a book is with a flatbed scanner.

T   F   17. Continuous word voice input systems are best for dictating large amounts of text.

T   F   18. A touch pad is used by moving it across a hard surface.

T   F   19. MIDI is the accepted standard for LCD screens.

T   F   20. To avoid flicker, a CRT screen needs to be refreshed often.

T   F   21. The most common use for a joystick is CAD/CAM applications.

T   F   22. Flat-panel displays can be found on desktop computers as well as laptop computers.

T   F   23. A laser printer uses nonimpact technology to produce characters.

T   F   24. A digital camera uses an embedded chip to focus the picture but records the picture on regular film.

T   F   25. The type of scanner that produces the highest quality image is the handheld scanner.

Fill-In

1. The written document that contains data to be keyed into the computer is called the _____.

2. LCD stands for _____.

3. The standard typeface read by OCR devices is known as _____.

4. A(n) _____ captures data where a retail sale takes place.

5. A(n) _____ is a pictorial screen symbol that represents a command or action.

6. MICR is most commonly used in the _____ industry.

7. TFT flat-panel displays are also known as _____ displays.

8. The term _____ describes collecting computer data at the point at which it is created.

9. The UPC is a(n) _____ used to identify grocery items.

10. A(n) _____ is a pointing device with which the user moves the pointer by rolling a ball with the fingers.

11. A(n) _____ is a single dot on the screen that can be addressed by software.

12. _____ uses a light beam to sense marks on machine-readable test forms.

13. The tabletop scanner that can handle a book page is the _____ scanner.

14. Which technology is more challenging: voice input or voice output? _____

15. A(n) _____ printer is an impact printer that uses a print head to create characters as a pattern of dots.

16. In synthesis by _____, speech is created by replaying stored spoken sounds.

17. _____ is a standard interface that enables digital musical devices to exchange data.

18. A(n) _____ terminal consists of a monitor and keyboard and has no processing capability.

19. _____ integrates CAD/CAM with the entire manufacturing process.

20. A screen that accepts input from a pointing finger is called a(n) _____.

 **ANSWERS**

Multiple Choice

1. c	6. d	11. a	16. a
2. b	7. a	12. b	17. b
3. b	8. d	13. d	18. a
4. c	9. c	14. a	19. c
5. a	10. c	15. a	20. c

True/False

1. F	6. F	11. F	16. T	21. F
2. T	7. T	12. T	17. T	22. T
3. F	8. T	13. F	18. F	23. T
4. F	9. F	14. T	19. F	24. F
5. F	10. T	15. F	20. T	25. F

Fill-In

1. source document
2. liquid crystal display
3. OCR-A
4. point-of-sale terminal
5. icon
6. banking
7. active-matrix
8. source data automation
9. bar code
10. trackball
11. pixel
12. OMR, or optical mark reading or mark sensing
13. flatbed
14. voice input
15. dot-matrix
16. analysis
17. MIDI
18. dumb
19. CIM, or computer-integrated manufacturing
20. touch screen

Planet Internet

FAQs and Help

When people begin to learn something new, they usually have many questions. In fact, many people who are being introduced to the same subject often have exactly the same questions. Rather than answer each question individually, it makes sense to keep the most frequently asked questions—FAQs—in a handy place that anyone can access. FAQs are a long-standing tradition on the Internet.

Where are the FAQs on the Internet?
The use of FAQs is so widespread that you are likely to come across them on many sites. However, some sites specialize in comprehensive Internet-related FAQs for beginners, notably the long-standing Web Browser Open FAQs. Another good place to start is Beginner's Central. Several sites, such as the Net Lingo site, offer lists of Internet-related definitions.

Where can I get some general information about the Internet?
Some sites include a history of the Internet as one of many offerings. Others, such as the Hobbes Internet Timeline, or the Little History of the World Wide Web (from CERN, the people who created it) and Internet101, offer a long and detailed history, with names, organizations, and timelines. You can get demographic information about the Internet—official and unofficial statistics—from sites such as InternetStats.com.

Where can I get some help on making a home page?
Advice abounds, usually with titles such as the Getting Started site. Most users who have an interest in making a Web page start with information about HTML. A good place to start would be the Beginner's Guide to HTML; actually, there are several sites with that exact name (just do a search on Yahoo!). There are dozens of useful HTML sites, such as Webmonkey. If you find one HTML site, it probably will have a list of links to others.

Anything else for making a page?
There are many sites that offer design advice and free clip art images. Getting Started is a popular home page advice site. David Seigel's HighFiveArchive.com contains the archived articles of the web magazine that has long been highly regarded for its excellent page design advice.

Where else can I get help?
There are several possibilities besides teaching yourself. Many colleges include home page creation as part of an Internet course. This may be via HTML or one of several authoring programs, such as FrontPage. Private firms advertise courses to teach you the basics in a few hours. Serious users, usually businesses that want a Web presence, may engage the services of consultants who can create a sophisticated Web site.

Internet Exercises:

1. **Structured exercise.** Begin with the URL http://www.prenhall.com/capron and link to the Web Browser Open FAQs. Provide the answer in your own words, in writing or

orally, to three questions that you found most helpful or to three questions that help a friend or family member who is curious about the subject.

2. **Free-form exercise.** Go to the Beginner's Guide to HTML and click on some of the links listed there. Explain in writing or orally the three most useful pieces of information you found for friends or family members who are thinking about setting up their own home page. Be sure to consider the reason your friends or family members want to have their own page.

3. **Advanced exercise.** Select a topic from one of the chapters in this book and write a short FAQ of at least five questions. Provide URLs from Web sites you've found that support the answers to these questions and provide additional information about the topic.

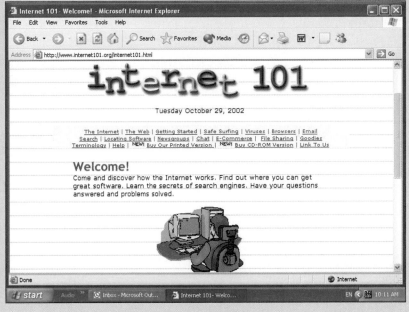

Storage and Multimedia:
The Facts and More

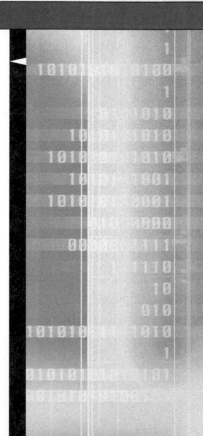

CHAPTER 6

LEARNING OBJECTIVES

List the benefits of secondary storage

Identify and describe storage media that are available for personal computers

Differentiate among the principal types of secondary storage

Describe how data is stored on a disk

Discuss the benefits of multimedia

Explain how data is organized, accessed, and processed

Dana Chiki, Colin Archibald, and Taylor Russell met in college, where they were studying to become architects. They did undergraduate and graduate work together and then went their separate ways into the work force. But they remained in the same metropolitan area and kept in touch.

Seven years later, at a professional conference, their casual conversation over dinner turned serious, and they began to consider forming their own architectural firm. The details of accomplishing this were complex and involved many months of planning. Of interest here is what they decided to do about computers, particularly computer storage.

Architectural drawings are made with special software; the software alone takes up many millions of bytes of storage. In addition, the architectural drawings themselves are storage hogs. The three architects did not hesitate to include hard disks with many gigabytes of storage.

Another issue was the need to produce computer-generated walk-through movies, simulated tours to show their clients the planned structure. For this they chose DVD-ROM, a type of high-capacity storage disk that can hold a full-length movie with room to spare.

Each of the architects already had a computer at home. They thought that they should upgrade the storage capacity of their individual computers so that they could bring work home. They also wanted some sort of transfer storage device so that they could carry drawings on disk between home and office; they settled on the Zip drive, which holds a high-capacity diskette.

The situation just described is more complicated than the ones most people face. However, it is true that disk storage is an ongoing issue for most users—we can never seem to get enough. A rule of thumb among computer professionals is to estimate disk needs generously and then double that amount. But estimating future needs is rarely easy.

▶ THE BENEFITS OF SECONDARY STORAGE

Picture the number of filing cabinet drawers that would be required to hold the millions of files of, say, tax records kept by the Internal Revenue Service or archives of employee records kept by General Motors. The record storage rooms would have to be enormous. Computers, by contrast, permit storage on tape or disk in extremely compressed form. Storage capacity is unquestionably one of the most valuable assets of the computer.

Secondary storage, sometimes just called storage, is separate from the computer itself, and is where software and data can be stored on a semipermanent basis. Because memory, or primary storage, loses its contents when power is turned off, secondary storage is needed to save both data and programs for later use.

The benefits of secondary storage can be summarized as follows:

- **Space.** Organizations may store the equivalent of a roomful of data on sets of disks that take up less space than a breadbox. A simple diskette for a personal computer can hold the equivalent of 500 printed pages, or one book. An optical disk can hold the equivalent of approximately 500 books.

- **Reliability.** Data in secondary storage is basically safe, because secondary storage is physically reliable. (You should note, however, that disks sometimes fail.) Also, it is more difficult for untrained people to tamper with data on disk than with data stored on paper in a file cabinet.

- **Convenience.** With the help of a computer, authorized users can locate and access data quickly.

- **Economy.** Together, space, reliability, and convenience indicate significant savings in storage costs. It is less expensive to store data on disk or tape (the principal means of secondary storage) than to buy and house filing cabinets. Data that is reliable and safe is less expensive to maintain than data that is subject to errors. But the greatest savings can be found in the speed and convenience of filing and retrieving data.

These benefits apply to all the various secondary storage devices, but some devices are better than others. The discussion begins with a look at the various storage media, including those used for personal computers, and then moves to what it takes to get data organized and processed.

▶ MAGNETIC DISK STORAGE

Diskettes (floppy disks) and hard disks are magnetic media; that is, they are based on a technology of representing data as magnetized spots on the surface of a spinning disk, with a magnetized spot representing a 1 bit and the absence of such a spot

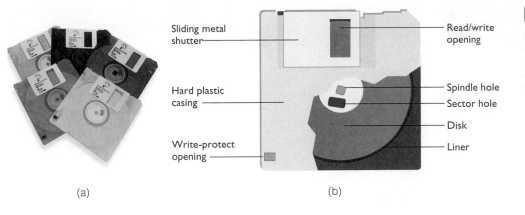

Sliding metal shutter

Hard plastic casing

Write-protect opening

Read/write opening

Spindle hole

Sector hole

Disk

Liner

(a)

(b)

◄ F I G U R E 6-1

Floppy disk. (a) These 3.5-inch floppy disks are protected by a rigid plastic exterior cover. (b) A cutaway view of a 3.5-inch disk.

representing a 0 bit. Reading data from the disk means converting the magnetized data to electrical impulses that can be sent to the processor. Writing data to disk is the opposite; it involves sending electrical impulses from the processor to be converted to magnetized spots on the disk.

Floppy disks

A floppy **disk** is made of flexible Mylar and coated with iron oxide, a substance that can be magnetized. A floppy disk can record data as magnetized spots on tracks on its surface. Floppy disks became popular along with the personal computer. Most computers use the 3.5-inch floppy disk, which has a capacity of 1.44MB of data (Figure 6-1). The floppy disk has the protection of a hard plastic jacket and fits conveniently in a shirt pocket or purse. The key advantage of floppy disks is portability. Floppy disks easily transport data from one computer to another. Workers, for example, carry their files from office computer to home computer and back on floppy disks instead of carrying stacks of papers in briefcases. Students use the campus computers but keep their files on their own floppy disks. Floppy disks are also a convenient vehicle for backup: it is easy to place an extra copy of a hard disk file on a floppy disk.

The venerable 3.5-inch floppy disk, a standard for a decade, is being challenged by three high-capacity drives. Sony's **HiFD** can store 200MB of data, while Imation's **SuperDisk** is available in 120MB and 240MB versions. Although each of these uses its own high-capacity disk, they both can read and write to standard floppy disks. Iomega's **Zip drive**, which is already installed by more than 20 million users, has by far the largest market share. The newest Zip drive has a capacity of 750MB, 520 times the capacity of traditional floppy disks (Figure 6-2). The disadvantage of the Zip drive is that it is not compatible with 3.5-inch floppy disks.

▼ F I G U R E 6-2

The Iomega Zip disk drive. Shown here is a separate drive unit, but many users have their Zip drive installed in a bay in the computer's housing.

Hard Disks

A **hard disk** is a rigid platter coated with magnetic oxide that can be magnetized to represent data. Hard disks come in a variety of sizes. Several platters can be assembled into a **disk pack.** There are different types of disk packs, the number of platters varying by model. Each disk in the pack has top and bottom surfaces on which to record data, although some drives do not record data on the top of the top platter or on the bottom of the bottom platter.

A **disk drive** is a device that enables data to be read from or written to a disk. A disk pack is mounted on a disk drive, which is a separate unit connected to the computer. Large computers have dozens or even hundreds of external disk drives; in contrast, the hard disk for a personal computer is contained within the computer housing. In a disk pack, all disks rotate at the same time, although only one disk is being read from or written to at any one time. The mechanism for reading or writing data to a disk is an **access arm;** it moves a read/write head into position over a particular

G E T T I N G   P R A C T I C A L

Floppy Disk and CD/DVD Care

Although floppy disks and CD/DVDs are fairly rugged, you should take precautions to protect them from damage.

General Guidelines

- CD/DVDs and floppy disks provide the best service if they are stored vertically. Don't stack them on top of each other or place heavy weight on them.

- Avoid extremes of temperature. The inside of a car on a hot, sunny day can be deadly.

- Insert and remove floppy disks and CD/DVDs carefully—never force them into a drive. If you encounter difficulty in insertion, remove the item and try again, gently. If you still have problems, get help from a service technician.

- Keep floppy disks and CD/DVDs away from food, drink, and smoke.

Floppy Disk Care

- Keep floppy disks away from magnets or anything that could generate a magnetic field. This includes stereo speakers and telephones.

- Don't touch the recording surface behind the slide.

- Be careful with disk labels. Loose labels or labels in several layers could become stuck inside the drive.

CD/DVD Care

- Store in a protective case, such as a jewel box or paper sleeve.

- Handle the CD/DVD by its edge. Avoid touching either surface.

- Don't write on the label side; you could destroy data.

- If necessary, clean the bottom (shiny) side with warm water and a soft cloth. Do not clean the label surface.

With proper care, CD/DVDs and floppy disks should have a long, trouble-free life. In the case of floppy disks and writable CD/DVDs, be sure to back up any data you can't afford to lose.

---

location (Figure 6-3a). The **read/write head** on the end of the access arm hovers a few millionths of an inch above the platter but does not actually touch the surface. When a read/write head accidentally touches the disk surface, it is called a **head crash** and data is destroyed. Data can also be destroyed if a read/write head encounters even minuscule foreign matter on the disk surface (Figure 6-3b). A disk pack has a set of access arms that slip in between the disks in the pack (Figure 6-3c). Two read/write heads are on each arm, one facing up to access the surface above it and one facing down to access the surface below it. All the arms move together as a unit; however, only one read/write head can operate at any one time.

Most disk packs combine the platters, access arms, and read/write heads in an airtight, sealed module. These disk packs are assembled in clean rooms so that even microscopic dust particles do not get on the disk surface.

Most hard disks for personal computers are sealed modules that mount in a 3½-inch bay within the computer's case (Figure 6-4). Hard disk capacity for personal computers has soared in recent years; older hard disks have capacities of hundreds of megabytes, but new ones offer tens of gigabytes of storage. Terabyte capacity is on the horizon. Although an individual probably cannot imagine generating enough output such as letters, budgets, reports, and pictures to fill a disk, software packages take up a lot of space and can make a dent rather quickly. Furthermore, graphics images and audio and video files require huge amounts of disk space. Perhaps more important than capacity is the speed advantage. Personal computer users find that accessing files on a hard disk is many times faster and much more convenient than accessing files on a floppy disk.

Removable hard disk systems are available for PCs. These systems consist of a drive that is installed either within the computer's case or in a separate case connected to

(a)

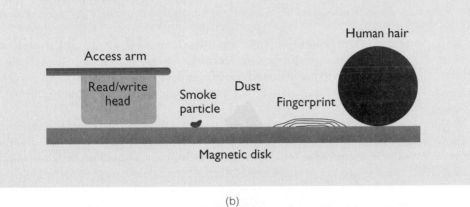

(b)

Read/write heads and access arms. (a) This photo shows a read/write head on the end of an access arm poised over a hard disk. (b) During operation, the read/write head comes very close to the surface of the disk. On a disk, particles as small as smoke, dust, a fingerprint, and a hair loom large. If the read/write head encounters one of these, a head crash occurs, destroying data and damaging the disk. (c) Note that there are two read/write heads on each access arm. Each arm slips between two disks in the disk pack. The access arms move as a unit, but only one read/write head operates at any one time.

(c)

(a)

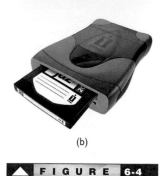

(b)

▲ **FIGURE** **6-4**

Hard disk for a personal computer. (a) The innards of a 3.5-inch hard disk with the access arm visible. (b) The Iomega Jaz hard disk drive with removable cartridge.

the computer via a cable. The disk itself is contained in a cartridge that can be removed from the drive. Although the capacity of the removable cartridges is much greater than that of the high-capacity floppy disks described previously (up to 2GB), they are not as spacious as the built-in hard disk systems on most PCs. Removable hard disk cartridges combine the portability advantages of floppy disks with access speed close to that of built-in systems. Their biggest disadvantage for home users is the expense of the cartridge—more than $100. The Iomega Jaz drive is one of the more popular removable hard drive systems (Figure 6-4b).

Recently, relatively inexpensive portable hard drives have been introduced. A 120MB portable drive for less than $300 can be used to transfer huge volumes of data, such as digital video, from system to system. The drives connect to the PC via a USB 2.0 port.

Hard Disks in Groups

No storage system is completely safe, but a **redundant array of independent disks (RAID)** comes close. RAID storage uses a group of two or more hard disks that work together as a unit. The most basic RAID system, RAID level 0, spreads data from a single file across several drives. This process is called **data striping** and enables the file to be read or written simultaneously by several drives, greatly increasing performance (Figure 6-5b).

RAID level 1 duplicates data on separate disk drives, a concept called **disk mirroring** (Figure 6-5c). This produces *fault tolerance;* if one drive fails, the system automatically switches to the backup and continues to operate. This process is reliable but expensive. However, expense may not be an issue when the value of the data is considered.

Higher levels of RAID combine data striping and data mirroring techniques to achieve both increased performance and fault tolerance. RAID is now the dominant form of storage for mainframe computer systems and is used extensively on network servers. Although available for desktop PCs, it is too expensive for most users.

How Data Is Organized on a Disk

Several characteristics determine how data is physically organized on a disk. The characteristics include tracks, sectors, clusters, and cylinders. Unless specifically noted, these concepts apply equally to floppy disks and hard drives.

TRACK   A **track** is the circular portion of the disk surface that passes under the read/write head as the disk rotates (Figure 6-6). The number of tracks on a particular disk's surface depends on how precisely the arm can position the read/write head. Whereas the standard 1.44MB floppy disk has 80 tracks on each of its two surfaces, a hard disk may have 1,000 or more tracks on each surface of several platters.

SECTOR   Each track on a disk is divided into **sectors** that hold a fixed number of bytes, typically 512 (Figure 6-7a). Data on the track is accessed by referring to the surface number, track number, and sector number where the data is stored.

The fact that a disk is circular presents a problem: the distance around the tracks on the outside of the disk is greater than that around the tracks on the inside. Data that takes up one inch of a track on the inside of a disk might be spread over several inches on a track near the outside of a disk. This means that the tracks on the outside are not storing data as efficiently.

Zone recording takes maximum advantage of the storage available by dividing a disk into zones and assigning more sectors to tracks in outer zones than to those in inner zones (Figure 6-7b). Because each sector on the disk holds the same amount of data, more sectors mean more data storage than there would be if all tracks had the same number of sectors.

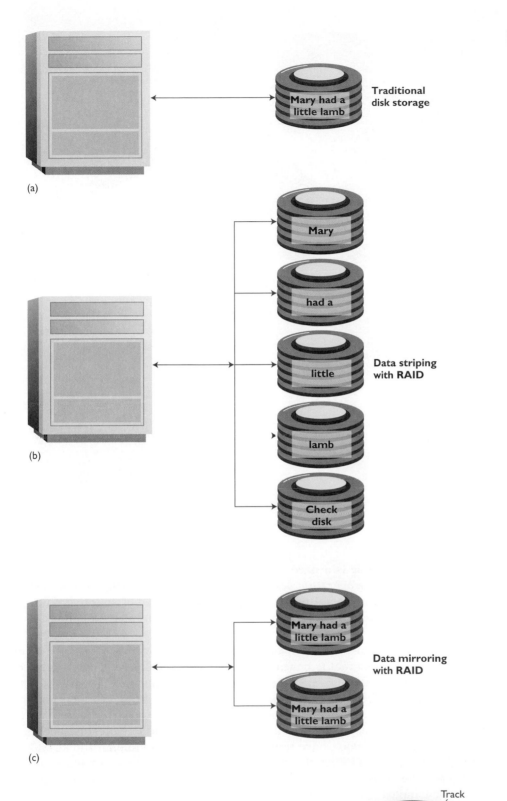

RAID storage. (a) Data is stored on disk in traditional fashion. (b) In a system called data striping with RAID, data is scattered among several disks. (c) Disk mirroring with RAID stores a duplicate copy of the data on a second disk.

(a)

Traditional disk storage

Mary

had a

little

lamb

Check disk

Data striping with **RAID**

(b)

Mary had a little lamb

Mary had a little lamb

Data mirroring with **RAID**

(c)

Track

Tracks. Each unique position of the read/write head results in a track on the disk surface. Each track contains the magnetic representation of the binary 1s and 0s.

Sectors and zone recording. (a) When data is organized by sector, the address is the surface, track, and sector where the data is stored. (b) If a disk is divided into traditional sectors, as shown here on the left, each track has the same number of sectors. Sectors near the outside of the disk are wider, but they hold the same amount of data as sectors near the inside. If the disk is divided into recording zones, as shown on the right, the tracks near the outside have more sectors than the tracks near the inside. Each sector holds the same amount of data, but because the outer zones have more sectors, the disk as a whole holds more data than the disk on the left.

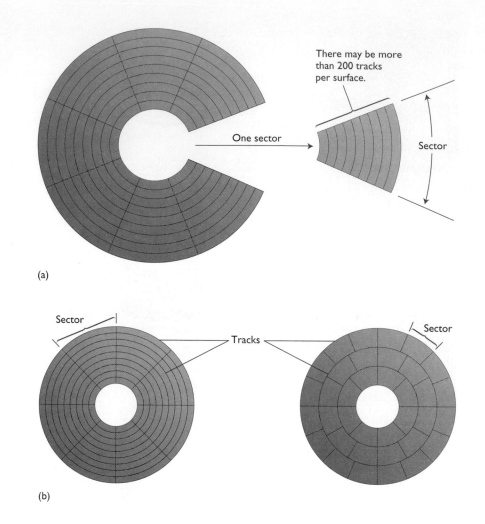

CLUSTERS   A **cluster** is a fixed number of adjacent sectors that are treated as a unit of storage by the operating system. Clusters typically contain two to eight sectors, depending on the operating system. Each file is stored in an integral number of clusters; even if a file is only a few bytes in length, it is allocated an entire cluster.

CYLINDER   On a hard disk that has multiple platters, a **cylinder** consists of the track on each surface that is beneath the read/write head at a given position of the read/write arms (Figure 6-8). When a file is larger than the capacity of a single track, the operating system stores it in tracks within the same cylinder, rather than spread it across tracks on the same platter. The purpose is to reduce the time it takes to move the access arms of a disk pack into position. Once the access arms are in position, they don't have to be moved to access additional tracks within the same cylinder.

Suppose you have an empty disk pack on which you want to store a large file. You might be tempted to record the data horizontally: start with the first surface and fill track 000, track 001, track 002, and so on, and then move to the second surface and again fill tracks 000, 001, 002, and so forth. Each new track and new surface requires movement of the access arms, a relatively slow mechanical process.

Recording the data vertically, on the other hand, substantially reduces access arm movement. The data is recorded on the tracks that can be accessed by one positioning of the access arms; that is, on one cylinder. Instead of moving the access arm to the next track each time a track is filled, the arm is moved only after all the tracks in a cylinder are filled. To visualize cylinder organization, pretend that a cylindrically shaped item, such as a tin can, is dropped straight down through all the disks in the disk pack. All the tracks encountered in the same position on each disk surface make up a cylinder.

Disk Access Speed

Three primary factors determine **access time,** the time needed to access data directly on disk:

- **Seek time: Seek time** is the time it takes the access arm to get into position over a particular track. Keep in mind that all the access arms move as a unit, so they are simultaneously in position over a set of tracks that make up a cylinder.

- **Head switching:** The access arms on the access mechanism do not move separately; they move together, all at the same time. However, only one read/write head can operate at any one time. **Head switching** is the activation of a particular read/write head over a particular track on a particular surface. Because head switching takes place at electronic speed, the time it takes is negligible.

- **Rotational delay:** After the access arm and read/write head are in position and ready to read or write data, the read/write head must wait for a short period until the desired data on the track rotates under it. On the average, this **rotational delay** is equal to one-half the time for a complete revolution of the disk.

Once the data has been found, the next step is **data transfer,** the process of transferring data between memory and the place on the disk track—from memory to the track if the computer is writing, from the track to memory if the computer is reading. One measure for the performance of disk drives is the average access time, which is usually measured in milliseconds (ms). On current hard disk drives, access time is faster than 10 ms. Another measure is the **data transfer rate,** which tells how fast data can be transferred once it has been found. This is usually stated in terms of megabytes of data per second.

Disk caching can improve the effective access time. When the disk drive reads data from a disk, it also reads adjacent data and stores it in an area of memory called the **disk cache.** When the next read instruction is issued, the drive first checks to see whether the desired data is in the disk cache. If it is, no physical read is necessary, greatly reducing access time. This is the same principle used in memory caching, which is discussed in Chapter 4.

▶ OPTICAL DISK STORAGE

The explosive growth in storage needs has driven the computer industry to provide inexpensive and compact storage with greater capacity. This demanding shopping list is a description of the **optical disk** (Figure 6-9). The technology works like this: a laser hits a layer of metallic material spread over the surface of a disk. When data is entered, heat from the laser produces tiny spots, or pits, on the disk surface. To read the data, the laser scans the disk, and a lens picks up light reflections from the spots. Optical storage technology is categorized according to its read/write capability. **Read-only media** are disks that are recorded by the manufacturer and can be read from but not written to by the user. Such a disk cannot be used for your files, but manufacturers can use it to supply software. An applications software package could include a dozen floppy disks or more; all these can fit on one optical disk with room to spare. Furthermore, software can be more easily installed from a single optical disk than from a pile of floppy disks.

Write-once, read-many media, also called **WORM media,** may be written to once. After it is filled, a WORM disk becomes a read-only medium. A WORM disk cannot be erased. For applications that require secure storage of original versions of

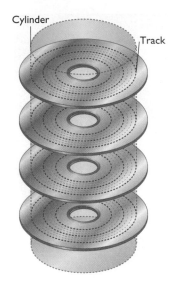

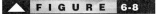

FIGURE 6-8

Cylinder data organization. To visualize a cylinder on disk, imagine dropping a cylinder such as a tin can straight down through all the disks in a disk pack. Within cylinder 150, the track surfaces are vertically aligned and are numbered from top to bottom.

(a)

(b)

▲ **FIGURE** **6-9**

Optical disks. (a) Optical disks store data using laser beam technology. (b) Many laptop computers include a CD-ROM drive. Laptop users can use CD-ROM applications to make on-the-road presentations or pop in a CD-ROM encyclopedia to find needed information.

valuable documents or data, such as legal records, the primary advantage of WORM disks is clear: after they are recorded, no one can erase or modify them.

A hybrid type of disk, called **magneto-optical** (**MO**), combines the best features of magnetic and optical disk technologies. A magneto-optical disk has the high-volume capacity of an optical disk but can be rewritten like a magnetic disk. The disk surface is coated with plastic and embedded with magnetically sensitive metallic crystals. To write data, a laser beam melts a microscopic spot on the plastic surface, and a magnet aligns the crystals before the plastic cools. The crystals are aligned so that some reflect light and others do not. When the data is later read by a laser beam, only the crystals that reflect light are picked up.

▶ COMPACT DISKS

Compact disk (CD) technology is an optical technology that uses the same media used for audio CDs. In fact, with the proper software, computer CD drives can play audio CDs. There are several types of CD drives, categorized according to their ability to read and write CDs.

CD-ROM   The **compact disk read-only memory** (**CD-ROM**) drive is capable only of reading data from CDs—it cannot record anything. CD-ROM has a major advantage over other optical disk designs: the disk format is identical to that of audio compact disks, so the same dust-free manufacturing plants that are stamping out digital versions of Wynton Marsalis or Jennifer Lopez can easily convert to producing anything from software to a digitized encyclopedia. Furthermore, CD-ROM storage is substantial, as much as 700 megabytes per disk, the equivalent of more than 450 standard 3.5-inch floppy disks. As the size of software applications has increased, CD-ROM has become the primary medium for software distribution.

CD-R   Although CD-ROMs are read-only, a different technology called **compact disc-recordable** (**CD-R**) enables writing on optical disks but just once; mistakes can-

---

▶ MAKING CONNECTIONS ◀   Internet Disk Drives

If you have ever used a PC on a local area network at school or work, you are probably familiar with the concept of network drives. A network drive is disk storage space located on a network server that is available for you to store data just as if it were on your own PC. Network drives enable you to back up data, share files with others on the network, and, in a school lab environment, access your files no matter which PC you use.

Several companies are making the ultimate network drive available, even to users who aren't connected to a local area network, as long as they have an Internet connection. Companies such as StoragePoint and X:drive provide you with disk space on their Internet servers that you can use as an extension of your hard drive. You can place your data on your Internet drive and get to it from anywhere you can get Internet access—work, school, or even the

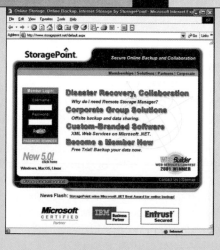

public library. You can also allow others access to some or all of the data on your virtual drive, providing an easy method of sharing files that are too large to transport via floppy.

Another use of your Internet drive is for off-site backup. Storing an extra copy of valuable data files, such as your financial records, your Ph.D. thesis, or that Great American Novel you've been working on for years, is great protection against a fire or flood that might destroy your PC and the backup copies stored on the shelf next to it. Although many of these companies used to provide limited free space, almost all now charge a monthly or yearly fee based on the amount of storage needed. One not-so-obvious limitation is the speed of your Internet connection; uploading and downloading multi-megabyte files can take quite a while with a 56kbps modem.

not be undone. CD-R technology requires a CD-R drive, special CD-R disks that look just like regular CDs except that they are marked CD-R, and the accompanying CD-R software. Once a CD-R disk is written on, it can be read not only by the CD-R drive but also by any CD-ROM drive.

CD-RW   Another variation, **compact disk-rewritable** (**CD-RW**), is more flexible, enabling you to erase and record over data multiple times. CD-RW technology requires a CD-RW drive, special CD-RW disks, and the CD-RW software. Some compatibility problems may be encountered in reading CD-RW disks on standard CD-ROM drives.

▶ DVD-ROM

The new storage technology that outpaces all others is **DVD-ROM**, for **digital versatile disk** (originally digital video disk). Think of a DVD, as it is called, as an overachieving CD-ROM. Although the two look the same, a DVD has up to a 4.7GB capacity, almost seven times more than that of the highest-capacity CD-ROM. And that is just the plain variety. DVDs have two layers of information, one clear and one opaque, on a single side; this double-layered DVD surface can hold about 8.5GB. Furthermore, DVDs can be written on both sides, bumping the capacity to 17GB. And a DVD-ROM drive can also read CD-ROMs. It is not surprising that DVD-ROM technology is seen as a replacement for CD-ROMs during the next few years.

Operating much like CD-ROM technology, DVD uses a laser beam to read microscopic spots that represent data. But DVD uses a laser with a shorter wavelength, enabling it to read more densely packed spots, thus increasing the disk capacity. The benefits of this storage capacity are many, including exquisite sound and the ability to hold full-length movies. Audio quality on DVD is even better than audio CDs. DVDs will eventually hold high-volume business data. Many new personal computers come equipped with a DVD-ROM drive as standard equipment.

Writable and rewritable versions of DVD are also available, although a single standard for either has not yet emerged. Three standards exist for writable DVDs: **DVD-RAM, DVD-R,** and **DVD+R.** There are two standards for rewritable DVDs: **DVD-RW** and **DVD+RW.** To add to the confusion, advances in laser technology have resulted in the Blu-ray Disc, which uses a blue-light laser rather than the red-light laser used in current CDs and DVDs. The shorter wavelength of the blue-light laser enables the Blu-ray Disc to hold about 27GB of data. When the market chooses among these competing standards and prices come down, there is little doubt that DVDs will replace CDs as the preferred optical media.

If you have a CD-ROM or a DVD-ROM drive, you are on your way to one of the computer industry's great adventures: multimedia.

▶ MULTIMEDIA

Multimedia stirs the imagination. For example, have you ever thought that you could see a film clip from *Gone with the Wind* on your computer screen? One could argue that such treats are already available on videocassette, but the computer version provides an added dimension for this and other movies, including reviews by critics, photographs of movie stars, lists of Academy Awards, and the possibility of user input. Software described as **multimedia** typically presents information with text, illustrations, photos, narration, music, animation, and film clips. Until the advent of the optical disk, placing this much data on a disk was impractical. However, the large capacity of optical disks means that the kinds of data that take up huge amounts of storage space, such as photographs, music, and film clips, can be readily accommodated.

Stamps from Your Computer

That's right—no more trips to the post office, no standing in line. Several sites on the Internet, including Stamps.com, let you pay for postage and store it right on your hard disk. When you need a stamp, you just print it on the envelope. Well, it does not look much like a real stamp, but the post office accepts it just the same.

Here is how it works. From your personal computer, you access a site that sells postage. You pay for postage, usually with a credit card. The postage company grants you permission to print a certain amount of postage, sending that amount and the stamp image to your vault, a file on your hard disk. (Alternatively, some companies keep your account on their own files, which you access via the Internet.) Then, just print and mail.

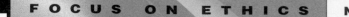

Multimedia Requirements

To use multimedia software, you must have the proper hardware. In addition to a CD-ROM or DVD-ROM drive, you need a sound card or sound chip (installed internally) and speakers, which may be internal (built into the computer housing) or external, connected to the computer via cables. Special software accompanies the drive and sound card. If full-motion video is important to you, be sure that your computer is equipped to handle **Motion Picture Experts Group** (**MPEG**), a set of widely accepted video compression standards. Another video-related issue is the speed of the drive: the faster the better. The higher the drive speed, the faster the transfer of data and the smoother the video showing on the screen.

Should your next computer be a multimedia personal computer? Absolutely. There is no doubt that multimedia is the medium of choice for all kinds of software.

Multimedia Applications

If you take a moment to peruse the racks of multimedia software in your local store, you see that most of the offerings come under the categories of entertainment or education, or possibly both. You can study and hear works by Stravinsky or Schubert. You can explore the planets or the ocean bottom through film clips and narrations by experts. You can be "elected" to Congress, after which you tour the Capitol, decorate your office, hire staff, and vote on issues. You can study the battle of Gettysburg, and even change the outcome. You can study the Japanese language, seeing the symbols and hearing the intonation. You can buy multimedia versions of reference books, magazines, children's books, and entire novels.

But this is just the beginning. Businesses are already moving to this high-capacity environment for street atlases, national phone directories, and sales catalogs. Coming offerings will include every kind of standard business application, all tricked out with fancy animation, photos, and sound. Educators will be able to draw on the new sight and sound capabilities for everything from human anatomy to time travel. And just imagine the library of the future, consisting not only of the printed word but also of photos, film, animation, and sound recordings—all flowing from the computer.

► MAGNETIC TAPE STORAGE

Magnetic tape storage has taken a subordinate role in storage technology. **Magnetic tape** looks like the tape used in music cassettes, plastic tape with a magnetic coating. As in other magnetic media, data is stored as extremely small magnetic spots. Tapes come in a number of forms, including 3½-inch tape wound on a reel, 3½-inch tape in data cartridges and cassettes, and tapes that look like ordinary music cassettes but are designed to store data instead of music. Tape capacity is expressed in

◄ **FIGURE** 6-10

Magnetic tape units. Tapes are always protected from outside dust and dirt by glass. These modern tape drives, called stackers, accept several cassette tapes, each with its own supply and take-up reel.

terms of **density,** which is the number of **characters per inch (cpi)** or **bytes per inch (bpi)** that can be stored on the tape.

Figure 6-10 shows a **magnetic tape drive** that might be used with a mainframe. The tape unit reads and writes data using a **read/write head.** When the computer is writing on the tape, the **erase head** first erases any data that was previously recorded on the tape.

Tape has a limited role in storage because disks have proved to be the superior storage medium. Disk data is quite reliable, especially within a sealed module. Furthermore, disk data can be accessed directly, in contrast to sequential data on tape, which can be accessed only by passing all the data ahead of it on the tape. Consequently, the primary role of tape today is as an inexpensive backup medium for data stored on disk systems.

► BACKUP SYSTEMS

Although a hard disk is an extremely reliable device, it is subject to electromechanical failures that cause loss of data, as well as physical damage from fire and natural disasters. Furthermore, data files, particularly those accessed by several users, are subject to errors introduced by users. There is also the possibility of errors introduced by software. With any method of data storage, a **backup system,** a way of storing data in more than one place to protect it from damage and errors, is vital. As we have already noted, magnetic tape is used primarily for backup purposes. For personal computer users, an easy and inexpensive way to back up a hard disk file is simply to copy it to a floppy disk or Zip disk whenever it is updated. But this is not practical for a system with many files or many users.

Personal computer users have the option of purchasing their own tape backup system to use on a regular basis for copying all data from hard disk to a high-capacity tape. Data thus saved can be restored to the hard disk later if needed. A key advantage of a tape backup system is that it can copy the entire hard disk to a single tape in minutes. Also, with the availability of gigabytes of hard disk space, it is not really feasible to swap floppy disks into and out of the machine. Furthermore, tape backup can be scheduled to take place when you are not going to be using the computer. CD-R and CD-RW media can also be used for backup, but they are limited to storing less than 1GB of data, whereas tape cartridges with more than 10GB of storage capacity are available at reasonable cost.

You're on File at Domino's

If you consider what items of personal information might be stored on disk files, you may think of your Social Security records or perhaps the information stored with your bank account. But small businesses also know about you. They store information you readily provide on their own disk files.

For example, if you phone a Domino's outlet to order a pizza, your name, address, phone number, and the product you ordered are recorded in the company's disk files. When you call again, this information can be retrieved quickly by keying in your phone number. This saves time and effort and can speed your pizza on its way.

► ORGANIZING AND ACCESSING STORED DATA

As users of computer systems, we offer data as we are instructed to do, such as entering our identification code at an automated teller machine or filling out a form with our name and address. But data cannot be dumped helter-skelter into a computer. Some computer professional—probably a programmer or systems analyst—has to have planned how data from users is received, organized, and stored and in what manner data is processed by the computer.

This kind of storage goes beyond what you may have done to store a memo created with word-processing software. Organizations that store data usually need a lot of data on many subjects. For example, a charitable organization might need detailed information about donors, names and schedules of volunteers, and a schedule of fund-raising events. A factory needs to keep track of inventory (such as name, identification number, location, and quantity of parts), the scheduled path of the product through the assembly line, records of quality-control checkpoints, and much more. All this data must be organized and stored according to a plan. First consider how data is organized.

Data: Getting Organized

To be processed by the computer, raw data is organized into characters, fields, records, files, and databases. First is the smallest element: the character.

- A **character** is a letter, digit, or special character (such as $, ?, or *).

- A **field** contains a set of related characters. For example, suppose that a health club is making address labels for a mailing. For each person, it might have a member number field, a name field, a street address field, a city field, a state field, a zip code field, and a phone number field.

- A **record** is a collection of related fields. On the health club mailing list, one person's member number, name, address, city, state, zip code, and phone number constitute a record.

- A **file** is a collection of related records. All the member records for the health club compose a file. Figure 6-11 shows how data for a health club member might look.

- A **database** is a collection of interrelated files stored together with minimum redundancy. Specific data items can be retrieved for various applications. For instance, if the health club is opening a new outlet, it can pull out the names of people with zip codes near the new club and send them an announcement. Database concepts are discussed in more detail in Chapter 13, Database Management.

Of particular interest is the **key field,** a unique identifier for a record. It might seem at first that a name of a person or a product would be a good key; however, because some names may be the same, a name field is not a good choice for a key. When a file is first computerized, existing description fields are seldom used as keys. Although a file describing people might use a Social Security number as the key, it is more likely that a new field will be developed that can be assigned unique values, such as customer number or product number.

In addition to organizing the expected data, a plan must be made to access the data on files.

The File Plan: An Overview

Now that you have a general idea of how data is organized, you are ready to look at the process used to decide how to place data on a storage medium. Consider this chain. (1) The application, such as payroll, airline reservations, or inventory control, determines how the data must be accessed by users. (2) After an access method has

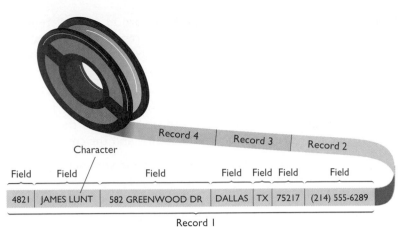

(a)

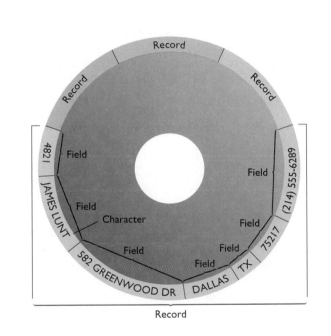

(b)

How data is organized.
Whether stored on tape or on disk, data is organized into characters, fields, records, and files. A file is a collection of related records. These diagrams represent (a) magnetic tape and (b) magnetic disk.

been determined, there are certain ways in which the data must be organized so that the needed access is workable. (3) The organization method, in turn, limits the choice of storage medium. The discussion about storing data begins with an appreciation of application demands, then moves to a detailed look at organization and access.

The following application examples illustrate how an access decision might be made:

- A department store offers its customers charge accounts. When a customer makes a purchase, a sales clerk needs to be able to check the validity of the customer's account while the customer is waiting. The clerk needs immediate access to the individual customer record in the account file.

- A major oil company supplies its charge customers with credit cards, which it considers sufficient proof for purchase. The charge slips collected by gas stations are forwarded to the oil company, which processes them in order of account number. Unlike the retail example, the company does not need access to any one record at a specific time but simply needs access to all customer charge records when it is time to prepare bills.

- A city power and light company employee accepts reports of burned-out streetlights from residents over the phone. Using a key made up of unique address

How Long Will It Last?
Although magnetic and optical media provide reliable long-term storage, they eventually deteriorate. The following figures represent a conservative estimate of media lifetime; proper care and a little luck can extend the life by quite a bit. For comparison, the Dead Sea Scrolls, written on papyrus, are more than 2,000 years old, and many books more than 400 years old can still be found in libraries' rare book collections.

- **Hard drive:** 3–5 years; mechanical components wear out

- **Floppy disk:** 1 year of regular use, somewhat longer with careful storage

- **Magnetic tape:** 3–5 years, as long as 25 years possible

- **CD-ROM:** 200 years (Obviously an estimate—it will be quite a while before we know for sure)

- **CD-R:** 100–200 years, only 5–10 years of shelf life before recording

- **CR-RW:** 30 years; proper temperature is critical, as is avoiding sunlight

- **DVD-ROM:** 200 years (estimated)

components, the clerk immediately finds the record for the offending streetlight and prints out a one-page report that is routed to repair units within 24 hours. To produce such quick service for an individual streetlight, the employee needs immediate access to the individual streetlight record

- Airline flight attendants' schedules for the next month are produced by computer monthly and delivered to the attendants' home-base mailboxes. The schedules are put together from information based on flight records, and the entire file can be accessed monthly at the convenience of the airline and the computer-use plan.

As you can see, the question of access comes down to whether a particular record is needed right away, as it was in the first and third examples. This immediate need for a particular record means that access must be *direct*. It follows that the data organization must also be direct, or at least *indexed*, and that the storage medium must be disk. Furthermore, the type of processing must be *transaction processing*. The critical distinction is whether immediate access to an individual record is needed. The following discussion examines all these topics in detail. Although the organization type is determined by the type of access required, the file must be organized before it can be accessed, so organization is the first topic.

File Organization: Three Methods

There are three major methods of organizing data files in secondary storage:

- Sequential file organization, in which records are stored in order by key

- Direct file organization, in which records are not physically stored in any special order

- Indexed file organization, in which records are stored sequentially but indexes are built into the file to enable a record to be accessed sequentially or directly

SEQUENTIAL FILE ORGANIZATION **Sequential file organization** means that records are stored in order according to a key field. As we noted earlier, a file containing information on people is in order by a key that uniquely identifies each person, such as Social Security number or customer number. If a particular record in a sequential file is wanted, all the prior records in the file must be read before the desired record is reached. Updating records in a sequential file requires that a new sequential file containing both the updated and unchanged records be created. Tape storage is limited to sequential file organization. Disk storage may be sequential, but records on disk can also be accessed directly.

DIRECT FILE ORGANIZATION **Direct file organization** (also called **random file organization**) enables **direct (random) access,** the ability to go directly to the desired record by using a record key; the computer does not have to read all preceding records in the file as it does if the records are arranged sequentially. Direct processing requires disk storage; in fact, a disk device is called a **direct-access storage device (DASD)** because the computer can go directly to the desired record on the disk. It is this ability to access any given record instantly that has made computer systems so convenient for people in service industries, for example, catalog order-takers determining whether a particular sweater is in stock, or bank tellers checking individual bank balances. An added benefit of direct-access organization is the ability to read, change, and return a record to its same place on the disk; this is called **updating in place.**

Obviously, if we have a completely blank area on the disk and can put records anywhere, there must be some predictable system for placing a record at a disk address and then retrieving the record at a subsequent time. In other words, after the record has been placed on a disk, it must be possible to find it again. This is done by choosing a certain formula to apply to the record key, thereby deriving a number to

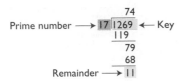

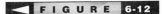

A hashing scheme.
Dividing the key number 1269 by the prime number 17 yields a remainder of 11, which can be used to indicate the address on a disk.

use as the disk address. The **hashing,** or **randomizing, algorithm** is the mathematical operation that is applied to a key to yield a number that represents the disk address. Even though the record keys are unique, it is possible for a hashing algorithm to produce the same disk address, called a **synonym,** for two different records; such an occurrence is called a **collision.** There are various ways to recover from a collision; one way is simply to use the next available record slot on the disk.

There are many different hashing schemes. Although the example in Figure 6-12 is far too simple to be realistic, it can give you a general idea of how the process works. An example of how direct processing works is provided in Figure 6-13.

INDEXED FILE ORGANIZATION   **Indexed file organization** is a third method of file organization, and it represents a compromise between the sequential and direct methods. It is useful in applications in which a file needs to be processed sequentially and access to individual records is needed.

An indexed file works as follows: records are stored in the file in sequential order, but the file also contains an index. The index contains entries consisting of the key to each record stored on the file and the corresponding disk address for that record. The

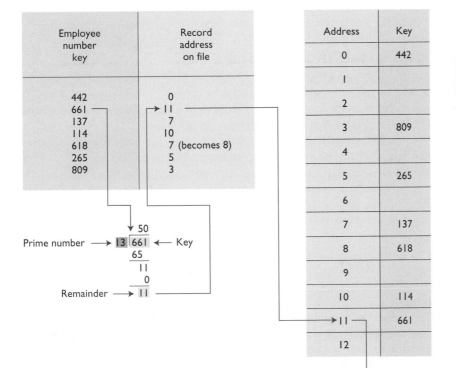

▲ **FIGURE** **6-13**

An example of direct access. Assume that there are 13 addresses (0 through 12) available in the file. Dividing the key number 661, which is C. Kear's employee number, by the prime number 13 yields a remainder of 11. Thus, 11 is the address for key 661. However, for the key 618, dividing by 13 yields a remainder of 7, a synonym, because this address has already been used by the key 137, which also has a remainder of 7. Hence the address becomes the next location, 8. Note that keys (and therefore records) need not appear in any particular order. (The 13 record locations available are, of course, too few to hold a normal file; a small number was used to keep the example simple.)

index is like a directory, with the keys to all records listed in order. For a record to be accessed directly, the record key must be located in the index; the address associated with the key is then used to access the record on the disk. Because the index is much smaller than the entire data file, it can often be loaded into memory, enabling fast address lookup. Accessing the entire file of records sequentially is a matter of bypassing the index and beginning with the first record, proceeding one at a time through the rest of the records.

► PROCESSING STORED DATA

After there is a plan for accessing the files, they can be processed. Most business file processing involves processing transactions to update a master file. A **transaction** is a business event that requires the business's records to be updated. A retail sale, the receipt of ordered goods, and the issuance of a paycheck are examples of transactions. A **master file** contains data that must be updated as transactions occur. Examples of master files are an inventory file, an employee file, and a customer file. There are several methods of processing data files in a computer system. The two main methods are batch processing (processing transaction data in groups at a more convenient later time) and transaction processing (processing transactions immediately, as they occur).

Batch Processing

Batch processing is a technique in which transactions are collected into groups, or batches, to be processed at a time when the computer may have few online users and thus be more accessible, often during the night. Unlike transaction processing, a topic discussed later in this chapter, batch processing involves no direct user interaction. For example, consider updating a health club address-label file, a list of all members of the health club and their addresses. The **transaction file** contains all changes to be made to the master file: additions (transactions to create new master records for new members), deletions (transactions with instructions to delete master records of members who have resigned from the health club), and revisions (transactions to change items such as street addresses or phone numbers in fields in the master records). Periodically, perhaps monthly or weekly, the master file is **updated** with the changes called for in the transaction file. The result is a new, up-to-date master file (Figure 6-14).

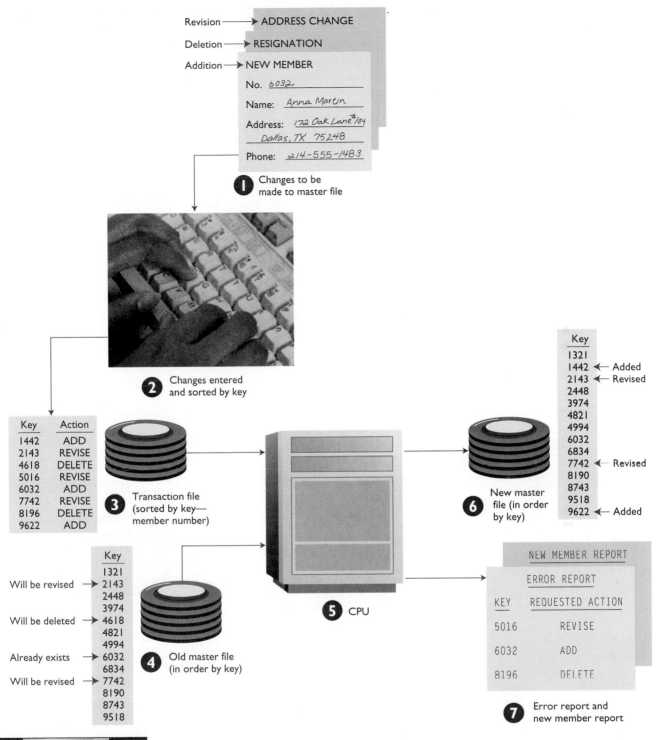

▲ **FIGURE** **6-14**

How batch processing works. The purpose of this system is to update the health club's master address-label file. The updating will be done sequentially. (1) Changes to be made (additions, deletions, and revisions) are input with (2) a keyboard, and then sorted and sent to a disk, where they are stored in (3) the transaction file. The transaction file contains records in sequential order, according to member number, from lowest to highest. The field used to identify the record is called the key; in this instance the key is the member number. (4) The master file is also organized by member number. (5) The computer matches transaction file data and master file data by member number to produce (6) a new master file, (7) an error report, and a new member report. Because this is a sequential update, the new master file is a completely new file, not just the old file updated in place. The error report lists member numbers in the transaction file that were not in the master file and member numbers already in the master file that were included in the transaction file as additions.

In batch processing, before a transaction file is matched against a master file, the transaction file must be sorted (usually by computer) so that all the transactions are in sequential order according to the key field used by the master file. In updating the health club address-label file, the key is the member number assigned by the health club. The records on the master file are already in order by key. After the changes in the transaction file are sorted by key, the two files can be matched and the master file updated.

During processing, the computer matches the keys from the master and transaction files, carrying out the appropriate action to add, revise, or delete. At the end of processing, a newly updated master file is created; in addition, an error report is usually printed. The error report shows actions such as an attempt to update or delete a nonexistent record or an attempt to add a record that already exists.

The biggest advantage of batch processing is its efficiency. The biggest disadvantage is that the master file is current only immediately after processing.

Transaction Processing

Transaction processing is a technique of processing transactions—a bank withdrawal, an address change, a credit charge—in random order; that is, in any order in which they occur. Although batch processing also uses transactions, they are grouped together for processing; in transaction processing, each transaction is handled immediately. Transaction processing is real-time processing. **Real-time processing** means that a transaction is processed fast enough for the result to come

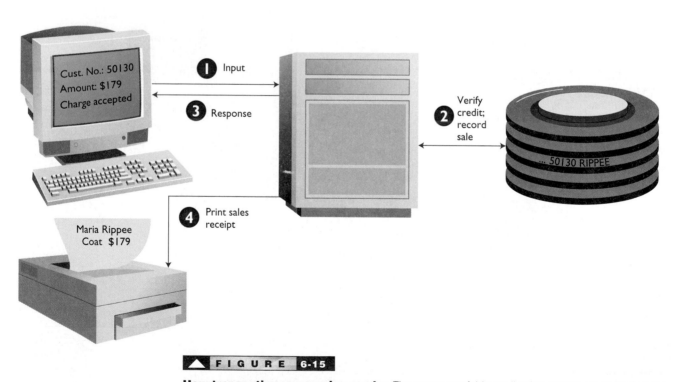

▲ **FIGURE** 6-15

How transaction processing works. The purposes of this retail sales system are to verify that a customer's credit is good, record the credit sale on the customer's record, and produce a sales receipt. Because customers may have the same name, the file is organized by customer account number rather than by name. Here Maria Rippee, account number 50130, wants to purchase a coat for $179. (1) The sales clerk uses the terminal to input Maria's account number and the sale. (2) When the computer receives the data from the clerk, it uses the account number to find Maria's record on the disk file, verify her credit, and record the sale so that she will be billed for it. (3) The computer returns an acceptance to the clerk's terminal. (4) The computer sends sales receipt information to the clerk's printer. All this is done within seconds while the customer is waiting. This example is necessarily simplified, but it shows a system that is real-time (immediate response) and online (directly connected to the computer).

back and be acted on right away. For example, a teller at a bank can find out immediately what your bank balance is. For processing to be real-time, it must also be **online;** that is, the terminals must be connected directly to the computer. Transaction processing systems use disk storage because disks enable direct access to the desired record.

Advantages of transaction processing are immediate access to stored data in the master file (and thus immediate customer service) and immediate updating of the master file. For example, a sales clerk could access the computer via a terminal to verify a customer's credit and also record the sale via the computer (Figure 6-15). Later, those updated records can be batch-processed to bill all customers.

Batch and Transaction Processing: The Best of Both Worlds

Numerous computer systems combine the best features of both methods of processing. Generally speaking, transaction processing is used for activities related to the current needs of people, such as workers and customers, as they go about their daily lives. Batch processing, by comparison, can be done at any time, even in the middle of the night, without worrying about the convenience of the people who are ultimately affected by the processing.

A bank, for instance, may use transaction processing to check your balance and individually record your cash withdrawal transaction during the day at the teller window or ATM. However, the deposit that you leave in an envelope in an instant deposit drop may be recorded during the night by means of batch processing. Printing your bank statement is also a batch process. Most store systems combine both methods: a point-of-sale terminal finds the individual item price as a sale is made and immediately updates inventory, whereas batch processing is used to produce daily and weekly sales reports.

Police license-plate checks for stolen cars work in the same way. As cars are sold throughout the state, the license numbers, owners' names, and other information are updated in the motor vehicle department's master file, usually via batch processing on a nightly basis. But when police officers see a car that they suspect may be stolen, they can radio headquarters, where an operator with a terminal uses transaction processing to check the master file immediately to find out whether the car has been reported missing. Some officers have a laptop computer right in the car and can check the information themselves.

Auto junkyards, which often are computerized big businesses, can make an individual inquiry for a record of a specific part needed by a customer who is waiting on the phone or in person. As parts are sold, sales records are kept to update the files nightly using batch processing.

As you can see from these examples, both workers and customers eventually see the results of transaction processing in the reports output by batch processing. Managers see further batch processing output in the form of information gathered and summarized about the processed transactions. Finally, new transaction processing is possible based on the results of previous batch processing.

▲

What is the future of storage? Perhaps it is holographic storage, which would be able to store thousands of pages on a device the size of a quarter and would be much faster than even the fastest hard drives. Whatever the technology, it seems likely that there will be greater storage capabilities in the future to hold the huge data files for law, medicine, science, education, business, and, of course, the government.

To have access to all that data from any location, we need data communications, the subject of the next chapter.

CHAPTER REVIEW

▶ Summary and Key Terms

- **Secondary storage,** sometimes called auxiliary storage, is storage that is separate from the computer itself and is where software and data can be stored on a semi-permanent basis. Secondary storage is necessary because memory, or primary storage, can be used only temporarily.

- The benefits of secondary storage are space, reliability, convenience, and economy.

- Floppy disks and hard disks are magnetic media, based on a technology of representing data as magnetized spots on the disk.

- **Floppy disks** are made of flexible Mylar. Advantages of floppy disks, compared with hard disks, are portability and backup. The 3.5-inch floppy disk standard may be challenged by Sony's **HiFD** or Imation's **SuperDisk,** new higher-capacity disks with drives that can handle both the new disks and the traditional 3.5-inch disk, or by Iomega's **Zip drive,** with a disk that is high capacity but not compatible with 3.5-inch floppy disks.

- A **hard disk** is a rigid platter coated with magnetic oxide that can be magnetized to represent data. Several platters can be assembled into a **disk pack.**

- A **disk drive** is a device that enables data to be read from a disk or written to a disk. A disk pack is mounted on a disk drive that is a separate unit connected to the computer. The disk **access arm** moves a **read/write head** into position over a particular track, where the read/write head hovers above the track. A **head crash** occurs when a read/write head touches the disk surface and causes data to be destroyed.

- A **redundant array of independent disks,** or **RAID,** uses a group of small, hard disks that work together as a unit. RAID level 0, **data striping,** spreads the data across several disks in the array, increasing performance. RAID level 1 duplicates data on separate disk drives, a concept called **disk mirroring,** which provides fault tolerance. Higher levels of RAID use both techniques to achieve increased performance and fault tolerance.

- A **track** is the circular portion of the disk surface that passes under the read/write head as the disk rotates.

- Each track is divided into **sectors** that hold a fixed number of bytes. Data on the track is accessed by referring to the surface number, track number, and sector number where the data is stored. **Zone recording** involves dividing a disk into zones to take maximum advantage of the storage available by assigning more sectors to tracks in outer zones than to those in inner zones.

- A **cluster** is a fixed number of adjacent sectors that are treated as a unit of storage by the operating system; it consists of two to eight sectors, depending on the operating system.

- On a hard disk that has multiple platters, a **cylinder** consists of the track on each surface that is beneath the read/write head at a given position of the read/write arms.

- Three factors determine **access time,** the time needed to access data directly from a disk: **seek time,** the time it takes to get the access arm into position over a particular track; **head switching,** the activation of a particular read/write head over a particular track on a particular surface; and **rotational delay,** the brief wait until the desired data on the track rotates under the read/write head. Once data is found, **data transfer,** the transfer of data between memory and the place on the disk track, occurs.

- Access time is usually measured in milliseconds (ms). The **data transfer rate,** which tells how fast data can be transferred after it has been found, is usually stated in terms of megabytes of data per second.

- Disk caching uses an area of memory called **disk cache** to temporarily store data from disk that the program might need soon. If desired data is found in the disk cache, time is saved because no actual read is necessary.

- **Optical disk** technology uses a laser beam to enter data as spots on the disk surface. To read the data, the laser scans the disk and a lens picks up different light reflections from the various spots. **Read-only media** are recorded on by the manufacturer and can be read from but not written to by the user. **Write-once, read-many media,** also called **WORM media,** may be written to once. A hybrid type of disk, called **magneto-optical (MO)**, has the large capacity of an optical disk but can be rewritten like a magnetic disk., **Compact disk read-only memory drive (CD-ROM)**, which has a disk format identical to that of audio compact disks, can hold as many as 700 megabytes per disk. **Compact disc-recordable (CD-R)** technology enables writing on optical disks. **Compact disk-rewritable (CD-RW)** technology is more flexible, enabling you to erase and record over data multiple times.

- **DVD-ROM,** for **digital versatile disk,** has a large storage capacity—as much as 17GB if both layers and both sides are used. Three standards exist for writable DVDs: **DVD-RAM, DVD-R,** and **DVD+R.** There are two standards for rewritable DVDs: **DVD-RW** and **DVD+RW.**

- **Multimedia** software typically presents information with text, illustrations, photos, narration, music, animation, and film clips. This is possible because of the large capacity of optical disks. **Motion Picture Experts Group (MPEG)** is a set of widely accepted video compression standards.

- **Magnetic tape** stores data as extremely small magnetic spots on tape similar to that used in music cassettes. Tape capacity is expressed in terms of **density,** which is the number of **characters per inch (cpi)** or **bytes per inch (bpi)** that can be stored on the tape.

- A **magnetic tape drive** reads and writes data using a **read/write head;** when the computer is writing on the tape, the **erase head** first erases any data that was previously recorded. Magnetic tape is used primarily as a backup medium.

- A **backup system** is a way of storing data in more than one place to protect it from damage and loss. Most backup systems use tape, but CD-R or CD-RW media can also be used.

- A **character** is a letter, digit, or special character (such as $, ?, or *). A **field** contains a set of related characters. A **record** is a collection of related fields. A **file** is a collection of related records. A **database** is a collection of interrelated files stored together with minimum redundancy; specific data items can be retrieved for various applications. A **key field** uniquely identifies each record.

- **Sequential file organization** means that records are stored in order according to the key field. If a particular record in a sequential file is wanted, then all the prior records in the file must be read before the desired record is reached. Tape storage is limited to sequential file organization.

- **Direct file organization** (also called **random file organization**) enables **direct (random) access**, the ability to go directly to the desired record by using a record key. Direct processing requires disk storage; a disk device is called a **direct-access storage device (DASD)**. Besides instant access to any record, an added benefit of direct-access organization is the ability to read, change, and return a record to its same place on the disk; this is called **updating in place.** The **hashing,** or **randomizing, algorithm** is the mathematical operation applied to a key to yield a number that represents the address. A hashing algorithm may produce the same disk address, called a **synonym,** for two different records; such an occurrence is called a **collision.**

- **Indexed file organization** stores records in the file in sequential order, but the file also contains an index of keys; the address associated with the key can be used to locate the record on the disk.

- A **transaction** is a business event that requires the business's records to be updated. A **master file** contains data that must be updated as transactions occur.

- **Batch processing** is a technique in which transactions are collected into groups, or batches, to be processed at a time when the computer has few online users and therefore is more accessible. A **transaction file,** sorted by key, contains all changes to be made to the master file: additions, deletions, and revisions. The master file is **updated** with the changes that are called for in the transaction file.

- **Transaction processing** is a technique of processing transactions in any order, as they occur. **Real-time processing** means that a transaction is processed fast enough for the result to come back and be acted upon right away. **Online** processing means that the terminals must be connected directly to the computer.

► Critical Thinking Questions

1. If you were buying a personal computer today, what would you expect to find as standard secondary storage? What storage might you choose as an option?

2. Can you imagine new multimedia applications that take advantage of sound, photos, art, and video?

3. Provide your own example to illustrate how characters of data are organized into fields, records, files, and databases. If you wish, you may choose one of the following examples: department store, airline reservations, or Internal Revenue Service data.

4. Provide your own examples of systems that combine batch and transaction processing.

5. Use the Internet to research the various formats of writable and rewritable DVDs. What are the advantages and disadvantages of each? What do you think might happen in the marketplace during the next year or two?

► STUDENT STUDY GUIDE

Multiple Choice

1. The density of data stored on magnetic tape is expressed as
   a. units per inch
   b. tracks per inch
   c. packs per inch
   d. bytes per inch

2. Storage is also referred to as
   a. cylinder storage
   b. ROM
   c. secondary storage
   d. memory

3. A magnetized spot on disk or tape represents
   a. cpi
   b. a zone
   c. MB
   d. a bit

4. A field contains one or more
   a. characters
   b. databases
   c. records
   d. files

5. Processing transactions in groups is called
   a. data transfer
   b. transaction processing
   c. head switching
   d. batch processing

6. A hard disk can be backed up efficiently by using
   a. zoning
   b. a tape system
   c. a transaction file
   d. CD-ROM

7. Data that must be updated as a result of business activity is contained in
   a. a field
   b. memory
   c. a transaction file
   d. a master file

8. DASD is another name for
   a. disk storage
   b. tape storage
   c. fields
   d. sorting

9. Optical disk technology uses which of the following to read and write data?
   a. a magnetic read/write head
   b. backup
   c. a laser beam
   d. RAID

10. Spreading data across several disks is a RAID technique called
    a. mirroring
    b. hashing
    c. data striping
    d. duplication

11. The time required to position a disk drive's access arm over a particular track is known as
    a. rotational delay
    b. seek time
    c. data transfer
    d. head switching

12. A way of organizing data on a disk pack to minimize seek time uses
    a. sequential files
    b. cylinders
    c. sequential order
    d. hashing

13. The speed with which a disk can find data being sought is called
    a. access time
    b. direct time
    c. data transfer time
    d. cylinder time

14. The disk storage that uses both magnetic and laser technology is called
    a. hashing
    b. CD-ROM
    c. magneto-optical
    d. WORM

15. The RAID method of duplicating data on multiple disks is called
    a. zoning
    b. the sector method
    c. data mirroring
    d. data striping

16. Before a sequential file can be updated, the transactions must first be
    a. numbered
    b. sorted
    c. labeled
    d. updated

17. Which of the following does a hashing algorithm use as input to produce a disk address.
    a. key
    b. file
    c. record
    d. character

18. Several small disk drives that work together as a unit are called a(n)
    a. CD-ROM
    b. WORM
    c. RAID
    d. MO

19. Assigning more sectors to outer disk tracks than to inner tracks is called
    a. zone recording
    b. data transfer
    c. randomizing
    d. sectoring

20. The ability to write a changed disk record back to its original location is called
    a. magneto-optical
    b. multimedia
    c. rotational delay
    d. updating in place

True/False

T F 1. Real-time processing means that a transaction is processed fast enough for the result to come back and be acted upon right away.

T F 2. CD-R technology permits writing on CD-ROMs.

T F 3. A field is a set of related records.

T F 4. A magnetic tape unit records data on tape but cannot retrieve it.

T   F   5. A transaction file contains records that are used to update the master file.

T   F   6. WORM media can be written once; and then becomes read-only.

T   F   7. A collision occurs when the hashing algorithm produces the same disk address for two different record keys.

T   F   8. Density is the number of characters per inch stored on magnetic tape.

T   F   9. The most common backup medium is CD-ROM.

T   F 10. Another name for randomizing is zoning.

T   F 11. Transaction processing systems are online systems.

T   F 12. Multimedia software can include film clips.

T   F 13. Hard disks have platters, access arms, and read/write heads in a sealed module.

T   F 14. Magneto-optical refers to a special type of tape that records data on cassettes.

T   F 15. A magnetic disk records data on concentric circular tracks.

Fill-In

1. Adding more sectors to the outer tracks of a disk is called _____.

2. Processing transactions in a group is called _____.

3. The primary advantage of optical disk technology lies in its _____.

4. The type of software that can offer photos, narration, and music is called _____.

5. DASD stands for _____.

6. The type of access that a file requires is determined by _____.

7. The two methods of file access are
   a. _____.
   b. _____.

8. If a read/write head touches a hard disk surface, this is called a _____.

9. CD-ROM stands for _____.

10. A(n) _____ is a group of disk sectors treated as a unit of storage.

11. The concept of using a group of small disk drives as a storage unit is called _____.

12. A(n) _____ is a unique identifier for a record.

13. The smallest unit of raw data is the _____.

14. A(n) _____ consists of the group of tracks beneath the read/write heads at one time.

15. Another name for a hashing algorithm is _____.

16. Four benefits of secondary storage are
   a. _____.
   b. _____.
   c. _____.
   d. _____.

17. The three kinds of components in a sealed data module are
   a. _____.
   b. _____.
   c. _____.

18. The three primary factors that determine access time for disk data are
   a. _____.
   b. _____.
   c. _____.

19. Three major methods of file organization are
   a. _____ .
   b. _____ .
   c. _____ .

20. Transactions must be _____ before being used to update a sequential file.

► ANSWERS

Multiple Choice

1. d	6. b	11. b	16. b
2. c	7. d	12. b	17. a
3. d	8. a	13. a	18. c
4. a	9. c	14. c	19. a
5. d	10. c	15. c	20. d

True/False

1. T	5. T	9. F	13. T
2. F	6. T	10. F	14. F
3. F	7. T	11. T	15. T
4. F	8. T	12. T	

Fill-In

1. zone recording
2. batch processing
3. capacity
4. multimedia
5. direct-access storage device
6. the application
7. a. sequential
   b. direct (random)
8. head crash
9. compact disk read-only memory
10. cluster
11. redundant array of independent disks (RAID)
12. key, or key field
13. character
14. cylinder
15. randomizing algorithm
16. a. space
    b. reliability
    c. convenience
    d. economy
17. a. disks
    b. access arms
    c. read/write heads
18. a. seek time
    b. head switching
    c. rotational delay
19. a. sequential
    b. direct
    c. indexed
20. sorted

Free or Not Free

Many people, especially those associated with schools and government organizations, have free access to the Internet. But is the information available on Internet sites also free? Often, the answer is yes. But remember that almost anything you find on the Internet is copyrighted and you must follow copyright law, unless the site specifically grants you exemption from the provisions of the copyright law.

What information is free and what isn't?

There are no uniform rules to guide you. Although some information providers make a blanket "help yourself" statement, much information is unaccompanied by a proprietary statement.

Other information best fits in an "almost free" category. The Copyright Web site discusses six categories of software availability. *Copyhoarding* involves creating software only for your own use and not distributing it to anyone else. *Licensing* is the standard "pay for use" deal, whereby you pay for the use of software under conditions specified by the owner. Generally, you are allowed to make a backup copy for personal use, but your rights to modify, share, or rearrange the code typically end there. *Shareware* is made available free for a trial period, generally on the honor system. If you like the software and want to use it after the trial period, you should send the specified payment to the software owner. *Freeware* is free. Both shareware and freeware software developers generally retain copyright and may place restrictions on use of the code. *Copylefting*, developed by the GNU Project with the Free Software Foundation, allows users to have free access to the source code of the software. Modifications may be made to the software. If a user makes improvements and modifications to the code, they must be made available to subsequent users.

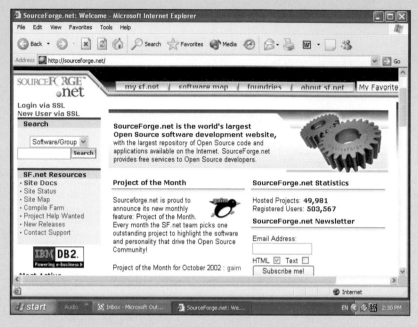

The last category is *public domain*, where all creative works will eventually end up. Users will then be free to modify at will; however, there is no provision that useful modifications will be easily available to other users, as with the Copylefting approach.

What quality differences exist among the six types of software discussed above?

Is licensed software consistently superior to the other categories? It depends on how the software was developed, tested, and maintained. Some shareware, freeware, and copylefted software is of excellent quality, even superior to newly licensed software, which is often far from bug-free. Some shareware programs, such as WinZip (originally known as PKZip), have been in use for many years and are extremely reliable. However, some shareware has not been well tested and might or might not always work correctly. Part of the goal of copylefted or Open Source software is to ensure well-written, freely available software; it is widely agreed that Linux software is as robust as widely available licensed software.

Can I download a copy of a computer image I found on the Web for my own use?

It depends on how you want to use the image and what additional uses the copyright owner might allow. Generally, you can save an image to use as the background on your computer, but you cannot add the image to your advertising brochure or club newsletter without permission. Many artists sell their works over the Internet and watermark their images to protect their copyright. A watermarked image will make it difficult, if not impossible, to remove identifying information about the owner of the artwork. Other Web sites deal with this issue by blocking the download of images using JavaScript or transparent overlays.

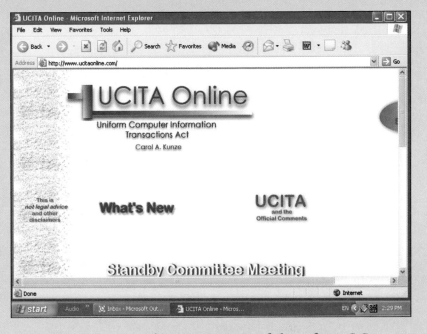

Internet Exercises:

1. **Structured exercise.** Read a Microsoft software license. Is it posted on the company's Web site and easily available for study before buying the product? What rights do you have as a user? What limitations does the license place on your use of the software? Can you sell it to someone else or install it on your mother's new computer? What will the company do if you have problems with the software; in particular, how does it handle bugs in its software?

2. **Free-form exercise.** Find a site that offers freeware or shareware. What is the licensing agreement? Is it posted on the Web site and easily available for study before downloading the product? What rights do you have as a user? What limitations does the license place on your use of the software? Can you sell it to someone else or install it on your mother's new computer? What will the company do if you have problems with the software; in particular, how does it handle bugs in its software?

3. **Advanced exercise.** Locate a copy of the Uniform Computer Information Transaction Act (UCITA) and read it carefully. The provisions discussed might well change your options for use of computer software in the future. What is its current status? How many states have passed it? Is your state considering a similar law? Be sure to check information from at least one site expressing concern about the impact of the proposed legislation as well as a site that strongly supports the proposed legislation. For example, check out UCITA Online and Kaner's Badsoftware site.

Planet Internet

Networking:
Computer Connections

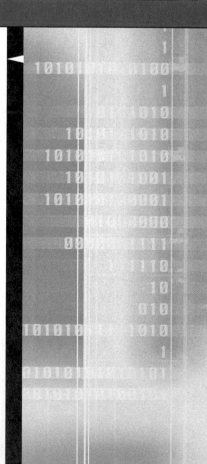

CHAPTER 7

Miguel Santora owns a small but growing wholesale office supplies business in the Miami area. From the very beginning 10 years ago, Miguel's business has used computers, but only as stand-alone desktop tools. His two salespeople use word processing to prepare customer proposals and a database program to keep track of customer information. The office manager uses a simple accounting package to prepare payroll checks and maintain the general ledger. Miguel himself uses a spreadsheet program to keep track of inventory and a database program to store supplier information.

Two years ago, Miguel signed up with an Internet service and had modems installed in the salespeople's computers to allow them to communicate with their customers via e-mail. Shortly thereafter, he decided to get a modem for his own computer so that he could more easily keep track of bid requests posted on the Internet by the various local governments that were a major part of his customer base. He had to add two more telephone lines as he and the salespeople began to spend more time online. He briefly considered installing a network to connect the company's computers, but dismissed the idea as too expensive and complicated.

Last month, Miguel's son Carlos graduated from college with a degree in business, with a minor in information systems. Carlos immediately saw the need for a network and used his knowledge of LAN technology to design and install a simple peer-to-peer LAN that allowed everyone in the office to communicate electronically with each other and to access the Internet at the same time without tying up the telephone lines.

You will not get enough detailed information from this chapter to design your own LAN as Carlos did, but you will gain an understanding of basic communications principals.

▶ DATA COMMUNICATIONS

Mail, telephone, TV and radio, books, newspapers, and periodicals—these are the traditional ways in which users send and receive information. However, **data communications systems**—computer systems that transmit data over communications lines, such as telephone lines or cables—have been evolving since the mid-1960s. This chapter takes a look at how they came about.

In the early days of computing, **centralized data processing** placed everything—processing, hardware, and software—in one central location. But centralization proved inconvenient and inefficient. All input data had to be physically transported to the computer, and all processed material had to be picked up and delivered to the users. Insisting on centralized data processing was like insisting that all conversations between people occur face-to-face in one designated room.

In the late 1960s, businesses began to use computers that were often at a distance from the central computer. These systems were clearly decentralized because the smaller computers could do some processing on their own, yet some also had access to the central computer. This new setup was labeled **distributed data processing,** which accommodates both remote access and remote processing. A typical application of a distributed data processing system is a business or organization with many locations—perhaps branch offices or retail outlets.

The whole picture of distributed data processing has changed dramatically with the advent of networks of personal computers. A **network** is a computer system that uses communications equipment to connect two or more computers and their resources. Distributed data processing systems are networks. Of particular interest in today's business world are local area networks (LANs), which are designed to share data and resources among several individual computer users in an office or building. Networking is examined in more detail in later sections of this chapter.

The next section previews the components of a communications system to give you an overview of how these components work together.

▶ PUTTING TOGETHER A NETWORK: A FIRST LOOK

Even though the components needed to transmit data from one computer to another seem quite basic, the business of putting together a network can be extremely complex. This discussion begins with the initial components and then moves to the list of factors that a network designer needs to consider.

Getting Started

The basic configuration—the way the components are put together—is straightforward, but there are a great variety of components to choose from, and the technology is ever changing. Assume that you have some data—a message—to transmit from one place to another. The basic components of a data communications system that are used to transmit that message are (1) a sending device, (2) a communications link, and (3) a receiving device. Suppose, for example, that you work at a sporting goods store. You might want to send a message to the warehouse to inquire about a Wilson tennis racket, an item that you need for a customer. In this case the sending device is your computer terminal at the store, the communications link is the phone line, and the receiving device is the computer at the warehouse. However, as you will see later, there are many other possibilities.

There is another often-needed component that must be mentioned in this basic configuration, as you can see in Figure 7-1. This component is a modem, which is usually needed to convert computer data to signals that can be carried by the communications channel and vice versa. Modems are discussed in detail shortly. (And, by the way, most modems now are internal, that is, plugged into an expansion slot within the computer's housing. We use the external variety in the illustration for clarity.)

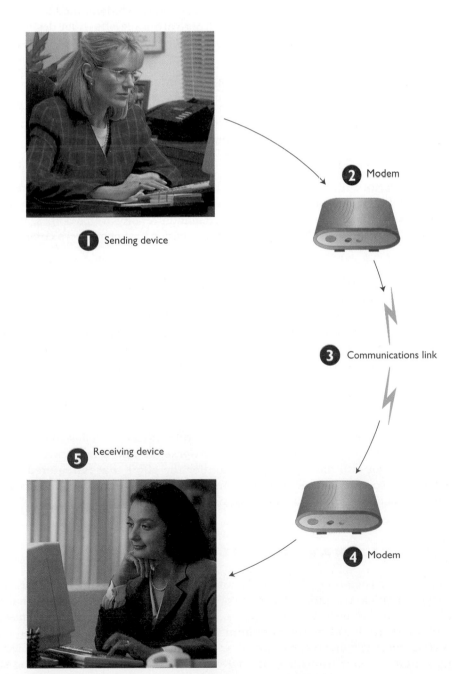

◄ **F I G U R E** **7-1**

Communications system components. Data originating from (1) a sending device is (2) converted by a modem to data that can be carried over (3) a communications link and (4) reconverted by a modem at the receiving end before (5) being received by the destination computer.

Network Design Considerations

The task of network design is a complex one, usually requiring the services of a professional specifically trained in that capacity. Although you cannot learn how to design a network in this brief chapter, you can ask some questions that can help you to appreciate what the designer must contemplate. Here is a list of questions that might occur to a customer who was considering installing a network; these questions also provide hints of what is to come in the chapter.

Question: I've heard that different kinds of modems and cables send data at different speeds. Does that matter?

Answer: Yes. The faster, the better. Generally, faster means lower transmission costs too.

Question: Am I limited to communicating via the telephone system?

Answer: Not at all. There are all kinds of communications media, with varying degrees of speed, reliability, and cost. There are trade-offs. A lot depends on distance, too. You wouldn't choose a satellite, for example, to send a message to the office next door.

Question: So the geographical area of the network is a factor?

Answer: Definitely. In fact, network types are described by how far-flung they are: A wide area network might span the nation or even the globe, but a local area network would probably be campuswide or cover an office.

Question: Can I just cable the computers together and start sending data?

Answer: Not quite. You must decide on some sort of plan. There are various standard ways, called topologies, to physically lay out the computers and other elements of a network. Also available are standard software packages, which provide a set of rules, called a protocol, that defines how computers communicate.

Question: I know one of the advantages of networking is sharing disk files. Where are the files kept? And can any user get any file?

Answer: The files are usually kept on a particular computer, one that is more powerful than the other computers on the network. Access depends on the network setup. In some arrangements, for example, a user might be sent a whole file, but in others the user would be sent only the particular records needed to fulfill a request. The latter is called client/server, a popular alternative.

Question: This is getting complicated.

Answer: Yes.

These and other related considerations are presented first, followed by an example of a complex network—or rather a set of networks. You need not understand all the details, but you will have an appreciation for the effort that is required to put together a network. Let us see how the components of a communications system work together, beginning with how data is transmitted.

▶ DATA TRANSMISSION

A terminal or computer produces digital signals, which are simply the presence or absence of an electric pulse. The state of being on or off represents the binary number 1 or 0, respectively. Some communications lines accept digital transmission directly, and the trend in the communications industry is toward digital signals. However, most telephone lines through which these digital signals are sent were originally built for voice transmission, and voice transmission requires analog signals.

The next section describes these two types of transmission and then modems, which translate between them.

Digital and Analog Transmission

Digital transmission sends data as distinct pulses, either on or off, in much the same way that data travels through the computer. However, some communications media are not digital. Communications media, such as telephone lines, coaxial cables, and microwave circuits, are already in place for voice (analog) transmission. The easiest choice for most users is to piggyback on one of these. Therefore the most common communications devices all use **analog transmission,** a continuous electrical signal in the form of a wave.

To be sent over analog lines, a digital signal must first be converted to an analog form. It is converted by altering an analog signal, called a **carrier wave,** which has alterable characteristics (Figure 7-2a). One such characteristic is the **amplitude,** or height, of the wave, which can be increased to represent the binary number 1 (Figure 7-2b). Another characteristic that can be altered is the **frequency,** or number of times a wave repeats during a specific time interval; frequency can be increased to represent a 1 (Figure 7-2c).

Conversion from digital to analog signals is called **modulation,** and the reverse process—reconstructing the original digital message at the other end of the transmission—is called **demodulation.** An extra device is needed to make the conversions: a modem.

Modems

A **modem** is a device that converts a digital signal to an analog signal and vice versa (Figure 7-3). Modem is short for modulator/demodulator.

TYPES OF MODEMS   The way modems connect to the telephone line varies. Most modems are directly connected to the phone system by a cable that runs from the modem to the wall jack. An **external modem** is separate from the computer. Its main advantage is that it can be used with a variety of computers. To have a modem that is literally out of sight, an **internal modem** board can be inserted into the computer; in fact, most personal computers today come with an internal modem as standard equipment.

Notebook and laptop computers without internal modems can use modems that come in the form of **PC cards,** originally known as PCMCIA cards, named for the Personal Computer Memory Card International Association. The credit-card–sized PC card slides into a slot in the computer (Figure 7-4). A cable runs from the PC card to

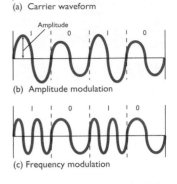

(a) Carrier waveform

(b) Amplitude modulation

(c) Frequency modulation

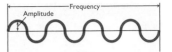

Analog signals. (a) An analog carrier wave moves up and down in a continuous cycle. (b) The analog waveform can be converted to digital form through amplitude modulation. As is shown, the wave height is increased to represent a 1 or left the same to represent a 0. (c) In frequency modulation, the amplitude of the wave stays the same, but the frequency increases to indicate a 1 or stays the same to indicate a 0.

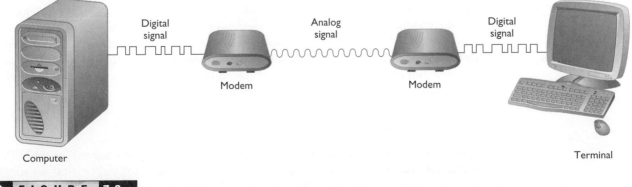

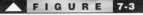

Modems. Modems convert—modulate—digital data signals to analog signals for sending over communications links, then reverse the process—demodulate—at the other end.

▲ **F I G U R E   7-4**

A PC card modem. This PC card modem, although only the size of a credit card, packs a lot of power: data reception at 56,000 bytes per second. The card, shown here resting against a laptop keyboard, is slipped into a slot on the side of the laptop. Look closely at the right end of the modem and you can see the pop-out jack. So it goes in this order: Slide in the card, pop out the jack, and snap in the phone cord.

the phone jack in the wall. PC cards and internal modems have given portable computers full connectivity capability outside the constraints of an office.

MODEM DATA SPEEDS The World Wide Web has given users an insatiable appetite for fast communications. This, as well as costs based on time use of services, provides strong incentives to transmit as quickly as possible. The old, standard modem speeds of 9600, 14,400, 28,800, and 33,600 **bits per second** (**bps**) have now been superseded by modems rated at 56,000 bps. Note, however, that because of FCC restrictions on power output, 56K modem receiving speeds are limited to 53Kbps while transmission speeds top out at 31.2Kbps. Line conditions and other variables often limit transmission to even lower speeds.

ISDN

As noted earlier, communication via phone lines requires a modem to convert between the computer's digital signals and the analog signals used by phone lines. But what if another type of line could be used directly for digital transmission? One technology is called **Integrated Services Digital Network,** usually known by its acronym, **ISDN.** The attraction is that an ISDN adapter can move data at 128,000 bps, more than double a standard modem. Another advantage is that an ISDN circuit includes two phone lines, so a user can use one line to connect to the Internet and the other to talk on the phone at the same time. Still, ISDN is not a panacea. Although prices are coming down, initial costs are not inexpensive. You need both the adapter and phone service and possibly even a new phone line, depending on your current service. Also, monthly fees may be significant. Furthermore, ISDN is unavailable in some geographic areas.

Digital Subscriber Line

Digital subscriber line (**DSL**) service uses advanced electronics to send data over conventional copper telephone wires. Like traditional analog modems, DSL modems translate digital computer messages to analog signals to send over the lines and then convert the message back to digital signals at the destination. However, DSL spreads the analog signals over a large range of frequencies, acting as though dozens of modems were sending signals at the same time. DSL is a catchall term for the varieties of DSL: ADSL, RADSL, and others. Because DSL lacks industry standards, various manufacturers are proposing their own variations. Currently, DSL service has a wide range of costs and speeds, depending on the variety and provider, but even the slowest speeds are many times faster than standard 56K modems. Also, a DSL connection is always live; you don't have to dial in to establish a connection. Some providers offer a range of speeds, with pricing for the higher speeds aimed at the business market. DSL service can also share the line—you can use your telephone at the same time that you are surfing the Web. This saves the cost of an extra telephone line for Web access. Although prices vary, and special equipment is needed, the cost of basic DSL service is not much more than the cost of your current Internet service plus the cost of an extra line. However, to get most varieties of DSL, you must be located within about three miles of your telephone company's switching office, and the DSL provider must have equipment installed in that office.

Cable Modems

Another approach, now available in most areas of the country served by cable TV, is the **cable modem,** a speedster that uses the coaxial television cables that are already in place without interrupting normal cable TV reception. Cable modems can be stunningly fast, receiving data at up to 10 million bps. As with DSL, a cable modem is always on; no dialing is necessary. However, all users on a cable segment share its capacity; as more households in a neighborhood go online, everyone's speed decreases. One other problem is security. With relatively inexpensive equipment, anyone on a cable segment can view all the data traveling on that segment.

Cellular Modems

Cellular modems can be used to transmit data over the cellular telephone system. Although this can be useful for people on the move, the transmission speed is generally less than half what it would be on the regular telephone system. Third generation (3G) digital cellular systems promise much higher speeds and greater capacity in the next few years, but will probably appear in Europe and Asia before they become available in the United States. The use of cellular modems to connect to the Internet is discussed in more detail in the next chapter.

Asynchronous and Synchronous Transmission

Sending data to a far destination works only if the receiving device is ready to accept it. But ready means more than just available; the receiving device must be able to keep in step with the sending device. Two techniques that are commonly used to keep the sending and receiving units dancing to the same tune are asynchronous and synchronous transmission.

When **asynchronous transmission** (also called **start/stop transmission**) is used, a special start signal is transmitted at the beginning of each group of message bits; a group is usually just a single character. Likewise, a stop signal is sent at the end of the group of message bits (Figure 7-5a). When the receiving device gets the start signal, it sets up a timing mechanism to accept the group of message bits. This type of transmission is typically used for low-speed communications.

Synchronous transmission is a little trickier because a large block of characters is transmitted together in a continuous stream (Figure 7-5b). There are no call-to-action signals for each character. Instead, the sending and receiving devices are synchronized by having their internal clocks put in time with each other via a bit pattern transmitted at the beginning of the message. Furthermore, error-check bits are transmitted at the end of each message to make sure all characters in the message were received properly. Synchronous transmission equipment is more complex and more expensive, but is much faster.

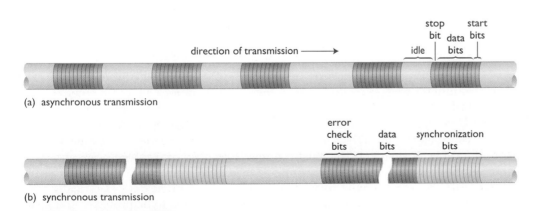

(a) asynchronous transmission

(b) synchronous transmission

◄ **FIGURE 7-5**

Asynchronous and synchronous transmission. (a) Asynchronous transmission uses start/stop signals surrounding each character. (b) Page-width constraints preclude showing the true amount of continuous data that can be transmitted synchronously between start and stop characters. Unlike asynchronous transmission, which has one start/stop set per character, synchronous transmission can send many characters, even many messages, between one start/stop set. Note that synchronous transmission requires a set of error-check bits to make sure all characters were received properly.

Simplex, Half-Duplex, and Full-Duplex Transmission

Data transmission can be characterized as simplex, half-duplex, or full-duplex, depending on permissible directions of traffic flow. **Simplex transmission** sends data in one direction only; everyday examples are television broadcasting and arrival/departure screens at airports. **Half-duplex transmission** allows transmission in either direction but only one way at a time. An analogy is talk on a CB radio. In a bank a teller using half-duplex transmission can send the data about a deposit, and after it is received, the computer can send a confirmation reply. **Full-duplex transmission** allows transmission in both directions at once. An analogy is a telephone conversation in which, good manners aside, both parties can talk at the same time. High-speed, computer-to-computer transmission usually occurs in full-duplex mode.

► COMMUNICATIONS MEDIA

The cost for linking widely scattered computers is substantial, so it is worthwhile to examine the communications options. Telephone lines are the most convenient communications channel because an extensive system is already in place, but there are many other options. A **communications medium** is the physical means of data transmission. The range of frequencies that a medium can carry is known as its bandwidth; **bandwidth** is a measure of the capacity of the link.

Types of Communications Media

There are several types of communications media. Some may be familiar to you already.

WIRE PAIRS   One of the most common communications media is the **wire pair,** also known as the **twisted pair.** Transmission of an electrical signal requires two conductors. In twisted pair wire, the two conductors are twisted around each other to reduce electrical interference and then sheathed in plastic. Multiple twisted pairs can be combined into a single cable (Figure 7-6a). Wire pairs are inexpensive. Furthermore, they are often used because they have already been installed in a building for other purposes or because they are already in use in telephone systems. However, they are susceptible to electrical interference, or noise. **Noise** is anything that causes distortion in the signal when it is received. High-voltage equipment, lightning, and even the sun can be sources of noise. Shielded twisted-pair wiring has a metallic protective sheath, which reduces noise and increases the transmission speed capability, but increases the cost.

COAXIAL CABLES   Known for sending a strong signal, a **coaxial cable** consists of a center conductor wire surrounded by a layer of insulation, which in turn is surrounded by a braided metallic outer conductor. The whole cable is then encased in a protective sheath (Figure 7-6b). Coaxial cable has much higher bandwidth and much less susceptibility to noise than does twisted-pair wire. The cable that connects your TV to the cable TV system is the most common type of coaxial cable.

FIBER OPTICS   Traditionally, most phone lines transmitted data electrically over wires made of metal, usually copper. These metal wires had to be protected from water and other corrosive substances. Fiber-optic technology eliminates this requirement (Figure 7-6c). Instead of using electricity to send data, **fiber optics** uses light. The cables are made of glass or plastic fibers, each thinner than a human hair, that can guide light beams for miles. Fiber-optic cable has much higher bandwidth than coaxial cable, yet the materials are substantially lighter and less expensive. Because it uses light rather than electricity, fiber-optic cable is immune to electrical noise and is much more secure; any attempt at intercepting a signal would be easy to notice.

(a)

(b)

(c)

▲ FIGURE 7-6

Communication links. (a) Twisted-pair cable consists of pairs of wires twisted together, then grouped to form a cable, which is then insulated. (b) A coaxial cable is a single conductor wire surrounded by insulation. (c) Fiber optics consists of hair-like glass fibers that carry voice and/or data signals.

MICROWAVE TRANSMISSION   Another popular medium is **microwave transmission,** which uses what is called line-of-sight transmission of data signals through the atmosphere (Figure 7-7a). Because these signals cannot bend to follow the curvature of the earth, relay stations—often antennas in high places, such as the tops of mountains and buildings—are positioned at points approximately 30 miles apart to continue the transmission. Microwave transmission offers high speed, cost-effectiveness, and ease of implementation. One problem is susceptibility to interference by weather conditions.

SATELLITE TRANSMISSION   **Satellite transmission** is a form of microwave transmission in which a satellite acts as the relay station. Its basic components are **earth stations,** which send and receive signals, and a satellite component called a transponder (Figure 7-7b). The **transponder** receives the transmission from an earth station (the uplink), amplifies the signal, changes the frequency, and retransmits the data to a receiving earth station (the downlink). (The frequency is changed so that the weaker incoming signals aren't impaired by the stronger outgoing signals.) This entire process takes only a fraction of a second.

If a signal must travel thousands of miles, satellites are often part of the link. A message being sent around the world probably travels by cable or some other physical link only as far as the nearest earth-satellite transmission station (Figure 7-8). From there it is beamed to a satellite, which sends it back to another transmission station near the data destination. Communications satellites are launched into space, where they are suspended about 22,300 miles above the earth. Why 22,300 miles? That is where satellites reach geosynchronous orbit—the orbit that allows them to remain positioned over the same spot on the earth. However, not all satellites are in geosynchronous orbit; some are much closer to the earth. These low-earth orbit (LEO) satellites are only about 1,000 miles above the earth and make a complete revolution every few hours, remaining visible for only a few minutes from any one location. Continuous coverage requires a number of satellites, and the antennas on the ground must track them across the sky. The big advantage of LEO satellites is the much lower cost of placing them in orbit.

WIRELESS TRANSMISSION   A group of technologies has recently emerged that transmit data over relatively short distances using **wireless transmission** techniques. **IrDA** uses infrared to transmit data a few feet between devices, such as a PDA and a desktop or a computer and a printer. Similar to a TV remote, IrDA requires a direct line-of-sight. **Bluetooth** is another short-distance technique (30 feet or less) that uses radio waves to connect mobile devices, such as handhelds, notebooks, and cell phones. See the Making Connections feature in this chapter for more information on Bluetooth.

For distances up to about 150 feet, the **802.11** family of standards governs wireless transmission. The first standard implemented, **802.11b,** allows transmission at up to 11Mbps. This standard is referred to as Wireless Fidelity or simply **Wi-Fi.** Wi-Fi capability is built into some notebook models, allowing them to easily join wireless LANs. **802.11a** and **802.11g** are the newest members of this family and allow transmission at speeds up to 54Mbps. The Local Area Network Components topic later in this chapter discusses the hardware components of a wireless network.

MIXING AND MATCHING   A network system is not limited to one kind of link and, in fact, often works in various combinations, especially over long distances. An office worker who needs data from a company computer on the opposite coast will most likely use wire pairs in the phone lines, followed by microwave and satellite transmission (Figure 7-9). Astonishingly, the trip across the country and back, with a brief stop to pick up the data, may take less than one second.

Protocols

A **protocol** is a set of rules for the exchange of data between a terminal and a computer or between two computers. Think of a protocol as a sort of precommunication agreement about the form in which a message or data is to be sent and receipt is to

Surf and Sleep

When you travel, what do you look for as the most important feature of a hotel room? A comfortable bed? A quiet room? Cable TV? Is a high-speed Internet connection on your list? If you travel on business a lot and have to maintain contact with your customers, your office, or your colleagues, it probably is.

By the time you read this, both the Hyatt International and Holiday Inn hotel chains say every room in their hotels will be provided with an Ethernet socket. All you have to do is plug your laptop's network card in to get a broadband Internet connection. If you run into any problems, both chains will have around-the-clock tech support available. These two chains are not the only ones planning to provide this service. One market research firm estimates that 80 percent of hotel rooms will be wired by 2004.

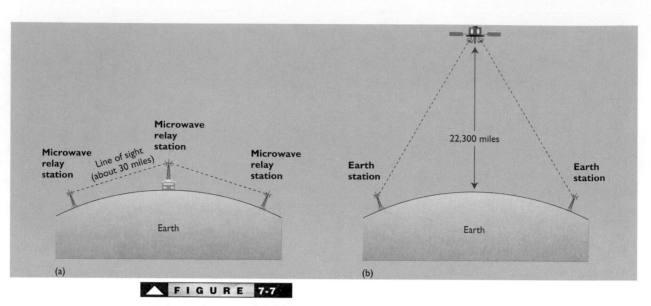

(a)

(b)

▲ **FIGURE** 7-7

Microwave and satellite transmission. (a) To relay microwave signals, dish-shaped antennas, such as these are often located atop buildings, towers, and mountains. Microwave signals can follow a line-of-sight path only, so stations must relay this signal at regular intervals to avoid interference from the curvature of the earth. (b) In satellite transmission, a satellite acts as a relay station and can transmit data signals from one earth station to another. A signal is sent from an earth station to the relay satellite, which changes the signal frequency before transmitting it to the next earth station.

► **FIGURE** 7-8

A satellite dish. A satellite dish is not usually the prettiest sight on the horizon, but a photographer has taken this shot of a dish with an exaggerating "fish-eye" lens, emphasizing the relationship between the dish and the signals that come from the satellite in space.

be acknowledged. Protocols are handled by hardware and software related to the network, so users need worry only about their own data.

PROTOCOL COMMUNICATIONS   Two devices must be able to ask each other questions: Are you ready to receive a message? Did you get my last message? Is there trouble at your end? They must also keep each other informed. (I am sending data now.) Of course, they use binary codes, not actual words. In addition, the two devices must agree on how data is to be transferred, including data-transmission speed and duplex setting. But this must be done in a formal way. When communication is desired among computers from different vendors (or even different models from the

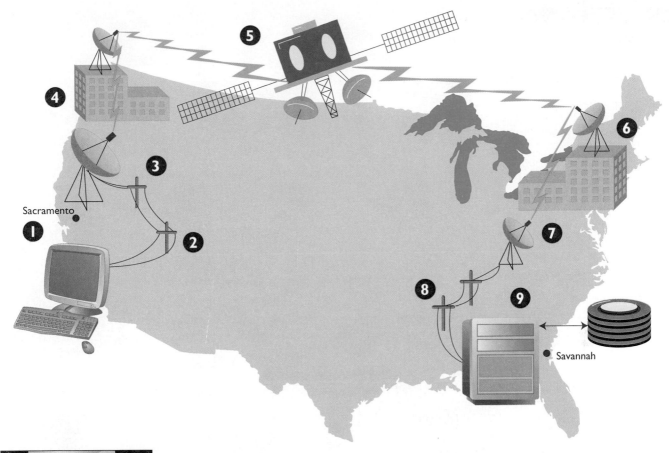

FIGURE 7-10

A variety of communications links. Say that an accountant working in the Sacramento office needs certain tax records from the headquarters computer files in Savannah. One possibility for the route of the user request and the response is as follows: (1) The accountant makes the request for the records, which (2) goes out over the local phone system to (3) a nearby microwave station, which transmits the request to (4) the nearest earth-satellite transmission station, where (5) it is re-layed to a satellite in space, which relays it back to earth (6) to an earth-satellite station near Savannah, where it is sent to (7) a microwave station and then (8) via the phone lines to (9) the headquarters computer. Once the tax records are retrieved from the Savannah computer files, the whole process is reversed as the requested records are sent back to Sacramento.

same vendor), the software development can be a nightmare, because different vendors use different protocols. Standards help.

SETTING STANDARDS   Standards are important in the computer industry; it saves money if users can coordinate effectively. Communications standards exist and are constantly evolving and being updated for new communications forms. Perhaps the most important protocol is the one that makes Internet universality possible. Called **Transmission Control Protocol/Internet Protocol (TCP/IP)**, this protocol permits any computer at all to communicate with the Internet. This is rather like everyone in the world speaking one language.

▶ NETWORK TOPOLOGIES

The physical layout of a network is called a **topology.** There are three common topologies: star, ring, and bus networks. In a network topology a component is called a **node,** which is usually a computer on a network. (The term *node* is also used to refer to any device that is connected to a network, including the server, computers, and peripheral devices, such as printers.)

► F I G U R E 7-10

Topologies. (a) The star network topology has a central computer that runs the network. (b) The ring network topology connects computers in a circular fashion. (c) The bus network topology connects all nodes in a line and can preserve the network if one computer fails.

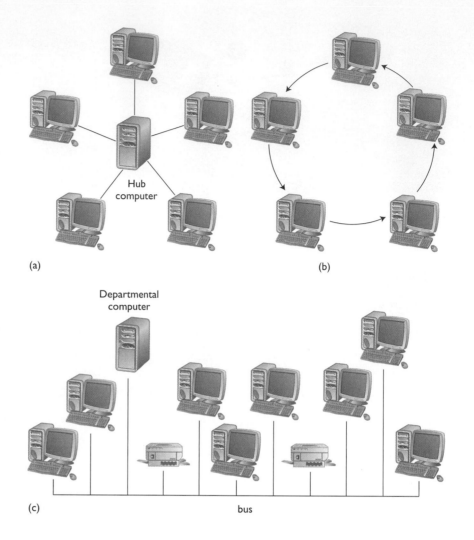

Hub computer

(a)

(b)

Departmental computer

(c)   bus

A **star network** has a central (hub) computer that is responsible for managing the network (Figure 7-10a). All messages are routed through the hub computer, which acts as a traffic cop to prevent collisions. Any connection failure between a node and the hub will not affect the overall system. However, if the hub computer fails, the network fails.

A **ring network** links all nodes together in a circular chain (Figure 7-10b). Data messages travel in only one direction around the ring. Each node examines any data that passes by to see whether that node is the addressee; if not, the data is passed on to the next node in the ring. Since data travels in only one direction, there is no danger of data collision. However, if one node fails, the ring is broken, and the entire network fails.

A **bus network** has a single line (the bus) to which all the network nodes are attached (Figure 7-10c). Computers on the network transmit data in the hope that it will not collide with data transmitted by other nodes; if a collision occurs, the sending node simply tries again. Nodes can be attached to or detached from the network without affecting the network. Furthermore, if one node fails, it does not affect the rest of the network.

► WIDE AREA NETWORKS

Networks can be classified by the geographical area they cover. The largest in scope is the **wide area network (WAN)**, which can span the world or just link computers across town. Some people refer to networks that cover a single city as a **Metropolitan Area Network (MAN)**. The concepts and components of a MAN are similar to those of a WAN.

► MAKING CONNECTIONS ◄   Bluetooth

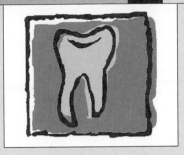

Notebook computers, cellular phones, and personal digital assistants have certainly been a boon for travelers, especially business professionals. No matter what your job is, or where it takes you, there is a device you can carry that will make connectivity easier. There is just one problem: For every device you add to your mobile computing arsenal, you must have another wire, cradle, or adapter of some sort to connect that device to your personal computer, as well as software to make the two devices talk to each other. But how much more can your briefcase take before it explodes in a mass of tangled wires?

Short-Range Radio Technology

Instead, you could do away with the wires and insert small chips—radio chips. Suppose now that those devices in your briefcase can communicate with each other—wirelessly. The ability to have wireless connectivity around the globe is a powerful concept, but getting connected across a room is equally important. That is the premise behind Bluetooth, the code name for a low-cost, wireless communications solution based on short-range radio technology.

Scenarios

What could you actually do with Bluetooth? Here are some possibilities:

- Imagine that you are in a meeting with your notebook computer open in front of you. Suddenly, the cursor begins to blink, and a new e-mail message is displayed on the screen. Your computer is not plugged into anything, and your cellular phone is in your briefcase under the table, but you are receiving e-mail over the wireless network. This is possible because your notebook is communicating with your cell phone, which in turn is communicating with the wireless network via the Bluetooth technology radio chip.

- You could walk into your office, put your briefcase down, and have the notebook computer inside it automatically sense that it is in range of your desktop and initiate the exchange of data to update both systems.

- You could walk into a meeting and automatically send copies of your presentation to the computers of everyone in the room.

- You could get off a plane with a cell phone in hand and a notebook computer in your carry-on luggage and transfer all the notebook's incoming and outgoing e-mail by simply pressing a couple of buttons on the phone. Data would be transferred between the notebook and the phone using Bluetooth; the phone would then transmit the notebook's data over the cellular phone network. You would not even need to remove the notebook from your carry-on bag.

How It Works

Bluetooth technology uses integrated radio transceivers built on tiny microchips about a half-inch square. Bluetooth chips are embedded into computer and communication devices. Thus begins the long-anticipated convergence of computing and communications. Bluetooth technology uses—bear with us for a minute—the 2.45-GHz ISM (Industrial Scientific Medical) frequency band of the radio spectrum, which is free and is not licensed by the Federal Communications Commission (FCC). This means that you will not have to get permission from the FCC to use the band and that Bluetooth devices can be used globally. Equipped with the radio chip, Bluetooth devices can talk to one another—exchanging voice and data information—at data speeds up to 1MB per second, within a range of about 30 feet. Unlike existing infrared networking, the radio-based technology of Bluetooth works when line of sight is not available; the connecting devices need not even be in the same room. Each device has a unique 48-bit address. Built-in encryption and verification will be provided.

Communication Services

A WAN typically uses communication services provided by **common carriers,** companies that are licensed by the Federal Communications Commission (FCC) to provide these services to the public. These services fall into two general categories: switched and dedicated. A **switched,** or **dial-up,** service establishes a temporary connection between two points when a call is placed. The connection remains in place for the duration of the call. When the call is ended, the connection is broken. The public telephone system, sometimes referred to as **plain old telephone service** (**POTS**), is the most common dial-up system. A **dedicated service** provides a permanent connection between two or more locations. Companies may build their own dedicated circuits using one or more of the media (cable, microwave, fiber optics, or satellite) described earlier, or they may lease dedicated circuits from a common carrier, in which case the circuits are referred to as **leased lines.** A company may lease standard telephone lines, ISDN or DSL lines, or larger-capacity digital lines. The two

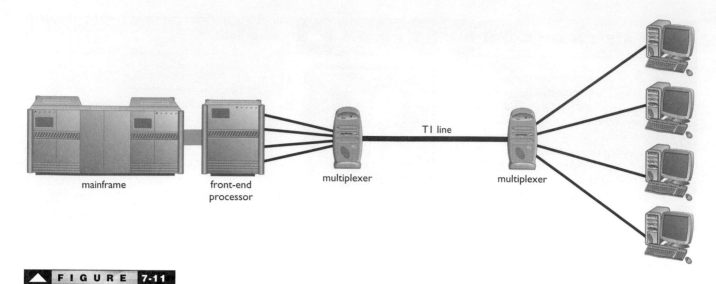

▲ **FIGURE** 7-11

Multiplexer. A multiplexer (MUX) combines the data from several slow-speed devices for transmission over a high-speed circuit.

most common high-capacity digital lines are the T1 and T3 lines. The T1 line has a capacity of 1.54Mbps, enough to carry 24 simultaneous voice connections. The T3 line combines the capacity of 28 T1 lines, or 43Mbps. These lines are quite expensive and are justified only for high-volume continuous traffic. Choosing among all these service options is a complex task, one performed by network design experts.

WAN Hardware and Software

WANs are normally controlled by one or more mainframe computers, called **host computers.** These host computers typically connect to the WAN through a **front-end processor (FEP)**, which is actually a computer in itself. Its purpose is to relieve the host computer of some of the communications tasks and thus free it for processing applications programs. In addition, a front-end processor usually performs error detection and recovery functions. The **multiplexer** is another device that is often found in WANs. A multiplexer combines the data streams from a number of slow-speed devices, such as PCs or terminals, into a single data stream for transmission over a high-speed circuit, such as a T1 line (Figure 7-11.) A multiplexer on the other end of the transmission would be necessary to break the high-speed stream into its component parts for processing.

In business, a personal computer sending data over a WAN is probably sending it to a mainframe computer. Because these larger computers are designed to be accessed by terminals, a personal computer can communicate with a mainframe only if the personal computer emulates, or imitates, a terminal. This emulation is accomplished by using **terminal emulation software** on the personal computer. The larger computer then considers the personal computer or workstation as just another user input/output communications device—a terminal.

When smaller computers are connected to larger computers, the result is sometimes referred to as a **micro-to-mainframe** link. If a personal computer is being used as a terminal, **file transfer software** permits users to download data files from the host or upload data files to the host. To **download** a file means to retrieve it from another computer. To **upload,** a user sends a file to another computer.

► LOCAL AREA NETWORKS

A **local area network (LAN)** is a collection of computers, usually personal computers, that share hardware, software, and data. In simple terms, LANs hook personal computers together through communications media so that each personal computer can share the resources of the others. As the name implies, LANs cover short distances, such as within a campus, building, or office.

Local Area Network Components

LANs do not use the telephone network. Networks that are LANs are made up of a standard set of components:

- All networks need some system for interconnection. In some LANs, the nodes are connected by a shared **network cable.** Low-cost LANs are connected with twisted-wire pairs, but many LANs use coaxial cable or fiber-optic cable, which may be more expensive but are faster. Some local area networks, however, are **wireless,** using low-power radio wave transmissions instead of cables. Wireless networks are easy to set up and reconfigure, because there are no cables to connect or disconnect, but they have slower transmission rates.

- A **network interface card,** sometimes called a **NIC,** connects each computer to the wiring in the network. On a desktop computer, a NIC is a circuit board that fits in one of the computer's internal expansion slots. The card contains circuitry that handles sending, receiving, and error checking of transmitted data. Notebook computers may have the NIC circuitry built-in, or may use a NIC in a PC card. A wireless NIC acts as a miniature transmitter/receiver to connect with a wireless access point, described below.

- Similar networks (those using the same protocol) can be connected by a **bridge,** a hardware/software combination that recognizes the messages on a network and passes on messages addressed to nodes in other networks. For example, a fabric designer whose computer is part of a department LAN for a textile manufacturer could send cost data, via a bridge, to someone in the accounting department whose computer is part of another company LAN, one used for financial matters. It makes sense for each department, design and finance, to maintain separate networks, because their interdepartmental communication is only occasional. A **router** is a special computer that directs communications traffic when several networks are connected. If traffic is clogged on one path, the router can determine an alternative path. More recently, now that many networks have adopted the Internet protocol (IP), routers are being replaced with **IP switches,** which are less expensive and, since no protocol translation is needed, faster than routers.

- A **gateway** is a collection of hardware and software resources that lets a node communicate with a computer on another dissimilar network. One of the main tasks of a gateway is protocol conversion. For example, a gateway could connect an attorney on a local area network to a legal service offered through a wide area network. Some routers can also perform gateway functions.

- A **wireless access point** (also called a **base station**) connects to a wired network and provides wireless transmit/receive capabilities over a radius of several hundred feet, even through non-metal walls. Computers with wireless NICs can connect to the network through these access points.

Now let us move on to the types of local area networks. Two ways to organize the resources of a LAN are client/server and peer-to-peer.

Client/Server Networks

A **client/server** arrangement involves a **server,** the computer that controls the network. In particular, a server has hard disks holding shared files and often has the highest-quality printer, another resource to be shared (Figure 7-12). The **clients** are the user workstations on the network. Under the client/server arrangement, the clients send requests for service to the server. The server fulfills the request and

The Networked Home

Networks aren't just for businesses anymore. As more and more families become multiple-PC households, the need for home networking grows.

Two possible approaches to home networking are borrowed from the office environment. You can connect all your computers with cables and set up a miniature Ethernet or you can set up a wireless Wi-Fi network using low-power, high-frequency radio transceivers on each PC. However, if you find stringing a mess of cables all over the house unappealing and the wireless approach is too pricey, consider two other alternatives that use existing home wiring. One approach uses the phone lines in your house to transmit data between computers without interfering with normal telephone use. If you don't have telephone jacks near all your computers, you can use your home's electrical wiring to connect your computers. Special adapters plug into the computer's parallel or USB port, then into any wall outlet. Whatever your choice, your local computer store will have reasonably priced packages containing all the hardware, software, and instructions you'll need to get that network up and running.

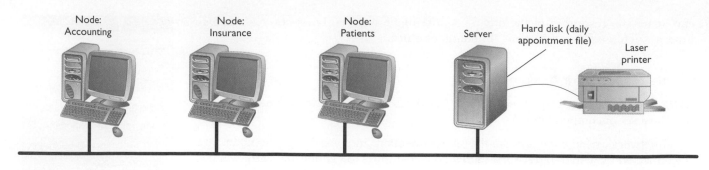

▲ FIGURE 7-12

Server and peripheral hardware. In this network for a clinic with seven doctors, the daily appointment records for patients are kept on the hard disk associated with the server. Workers who, using their own computers, deal with accounting, insurance, and patient records can access the daily appointment file to update their own files.

sends results back to the client. A computer that has no disk storage ability and is used basically to send input to the server for processing and then receive the output is called a **thin client.** Sometimes the server and the client computer share processing. For example, a server, on request from the client, could search a database of cars in the state of Maryland and come up with a list of all Jeep Cherokees. This data could be passed on to the client computer, which could process the data further, perhaps looking for certain equipment or license plate letters. In this example, the server is providing database service. This method can be contrasted with a **file server** relationship, in which the server transmits the entire file to the client, which does all its own processing. In the Jeep example, the entire car file would be sent to the client, instead of just the extracted Jeep Cherokee records (Figure 7-13). Other types of services that a server might provide to clients include print services and file storage services. In large LANs, separate servers might provide each of these services.

Client/server has attracted a lot of attention, because a well-designed system reduces the volume of data traffic on the network and allows faster response for each client computer. Also, because the server does most of the heavy work, less-expensive computers can be used as nodes.

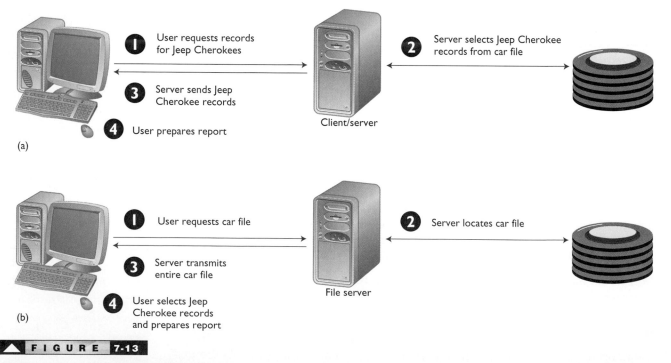

▲ FIGURE 7-13

Client/server contrasted with file server. (a) In a client/server relationship, (1) a user makes a request to the server to select only Jeep Cherokee records from a state car file; (2) the server does so and (3) sends the records back to the user, who (4) uses those specific records to prepare a report. (b) In a file server relationship, (1) a user asks for the entire state car file, which (2) the server locates and then (3) transmits to the user, who then (4) selects the Jeep Cherokee records and prepares a report. The client/server setup places most of the processing burden on the more powerful server and also significantly reduces the amount of data being transferred between server and user.

Everything You Always Wanted to Know About E-Mail

I know generally what hardware and software need to be in place for e-mail, but how do I get in on the action? You must first sign up with an online service, Internet service provider, or e-mail service, probably giving a credit card number for monthly payments and then being prompted to make up your own e-mail address and password. Thus established, you will probably click a screen icon to invoke your e-mail service whenever you want it.

I don't know how I actually send e-mail. Your e-mail service or e-mail software will provide menus of choices, one of which is to write e-mail. The look of the screen may vary, but generally, all e-mail write systems have the same elements: a place for the e-mail address of the recipient, a place to put the message title, and a place for you to type your message. You can see these three elements on the America Online (AOL) screen shown here.

That's it? Well, some e-mail software will let you get a bit fancier if you wish. For example, as you can see here, AOL offers buttons for changing fonts, checking spelling, adding a photo, and so on.

How does my message get to the recipient? First, you click a Send button, in this case, Send Now if you are online (connected to AOL) or Send Later if you are offline. AOL, or whatever service you are using, takes care of delivery.

How do I know someone's e-mail address? Just ask. You will have a collection of your friends' and colleagues' addresses in no time. And since you are not expected to memorize them, just keep them in the clickable address book. There are also several Internet e-mail directories where you can look up people's e-mail addresses.

How do I get my own e-mail? It varies by the service, of course, but generally, when you go online, you will be informed that you have mail; AOL intones the famous "You've got mail!" In offices where users are online to their company servers all day, a quiet chiming sound may indicate that new mail has arrived. Other systems simply display a small window on the screen, with a message that mail has arrived. You click the list of mail and click each item to read it. You may also, of course, choose to ignore it.

Can I just stay online for hours writing e-mail? Theoretically, yes, but it is not a good idea if you have a dial-up connection. You would be tying up a connection unnecessarily. You can write your e-mail offline and then, when the mail is ready, go online and send it. Most people write and read their e-mail offline.

Can I get free e-mail? Probably. You may be able to hook up to your college system. You will likely have e-mail at your place of work, although your employer may limit personal messages. You can get free e-mail on your personal computer from several sources, notably Mail.com, which will set you up on its own server in return for supplying some personal information used for marketing.

Peer-to-Peer Networks

All computers in a **peer-to-peer** arrangement have equal status; no one computer is in control. With files and peripheral devices distributed across several computers, users share one another's data and devices as needed. Peer-to-peer networks are common in small offices with perhaps a dozen or fewer personal computers. The main disadvantage is lack of speed; peer-to-peer networks slow down under heavy use. Many networks are hybrids, containing elements of both client/server and peer-to-peer arrangements. Peer-to-peer concepts have also been applied over the Internet. Napster and Gnutella are examples; they enable users to access files on other users' computers. Unfortunately, in Napster's case, the files being shared contained copyrighted material, and legal action shut the service down.

Local Area Network Protocols

As already noted, networks must have a set of rules—protocols—that are used to access the network and send data. Recall that a protocol is embedded in the network software. The two most common network protocols for LANs are Ethernet and the Token Ring network.

   Ethernet, the network protocol that dominates the industry, uses a either a bus topology (coaxial cable) or star topology (twisted-pair or fiber cable) and is inexpensive

Sip and Surf

Now you can check your e-mail, watch a live Webcast, or listen to streaming audio while sipping an Iced Caramel Macchiato espresso at your local Starbucks. Starbucks has partnered with T-Mobile HotSpot to offer high-speed wireless network access at over 70 percent of its stores using the Wi-Fi (802.11b) standard. The wireless access points installed at each location enable anyone with a Wi-Fi-enabled device, such as a laptop or PDA, to connect to the Internet at speeds approaching 10Mbps.

Of course, there's a cost involved. Customers will be able to pay for a package of minutes at the store or subscribe to a variety of monthly usage plans. T-Mobile HotSpot also offers the service at major airports and plans on expanding coverage to many other locations over the next few years.

and relatively simple to set up. Because all computers in a LAN share the network bandwidth, they must follow a set of rules about when to communicate; otherwise, two or more computers could transmit at the same time, causing garbled or lost messages. Operating much like a party line, a computer "listens" to determine whether the cable is in use before transmitting data. If the cable is in use, the computer must wait. When the cable is free from other transmissions, the computer can begin transmitting immediately. This transmission method is called by the fancy name **carrier sense multiple access with collision detection,** or **CSMA/CD.**

If by chance two computers transmit data at the same time, the messages collide. When a **collision** occurs, the data is destroyed and the resulting electrical noise is sensed by the transmitting computers. Each computer waits a random period of time (a small fraction of a second) and then transmits again. Since the wait period for each computer is random, it is unlikely that they will begin transmitting again at the same time. However, either may have a collision with another transmitting computer. When too many computers are attempting to transmit too many messages, many collisions occur, and performance is degraded.

A **Token Ring network,** which is closely associated with IBM, works on the concept of a ring network topology, using a token—a kind of electronic signal. The method of controlling access to the shared network cable is called **token passing.** The idea is similar to the New York City subway: If you want to ride—transmit data— you must have a token. However, unlike the subway, only one token is available. The token circulates from computer to computer along the ring-shaped LAN.

When a computer on the network wishes to transmit, it waits for an empty token; then it attaches its message to the token and transmits. The receiving computer strips the token from the message and sends the token back onto the network. Because only one token is circulating around the network, only one device can access the network at a time. Some larger networks allow for multiple tokens, permitting more than one message at a time to be transmitted.

► THE WORK OF NETWORKING

The use of automation in the office is as varied as the offices themselves. As a general definition, however, **office automation** is the use of technology to help people do their jobs better and faster. Much automated office innovation is based on communications technology. This section begins with several important office technology topics: e-mail, facsimile technology, groupware, teleconferencing, and electronic data interchange.

Electronic Mail

Electronic mail, or **e-mail,** is the process of sending a message directly from one computer to another, where it is stored until the recipient chooses to receive it. A user can send data to a colleague downstairs, a message across town to that person who is never available for phone calls, a query to the headquarters office in Switzerland, and even memos simultaneously to regional sales managers in Chicago, Raleigh, and San Antonio. E-mail users shower it with praise. It can reach many people with the same message, it reduces the paper flood, and it does not interrupt meetings the way a ringing phone does. Because e-mail does not require both participants to be present at the time of transmission, it is a boon to people who work on the same project but live in different time zones.

Facsimile Technology

Operating something like a copy machine connected to a telephone, **facsimile technology** uses computer technology and communications links to send graphics, charts, text, and even signatures almost anywhere in the world. The drawing—or

---

FOCUS   ON   ETHICS   **What's in a Name?**

Internet domain names such as www.prenhall.com are valuable commodities. Businesses want short, memorable names that Web surfers will clearly connect to their company name or their products. Suppose you were appointed to the Internet Committee on Assigned Names and Numbers (ICANN) and were asked to decide who should get to control various domain names. How would you decide the following cases? Why?

1. Two long-established organizations have competing claims to a domain name that contains their initials. For example, the World Wrestling Federation and the World Wildlife Fund might both want wwf.com.

2. Someone has registered a domain name identical to that of a well-established company, except that the new name takes advantage of a common typo. For instance, imagine that a company wants to register www.prenhill.com to collect "hits" from readers of this text who make typographical errors.

3. A group of disgruntled customers of MegaMerger Corporation want to register www.megamergercorpstinks.com. MegaMerger says this should be stopped.

4. MegaMerger Corporation wants to buy 150 domain names (www.megamergerisevil.com, www.megamergeristoobig.com, and so on) to prevent unhappy customers, disgruntled employees, or Internet troublemakers from using them.

---

whatever—is placed in the facsimile machine at one end, where it is digitized. A built-in modem converts the digital signal to analog form and transmits it through the telephone system, where it is received and reassembled at the other end to form a nearly identical version of the original picture. All this takes only minutes—or less. Facsimile is not only faster than overnight delivery services, it is also less expensive. Facsimile is abbreviated **fax,** as in "I sent a fax to the Chicago office." The word "fax" is also used as a verb, as in "I faxed her the contract."

Personal computer users can send and receive faxes directly by means of a **fax modem,** which also performs the usual modem functions. Virtually all modems sold today have fax capability. A user can send computer-generated text and graphics as a fax, without first printing it. When a fax comes in, it can be reviewed on the computer screen and printed out only if necessary. Be aware that a fax transmission is basically a "picture" of the original. For the recipient of a faxed document to process it with word-processing software, the document must first be converted into text using optical character recognition (OCR) software.

Groupware

Groupware is any kind of software that lets a group of people share things or track things together. The data that the workers share is in a database on disk. But the key to their being able to share that data is their access to it via communications lines. We mention groupware to emphasize the role of communications systems in letting people, who may be in far-flung locations, work together.

Teleconferencing

An office automation development with cost-saving potential is **teleconferencing,** a method of using technology to bring people and ideas together despite geographic barriers. There are several varieties of teleconferencing, but most common today is videoconferencing; its components usually include a large screen, video cameras that can send live pictures, and an online computer system to record communication among participants (Figure 7-14). Although this setup is expensive to rent and even more expensive to own, the costs seem trivial when compared with travel expenses—airfare, lodging, meals, lost productivity—for in-person meetings.

Videoconferencing has some drawbacks. Some people are uncomfortable about their appearance on camera. A more serious fear is that the loss of personal contact will detract from some business functions, especially those related to sales or negotiations.

A videoconferencing system. Geographically distant groups can hold a meeting with the help of videoconferencing. A camera transmits images of local participants for the benefit of distant viewers.

Electronic Data Interchange

Businesses use a great deal of paper in transmitting orders. One method that has been devised to cut down on paperwork is **electronic data interchange (EDI)**. EDI started out as a series of standard formats that allow businesses to transmit invoices, purchase orders, and the like electronically. Current versions of EDI use XML, a Web standard for describing data, to define business documents. In addition to eliminating paper-based ordering forms, EDI can help eliminate errors in transmitting orders that result from transcription mistakes made by people. Since EDI orders go directly from one computer to another, the tedious process of filling out a form at one end and then keying it into the computer at the other end is eliminated. Many firms use EDI to reduce paperwork and personnel costs. Some large firms, especially discounters, such as Wal-Mart, require their suppliers to adopt EDI and, in fact, have direct computer hookups with their suppliers.

Electronic Fund Transfers: Instant Banking

Using electronic fund transfer (EFT), people can pay for goods and services by having funds transferred from various accounts electronically, using computer technology. One of the most visible manifestations of EFT is the **ATM**—the **automated teller machine** that people use to obtain cash quickly. A high-volume EFT application is the disbursement of millions of Social Security payments by the government directly into the recipients' checking accounts. The U.S. Federal Reserve Bank uses EFT to transfer large sums of money between member banks on a daily basis.

Telecommuting. Using CAD/CAM software, this architect works at home four days a week. He goes in to the office one day a week for meetings and conferences.

Computer Commuting

A logical outcome of computer networks is **telecommuting,** the substitution of communications and computers for the commute to work (Figure 7-15). A telecommuter works at home on a personal computer and probably uses the computer to communicate with office colleagues or customers. In fact, many telecommuters are able to link directly to the company's

network. Many telecommuters stay home two or three days a week and come in to the office the other days. Time in the office permits the needed face-to-face communication with fellow workers and also provides a sense of participation and continuity. Over 30 million people in the United States telecommute at least one day per week.

The Internet

The Internet is not just another online activity. The other topics discussed in this section pale in comparison. The Internet is considered by many to be the defining technology of the beginning of the twenty-first century, and it may well hold that status for several years. Since we are devoting separate chapters and features exclusively to the Internet, we mention it here only to make the list complete.

► THE COMPLEXITY OF NETWORKS

Networks can be designed in an amazing variety of ways, from a simple in-office group of three personal computers connected to a shared printer, to a global spread including thousands of personal computers, servers, and mainframes. The latter, of course, would not be a single network but, instead, a collection of connected networks. You have already glimpsed the complexity of networks. Now let us consider a set of networks for a toy manufacturer (Figure 7-16).

The toy company has a bus LAN for the marketing department, consisting of six personal computers, a modem used by outside field representatives to call in for price data, and a server with a shared laser printer and shared marketing program and data files. The LAN for the design department, also a bus network, consists of three personal computers and a server with shared printer and shared files. Both LANs use the Ethernet protocol and have client/server relationships. The design department sometimes sends its in-progress work to the marketing representatives for their evaluation; similarly, the marketing department sends new ideas from the field to the design department. The two departments communicate, one LAN to another, via a bridge. It makes sense to have two separate LANs, rather than one big LAN, because the two departments need to communicate with each other only occasionally.

In addition to communicating with each other, users on each LAN, both marketing and design, occasionally need to communicate with the mainframe computer, which can be accessed through a gateway. All communications for the mainframe are handled by the front-end processor. Users in the purchasing, administrative, and

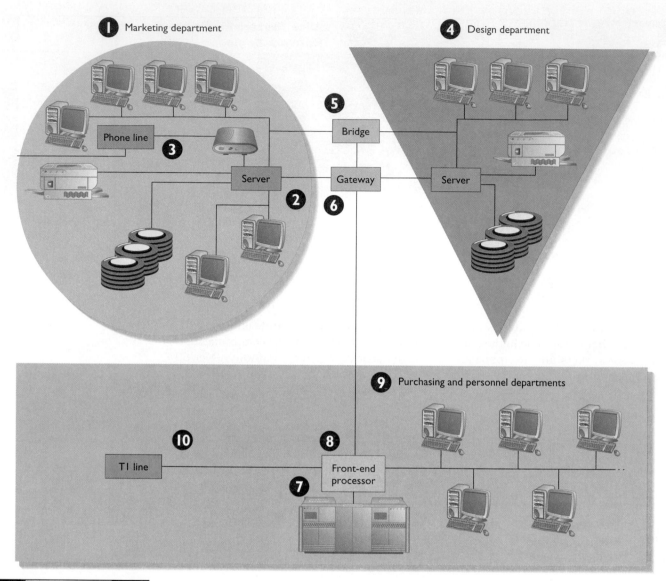

▲ FIGURE 7-16

Example of a network. In this set of networks for a toy manufacturer, (1) the marketing department has a bus LAN with six personal computers that use a shared printer. Both program and data files are stored with the (2) server. Note (3) the modem that accepts outside inquiries from field representatives. (4) The design department, with just three personal computers, has a similar LAN. The two LANs can communicate via (5) a bridge. Either LAN, via (6) a gateway, can access (7) the mainframe computer, which uses (8) a front-end processor to handle communications. Users in (9) the purchasing and personnel departments have terminals attached directly to the mainframe computer. The mainframe computer also has (10) a T1 connection to the mainframe at the headquarters office in another state.

personnel departments have terminals that connect directly to the mainframe computer. The mainframe also has T1 connection to the Internet, which it uses to communicate with the mainframe computer at corporate headquarters in another state.

Network factors that add to complexity but are not specifically addressed in Figure 7-16 include the electronic data interchange setups between the toy manufacturer's purchasing department and seven of its major customers and the availability of e-mail throughout the networks.

▲

The near future in data communications is not difficult to see. The demand for services is just beginning to swell. E-mail already pervades the office and the campus and is growing rapidly in the home. Expect instant access to all manner of information from a variety of convenient locations. Prepare to become blasé about communications services available in your own home and everywhere you go.

CHAPTER REVIEW

► Summary and Key Terms

- **Data communications systems** are computer systems that transmit data over communications lines, such as telephone lines or cables.

- **Centralized data processing** places all processing, hardware, and software in one central location.

- Businesses with many locations or offices often use **distributed data processing,** which allows both remote access and remote processing. Processing can be done by the central computer and the other computers that are hooked up to it.

- A **network** is a computer system that uses communications equipment to connect two or more computers and their resources.

- The basic components of a data communications system are a sending device, a communications link, and a receiving device.

- **Digital transmission** sends data as distinct on or off pulses. **Analog transmission** uses a continuous electric signal in a **carrier wave** with a specific amplitude and frequency.

- Digital signals are converted to analog signals by **modulation** (change) of a characteristic, such as the **amplitude** (height) or **frequency** of the carrier wave. **Demodulation** is the reverse process; both processes are performed by a device called a **modem.**

- An **external modem** is not built into the computer and can therefore be used with a variety of computers. An **internal modem** is on a board that fits inside a personal computer. Notebook and laptop computers often use a **PC card modem** that slides into a slot in the computer.

- Modem speeds are usually measured in **bits per second** (**bps**).

- An ISDN adapter, based on **Integrated Services Digital Network** (**ISDN**), can move data at 128,000 bps, a vast improvement over any modem.

- **Digital subscriber line** (**DSL**) service uses advanced electronics to send data over conventional copper telephone wires many times faster than a conventional modem.

- **Cable modems** use the cable TV system to transmit data at high speeds. The actual speed depends on the number of subscribers in a neighborhood using the service.

- **Cellular modems** can be used to transmit data over the cellular telephone system.

- Two common methods of coordinating the sending and receiving units are **asynchronous transmission** and **synchronous transmission.** The asynchronous, or start/stop, method keeps the units in step by including special signals at the beginning and end of each group of message bits; a group is usually a character. In synchronous transmission, the internal clocks of the units are put in time with each other at the beginning of the transmission, and the block of characters is transmitted in a continuous stream.

- **Simplex transmission** allows data to move in only one direction (either sending or receiving). **Half-duplex transmission** allows data to move in either direction but only one way at a time. With **full-duplex transmission,** data can be sent and received at the same time.

- A **communications medium** is the physical means of data transmission. **Bandwidth** refers to the range of frequencies that a medium can carry and is a measure of the capacity of the link. Common communications media include **wire pairs** (or **twisted pairs**), **coaxial cables, fiber optics, microwave transmission,** and **satellite transmission.** In satellite transmission, which uses **earth stations** to send and receive signals, a **transponder** in the satellite ensures that the stronger outgoing signals (the **downlink**) do not interfere with the weaker incoming (**uplink**) ones. **Noise** is anything that causes distortion in the received signal.

- The following **wireless transmission** techniques are used to transmit data over short distances: **IrDA** uses infrared to transmit data a few feet. **Bluetooth** uses radio waves to connect mobile devices over distances less than 30 feet. The **802.11** family of standards is used for transmission up to about 150 feet and includes **802.11b** (also known as **Wi-Fi**), **802.11a**, and **802.11g.**

- A **protocol** is a set of rules for exchanging data between a terminal and a computer or between two computers. The protocol that makes Internet universality possible is **Transmission Control Protocol/Internet Protocol** (**TCP/IP**), which permits any computer at all to communicate with the Internet.

- The physical layout of a local area network is called a **topology.** A **node** usually refers to a computer on a network. (The term *node* is also used to refer to any device that is connected to a network, including the server, computers, and peripheral devices, such as printers.) A **star network** has a central computer, the hub, that is responsible for managing the network. A **ring network** links all nodes together in a circular manner. A **bus network** has a single line, to which all the network nodes and peripheral devices are attached.

- Computers that are connected so that they can communicate among themselves are said to form a network. A **wide area network** (**WAN**) is a network of geographically distant computers and terminals. A **metropolitan area network** (**MAN**) uses similar technologies, but is limited to a single metropolitan area. WANs typically use communication services provided by **common carriers.** These services fall into two general categories: **switched,** or **dial-up,** and **dedicated.** The public telephone system, sometimes referred to as **plain old telephone service** (**POTS**), is the most common dial-up system. Common carriers provide dedicated service over **leased lines.**

- WANs are normally controlled by one or more mainframe computers, called **host computers.** These host computers typically connect to the WAN through a **front-end processor** (**FEP**) that handles communications tasks. A **multiplexer** combines the data streams from several slow-speed devices into a single data stream for transmission over a high-speed circuit.

- To communicate with a mainframe, a personal computer must employ **terminal emulation software.** When smaller computers are connected to larger computers, the result is sometimes referred to as a **micro-to-mainframe** link. In a situation in which a personal computer or workstation is being used as a network terminal, **file transfer software** enables a user to **download** files (retrieve them from another computer and store them) and **upload** files (send files to another computer).

- A **local area network** (**LAN**) is usually a network of personal computers that share hardware, software, and data. The nodes on some LANs are connected by a shared **network cable** or by wireless transmission. A **network interface card** (**NIC**) may be inserted into a slot inside the computer to handle sending, receiving, and error checking of transmitted data.

- If two LANs are similar, they may send messages among their nodes by using a **bridge.** A **router** is a special computer that directs communications traffic when several networks are connected together. Because many networks have adopted the Internet protocol (IP), some use **IP switches,** which are less expensive and faster than routers. A **gateway** is a collection of hardware and software resources that connects two dissimilar networks, including protocol conversion.

- A **wireless access point** (also called a **base station**) connects to a wired network and provides wireless transmit/receive capabilities over a radius of several hundred feet.

- A **client/server** arrangement involves a **server,** a computer that controls the network and provides services to the **client** workstations. The server has hard disks that hold shared files and often has the highest-quality printer. the server usually performs the processing, and only the results are sent to the node. A computer that has no disk storage capability and is used basically for input/output is called a **thin client.** A **file server** transmits an entire file to the node, which does all its own processing.

- All computers in a **peer-to-peer** arrangement have equal status; no one computer is in control. With all files and peripheral devices distributed across several computers, users share each other's data and devices as needed.

- **Ethernet** is a type of network protocol that accesses the network by first "listening" to determine whether the cable is free; this method is called **carrier sense multiple access with collision detection,** or **CSMA/CD.** If two nodes transmit data at the same time, a **collision** occurs. A **Token Ring network** controls access to the shared network cable by **token passing.**

- **Office automation** is the use of technology to help people do their jobs better and faster. **Electronic mail (e-mail)** allows workers to transmit messages to other people's computers. **Facsimile technology (fax)** can transmit text, graphics, charts, and signatures. **Fax modems** for personal computers can send or receive faxes and handle the usual modem functions.

- **Groupware** is any kind of software that lets a group of people share or track things, often using data communications to access the data.

- **Teleconferencing** is usually videoconferencing, in which computers are combined with cameras and large screens. **Electronic data interchange (EDI)** enables businesses to send common business forms electronically.

- In **electronic fund transfer (EFT)**, people pay for goods and services by having funds transferred from various checking and savings accounts electronically, using computer technology. **The ATM—the automated teller machine**—is a type of EFT.

- In **telecommuting,** a worker works at home and uses a personal computer to communicate with office colleagues and customers.

► Critical Thinking Questions

1. Suppose you ran a business out of your home. Pick your own business or choose one of the following: catering, motorcycle repair, financial services, a law practice, roofing, or photo research. Now, assuming that your personal computer is suitably equipped, determine the purposes for which you might use one or more—or all—of the following: e-mail, fax modem, the Internet, electronic fund transfers, and electronic data interchange.

2. Discuss the advantages and disadvantages of telecommuting versus working in the office.

3. Do you expect to have a computer on your desk on your first full-time job? Do you expect it to be connected to a network?

4. What benefits do wireless networks have over wired networks? Search the Internet to locate information about organizations using wireless networks.

5. Amplitude modulation and frequency modulation used to alter an analog carrier wave to carry digital data are the same basic techniques used to transmit AM and FM radio broadcasts. From what you know about the differences between AM and FM radio, draw some conclusions about the susceptibility of amplitude modulation and frequency modulation to interference by electrical noise.

▶ STUDENT STUDY GUIDE

Multiple Choice

1. _____ is the protocol that governs communications on the Internet.
   a. EFT
   b. TCP/IP
   c. MAN
   d. EDI

2. What is a computer that has no hard disk storage but sends input to a server and receives output from it called?
   a. thin client
   b. host
   c. MAN
   d. transponder

3. What are devices that send and receive satellite signals called?
   a. modems
   b. earth stations
   c. tokens
   d. servers

4. Housing all hardware, software, storage, and processing in one site location is called
   a. time-sharing
   b. a distributed system
   c. centralized processing
   d. a host computer

5. Transmission permitting data to move both directions but only one way at a time is called _____.
   a. half-duplex
   b. full-duplex
   c. simplex
   d. start/stop

6. What is the process of converting from analog to digital called?
   a. modulation
   b. telecommuting
   c. line switching
   d. demodulation

7. Which device is used with satellite transmission and ensures that strong outgoing signals do not interfere with weak incoming signals?
   a. microwave
   b. cable
   c. transponder
   d. modem

8. Which medium is least susceptible to noise?
   a. twisted pair
   b. fiber optics
   c. microwave
   d. cellular phone

9. What method does an Ethernet network use to control access to the network?
   a. CSMA/CD
   b. ISDN
   c. a bus
   d. token passing

10. The arrangement in which most of the processing is done by the server is known as _____.
    a. simplex transmission
    b. a file server
    c. electronic data interchange
    d. a client/server relationship

11. What is distortion in a signal called?
    a. phase
    b. IP switch
    c. noise
    d. amplitude

12. Two or more computers connected to a hub computer is a _____.
    a. ring network
    b. CSMA
    c. node
    d. star network

13. Which of the following provides a connection between similar networks?
    a. router
    b. bridge
    c. gateway
    d. fax

14. What is the physical layout of a LAN called?
    a. topology
    b. link
    c. contention
    d. switch

15. In which of the following network types do all computers have equal status?
    a. a communications link
    b. WAN
    c. peer-to-peer
    d. a gateway

16. Which of the following types of modulation changes the strength of the carrier wave?
    a. frequency
    b. amplitude
    c. phase
    d. prephase

17. In which of the following networks are all nodes connected to a single network cable?
    a. star
    b. switched
    c. ring
    d. bus

18. Signals produced by a computer to be sent over standard phone lines must be converted to _____.
    a. modems
    b. digital signals
    c. analog signals
    d. microwaves

19. Which device is used to transfer messages between LANs that use the Internet protocol?
    a. bus
    b. gateway
    c. IP switch
    d. token

20. Microwave transmission, coaxial cables, and fiber optics are examples of _____.
    a. modems
    b. routers
    c. communication media
    d. ring networks

21. What is a network of geographically distant computers and terminals called?
    a. bus
    b. ATM
    c. WAN
    d. LAN

22. Two dissimilar networks can be connected by a _____.
    a. gateway
    b. bus
    c. node
    d. server

23. Graphics and other paperwork can be transmitted directly by using _____.
    a. CSMA/CD
    b. facsimile
    c. token passing
    d. transponder

24. Which of the following refers to the range of frequencies that can be carried on a transmission medium and is a measure of the capacity of the medium?
    a. WAN
    b. bandwidth
    c. EFT
    d. EDI

25. Which of the following software is used to make a personal computer act like a terminal?
    a. fax
    b. bridge
    c. videoconferencing
    d. emulation

True/False

T F   1. DSL modems use the cable TV network for data transmission.

T F   2. Local area networks are designed to share data and resources among several computers in the same geographical location.

T F   3. A WAN is usually limited to one office building.

T F   4. A front-end processor is a specialized computer.

T F   5. A thin client usually has no disk storage.

T F   6. An internal modem can be used with a variety of computers.

T F   7. A modem is used for both modulation and demodulation.

T F   8. Synchronous transmission sends many characters in a single block.

T F   9. A satellite transponder ensures that the stronger incoming signals do not interfere with the weaker outgoing ones.

T F 10. Full-duplex transmission allows transmission in both directions at once.

T F 11. A multiplexer combines several slow-speed transmissions into a single high-speed stream.

T F 12. A standard modem can transmit data faster than ISDN can.

T F 13. The 802.11b standard is also known as Wi-Fi.

T F 14. A digital signal can be altered by frequency modulation.

T F 15. Synchronous transmission is also called start/stop transmission.

T F 16. Interactions among networked computers must use a protocol.

T F 17. The term "node" may refer to any device that is connected to a network.

T F 18. Ethernet and Token Ring are identical protocols.

T F 19. A ring network has no central host computer.

T F 20. A file server usually transmits the entire requested file to the user.

T F 21. A gateway connects two similar computers.

T F 22. A bus network uses a central computer as the server.

T F 23. Fax modem boards can be inserted inside computers.

T F 24. Ethernet systems "listen" to determine whether the network is free before transmitting data.

T F 25. Telecommuting is a type of information utility.

Fill-In

1. _____ are computer systems that transmit data across telephone lines or cables.

2. TCP/IP stands for _____.

3. The kind of signal that most telephone lines require is _____.

4. A(n) _____ converts a digital signal to an analog signal and vice versa.

5. _____ technology enables you to send a copy of an image across telephone lines, where it can be printed out at the other end.

6. Distortion in the received signal is called _____.

7. The ranges of frequencies that can be transmitted on a medium at one time is referred to as _____.

8. _____ refers to the use of technology in the office.

9. A(n) _____ is a company that is licensed by the FCC to provide communications services to the public.

10. _____ is a wireless technology used to connect devices over distances less than 30 feet.

11. A(n) _____ allows laptops with wireless NICs to connect to a network.

12. _____ software allows a PC to communicate with a main frame as if it were a terminal.

13. _____ lines are dedicated lines provided by a common carrier.

14. POTS stands for _____.

15. A(n) _____ is the device used to connect a PC to the network.

► ANSWERS

Multiple Choice

1. b	6. d	11. c	16. b	21. c
2. a	7. c	12. d	17. d	22. a
3. b	8. b	13. b	18. c	23. b
4. c	9. a	14. a	19. c	24. b
5. a	10. d	15. c	20. c	25. d

True/False

1. F	6. F	11. T	16. T	21. F
2. T	7. T	12. F	17. T	22. F
3. F	8. T	13. T	18. F	23. T
4. T	9. F	14. F	19. T	24. T
5. T	10. T	15. F	20. T	25. F

Fill-In

1. data communications systems
2. Transmission Control Protocol/Internet Protocol
3. analog
4. modem
5. facsimile (fax)
6. noise
7. bandwidth
8. office automation
9. common carrier
10. Bluetooth
11. wireless access point *or* base station
12. terminal emulation
13. leased
14. plain old telephone service
15. network interface card

Online Privacy

"Privacy is dead. Get over it." It's certainly not the first controversial statement from Sun Microsystems CEO Scott McNealy. After all, a guy who plays in pickup ice hockey games with his employees is unlikely to take a purely conventional stand on much of anything. Still, McNealy's comments on privacy symbolize the face-off between governments, corporations, privacy advocates, and individuals over how information should be collected and shared over the Web.

Who's collecting information about my Web browsing?

The short answer is "Almost everyone." Web site operators, e-commerce businesses, ISPs, Internet "information merchants," and even government agencies all may have recorded information about your browsing habits.

Web site operators want to collect information about who is using their pages so as to attract more advertisers. E-commerce sites are very interested in your browsing and purchasing habits, with the aim of better targeting advertising and promotions. Some Internet businesses specialize in collecting and reselling information about your Web browsing and shopping habits. Some "information merchants" have even used surreptitious measures such as secret backdoors in popular shareware packages and tracking programs hidden in HTML. Thirteen government sites recently acknowledged that they use browser cookies for tracking users who browse there.

Your e-mail or Web page views may even have been tracked by the FBI's Carnivore system, even if you are not guilty of a crime, if you have sent e-mail to or received e-mail from, someone who is being monitored.

Why should I be concerned if some company knows what pages I went to? They don't know who I am anyway.

Information merchants can and do know who you are. The problem is not so much the knowledge that a single Web site or e-commerce site has about you. Surely they have to know whose credit card is being used, and it may be a real benefit to have an e-commerce site "remember" your typical purchases and offer related specials from time to time. The problem lies more in the sharing of information between enterprises and the personally identifying and reveal-

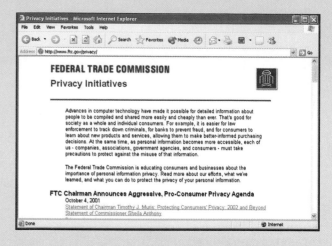

ing patterns that emerge when information from multiple sites is combined into a single database.

For example, you might believe that you are browsing health care sites anonymously, but the lack of clear guidelines and the availability of tracking information in the form of browser cookies means that your health-related inquiries on HIV risk, for instance, could be made available to potential insurers. Your records of day-trading stocks and subsequent Internet searches for "debt restructuring OR bankruptcy" are probably not information that you would care to see in the hands of potential employers either.

Most consumers would rightly be concerned about the distribution of the very kinds of personal information that we work so hard to protect in other contexts if they were aware of the information collection facilities that exist now.

The government protects my online privacy, right?

Not yet. Although concern is clearly evident in government, little concrete action has emerged as yet. The Federal Trade Commission has said that it is studying privacy issues on the Web, some congressional action has been proposed, and a few states have enacted legislation, little of which is yet in force. As in so many other contexts, our technological advances have outstripped the pace of legislation and consumer awareness.

What is the situation in other countries?

Policies about the protection of personal information vary widely from one country on the Internet to another. However a notable example of privacy policies that are significantly stronger and clearer than those in the United States are the guidelines produced by the European Union. These guidelines state five basic principles that must be satisfied not only among member nations, but also by global trading partners such as the United States. They include limitations on the transfer and reuse of collected data, standards for data accuracy and fairness, requirements that the purpose of collection and the identify of the collector be revealed, guarantees that the information collected is held securely, and procedures for challenges and corrections to the data. Delays in adopting these policies by the United States for commerce with the European Union have been the subject of much negotiation and concern.

What can I do to protect my on-line privacy?

Short-term solutions include the following:

- Become more aware of the privacy policies (or the lack of privacy) at the e-commerce sites you use.

- Disable the unquestioning acceptance of "cookies" by your browser.

- Use programs to find and remove cookies from your computer.

- Turn off "one-click" ordering on e-commerce sites, where available.

- Consider using strong encryption for e-mail or other transactions that you wish to remain private.

- Learn about the available anonymous browsing tools on the Internet.

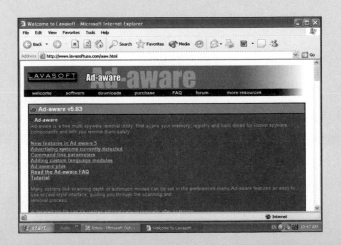

- Scan software reviews to find out whether shareware or freeware you have downloaded is known to secretly upload information about your browsing or downloads to third parties.

- Consider using a spyware removal service, such as AdAware, to detect and delete the programs that carry out this sort of information reporting.

Longer-term solutions include the following:

- Contact e-commerce sites where you shop and ask them to beef up their information privacy policies and to limit information sales to third parties as a condition of your continued business.

- Write or e-mail the Federal Trade Commission and your local senators or members or Congress to express your concern about Internet privacy.

Internet Exercises

1. **Structured exercise.** Using this text's Web site as a starting point, examine the privacy policies of one or more e-commerce sites you select. Evaluate the e-merchant's privacy policy in light of the guidelines from the European Union mentioned above. More detailed explanations of the European Union's guidelines are also available from URLs listed at http://www.prenhall.com/capron.

2. **Free-form exercise.** Compare the number of privacy-related Internet articles this year compared to last. You might use a search engine to form a query for "privacy and policy" with appropriate date ranges or use the search feature built into various Internet news pages such as CNN or MSNBC. Do interest and controversy over privacy seem to be decreasing or increasing? Try to categorize the privacy-related postings. How many concern theft of information, how many concern governmental monitoring, how many concern disbursement of medical or other personal information?

3. **Advanced exercise.** Use a tool such as Cookie Pal to examine the cookies on your own or the school's computer. Links to these tools are available at http://www.prenhall.com/capron. How many cookies did you find? Which Web sites did you recognize? Evaluate how the information from some of the Web sites identified from these cookies could be used to profile the user.

Planet Internet

The Internet:
At Home and In the Workplace

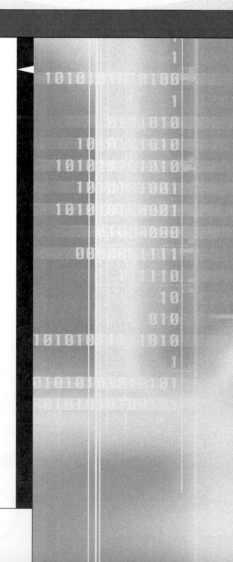

CHAPTER 8

LEARNING OBJECTIVES

Briefly describe the history of the Internet

Explain what is needed to get on the Internet

Describe generally what an Internet service provider does

Describe the rudimentary functions of a browser

Describe how to search the Internet

List and describe the non-Web services of the Internet

Describe the various types of e-commerce

Discuss e-commerce payments and taxes

Describe how advertising is done on the Internet

Describe what an intranet is and how a business uses it

Her friends, only half-teasing, tell everyone that Kathleen Cameron is "browsing for housing." Although Kathleen and her husband, John, are mildly amused, they actually see their approach as practical. They are buying a house on the Internet.

The adventure began in San Francisco, where Kathleen and John were living when he took a new job with a venture capital firm in Atlanta. Kathleen, a photo researcher, had plenty of experience searching the Internet and figured that was a good place to get a head start on house hunting.

When real estate professionals dream of the ideal customer, they may have someone like the tech-savvy Kathleen in mind. She is the harbinger of the future: a user of the houses-on-computers system that has taken many dollars to put in place. Both national and local real estate Web sites are racing to attract customers.

The National Real Estate Association estimates that there are approximately 100,000 real estate and related Web sites. Many sites offer an amazing amount of information, including maps of cities and neighborhoods, listings showing the outside of the house, and even a virtual tour through the inside of the house. Kathleen is particularly interested in the search feature that allows her to narrow her focus by zip code, price, number of bedrooms, view, schools, and more. Most sites also offer help with calculating home financing.

Before Kathleen and John made the cross-country trip to go house hunting in person, they already knew what neighborhood they wanted to live in and had preselected seven possible houses. They enlisted the aid of a local real estate agent, chose one of the preselected houses, and closed the deal—all within three days.

Real estate sales are, in fact, a local activity requiring in-person encounters, so perhaps to say that you can "buy a house on the Internet" is a bit of an exaggeration. But this is about as close as one can get. Home buying is just one of many business activities on the Internet.

▶ THE INTERNET AS A PHENOMENON

The Internet exploded into the public consciousness in the mid-1990s. Because of its nature, it is impossible to determine exactly how many people are connected, but all estimates agree that the growth rate of Internet sites and Internet users can only be described as unprecedented. One reliable study stated that the number of host computers on the Internet grew from 72 million in 2000 to 162 million in 2002, a 125 percent increase in two years! Another study estimated the number of individuals using the Internet worldwide in 2002 to be about 567 million, with projections for 780 million users in 2003. Consider that the telephone took 91 years to reach 100 million users and television took 54 years to reach the same level, while the Internet more than quintupled that number of users in its first 12 years of public availability.

These are dramatic numbers, but the effect on people's lives is, and will be, even more dramatic. E-commerce is growing rapidly. Busy people can do much of their shopping online, even buying groceries for next-day delivery in many areas. Many workers telecommute via the Internet at least a few days a week. By some estimates, information technology and Internet-based development have accounted for over half the economic growth in the United States in the past several years. This chapter will look at the technologies involved in individual and business uses of the Internet and discuss some of the trends for its future.

▶ A (VERY) BRIEF HISTORY OF THE INTERNET

The history of the Internet bears telling. It is mercifully short. The reason that there is little to say is that the Internet slumbered and stuttered for approximately 20 years before the general public even knew it existed. It was started by obscure military and university people as a vehicle for sharing information on defense-related research projects. They never in their wildest dreams thought that it would become the international giant it is today. Let us look back briefly, to understand their point of view.

A Quick Timeline

In the 1960s, computer networking was in its infancy. The few networks that existed were based upon proprietary hardware and software standards developed by the various computer manufacturers. Interconnecting these networks using existing technology was virtually impossible. The Defense Advanced Projects Research Agency (DARPA) sponsored a project to develop a network technology that would allow researchers at various locations throughout the country to share information and that would also be resistant to disruption. The result of this project, **ARPANET**, debuted in September, 1969, connecting computers at four locations—UCLA, the Stanford

Research Institute, UC Santa Barbara, and the University of Utah. Over the next few years, the number of connected computers grew quickly, and in 1972, e-mail capability was introduced and quickly became the largest network application. In 1973, ARPANET went international with the connection of the University College of London, UK, and the Royal Radar Establishment in Norway.

In 1986, the National Science Foundation connected its large network, **NSFnet**, to ARPANET, and the resulting network became known as the Internet. The NSFnet **backbone** (the high-speed transmission circuits analogous to the interstate highway system) initially carried the bulk of Internet traffic, but companies such as PSI, UUNET, Sprint, and others quickly developed capacity. In 1995, NFSnet ceased operating its backbone network, leaving the commercial carriers to bear the load.

Tim and Marc

Tim Berners-Lee is arguably the pivotal figure in the surging popularity of the Internet: He made it easy. In 1990 Dr. Berners-Lee, a physicist at a laboratory for particle physics in Geneva, Switzerland, perceived that his work would be easier if he and his far-flung colleagues could easily link to one another's computers (Figure 8-1). He saw the set of links from computer to computer to computer as a spider's web; hence the name **Web**. The **CERN site**, the particle physics laboratory where Dr. Berners-Lee worked, is considered the birthplace of the **World Wide Web**.

A **link** (also called a **hyperlink**) on a Web site is easy to see: It is either underlined and colored text or an icon or image. (Figure 8-2). The pointer changes to a pointing hand when it is positioned over a link. A mouse click on the link appears to transport the user to the site represented by the link, and in common parlance one speaks of moving or transferring to the new site; actually, data from the new site is transferred to the user's computer.

A **browser** is interface software that is used to explore the Internet. **Marc Andreessen** was a college student when, in 1993, he led a team that invented the first graphical browser (Figure 8-1). Until then, browsers such as Lynx were text-only. Andreessen's browser, named **Mosaic**, featured a graphical interface so that users could see and click on pictures as well as text. This made Web page multimedia possible. For the viewing public, the Internet now offered both easy movement

(a)

(b)

◄ FIGURE 8-1

(a) **Dr. Tim Berners-Lee.** Working at the CERN particle physics lab in Geneva, Switzerland, Dr. Berners-Lee invented a method of linking from site to site so that he could easily communicate with his colleagues worldwide. Thus was born the World Wide Web or, simply, the Web. (b) **Marc Andreessen**. As a student, Marc Andreessen led a team of college students that developed the first graphical browser, called Mosaic. He later developed a commercial product, the Netscape Navigator browser (later Netscape Communicator), which was an instant success.

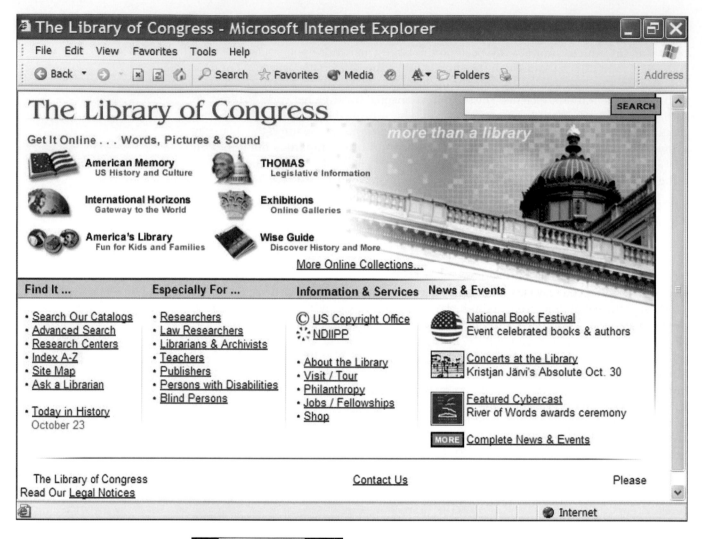

▲ FIGURE 8-2

Links. On this screen showing the Library of Congress' home page, the underlined words and the images on the upper left are links.

with Dr. Berners-Lee's links and attractive images and a graphical interface provided by Mosaic. Today the most used browser is Microsoft's Internet Explorer, although Netscape Communicator, produced by a company founded by Marc Andreessen and others (and later acquired by AOL) is still popular.

► GETTING STARTED

History is interesting, but most people want to know how to use the Internet, or at least how to get started. We cannot be specific here because many factors—computers, servers, browsers, and more—vary from place to place and time to time. But we can talk about overall strategy and what the various services and software applications have to offer.

A Little About the Technology

A message to be sent over the Internet is divided up into uniformly sized **packets**, each labeled with its destination address. Each packet winds its way individually through the network, probably taking a different route from the other packets but each heading in the direction of its destination and eventually being reconstituted into the original message at the end of the journey. A packet can travel a variety of paths; the chosen path does not matter as long as the packet reaches its destination. The software that takes care of the packets is **Transmission Control Protocol/ Internet Protocol (TCP/IP)**. TCP does the packeting and reassembling of the message. The IP part of the protocol handles the addressing, seeing to it that packets are routed across multiple computers to their ultimate destination.

The Internet Service Provider and the Browser

An Internet user needs a computer with a modem (dial-up, cable, or DSL) or a network connection and the related software, an Internet service provider, and a browser. An **Internet service provider (ISP)** provides the server computer and the software to connect to the Internet. If you are accessing the Internet from a school, an organization, or a workplace, it is likely that these elements are already in place. Your only task would be to activate the browser and know how to use it.

If you wish to access the Internet from your own personal computer, one possibility is to sign up for an **online service**, (also called an **information utility**) such as America Online, that includes Internet access. Internet service and a browser are included in the package, and thus Internet access is available to you as soon as you have signed up for the online service. The main difference between an ISP and an online service is that an ISP is a vehicle to access the Internet, but an online service offers, in addition, members-only services and information. Online services provide content on every conceivable topic, all in a colorful, clickable environment that even a child can use. Content includes news, weather, shopping, games, educational materials, electronic mail, forums, financial information, and software product support. You will probably prefer an online service over an ISP if you are new to the online experience, if most of your friends and colleagues use the same online service, if people of different skill levels will use your computer to go online, or if you want to control what your children see online.

If you elect to go directly to an Internet service provider, you will first need to select one. Some people seek advice from friends; others begin with advertisements in their phone books or the business section of the newspaper. Note the Getting Practical feature called "Choosing an Internet Service Provider." Once you have arranged to pay the fees (possibly an installation fee and certainly a monthly fee), you will set up your ISP interaction according to your provider's directions. The ISP may provide a disk that, once inserted into your computer's disk drive, will automatically set up the software, connect to the ISP, and set up your account, all with minimal input from you.

The Browser in Action

As we mentioned earlier, a browser is software used to explore the Internet. When they first came on the scene, graphical browsers were a great leap forward in Internet friendliness. Several browsers are available, some better organized and more useful than others. Microsoft's Internet Explorer is by far the most popular browser, probably because it is included with Windows, but others such as Netscape, Opera, and Mozilla are available. If you connect through an online service, that service will probably provide you with its own browser, often a modification of a popular commercial browser.

The browser screen display is divided into three sections (Figure 8-3). The top section is the browser control panel, consisting of lines of menus and buttons. The middle section, by far the largest part of the screen, is the browser display window. At the very bottom of the screen is a status line, which indicates the progress of data being transferred as you move from site to site. The status line may also show other messages, depending on the browser. The browser control panel at the top stays the same—except for the changing address of the visited site—as you travel from site to site through the Web; the browser display window changes, showing, in turn, each new Internet site you visit. Note, by the way, that it is common to refer to "going to a site," but in actual fact you are going nowhere; the information from the site is coming

Browser control panel. Most browsers offer pretty much the same functions; the example here is a popular browser called Internet Explorer. Just below the browser's title, showing the name of the Web site and browser display, is a set of pull-down menus; each such menu has several submenus. Just below the menus is a line of buttons. The buttons grouped to the left refer to the current Web site in the browser display window: Back (go to the previous site), Forward (go forward to the next site, assuming you already went back), Stop (stop an incoming site that is taking too long to load or that, after just a brief look, you wish to see no further), Refresh (reload the current site), and Home (return to browser's home page). The middle buttons are Search (find sites on the Web), Favorites (keep a list of sites to which one might return), and History (lists of sites you visited, by week and by day). The buttons on the right are Print (print the content of the current site), Mail (get e-mail if you are set up on an account), and Fullscreen (let the browser display window take up the entire screen). Below the button line is the Address window, which contains the URL of the site in the browser display window. You can type a new site address into the Address window and press Enter to go to that site.

to you. The data from the "visited" site is sent from its host computer across the Internet to your computer.

When you start your browser software, it will display either the **home page**—initial page—of the Web site for the company that created your particular browser or some other site designated by your ISP. However, most browsers allow you to change the first page you see when you sign on to one of your own preference. If the whole page doesn't fit on your screen, it can be scrolled—moved up and down—by using the scroll bar on the right; simply press your mouse button over a scroll bar arrow to see the page move. A scroll bar at the bottom indicates that the site display is wider than your screen and it allows you to move the page right and left. As you move the page,

GETTING PRACTICAL

Choosing an Internet Service Provider

If you have decided that you want to connect your computer to the Internet directly via an Internet service provider, you have to choose among many offerings. Many ISPs are national in scope; others are regional or local services. The best rates generally come from local ISPs. Local ISPs are usually what are called retail ISPs; that is, they deal primarily with individuals and small businesses.

You can begin by checking the Yellow Pages of your local phone directory, which probably has listings under "Internet." Also check out ISP advertisements in monthly computer magazines and, in urban areas, in your local newspaper. Many advertisements include a toll-free number that you can call for free software and a free trial subscription of a month or of a certain number of online hours.

An online resource called The List is by far the most comprehensive and useful list of ISPs (http://www.thelist.com). It is, of course, available only to people who are already able to get online, but you should be able to access it through your school or local library Internet connections. It features thousands of ISPs and is searchable by state, province (in Canada), and telephone area code.

If you are willing to put up with advertisements appearing on your screen as you surf, consider one of the free ISPs. A search of "free ISP" on any of the search engines should turn up a number of candidates. Check their Web pages to see if they have local access numbers in your area.

Here are some further tips:

- Look for an ISP whose access is only a local phone call away. Otherwise, long-distance charges will figure prominently in your monthly phone bill. Even if a seemingly toll-free number is offered, the provider will recoup the cost in charges to you.

- If you plan on traveling with a laptop, consider one of the national ISPs that have local numbers all over the country.

- If you plan on using one of the faster access methods, such as ISDN, DSL, or cable modem, you need to find out whether the ISP offers that service.

- Ideally, find a provider with software that will automate the registration process. Configuring the right connections on your own is not a trivial task.

- Figure out how likely you are to want to get help. At the very least, ask for the phone numbers and hours of the help line. If help is available only via e-mail, take your business elsewhere.

- ISPs are volatile. Make sure your contract includes terms that let you opt out if your ISP wants to transfer your account to a different ISP or if your ISP is bought out. For that matter, make sure you can opt out for your own reasons.

Finally, don't fall for an unrealistic bargain. Like anything else, if it sounds too good to be true, it probably is. You will probably find that a "bargain" service is oversubscribed, underpowered, and prone to busy signals. Even worse, your call for technical help may garner only a "this number has been disconnected" message. Stability is worth something.

---

note that the browser control panel stays in place; it is always available no matter what the browser display window shows.

Browser Functions and Features

Next, let us examine the functions of the browser control panel. You can follow along on Figure 8-3 as you read these descriptions. Again, this discussion is necessarily generic and may vary from browser to browser.

MENUS AND BUTTONS   Using a mouse lets you issue commands through a set of **menus**, a series of choices normally laid out across the top of the screen. The menus are called **pull-down menus** because each initial choice, when clicked with a mouse, reveals lower-level choices that pull down like a window shade from the initial selection at the top of the screen. You can also invoke commands using **buttons** for functions such as Print to print the current page, Home to return to the browser home page, and—perhaps the ones you will use the most—Back and Forward to help you retrace sites you have recently visited. If you rest the cursor over a button for just a few seconds, a small text message called a **screen tip** will reveal its function. Note

```
URL:
http://www.intel.com/pressroom/index.asp
```

Protocol   Host computer address   Path, directory,
                       (domain)   file name

that all functions are listed in the pull-down menus; the buttons are just convenient shortcuts for the most commonly used functions.

URL   The address window just below the toolbar buttons will usually contain a **Uniform Resource Locator** (**URL**), a rather messy-looking string of letters and symbols, which is the unique address of a Web page or file on the Internet. An URL (pronounced "earl" or, alternatively, "U-R-L") has a particular format (Figure 8-4). A Web page URL begins with the protocol *http*, which stands for **HyperText Transfer Protocol**. This protocol is the means of communicating by using links, the clickable text or image that transports a user to the desired Web site. Next comes the **domain name**, which is the address of the site's host computer. The last part of the domain name, "com" in Figure 8-4, is called a **top-level domain** and represents the purpose of the organization or entity—in this case, "com" for "commercial." In some cases, the top-level domain name is a two-letter code that stands for the country of origin. Note the usage of top-level domain names in Figure 8-5. The last part of the URL, often the most complex, contains directories and file names that specify the exact location of the Web page on the host computer. Parts of the URL to the right of the domain, that is, the directory and file names, are case-sensitive; you must type uppercase or lowercase characters exactly as indicated.

Most sites have a home page that acts as a directory by linking to what are often numerous pages of content. That home page is typically accessed by using a short URL that ends with the domain name. Also, many advertised URLs neglect to even mention the "http://" part of their address, partly because most browsers will supply the "http://" for you.

No one likes to type URLs. There are several ways to avoid it. The easy way, of course, is simply to click links to move from one site to another. Another way is to click a pre-stored link on your browser's **hot list**—called Bookmarks, Favorites, or something similar—where you can store your favorite sites and their URLs.

PLUG-INS   In addition to the browsers themselves, various vendors offer **plug-ins**, software that enhances the value of a browser by increasing its functionality or features. Typical plug-ins can enhance a site's audio-video experience or improve image viewing. Most plug-ins can be downloaded from their own Web sites. Once the plug-in is downloaded and installed, usually a simple procedure, the browser can automatically handle the newly enabled features. An example of a plug-in is Adobe Acrobat Reader, which is used to display and print documents that have been created in Portable Document Format (PDF). Since everything from product descriptions to IRS forms is on the Web in PDF, it is important that a browser be equipped to handle the format. Perhaps the most popular plug-in is Shockwave, from a company named Macromedia. Shockwave permits viewing sites that include quality animation and other effects.

WEB PAGE PROGRAMS   In the early days of the Web, everything presented on a Web page was static, composed of material that had already been prepared. A user was basically accessing the electronic version of a printed page. Even though that access was certainly a convenience, the content of the Web page offered nothing innovative—until it became possible to include small programs in the pages downloaded to your browser. These programs allow Web pages to perform virtually any task—display animations, receive input, perform calculations, and so forth. They also provide the possibility of dynamic interaction, in which the user can receive immediate feedback and the programs actually do things on their own.

Distribution of Top-level Domains

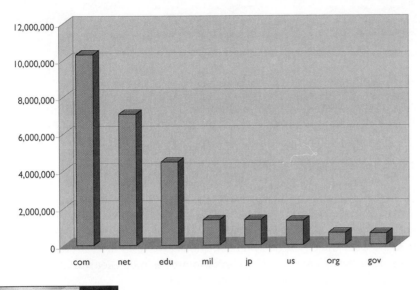

Distribution of top-level domain names. A glance at the chart shows that the majority of Web sites, worldwide, have the top-level domain "com"; that is, they are business sites. Sites using "net" are often business sites too. The other domains shown here are "edu" for education; "mil" for military (U.S. only); "org" for nonprofit organizations; "gov" for U.S. government (U.S. only); "jp" for Japan; and "us" for United States, for those wishing to distinguish it from sites in other countries. Country domains use two letters; typical examples are "fi" (Finland), "uk" (United Kingdom), "de" (Germany), "ca" (Canada), "au" (Australia), "nl" (Netherlands), and "se" (Sweden). In November 2000, the following new top-level domain names were approved for use: ".biz" for business sites; ".pro" for professionals such as lawyers, doctors and accountants; ".name" for personal sites; ".aero"; ".coop"; ".info"; and "museum." Currently, the number of sites using these new domains is too small to register on this chart. (Source: Internet Software Consortium (http://www.isc.org))

These programs come in several different forms. **JavaScript** (from Netscape) and **VBScript** (a subset of the Visual Basic programming language from Microsoft) are scripting languages that are used to produce a series of instructions to be interpreted and executed by your browser. Java **applets** and **ActiveX controls** (from Microsoft) are small programs embedded in a Web page that run when your browser loads the page ((Figure 8-6). To benefit from these scripts and programs, a user must have a browser that is capable of running them, as, indeed, the most popular browsers are. If you are thus equipped, you will doubtless see many applets and controls in action as you cruise the Web. One word of caution: all of these present some security risks, so many users set their browsers to deactivate them.

Wireless Internet Access

In the last year there has been explosive growth in the number of people using mobile handheld devices to access the Internet. These devices include text pagers, personal digital assistants (PDAs), pocket computers, and even Web-enabled cellular phones. Some use a pen-based system to enter characters through the screen, while others are equipped with a miniature keyboard. All have a limited display area that makes it difficult to browse the Web as you would with your PC. However, they are adequate for sending and receiving e-mail, checking weather forecasts, making airline reservations, and many other functions that mobile professionals find useful. To access the Web with these devices, you must establish an account with a wireless access service provider and, if your device is not already so equipped, buy a cellular modem card or adapter. Many wireless access providers use the **Wireless Application Protocol (WAP)** to convert Web pages into a format that is more compatible with the limited capabilities of handheld devices. Access speeds are much slower than even a basic telephone modem connection,

Army or Education? Both!

The U.S. Army's strongest competitors for recruits are institutions of higher learning. Rather than fighting them, the Army has decided to join them—in a big way! Its Army University Access Online project provides all one million of its soldiers with access to a comprehensive array of college and university online courses from 21 colleges and universities. In addition, each soldier receives a laptop computer, a printer, and an ISP account, enabling soldiers to pursue their education wherever duty takes them. In addition to attracting recruits who might otherwise bypass military service, the Army hopes to have its forces better prepared for the battlefield of the future.

but since very few graphics are transmitted, most users find the speed adequate. Evolving wireless standards promise significant speed increases in the near future.

► SEARCHING THE INTERNET

Although a browser, true to its name, lets a user browse by listing clickable categories of information—sports, business, kids, whatever—most users soon want to find something specific. A **search engine** is software, usually located at its own Web site, that lets a user specify search terms; the search engine then finds sites that fit those terms. A browser usually offers links to one or more search engines, or a user can simply link to the site of a favorite search engine.

A search engine does not actually go out to the Web and "look around" each time a search is requested. Instead, the search engine, over time, builds an index, or database of searchable terms that can be matched to certain Web sites. To build this database, a search engine uses software called a **spider** (also called a crawler or bot) to follow links across the Web, calling up pages and automatically indexing to its database some or all the words on the page. In addition, sites are submitted by their owners to the search engine, which indexes them.

As the result of a search request, the search engine will present a list of sites in some format, which varies by search engine. In fact, the nature of the search varies according to the search engine. Initially, users are astonished at the number of sites found by the search engine, often thousands and perhaps tens of thousands.

Hot Search Engines

The title of this section is somewhat facetious, since a new "hot" search engine can show up overnight. Furthermore, some early search engines, less than half-a-dozen years old, are considered hackneyed and dull. Nevertheless, of the dozens of search engines in existence, a list of a few useful search engines is appropriate. Note that the use of these search engines is free, although you will, of course, encounter some advertising. Table 8-1 offers a comparison chart.

Although it might seem that the same search query ought to produce the same list of sites no matter what the search engine, this is hardly the case. Search engines vary widely in size, content, and search methodology. Keeping this in mind, serious researchers sometimes put the same query to each of several search engines and expect to be given a somewhat different list of sites from each. The ultimate search method, called a **metasearch**, uses software that searches the search engines. That is, it runs your query on several different search engines, probably the top seven or eight, simultaneously, then combines the results into a single list. Table 8-1 also lists several of the metasearch engines.

Internet Directories

Yahoo, one of the most popular "search engines" on the Internet, really isn't a search engine at all, but rather a directory. A **directory** is the work of human researchers, who sift through sites and organize them by content categories, allowing you to quickly focus on a group of sites that interest you. Many smaller directories concentrate on specific content areas, such as art and artists, and even rate listed sites for quality. Of course, any rating is the subjective judgment of the people who compile the directory. Several directories are included in Table 8-1.

TABLE 8-1	A selection of Internet search tools	
Directories		
About	About	Human experts, called Guides, compile directories organized around specific topics.
Yahoo!	Yahoo!	Well-organized categories let the user switch from browsing to searching in a certain area; but finds only keywords, not any word on a site
Search Engines		
alltheweb	AlltheWeb	Fast; supports a large number of languages; can limit results to specific domains
altavista	AltaVista	Very fast; indexes every word on every page of every site; searches Usenet too; excellent for custom searches
Google	Google	Results ranked by algorithm based on number of links from other pages
HotBot	HotBot	Fast; unique search options let you restrict searches; very comprehensive; excels at finding current news
Lycos	Lycos	Numerous search options, a comprehensive directory, and good returns on simple searches.
Metasearch Sites		
metacrawler	MetaCrawler	Accepts search terms and submits to several popular search engines; eliminates duplicates and ranks by relevancy
DOGPILE	Dogpile	Well-designed, easy-to-use interface; can search Usenet

► **BRANCHING OUT**

Although the World Wide Web is usually the focus of any Internet discussion, there are other parts of the Internet that deserve attention. All of them, in fact, predate the Web. One way to identify such sites is to observe the protocol. Instead of *http*, which you may be accustomed to seeing used for Web sites, you may see *news* or *ftp*.

Newsgroups

Usenet is an informal network of computers that allows the posting and reading of messages in groups that focus on specific topics. A more informal name is simply **newsgroups**. Topics of newsgroup discussions cover almost any conceivable subject. Today there are more than 20,000 newsgroups. Participating in newsgroups requires software called a **newsreader**. This software is included in most browsers, but some newsgroup participants prefer to use stand-alone newsreaders with lots of extra features.

Think of a Usenet as a series of bulletin boards, each devoted to a specific topic. If you happen along, you can read other people's postings. If you wish to respond to a message or just contribute your own original thought, you leave a message. Before participating in a discussion, you should familiarize yourself with the newsgroup's content by browsing its **FAQs**, or list of **frequently asked questions**, to avoid rehashing topics that have already been addressed. You should also become familiar with the general rules of good behavior on the Internet, referred to as **netiquette**.

In many newsgroups anyone can post messages about anything, whether or not it relates to the topic of the newsgroup. Some people take perverse delight in posting messages attacking others, often in the crudest terms. This type of message, referred to as a **flame**, can provoke a **flame war**, back-and-forth exchanges of flames. To

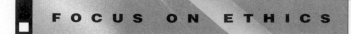

FOCUS ON ETHICS — High Speed Pump and Dump?

The speed with which information can be communicated via the Internet has led to new twists on old scams. One teenager grossed $800,000 in an investment scheme known as "pump and dump." After buying large blocks of low-priced stocks, the teen then talked up the prospects for the stock on financial message boards and in chat rooms. When the stock price rose, he was able to sell the stock at a very significant profit.

After an investigation by the Securities and Exchange Commission (SEC) this individual was fined $285,000 dollars, which left him with a profit of about $500,000. He received no further punishment, and he bought his parents expensive cars with the profits.

Answer the following questions:

1. Was the behavior ethical? Why or why not?
2. If this behavior was unethical, how would you distinguish "pump and dump" from regular stock trading?
3. The teen made frequent use of multiple screen-names to make it appear that his "buy" recommendations were coming from more than one person. Does this affect your evaluation of the ethical situation in this case?
4. What lessons would you draw for online investing from this case?

avoid problems with flames and other inappropriate material, some newsgroups are moderated. In a **moderated newsgroup**, all postings are first sent to a **moderator**, who decides whether the message is appropriate for posting.

FTP: Downloading Files

You already know that you can access files that reside on remote computers through the Internet and view them on your own computer screen. That is, you are allowed to look at them. But what if you wanted to keep a file; that is, what if you wanted your own copy of a file on your own computer? It may be possible to download—get—the file from the distant computer and place it on the hard disk of the computer you are using. All kinds of files—programs, text, graphics images, even sounds—are available to be copied without restriction. The free files are public archives, often associated with an educational institution or government.

Computers on the Internet have a standard way to transfer copies of files, a program called **FTP**, for **file transfer protocol**. The term has become so common that FTP is often used as a verb, as in "Jack FTP-ed that file this morning." Computers that maintain collections of downloadable files are called **FTP servers**. Most downloading is done by a method called **anonymous FTP**. This means that instead of having to identify yourself with a proper account on the remote computer, you can simply log in as Anonymous. Also, instead of a password, you just use your e-mail address. All of this can easily be done through your browser.

Telnet: Using Remote Computers

Many applications on large systems require users to access a host computer through a terminal. **Telnet** is a protocol that allows remote users to use their PC to log onto a host computer system over the Internet and use it as if they were sitting at one of that system's local terminals. Usually, the user has to have an account on the host system and enter an appropriate user ID and password. However, some systems are set up to allow guest logins, for which no prior account is necessary. Most Web browsers include Telnet capability.

E-mail

E-mail, already discussed in the chapter on networking, is the most-used feature of the Internet, used by even more people than the Web. Before the Internet, e-mail users were limited to communicating only with others on the same network. As a network of networks, the Internet has made it possible for any user connected to the Internet to send e-mail to anyone else on the Internet. This is similar to the telephone system. No matter what company provides your local telephone service, you can call anyone in the world, since all telephone companies are now connected to each other.

If you are connected to the Internet through your employer's or school's network, that network will provide a **mail server** that collects and stores your e-mail in a **mailbox** that you can access at your convenience. On some networks, you will receive an audible alarm (usually a soft chime) or see a small message box on your screen for a brief period when new mail arrives. If you connect to the Internet through an ISP, the mail server resides on the ISP's computer, and you will have to check periodically for new mail. Your **e-mail address** consists of the user name assigned to you by your ISP or network administrator, followed by the @ symbol, then the domain name of your mail server.

E-mail client software on your PC allows you to retrieve, create, send, store, print, and delete your e-mail messages. Additional features include an address book, from which you can select addressees for new mail, and the ability to attach files containing graphics, audio, video, and computer programs to your e-mail. Be aware, however, that for security reasons, some networks will block some or all attachments from incoming messages. Basic e-mail client software is included with most browsers, but many people use separate e-mail software that includes advanced features such as **filters** that can direct incoming e-mail to specific folders and even reject **spam**, that unsolicited junk e-mail that can overwhelm a users in-box.

► THE WORLD OF E-COMMERCE

The world of **electronic commerce**, or, more commonly, **e-commerce**, buying and selling over the Internet, represents nothing less than a new economic order. Even the word "retail" is evolving to "e-tail," short for "electronic retail." With a few clicks of your mouse, you can buy a suit in Thailand, an out-of-print biography, a particular used car, or a bargain airline ticket. Or, considering more mundane items, you can buy music CDs, videos, clothes, computers, baby equipment, jewelry, sporting goods, office supplies, cosmetics, flowers, gifts, and your weekly groceries—still with just a few clicks. Businesses are also finding it faster and cheaper to deal with their suppliers and business customers electronically.

Business-to-Consumer E-commerce

In Internet jargon, retail activity is referred to as **business-to-consumer (B2C)** e-commerce. B2C e-commerce has gotten the lion's share of media attention: outlandishly expensive Superbowl commercials, .com addresses at the bottom of almost every newspaper ad and TV commercial, and numerous news stories concerning the successes and notable failures among the major players. Although there have been some spectacular failures among Internet retailers in the last several years, analysts agree that B2C e-commerce will continue to grow rapidly. Some reliable estimates have U.S. online sales growing from $48 billion in 2002 to over $130 billion by 2006. In case you thought e-commerce was a U.S. phenomenon, these same sources estimate that more than half of all online sales will take place outside the United States by 2005.

Several types of businesses engage in B2C e-commerce. Many retailers, such as Amazon.com, do business exclusively over the Internet and are referred to as **pure-play** retailers (Figure 8-7). Some of these companies have their own warehouses from which they fill customer orders, while others simply relay orders directly to the manufacturer or wholesaler, who then ships the items to the customer. In either case, the pure-play retailers avoid the salespeople salaries, store rental costs, and other expenses involved in maintaining physical stores in multiple locations, enabling them (theoretically) to charge lower prices for their goods.

In the last few years, many traditional retail outlets, referred to as "bricks and mortar" companies, have established sites on the Internet, thus becoming known as **bricks-and-clicks** retailers. These companies, such as J.C. Penney and Macy's, have the advantage of a well-known brand name and a loyal customer base (Figure 8-8).

Online Travel Resources

Planning a trip? Most people are aware of the on-line reservation systems of the airlines, major hotel chains, and car rental agencies. But the Internet can aid your travel plans in many other ways. For instance, if the major hotels don't interest you, try the Bed & Breakfast Channel (bbchannel.com)—it lists over 19,000 bed-and-breakfast inns throughout the United States, most including photos. If your plans include overseas travel, check out the Centers for Disease Control Travel Advisory (www.cdc.gov/travel) for required inoculations and strategies to avoid any local health problems at your destination. You also might want to visit the Universal Currency Converter site (xe.net/currency) to find out the current rate of monetary exchange and Travlang (travlang.com) to pick up some useful foreign words and phrases. Travlang even supplies sound clips to help with the proper pronunciation.

► FIGURE 8-7

Pure-play retailers.
Amazon.com sells exclusively over the Internet and is referred to as a pure-play retailer.

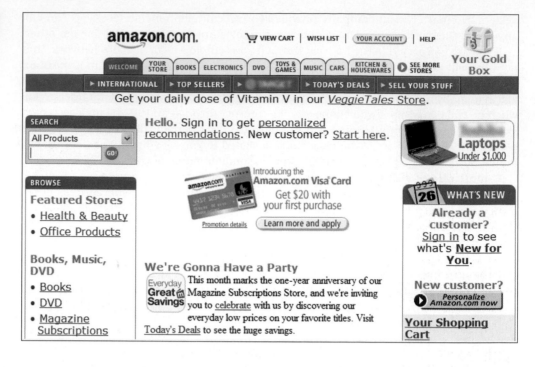

Mail-order retailers, such as L.L. Bean and Land's End, have also embraced the Internet. Although this type of retailer often maintains a few traditional retail outlets, most of their business has been done via catalogs mailed to customers, who then place orders over the telephone or by mail. Presenting their catalog online and accepting online orders is a relatively small step that allows these retailers to reach many more customers. These companies have been referred to as **flips-and-clicks** retailers (Figure 8-9).

Business-to-Business E-commerce

Business-to-business (B2B) e-commerce involves one business providing another business with the materials and supplies it needs to conduct its operations. You don't read much about this type of e-commerce because, as one writer put it, "A story about companies bidding against one another for contracts to supply nuts and bolts to create agricultural machinery is not hot copy." However, the numbers show that B2B e-commerce has a much greater impact on the economy than the B2C variety: worldwide B2B e-commerce is expected to grow from $1.9 trillion in 2002 to $8.5 trillion by 2005.

Although much B2B e-commerce currently takes place directly between a business and its suppliers, B2B **Internet exchanges** are being developed to provide electronic marketplaces for buyers and sellers in many industries. For example, the big three U.S. automakers (GM, Ford, and Chrysler) are backing an exchange for auto industry suppliers. On a global scale, a number of sites provide opportunities for companies worldwide to buy and sell chemical products (Figure 8-10). Advantages for buyers include reduced costs of procurement and the ability to consider a larger number of suppliers. Possible problems include security—a hacker attack on a major B2B exchange could bring an entire industry to its knees—and antitrust concerns that the exchanges could lead to price fixing within an industry.

Consumer-to-Consumer E-commerce

Consumer-to-consumer (C2C) e-commerce takes place over the many online auction sites. Before these sites debuted, selling one-of-a-kind items was a hit-or-miss proposition. Would you be able to connect with the few people who might be interested in what you had to sell? The newspaper classified ads were your best bet, but they reach a lim-

◄ **F I G U R E** **8-8**

Bricks-and-clicks.
Companies such as Macy's and Sears started out as tradtional retailers, but have developed a presence on the Internet. They are referred to by the term *bricks-and-clicks*.

ited geographical audience. Now, on sites such as eBay (Figure 8-11), your item is visible to anyone in the world with an Internet connection. These sites make buying and selling so easy that many people have set up home businesses trading over auction sites.

All is not rosy in this area, however. Between 40 percent and 50 percent of all reported Internet fraud takes place on online auctions. With over $3.1 billion in goods sold over eBay in the first quarter of 2002 alone, even their reported "less than 0.1 percent" rate of fraudulent transactions results in a significant number of fraud victims.

▶ PAYMENTS AND TAXES

You have seen the ads and perused the site, and now you want to make a purchase. How will you pay for it? And must you pay taxes on your purchase? These simple questions have rather complex answers that have kept the industry's attention since the beginning of online sales.

► **F I G U R E** **8-9**

Flips-and clicks. Many mail order retailers such as L. L. Bean and Land's End have expanded onto the Internet, resulting in the term *flips-and-clicks*.

E-commerce Payments

Some retail sites give you the option of phoning or faxing your order. Others allow you to place the order online, then call with your credit card number. They do this because they know that some people are leery of submitting their credit-card numbers over the network to an online retail site. These people fear that the card number may be intercepted in transit and then used illicitly to run up charges on the card. Although this is theoretically possible, it is highly unlikely. To begin with, the messages between the buyer and reputable online retailers are encrypted—encoded—so that they are not readable to the casual observer. It would take a skilled programmer to undo the encryption; frankly, there are more fruitful places to attack. The de facto standard for online transaction payments is the **Secure Sockets Layer** (**SSL**) protocol. However, most sites simply refer to it as "our secure server," and many customers have become comfortable using it. Unfortunately, some retail sites aren't as careful with your credit card information after they've received it. As recent media reports have highlighted, hackers have penetrated the security of several sites and stolen thousands of credit card numbers.

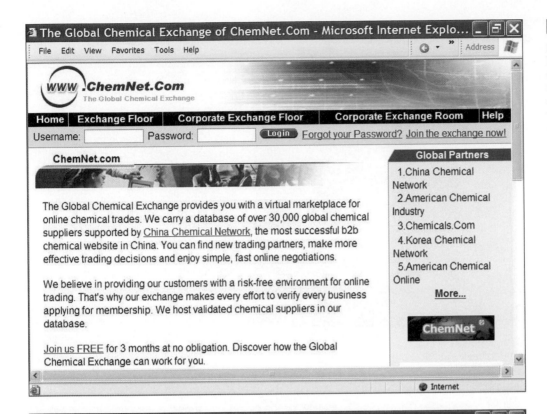

B2B Internet exchanges.
B2B Internet business exchanges provide electronic marketplaces for buyers and sellers in many industries. A worldwide chemical products exchange is shown here.

C2C e-commerce. Auction sites such as eBay allow consumers to both buy and sell from other consumers.

E-commerce Taxes

One of the little thrills of catalog shopping is that you might not have to pay local sales taxes on articles purchased. Under U.S. federal law, if a mail-order company from which you order is located out of state, it has to collect sales taxes for your state only if the company has some sort of physical presence (sometimes called a nexus) in your state, such as a branch store or a warehouse. Now try to apply that to Internet

► MAKING CONNECTIONS ◄ Free Internet E-mail Accounts

You probably already have an e-mail account provided by your ISP, employer, or school. So why do you need another one? Consider the following:

- You graduate from college, change employers, or decide to find a better ISP. All three situations result in a change of e-mail address and the resulting bother and possible confusion in notifying all your correspondents.

- Your employer doesn't approve of employees using business e-mail accounts for personal communications. And remember, most employers keep e-mail messages in log files, even after you delete them.

- You would like the convenience of checking your e-mail no matter where you are—a friend's house, the library, home, or at work.

- You don't have your own Internet access or e-mail address, relying instead on friends' computers or those at the local library.

In all of these situations a free Internet e-mail account could be just the answer. A number of sites now provide these accounts. The granddaddy of all is Hotmail, now offered by MSN. Most Internet portals, such as Yahoo! and Excite, include free e-mail to encourage you to keep returning. And some other sites, such as Ziplip, exist for the sole purpose of providing free e-mail.

To establish your free account, visit the site and click on the link that says, "Register for free e-mail" or something similar. The resulting screen(s) will ask you to enter registration information, including your choices for a user name and password. Unless it's a brand-new service, don't expect to find any neat names left—they're already spoken for. If you choose a user name that somebody else already has, you'll be asked to choose again, often with some alternatives offered. Once you settle on an available name and fill in the required registration information, you're all set. You can send and retrieve e-mail from any computer that is logged onto the Internet just by visiting your e-mail site and signing on with your user name and password.

The following are some things to look for in choosing a free e-mail provider:

- What is their privacy policy? What do they do with the personal data you provide when you register? Most use that data to provide targeted ads when you visit the site, but some may sell the data (including your e-mail address) to others. Some, such as Ziplip, require no personal data at all. There should be a link labeled "Privacy Policy" or something similar on the site. Read it!

- How easy is the service to use? Some are easy and intuitive; others require a lot more work to understand. All have a Help link, but not all Help is that helpful. The easiest way to evaluate ease of use is to sign up for an account and use it several times. After all, it's free. If you find it doesn't suit you, you can try another service.

- What features are supported? Some providers allow you to create a group address, so that a single message will be sent to everyone in the group. Providers also vary in the amount of storage provided for old e-mail. If you save everything, this could be important.

commerce, whose sellers are likely to be far away and whose "presence" any place is debatable. But that is just the beginning of the long-running debate on taxing the Internet. Some folks want to tax even using the Internet.

There are approximately 30,000 taxing entities—states, counties, cities—in the United States. If all of them were to be turned loose to get their slice of the pie, the Internet would be seriously burdened and perhaps irreparably harmed. The compromise, passed into law in October 1998, is called the **Internet Tax Freedom Act**. The act has four basic components:

1. It prohibits state and local governments from imposing taxes on Internet access charges, such as those billed by America Online or an Internet service provider.

2. It prohibits taxes from being imposed on out-of-state businesses through strained interpretations of "presence."

3. It creates a temporary commission to study taxation of Internet commerce and report back to Congress on whether the Internet ought to be taxed.

4. It calls on the executive branch to demand that foreign governments keep the Internet free of taxes and tariffs.

In summary, the act provides that the Internet be free of new taxes for three years while a committee determines whether taxes should be imposed and, if so, how to do so in a uniform way. Further, notice that nothing has changed in regard to imposing sales taxes. The act refers only to new taxes or to trying to interpret "presence" in some new way. State and local governments are allowed to impose sales taxes on Internet sales, provided that the tax is the same as that which would be imposed on the transactions if they were conducted in a more traditional manner, such as over the phone or through mail order. Although the act was set to expire in 2001, the **Internet Non-Discrimination Act**, passed in 2000, extends these provisions through 2005.

▶ PORTALS AND ADVERTISING

You know how network television earns money: Although broadcasts are free to viewers, the networks collect revenues from advertisers. Furthermore, the amount of money the networks charge advertisers is directly related to how popular the show is, that is, how many viewers are on hand to see the advertising. Now apply this technique to Web sites. Web sites that carry advertisements can charge for them at rates that are directly related to the number of visitors to the site: The more visitors, the higher the advertising rates.

Thus it is that a Web site wants to be your **portal** to the Internet—your everyday first stop, your neighborhood, your hangout. The site owners want you to come early and often. But, most of all, they want to persuade you to use them as your guide to the rest of the Internet.

Getting Personal

To be a good guide, the portal site begins by presenting content and links on a wide variety of topics, from health to movies to shopping. But to be a good guide to you personally, the portal site needs some information from you that it can use to personalize your use of the site. You will see a link on the portal site saying something like "My _____" (fill in the site name), or perhaps "Personalize" or "Customize." On the basis of the personal data you supply, the site can present local weather conditions, local news and sports scores, and even a portfolio of stocks you own. The more the portal offers you, the greater the likelihood that you will drop by often. Some portals go further, offering instructions on how to make the portal site the "home page" that appears each time you activate your browser to begin surfing the Internet.

Another Source of Money

Referral fees provide an even more significant revenue stream for portal Web sites. The portal Web site offers the news, sports, shops, and so forth from sources called **affiliates**, which the portal chooses. The affiliates—based on deals made with the portal—pay for the privilege. They may pay only for being listed on the portal site or—more likely—pay a percentage of a sale to any visitor who has clicked there from the portal site. For example, if a visitor at the Yahoo! site clicks on Clifford's Flowers, and then sends balloons from Clifford's to her sister across the country, Yahoo! will get a percent of the profit from that sale, simply because it made the referral.

Just who are these portal sites? Most are familiar names to Web surfers. Many started out as search engines and then expanded their content and retail connections. A well-known portal is Yahoo!, which was begun as a search site by two college students (Figure 8-12). (By the way, they named it Yahoo! as an acronym for "Yet Another Hierarchical Officious Oracle," although no one bothers with that windy title anymore.) Yahoo!'s advertising campaign has been so successful that it is familiar even to people who have never used the Internet. Other content-rich portals are MSN, Excite, Netscape, Go Network, and America Online. The America Online site is indeed the first site seen by AOL customers jumping from AOL-specific content to the

Web Site Analysis

You have probably seen Web sites that include a counter with phrasing such as "2,307 people have visited this site" or perhaps "You are visitor 471." But you are unlikely to see such notices on a professionally produced business site. Why? Probably two reasons. One is that these Web sites want you to assume that they are a popular stopover and, of course, have many visitors. Why tell you—or the competition—just how many? A second reason is that they already have this information, and much more, via Web site analysis software.

Web analysis software runs in the background of a site. As a visitor, you are not aware of its existence. But the analysis software makes note of everything it can about you: from which site you came and at what time of day, how long you stayed, what parts of the site you visited, what files you downloaded, and much more.

This information is collected on an ongoing basis and presented in useful reports and charts to the Web site owner. Suppose, for example, that the analyzed site had posted advertising banners on several different sites. If the Web site analysis report shows that several hundred visitors came directly from site A, but hardly any came from site B, then advertising dollars are better spent on site A and perhaps should be withdrawn from site B.

▶ **FIGURE 8-12**

A portal. Portal sites hope to be your main site, the place where you jump off to the rest of the Web. Yahoo!, shown here, is a popular portal site.

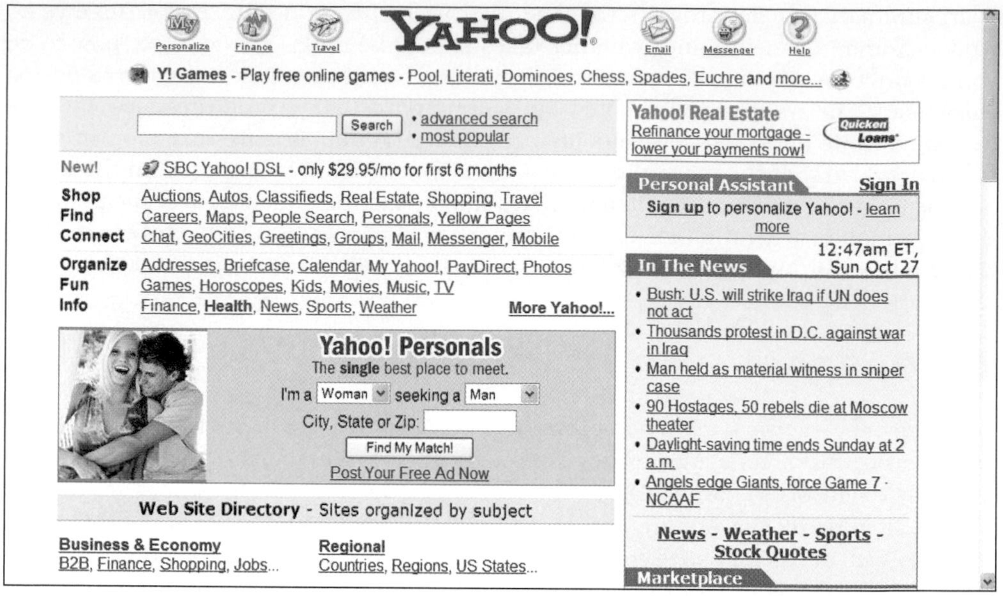

Internet, but it is also a portal site in its own right that often is accessed by people who are not members of AOL.

Portals continue to grow in number and in content. The ultimate goal of each portal is to make its site your one-stop site on the Internet. Surfers would never settle for one site, of course, but it seems likely that they will settle on one site as their personalized—and often-visited—home page.

More Advertising

We have lived with advertising all our lives. It can be intrusive and annoying, but often it is informative, interesting, or even funny. For the most part, however, it is just in the background. For the user, the main advantage of advertising is that it pays all or most of the costs of the message on radio and television, in magazines and newspapers, and on the Internet.

Many advertisements on Web sites are in the form of **banner ads**, which were originally in the shape of a long rectangle. Advertisers pay the host site for the privilege of showing their ad on the site; it is their hope, of course, that users will be sufficiently attracted to the ad that they will click on the banner and thus be transported to the site of the advertiser. Many small ads are, in fact, in a variety of shapes. Some of them are little applets, showing some sort of motion to get our attention.

Banners do not work as well as advertisers would like because users are often reluctant to click through, that is, leave the current site, in which they are presumably interested, and go to the advertised site. One solution to this problem is the live banner, which includes audio and video to give the user more product information without leaving the site. This approach has proved popular but is not without drawbacks: The live banners work slowly, especially with slower modems, and are expensive to develop.

The most annoying advertisements on the Web are the **pop-over ads**, which open a new window on top of your current window, and **pop-under ads**, which open a new window underneath your current window and only become visible when you close the window you are viewing. Both types require extra mouse movement and clicking to delete and distract the user from the business at hand.

The most effective Web advertisements are **context-sensitive**; that is, the ad is related to the subject matter on the screen. As the advertisers put it, there is greater "click through and conversion," meaning that the ad is more likely to be clicked and, once at the advertised site, the user is more likely to buy something. Notice, for example, in Figure 8-13, that choosing the topic Cruises elicits ads about cruises, whereas choosing the topic Entertainment summons ads for DVD rentals. Since the

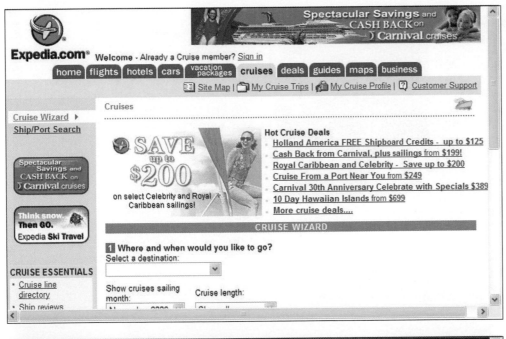

(a)

(b)

user is in control of the path through the Web, it is reasonable to assume that he or she is more receptive to ads on his or her chosen topic.

Web site ads have disadvantages for users. One is that they often have graphics and perhaps even applets, both of which take time to load. Another disadvantage is that as the page is loading on the screen, the ads load first, or at least early, so that you will not see the entire page until the ads are in place. That is, the site manager wants to make sure that you see the advertisements before you go clicking off somewhere else.

▶ INTRANETS

Although many businesses use the Internet to promote their products and services to the public, they are finding that an even more useful application is for their internal—company-only—purposes, hence the intranet.

Not all IT professionals work hands-on with the computers that are their responsibility. Take Greg, for instance. Greg works Tier Two technical support for an Internet service provider. Tier Two means that Greg gets to speak with the clients having the really difficult problems, but at least he has more time at his disposal to do so.

Solving problems for someone when the computer is hundreds or thousands of miles away can require a lot of patience. "You just really have to know your stuff," says Greg. "Sometimes I have to close my eyes, and try to see the client's computer on the other end of the line." He has to know all the ISP's software by heart, as well as all of the most common Internet applications.

"That's the real trick to getting to the bottom of a problem. If you know what you're talking about, it's easy to get the answers you need from someone who might be new to the Internet. If I can describe to the client what he or she should be seeing on the screen, that helps me guide him or her to find the answers I need so that we can fix it."

Greg works on things from both sides of the problem. Not only does he enlist his clients' help to find out what is shown on their computers, he also looks to the ISP's network technicians to help him determine exactly where the problem lies. For instance, examining an e-mail problem right at the e-mail server can often give that last bit of insight needed to close the case.

Vendors promoting their intranet software products in magazine advertisements often make a play on the word—perhaps InTRAnet or even Intranet. They do not want you to think that they are simply misspelling "Internet." In fact, an **intranet** is a private Internet-like network that is internal to a certain company. The number of intranets has been growing rapidly. Every Fortune 500 company either has an intranet or is planning one. Part of the reason for the phenomenal growth is the relative ease of setting up an intranet.

Setting Up an Intranet

It's fast, it's easy, it's inexpensive—relatively speaking, of course. The components of an intranet are familiar ones: the same ones that are used for the Internet. Hardware requirements include a server and computers used for access. These probably exist because most companies already have local area networks; this is why setting up an intranet is fast, easy, and inexpensive. The Internet TCP/IP protocols must be in place. The server, which will act as a clearinghouse for all data regardless of source, needs its own software. The server will process requests and also perhaps pull data from traditional sources such as a mainframe computer. As on the Internet, each access computer needs a browser.

The intranet developers will doubtless devote the most time and attention to writing the Web pages that employees will see and use. The pages must be well designed and easy to follow, opting for function over glitz. A typical opening page would probably have an attractive company logo and several clickable generic icons to represent functions. One click would lead to a more detailed page and so on. By presenting information in the same way to every computer, the developers can pull all the computers, software, and data files that dot the corporate landscape into a single system that helps employees find information wherever it resides.

Intranets at Work

A well-designed intranet can be used by most employees from day one. They can point and click and link to sites that contain information previously locked away behind functionaries and forms. Suppose, for example, that an employee needs to check on the status of her benefits. Traditionally, she would probably have to find the right form, fill it out correctly, submit it, and wait a few days for a response. Now all she has to do is point and click, give some identifying information such as Social Security number, and the information shows up on the screen and can be printed.

Employee information is just the beginning. Typical applications are internal job openings, marketing, vacation requests, corporate policy information, and perhaps company training courses. Some even include the local weather report and the daily cafeteria menu. Intranets even cut down on the flow of e-mail. Management can, instead of sending out mass e-mail to employees, post notices on a Web page and leave it to employees to check it regularly or use push technology to send information to them as needed.

The Internet Too

An intranet can remain private and isolated, but most companies choose to link their intranets to the Internet. This gives employees access to Internet resources and to other employees with their own intranets in geographically dispersed places. The employee access to the public Internet should not be confused with public access to the company intranet; the intranet is private.

However, companies may choose to provide access to their intranets to selected customers and suppliers. Such an arrangement is called an **extranet**. Some companies are finding that their long-standing relationships with customers and suppliers can be handled more easily and more inexpensively with an extranet than with more traditional electronic data interchange—EDI—systems.

► VIRTUAL PRIVATE NETWORKS

A **virtual private network** (**VPN**) provides technology that uses the public Internet as a channel for private data communication. A VPN essentially carves out a private passageway through the Internet. Thus a VPN allows remote offices, company road warriors, and even business partners or customers to use the Internet, rather than pricey private lines, to reach company networks. The idea of the VPN is to give the company the same capabilities at a much lower cost by sharing the public infrastructure.

Virtual private networks may be new, but the tunneling technology on which they are based is well established. **Tunneling**, also called **encapsulation**, is a way to transfer data between two similar networks over an intermediate network. Tunneling software encloses one type of data-packet protocol into the packet of another protocol. **Point-to-Point Tunneling Protocol** (**PPTP**) is the standard protocol for the packet that is doing the tunneling. The original protocol, the one holding the tunnel, is the standard Internet TCP/IP protocol. Thus organizations can use the Internet to transmit data "privately" by embedding their own network protocol—PPTP technology—within the TCP/IP packets carried by the Internet.

VPN tunneling adds another dimension to the tunneling procedure. Before encapsulation takes place, the packets are encrypted—encoded—so that the data is unreadable to outsiders. The encapsulated packets travel through the Internet until they reach their destination; the packets are then separated and returned to their original format. Authentication technology is used to make sure the client has authorization to contact the server.

By replacing expensive private network bandwidth with relatively low-cost Internet bandwidth, a company can slash operating costs and simplify communications. No longer needed are the 800 lines and long-distance charges; employees simply place local or toll-free calls to Internet service providers (ISPs) to make the connection. Employees working from home can use VPN technology to communicate with their company's intranet. VPNs also reduce in-house network management responsibilities because much of the remote communications burden is turned over to ISPs.

▲

We have said that the Internet is interesting and fun, and it is. But it is much more than that. The Internet represents a new and important business model and, indeed, an entire new way of looking at industry and commerce.

CHAPTER REVIEW

► Summary and Key Terms

- In 1969 the Defense Department set up a connected group of geographically dispersed computers called **ARPANET**, for Advanced Research Projects Agency Network.

- In 1986, the National Science Foundation connected its large network, **NSFnet**, to ARPANET, and the resulting network became known as the Internet.

- The Internet **backbone** (the high-speed circuits that carry the bulk of Internet traffic), was originally provided by NSFnet, but in 1995, NFSnet withdrew, leaving commercial carriers to bear the load.

- In 1990 Tim Berners-Lee made getting around the Internet easier by designing a set of links for one computer to connect to another. He saw the set of links as a spider's web; hence the name **Web**. Berners-Lee's laboratory at the **CERN site** is considered the birthplace of the **World Wide Web**.

- A **link** on a Web site is easy to see: It is either colored text called hypertext or image that causes the pointer to change to a pointing hand as it passes over the link. A mouse click on the link transports the user to the site represented by the link.

- A **browser** is interface software used to explore the Internet. As a student in 1993, **Marc Andreessen** led a team that invented Mosaic, the first graphical browser.

- A message to be sent to another computer is divided up into **packets**, each labeled with its destination address; the packets are reassembled at the destination address. The software that takes care of the packets is **Transmission Control Protocol/Internet Protocol** (**TCP/IP**). TCP does the packeting and reassembling of the message. The IP part of the protocol handles the addressing, seeing to it that packets are routed across multiple computers.

- An Internet user needs a computer with a modem and its related software, an Internet service provider, and a browser. An **Internet service provider** (**ISP**) provides the server computer and the software to connect to the Internet. An **online service** (also called an **information utility**) also provides an Internet connection but additionally includes extensive members-only content.

- When you start your browser software, it will display either the **home page**—initial page—of the Web site for the company that created your particular browser or some other site designated by your ISP. The browser shows three parts on the screen: the browser control panel, consisting of lines of menus and buttons; the browser display window to show the current site; and a status line at the bottom. The page can be scrolled—moved up and down—by using the scroll bar on the right.

- Using a mouse permits commands to be issued through a series of **menus**, a series of choices that are normally laid out across the top of the screen. The menus are called **pull-down menus** because each initial choice, when clicked with a mouse, reveals lower-level choices. **Buttons** can also invoke commands. If you rest the cursor over a button for just a few seconds, a small text message called a **screen tip** will reveal its function.

- The **Uniform Resource Locator** (**URL**) is a string of letters and symbols that is the unique address of a Web page or file on the Internet. A Web page URL begins with the protocol http, which stands for **HyperText Transfer Protocol**, the means of communicating using links. Next comes the **domain name**, which is the address of the Internet service provider or other host. The last part of the domain name is called a **top-level domain** and represents the purpose of the organization or entity or its country of origin. The last part of the URL, often the most complex, specifies the exact location of the Web page on the host computer.

- A **hot list**—called Bookmarks, Favorites, or something similar—stores favorite sites and their URLs.

- A **plug-in** is software that can be added to a browser to enhance its functionality.

- **JavaScript** and **VBScript** are scripting languages that are used to produce a series of instructions included with a Web page that are interpreted and executed by your browser. Java **applets** are small programs that provide multimedia effects and other capabilities on Web pages. Microsoft's **ActiveX controls** provide similar functionality.

- The **Wireless Application Protocol** (**WAP**) is used by wireless access providers to format Web pages for viewing on mobile handheld devices.

- A **search engine** is software that lets a user specify search terms; the search engine then finds sites that fit those terms. A **spider** program follows links throughout the Web, indexing the pages it finds in the search engine's database. A **metasearch** uses software that automatically runs your query on several search engines. An Internet **directory** employs human researchers to organize and categorize Internet sites.

- **Usenet**, or **newsgroups**, is an informal network of computers that allow the posting and reading of messages in newsgroups that focus on specific topics. **Newsreader** software, included in most browsers, is used to participate in newsgroups. A list of frequently asked questions (**FAQs**) provides information on topics already covered in the newsgroup. **Netiquette** refers to the general rules of good behavior on the Internet. An abusive message attacking someone is called a **flame**. A **flame war** is an exchange of flames. **Moderated newsgroups** are controlled by a **moderator**, who determines what messages are posted.

- Computers on the Internet have a standard way to transfer copies of files, a set of rules called **FTP**, for **file transfer protocol**. Computers that maintain collections of downloadable files are called **FTP servers**. Most downloading is done by a method called **anonymous FTP**, meaning that a user can be named Anonymous and the password can be simply the user's e-mail address.

- **Telnet** is a protocol that allows remote users to use their PC to log onto a host computer system over the Internet and use it as if they were sitting at a local terminal on that system.

- **E-mail** is the most-used feature of the Internet. E-mail is provided through a **mail server** maintained by your network or ISP that provides you with an **e-mail address**, consisting of your user name and the mail server's domain name, and a **mailbox** to store your messages. **E-mail client software** on your PC allows you to retrieve, create, send, store, print, and delete your e-mail messages. E-mail **filters** can direct incoming e-mail to specific folders and even reject **spam**, unsolicited junk e-mail that can overwhelm a users in-box.

- The world of **electronic commerce**, or, more commonly, **e-commerce**, buying and selling over the Internet, represents a new economic order. Customers can buy just about anything on the Internet.

- **Business-to-consumer** (**B2C**) e-commerce refers to retail transactions between an online business and an individual. **Pure-play** retailers do business exclusively over the Internet, **bricks-and-clicks** retailers are traditional retailers who have established Internet sites, and **flips-and-clicks** retailers are mail-order retailers who have embraced the Internet.

- **Business-to-business** (**B2B**) e-commerce involves one business providing another business with the materials and supplies that it needs to conduct its operations. B2B **Internet exchanges** are electronic marketplaces to connect buyers and sellers in many industries.

- **Consumer-to-consumer** (**C2C**) e-commerce takes place between consumers over the many online auction sites.

- Since many people are concerned about the security of online transactions, some retail sites give you the option of phoning or faxing your order. Others allow you to place the order online, then call with your credit card number. Most online transaction payments use the **Secure Sockets Layer** (**SSL**) protocol to encrypt credit card numbers and other personal information.

- The **Internet Tax Freedom Act** imposed a three-year moratorium (which began in October 1998) on taxes imposed on the Internet and called for a committee to study the matter. The **Internet Non-Discrimination Act** extended the moratorium until 2005.

- A Web site that is used as a gateway or guide to the Internet is called **affiliate** sites and **banner ads** placed on the portal's Web page.

- Users who leave the current site for an advertised site are said to click through; to get business from users who will not click through, a live banner, which lets a user get more information about a product without leaving the current site, may be used.

- Other types of Web advertisements include **pop-over ads**, which open a new window on top of your current window, and **pop-under ads**, which open a new window underneath your current window and only become visible when you close the window you are viewing.

- The most effective Web advertisements are **context-sensitive**; that is, the ad is related to the subject matter on the screen.

- An **intranet** is a private Internet-like network that is internal to a certain company. Companies may choose to provide access to their intranets to selected customers and suppliers. Such an arrangement is called an **extranet**.

- A **virtual private network** (**VPN**) provides technology that uses the public Internet backbone as a channel for private data communication. **Tunneling**, also called **encapsulation**, is a way to transfer data between two similar networks over an intermediate network by enclosing one type of data packet protocol into the packet of another protocol. **Point-to-Point Tunneling Protocol** (**PPTP**) is a standard tunneling protocol.

▶ Critical Thinking Questions

1. After he left school, Marc Andreessen, in his own words, wanted to make a "Mosaic killer." He felt that he had not been given sufficient credit for his college efforts and set out to make his fortune commercially with Netscape Navigator, the forerunner of Netscape Communicator. He did. Dr. Tim Berners-Lee, however, rejected numerous commercial offers. He felt that if he cashed in on his invention, it would compromise the Web, which he wanted to be available to everyone. Are both these positions defensible? Comment.

2. How reliable are search engines? Why might one search engine give a different set of results than another?

3. Some established companies fret over whether or not to offer their goods and services over the Internet, possibly in competition with their traditional outlets. If the decision were up to you, at what point might you go forward with a complete retail site?

4. What is your opinion of the advertisements that frequently appear on Web sites? The answer is not as simple as it may first appear. Keep in mind that just as commercials pay for free television, Web advertisements pay for the Internet. In answering this question, ignore the access fees—cable or satellite fees for television and ISP or online service fees for the Internet. In other words, would you be willing to pay a small fee every time that you visit a site that contains no advertisements? How do you think these fees would be charged and collected?

5. Some businesses, organizations, and educational institutions place information about themselves on the Internet as well as on their company, organizational, or institutional intranets. Describe the types of information that a company, organization, or institution might place on their Internet site, and the types of information that they would place on their intranet. Does your school use the Internet and have an intranet? If it has an intranet, can students, faculty, and staff access it from both on-campus computers as well as from off-campus computers?

► STUDENT STUDY GUIDE

Multiple Choice

1. The creator of the Web was
   a. Rand Corporation
   b. ARPANET
   c. Tim Berners-Lee
   d. Marc Andreessen

2. The protocol for downloading files over the Internet carries the abbreviation
   a. HTTP
   b. FTP
   c. ISP
   d. URL

3. The software on a user's computer that provides a graphical interface to access the Internet is called a(n)
   a. URL
   b. FTP
   c. ISP
   d. browser

4. A message to be sent to another computer over the Internet is divided into
   a. URLs
   b. hyperregions
   c. packets
   d. frames

5. ISP stands for
   a. Internet Serial Port
   b. Internet Switching Protocol
   c. Internet Service Provider
   d. none of the above

6. A Web site's initial page is called a(n)
   a. home page
   b. mother page
   c. primary page
   d. entry page

7. The first major network of computers was
   a. World Wide Web
   b. BIGnet
   c. EarthNet
   d. ARPANET

8. The most used top-level domain is
   a. .net
   b. .edu
   c. .com
   d. .gov

9. Microsoft adds functionality to Web pages by using which of the following?
   a. Java
   b. Helper Apps
   c. JavaScript
   d. ActiveX controls

10. A newsreader is
    a. a person who reads a newspaper
    b. software that is used for Usenet
    c. a device used by the visually impaired
    d. none of the above

11. Another name for tunneling is
    a. portal
    b. cabling
    c. encapsulation
    d. bandwidth

12. A Web site that is used as a gateway or guide to the Internet is a(n)
    a. portal
    b. backbone
    c. ISDN
    d. extranet

13. The term that is used to describe the high-speed communication circuits that carry the bulk of Internet traffic is
    a. encapsulation
    b. backbone
    c. tunneling
    d. e-commerce

14. A technology that uses the public Internet as a channel for private data communications is known as
    a. e-commerce
    b. DSL
    c. VPN
    d. ISDN

15. America Online is the largest
    a. Wide Area Network (WAN)
    b. online service
    c. phone company
    d. manufacturer of modems

16. Users who leave the current site by clicking on a banner ad are said to
    a. push
    b. tunnel
    c. stream
    d. click through

17. An advertisement that is related to what is currently showing on the Web page is called
    a. encapsulation
    b. context-sensitive
    c. a portal
    d. the backbone

18. Which of the following allows remote users to access a company network from their PC as if they were at a local terminal?
    a. IRC
    b. FTP
    c. Usenet
    d. Telnet

19. Which factor was NOT a major contributor to the emergence of the Internet?
    a. links
    b. browsers
    c. banner ads
    d. TCP/IP

20. Which of the following uses human researchers to organize and categorize information on the Internet??
    a. search engines
    b. directories
    c. metasearch sites
    d. all of the above

True/False

T   F   1. Browser software is kept on the host computer.

T   F   2. In an URL, the domain name is the address of the host computer for the Web site.

T   F   3. The inventor of the graphical browser is Marc Andreessen.

T   F   4. TCP/IP is the standard Internet protocol.

T   F   5. Plug-ins increase the functionality of browsers.

T   F   6. States are not permitted to assess taxes on Internet purchases.

T   F   7. A link on a Web site is usually colored text or an image or icon.

T   F   8. Spamming means sending a message that attacks others.

T   F   9. The anonymous Telnet protocol is used to upload and download files.

T   F   10. E-mail is the most used feature of the Internet.

T   F   11. Most browsers no longer require users to enter http:// in Web addresses.

T   F   12. Java is the name of the newest Internet browser.

T   F   13. Two companies associated with the Internet backbone are DSL and ISDN.

T   F   14. An intranet is a public network and an extranet is a private network.

T   F   15. A live banner ad lets a user see advertised information without leaving the current site.

T   F   16. Encapsulation is related to virtual private network technology.

T   F   17. E-commerce sites display their wares but do not permit actual purchases of goods via the Internet.

T   F   18. An affiliate site shares the profit from a sale with the site that made the referral.

T   F   19. One problem with banner ads is that users are often reluctant to leave the current site to go to the advertised site.

T   F   20. B2C e-commerce has a much larger dollar volume than B2B e-commerce.

Fill-In

1. _____ is the protocol that uses links to move from one site to another on the Internet.

2. Java _____ are small programs that can be included in Web pages to provide animation effects.

3. _____ is a protocol that formats Web pages for viewing on handheld devices.

4. A(n) _____ runs your search request on several search engines simultaneously.

5. _____ is an informal network of computers that allows the posting and reading of messages that focus on specific topics.

6. Appropriate behavior in network communications is referred to as _____.

7. A(n) _____ newsgroup is controlled by an individual who determines which messages get posted.

8. Search engines use a _____ program that follows links through the Web to indcx sites for the search engine's database.

9. The _____ is a string of letters and symbols that is the unique address of a Web page or file on the Internet.

10. A URL consists of three main components: _____, _____, and _____.

11. A hot list of favorite sites is also known as _____ or _____.

12. The last part of the domain name is called the _____ and represents either the purpose of the organization or its country of origin.

13. The major communication circuits that connect Internet servers across wide geographical areas and carry the bulk of traffic are collectively called the Internet _____.

14. A private Internet-like network that is internal to a company is called a(n) _____.

15. In the context of a VPN, another word for encapsulation is _____.

16. Portal sites collect money from sites to which they refer visitors; these sites are called _____.

17. A Web site that is used as a gateway or guide to the Internet is called a(n) _____.

18. A(n) _____ is software added to a browser to increase its functionality.

19. A(n) _____ is an abusive message attacking someone posted in a newsgroup.

20. _____ retailers do business exclusively over the Internet.

21. Internet _____ are electronic marketplaces that allow businesses in an industry to buy from and sell to each other.

22. _____ e-commerce takes place between consumers over online auction sites.

23. _____ is a protocol that uses encryption to protect personal information traveling across the Internet.

24. The term _____ refers to an arrangement where a company's customers and suppliers are allowed access to its internal network over the Internet.

25. E-mail client software often includes _____, which allow you to direct incoming messages to specific folders and even delete spam.

► ANSWERS

Multiple Choice

1. c	6. a	11. c	16. d
2. b	7. d	12. a	17. b
3. d	8. c	13. b	18. d
4. c	9. d	14. c	19. c
5. c	10. b	15. b	20. b

True/False

1. F	6. F	11. T	16. T
2. T	7. T	12. F	17. F
3. T	8. F	13. F	18. T
4. T	9. F	14. F	19. T
5. T	10. T	15. T	20. F

Fill-In

1. HTTP
2. applets
3. WAP
4. metasearch
5. Usenet
6. netiquette
7. moderated
8. spider
9. URL
10. protocol, domain name, path/directory/filename (location on host)
11. bookmarks, favorites
12. top-level domain
13. backbone
14. intranet
15. tunneling
16. affiliates
17. portal
18. plug-in
19. flame
20. pure play
21. exchanges
22. C2C
23. SSL
24. extranet
25. filters

Planet Internet

Let's Chat

Want to send text messages to a distant friend in real-time? Want to participate in discussions on one of over 12,000 topics while chatting on the equivalent of the old-time "party line" telephone? Want to enter the world of nicks, ops, IRC cops, and bots? Then Internet Relay Chat (IRC) is for you.

What is IRC?

IRC is an old medium by Internet standards. Originally developed in 1988, IRC messages were already whizzing around the Net well before the invention of the graphical Web browser. IRC is organized into channels, each of which is transmitted worldwide by one or more servers.

How do I get started?

To get started on IRC, you need to download a client. This is a program that lets you connect to an IRC server and exchange messages. Two of the most popular clients are mIRC and pirch.

Once you install the client, you choose a "nick," or nickname, that identifies you online. Then you can choose from a list of servers to which you can connect.

Some servers are part of networks, host computers that all carry the same channels. The channel #chat on one Efnet network server will be the same #chat as on another Efnet server. Larger servers

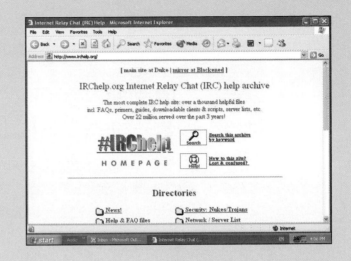

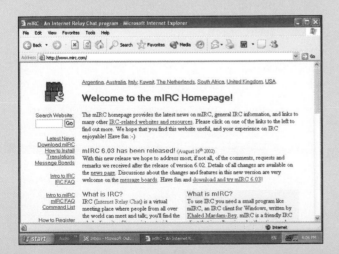

may have over 30,000 simultaneous users spread over the channels they carry.

What's next?

To find a channel of interest, type /list. You will be shown a list of channels you can enter, the number of users currently in that channel, and their nominal topic. You will quickly note that the channel names (preceded by #) will not necessarily have anything to do with their current content. Channels don't always have to stick to a specific topic; you might find people in #windows talking about football teams, for instance.

Caution.

Keep in mind that the content of some channels is not appropriate for all audiences, and parents should be particularly careful not to allow young children unsupervised access. Anonymity is one of the key features of IRC, so take advantage of it by never revealing personally identifying information such as your street address or credit information.

Instant Messaging.

Another way to chat with friends over the Internet is by using instant messaging software.

Instant messaging is similar to IRC chatting in that you still type a message to another person, who sees it instantly, and can reply right away in turn.

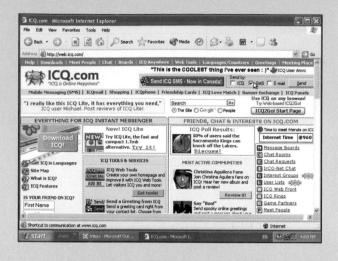

The main difference with instant messaging is that you're not broadcasting your message in a public forum—it's going directly to the person on the other end. The three most popular instant messaging applications for PC are: AOL Instant Messenger (AIM), ICQ, and Microsoft Messenger. For example, in the image above, the little yellow "note" icon in the system tray blinks to indicate a waiting ICQ message, while the green flower shows that the user is connected to the ICQ network.

The other key difference is that with an instant messaging application, you have to know who you're sending the message to before you can send it. Like e-mail, this is usually done by giving someone your instant messaging account number (or name), but most messaging networks will also allow you to search their database of accounts for people.

Each instant messaging application uses its own network, so you can only chat with people who are using the same application. If you want to start using an instant messenger, make sure to check with your friends and colleagues first to find out which one is most commonly used. That way, you'll be sure to communicate with the largest number of people.

Instant messaging applications also let you know who is online, and who isn't, so you know when you can send a message to someone.

Like IRC, some instant messaging services do have public chat forums that you can log into and chat with just anybody. However, the focus and advantage of instant messaging has always been that it's a fast way of checking to see if a contact is online, and then sending that person a message. . . . instantly!

Internet Exercises:

1. **Structured exercise.** Browse to one of the introductory IRC pages linked from http://www.prenhall.com/capron. Answer the following questions:

   - How would you "wave" to someone on IRC?

   - How do you change your "nick" on IRC?

   - What IRC client program would be required for your own, or your school's computer?

2. **Free-form exercise.** Find the code of conduct, chat rules, or etiquette guidelines for an IRC chat server or channel. For what specific behaviors, over and above those that are clearly illegal in your country, can a user be kicked or banned from the server?

3. **Advanced exercise.** Using an IRC client program, or one of the browser-based chat programs, enter a channel of your choice and note the following:

   - Which channel did you choose? Why?

   - Did the majority of participants stick to the nominal topic of the channel?

   - How many users were in the channel when you were there?

   - What conduct, if any, did you see that seemed to violate the server rules?

   - How helpful, educational, or entertaining would you rate your experience?

Social and Ethical Issues in Computing:
Doing the Right Thing

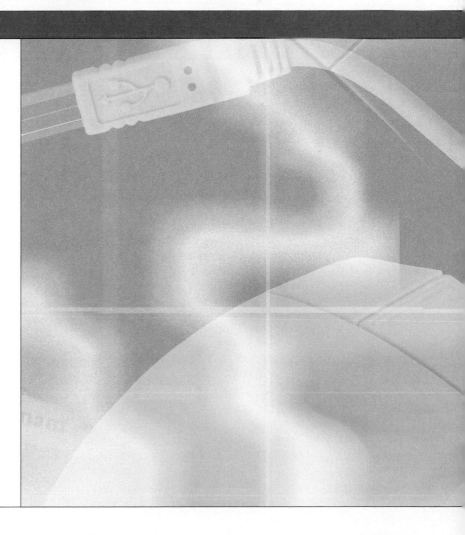

Social and Ethical Issues in Computing:
Doing the Right Thing

CHAPTER 9

Lynn Stinson works as an accounts receivable clerk at a small company. Her workday revolves around resolving customer problems with billing statements and contacting customers with overdue balances to convince them to make payment arrangements. Twenty-two years ago she graduated from a community college with an A.S. degree in Accounting and took a position as a bookkeeper. After working for several years, Lynn quit to raise her two daughters. When the younger daughter left for college two years ago, she reentered the workforce, quickly finding her current position.

Although Lynn enjoys dealing with customers and helping them solve their problems, she didn't see much opportunity for advancement. Last year, she decided to return to school in the evenings to pursue a B.S. degree in management. One of the courses she was required to take was a business computing course that covered the basics of several common computer applications (word processing, spreadsheets, and databases) as well as general computer concepts. One evening the professor was discussing the topic of ergonomics, adapting equipment to better meet human needs, and pointing out some of the symptoms that result from poor workplace design.

Lynn realized that she had been experiencing some of those symptoms herself. She often finished the day with a stiff neck and shoulders and had begun experiencing lower back pain. When she checked with several coworkers, she found that they, too, had been having similar problems. She did some research on the Internet about ergonomic workplace design, documenting the costs involved and the benefits that employees would experience, including fewer health problems and increased productivity. Many of the changes were inexpensive, such as using wrist rests while keying and adjusting room lighting. Others, such as purchasing ergonomically designed furniture, were more expensive.

Lynn approached her boss with her findings. Impressed with the quality and detail of her work, he told her that the company was in the early stages of planning an office remodeling project and invited her to join the project team.

▶ A FIRST LOOK AT SOCIAL ISSUES AND ETHICS IN COMPUTING

Not too many years ago, most people were able to ignore computers and computing entirely. That is no longer possible. Almost every aspect of our lives involves computers in some way. Looking through help wanted ads, you'll find that most jobs require at least a minimum level of computer skills; the higher the pay, the higher the skill level required. Our entire transportation system relies on computers, from air traffic control to computer-controlled traffic lights. Medical care revolves around computers: scheduling appointments, filing insurance claims, billing patients, and even assisting doctors with the latest medical procedures.

With this high level of integration of computing into society, it is no longer desirable to leave the social and ethical issues of computing to the experts; everyone must become knowledgeable and involved. This chapter considers many of the issues with which you should become familiar.

▶ THE DIGITAL DIVIDE

One of the major issues confronting society today is the growing **digital divide** that separates the computing haves from the have-nots. As those with access to computers and the Internet take advantage of the personal and economic opportunities provided by that access, those without access fall further and further behind. Within individual countries, the major divisions occur between urban and rural, rich and poor. Worldwide, the divide is between industrialized and non-industrialized nations.

Within the United States, several initiatives have been taken to narrow the divide. The FCC administers the **Universal Service Fund** that helps service providers with the higher costs of providing communication services to rural areas. The Federal **E-Rate** program adds a little to everyone's telephone bill to provide rate subsidies for Internet access for schools and libraries. The subsidies range from 20 percent to 90 percent, depending on economic factors. CTCNet, a nonprofit organization dedicated to providing computing resources to disadvantaged neighborhoods, has received millions of dollars in grants from the National Science Foundation and many private corporations to set up community technology centers where children and adults can take advantage of computers and Internet access.

Worldwide, thousands of initiatives exist within disadvantaged regions and countries to improve access to the digital world. Africa ONE is a project that is creating a fiber-optic network to connect the nations of Africa to each other and provide increased connectivity to the rest of the world. One other example is the Peruvian Telecentre Franchises project, which is establishing a franchise structure to provide telephone and Internet access to small towns and rural areas throughout Peru.

► WORKPLACE ISSUES

As workers spend more and more of their time using computers, several workplace computing issues have become important. Physical stress caused by computer use affects many employees. Employer monitoring has caused controversy and raised the level of mental stress among employees. The environmental impact of businesses' use of computers has become significant.

Healthy Computing

Can all this computing be good for you? Are there any unhealthy side effects? The computer seems harmless enough. How bad can it be, sitting in a padded chair in a climate-controlled office? Health questions have been raised by the people who sit all day in front of computer screens. Does the monitor produce harmful emissions? What about eyestrain? And what about the age-old back problem? Then there is repetitive strain injury (RSI), which may affect workers who hold their hands over a keyboard. RSI is caused by speed, repetition, awkward positioning, and holding a static position for a long period of time. Carpal tunnel syndrome is the most prevalent RSI.

Ergonomic Equipment

Workers can do a number of things to take care of themselves. A good place to begin is with an ergonomically designed workstation. In its formal sense, **ergonomics** is the use of research in designing systems, programs, or devices that are appropriate to use for their intended purposes. In the context of computers, ergonomics refers to human factors related to the use of computers. Begin with a pneumatically adjustable chair with five feet at its base, a keyboard platform set to the proper height, and a monitor that can be raised, lowered, tilted, and swiveled to suit the user. Lighting should be adjusted to minimize glare on the screen. A properly designed workstation takes a variety of factors into account, such as the distance from the eyes to the screen and the angle of the arms and wrists (Figure 9-1). Of course, none of this does any good unless the user is trained in the effective use of the workstation.

Although numerous tests have failed to show any harmful effects from the small amount of radiation produced by a typical computer monitor, many people remain concerned. Actions you can take to minimize your radiation exposure include sitting directly in front of the screen (most radiation is emitted from the sides and back), sitting as far as possible from the screen (the level of radiation decreases dramatically as distance increases), and using an anti-radiation screen cover (Figure 9-2). Also, LCD and gas plasma monitors produce much lower emission levels than do CRTs.

Ergonomic Behavior

In addition to using properly designed and configured equipment, workers must use the equipment correctly to prevent injury. The following are some guidelines to follow to ensure the best results.

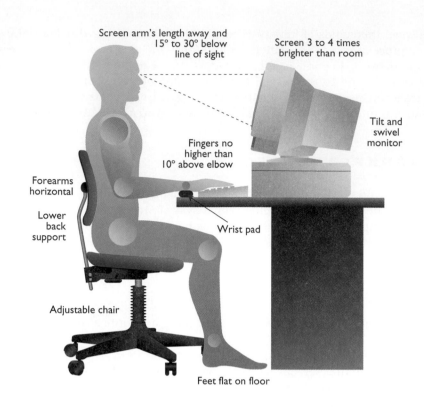

An ergonomically designed workstation. Start with the right equipment, such as an adjustable chair and a monitor that can be tilted and swiveled. It is up to the worker to sit in the proper manner—back supported, feet flat on the floor, and so forth.

Screen arm's length away and 15° to 30° below line of sight

Screen 3 to 4 times brighter than room

Tilt and swivel monitor

Fingers no higher than 10° above elbow

Forearms horizontal

Lower back support

Wrist pad

Adjustable chair

Feet flat on floor

Take That Break!

One of the best ways for computer users to avoid repetitive strain injuries is to take frequent rest breaks. Unfortunately, many of us get so wrapped up in our work that we neglect this important preventive measure. A program called Ergonomic Timer by Tropical Software is just what the doctor ordered. This program monitors mouse clicks, keystrokes, and elapsed work time to remind you when a break is due. A countdown timer even lets you know when the break is over.

- Turn the screen away from the window to reduce glare, and cover your screen with a glare deflector. Turn off overhead lights; illuminate your work area with a lamp.

- Place the keyboard low enough to avoid arm and wrist fatigue. Your elbow should be bent at a right angle and your forearm should be parallel to the floor.

- Do not bend your wrists when you type. Use an inexpensive raised wrist rest. Do not rest your wrists on a sharp edge.

- Position the seat back so that your lower back is supported.

- Sit with your feet firmly on the floor. Shorter people might need to use an angled footrest.

- Enlarge fonts so that they are easier to see; you can return them to their normal size before printing the document.

- Most important of all, take a break. At the least, exercise at your desk, occasionally rotating your wrists, rolling your shoulders, and stretching. Better yet, get up and walk around at regular intervals.

- Finally, keep your fingernails short, or at least not too long.

Repetitive strain injuries seem to be aggravated by overall job stress. Among the psychological and environmental factors that increase risk are long commutes, dissatisfaction with management, and the occurrence of stressful events in one's personal life. Even so, most computer-related health problems can be avoided with proper attention to your physical well-being at the computer.

Employee Monitoring

The next chapter discusses employer monitoring of employee actions from a privacy perspective. Here, the concern is with monitoring for performance evaluation. In any

◄ **FIGURE 9-2**

Anti-radiation protection.
Not only does this protective
screen block radiation, it also
minimizes glare on the screen.

case when the majority of an employee's duties involve the computer, various tools
allow an employer to record and evaluate those activities.

If a job involves intensive keying, such as word processing or data entry, a key-
stroke monitoring system can tell the manager how many keystrokes per hour each
employee is producing and may even place a window on the employee's monitor
telling him whether he is above or below the expected standard. Some studies have
shown that this type of monitoring causes higher stress levels and increased risk
of RSI.

Other software tools allow employers to keep track of how long an employee is
away from the computer, what files are stored on the hard drive, and what sites the
employee is visiting on the Internet.

Although there are no federal laws limiting performance monitoring, or even requiring employers to notify employees that is taking place, more enlightened organizations have policies in place to inform employees of monitoring practices through
employee handbooks or periodic memos. Also, some union contracts contain limitations on employee monitoring.

Environmental Concerns

Computers can affect the environment through the power they consume, the supplies required in their use, and disposal of obsolete equipment. **Green computing**
refers to addressing these factors in an environmentally responsible manner.

POWER CONSUMPTION. The Environmental Protection Agency (EPA) has
calculated that reducing the power consumption of all PCs by one-half would save
enough electricity to provide power for the states of Maine, Vermont, and New
Hampshire, cut U. S. power bills by over $2 billion, and reduce carbon dioxide
emissions equivalent to the amount produced by 5 million automobiles! With numbers like these, it is easy to see how seemingly insignificant actions can save a

▲ **F I G U R E 9-3**

Energy Star logo. Computer products displaying this logo have been designed with energy conservation in mind.

significant amount of electricity if taken by enough people. To encourage power conservation, the EPA has developed the **Energy Star** standards for computers to limit the power that system components consume while idle. Equipment complying with these standards displays the Energy Star logo (Figure 9-3). Many organizations require all newly purchased computer equipment to meet Energy Star standards.

Current operating systems contain many **energy management features**. Laptops have long used these features to prolong battery life, but now desktop systems also use them for power conservation. Power settings enable you to specify the length of time a system will wait before turning off the monitor, turning off the disk drive, and putting the system into standby or hibernate modes (Figure 9-4). Contrary to popular belief, a screen saver does not save electricity. Screen savers were originally designed to prevent the phosphors on the tube of a CRT monitor from "burning in" and leaving a ghost image when a stationary image remained on the screen for an extended period, but current CRTs don't have that problem. Now, screen savers provide a way for users to personalize their systems, but require as much power as normal use.

You may have heard that frequently turning your system on and off can cause it to wear out prematurely. For this reason, many people leave their system on all the time, or perhaps just turn it on when they arrive at work and leave it on until the end of the day. However, current systems will not suffer any damage from occasionally turning them off and on. If you aren't going to be using your system for 16 minutes or more, you'll save electricity by turning it off.

► **F I G U R E 9-4**

Energy management features. This Windows XP dialog box enables you to choose settings that optimize your notebook computer's use of power.

Power Options Properties   ? ✕

| Power Schemes | Alarms | Power Meter | Advanced | Hibernate |

Select the power scheme with the most appropriate settings for this computer. Note that changing the settings below will modify the selected scheme.

Power schemes

Max Battery ▼

Save As...   Delete

Settings for Max Battery power scheme

When computer is:	🔌 Plugged in	🔋 Running on batteries
Turn off monitor:	After 15 mins ▼	After 1 min ▼
Turn off hard disks:	Never ▼	After 3 mins ▼
System standby:	After 20 mins ▼	After 2 mins ▼
System hibernates:	After 45 mins ▼	After 1 hour ▼

OK   Cancel   Apply

COMPUTER SUPPLIES.   Computer users consume supplies such as paper and toner cartridges. Much of these supplies eventually end up as waste. Sound management of supplies will not only reduce environmental impact but will also save a company money.

You can use the following strategies to reduce the amount of paper waste you generate.

- Don't print out everything.

- Use e-mail rather than sending a fax or a memo.

- Use the back of already used paper for draft copies.

- Save the expensive heavyweight bond paper for critical items and use recycled paper for most of your printing needs.

- Finally, make sure that the used paper is recycled, rather than dumped with the rest of the trash.

Ink-jet cartridges and toner cartridges from laser printers and copiers can be refilled and reused. Do-it-yourself kits are available, but most experts recommend sending cartridges to one of a number of companies that accept them for remanufacture. The remanufactured cartridges are guaranteed to perform as well as or better than the original and cost much less.

PC DISPOSAL.   What do you do with a PC that has outlived its usefulness? First, you should investigate ways to prolong the PC's life. By upgrading key components such as memory and hard drive, you may be able to delay the need to replace the entire system. If that's not possible, perhaps someone else in your organization with more limited computing needs can use it. When you do buy a new system, keep components, such as the keyboard and monitor, that don't need to be replaced. Investigate the possibility of donating usable equipment to charitable organizations.

Ultimately, though, you will need to dispose of obsolete equipment. A National Safety Council study estimates that over 315 million PCs will be discarded by 2004. Because PCs contain a number of toxic substances, such as lead, cadmium, and mercury, they should never be discarded in a landfill. The state of Massachusetts has even banned computers and TVs from landfills, imposing a $25,000 fine on any landfill operator who knowingly accepts these items. Several groups are bringing pressure on computer manufactures to address this problem by designing computers using fewer toxic materials and by establishing recycling programs to recover usable material and neutralize toxicity from junked PCs. As a last resort, recycling companies accept discarded equipment for a fee based on the age and the number of systems recycled.

► LEGAL ISSUES

The world-wide reach of the Internet presents many interesting and important legal issues. Those involving intellectual property—copyrights, trademarks, and patents—are covered in a later section. Here we will discuss one of the thorniest legal issues facing the Internet, that of jurisdiction. If you purchase a product that doesn't work from a local store, and the store refuses to replace it or refund your money, your legal remedy is fairly straightforward: You take the dispute to your local small claims court. The situation is a lot different, however, if you purchased the product from a vendor in another country over the Internet. Whose laws apply, yours or the vendor's? There are no cut and dried answers to this jurisdictional problem, as the following examples show.

Home Page Snoops

Notice that this little item is not accompanied by a real family photo; we do not want to make things worse than they already are. Some Web sites say, "Click my picture to find out more about me." The plain fact is that people are abandoning privacy on their own Web pages. Pictures of children, provided by proud parents, can give valuable information, starting with appearance and names, that might be used to harm a child.

Identity thieves, who would like to pose as you and run up a mountain of debt in your name, can often find name, birth date, occupation, degrees, and maybe even your address. Think about it. A name, birth date, and birthplace will get a birth certificate. A driver's license, the de facto identifier, is not far behind, and it unlocks the keys to credit cards.

Suppose you are interested in genealogy and include part of the family tree on your site. So there is mother's maiden name, right? Bingo! That is a major identifier used by banks and other security-conscious organizations. You just compromised your bank account. Enough said.

International Jurisdictional Issues

In 2000, two French organizations brought suit in France to force Yahoo to prevent French citizens from accessing Yahoo auction pages featuring Nazi memorabilia. France has strict laws forbidding the sale of Nazi memorabilia and any other items likely to incite racial hatred. Yahoo countered that sale of the items was perfectly legal in the United States where its headquarters and servers are based, and that the French court had no legal jurisdiction. In May 2000, a French judge ruled against Yahoo, ordering it to implement technology to prevent such access and giving it two months to comply. Yahoo responded by claiming that current technology would not allow it to block access from French citizens with any degree of reliability. As the dispute wound its way through the French legal system, Yahoo brought suit within the U.S. to have the case dismissed. In November 2001, a U.S. District Court judge ruled that Yahoo was not bound by the French court's decision, because that would be a violation of Yahoo's First Amendment rights. However, in January of 2002, Yahoo bowed to international pressure and removed the items in question from its site, making them unavailable to everyone. The jurisdictional conflict between French and U.S. courts remains unresolved.

A similar jurisdictional issue arose in Germany. The manager of CompuServe's German subsidiary was convicted of pornography charges that were brought based on images carried on the parent company's U.S. site. Although these images were deemed pornographic under German law, they were acceptable under the more liberal U.S. law. After a two-year journey through Germany's appeal system, the verdict was finally overturned, based on the fact that the German manager had no control over the content on the U.S. site and could not have prevented German subscribers from accessing that site.

The High Court of Australia ruled that an Australian citizen could sue Dow Jones & Co. Inc., (a U.S. corporation) in Australian courts under Australian law for defamation of character based on an article published on Dow Jones' U.S. Web site. Dow Jones argued that any lawsuit should be brought in the state of New Jersey in the U.S., since that is where its servers are located and where the article in question was published. The High Court disagreed, pointing out that Dow Jones advertised and sold subscriptions in Australia, thereby subjecting itself to Australian laws.

These examples serve to emphasize the point that the application of national laws to a world-wide medium like the Internet is a difficult process at best. Imagine the confusion and expense that would result if each organization had to check the content of every one of its Web pages to ensure that each was legal according to the laws of every country in the world. Much work remains to be done in this area to resolve the cultural differences causing the legal conflicts and to establish international agreements for conflict resolution.

National Jurisdictional Issues

Jurisdictional questions are not just an international issue. Similar conflicts can arise within countries. The movie industry trade group DVD-CCA filed suit in a California court, where it is based, against a number of defendants for posting software on the Internet that broke DVD copy protection. One of the defendants, a Texas resident who posted the software on a Web site in Indiana where he was a college student, contested the jurisdiction of the California court. The California Supreme Court, overruling lower courts, stated that the student couldn't be forced to stand trial in California, because he had no connection to that state. The case has been appealed to the U.S. Supreme Court, which has agreed to hear it.

Another jurisdictional issue within the United States involves the imposition of sales taxes on Internet transactions. Currently, a merchant is required to charge state or local sales tax on a sale only if it has a physical presence, such as a store or warehouse, in the community. This is the same law that applies to catalog retailers.

Technically, consumers are required to report their purchases and send in the applicable tax, but that seldom happens. As the volume of Internet sales transactions increases dramatically, state and local officials have been lobbying to have all transactions subjected to sales tax. They see large amounts of revenue being lost and local merchants being put at a severe price disadvantage. A study by the University of Tennessee reports that states, cities, and counties nationwide lost $13.3 billion in revenue last year from uncollected e-commerce sales taxes. On the other side of the issue, Internet merchants point to the hodgepodge of state and local taxes throughout the country and complain of the difficulty and expense of determining the proper tax rate and the procedures for sending the taxes they collect to the appropriate governments.

At the national level, Congress has been reluctant to impose any new taxes on the Internet, fearing that its growth could be curtailed. The current moratorium on Internet taxes, titled the **Internet Nondiscrimination Act,** carries through 2005 and prohibits any new taxes that single out Internet transactions, such as taxes on Internet service, double taxation by two different states for products purchased via the Internet, or taxes that treat Internet purchases differently from other types of sales. However, it does not prohibit states and localities from imposing the same taxes on Internet purchases that that they impose on any other purchase. The difficulty is in collecting those taxes.

► PROTECTING CHILDREN ON THE INTERNET

The Internet has opened up wonderful new opportunities for children—help with homework, dazzling new adventure games, and a chance to strike up conversations with new friends in other countries. Millions of youngsters are surfing and chatting and e-mailing. But cyberspace can be a mixed blessing for children, who may also be exposed to its less savory elements. Concerned parents are taking steps to monitor their children's use of the Internet.

The most widely used online service, America Online, gives parents control of usage. The parent can create extra sign-in names and tailor privileges to each child. Younger children, for example, can be limited to AOL's kids' area, which includes its own children's Web browser. Another possibility is **blocking software,** a product that tries to act as a high-tech chaperone (Figure 9-5). Blocking software typically keeps children away from its own updatable list of objectionable sites and avoids sites with other objectionable material, such as foul language or sites requesting name, phone number, or credit card number. Blocking software cannot be totally effective because the Web changes too fast for software staff to maintain a complete list of objectionable sites. Also, some blocking software has been criticized for being overzealous, blocking access to innocuous sites. One product even blocked access to the infant care site BabyZone.

The best monitoring technique may be to avoid having a computer in a child's bedroom. Instead, the computer might be located in a more public, high-traffic location, such as the family room or kitchen (Figure 9-6).

Congress passed the **Communications Decency Act** in 1996, attempting to target, in particular, people who preyed on children on the Internet. The law caused a firestorm on the Internet, with many sites displaying the "blue ribbon" of free speech in protest. The U.S. Supreme Court struck down the law for vagueness.

But more laws have been passed since that time, and others are likely to follow. The **Children's Online Privacy Protection Act (COPPA)** requires Web sites that target children under age 13 to post a privacy policy that clearly states what information they collect and set up parental notification and consent systems before gathering information from the children. Its provisions took effect in April 2000.

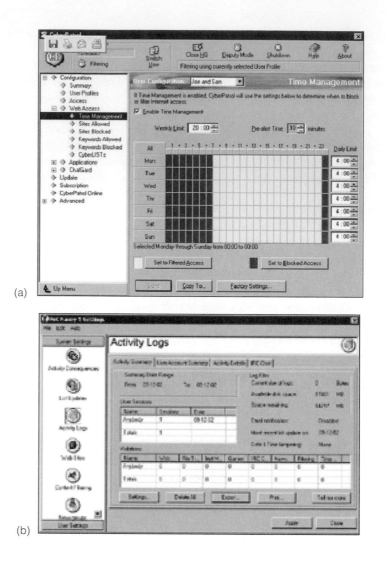

► FIGURE 9-5

Blocking software. Both (a) Cyber Patrol and (b) Net Nanny software let parents control on-line access and block entry to objectionable sites.

(a)

(b)

The **Children's Internet Protection Act** (**CIPA**), which went into effect in April 2001, requires libraries receiving any type of federal funding to implement technology that blocks or filters certain material from being accessed through the Internet. A closely related law, the **Neighborhood Children's Internet Protection Act** (**NCIPA**), was enacted at the same time and requires libraries receiving the E-Rate discount to establish an Internet safety policy that addresses five issues:

● Access by minors to "inappropriate matter"

● Safety and security of minors when using e-mail, chat rooms, and other forms of direct electronic communication

● Unauthorized access, including hacking and other unlawful online activities by minors

● Unauthorized disclosure of personal identification information of minors

● Measures designed to restrict minors' access to harmful materials.

In May of 2002, a panel of District Court judges blocked enforcement of CIPA, ruling that it would force libraries to violate the First Amendment rights of their patrons. The judges stated that, "because of the inherent limitations in filtering technology, public libraries can never comply with CIPA without blocking access to a substantial amount of speech that is both constitutionally protected and fails to meet even the filtering companies' own blocking criteria." The Justice Department appealed the ruling to the U.S. Supreme Court, which agreed to hear the case in March, 2003.

Taking a different approach, in November 2002 Congress established a new second-level .kids Internet domain under the .us country domain. The *.kids.us* domain is designed to create a safe haven on the Internet for children, where parents can be assured that Web sites are free of pornography and other material not suitable for youngstcrs. Any sitcs in this domain are prohibited from linking to sites outside the domain. The domain will be made available by the end of 2003 and will be monitored by a private company under government contract to ensure that all material is suitable for children 13 and under.

► **FIGURE** **9-6**

Child monitoring. One of the best ways to monitor a child's Internet use is to place the computer in a high-traffic area of the house.

► ETHICS IN COMPUTING

Ethics refers to standards of moral conduct. People use ethical principles to help them to determine the proper course of action to take in difficult situations. Many philosophers have proposed a series of ethical principles, and most world religions put forth ethical and moral guidelines, but the most concise statement of ethical behavior is known as the Golden Rule, typically stated as, "Do unto others as you would have them do unto you." The Computer Ethics Institute, founded by the Brookings Institution, IBM, the Washington Consulting Group, and the Washington Theological Consortium, has applied the general principles of ethics to the world of computing to develop the Ten Commandments Of Computer Ethics, shown in Figure 9-7, as guidelines for anyone involved with computing, be they computer professionals, managers, or users of computer systems. It is important to note that, although unethical acts may be immoral, they are not always illegal, although illegal acts are almost always unethical. This is especially true in the field of information technology, where laws have trouble keeping up with the rapidly advancing technology.

Ten Commandments Of Computer Ethics

1. Thou Shalt Not Use A Computer To Harm Other People.
2. Thou Shalt Not Interfere With Other People's Computer Work.
3. Thou Shalt Not Snoop Around In Other People's Computer Files.
4. Thou Shalt Not Use A Computer To Steal.
5. Thou Shalt Not Use A Computer To Bear False Witness.
6. Thou Shalt Not Copy Or Use Proprietary Software For Which You have Not Paid.
7. Thou Shalt Not Use Other People's Computer Resources Without Authorization Or Proper Compensation.
8. Thou Shalt Not Appropriate Other People's Intellectual Output.
9. Thou Shalt Think About The Social Consequences Of The Program You Are Writing Or The System You Are Designing.
10. Thou Shalt Always Use A Computer In Ways That Insure Consideration And Respect For Your Fellow Humans.

© Copyright 1992 Computer Ethics Institute

▶ PROFESSIONAL ETHICS

Computer users are people who use the computer as a tool in performing their everyday job duties. On the other hand, **computer professionals** are people whose work focuses on the computer systems themselves, people with titles such as programmer, systems analyst, network administrator, and computer operator. Computer professionals need to consider the ethical implications of their actions in developing and administering computer systems. Several professional organizations involved in various aspects of information technology have developed their own codes of ethics. One of the most well known is the Code of Ethics and Professional Conduct developed by the Association for Computing Machinery, a worldwide organization for information technology professionals and students. An outline of a portion of this detailed and comprehensive code is shown in Figure 9-8. The sections shown here include a general set of principles, referred to in the Code as general moral imperatives, a more specific set of professional responsibilities, and a set of guidelines for organizational leaders in the use of computer systems. In the full Code, each of these headings is followed by one or more paragraphs of explanatory material. The complete Code can be viewed on the ACM Web site, www.acm.org.

Programmer Responsibility

What are a programmer's ethical responsibilities for the operation of a computer system that he or she has developed? Imagine that you are the lead programmer on a large, complex application project that, after more than a year, is almost completed. You have been testing the system for a several months and have corrected all the major bugs that have been discovered. The few remaining known problems are minor, but you are concerned that, without further testing, some major undiscovered bugs may still exist. However, your boss, the project manager, says that upper management has notified her that a competitor is about to release a similar application and that this product must be released immediately. She (your boss) directs you to certify that testing has been completed, so that the product may be shipped to customers.

ACM Code of Ethics and Professional Conduct

GENERAL MORAL IMPERATIVES.
As an ACM member I will ....
1. Contribute to society and human well-being.
2. Avoid harm to others.
3. Be honest and trustworthy.
4. Be fair and take action not to discriminate.
5. Honor property rights including copyrights and patent.
6. Give proper credit for intellectual property.
7. Respect the privacy of others.
8. Honor confidentiality.

MORE SPECIFIC PROFESSIONAL RESPONSIBILITIES.
As an ACM computing professional I will ....
1. Strive to achieve the highest quality, effectiveness and dignity in both the process and products of professional work.
2. Acquire and maintain professional competence.
3. Know and respect existing laws pertaining to professional work.
4. Accept and provide appropriate professional review.
5. Honor contracts, agreements, and assigned responsibilities.
6. Improve public understanding of computing and its consequences.
7. Access computing and communication resources only when authorized to do so.

ORGANIZATIONAL LEADERSHIP IMPERATIVES.
As an ACM member and an organizational leader, I will ....
1. Articulate social responsibilities of members of an organizational unit and encourage full acceptance of those responsibilities.
2. Manage personnel and resources to design and build information systems that enhance the quality of working life.
3. Acknowledge and support proper and authorized uses of an organization's computing and communication resources.
4. Ensure that users and those who will be affected by a system have their needs clearly articulated during the assessment and design of requirements; later the system must be validated to meet requirements.
5. Articulate and support policies that protect the dignity of users and others affected by a computing system.
6. Create opportunities for members of the organization to learn the principles and limitations of computer systems.

► **FIGURE** **9-8**

A portion of the ACM Code of Ethics and Professional Conduct.

She says that the known minor bugs can be acknowledged, with notice to the customers that the bugs will be fixed in the near future. Should you agree to your employer's wishes or should you refuse, knowing that the possibility of major problems still exists, due to the shortened testing period (and that you would probably be fired)? Would your decision be influenced by the type of application (accounting versus medical management) involved? There are no pat answers to questions like these. You must apply ethical principles and come to your own decision. One way that has been suggested to help you decide whether you've made the right decision is to ask yourself how you would feel if your actions made the front page of the local newspaper.

Computer software is extremely complex. In all but the simplest systems, it is impossible to determine that no mistakes exist. According to Edsger Dijkstra, a pioneer is software design, testing can only show the presence of bugs, not their absence. With this in mind, programmers should design programs to limit the harm that could come from program errors. How to accomplish this is a topic for a course in software design.

The Hippocratic Database

Medical doctors use the Hippocratic oath as the ethical guideline governing their practice of medicine. The oath contains a statement on privacy that reads, "Whatever in connection with my professional practice or not in connection with it I may see or hear in the lives of my patients. . . . I will not divulge, reckoning that all such should be kept secret." IBM researchers are developing a database design that would apply the same principle to storing and retrieving data. The database owner would define the storage and retrieval policies and owners of data could review the policies before allowing their data to be stored in the database. Controls would also be placed on queries to the database, ensuring that each query would have access only to the necessary data. The Hippocratic database design has great potential to protect consumers' privacy.

▶ ETHICAL USE OF COMPUTERS

How should ethical principles be applied to the use of computers in a business environment? While computer professionals are responsible for the design and development of computer systems, nonprofessionals are normally responsible for their everyday use and must be familiar with the applicable ethical principles. One major concern is the accuracy of information stored in a computer. Users must be responsible for implementing procedures that continually monitor the accuracy of information being entered into the system and provide a means of correcting inaccurate information.

Businesses also have the ethical and, in many cases legal, responsibility to protect the privacy of customers' personal data stored on their computers. They must develop privacy policies that explain how the data will be used and who has access to it and implement procedures to enforce those policies. Customers should be given the option of preventing their data from being released to third parties. From an individual's point of view, an opt-in policy is preferred. Under an **opt-in policy,** customers are notified of the privacy policy and must specifically agree before their data can be released. Many businesses use the **opt-out** approach, in which customers are assumed to have agreed to the release of their data unless they specifically request to have it kept private.

In addition to establishing policies concerning the collection and retention of personal data, companies have the responsibility to protect the data from unauthorized access while it is stored on their system. Many of the cases involving theft of personal data over the Internet have been traced to lax security procedures on the part of the victimized companies, including actions as obvious as failing to apply patches to announced vulnerabilities in their operating systems.

The ability of computers to alter reality also imposes certain ethical obligations. Is it ethical for news organizations to use digitally altered photographs? The most famous occurrence in this area happened when Time magazine altered the mug shot photo of O. J. Simpson for their cover by darkening it to make Simpson look more sinister (Figure 9-9). Some groups believe that alteration is permissible as long as the content and meaning is not altered, whereas others feels that any alteration is unethical.

▶ INTELLECTUAL PROPERTY RIGHTS IN A DIGITAL WORLD

Intellectual property (**IP**) refers to results of intellectual activity in the industrial, scientific, literary, or artistic fields. It typically refers to such items as literary and artistic works, which include written material, music, drama, and paintings; inventions; and commercial identities, such as logos and brand names. The owner of IP controls its use and is entitled to any benefits arising from such use. IP rights are legally protected in several ways, depending on the form of the property. The **U.S. Copyright Act** protects literary and artistic works. Patents protect inventions, and trademark law protects the rights of businesses to their identity. All of these concepts have been around far longer than computers have, but the predominance of digital representation of these forms of IP has led to many issues that need to be considered here. Each of the areas mentioned (copyrights, trademarks, and patents) is discussed in the following sections.

Copyrights

Copyright protection provides the creator of a literary or artistic work control over the use and distribution of that work. The digital age has presented a number of

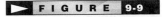

new issues in the area of copyright enforcement. Digital representation has led to new forms of IP, made the copying and distribution of existing IP much easier, and made policing of IP rights much more difficult. Much controversy has resulted from the widespread distribution of pirated copies of music and video over the Internet. Prior to digital technology, you could make analog copies of cassettes or videotape. However, distribution and quality issues minimized the piracy problem. With analog copying, each subsequent copy is slightly reduced in quality. So if you make a copy of a friend's copy of the original audiocassette, your copy's quality is noticeably inferior to the original. Moreover, making and distributing enough copies to seriously impact the music companies' sales was a daunting task, suitable only for commercial pirates, who could be targeted and legally prosecuted. Digital copying removes both barriers to piracy. Digital copies are exact duplicates of the original and can be posted on and downloaded from the Internet with ease. With thousands of individuals performing these illegal actions, detection and prosecution is difficult and expensive.

One point of contention has been with the concept of fair use. Under the **fair use** provision of the U.S. Copyright Act, you are permitted to make use of copyrighted works for limited purposes, including criticism, news reporting, education, and research, provided such use falls within guidelines specified in the Act that limit the commercial impact of the fair use. Also, courts have ruled that copying done for personal use, such as recording a TV show to watch at a later time or copying a CD to cassette so that you can listen to it in your car, falls under the fair use provisions of the Act. The controversy arises when the efforts of the content providers to protect their products from piracy interfere with the fair use rights of the consumer.

DIGITAL CONTENT.   In an attempt to prevent digital piracy, digital content developers have come up with numerous copy-protection schemes designed to make it impossible to copy original CDs, DVDs, and other digital formats. As fast as the copy protection schemes are developed, hackers discover methods of breaking the protection schemes and publish them on the Internet. The hackers claim that their purpose is to permit users to exercise their fair use rights; whereas the content publishers (primarily the music and video industries) claim that the purpose is to enable piracy. In 1998, Congress passed the **Digital Millennium Copyright Act (DMCA)**, which makes it illegal to use, develop or publish methods of breaking antipiracy protections added to copyrighted works and bans devices designed for that purpose. Critics complain that this law prevents users from exercising their fair use rights. The two following cases illustrate the controversy.

► MAKING CONNECTIONS ◄   Working in the Age of Connectivity

As access to high-speed Internet connections becomes more common, the nature of work promises to change dramatically. The ability to access information and services online will lead to many changes. Here are some guesses about our future:

- Using a computer and online services will be akin to using a phone. Everyone in or out of an office will know how.

- Because most workers will telecommute most of the time, work will be less central to people's lives. Work will become less of a place to go and more of a thing to do. And, as the feet-up architect shown here can attest, the attire, and even the posture, will be casual. On the other hand, workaholics will have even more difficulty separating work from family life.

- A telecommuting society means we will stop building skyscrapers to house office workers. However, some people may go to a "work center" just to hang out with

other humans and not feel isolated. Since most workers will be at home, the importance of family and community will increase.

- Large public companies will be replaced by hundreds of smaller entrepreneurial companies that will survive nicely by ordering supplies online, advertising their goods and services online, and selling directly to their customers via the Internet and home computers.

- Workers will use their computers to access information and services related to accounting, the law, and medicine. Thus, since these services will become less labor-intensive, their prices to the consumer will drop significantly.

- People working at home will use their online computer services for activities beyond their work—to bank, vote, send gifts, get advice, download entertainment, and chat with friends.

In July 1996, the Contents Scramble System (CSS) was developed to prevent copying of DVDs. In 1999, a Norwegian high school student developed a method of defeating CSS so that he could view his own legally purchased DVDs on his Linux-based computer. He published his method, called DeCSS, on the Internet and was awarded a Norwegian national prize for making a significant contribution to society outside of school. In January 2002, at the urging of the U.S. Motion Picture Association, the Norwegian government indicted him under a Norwegian law that made it a crime to break into someone's locked property (even though he owned the DVDs). In January 2003, the teenager was acquitted of the charges, with the court stating that he hadn't broken any Norwegian laws, because he hadn't used his software to make illegal copies. U.S. legal experts warned that he probably would have been found guilty under U.S. laws, because the DCMA makes it illegal to use or publish the software, even if no copyright violations occur. A Norwegian appeals court has agreed to hear the prosecutor's appeal of the acquittal and is expected to decide the case by the end of 2003.

In July 2001, Russian programmer Dmitry Sklyarov was arrested while in the United States to make a presentation at a professional conference. He was accused of working with his employer, the Russian company ElcomSoft Co. Ltd, to develop a program that allowed owners of electronic books created in Adobe's eBook format to convert them into Adobe Portable Document Format (.pdf) files. This conversion removed restrictions on copying the e-books that were embedded into the files by e-book publishers, thus violating the DCMA. His defenders said that the software he developed had many legitimate uses and that Sklyarov was never accused of infringing any copyrighted e-book, or of assisting anyone else to infringe copyrights. The software he helped develop violated no laws in Russia, where it was created and marketed. Charges against Skylarov were dropped on the condition that he testify against his employer. In December 2002, ElcomSoft was acquitted by jury verdict.

SOFTWARE.   Computer software is classified as copyrightable intellectual property. Most forms of software discussed in Chapter 2, including freeware, shareware, and commercial software, are copyrighted. Only public-domain and open-source software fall outside copyright restrictions. When you purchase software, you are bound by the terms of the license accompanying the software. This can be an individual, site, or network license, as explained in Chapter 2. In most cases, the license grants you the right to use the software, but you are not permitted to modify, sell, or give it away (shareware licenses do allow you to freely distribute copies). Those rights remain with the copyright holder. One loophole in the Copyright Act required proof of financial gain for a criminal violation to be proven. As a result, people who had posted copies of games and other copyrighted software on the Internet could not be prosecuted if they received no money for doing so. In 1997, the **No Electronic Theft (NET) Act** closed this loophole, authorizing criminal prosecutions against anyone who willfully reproduces or distributes copyrighted material by electronic means, regardless of the purpose or motive.

A new form of control over software rights, called **copyleft,** has been developed by Richard Stallman, a former MIT Artificial Intelligence Center employee, who believes that all software should be free. The term *free* in this context refers not to the price of the software, but to the freedom of the programmer to use it as he sees fit. Under the copyleft approach everyone has permission to run, copy, or modify the program, and to distribute modified versions, but not permission to add restrictions of their own. This is achieved by first stating that it is copyrighted; then adding distribution terms, which give everyone the rights to use, modify, and redistribute the program's code or any program derived from it but only if the distribution terms are unchanged.

DIGITAL IMAGES.   Another aspect of digital copyright applies to digital images, whether cartoon-like line art, photographs, or complex images developed with sophisticated graphics software. Unless an image is specifically exempted, copyright protection automatically exists when the image is created. The fair use concept allows you to use a downloaded image as your screen saver, but you are not permitted to distribute the image or post it on your own Web site. Merely crediting the source of the image is not sufficient; you must obtain permission from the copyright owner.

PLAGIARISM.   One copyright issue that deserves special attention in a college text is **plagiarism,** the representation of someone else's words or ideas as your own. Always a problem, plagiarism has become epidemic on college campuses with the advent of the Internet. From a copyright perspective, fair use allows you to include a portion of another's work within your own, but only if you properly cite, or identify, the source. Violation of copyright laws and the subsequent legal penalties are usually not the major problem for college students caught plagiarizing. Many institutions have academic penalties that range from receiving a grade of zero on the assignment all the way up to expulsion for the first offense.

Patents

Patents are designed to protect inventions and encourage inventors to innovate by granting the patent holder exclusive rights to the invention for 20 years. In the early 1980s, the courts extended patent protection to computer software algorithms and techniques, and in the subsequent years, the Patent Office has been granting software patents at an ever-increasing pace. Patents have even been granted for business methods implemented in software, such as Amazon.com's one-click purchase process. Organizations wishing to use the algorithm or business method within their systems must obtain a license and pay royalties to the patent holder.

DAY IN THE LIFE
Geoff Kehler, *IT Assistant*

As the programmer responsible for writing and maintaining the server-side components for an e-commerce Web site, Edgar knows pressure. He has to write his software in three different programming languages, but most importantly, he has to design it to interact with the other software his company uses for creating and tracking orders. Edgar uses Perl for the user interface on the Web site, C++ to create the components that handle company procedures for order placement, and most recently, C# to talk to the database of merchandise on the company's internal network.

Each component needs to be secure, and must quickly and reliably transmit the information provided by the customer to the appropriate department within the company. He interacts every day with the Web site designers on one side, and the other system programmers on the other.

A job is never over simple when a program is first finished. In addition to debugging his programs if they don't work exactly the way they are supposed to, Edgar is also constantly rewriting the existing software components to take into account changes to the company's Web site, new procedures within the company, and changes to the company's products.

So what does it feel like to keep building and rebuilding software like Edgar does? He laughs.

"I'm never bored, that's for sure."

Trademarks

A **trademark** is a word, name, symbol, or device used to distinguish one company and its products from another. Two issues arise over the use of trademarks in the digital arena. First, Web developers must be careful of infringing on trademark rights by unauthorized use of a company's trademarks on their site or by use of words or symbols that could easily be confused with a company's trademarks.

A second issue can occur when someone obtains a domain name that includes another company's trademark. One practice that was common in the mid 1990s, referred to as **cybersquatting,** involves registering common words and phrases as domain names, with the intention of selling the domain name at a profit to a company that wants a catchy, easily-remembered URL. For instance, wallstreet.com was sold for $1 million in 1999. A variation on this practice was to register a company's trademark before they thought of doing it themselves (in the early and mid 90s, many large companies seemed oblivious to the presence of the Internet), then offering to sell the name to them at a high price. In 1999, Congress passed the **Anti-Cybersquatting Consumer Protection Act,** with civil penalties up to $100,000 for anyone registering a domain name using someone else's trademark. Trademark owners can use this law to force site owners to relinquish domain names that sound similar to or contain a trademark. For example, Ford Motor Co. could proceed against the owner of fordcars.com.

CHAPTER REVIEW

▶ **Summary and Key Terms**

- With the high level of integration of computing into society, it is no longer desirable to leave the social and ethical issues of computing to the experts; everyone must become knowledgeable and involved.

- One of the major issues confronting society today is the growing **digital divide** that separates the computing haves from the have-nots. To narrow the divide within the United States, the FCC administers the **Universal Service Fund** that helps service providers with the higher costs of providing communication services to rural areas. The Federal **E-Rate** program adds a little to everyone's telephone bill to provide rate subsidies for Internet access for schools and libraries. Worldwide, thousands of initiatives exist within disadvantaged regions and countries to improve access to the digital world.

- **Ergonomics** is the use of research in designing systems, programs, or devices that are appropriate to use for their intended purposes. In the context of computers, ergonomics refers to human factors related to the use of computers.

- Many software tools exist that allow employers to monitor the computer activities of employees. Although there is no requirement to notify employees of such monitoring, more enlightened organizations have policies in place to inform employees of monitoring practices.

- **Green computing** refers to addressing the environmental impact of computers use in an environmentally responsible manner. Many organizations require all newly purchased computer equipment to meet the EPA's **Energy Star** standards for limiting power requirements.

- Current operating systems contain many **energy management features** that reduce the power requirements of computer systems.

- Computer users should make every effort to reduce the amount of paper waste generated and to recycle laser printer toner cartridges.

- Make every effort to prolong the useful life of your computer. When you must dispose of it, use an environmentally responsible recycling company.

- One of the biggest legal problems facing the Internet is the issue of international jurisdiction. When a dispute arises between individuals and organizations from several countries, whose laws apply? The application of national laws to a worldwide medium like the Internet is a difficult process.

- Within the United States similar jurisdictional issues exist between states. The imposition of state and local sales taxes on Internet transactions is a major concern. The **Internet Nondiscrimination Act** prohibits states from imposing any new taxes that single out Internet transactions, but doesn't prohibit the states from taxing Internet transactions the same way they tax any other transaction.

- The Internet can be a dangerous place for children. **Blocking software** attempts to prevent children from accessing objectionable sites. The **Communications Decency Act** attempted to prevent people from preying on children on the Internet, but was struck down by the Supreme Court. The **Children's Online Privacy Protection Act** (**COPPA**) requires Web sites that target children under age 13 to post a privacy policy that clearly states what information they collect and set up parental notification and consent systems before gathering information from the children.

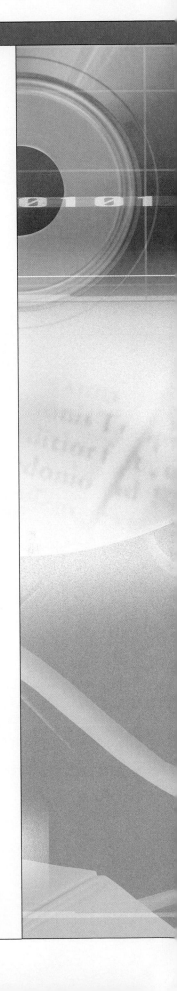

- The **Children's Internet Protection Act (CIPA)** requires libraries receiving any type of federal funding to implement technology that blocks or filters certain objectionable material on the Internet. The **Neighborhood Children's Internet Protection Act (NCIPA)** requires libraries receiving the E-Rate discount to establish an Internet safety policy to protect children. Enforcement of CIPA has been blocked by the courts.

- Congress has taken a different approach to child protection by establishing the **.kids.us** domain that will prohibit content that is unsuitable for children.

- **Ethics** refers to standards of moral conduct. Although unethical acts may be immoral, they are not always illegal, although illegal acts are almost always unethical.

- **Computer professionals** are people whose work focuses on the computer systems themselves, people with titles such as programmer, systems analyst, network administrator, and computer operator. A number of professional organizations involved in various aspects of information technology have developed their own codes of ethics.

- Nonprofessionals are normally responsible for the everyday use of computers and must be familiar with the applicable ethical principles.

- Businesses have the ethical and, in many cases legal, responsibility to protect the privacy of customers' personal data stored on their computers. Under an **opt-in policy,** businesses notify customers of their privacy policy, and the customers must specifically agree before the business can release their data to third parties. With an **opt-out** approach, customers are assumed to have agreed to the release of their data unless they specifically request that the business keep it private.

- The ability of computers to alter reality imposes certain ethical obligations on news organizations.

- **Intellectual property (IP)** refers to results of intellectual activity in the industrial, scientific, literary, or artistic fields. IP is legally protected in several ways. The **U.S. Copyright Act** protects literary and artistic works. Patents protect inventions, and trademark law protects the rights of businesses to their identity.

- **Copyright** protection provides the creator of a literary or artistic work control over the use and distribution of that work. Digital representation of IP makes it much easier to violate copyright law. The concept of fair use allows you to make use of copyrighted works for limited purposes, including criticism, news reporting, education, and research, provided such use falls within specific guidelines.

- The **Digital Millennium Copyright Act (DMCA)** makes it illegal to use, develop, or publish methods of breaking antipiracy protections added to copyrighted works and bans devices designed for that purpose. Critics complain that this law prevents users from exercising their fair use rights.

- Computer software is classified as copyrightable intellectual property. The software license specifies the rights of the purchaser, but generally prohibits selling or giving away copies. The **No Electronic Theft (NET) Act** prohibits reproducing or distributing copyrighted material by electronic means, regardless of the purpose or motive.

- **Copyleft** is an alternative means of controlling software rights in which everyone has permission to run, copy, or modify the program, and to distribute modified versions, but not permission to add restrictions of their own.

- Digital images are protected by copyright. You must have permission to distribute an image or use it on your Web site.

- **Plagiarism** is the representation of someone else's words or ideas as your own. Fair use allows you to include a portion of another's work within your own, but only if you properly cite, or identify, the source.

- **Patents** protect inventions by granting the patent holder exclusive rights to the invention for 20 years. Business methods implemented in software may be patented.

- A **trademark** is a word, name, symbol, or device used to distinguish one company and its products from another.

- **Cybersquatting** involves registering common words and phrases as domain names, with the intention of selling the domain name at a profit to a company that wants a catchy, easy-to-remember URL.

- The **Anti-Cybersquatting Consumer Protection Act** provides penalties up to $100,000 for anyone registering a domain name using someone else's trademark.

► Critical Thinking Questions

1. Ergonomic workplace furniture can be much more expensive than standard desks and chairs. How might you justify a request for ergonomic furniture to your employer? If you were the employer, how might ethics influence your response to such a request?

2. As a college student, how might you incorporate green computing concepts into your use of computers?

3. Software publishers employ technical support representatives to respond to customer questions over the telephone and through email. Many publishers use computerized systems to monitor the length of time the representatives spend on each inquiry and the number of inquires processed per hour. How might such monitoring benefit the company? How might it harm the company?

4. Do you think that consumers should have to pay sales tax on Internet purchases? Why or why not?

5. The DMCA makes it illegal to use, develop, or publish methods of breaking antipiracy protections, even if those acts do not result in copyright violations. Content publishers claim that these provisions are necessary to prevent digital piracy and without them it would not be economically feasible to produce new music and movies. Critics argue that this law prevents consumers from exercising their fair use rights. Elaborate on each side's position and indicate which you favor.

► **STUDENT STUDY GUIDE**

Multiple Choice

1. Which of the following is designed to address the digital divide issue?
   a. Energy Star standards
   b. DCMA
   c. E-Rate program
   d. NET Act

2. Which of the following is not good ergonomic behavior when working on your computer?
   a. Work in a brightly lighted room.
   b. Don't bend your wrists when you type.
   c. Set the keyboard at a height that allows your arms to remain parallel to the floor.
   d. Take frequent short breaks.

3. Carpal tunnel syndrome is an example of which of the following?
   a. energy management feature
   b. copyright violation
   c. RSI
   d. jurisdictional issue

4. Which of the following prohibits taxes that single out Internet transactions?
   a. blocking software
   b. Internet Nondiscrimination Act
   c. COPPA
   d. CIPA

5. Which of the following requires libraries receiving the E-Rate discount to establish an Internet safety policy addressing protection of minors.
   a. COPPA
   b. DCMA
   c. Communications Decency Act
   d. NCIPA

6. Which of the following would provide protection against having images from your Web site used by someone else without your permission?
   a. copyright
   b. trademark
   c. copyleft
   d. patent

7. Which of the following is not a strategy for reducing paper waste?
   a. Print all your documents and file them, so you won't have to print them again.
   b. Use e-mail rather than send memos.
   c. Recycle paper waste.
   d. Print draft copies on the back of already used paper.

8. Which of the following means of legal protection allows you to modify and distribute a protected program as long as you don't add restrictions of your own?
   a. copyright
   b. copyleft
   c. patent
   d. trademark

9. Which of the following can allow you to protect a business method implemented in software?
   a. copyright
   b. copyleft
   c. patent
   d. trademark

10. Which of the following is not protected by copyright?
    a. a novel
    b. a music CD
    c. a computer program
    d. a brand name

True/False

T   F   1. An ergonomically designed workplace allows the user to adjust the equipment and furniture to meet her needs.

T   F   2. It is important to take regular breaks while working at your computer.

T   F   3. It is illegal for employers to monitor employees' computer use without notifying them.

T   F   4. Some union contracts place limits on employee monitoring.

T   F   5. Computers consume an insignificant amount of electrical power.

T   F   6. Screen savers are not designed to save electricity.

T   F   7. Turning computers on and off more than once a day can cause damage.

T   F   8. Although remanufactured toner cartridges are cheaper than new cartridges, they don't perform as well.

T   F   9. PCs contain toxic substances and should not be discarded in landfills.

T   F   10. The Internet Nondiscrimination Act prohibits states and localities from charging sales taxes on Internet transaction.

T   F   11. Blocking software is designed to prevent children from accessing objectionable Web sites.

T   F   12. Enforcement of the CIPA was blocked by the courts on the premise that it would force libraries to violate the First Amendment rights of their patrons.

T   F   13. The .kids.us domain was created by Congress to establish a safe haven on the Internet for children.

T   F   14. A company should patent its product names to prevent them from being used improperly by others.

T   F   15 It is permissible to use an image copied from another Web site on your Web site as long as you credit the source of the image.

Fill-In

1. The term _____ refers to the practice of registering common words and phrases as domain names in the hope that you can sell them for a profit.

2. The EPA has developed the _____ standards for computers to limit the power that system components consume while idle.

3. _____ is the use of research in designing systems, programs, or devices that are appropriate to use for their intended purposes.

4. The _____ separates the computer haves from the have-nots, within the United States and world-wide.

5. The term _____ refers to literary and artistic works, inventions, and commercial identities.

6. The _____ provision of the U.S. Copyright act would allow you to make a copy of a copyrighted item for your personal use.

7. _____ is the representation of someone else's words or ideas as your own.

8. A(n) _____ provides an inventor exclusive rights to the invention for a period of 20 years.

9. The _____ program provides rate subsidies for Internet access for libraries and schools.

10. _____ refers to addressing the environmental impact of computers use in an environmentally responsible manner.

► ANSWERS

Multiple Choice

1. c	5. d	9. c
2. a	6. a	10. d
3. c	7. a	
4. b	8. b	

True/False

1. T	6. T	11. T
2. T	7. F	12. T
3. F	8. F	13. T
4. T	9. T	14. F
5. F	10. F	15. F

Fill-In

1. cybersquatting
2. Energy Star
3. ergonomics
4. digital divide
5. intellectual property (IP)
6. fair use
7. plagiarism
8. patent
9. E-Rate
10. green computing

Planet Internet

Shopping Tour

Shopping conveniences have existed since catalogs were invented. Convenience is at a high point today, because computer shopping offers goods and services handily bundled together.

Consolidation continues among the various shopping sites on the Web, with many sites opening and closing within a year, as often happens with small bricks-and-mortar businesses. Although you may be interested in finding the cheapest price for your product for a one-time purchase, you might want to consider paying a little more to support a site offering products you would like to purchase regularly (just as you might support a local bricks-and-mortar specialty shop.) If you really just want the best price, go to specialized price-comparison search engines, such as PriceGrabber and Buy.com.

Electronic Mall or Specialty Site?

You know your shopping needs best. You can shop directly from AOL or Amazon for a wide variety of products. Your favorite mail order catalog may now have a Web site, which they update on a weekly basis to keep it current. If you don't know what's available on the Web, start with a search engine request, or check out vendor links on your favorite hobby Web site.

Is Online Shopping Safe and Secure?

First, check to see whether the site states that it handles secure transactions. If so, shoppers generally have few problems. You can also check the status bar of your Web browser for security when submitting your purchase information. A lock symbol indicates that the connection is secure. Most major credit cards guarantee you the same stolen-number limits as with any other credit card purchase. However, many sites also provide you with a phone number or even a printable mail order form if you feel more comfortable with those methods. Most offer order confirmation and receipts via e-mail, and some follow up with a hardcopy receipt. Your instructor could order reprints of a Harvard Business Review Case for the class, as a downloadable file, receive e-mail confirmation and a hardcopy receipt in the mail a week or so later. Web sites that expect to keep your business should provide accurate information about backorders, shipping delays, and the like.

What about Shipping Charges and Sales Tax?

Sites that offer goods at essentially the same basic price may differ greatly in shipping charges. There may be a minimum $10 shipping charge even for a $5 purchase (and if that's the only way to obtain your daughter's favorite stuffed toy for her birthday, you may be willing to pay $15 for a $5 toy). Not all specialized price-comparison search engines include shipping charges in their charts, so be sure to check before purchasing. Some companies regularly collect sales tax; many do not. The federal government has not decided how best to handle sales tax issues on the Internet on a national basis. Of course, you are responsible for state and local taxes as specified by your locale.

Do Online Merchants Have Special Discounts for Specific Categories of Customers, as Happens Sometimes with Mail-Order Catalogs?

It's possible, but it's likely that most clearly specify the criteria for discounts and promotions as a result of the Amazon "pricing experiment." Amazon conducted a pricing experiment that was discovered by users and widely published where the same customer pricing the same product at a different time of the day or using a

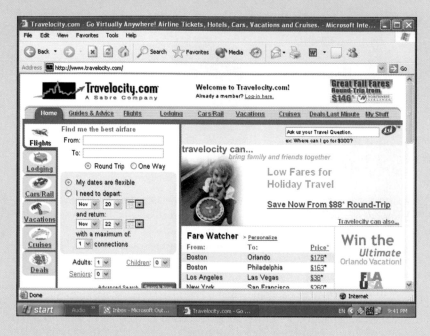

different username was quoted (and sometimes charged) differing prices. Amazon refunded the difference between the lowest price and the sales price to affected customers and assured customers they would not conduct similar pricing experiments in the future.

Internet Exercises

1. **Structured exercise.** Go to http://www.prenhall.com/capron and use the links there to compare prices for a product using the specialized price-comparison sites provided.

2. **Freeform exercise.** Compare the price for a specified item on popular auction sites to the price for the same merchandise on another e-commerce site. What do you see as the most important differences between buying at auction sites versus buying from other e-commerce sites? Things to consider include price, availability, how long it takes to receive the item, payment and shipping options and security.

3. **Advanced exercise.** Working alone or with a group, make a short shopping list of familiar items. Compare prices and ease of shopping using an online retailer with those at local stores where you regularly shop. Be sure to log the time spent gathering information online and from the local stores (or from their sales flyers). Don't forget to include shipping and sales tax as appropriate.

Planet Internet

Security and Privacy:
Computers and the Internet

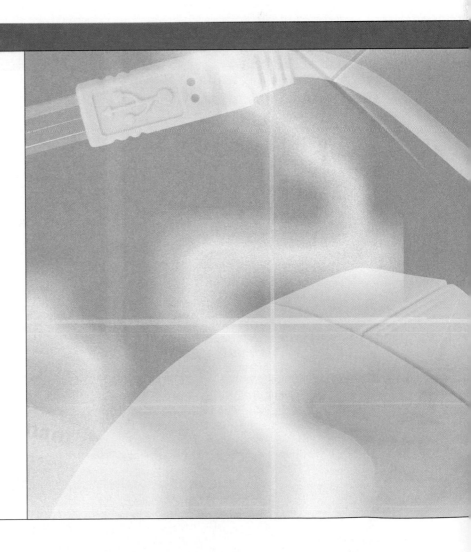

Security and Privacy:
Computers and the Internet

CHAPTER 10

LEARNING OBJECTIVES

Explain the different types of computer crime and the difficulties of discovery and prosecution.

Describe the aspects of securing corporate data, including software and data security, disaster recovery plans, and security legislation.

Describe in general terms how viruses work, the damage they can cause, and procedures used to prevent this damage.

Explain the threats to personal privacy posed by computers and the Internet. Describe actions you can take to maximize your privacy.

At Wolfe-Straus, a company that manufactures particleboard, there is a high awareness of computer security. Potential hires are carefully screened. Employees know better than to reveal their computer passwords. Diskettes holding data are never left lying around. Important files are backed up on a regular basis. Outdated reports with sensitive data are fed to the shredder. It seems as if they're doing everything right.

How is it, then, that a thief was able to walk off with the entire employee personnel file? Stolen reports? Illicit Internet access? No, it was really a simple matter. Using a screwdriver, the thief was able to remove and steal the entire hard drive from a personal computer.

The file contained employee names, addresses, birth dates, Social Security numbers, salaries, and home phone numbers. The company had to warn its 577 employees that their personal data had been compromised. That information could be used to apply for fraudulent credit cards in the employees' names or to gain access to other information about them. Even worse, the stolen hard disk contained the bank account numbers of retired workers who opted for direct-deposit pension checks. Managers could only shake their heads and hope that they were faced with a relatively stupid criminal who wanted just the $200 hardware, rather than a smart criminal who would recognize that the data could be worth hundreds of thousands of dollars.

Security personnel considered several options to prevent such incidents in the future, including keeping all data on server disks in locked rooms, applying a password to all files, using hard drives that required special tools for detachment, and placing cages around desktop machines when not in use. They settled on a triple plan: using file passwords, placing important files on servers only, and placing other personal computer files on removable hard drives that could be locked away at night.

▶ A FIRST LOOK AT SECURITY AND PRIVACY

There was a time when security and privacy issues related to computers were easily managed: You simply locked the computer room door. Those centralized days are, of course, long gone. Now, in theory, anyone can hook up to any computer from any location. In light of data communications access, the first issue is security. The vast files of computer-stored information must be kept secure—safe from destruction, accidental damage, theft, and even espionage.

A second issue is privacy. Private data—salaries, medical information, Social Security numbers, bank balances, and much more—must be kept from prying eyes. The problems are many, and the solutions complex. The escalating expansion of the Internet has only heightened the existing problems and added new problems of its own. These issues and more will be addressed in this chapter.

▶ COMPUTER CRIME

It was 5 o'clock in the morning, and 14-year-old Randy Miller was startled to see a man climbing in his bedroom window. "FBI," the man announced, "and that computer is mine." So ended a computer caper in San Diego in which 23 teenagers, ages 13 to 17, had used their home computers to invade computer systems as far away as Massachusetts. The teenagers were **hackers,** people who attempt to gain access to computer systems illegally, usually from a personal computer, via a data communications network.

The term *hacker* was originally used among computer enthusiasts as a term of recognition for a person with a very high level of computer expertise, but somewhere along the way, a journalist referred to someone who was breaking into computers via the Internet as a hacker and the meaning stuck. Experts prefer the term **cracker** for persons engaging in illegal activities. In this case, the hackers did not use the system to steal money or property. But they did create fictitious accounts and destroyed or changed some data files. The FBI's entry through the bedroom window was calculated: The agents figured that, given even a moment's warning, the teenagers were clever enough to alert each other via computer.

This story—except for the boy's name—is true. Hackers ply their craft for a variety of reasons but most often to show off for their peers or to harass people they do not like.

You will probably not be surprised to learn that hackers have invaded Web sites. These vandals show up with what amounts to a digital spray can, defacing sites with taunting boasts, graffiti, and their own private jokes. Although the victims feel violated, the perpetrators view their activities as mere pranks. In reality, such activity is antisocial and can result in great expense for the victims.

Hackers and Other Miscreants

Hacking has long been thought the domain of teenagers with time on their hands. The pattern is changing, however. A recent government survey showed that the computer systems of over half of the largest U.S. corporations had been invaded, but not by teenagers. Most intruders were competitors attempting to steal proprietary information. Even more astounding, federal investigators told a U.S. Senate hearing that the U.S. Department of Defense computers are attacked more than 200,000 times per year. Most worrisome is the emerging computer attack abilities of other nations, which, in a worst-case scenario, could seriously degrade the nation's ability to deploy and sustain military forces.

- Many hackers ply their craft by surprisingly low-tech means. Although some use sophisticated methods to attack network security, many simply use what is called **social engineering,** a tongue-in-cheek term for con artist actions, to persuade unsuspecting people to give away their passwords over the phone. Recognizing the problem, employers are educating their employees to be alert to such scams.

- Hackers are only a small fraction of the security problem. The most serious losses are caused by electronic pickpockets, who are usually a good deal older and not so harmless.

Consider these examples:

- A brokerage clerk sat at his terminal in Denver and, with a few taps of the keys, transformed 1700 shares of his own stock, worth $1.50 per share, to the same number of shares in another company worth 10 times that much.

- A keyboard operator in Oakland, California changed some delivery addresses to divert several thousand dollars' worth of department store goods into the hands of accomplices.

- A ticket clerk at the Arizona Veteran's Memorial Coliseum issued full-price basketball tickets for admission and then used her computer to record the sales as half-price tickets and pocketed the difference.

These stories illustrate that computer crime is not always flashy, front-page news about geniuses getting away with millions of dollars. These people were ordinary employees in ordinary businesses—committing computer crimes.

The problem of computer crime has been aggravated in recent years by increased access to computers. More employees now have access to computers on their jobs. In fact, computer crime is often just white-collar crime with a new medium: Every time an employee is trained on the computer at work, he or she also gains knowledge that—potentially—could be used to harm the company.

The Changing Face of Computer Crime

Computer crime once fell into a few simple categories, such as software theft or data destruction. The dramatically increased access to networks has changed the focus to damage that can be done by unscrupulous people with online access. The most frequently reported computer crimes fall into these categories:

- **Credit card fraud.** Customer numbers are floating all over public and private networks, in varying states of protection. Some are captured and used fraudulently.

- **Data communications fraud.** This category covers a broad spectrum, including piggybacking on someone else's network, the use of an office network for personal purposes, and computer-directed diversion of funds.

G E T T I N G   P R A C T I C A L   **Protecting Your PC**

How vulnerable is your PC to a hacker attack? If you connect to the Internet via a dial-up line to your ISP and spend an hour or two at a time surfing and checking e-mail, you aren't in too much danger. But if you have a cable or DSL connection and leave your computer running most of the time, your PC is a prime target, especially if you use Windows XP.

When you are online, your computer's IP address allows it to receive data. ISPs assign a temporary IP address each time a dial-up connection is established. This makes it difficult for hackers to find you. However, because cable and DSL connections are always on whenever your computer is powered up, your ISP may assign you a permanent IP address, making you an easy target. Also, Windows XP security is notoriously weak, especially in its standard configuration. Its many shortcomings are well known to hackers.

So what can you do to protect yourself? First, install a strong personal firewall. A firewall is software that blocks attack attempts via the Internet. Until recently, firewalls were expensive, complex software packages used to protect company networks from intrusion. But recently, several good, inexpensive (less than $50) firewall programs for PCs have become available.

Second, plug the security holes in Windows. An Internet search using Windows and security as keywords will turn up several good Internet sites that describe how to tweak the network and file-sharing settings in Windows and eliminate the major security problems.

Third, use passwords on your system. By picking longer passwords that combine numbers and letters and changing them monthly, you can make it much more difficult for any hacker who manages to breach your defenses.

As small home networks become more common, the future trend is for firewalls that run on dedicated hardware devices connected between the Internet and the network. These will be much more secure than firewall software on a general-purpose PC.

- **Unauthorized access to computer files.** This general snooping category covers everything from accessing confidential employee records to the theft of trade secrets and product pricing structures.

- **Unlawful copying of copyrighted software.** Whether the casual sharing of copyrighted software among friends or assembly-line copying by organized crime, unlawful copying incurs major losses for software vendors.

Some "Bad Guy" Tricks

Although the emphasis in this chapter is on preventing rather than committing crime, being familiar with the terms and methods computer criminals use is part of being a prudent computer user. Many of these words or phrases have made their way into the general vocabulary.

- **Bomb.** A **bomb** causes a program to trigger damage under certain conditions; it is usually set to go off at a later date—perhaps after the perpetrator has left the company. Bombs are sometimes planted in software that is to be used by the general public. Shareware, which is less rigorously monitored than commercial software, has been known as a source of bombs.

- **Data diddling.** The unattractive term, **data diddling,** refers to changing data before or as it enters the system—for example, a course grade or hours worked. Auditors who are monitoring a computer system cannot limit themselves to the computer processing itself; they must verify the accuracy of the source data.

- **Denial of service (DoS) attack.** A **DoS attack** occurs when hackers bombard a site with more requests for service that it can possibly handle, preventing legitimate users from accessing the site. Through the use of Trojan horse programs planted on unsuspecting sites around the Internet, hackers can cause the attacks to come from many different sites simultaneously. During a four-day period in February 2000, DoS attacks crippled the servers of such sites as Yahoo!, Amazon.com, eBay, CNN.com, and E*Trade for up to four hours each.

- **Piggybacking.** The term fits: In **piggybacking,** an illicit user "rides" into the system on the back of another user. The original user gives some sort of identification, probably a password, to access the system. Then, if the legitimate user does not exit the system properly, the intruder may have access to systems and files by simply continuing where the original user has left off.

- **Salami technique.** The name **salami** given to this embezzlement technique reflects the small "slices" of money that may be squirreled away undetected from a large financial system. In one famous case, a bank employee commandeered the extra amounts when accounts were rounded to dollars and cents after interest was computed. For example, if interest was computed to be $77.0829, the interest was reported as $77.08, and the $0.0029 added to the unauthorized salami account. Done hundreds of times over thousands of accounts, these small amounts add up. This particular scheme, by the way, would not work today; bank auditors are much too savvy for anything this obvious.

- **Scavenging.** The simple approach of **scavenging** is still all too common, even in this day of shredders. Scavengers simply search company trash cans and dumpsters for printouts containing not-for-distribution information, perhaps even a gold mine of credit card numbers. It is not unusual for thieves to get account numbers and other information from the garbage and recycling bins of individuals, hence the popularity of personal home shredders.

- **Trapdoor.** A **trapdoor** is an illicit program that is left within a completed legitimate program. It allows subsequent unauthorized—and unknown—entry by the perpetrator, who then has the ability to make changes to the program. This technique is not available to the average person. The programmer who has the skills to do it can cause great damage, from altering the method of program processing to destroying records and files.

- **Trojan horse.** A **Trojan horse** involves illegal instructions covertly placed in the middle of a legitimate program. The program does do something useful, but via the Trojan horse instructions, does something destructive in the background.

- **Zapping.** The generic term **zapping** refers to a variety of software, probably illicitly acquired, designed to bypass all security systems.

In summary, there are multiple opportunities for scoundrels to cause havoc in and around computer systems. It is up to employees and individuals at all levels to recognize the danger and protect their assets.

White-Hat Hackers

Perhaps you saw the movie *Sneakers*, in which Robert Redford, in the opening scene, appears to be in the process of robbing a bank. But, no, Mr. Redford is actually executing a test of the bank's security system. This is a common scene at today's banks and in any other organization that depends on computer networks.

Faced with threats on every side, most network-laced companies have chosen a proactive stance. Rather than waiting for the hackers, snoops, and thieves to show up, they hire professionals to beat them to it. Called **white-hat hackers,** tiger teams, or sometimes intrusion testers or hackers for hire, these highly trained technical people are paid to try to break into a computer system before anyone else does.

Using the same kind of finesse and tricks that a hacker might, white-hat hackers exploit the system weaknesses. After chinks are revealed, they can be sealed or protected. The hacker's first approach, typically, is to access the company's system from the Internet. The quality of security varies from company to company. Sometimes security is fairly tight; other times, as one hacker put it, "It's a cakewalk."

Sometimes companies hire one company to establish security and then hire white-hat hackers to try to defeat it. The company might not even alert its own employees to the hacker activities, preferring to see whether the intrusions are detected and, if so, how employees react.

Discovery and Prosecution

Prosecuting the computer criminal is difficult for several reasons. To begin with, discovery is often difficult. Many times the crime simply goes undetected. In addition, crimes that are detected are—an estimated 85 percent of the time—never reported to the authorities. By law, banks have to make a report when their computer systems have been compromised, but other businesses do not. Often these businesses choose not to report such crimes, because they are worried about their reputations and credibility in the community.

Even if a computer crime is detected, prosecution is by no means assured. There are a number of reasons for this. First, some law enforcement agencies do not fully understand the complexities of computer-related fraud. Second, few prosecutors are qualified to handle computer crime cases. Third, judges and juries are not always educated about computers and might not understand the nature of the violation or the seriousness of the crime.

In short, the chances of having a computer crime go undetected are, unfortunately, good. And if it is detected, the chances that the criminal will suffer no consequences are also good: A computer criminal might not go to jail, might not be found guilty if prosecuted, and might not even be prosecuted.

But this situation is changing. Since Congress passed the **Computer Fraud and Abuse Act** in 1986, awareness of computer crime has grown on the national level. This law is supplemented by state statutes; most states have passed some form of computer crime law. Computer criminals who are successfully prosecuted are subject to fines, jail time, and confiscation of their computer equipment.

Computer Forensics

"I'll lose my job if they find out what I sent you." Most companies keep copies of all e-mail that is sent and received, and most do spot checks of the contents. When the above statement was discovered among an employee's outgoing messages, a company security officer wondered whether she had uncovered corporate espionage. Was the message sender giving away—or perhaps selling—company secrets? In this case it was easy to find out: The security officer simply extracted the attachment that had been sent with the message. It turned out to be pornographic material—and the employee did indeed lose his job over this incident.

Checking an already-identified e-mail message stored on disk is relatively straightforward, but finding other kinds of data is trickier. The data of interest may be in a deleted file or stored with a phony file name or disguised in some other manner. But such data is not safely hidden from professionals known as forensic experts. A relatively new field, **computer forensics** refers to uncovering computer-stored information suitable for use as evidence in courts of law.

Computer forensics has been used in both criminal and civil cases, in applications as varied as murder, blackmail, and counterfeiting. Each computer forensic examination is unique in its purpose and, possibly, method of approach. One company might need to trace missing inventory; whereas another might be responding to a court-ordered subpoena for e-mail messages containing sexual harassment language.

An unsophisticated perpetrator might get a tip that he or she is being investigated and delete the related files before anyone can examine the computer. This is a plaintiff's (or prosecutor's) delight: Not only can the deleted files be reconstructed; the accused party has displayed guilty behavior.

Some computer forensics experts have set up shop and are for hire, perhaps even advertising on their own Web sites (Figure 10-1). But most such experts are on the staffs of police departments and law firms.

► SECURITY: PLAYING IT SAFE

As you can see from the previous sections, companies and organizations have been vulnerable in the matter of computer security. **Security** is a system of safeguards designed to protect a computer system and data from deliberate or accidental damage or access by unauthorized persons. That means safeguarding the system against such threats as natural disasters, fire, accidents, vandalism, theft or destruction of data, industrial espionage, and hackers.

Identification and Access: Who Goes There?

How does a computer system detect whether you are the person who should be allowed access to it? Various means have been devised to give access to authorized people without compromising the system. These means fall into four broad categories: what you have, what you know, what you do, and what you are.

- **What you have.** You might have a key, badge, token, or plastic card to give you physical access to the computer room or to a locked-up terminal or personal computer. A card with a magnetized strip, for example, can give you access to your

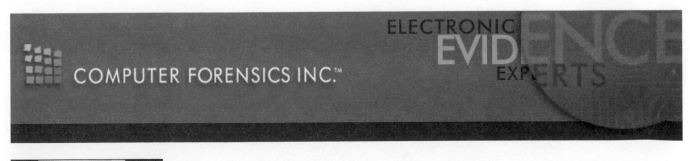

▲ **FIGURE** **10-1**

Forensics experts. Computer Forensics Inc. offers its services to large corporations and law firms.

▼ F I G U R E   10-2

BioMouse Plus. The BioMouse Plus, a product of Activcard, uses fingerprint scanning and smart-card reading to authenticate the user. The system consists of a mouse/scanner/smart card reader, shown here, and related software.

bank account via a remote cash machine. Taking this a step further, some employees begin each business day by donning an **active badge,** a clip-on identification card with an embedded computer chip. The badge signals its wearer's location—legal or otherwise—by sending out radio signals, which are read by sensors sprinkled throughout the building.

- **What you know.** Standard what-you-know items are a password or an identification number for your bank cash machine. Cipher locks on doors require that you know the correct combination of numbers.

- **What you do.** In their daily lives people often sign documents as a way of proving who they are. Although a signature is difficult to copy, forgery is not impossible. Today, software can verify both scanned and online signatures.

- **What you are.** Now it gets interesting. Some security systems use **biometrics,** the science of measuring individual body characteristics. Fingerprinting might seem to be old news, but not when you simply insert your finger into an identification machine (Figure 10-2). Some systems use the characteristics of the entire hand. Another approach is identification by voice pattern. Even newer is the concept of identification by the retina of the eye, which has a pattern that is harder to duplicate than a voiceprint, or by the entire face, which draws its uniqueness from heat radiating from blood vessels (Figure 10-3).

When Disaster Strikes: What Do You Have To Lose?

Computer installations of any kind can be struck by natural disasters or by disasters of human origin, which can lead to security violations. What kinds of problems might this cause an organization?

Your first thoughts might be of the hardware—the computer and its related equipment. But loss of hardware is not a major problem in itself; the loss is probably covered by insurance, and the hardware can be replaced. The true problem with hardware loss is the diminished processing ability that exists while managers find a substitute facility and return the installation to its former state. The ability to continue processing data is critical. Some information industries, such as banking, would go out of business in a matter of days if their computer operations were suspended. Loss of software should not be a problem if the organization has heeded industry warnings—and used common sense—to make backup copies of program files.

A more important problem is the loss of data. Imagine trying to reassemble lost or destroyed files of customer records, accounts receivable, or design data for a new airplane. The costs would be staggering. Software and data security are presented in more detail later in this chapter. First, consider an overview of disaster recovery, the steps to restoring processing ability.

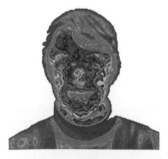

▲ F I G U R E   10-3

Identification. A person's entire face is used for identification in some security systems. Identification is based on a unique pattern of heat radiating from an individual's facial blood vessels.

Disaster Recovery Plan

A **disaster recovery plan** is a method of restoring computer processing operations and data files if operations are halted or files are damaged by major destruction. There are various approaches. Some organizations revert temporarily to manual services, but life without the computer can be difficult indeed. Others arrange to buy time at a service bureau, but this is inconvenient for companies in remote or rural areas. If a single act, such as a fire, destroys your computing facility, it is possible that a mutual aid pact will help you get back on your feet. In such a plan, two or more companies agree to lend each other computing power if one of them has a problem. This would be of little help, however, if there were a regional disaster and many companies needed assistance.

Banks and other organizations with survival dependence on computers sometimes form a **consortium,** a joint venture to support a complete computer facility. Such a facility is completely available and routinely tested but used only in the event of a disaster. Among these facilities, a **hot site** is a fully equipped computer center, with hardware, environmental controls, security, and communications facilities. A **cold site** is an environmentally suitable empty shell in which a company can install its own computer system.

The use of such a facility or any type of recovery at all depends on advance planning—specifically, the disaster recovery plan. The idea of such a plan is that everything except the hardware has been stored in a safe place somewhere else. The storage location should be several miles away so that it will not be affected by local physical forces, such as a flood or tornado. Typical items stored at the backup site are program and data files, program listings, program and operating systems documentation, hardware inventory lists, output forms, and a copy of the disaster plan manual.

The disaster recovery plan should include a list of priorities identifying the programs that must be up and running first, plans for notifying employees of changes in locations and procedures, a list of needed equipment and where it can be obtained, a list of alternative computing facilities, and procedures for handling input and output data in a different environment.

Software Security

Software security has been an industry concern for years. Initially, there were many questions: Who owns custom-made software? Is the owner the person who wrote the program or the company for which the author wrote the program? What prevents a programmer from taking copies of programs from one job to another? The answer to these questions is well established. If the author of the software—the programmer—is in the employ of the organization, the software belongs to the organization, not the programmer. The programmer may not take the software along to the next job. If the programmer is a consultant, however, the ownership of the software that is produced should be specified in the contract; otherwise, the parties enter extremely murky legal waters.

Data Security

We have discussed the security of hardware and software. Now consider the security of data, which is one of an organization's most important assets. Here too there must be planning for security. Usually, security officers, who are part of top management, do this planning.

What steps can be taken to prevent theft or alteration of data? There are several data protection techniques; these will not individually (or even collectively) guarantee security, but they make a good start.

- **Secured waste.** Discarded printouts, printer ribbons, and the like can be sources of information to unauthorized people. This kind of waste can be made secure by the use of shredders or locked trash barrels.

- **Internal controls.** Internal controls are controls that are planned as part of the computer system. One example is a transaction log. This is a file of all accesses or attempted accesses to certain data.

- **Auditor checks.** Most companies have auditors go over the financial books. In the course of their duties, auditors frequently review computer programs and data. From a data security standpoint, auditors might also check to see who has accessed data during periods when that data is not usually used. Today auditors can

Cyberwarfare

Many science fiction authors have written about wars conducted primarily by computers, but most of their tales have been set far into the future. This type of conflict, dubbed cyberwarfare, could happen sooner than most people think.

All major countries and many smaller ones have been developing cyberwarfare capabilities for a number of years. The United States has consolidated its offensive cyberwarfare programs at the U.S. Space Command in Colorado. China is considering creation of a fourth branch of its armed forces devoted to information warfare. And a Russian general has compared the disruptive effects of a computer attack on a transportation or electrical grid to that of a nuclear weapon.

Smaller countries have already begun employing cyberattacks to disrupt their enemies. Myanmar's military junta has used (ineffectively, at best) an e-mail virus to attempt to disrupt dissidents' Web activities. Azerbaijan, a former Soviet republic, has been identified as the source of attacks on Armenian Web sites. Since Internet access in Azerbaijan is tightly controlled, government responsibility for the attacks was

continued

strongly suspected. Armenian retaliation against Azerbaijani sites followed quickly.

Even China has been actively testing its capabilities. When the U.S. Department of Transportation computers came under a denial-of-service (DoS) attack, officials quickly identified several Falun Gong (a religious movement in China) sites around the world as the apparent source. Further investigation, however, traced the true source to a computer belonging to the Chinese secret police.

use off-the-shelf audit software, programs that assess the validity and accuracy of the system's operations and output.

- **Applicant screening.** The weakest link in any computer security system is the people in it. At the least, employers should verify the facts that job applicants list on their résumés to help weed out dishonest applicants before they are hired. Employees who are hired for sensitive positions should undergo complete background checks.

- **Passwords.** A password is a secret word, number, or combination of the two that must be typed on the keyboard to gain access to a computer system. Cracking passwords is the most prevalent method of illicit entry to computer systems.

- **Built-in software protection.** Software can be built into operating systems in ways that restrict access to the computer system. One form of software protection is a system that matches a user number against a number assigned to the data being accessed. If a person does not get access, it is recorded that he or she tried to tap into some area for which that person was not authorized. Another form of software protection is a user profile: Information is stored about each user, including the files to which the user has legitimate access.

Personal Computer Security

One summer evening two men in coveralls with company logos backed a truck up to the building that housed a university computer lab. They showed the lab assistant, a part-time student, an authorization slip to move 23 personal computers to another lab on campus. The assistant was surprised but not shocked, since lab use was light in the summer semester. The computers were moved, all right, but not to another lab.

There is an active market for stolen personal computers and their internal components. As this unfortunate tale indicates, personal computer security breaches can be pretty basic. One simple, but not foolproof, remedy is to secure personal computer hardware in place with locks and cables (see Figure 10-4). Also, most personal computers have an individual cover lock that prevents access to internal components.

Although personal computers aren't as environmentally sensitive as larger computers, users should avoid eating, drinking, and smoking around them. Occasional cleaning, such as vacuuming the keyboard, is recommended.

Several precautions can be taken to protect disk data. One is to use a **surge protector,** a device that prevents electrical problems from affecting computer data files. The computer is plugged into the surge protector, which is plugged into the outlet (Figure 10-5a). An **uninterruptible power supply** (**UPS**) includes surge protection and battery backup, which enables you to continue operating your PC during power loss or brownouts (Figure 10-5b). Inexpensive UPSs provide five to ten minutes of

▼ FIGURE 10-4

Cable lock. Physical security is provided by using a cable lock to fasten the PC to the desktop.

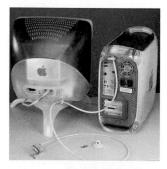

► FIGURE 10-5

Protection from power problems. (a) A surge protector protects the computer from overvoltages caused by power surges. (b) An uninterruptible power supply (UPS) provides battery backup in case of brownouts or power failures.

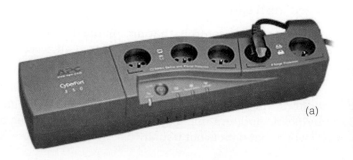
(a)

(b)

battery power, enough to allow you to save and close all files and shut down the system without loss of data. More expensive units can supply power for a half-hour or more. Diskettes should be under lock and key. The most critical precaution, however, is to back up your files regularly and systematically.

Prepare for the Worst: Back Up Your Files

Although organizations recognize the value of data and have procedures in place for backing up data files on a regular basis, personal computer users are not as devoted to this activity. In fact, one wonders why, with continuous admonishments and readily available procedures, some people still leave their precious files unprotected.

WHAT COULD GO WRONG? If you use software incorrectly or simply input data incorrectly, it might be some time before the resulting erroneous data is detected. You then need to go back to the time when the data files were still acceptable. Sometimes the software itself can harm data, or a hard disk could physically malfunction, making your files inaccessible. Although none of these mishaps are too likely, they certainly do happen. It is even less likely that you would lose your hard disk files to fire or flood, but this is also possible. The most likely scenario is that you will accidentally delete some files yourself. (Deleted files can probably be recovered using utility software if the action is taken right away, before other data is written over the deleted files.) Finally, there is always the possibility of your files being infected with a virus. Experts estimate that average users experience a significant disk loss once every year.

WAYS TO BACK UP FILES. Some people simply make another copy of their hard disk files on diskette.

A better way is to back up all your files on a tape. Backing up to a tape drive, CD-RW, or DVD-RAM is safer and faster. You can also use software that will automatically back up all your files at a certain time of day, or on command. Sophisticated users place their files on a mirror hard disk, which simply makes a second copy of everything you put on the original disk; this approach, as you might expect, is expensive.

Backup software generally provides three types of backup. A **full backup** copies everything from the hard drive. A **differential backup** copies all files that have been changed since the last full backup. An **incremental backup** copies only those files that have been changed since either the last full backup or the last incremental backup. A comprehensive backup plan involves periodic full backups, complemented by either incremental or differential backups. With the differential approach, the restoration process requires the use of two backup files: the last full backup followed by the most recent differential backup. Restoration using the incremental approach can require a number of files—the last full backup followed by each incremental backup performed since the full backup.

► VIRUSES: NOTORIOUS PESTS

Worms and viruses are unpleasant terms that have entered the jargon of the computer industry to describe some of the insidious ways in which computer systems can be invaded.

A **worm** is a program that transfers itself from computer to computer over a network and plants itself as a separate file on the target computer's disks. Worms are rare, however. The ongoing nuisance is the virus, which, as its name suggests, is contagious. A **virus** is a set of illicit instructions embedded in a file that passes itself on to other files with which it comes into contact. In its most basic form, a virus is the digital equivalent of vandalism. It can change or delete files, display words or obscene messages, or produce bizarre screen effects. In its most vindictive form, a virus can slowly sabotage a computer system and remain undetected for months, contaminating data or, in the case of the famous Michelangelo virus, wiping out your entire hard drive. A virus may be dealt with by means of a **vaccine,** or **antivirus,** a computer program that stops the spread of a virus and often eradicates it. However, a **retrovirus** has the ability to fight back and may even delete or disable antivirus software.

You might wonder who produces viruses. At one point, the mischief-makers were mostly curious young men. Now, virus makers are older and actually trade notes and tips on the Internet. They do what they do, psychologists say, mostly to impress their friends. Experts have estimated that hundreds of virus writers exist worldwide. However, although there are thousands of known viruses, most of the damage is caused by only a dozen or so (Table 10-1).

T A B L E 1 0 - 1 Typical Viruses and Worms	
Name	**Unpleasant Consequences**
CodeRed	A worm that infects computers running Microsoft's IIS Server. Its original payload used the infected computer to launch a DoS attack on the White House Web site, but a variant, CodeRed II, allows a hacker to have full remote access to the infected computer.
Nimda	A mass-mailing worm that utilizes multiple methods to spread itself. On infected machines files are modified, security settings are altered, and system performance degrades.
SirCam	Distributed as an e-mail attachment. Infected computers may have files deleted, performance may be degraded, and random files may be sent from the hard drive to anyone in the address book.
Form	Causes a clicking noise in the computer's keyboard on the 18th day of the month; it may also corrupt data on diskettes.
Melissa	A macro virus distributed as an e-mail attachment that, when opened, disables a number of safeguards in Word 97 or Word 2000, and, if the user has the Microsoft Outlook e-mail program, causes the virus to be resent to the first 50 people in the user's address book.
Ripper	Corrupts data written to a hard disk approximately one time out of a thousand.
MDMA	Affects Microsoft Word files; can delete files.
Concept	Transferred from one Microsoft Word file to another if both are in memory at the same time; also transferred by e-mail attachments. Causes a file to be saved in the template directory instead of where it belongs; confuses users, who do not know what happened to the most recent version of the file.
One_Half	Encrypts the hard disk so that only the virus can read the data there; when the encryption is half completed, it flashes One_Half on the screen. If you try to remove the virus without the proper antivirus software, you lose the encryption key and thus your data.
Michelangelo	Destroys all data on the hard disk on March 6, Michelangelo's birthday.
Cascade	Picks random text characters and drops them to the bottom of the screen.
Jerusalem	Deletes any program executed on Friday the 13th.

Transmitting a Virus

Consider this typical example. A programmer secretly inserts a few viral instructions into a game called Kriss-Kross, which she then offers free to others via the Internet. Any takers download the game to their own computers. Now each time a user runs Kriss-Kross—that is, loads it into memory—the virus is loaded too. The virus stays in memory, infecting any other program that is loaded until the computer is turned off. The virus has now spread to other programs, and the process can be repeated again and again. In fact, each newly infected program becomes a virus carrier. Although many viruses are transmitted in just this way via networks, another common method is by passing diskettes from computer to computer (Figure 10-6).

Here is another typical scenario. An office worker puts a copy of a report on a diskette and slips it into her briefcase to take home. After shooing her children away from the new game they are playing on the computer, she sits down to work on the report. She does not know that a virus, borne by the kids' new software, has infected the diskette. When she takes the diskette back to work, the virus is transmitted from her computer to the entire office network.

The most insidious viruses attach to the operating system. One virus, called Cascade, causes random text letters to "drop" to a pile at the bottom of the screen. Viruses attached to the operating system itself have greater potential for mischief.

A relative newcomer to the virus scene is the macro virus, which uses a program's own macro programming language, often Microsoft Word, to distribute itself. A macro virus infects a document by being carried as a macro program. When you open the document that has the virus, any other documents that are opened in the same session may become infected by the virus. This also applies to an infected document that you may have received as an e-mail attachment. The Melissa virus is one of the most notorious macro viruses (Figure 10-7).

Damage from Viruses

Some viruses are benign, more on the order of pranks, but many cause serious damage. Even the benign ones can cause confusion and possibly panic, leading to lost time and effort. Many viruses remain dormant until triggered by some activity. For

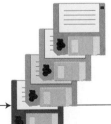

ORIGINATION
A programmer writes a tiny program —the virus—that has destructive power and can reproduce itself. The virus is introduced to the computer via disk or downloading.

TRANSMISSION
Most often, the virus is attached to a normal program; unknown to the user, the virus spreads to other software.

REPRODUCTION
The virus is passed to other users who use other computers. The virus remains dormant as it is passed on.

INFECTION
At a predetermined time, prompted by the computer's internal clock, the attack begins: A benign virus may just print an unexpected message, but a vicious virus may destroy data files and gobble up memory.

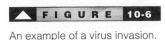

▲ FIGURE 10-6

An example of a virus invasion.

► FIGURE 10-7

The Melissa virus. The Melissa virus is an MS Word macro virus that sends the infected document to the first 50 addresses in your Outlook address book. There are a number of variants. One of them has the following effects: (a) On December 25, this message will appear on your screen and insert random colored shapes (b) into the current document. It will also attempt to reformat the C: drive the next time your system is booted.

example, a virus called Jerusalem B activates itself every Friday the 13th and proceeds to erase any file you try to load from your disk. Another virus includes instructions to add 1 to a counter each time the virus is copied to another disk. When the counter reaches 4, the virus erases all data files. This is not the end of the destruction, of course; the three other copied disks have also been infected.

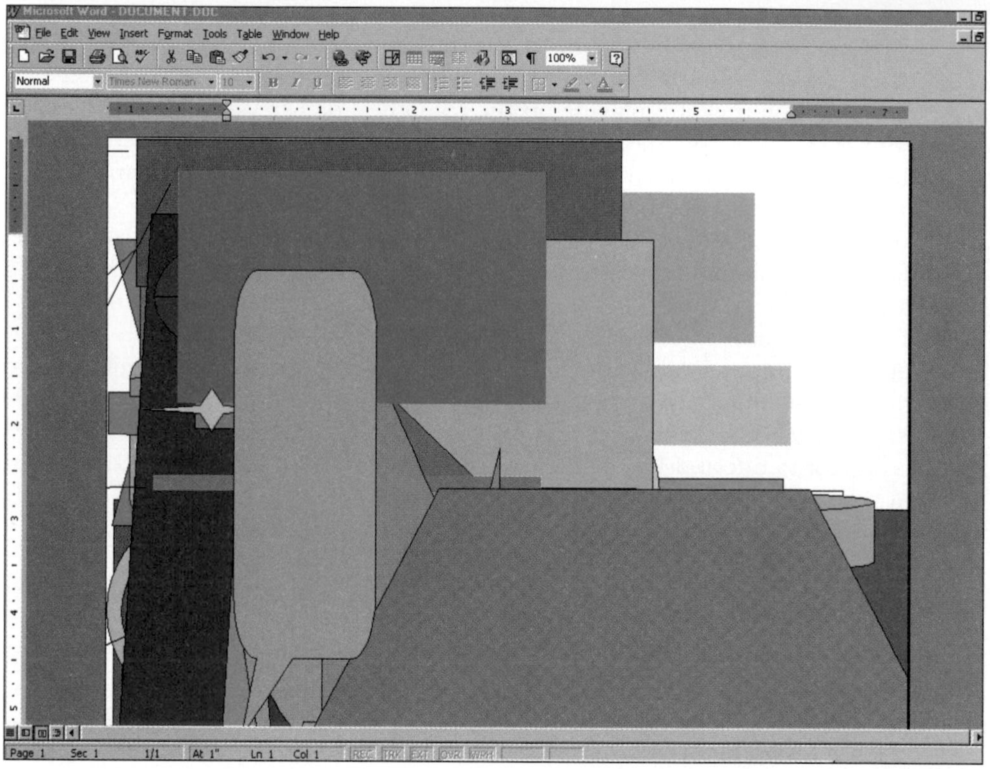

Virus Myths

Viruses are merely programs written to create copies of themselves and to attach these copies to other programs. The only way any virus can infect your computer is by executing one of these programs or by booting from a diskette containing an infected boot sector. Almost no one boots from a disk, preferring instead to use the operating system on the hard disk. However, it is fairly common to boot the computer when a disk is accidentally left in the drive. Even though you receive the "Non-system disk" error message and remove the diskette, the damage may have been done.

Keeping in mind that a virus must be in an executable program (including an executable macro program within a document) or booted from a disk, it is possible to debunk some virus myths:

No privacy on the company e-mail, that is. Your employer can snoop into messages you send or receive even if you think you erased them. You have erased them only from their current hard drive location; copies are still in the company's computer files. In fact, most companies archive all such files on tape and store them for the foreseeable future. Companies may fail to convey to employees the message that e-mail, as a company communications channel, is not private. Employees are often startled, after the fact, to discover that their messages have been intercepted.

Furthermore, some people specialize in extracting deleted messages for use as evidence in court. E-mail can be a dangerous time bomb, because litigators argue that more than any other kind of written communication, e-mail reflects the real, unedited thoughts of the writer. This candid form of corporate communication increasingly is providing the most incriminating evidence used against companies in litigation. In fact, internal company e-mails provided some of the most damaging evidence in the government's antitrust case against Microsoft.

What to do? It is certainly degrading to have something you thought was private waved in front of you as evidence of malingering. As one computer expert put it, if nothing is private, just say so. Companies have begun doing exactly that. The company policy on e-mail is—or should be—expressed in a clear, written document and routinely disseminated to all employees. However, even that step is probably insufficient. People tend to forget or get complacent. Reminders should be given through the usual company conduits—bulletin boards, posters, and so forth.

What about the e-mail you send and receive at home—do you at least have privacy in your own home? Maybe not. You certainly cannot count on it if the computer of the party at the other end is in an office. And keep in mind that messages sent across the Internet hop from computer to computer, with (depending on the service used) the sender having little say about its route. There are many vulnerable spots along the way. Also, your ISP will keep backup tapes of e-mail for some period of time, during which your e-mails would be subject to subpoena by the authorities.

- You cannot get a virus by simply being online, by surfing the Internet, or even from your own local area network. You could, of course, download a program and then, by executing it, get a virus.

- Although most e-mail viruses are in attachments that must be opened, it is possible for a virus to be activated in some versions of Microsoft Outlook by simply viewing an e-mail.

- Data is not executed, so you cannot get a virus from data, including graphics files. However, beware of graphics files that include a viewer program; that program could contain a virus.

Virus Prevention

A word about prevention is in order. The most powerful weapon at your disposal is antivirus software. Antivirus software uses several techniques to detect viruses, but the most common technique is to search for **virus signatures.** Each virus can be identified by a unique string of bits called its signature. When a new virus is detected, experts immediately examine it to determine its signature. Then they add this signature to a file of known virus signatures. Companies that publish antivirus software, such as Symantec and McAfee, maintain Web sites that contain the latest signature files. Because new viruses appear regularly, it is important that you visit your antivirus publisher's site frequently to download these signature files.

Antivirus software scans your hard disk every time you boot the computer or, if you prefer, at regularly scheduled intervals.

Although there have been isolated instances of viruses in commercial software, viruses tend to show up on free software or software acquired from friends or the Internet. Use a commonsense approach to new files. Never install a program unless the diskette comes in a sealed package. Be especially wary of software that arrives unexpectedly from companies with which you have not done business. Use virus-scanning software to check any file or document, no matter what the source, before loading it onto your hard disk. If your own diskette was used in another computer, scan it to see whether it caught a virus. Avoid using programs that may be stolen or whose origin is unclear.

Currently, the most common method of virus infection is through e-mail attachments. Attached documents created by programs, such as Microsoft Word, may contain macro viruses. Executable files may be disguised as innocuous text files attached to e-mails from your friends. After these files infect your system, they can use your e-mail program to send themselves to everyone in your address book, just as your friends unknowingly sent them to you. Most antivirus software can be set to scan incoming e-mail attachments, but you should still be wary of opening any unexpected attachments, no matter who they're from.

► PRIVACY: KEEPING PERSONAL INFORMATION PERSONAL

Think about the forms you have willingly filled out: paperwork for loans or charge accounts, orders for merchandise through the mail, magazine subscription orders, applications for schools and jobs and clubs, and on and on. There may be some forms you have filled out with less delight—tax forms, military draft registration, a court petition, an insurance claim, or a form for a stay in the hospital. And remember all the people who got your name and address from your check: fundraisers, advertisers, and petitioners. These lists don't cover all the ways in which you have supplied data, but you can know with certainty where it all goes: straight to computer files.

Passing Your Data Around

Where is your data now? Has it been shared, rented, or sold? Who sees it? Will it ever be deleted? Or, to put it more bluntly, is anything private anymore? In some cases you can only guess at the answers. It is difficult to say where your data is now, and bureaucracies are not eager to enlighten you. The data may have been moved to other files without your knowledge. In fact, much of the data is most definitely passed around, as anyone with a mailbox can attest. Even some online services sell their subscriber lists, neatly ordered by ZIP code and computer type.

As for who sees your personal data, the answers are not comforting. Government agencies, for example, regularly share data that was originally filed for some other purpose. Consider IRS records, which are compared with student loan records to intercept refunds to former students who have defaulted on their loans. The IRS created a storm of controversy by announcing a plan to use commercial direct-mail lists to locate tax evaders. Many people are worried about the consequences of this kind of sharing (Figure 10-8). For one thing, few of us can be certain that data about us, good or bad, is deleted when it has served its legitimate purpose.

The unfortunate fact is that for very little money, anybody can learn anything about anybody through massive databases. Some matters you want to keep private. You have the right to do so. Although you can do little to stop data about you from circulating through computers, there are some laws that give you access to some of it. Let us see what kind of protection is available to help preserve privacy.

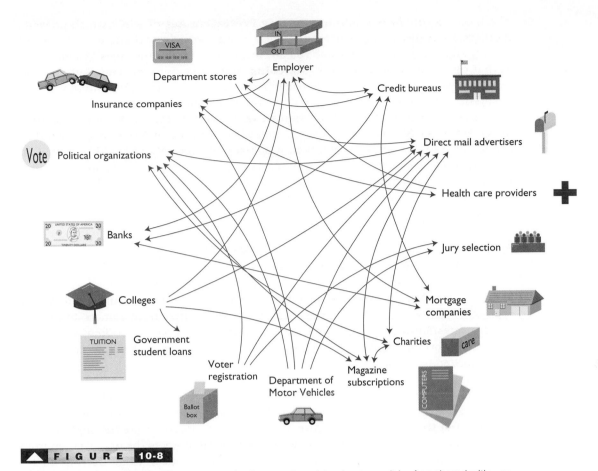

▲ **F I G U R E 10-8**

Potential paths of data. When an organization acquires data about you, it is often shared with—or sold to—other organizations.

Privacy Legislation

Significant legislation relating to privacy began with the **Fair Credit Reporting Act** in 1970. This law allows you to have access to and gives you the right to challenge your credit records. In fact, this access must be given to you free of charge if you have been denied credit. Businesses usually contribute financial information about their customers to a credit bureau, which gives them the right to review a person's prior credit record with other companies. Before the Fair Credit Reporting Act, many people were—without explanation—turned down for credit because of inaccurate financial records about them. Because of the act, people may now check their records to make sure they are accurate.

The **Freedom of Information Act** was also passed in 1970. This landmark legislation allows ordinary citizens to access data about them that was gathered by federal agencies, although sometimes a lawsuit has been necessary to pry data loose.

The most significant legislation protecting the privacy of individuals is the **Federal Privacy Act** of 1974. This act stipulates that there can be no secret personal files; individuals must be allowed to know what is stored in files about them and how the data is used, and they must be able to correct it. The law applies not only to government agencies but also to private contractors dealing with government agencies. These organizations cannot obtain data willy-nilly for no specific purpose; they must justify the need to obtain it.

A more recent law is the **Video Privacy Protection Act** of 1988, which prevents retailers from disclosing a person's video rental records without a court order; privacy supporters want the same rule for medical and insurance files. Another step in that direction is the **Computer Matching and Privacy Protection Act** of 1988, which prevents the government from comparing certain records in an attempt to find a match. However, most comparisons are still unregulated.

In 1996, Congress enacted the **Health Insurance Portability and Accountability Act** (**HIPAA**), which protects employees' health-insurance coverage when they change or lose their jobs. In addition, it governs the security of health information records and transactions, requiring employers, health care providers, and insurance companies to take appropriate steps to protect the privacy of individuals' medical records. Its provisions take effect in phases between 2001 and 2004.

► THE INTERNET: SECURITY AND PRIVACY PROBLEMS

Networks, whether connected to the Internet or not, pose unique security and privacy problems. Many people have access to the system, often from remote locations. Clearly, questions arise: If it is so easy for authorized people to get data, what is to stop unauthorized people from tapping it? Organizations must be concerned about unauthorized people intercepting data in transit, whether hackers, thieves, or industrial spies.

One fundamental approach to network security is to set up a firewall. A **firewall** is a combination of hardware and software that sits between an organization's internal network and the Internet (see Figure 10-9). All traffic between the internal network and the Internet goes through the firewall. The firewall protects the organization from unauthorized access and can also be configured to prevent internal users from accessing inappropriate Internet sites.

► FIGURE 10-9

Firewall. A firewall protects an organization from unauthorized access and can also be configured to prevent internal users from accessing inappropriate Internet sites.

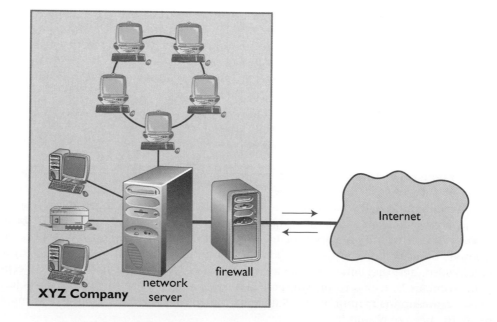

Encryption

Data being sent over communications lines may be protected by scrambling the messages—that is, putting them in code that only the person receiving the message can break. The scrambling process is referred to as **encryption** and uses a code called the **encryption key** to convert the message into an unreadable form. Only someone with the proper key can decrypt the message. The American National Standards Institute has endorsed a process called the **Data Encryption Standard** (**DES**), a standardized **private key encryption** system by which senders and receivers encrypt and decrypt their messages using the same shared key. One problem with this type of encryption is the difficulty of safely arranging for both parties to share a key without having it intercepted by third parties.

Public key encryption systems solve this problem by using a pair of keys generated by the encryption software. Messages that are encrypted by one of the keys can be decrypted only by the other key of the pair. The receiver keeps one key private and makes the other public. Anyone can encrypt a message to the receiver using the public key. Only the receiver can decrypt the message using the private key. Also, a sender can use his private key to encrypt a message and if the recipient can decode it using the sender's public key, the recipient knows that message actually originated with that sender and not someone pretending to be the sender. **RSA,** named after its inventors, Rivest, Shamir, and Adleman, is the most common public key encryption system. In addition to being used in several encryption programs, RSA technology is also built into the latest versions of Microsoft Internet Explorer and Netscape Navigator.

Privacy Problems for Networked Employees

Although employees do not have expectations of total privacy at the office, they are often shocked when they discover that the boss has been spying on them via the network, even their comings and goings on the Internet. The boss, of course, is not spying at all, merely "monitoring." This debate has been heightened by the advent of software that lets managers check up on networked employees without their ever knowing that they are under surveillance. With a click of a mouse button, the boss can silently pull up an employee's current computer screen.

Surveillance software is not limited to checking screens. It can also check on e-mail, count the number of keystrokes per minute, note the length of a worker's breaks, and monitor which computer files are used and for how long.

Worker associations complain that workers who are monitored suffer much higher degrees of stress and anxiety than unmonitored workers. However, vendors defend their products by saying that they are not spy software but rather products designed for training, monitoring resources, and helping employees. Privacy groups are lobbying legislators at the state and federal levels to enact legislation that requires employers to at least alert employees that they are being monitored.

People who feel invaded at work might be shocked to find out that they are also being watched when online—in the supposed privacy of their homes. This time it is not the boss but the Web site owners who are watching.

You Are Being Watched

It might seem to be the ultimate in privacy invasion. When you visit a Web site, it can easily collect the city you are calling from, the site from which you just came, and, of course, everything you do while you are at the site. Software can also discover and record the hardware and software you use. Software can even monitor a user's **click stream,** the series of mouse clicks that link from site to site. Thus a history of what a user chooses to view on the Web can be recorded and used for a variety of purposes by managers and marketers.

Do Privacy Policies Really Work?

When Toysmart.com, a company selling educational and nonviolent children's toys online, ran into financial difficulty in the summer of 2000, it attempted to sell all its assets. The major asset was its customer database, which included names, addresses, billing information, shopping preferences, and family profiles that contained children's names and birth dates.

Over a year earlier, Toysmart had posted a privacy policy on its Web site stating that information collected from customers would never be shared with third parties. The FTC filed a lawsuit to prevent the sale of the customer database and soon reached an agreement with Toysmart that would allow the sale only as part of a sale of the entire Web site to a qualified buyer that would continue to operate the business.

Although most privacy advocates hailed the FTC's prompt action to protect customer privacy, some thought that, given the original policy statement, customers should have been given notice of any sale of their information and have the opportunity to decline.

Many Web servers store information about you in a small text file called a **cookie.** This file is actually stored on your own hard drive and sent back to the server by your browser each time you revisit that site. Cookies can be used to store your viewing preferences so that the server can personalize the Web site appearance each time you access the site. Online shopping sites use cookies to keep track of your shopping cart contents until you check out, and some allow you to maintain wish lists for up to 90 days. Secure sites, such as online brokerages, put a temporary cookie on your system when you log on using your password. This allows you to access multiple pages at that site during a single visit without having to reenter your password for each page. These uses for cookies are beneficial.

A more controversial use of cookies involves tracking your surfing habits so that you can be targeted for certain types of advertisements. Advertising companies, such as Doubleclick, have agreements with many Web sites allowing them to place cookies on your computer whenever you visit any of the affiliated sites. By examining the cookies it has placed on your system, Doubleclick can determine which sites you have visited, deduce your interests and preferences, and choose the advertisements you see when you visit a site. For instance, if you have just looked at several sites selling ski equipment and are now at an airline reservations site looking at flights to Colorado, you might very well see an ad for an Aspen ski resort in one corner of your screen.

Browser preferences can be set to refuse all cookies or to warn you when a site attempts to store a cookie on your computer and allow you to choose whether to accept it, but most users are unaware of this feature. You can also download software that lets you manage the cookies on your hard drive, deleting the ones placed there by advertising companies.

To combat perceived threats to the Internet user's privacy, the World Wide Web Consortium (W3C—the group responsible for developing Web standards) has approved the **Platform for Privacy Preferences Project (P3P)**, a set of standards that allows a Web site server to transmit its privacy policies electronically to the user. Users can configure their software with their privacy preferences, including what personal information they are willing to provide, and the software determines whether the Web site meets the users' requirements. A pantheon of Internet giants, including Microsoft, Netscape, America Online, IBM, AT&T, Hewlett-Packard, and many others support P3P. However, participation by Web sites is voluntary, and no laws force sites to follow the privacy policies they post. Only time will tell whether P3P will inspire sufficient confidence among users to become a lasting standard.

Junk E-mail

Privacy invasion in the form of junk e-mail has become, unfortunately, a common event. The volume of junk e-mail will only soar as more marketers discover how cheap it is. A postal mailing to a million people costs about $800,000, including postage and printing. Internet marketers can reach the same number of people by making a phone call and paying a few hundred dollars for time spent online. The software that makes mass advertising—called **spamming**—possible gathers e-mail addresses and sends e-mail messages for marketers: thousands and thousands every day. One of the most annoying aspects of e-mail is that, unlike postal junk mail, which at least arrives at no cost to you, a user who pays for online usage may be paying for part of the cost of junk e-mail delivery. Furthermore, the spammers are often devious, using subject lines that appear to indicate personal messages or a reply to "Your request for information."

Enraged spam recipients sometimes respond to the perpetrator by **flaming,** sending insulting messages in return. Experienced spammers, however, have probably already abandoned the originating site and moved to another one. Also, many

DAY IN THE LIFE | Marty Lefebvre, *IT Technician*

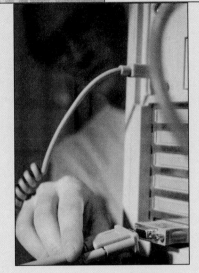

Viruses are the scourge of the computer world, which is why businesses must remain especially vigilant against them. All you need to do is read the news reports on the latest virus making the rounds to see the ways in which they can cost businesses money. This is why making antivirus efforts a part of IT duties isn't just smart, it's a necessity.

Marty is an IT technician who, in addition to his other duties, takes care of the antivirus software for his company. There's more to consider than just making sure the software is installed on every computer in the office. Marty has to ensure that each is programmed to automatically check for viruses daily, and update the virus definitions just as

often. Now, in a business with over sixty workstations, that could create a lot of Internet traffic. So Marty simply downloads the virus definitions once every day and stores them on a specific place on the internal network. The antivirus software on each workstation is configured to fetch the definitions from there, saving the Internet bandwidth by keeping the traffic confined to the internal LAN.

Now known as Mr. Virus to the rest of the company, Marty even maintains a virus newsletter, which he sends out once a week. In it, he describes not only the real viruses on the prowl, but also the most common virus hoaxes currently making the rounds.

spammers use software that creates a phony source address for the spam. If you want to maximize your privacy and reduce your chances of getting junk e-mail, be careful where you leave your e-mail address. A prime source of e-mail addresses is newsgroup messages, whose e-mail addresses will likely be gathered up and sold. Furthermore, Internet business sites entice visitors to supply personal data that can be used for marketing and promotion. An e-mail address is their most treasured commodity.

There is no sure protection from junk e-mail, but there are ways to minimize it. One approach is to use **filter software,** which gives you some control over what messages will be accepted. The filter software already knows that you do not want messages whose titles are "Lose 30 pounds in 10 days!!!" or "Earn $$$$ at home!" In addition to eliminating the obvious, you may add your own list of screening words. You may even state the exact e-mail addresses from which you will accept mail. Some ISPs provide easy-to-use filters for customers who want to reduce the amount of unwanted e-mail they receive.

Your online service may let you make up several online names. Most experts recommend that you use a separate name for surfing the Internet and ignore any mail that comes in for that name. More spam-fighting advice from experts includes never filing a member's profile with your online service, not filling in registration forms at Web sites unless the purveyor promises not to sell or exchange your information, and never, never responding to a spammer. Don't even reply to messages that promise to remove your name from their mailing list; spammers use such replies to verify working e-mail addresses, and your response could lead to more spam.

The federal government has been unable to produce anti-spamming legislation, but the individual states are starting to take up the slack. The first such law with teeth was passed by the state of Washington in 1998. The law specifically bans unsolicited commercial e-mail that has misleading information in the subject line, disguises the path it took across the Internet, or contains an invalid reply address. Suits brought by the state have sought $2000 for each piece of unsolicited commercial e-mail sent to Washington residents in violation of the law. In 2002 in the state of Virginia, AOL won a $7 million award against a spammer thanks to the Virginia

Computer Crimes Act. Many other states have also passed anti-spamming legislation, but results have been limited so far.

▲

The issues raised in this chapter are often the ones that we think of after the fact, when it is too late. Security and privacy factors are somewhat like insurance that we wish we did not have to buy. But we do buy insurance for our homes, cars, and lives because we know that we cannot risk being without it. The computer industry also knows that it cannot risk being without safeguards for security and privacy. As a computer user, you will share responsibility for addressing these issues.

CHAPTER REVIEW

► **Summary and Key Terms**

- The word **hacker** originally referred to a person with a high level of computer expertise, but now the term usually describes a person who gains access to computer systems illegally. Experts prefer the term **cracker** for persons engaging in illegal activities. Using **social engineering,** a tongue-in-cheek term for con artist actions, hackers persuade unsuspecting people to give away their passwords over the phone.

- Tricks employed by unscrupulous computer users can involve various devices, including a **bomb,** which causes a program to trigger damage under certain conditions; **data diddling,** or changing data before or as it enters the system; a **denial of service (DoS) attack,** in which a site is bombarded with so many requests that legitimate users cannot access it; **piggybacking,** which is accessing a system via a legitimate user; **salami,** or embezzling small "slices" of money; **scavenging,** or searching company trash cans and dumpsters; a **trapdoor,** which allows subsequent unauthorized entry to a legitimate program; a **Trojan horse,** which places illegal instructions in the middle of a legitimate program; and **zapping,** or using software to bypass security systems.

- **White-hat hackers,** also known as tiger teams, intrusion testers, or hackers for hire are highly trained technical people who are paid to try to break into a computer system before anyone else does.

- Prosecution of computer crime is often difficult because law enforcement officers, attorneys, and judges are unfamiliar with the issues involved. However, in 1986 Congress passed the latest version of the **Computer Fraud and Abuse Act,** and most states have passed some form of computer crime law.

- **Computer forensics** refers to uncovering computer-stored information suitable for use as evidence in courts of law.

- **Security** is a system of safeguards designed to protect a computer system and data from deliberate or accidental damage or access by unauthorized persons.

- The means of giving access to authorized people are divided into four general categories: what you have (a key, badge, or plastic card); what you know (a system password or identification number); what you do (such as signing your name); and what you are (your fingerprints, voice, and retina, as known through **biometrics,** the science of measuring individual body characteristics). An **active badge,** a clip-on employee identification card with an embedded computer chip, signals its wearer's location by sending out infrared signals, which are read by sensors throughout the building.

- A **disaster recovery plan** is a method of restoring data processing operations if they are halted by major damage or destruction. Common approaches to disaster recovery include relying temporarily on manual services; buying time at a computer service bureau; making mutual assistance agreements with other companies; or forming a **consortium,** a joint venture with other organizations to support a complete computer facility to be used only in the event of a disaster.

- A **hot site** is a fully equipped computer facility with hardware, environmental controls, security, and communications equipment in place. A **cold site** is an environmentally suitable empty shell in which a company can install its own computer system.

- Personal computer security is based on such measures as locking hardware in place; providing an appropriate physical environment; and using a **surge protector,** a device that prevents electrical problems from affecting computer data files. An **uninterruptible power supply** (**UPS**) includes surge protection and battery backup, which enables you to continue operating your PC during power loss or brownouts.

- Backups protect the user from destruction of data and software files. There are three types of backup: A **full backup** copies everything from the hard drive. A **differential backup** copies all files that have been changed since the last full backup. An **incremental backup** copies only those files that have been changed since the last full or incremental backup.

- A **worm** is a program that transfers itself from computer to computer over a network, planting itself as a separate file on the target computer's disks. A **virus** is a set of illicit instructions that passes itself to other programs with which it comes in contact. A **retrovirus** can fight back and may delete or disable antivirus software.

- A **vaccine,** or **antivirus,** is a computer program that stops the spread of the virus and eradicates it. Antivirus software searches for **virus signatures,** unique strings of bits that identify each virus. Users must frequently download the latest virus signature files from the publisher's Web site to maintain the proper level of protection.

- The security issue extends to the use of information about individuals that is stored in the computer files of credit bureaus and government agencies. The **Fair Credit Reporting Act** allows individuals to check the accuracy of credit information about them. The **Freedom of Information Act** allows people access to data that federal agencies have gathered about them. The **Federal Privacy Act** allows individuals access to information about them that is held not only by government agencies but also by private contractors working for the government. Individuals are also entitled to know how that information is being used. The **Video Privacy Protection Act** and the **Computer Matching and Privacy Protection Act** have extended federal protections. The **Health Insurance Portability and Accountability Act** (**HIPAA**) contains provisions requiring employers, health care providers, and insurance companies to take appropriate steps to protect the privacy of individuals' medical records.

- A **firewall** is a combination of hardware and software that controls the traffic moving between an organization's internal network and the Internet.

- The process of scrambling messages is referred to as **encryption** and uses a code called the **encryption key** to convert the message into an unreadable form. The **Data Encryption Standard** (**DES**) is a standardized private key encryption system that requires senders and receivers to use a shared key to encrypt and decrypt messages. **RSA** is a **public key encryption system** that uses a pair of keys: one to encrypt a message and the other to decrypt it. The sender uses the receiver's public key to encrypt the message, and the receiver uses the matching private key to decrypt it.

- Software can monitor a user's **click stream,** the series of mouse clicks that link from site to site and provide a history of what that user chooses to view on the Web.

- Web servers can store information about you in **cookies,** small text files that are stored on your hard drive. Your browser sends the information in the cookie back to the server when you revisit the site. Browsers can be set to refuse cookies or to warn you when a cookie is being stored on your system and allow you to accept or refuse it.

- The **Platform for Privacy Preferences Project** (**P3P**) is a proposed set of standards that allows a Web site server to transmit its privacy policies electronically to the user.

- Privacy invasion in the form of junk e-mail has become a common event and will get worse because junk e-mail is inexpensive to send. Mass advertising on the Internet is called **spamming,** Enraged spam recipients sometimes respond to the perpetrator by **flaming,** sending insulting messages in return. **Filter software** offers some control over which e-mail messages will be accepted.

► Critical Thinking Questions

1. Before accepting a particular patient, a doctor might like access to a computer file listing patients who have been involved in malpractice suits. Before accepting a tenant, the owner of an apartment building might want to check a file that lists people who have previously sued landlords. Should computer files be available for such purposes?

2. Discuss the following statement: An active badge may help an organization maintain security, but it also erodes the employee's privacy.

3. Spammers claim that anti-spamming legislation violates their First Amendment rights to free speech. Is this a legitimate argument? Why or why not?

4. Why might businesses be reluctant to report computer crimes committed against them?

5. If you have worked for a company that provided you access to its computer network, describe the security procedures used on that network and evaluate their effectiveness.

► STUDENT STUDY GUIDE

Multiple Choice

1. Persuading people to divulge their passwords is called
   a. social engineering
   b. flaming
   c. biometrics
   d. encryption

2. The history of a user's movements from site to site is in the
   a. worm
   b. vaccine
   c. consortium
   d. click stream

3. One safeguard against theft or alteration of data is the use of
   a. DES
   b. the Trojan horse
   c. antivirus software
   d. data diddling

4. The legislation that prohibits government agencies and contractors from keeping secret personal files on individuals is the
   a. Federal Privacy Act
   b. Computer Abuse Act
   c. Fair Credit Reporting Act
   d. Freedom of Information Act

5. Uncovering computer data that might be useful in a court of law is called
   a. spamming
   b. computer forensics
   c. social engineering
   d. flaming

6. Computer crimes are usually
   a. easy to detect
   b. blue-collar crimes
   c. prosecuted
   d. committed by insiders

7. The "what you are" criterion for computer system access involves
   a. a badge
   b. a password
   c. biometrics
   d. a magnetized card

8. The key problem for a computer installation that has met with disaster is generally
   a. equipment replacement
   b. insurance coverage
   c. loss of hardware
   d. loss of data

9. In anticipation of physical destruction, every computer organization should have a
   a. biometric scheme
   b. DES
   c. disaster recovery plan
   d. set of active badges

10. A file with a record of Web site activity is called a(n)
    a. hot file
    b. cookie file
    c. filter file
    d. active file

True/False

T   F   1. A mutual aid pact would be most useful in the case of a regional disaster.

T   F   2. Vaccine is another name for antivirus software.

T   F   3. The Trojan horse is an embezzling technique.

T   F   4. If a computer crime is detected, prosecution is assured.

T   F   5. Web site adherence to the P3P standards is required by Federal law.

T   F   6. Fingerprints are an example of biometrics.

T   F   7. The actual loss of hardware is a major security problem because of its expense.

T   F   8. Backup files should always be stored onsite so that files and programs can be quickly restored in case of problems.

T   F   9. Victims of mass advertising often respond by flaming.

T   F 10. Most computer crimes are not detected.

T   F 11. A private key encryption system uses a pair of keys for encryption and decryption.

T   F 12. RSA is a public key encryption system.

T   F 13. After you purchase and install virus protection software, you are protected from viruses with no further action required on your part.

T   F 14. Cookies are small text files that Web sites install on your hard drive.

T   F 15. A firewall protects a business's network from attacks via the Internet.

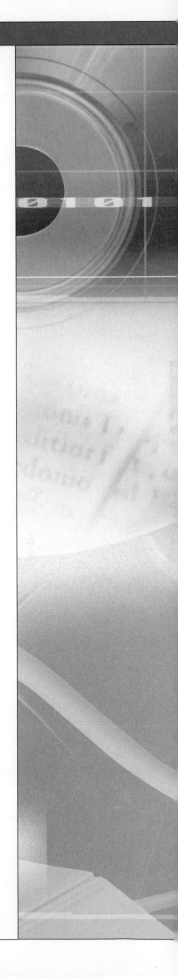

Fill-In

1. An environmentally suitable empty shell into which a computer organization can put its computer system is known as a(n) _____.

2. A system of safeguards to protect a computer system and data from damage or unauthorized access is called a(n) _____ system.

3. Bypassing security systems with an illicitly acquired software package is called _____.

4. The field that is concerned with the measurement of individual body characteristics is known as _____.

5. A fully equipped computer center to be used in the event of a disaster is called a(n) _____.

6. The assurance to individuals that personal information will be used properly is called a(n) _____.

7. A person who gains access to a computer system illegally is called a(n) _____.

8. A standardized private key system by which senders and receivers can scramble and unscramble their messages is the _____.

9. A device that prevents electrical problems from affecting computer files is the _____.

10. The file on your own hard drive that has records of Web activity is called a(n) _____.

11. A(n) _____ copies all files that have changed since the last full backup.

12. A virus _____ is a unique string of bits that identifies the virus.

13. _____ is a proposed set of standards that allows a Web site server to transmit its privacy policies electronically to the user.

14. _____ is the process of scrambling a message so that only the intended receiver can unscramble it.

15. A(n) _____ is a combination of hardware and software that sits between an organization's network and the Internet for the purpose of preventing unauthorized access to the network.

► ANSWERS

Multiple Choice

1. a	6. d
2. d	7. c
3. a	8. d
4. a	9. c
5. b	10. b

True/False

1. F	6. T	11. F
2. T	7. F	12. T
3. F	8. F	13. F
4. F	9. T	14. T
5. F	10. T	15. T

Fill-In

1. cold site
2. security
3. zapping
4. biometrics
5. hot site
6. privacy policy
7. hacker, or cracker
8. Data Encryption Standard (DES)
9. surge protector, or UPS
10. cookie
11. differential backup
12. signature
13. Platform for Privacy Preferences Project (P3P)
14. encryption
15. firewall

Planet Internet

Hackers, Crackers, and Trojans

Unless you've been living in a cave for the past few years, you have heard about computer hackers and their exploits. The conviction of Kevin Mitnick, break-ins at NASA computers, and denial-of-service attacks on yahoo.com all have occasioned concern, legislation, and an increased awareness of security. But who are hackers and how much of a threat do they pose to the average Internet surfer?

What Is a Hacker?

Originally, the term *hacker* had positive connotations and was akin to calling someone a *computer geek*—not exactly flattering but indicating someone with a deep and abiding interest in the internals of computer hardware

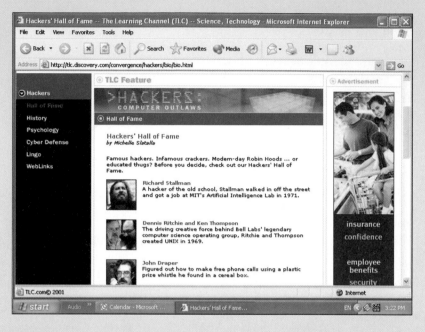

and software and certainly not a criminal. A few folks who still fancy themselves hackers in some positive sense maintain that those who use their hacking skills to commit computer crimes should be known as *crackers* instead. This distinction proves slippery in practice, as legislation increasingly broadens the definitions of a computer crime.

Will Hackers Attack My Computer?

Most hackers or crackers are interested in targets more challenging and more valuable than your personal computer. The majority of hacker attacks are directed at government and corporate targets and at e-commerce Web sites. Motives may range from a modern variant of boyish pranks to organized efforts to steal credit information for fraudulent reuse.

If you access the Internet via a dial-up connection, the odds are that you will never encounter a hacker at your computer's doorstep. The limited duration of contact and the fact that your computer's IP address—its identifier on the Internet—is likely to be different on each call make it unlikely that a hacker will find or penetrate your computer, even if you have no additional security in place.

Your data probably isn't interesting to a hacker, and the relatively slow speed at which your computer accesses the Internet over its modem doesn't make yours a good platform for launching denial-of-service attacks on others.

Users who have high-speed, always-on connections to the Internet, such as those offered by cable modems and DSL links, do face a more significant risk, and understanding this risk sheds important light on the nature of hacking.

Who Is the Average Hacker?
What Does He or She Do?

If there can be said to be a romantic image of the hacker, it's probably of a young, computer-savvy guy, sitting atop a stack of computer magazines, surviving sleep deprivation and junk food, elegantly improvising code on the fly to access your computer. Most of the time, this is an unlikely scenario. Instead, imagine much less knowledgeable young men and women starting a program on their shiny new PCs that scans the Internet for thousands of computers a night while they do their homework. Rather than trial-and-error coding, these script kiddies use programs they downloaded from Web sites to automatically find weaknesses in the thousands of computers scanned and then to enable breaking in just by typing a couple of commands in a window.

What would a successful script kiddie do with access to your computer? Probably download a Trojan, or back door program, onto your computer. With names like Back Orifice, Trinity, and even Stacheldracht (German for barbed wire), these programs enable the script kiddies to control your computer remotely. Your PC might be commanded to act as a relay for spam e-mail, a platform for attacks on other computers, an agent in a distributed denial of service attack, or simply as an IRC server for online hacker chats. The first you'd hear of the problem would be when you started getting irate e-mail from system administrators asking why your computer is attacking theirs.

What Can I Do To Safeguard My Computer?

Fortunately, these scenarios are largely preventable with a few hardware or software precautions. Firewall software—whether purchased or freeware—can detect and prevent the most common automated attacks. For under $100, users of high-speed Internet connections can purchase a screening router that blocks errant connection attempts.

The growing sophistication and availability of automated break-in tools (the script for the script kiddies) has made hacking less of an elite hobby and more available to the general public. At the same time the larger number of Internet users with reliable, high-speed Internet connections increases the number of target computers markedly. It is likely that you'll never be a victim or target of a hacker attack, but given the costs in aggravation, service disruption, data loss, and possible legal consequences, precautions, such as firewalls, seem to be in order.

Internet Exercises

1. **Structured exercise.** Search the security vulnerabilities database linked to on the Prentice Hall Web site for two or three popular programs available on your computer—a browser, a word processor and a game program. Did you find any reported vulnerabilities for these programs?

2. **Freeform exercise.** Browse Internet news sites for cases of computer hackers who have been tried and convicted or who have pled guilty. What penalties did they receive? How do the penalties the hacker or hackers received compare with the penalties for vandalism? For robbery? Did you find differences depending on what country prosecuted the individuals?

3. **Advanced exercise.** Browse to one of the pages reachable from the Prentice Hall Web site and examine a specific computer break-in or security flaw described there. Answer the following questions:

   - Which operating system or program has reported the vulnerability?

   - How serious is the described problem? Reports of vulnerabilities usually describe severity by stating what an attacker using that exploit could do with or to the vulnerable computer.

   - What steps are described for fixing the vulnerability?

Planet Internet

Word Processing and Desktop Publishing:
Printing It

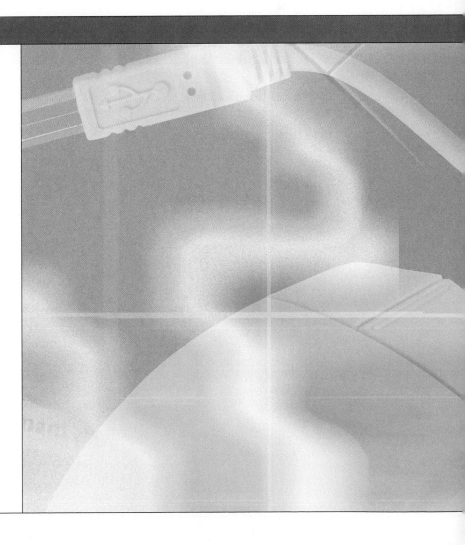

Word Processing and Desktop Publishing:
Printing It

C H A P T E R

11

LEARNING OBJECTIVES

Explain the need for word processing

List and describe the basic features of word processing programs

Describe how spelling checkers and thesaurus programs work

Explain the value of collaboration using word processing and the Web

Describe the advantages of desktop publishing

Define desktop publishing terminology

Mildred Franceschi, a physical therapist in the Mount Tahoma School District, appreciates the interaction between her students and computers. In particular, she has observed them using software that was designed to help physically challenged students communicate.

Until recently, however, Mildred has done most of her own paperwork by hand. Other items, primarily the dreaded end-of-year reports, were typed and retyped by a secretary using a typewriter. For Mildred everything changed the day the district administrators announced that professional employees would get their own computers to take home with them. The administrators also required them to take a series of classes on how to use the computer-software.

Mildred learned word processing, software that let her prepare and print text documents, such as memos and reports. She made her first tentative foray into word processing by typing a memo. She was not concerned about typing mistakes she made but simply corrected them on-screen before she printed the memo.

That was the beginning. With a speed that surprised her, Mildred found herself moving all her paperwork to the computer: individualized child service plans, bus schedules, academic and physical progress reports, and her own time records for each child. At first Mildred composed what she wanted to communicate on paper and then keyed it into the word-processing program. Before long, she became comfortable enough to compose directly on the computer. Furthermore, she saw her overall communication improve as she wrote memos to parents, teachers, doctors, and staff members.

A few months later Mildred decided to use her word-processing skills to tackle the annual grant proposal document. In past years the entire proposal, running some 40 pages, had to be typed from scratch. This was true even though much of the proposal was the same from year to year. A word-processed document can be handled differently: Only new or changed material has to be keyed in, and then the entire document can be printed as if new. Relishing the thought of how easy it was going to be next year, Mildred set out to produce the grant proposal in word-processed form.

Mildred could also improve the document's attractiveness by using features such as boldface, underlining, and even graphics. Best of all, she could make the document look professionally printed by choosing an attractive typeface—font—from her word-processing package.

Mildred is still a busy physical therapist. But thanks to her computer and its word processing software, she has more time for her first love: children.

▶ WORD PROCESSING AS A TOOL

Word-processing software lets you create, edit, format, store, retrieve, and print a *text document*. Let us examine each part of the definition. A text document is any text that can be keyed in, such as a memo or report. *Creation* is the original composing and keying in of the document. *Editing* is making changes to the document to fix errors or improve its content—for example, deleting a sentence, correcting a misspelled name, or moving a paragraph. *Formatting* refers to adjusting the appearance of the document to make it look appropriate and attractive. For example, you might want to center a heading, make wider margins, or use double spacing. *Storing* the document means saving it on disk so that it can be accessed on demand. (Although beginners usually think only in terms of saving the completed document, all users, whether experienced or inexperienced, should save a document at regular intervals while they are keying it to avoid losing work if something should go wrong.) *Retrieving* the document means bringing the stored document from disk back into computer memory so that it can be used again or changed in some way. *Printing* is producing the document on paper, using a printer connected to the computer.

A word-processing package is a sophisticated tool with many options. This chapter discusses several of them. First, here is an overview of how word processing works.

▶ AN OVERVIEW: HOW WORD PROCESSING WORKS

Think of the computer's screen as a page of typing paper. When you type, you can see the line of text you are typing on the screen; it looks just like a line of typing on paper. You are not really typing on the screen, of course; the screen merely displays what you are entering into memory. As you type, the program displays the **insertion point,** or **cursor,** to show where the next character you type will appear on the screen. The insertion point is usually an underscore, rectangle, or vertical line that you can easily see. Although this chapter examines word processing in a general way that applies to any word-processing software, occasionally, as here, a point will be demonstrated with Microsoft Word 2002 (Figure 11-1).

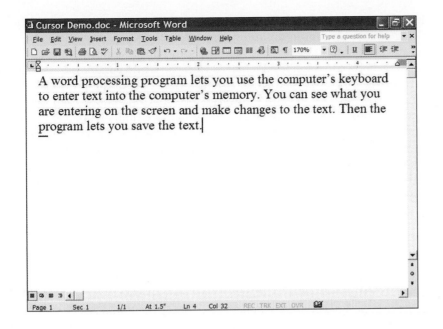

◄ F I G U R E 11-1

Entering text with word processing software. As you type in your text, the position of the cursor (the vertical line just to the right of the last word on the screen) shows where the next character will be placed.

Scrolling

A word-processing program lets you type page after page of material. Most programs show a horizontal line on the screen to mark where one printed page ends and another begins; this line does not appear on the printed document. Most word-processing programs also display, at the bottom of the screen, the number of the page on which you are currently typing and also an indicator of the line you're on, either by line number or by inches from the top of the printed page. Although the screen display size is limited, your document size is not. As you add new lines at the bottom of the screen, the lines you typed earlier move up the screen. Eventually, the first line you typed disappears off the top of the screen. However, the line has not disappeared from the document or from the computer's memory.

To see lines that have disappeared from the top, you can move the cursor to the top of the screen and press the up arrow key; lines that had disappeared drop back down onto the screen. You can also use a mouse to accomplish the same thing by clicking over the up arrow of the scrollbar on the right side of the window. You can use opposite movements to send screen lines in the upward direction. This process, called **scrolling,** lets you see any part of the document—but only one screen at a time.

No Need to Worry about the Right Side

After you start to type the first line of a document, you will eventually get to the right edge of the document. If there is not enough room at the end of a line to complete the word you are typing, the program automatically moves that word to the left margin of the next line down. This feature is called **word wrap.** With word wrap you do not have to push a carriage return key (on the computer, the Enter key) at the end of each line as you would with a typewriter; in fact, you should not press Enter at the end of a line. If you do so, the word wrap feature does not work properly. You should press Enter only when you want a blank line or to signal the end of a paragraph.

Easy Corrections

What if you make a mistake while you are keying? No problem: Move the cursor to the position of the error and make the correction. Use the **Backspace key** to delete characters to the left of the cursor, or use the **Delete key** to delete the character under the cursor or just to the right of the cursor. Word-processing programs let you delete characters or whole words, lines, or paragraphs that you have already typed; the resulting spaces are closed up automatically.

Sometimes people delete parts of a document and immediately regret it. Accidental or incorrect deletions can usually be repaired with the **Undo command,** usually shown as a reverse arrow on the toolbar. Undo reverses the effect of the previous action and returns the document to its condition just before that operation. High-performance word-processing programs offer the ability to undo more than one previous operation.

You can also insert new characters in the middle of a line or a word without typing over (and erasing) the characters that are already there. The program automatically moves the existing characters to the right of the insertion as you type the new characters and rewraps the text. However, if you wish, the word processing program also lets you *overtype* (replace) characters you typed before.

Menus and Buttons: At Your Command

Most word-processing packages permit commands to be given via **menus,** a set of choices normally laid out across the top of the screen. The menus are called **pull-down menus** because each initial choice, when clicked with a mouse, reveals lower-level choices that pull down like a window shade from the initial selection at the top of the screen. For example, an initial selection of Format may reveal several submenus; the submenu Bullets and Numbering has its own set of selections (Figure 11-2a). A mouse user can also invoke commands by using **buttons.** A **toolbar** is a collection of such buttons, usually shown across the top of the screen just below the pull-down menus (Figure 11-2). There are different kinds of toolbars for different application programs and even a variety of toolbars within the same software. As an example of button functions, the top-left buttons on the screen in Figure 11-2b let you begin a new

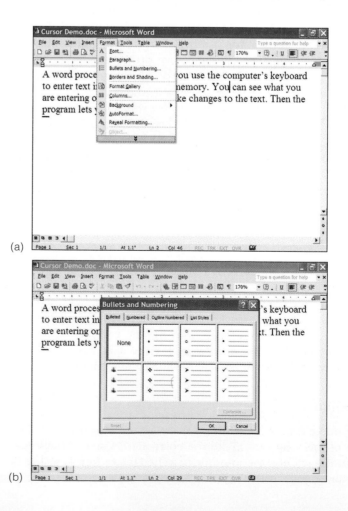

► **FIGURE 11-2**

Pull-down menus. (a) When the Format menu is clicked with a mouse, a submenu of choices appears. If the third choice on the pull-down menu, Bullets and Numbering, is clicked, the submenu shown in part (b) appears. (b) Some submenus have their own submenus; here, the submenu Bullets and Numbering has further selections. Note also the vertical scrollbar on the right side of the screen. When you click the upward-pointing triangle at the top of the scrollbar or the downward pointing triangle at the bottom of the scrollbar, the document moves up or down, respectively. You can also use the mouse to drag the rectangle within the scrollbar up and down, and the document will scroll accordingly.

(a)

(b)

► **M A K I N G   C O N N E C T I O N S** ◄   **The Virtual Office**

The word *virtual* is applied in various computer settings, but it always means the same thing: the appearance of something that really does not exist. The computer somehow masks the reality and permits benefits similar to those offered by the real thing. In this discussion of the virtual office, the office as we know it—a physical place with a desk and a chair and office supplies—does not actually exist. But its functions do exist.

Consider the way Nora Mathison runs her sprinkler installation business in Phoenix. She relies on a toll-free phone number, voice mail, a cellular phone, and a notebook computer with a fax modem. No building, no office, no desk.

Nora advertises her toll-free number in the Yellow Pages; potential customers in the urban/suburban area can call the number without charge. When they do, they are advised to leave a voice mail message. Nora, working on site in some customer's yard, can retrieve her voice mail messages and return the calls on her cell phone. She can use software on her notebook computer to work up a bid right at a customer site, or she can do the work later and fax the results to the customer. She also uses the notebook computer for scheduling, work flow, and billing.

In addition to convenience the virtual office can minimize start-up costs for fledgling entrepreneurs. For business people who spend most of their time out of the office anyway, the virtual office is an ongoing asset.

document (the white paper button), open an existing document (the file folder button), or save a document (the diskette button). You can discover the meaning of any button by resting your mouse on it; an explanatory phrase will soon appear.

► WORD-PROCESSING FEATURES

All word processing users begin by learning the basics: Invoke the word-processing software, key in the document, change the document, and save and print the document. However, most users also come to appreciate the various features offered by word processing software (Figure 11-3).

Formatting

The most commonly used features are those that control the **format**—the physical appearance of the document. Format refers to centering, margins, tabs and indents, justification, line spacing, emphasis, and all the other factors that affect appearance. Note the examples in Figure 11-3 as some formatting options are described:

VERTICAL CENTERING   A short document, such as a memo, starts out bunched at the top of the page. **Vertical centering** adjusts the top and bottom margins so that the text is centered vertically on the printed page. This eliminates the need to calculate the exact number of lines to leave at the top and bottom, a necessary process if you are using a typewriter.

LINE CENTERING   Any line can be individually **centered** between the left and right margins of the page. Headings and titles are usually centered; other lines, such as addresses, may also be appropriately centered.

Enlarged typeface

Line graphic

Underline

Block indent

Numbered outline

Boldface

Superscript

Bulleted checklist

Footnote

Header

Centered heading

Sans serif typeface

Reference to footnote

Ragged right text

Fully justified text

Inserted graphic image

Italic

Pagination

Chapter 1

COMMUNITY CRIME PREVENTION AND SAFETY

<u>Statement of goals:</u> Citizens must share the responsibility for prevention of crime and for their own safety. Law enforcement and government agencies cannot and should not handle it alone.[1]

I. Home Security
    A. Outside your home
    B. Doors and windows
    C. Locks
    D. Property marking
    E. Inventory sheet
II. General Safety
    A. Safety in your home
    B. Safety in your neighborhood
    C. Going on vacation

Security overview. Burglary is a crime of opportunity—perhaps a weak door or an unlocked window. Most burglars use unsophisticated methods to gain entry, using simple force on an easy target. Citizens can use preventive strategies to make their homes secure.

Safety overview. Safety is a broad topic, running the gamut from keeping your chimney clean to having a fire escape plan to wrapping your water pipes when the temperature dips below $32°$. Safety is of particular concern when people are going on vacation. Planning ahead will prevent many problems.

HOME SECURITY CHECKLIST

☐ Strong exterior doors
☐ Deadbolt locks
☐ Door peephole
☐ Windows secured
☐ Timed lights
☐ Lighted entrances
☐ Shrubs trimmed

---

[1] *Blockwatch: Community Crime Prevention,* Seattle Police Department Crime Prevention Division, 2001.

I

▲ FIGURE 11-3

Word-processing features. Although it is not possible to show all word-processing features on a single page, this page illustrates many of the capabilities that are available.

MARGINS Some settings, called **default settings,** are used automatically by the word-processing program; they can be overridden by the user. The default left and right margins are usually 1.25 inches wide. Documents are often typed using the default margin settings. However, if the document would look better with narrower or wider margins, you can change the margin settings. When the margin settings are changed, word-processing software automatically adjusts the text to fit the new margins. This process is called **automatic reformatting.**

TABS AND INDENTATION It is common to **tab** just once to begin a paragraph. Some users need a set of tab positions across the page to make items align. It is also possible to **indent** an entire paragraph and even to indent it from two sides so that it stands out.

JUSTIFICATION The evenness of text at the side margins is called **justification.** A document of several paragraphs is often most attractive if it is **fully justified,** that is, has an even margin down each side. The program adjusts each line so that it ends exactly at the right margin, spacing the words evenly. On occasions—perhaps to spot any unintentional spaces—only left justification is desired; this is sometimes referred to as **ragged-right** text because of the uneven appearance of the unjustified right side. It is also possible to right-justify text; that is, have the right margin even and the left margin ragged, but this effect is seldom used.

LINE SPACING Most of the time you will want your documents—letters, memos, reports—to be single-spaced. But on occasion you will find that it is convenient or necessary to double space or even triple space a document. Word processing lets you do this with ease.

BOLDFACE, ITALIC, AND UNDERLINING Certain words or phrases, or even entire paragraphs, can be given emphasis by using a darker text known as **boldface** text, or by using the slanted type called *italic*, or by <u>underlining</u> important words. Some style guidelines still require underlining in special circumstances, and all modern word-processing programs support it. However, underlining is something of an anachronism, given the italics, boldface, and special font features of modern word processing programs. Italics or boldface is probably a better choice than underlining for emphasizing text.

FONTS Most word-processing packages offer dozens of fonts. In fact, you can easily see what they look like by using a pull-down menu (Figure 11-4). A **font** is a set of characters—letters, punctuation, and numbers—of the same design. Figure 11-5 shows some fonts in a large enough size that you can get a better idea of the variety. Everyday fonts can generally be grouped into serif and sans serif fonts (*sans* means *without*). In a **serif** font, each character includes serifs, short horizontal lines added to the tops and bottoms of letters, which are thought to help the eye travel more easily from character to character, making reading easier. A **sans serif** font is clean and stark, with no serif marks (Figure 11-6). In this book the main text uses a serif font, but the margin notes and figure captions use a sans serif font.

Most fonts available today are **scalable** fonts. This means that they can be set to almost any size without the individual letters appearing ragged or irregular. Fonts that use the trade name TrueType are always scalable. Most word-processing programs let you dress up your text by adding color and three-dimensional effects (Figure 11-7).

Squeezing or Stretching a Document

At times you want text to fit into a specific space. For example, an instructor could suggest that a term paper be at least 10 double-spaced pages, or a potential employer

Pull-down fonts. Notice that the font name is written in the style of the font, an easy way to see what you are getting.

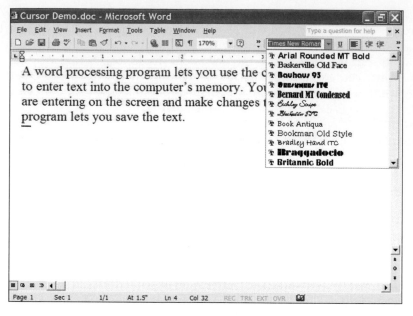

Various fonts. These fonts, just ten of hundreds of possibilities, can serve a purpose or just whimsy. As you can see, some are easier to read than others are.

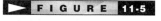

this font is called *Hogarth*

this font is called *Surf Style*

this font is called City

this font is called Commerce Lean

this font is called *Rage*

this font is called Arriba Arriba

THIS FONT IS CALLED BANG

this font is called Laser Chrome

this font is called Gotisch

this font is called Journal Ultra

Comparing serif and sans serif fonts. (a) This popular serif font is called Times New Roman. (b) This sans serif font is called Helvetica Light.

(a) The quick brown fox jumped over the lazy dog.

(b) The quick brown fox jumped over the lazy dog.

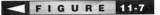

WordArt Gallery

could request a résumé of no more than two pages. Or perhaps the problem is something as simple as taking a memo that runs three pages plus two lines and reducing it to three pages. There are several ways to use word-processing features to adjust the length of a document:

- Adjust the margins, both sides and top and bottom, making them larger to stretch the number of pages or smaller to reduce the number.

- Try different line spacing. One-and-a-half line spacing, available with most word-processing programs, looks quite similar to double spacing.

- Experiment with fonts. Some take up less room than others at the same point size. And, of course, point size is a variable that you can adjust.

Note the variation in size in the two versions of the letter in Figure 11-8.

Printing Envelopes

After printing your computer-produced letter, you carefully fold it in thirds with nice even creases, slip it into an envelope that matches the paper, and then proceed to chicken-scratch the address onto it. The professional look falls through in this scenario. Using your computer to address and print the envelope adds that finishing touch.

It is not that difficult to do. Every word-processing program offers a way to produce envelopes that look as good as the letters they contain. Here, generally, is how it is done. Find the Envelope command on one of your program's pull-down menus (Figure 11-9a). That command opens a window (Figure 11-9b), giving you the opportunity to type the recipient's address; the address will be there automatically if you highlighted it in the letter before you invoked the Envelope command. There is also space to type your return address. You can set your address as the default return address and not have to type it each time; this can, of course, be overridden when you need to use another address. You can omit the return address altogether if you are using an envelope with a preprinted return address. Most word-processing programs also include the postal bar code that provides automatic routing of your letter to its destination.

The software offers a variety of options, such as different fonts and font sizes, envelope size, and the manner in which the envelope is fed into the printer. The tricky

► F I G U R E   **11-8**

Stretching a document. It is fairly easy to stretch or compress a document by varying margins, fonts, and line spacing. (a) This document is bunched at the top and poorly presented altogether. (b) The same document has been arranged more suitably on the page by making the side and top margins wider and increasing the font size from 12 to 14. While we were at it, we used full justification, moved the image to the center of the document, and made the title more attractive using the program's WordArt feature. We also centered the title.

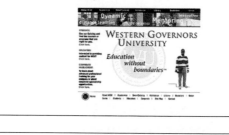

Internet University
Learning from a distance is already available on the Internet in a variety of forms. But there is also something different, something more grand: a virtual university. This university goes beyond a course or two; it offers four-year degrees. The school is sponsored by ten western states (excluding California), created in response to the high costs of educating college students on-site. Called the Western Governors University, the school is an accredited regional university that exists solely in cyberspace. The key here is *accredited*, meaning that the degree will be recognized by other institutions, including graduate schools, throughout the country.

Western Governors University is a real university, just without a physical campus. The school is based on a simple idea: In the real world, people have jobs and lives and responsibilities that do not always allow them to sit in a university classroom. Students can take courses from institutions all across the country without ever leaving home. WGU does not offer instruction itself. Rather, it brokers instruction provided by affiliated colleges, universities, and corporations.

Using technology like the World Wide Web, e-mail, satellite broadcasts and more, WGU makes it possible for students to earn degrees or certificates in several different college and university study programs, no matter where they live or what their schedules.

As the WGU site, shown here, notes: WGU isn't your average university. But then again, who ever wanted to be average?

(a)

(b)

part is getting the envelope into the printer correctly; refer to the manual that matches your printer—or, even better, have someone show you. When everything is ready, click the Print button in the Envelope window shown in Figure 11-9b. The envelope comes out of the printer ready to be stamped and mailed.

Other Important Features

Popular word-processing packages offer more features than most people use. Although it is not possible to discuss every feature here, this list contains a few that you might find handy.

SEARCH Imagine that you are working with a 97-page study called "Western Shorebirds," all nicely prepared as a word-processed document. There has been an additional sighting of the white-rumped sandpiper, and it has fallen to you to make a

(a)

(b)

◄ **FIGURE** **11-9**

Printing an envelope. To print an envelope, (a) find the Envelope command on a menu, (b) invoke the command to see the window for addresses and options, and after completing the necessary steps, click Print to produce the printed envelope.

change in the report. You could, of course, leaf through the printed report to find out where to put the change. Alternatively, you could scroll the report on the screen, hoping to see the words "white-rumped sandpiper." The fast and easy way, however, is to use the **search command,** also called the **find command.** Just invoke the search command, type the word or words you are looking for, and the exact page and place where it is located appears on the screen.

FIND AND REPLACE   Suppose you type a long report in which you repeatedly and incorrectly spell the name of a client as "Mr. McDonald." To make a change, you could search for each individual occurrence of "McDonald," replacing each incorrect "Mc" with the correct "Mac." There is, however, a more efficient way—using the **find-and-replace** feature. You make a single request to replace one word or phrase with another. Then the find-and-replace command quickly searches through the entire document, finding each instance of the word or phrase and replacing it with the word or phrase that you designated. Most word-processing programs also offer **conditional replace,** which asks you to verify each replacement before it is carried out.

PAGINATION   Displaying page numbers in a document is a normal need for most users. Word-processing programs offer every imaginable paging option, permitting the page number to be located at the top or bottom of the page and to the left, right, or center, or even alternating left and right.

PRINT PREVIEW   Many users call print preview their favorite feature. With a single command a user can view on the screen in reduced size an entire page, two facing

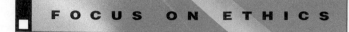

pages, or even several consecutive pages. This gives a better overall view than the limited number of lines available on a screen.

FOOTNOTES   To insert a **footnote,** you need only give the footnote command and type the footnote text. The word processing program keeps track of space needed and automatically renumbers if you add a new footnote. Footnotes can easily be converted to endnotes and vice versa.

HEADERS AND FOOTERS   Unlike footnotes, which appear only once, **headers** (top of the page) and **footers** (bottom of the page) appear on every page of a document (see Figure 11-3). Several variations are available, including placement, size, and font. Footers are commonly used for the page number. In addition to page numbers, most word processing programs can automatically insert other useful information into headers or footers. Examples include the date and time the document was last modified and the filename under which the document is stored on disk.

Text Blocks: Moving, Copying, and Deleting

Text block techniques comprise a powerful set of tools. A **text block** is a unit of text in a document. A text block can consist of one or more words, phrases, sentences, paragraphs, or pages. Text blocks can be moved, copied, or deleted.

Consider this example. Robert Merino is the manager of the Warren Nautilus Club, a fitness center seven blocks from the state university he attends. Last December, just before the student holidays, Robert used word processing to dash off a notice to the members, informing them of changes in the holiday schedule (Figure 11-10a).

Now, four months later, Robert wants to produce a similar notice regarding schedule changes during spring break. Rather than beginning anew, Robert will retrieve his old document from the disk and key in the changes. After Robert has given the command to retrieve the document, the current version of the notice, just as he saved it on disk, is loaded into memory and displayed on the screen. Robert plans to make changes so that the new notice will be as shown in Figure 11-10b. In particular, Robert uses text block commands to move a paragraph.

MARKING A TEXT BLOCK   Whenever action is to be taken on a block of text, that block must first be **marked,** which is a form of identification. Marking a block is sometimes called **selection,** because you are selecting text with which to work. A block is usually marked by placing the mouse at the beginning of the block, holding the mouse button down, and dragging the mouse to the end of the block. In Robert's memo the block to be marked is the paragraph with the special offer. On

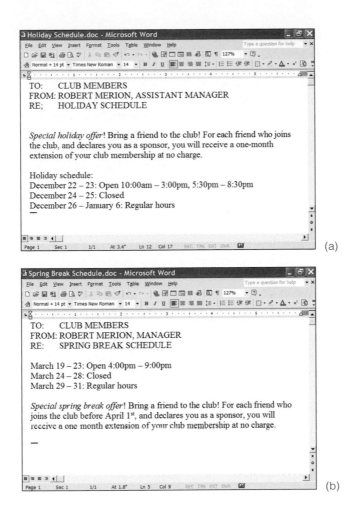

(a)

(b)

◄ **F I G U R E   11-10**

Moving a text block.
(a) Robert's original memo.
(b) Robert begins by deleting "ASSISTANT" so that his title reflects his recent promotion to manager. He next uses the find-and-replace command to change each mention of December to March. He takes a few moments to delete the old dates and times, add the new ones, and add April 1 as the deadline for the new member promotion. Finally, because the notice is supposed to be about the changed schedule, he uses text block commands to move the special offer paragraph to the end of the notice. The result is the revised memo shown here.

the screen the marked block is now highlighted, probably by **reverse video**—the print in the marked text is the color of the normal background and the background is the color of the normal text. After the block is marked, it can be moved, copied, or deleted.

MOVING A TEXT BLOCK   Moving a block of text removes it from its original location and places it in another location. The block still appears only once in the document. Moving a block from one location to another is also called **cutting and pasting,** a reference to what you would have to do if you were working with a document on paper. Most word processing programs use the actual words *Cut* and *Paste* as command names: The Cut command removes the block from its old location, and the Paste command places the block in its new location, as indicated by the cursor location. To summarize the move operation: (1) Mark the block. (2) Cut. (3) Move the cursor to the new destination, and (4) paste.

COPYING A TEXT BLOCK   The Copy command leaves the block intact in its original location but also inserts it in a designated new location, creating two copies of the block. Typical commands for copying a block are Copy and Paste. To summarize the copy operation: (1) Mark the block. (2) Copy. (3) Move the cursor to the new destination, and (4) paste.

DELETING A TEXT BLOCK   Deleting a block of text is easy. In fact, it has already been described. After a block is marked and cut, it is effectively deleted. An easy alternative is to mark a block and press the Delete key.

► SPELLING CHECKER AND THESAURUS PROGRAMS

A **spelling checker** program finds spelling errors you might have made when typing a document. The program compares each word in your document to the words it has in its dictionary. If the spelling checker finds a word that is not in its list, it assumes that you have misspelled or mistyped that word. The spelling checker draws attention to the offending word in some way, perhaps by reversing the screen colors or underlining in a different color. When you position the cursor on that word, the spelling checker displays words from its dictionary that are close in spelling or sound to the word you typed (Figure 11-11). If you recognize the correct spelling of the highlighted word in the list you are given, you can replace the incorrect word with the correct word from the list.

Spelling checkers often do not recognize proper names (such as Ms. Verwys), acronyms (for example, NASA), or technical words specific to some disciplines, such as orthotroid. So you must decide whether the word is actually misspelled. If it is, you can correct it easily with the word-processing software. If the word is correct, the software lets you signal that the word is acceptable and, if you want you can add it to the dictionary.

A **thesaurus** program offers synonyms (words with the same meaning) and antonyms (words with the opposite meaning) for common words. Suppose you find a word in your document that you have used too frequently or that does not seem suitable. Place the cursor on the word. Then click the menu command or button that activates the thesaurus program. The program provides a list of synonyms for the word you want to replace (Figure 11-12). A click on the chosen new word replaces the word in your document with the synonym you prefer. It is easy, and even painlessly educational.

► WORD PROCESSING AND THE WEB

The World Wide Web can be used as a universal communications vehicle because all computers use the same protocol. Users can send messages to one another despite differences among their computers. However, instead of just relaying messages, users have taken the next logical step: collaboration on the same document by using the Web.

► FIGURE 11-11

Spelling checker. The highlighted word, *greem*, is misspelled, so the spelling checker offers a list of alternatives in the suggestion window. In this case, highlighting *green* and selecting Change replaces the misspelled word with the correct spelling.

GETTING PRACTICAL   Getting Help

Sooner or later, most computer users need some help with hardware or software. Help is usually available in a variety of forms. All reputable vendors, whether of hardware or software, have their own Web sites to offer support, such as the one shown here for Dell. Vendors encourage users to go first for help to their Web sites. A support site typically offers lists of frequently asked questions (with answers), software fixes that can be downloaded, and an e-mail service you can use to send specific questions to their technical staff.

Many users prefer to get help directly over the phone from staff employed by the hardware or software maker. Typically, assistance is free for a certain time period, perhaps 90 days from the first phone call, but later there is a charge to the user. However, if the help line is not a toll-free number, you may run up long-distance charges. To make the best use of your time on the phone, do some advance preparation. Before you call, do the following:

- Place your phone near your computer and be sitting at your computer as you call.

- If you are an established customer, have your customer number handy.

- Know your computer type, model, and serial number and the version of your software package.

- Write down the exact wording of any error messages.

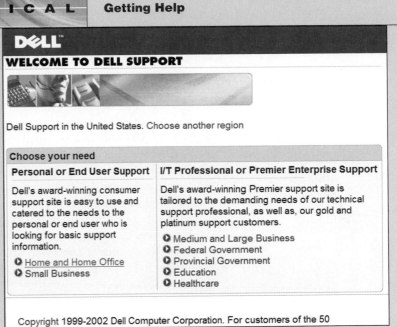

Dell Support in the United States. Choose another region

Choose your need

Personal or End User Support	**I/T Professional or Premier Enterprise Support**
Dell's award-winning consumer support site is easy to use and catered to the needs to the personal or end user who is looking for basic support information.	Dell's award-winning Premier support site is tailored to the demanding needs of our technical support professional, as well as, our gold and platinum support customers.

- Home and Home Office
- Small Business

- Medium and Large Business
- Federal Government
- Provincial Government
- Education
- Healthcare

Copyright 1999-2002 Dell Computer Corporation. For customers of the 50

- Be prepared to press phone buttons in response to directions and then to wait—perhaps many minutes—to be connected to a live person who can help you.

When you call, do the following:

- Give identifying information when asked.

- State the problem clearly.

- Tell the technician what you have already tried.

- Be ready to explore solutions on the computer as you talk.

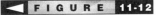

► **FIGURE 11-12**

A thesaurus program.
The words on the list are synonyms for the highlighted word, *exclusively*.

Suppose, for example, that three nutritionists, in different offices, are working on a paper to show the results of their joint study. They want to be able to massage the document as it is passed among them over the Web. They do not want to learn HTML, the language of Web pages. They just want to work in the usual way, writing a word-processed document. There are ways to use e-mail to collaborate on word-processed documents, but an easier way is to use the HTML feature provided by the word-processing programs themselves. In short, write the text in the usual way, but click a couple of extra buttons to save it as a Web page that others can easily access.

Figure 11-13a shows a word-processed document. With a different save option, the document can be saved as a Web page (Figure 11-13b). When the document is made available on a Web page, others can access it and view it as a regular word-processed document while making changes or adding comments. One approach is to have the originator password-protect the document in such a way that viewers can add comments but not change the original content.

Web options in word-processing and other applications programs can be quite powerful. The details of the topic are beyond the scope of this book. For now, you simply need to be aware of the possibilities.

▶ **F I G U R E 11-13**

Word processing and the Web. Look-alikes? Not quite. Look in the upper-left corners for the clue, and then compare the toolbars. (a) This is the original text, saved as a word-processed document. (b) This is the same document, saved as a Web page.

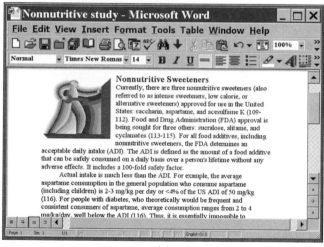

(a)

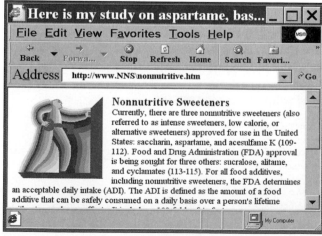

(b)

DAY IN THE LIFE

Sara Beltran,
Systems Administrator

The title, Systems Administrator, means something different from business to business. At Sara's place of employment, it means that she is responsible for administrating the file server that the company uses for its office projects. This server has many uses, such as enabling other users in the company to collaborate on projects remotely, as well as being the repository for all the company's document templates. As part of her duties, whenever a department creates a template document, Sara first has to review it for security. This means verifying that there are no viruses, no problems with macros, and so on. She then takes the file and makes it available to all the departments who should have access to it.

This means that each time a person working in that department needs to make a document based on that template, he or she simply opens the new file section of their word processor or spreadsheet software, and the template is already waiting there.

► DESKTOP PUBLISHING: AN OVERVIEW

Would you like to be able to produce well-designed pages that combine elaborate charts and graphics with text and headlines in a variety of fonts? You can, with a technology called **desktop publishing.** You can use desktop publishing software to design sophisticated pages and, with a high-quality printer, print a professional-looking final document (Figure 11-14).

Unlike word processing, desktop publishing gives you the ability to decide where you want text and pictures on a page, what fonts to use, and what other design elements to include. Desktop publishing fills the gap between word processing and professional typesetting (Figure 11-15).

◄ **FIGURE 11-14**

Desktop publishing. With desktop publishing software and a high-quality laser printer, you can create professional-looking newsletters and documents.

▶ **F I G U R E** **11-15**

High-end desktop publishing. The cover of this book was produced with the latest computer technology.

Personal Greetings

Computers have opened up all sorts of possibilities for "homemade" personal greetings. Several software packages are available to help you make banners, flyers, calendars, and greeting cards. You need not have any artistic talent; many images and preplanned designs are available as part of the software. In fact, all you really need in addition to a computer is some software and a color printer.

Even more popular are the many Web sites that offer postcards and greeting cards that you can send online to a friend. These free services let you choose a card (such as the balloons shown here, from the Acme Postcard site), select a message from their list (Happy Birthday, Congratulations, and so forth), and personalize it with your own message. Most sites also let you include music to be delivered with the card.

▶ THE PUBLISHING PROCESS

Desktop publishing gives the user full control over the editing and design of the document. Desktop publishing also eliminates the time-consuming measuring and cutting and pasting that are involved in traditional production techniques.

The Art of Design

One part of the design of a document is **page layout**—how the text and graphics are arranged on the page. For example, magazine publishers have found that text organized in columns and separated by a solid vertical line is an effective page layout. If pictures are used, they must be inserted into the text. Picture size needs to be adjusted for proper fit on the page. In addition to page layout, designers must take into account such factors as headings, type sizes, and fonts. Are general headings used? Do separate sections or articles need their own subheadings? Does the size of the type need to be increased or decreased to fit a story into a predetermined space? What is the best font to use? Should more than one kind of font be used on a page?

To help you understand how some of these decisions are made, it is necessary to discuss some of the publishing terminology involved.

Fonts: Sizes and Styles

The type that a printer uses is described by its size, font, weight, and style. **Type size** is measured by a standard system that uses points. A **point** equals 1/72 inch. Point size is measured from the top of the letter that rises the highest above the baseline (a letter such as h or l) to the bottom of the letter that descends the lowest (a letter such as g or y). Figure 11-16 shows type in different sizes.

The font selected determines the shapes of the letters and numbers in a published document. Recall that a font is a set of characters of the same design. A font can be printed in a specific **weight,** such as boldface, which is heavier or darker than usual, or in a specific **style,** such as italic. Changes in font provide emphasis and variety.

As shown in Figure 11-17a, varying the size and style of the type used in a publication can improve the appearance of a page and draw attention to the most important sections. However, using too many different fonts or using clashing fonts can create a page that is unattractive and hard to read (Figure 11-17b). Combine fonts with discretion.

Most printers used in desktop publishing store a selection of fonts in a ROM chip in the printer. These are called the printer's **internal fonts.** Also, most desktop pub-

Times New Roman (12)

Times New Roman (18)

Times New Roman (24)

Times New Roman (36)

Times New Roman (48)

▲ **FIGURE** 11-16

Different point sizes. This figure shows a variety of different point sizes in a popular font called Times New Roman. The smallest shown here, point size 12, is often used for long text passages, such as correspondence. The larger sizes probably would be used only for headings or titles.

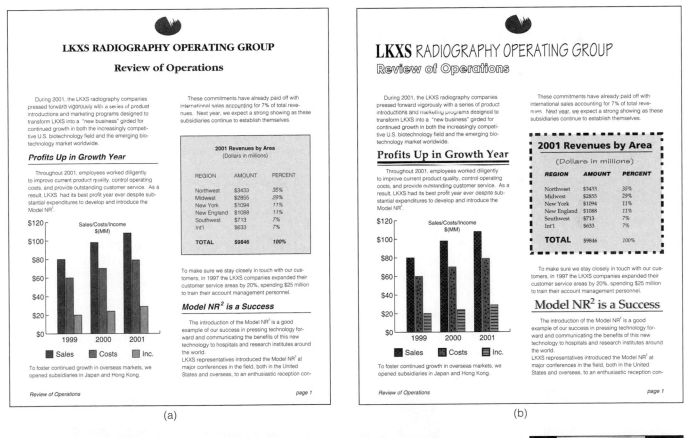

(a)   (b)

▲ **FIGURE** 11-17

Sample designs. (a) This example uses complementary fonts to produce a professional-looking document. (b) The same page created with clashing fonts and other distractions.

lishing programs provide a **font library** on a disk. A font library contains a selection of fonts called **soft fonts.** A soft font can be sent, or downloaded, from the font library on the hard drive to the computer, from which it then can be sent to the printer.

Principles of Good Typography

Word-processing and desktop-publishing programs put many fonts at your disposal, but you can overwhelm a document if you use overly fancy fonts or too many fonts. A general rule is less is better. The guidelines that follow promote a clean and attractive look for your document:

- Use only two or three fonts in a document.

- Be conservative: Limit the use of decorative or unusual fonts. In particular, use stylized fonts such as Benguiat, *Brush*, or Lemonade only for signs and titles, never for passages of text.

- Use different sizes and styles of one font to distinguish between heading levels, rather than using different fonts.

- Never type text body in all capital letters.

- Do not use type that is too small to read easily just to fit everything on one page.

- Use a sans serif font only for short text passages; for long passages use a serif font, which is easier to read.

- Use italic or boldface, rather than underlining, for emphasis.

These simple guidelines almost guarantee an attractive document.

Leading and Kerning

Two terms that you will encounter when you begin desktop publishing are *leading* and *kerning*. **Leading** (pronounced *ledding*) refers to the spacing between the lines of type on a page. Leading is measured vertically from the base of one line of type to the base of the line above it. The greater the leading, the more white space there is between lines. Leading, just like type size, is measured in points.

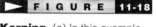

FIGURE 11-18

Kerning. (a) In this example, the space between the characters is not altered. (b) Kerning, or adjusting the space between the characters, can improve the overall appearance of the word.

(a) Unkerned: WAVE (b) Kerned: WAVE

Kerning refers to adjusting the space between the characters in a word. In desktop-publishing software, each font has a default kerning. An example of kerning is shown in Figure 11-18.

Halftones

Halftones, which resemble photographs, appear in newspapers, magazines, books, and documents produced by desktop publishing. Halftones are representations made up of black dots printed on white paper. Varying the number and size of dots in a given space produces shades of gray. As you can see in Figure 11-19, the smaller the dot pattern used, the clearer the halftone.

Using Desktop Publishing Software

The page composition program is the key ingredient of a desktop-publishing system. **Page-composition programs,** also called **page-makeup programs,** let you design

FIGURE 11-19

Halftones. Halftones consist of a series of dots. Reducing the size of the dots makes the resulting halftone clearer.

▲ **F I G U R E** 11-20

Clip art. Word-processing and desktop-publishing programs include clip art with the software and make additional art available for downloading from an affiliated Web site. Clip art can also be purchased separately from other vendors. Much clip art is mundane—primitive sketches of familiar items, such as pencils, stars, and grinning pumpkins. However, software makers have hired commercial artists to improve the look of clip art, resulting in a greater sophistication and variety.

each page on the computer screen. You can determine the number and the width of the columns of text to be printed on the page. You can also indicate where pictures, charts, graphs, and headlines are to be placed. After you create the page design, you can use the page-composition program to insert text and graphics into it. Text may be keyed as you prepare the page or imported as a file created by a word-processing program. Page-composition programs also let you move blocks of text and pictures around on your page. If you are not satisfied with the way the page looks, you can change the size of the type or the pictures.

Most desktop publishing programs offer **templates,** predetermined page designs that you can use quickly by filling in your own text. Templates that are typically offered include those for newsletters, flyers, greeting cards, banners, calendars, and even business forms. Page-composition programs can also integrate **clip art**—images available for public use—into your publication to enliven your text. Most desktop-publishing programs include a clip art library. You can purchase disks of additional clip art or find clip art for free or a small fee on many Web sites. Figure 11-20 shows examples of illustrations in a clip art library.

▲

By now you should be convinced that familiarity with word processing is essential for your career and that desktop publishing is a valuable tool for individuals as well as businesses. The next chapter covers spreadsheet software, another important personal productivity application.

CHAPTER REVIEW

▶ Summary and Key Terms

- **Word processing** is the creating, editing, formatting, storing, retrieving, and printing of a text document.

- A text document is any text that can be keyed in, such as a memo. *Creation* is the original composing and keying in of the document. *Editing* is making changes to the document. *Formatting* is adjusting the appearance of the document. *Storing* is saving the document to disk. *Retrieving* is bringing the stored document from disk back into computer memory, and *printing* is producing the document on paper.

- The **insertion point,** or **cursor,** usually a blinking underscore or rectangle, shows where the next character you type will appear on the screen.

- **Scrolling,** done by moving the cursor, lets you display any part of the document on the screen.

- **Word wrap** automatically starts a word on the next line if it does not fit on the previous line.

- Use the **Backspace key** to delete characters to the left or the **Delete key** to delete the character under the cursor or to the right of the cursor. Accidental or incorrect deletions can usually be repaired with the **undo command,** which reverses the effect of the previous action.

- Mouse users issue commands through a series of **menus,** called **pull-down menus,** which offer initial choices and submenus, or by using **buttons** at the top of the screen. The **toolbar** is a collection of such buttons.

- The **format** is the physical appearance of the document.

- **Vertical centering** adjusts the top and bottom margins so that the text is centered vertically on the printed page.

- Any line can be individually **centered** between the left and right margins of the page.

- Settings automatically used by the word-processing program are called **default settings.**

- When the margin settings are changed, word-processing software adjusts the text to fit the new margins; this process is called **automatic reformatting.**

- Users can **tab** just once to begin a paragraph or can **indent** an entire paragraph.

- **Justification** refers to the evenness of the text at the side margins. A document is **fully justified** when it has an even margin down each side. Left justification causes an unjustified right side, which is referred to as **ragged-right** text.

- **Line spacing** variations include single-spaced, double-spaced, and even triple-spaced.

- Specific words, phrases, or entire paragraphs can be given special emphasis by using a darker text known as **boldface** text, by using the slanted type called *italic,* or by <u>underlining.</u>

- A **font** is a set of characters—letters, punctuation, and numbers—of the same design. On a **serif** font, each character includes small horizontal lines, known as serifs. A **sans serif** font is clean and stark, with no serif marks. Most fonts available today are **scalable,** meaning that they can be set to almost any size.

- The **Search command,** also called the **Find command,** displays on the screen the exact page and place where a word or phrase is located. The **Find-and-Replace feature** finds each instance of a certain word or phrase and replaces it with another word or phrase. A **conditional replace** asks the user to verify each replacement.

- Word-processing programs offer **pagination** options, permitting the page number to be located at the top or bottom of the page and to the left, right, or center, or even alternating left and right.

- With a single command, you can see in reduced size a **print preview** of an entire page or two facing pages or even several consecutive pages.

- A word-processing program keeps track of space needed for a **footnote** and automatically renumbers if a new footnote is added.

- **Headers** (top) and **footers** (bottom) appear on every page of a document. Variations are available, including placement, size, and font.

- A **text block** can be moved, copied, or deleted. To manipulate a block of text, you must first **mark** (or **select**) the block, which then usually appears in **reverse video** (in which the background color becomes the text color and vice versa). The block move command, also known as **Cut and Paste,** moves the text to a different location. The block copy command copies the block of text into a new location, leaving the text in its original location as well. Block delete removes the block entirely.

- A **spelling checker** program includes a built-in dictionary. A **thesaurus** program supplies synonyms and antonyms.

- A **desktop-publishing program** lets you produce professional-looking documents containing text and graphics.

- One part of the overall design of a document is **page layout**—how text and pictures are arranged on the page.

- Type is described by **type size,** font, **weight,** and **style.** Type size is measured by a standard system based on the **point,** a unit of measure equal to 1/72 of an inch.

- Most printers used in desktop publishing contain **internal fonts** stored in a ROM chip. Most desktop publishing programs provide a **font library** on disk, containing additional fonts called **soft fonts.**

- **Leading** refers to the spacing between the lines of type on a page. **Kerning** refers to adjusting the space between the characters in a word.

- A **halftone** is a photographic representation made up of dots.

- **Page-composition programs,** also called **page-makeup programs,** let you design the page layout. Most desktop program packages offer templates, predetermined page designs. Page-composition programs also allow the incorporation of electronically stored **clip art**—professionally produced images for public use.

► Critical Thinking Questions

1. You are producing a monthly newsletter for your volunteer organization, which helps illiterate adults learn to read. You prepare the first two issues using word processing, and these seem adequate. But you have seen newsletters that are more sophisticated and discover that they are made with desktop-publishing software, something with which you are not familiar. Assuming that the cost of the software is not a problem, what would it take for you to make the switch?

2. List all the uses you might make of desktop publishing at home.

Consider, for example, items such as birthday cards and banners.

3. Suppose you are an editorial assistant at a publishing house. As part of your job, you prepare the schedule for book development and production. You circulate your first cut of the schedule to various editors and designers (usually about six people), who return their copies with changes for you to incorporate. Contrast the differences in this process between using simple word processing and using the word-processing feature that makes the shared papers into Web pages.

► STUDENT STUDY GUIDE

Multiple Choice

1. A set of choices on the screen is called a(n)
   a. menu
   b. reverse video
   c. editor
   d. template

2. A program that provides synonyms is called a(n)
   a. indexing program
   b. form letter program
   c. editing program
   d. thesaurus program

3. An image made up of dots is called a
   a. pull-down menu
   b. block
   c. header
   d. halftone

4. A type of menu that shows additional subchoices is a
   a. reverse menu
   b. scrolled menu
   c. pull-down menu
   d. wrapped menu

5. The feature that automatically moves you to the next line when the current line is full is
   a. find and replace
   b. word wrap
   c. ragged right
   d. right-justified

6. Verification with the Find-and-Replace feature is called
   a. verified replace
   b. conditional replace
   c. questionable replace
   d. "what-if" replace

7. The feature that allows viewing of any part of a document on the screen is called
   a. searching
   b. scrolling
   c. pasting
   d. editing

8. Transferring text to another location without deleting it from its original location is called
   a. scrolling
   b. searching
   c. copying
   d. moving

9. Ragged right means the right margin is set to be
   a. uneven
   b. variable
   c. even
   d. wide

10. Spelling checker programs use
    a. tab settings
    b. pasting
    c. pagination
    d. a dictionary

True/False

T   F   1. Formatting refers to the physical appearance of a document.

T   F   2. A thesaurus program supplies synonyms and antonyms.

T   F   3. A spelling checker program can detect spelling errors and improper use of language.

T   F   4. Right-justified means that the right margin will be ragged.

T   F   5. The Move command moves text to another location and deletes it from its original location.

T   F   6. A footer appears on the bottom of each page of the document.

T   F   7. The feature that word processing and typing have in common is that permanent marks are made on paper as the document is keyed.

T   F   8. When margin settings are changed, automatic reformatting adjusts the text to fit the new margins.

T   F   9. The Copy command moves text to another location and deletes it from its original location.

T   F   10. A template is a set of clip art.

T   F   11. A pull-down menu can be clicked with a mouse to show submenus.

T F 12. Text is centered vertically by adjusting the right margin.

T F 13. Clip art is art that is designed by the user of a desktop-publishing program.

T F 14. A conditional replace asks a user to verify each replacement.

T F 15. Another phrase for marking a text block is selecting a text block.

T F 16. Print preview permits a user to view one or more pages on-screen before printing.

T F 17. A sans serif font is clean, with no serif marks.

T F 18. Another name for the Search command is the Find command.

T F 19. Internal fonts are stored on hard disk.

T F 20. The cursor is usually a blinking underline, rectangle, or vertical line.

Fill-In

1. Settings that are automatically used by the word-processing program unless overridden by the user are called _____ settings.

2. A line that prints on the top of each page of the document is called the _____.

3. Another term for the Move command is _____.

4. The _____ feature permits a user to view any part of a document on the screen, about 20 lines at a time.

5. Resetting _____ will make a document shorter and wider.

6. The _____ feature finds and changes text.

7. Words printed in darker type arc said to be in _____.

8. Before a block of text can be copied or moved, the user must _____.

9. A(n) _____ documcnt has even left and right margins.

10. The verification feature with find and replace is called _____.

11. Synonyms and antonyms can be supplied by a(n) _____.

12. A set of drawings stored on disk is called _____.

13. Printers used for desktop publishing usually have _____ software on a ROM chip.

14. The fonts stored on the hard drive are called _____.

15. _____ programs let the user design the page layout.

16. Adjusting the space between characters in a word is called _____.

17. Italic is an example of the _____ font characteristic.

18. Boldface is an example of the _____ font characteristic.

19. A set of characters of the same design comprise a(n) _____.

20. The feature that automatically moves a word to the next line if it does not fit on the previous line is known as _____.

► **ANSWERS**

Multiple Choice

1. a   6. b
2. d   7. b
3. d   8. c
4. c   9. a
5. b   10. d

True/False

1. T   6. T   11. T   16. T
2. T   7. F   12. F   17. T
3. F   8. T   13. F   18. T
4. F   9. F   14. T   19. F
5. T   10. F   15. T   20. T

Fill-In

1. default
2. header
3. cut and paste
4. scrolling
5. margins
6. find and replace
7. boldface
8. mark (or select) the text
9. fully justified
10. conditional replace
11. thesaurus program
12. clip art
13. internal fonts
14. soft fonts
15. page composition or page makeup
16. kerning
17. style
18. weight
19. font
20. word wrap

Planet Internet

Entertainment

Entertainment on the Internet falls into two broad categories. The first and larger category comprises sites *about* entertainment—sports, music, television, movies, and more. The second category includes the sites that actually *provide* online entertainment, notably games, music, children's sites, and humor. Entertainment on the Internet is so popular that it has spawned at least two cable TV shows: *Internet Tonight* and *You Made It!* on TechTV.

What About Music?

Music fans of any genre can find sites devoted to the history, current events, tours, personal lives, and anything else the artist or fans of the artist care to

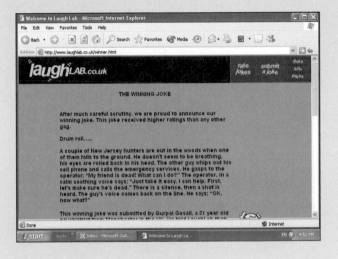

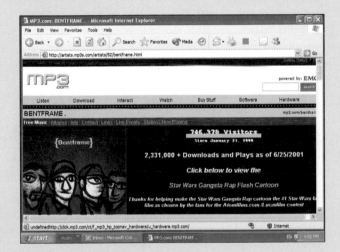

share online. Regardless of your taste—rock, classical, jazz, country, whatever—it's all on the Internet. Web sites allowing you to sample, download, and share music with others in MP3 format are extremely popular.

Internet music distribution has been a particular boon to groups that have a narrow, focused appeal. These artists, who would be unable to get distribution through traditional means because of their limited audience, thrive on the Net. The group Bentframe, for example, has achieved a degree of Internet fame from their hit *The Star Wars Gangsta Rap*. That's not one you'll see in the bricks-and-mortar music stores.

Online Humor

The Internet has been a hotbed of humor from the beginning. E-mail has done a lot to revive the dying oral tradition of joke retelling. In fact, an English university professor recently conducted a year-long survey online to find out what the world considers the funniest joke to be. The survey is now over, but you can read the winner on the Laugh Lab Web site (see the previous screenshot). The Net also seems an ideal vehicle for satire. For a classic satirical piece, search the Internet for the purported news story about Microsoft acquiring the Vatican in exchange for stock options—there are many copies of

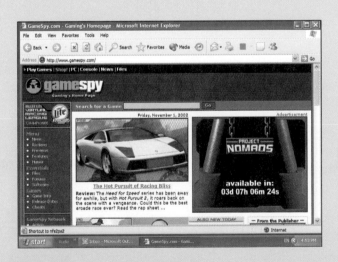

it still to be found online, despite the fact that it is over ten years old! Other interesting sites include The Onion, or Satirewire.

I Like to Follow Sports. What's on the Net?
You can follow any sport that captures your interest. The sites for the most popular sports—basketball, American football, soccer, and baseball—compete with one another to offer the most complete account of scores, player statistics, schedules, standings, and even player injuries.

Games
Games range from free Java, JavaScript, and Flash-based animated Web pages to detailed buy-ware (purchased via credit card) shoot-em-ups, and lavish role-playing games.

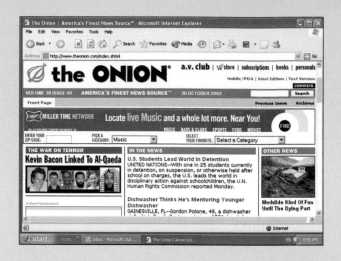

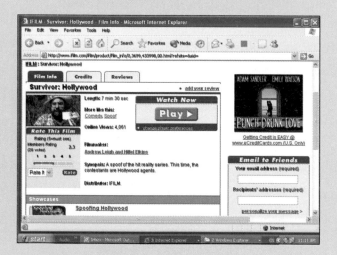

You can find any type of game imaginable (and some you probably never imagined) on the Internet. Even if you're a fan of silly games, you might not have anticipated a variation on Whack-a-Mole featuring Britney Spears. The Internet Tonight site features a different, and usually wacky, game each week.

I Like Cinema or Books. What's on the Net for Me?
You can find entire "movies" made for the Internet; they range from serious drama, to science fiction, and into the just plain silly. The Bijou Cafe offers a Net twist to the art film, and all major motion pictures have lavish promotional sites offering trailers,

endless "the making of" documentaries, cast interviews, and more. Cartoons abound, and as with Internet humor, parodies seem to be everywhere. The Comedy section of the Ifilms site has many of these; for example, a parody of reality show Survivor where all the contestants are Hollywood agents.

Of course, the Web is a great place to buy books, but even the traditional bricks-and-mortar booksellers have augmented their sites with reviews, excerpts, and even a few free samples. Internet magazines or zines are commonplace and range from idiosyncratic musings and sociopathic ruminations to excellent contemporary journalism in the likes of Wired and Salon.

1. **Structured exercise.** Begin with the URL http://www.prenhall.com/capron and check out one or more sites from at least two of the previously mentioned categories. How would you rate the quality of the entertainment provided? Who would be the audience for the Web sites you reviewed?

2. **Free-form exercise.** Find four entertainment sites not listed on your text's Web page. Write a review of these sites to share with your classmates.

3. **Advanced exercise.** Create a review/rating evaluation sheet for online humor or Internet cinema sites, including at least six criteria (for example. excessive vulgar language). Rate two sites using your own criteria, revise your evaluation form as needed and have classmates rate two sites each using your criteria.

Spreadsheets and Business Graphics:
Facts and Figures

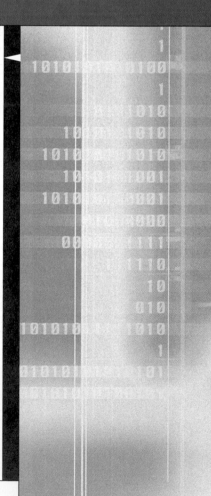

CHAPTER 12

In his first year in college, Dale Husbands took an introductory computer class that included a hands-on component for word processing, spreadsheets, and databases. He breezed through the word processing part, but he didn't get spreadsheets at first. What did rows and columns of numbers have to do with anything in the real world? And who wants to key in a whole bunch of numbers?

Dale came to understand two important notions. The first was that spreadsheets were good for helping plan ahead, because numbers in a spreadsheet can be changed to see what results the changes might cause—the famous "What if . . ." approach. The second, and even more attractive, fact was that he could get the computer to do most of the work.

Dale needed a secondhand car. He decided to see how the spreadsheet could help him predict how much money he would have, varying the amount he might use from his current bank savings, the amount he might put away per month, and the number of months he would have to save. The spreadsheet here shows the results. Dale typed in the first two columns, and the computer produced the results in the last two columns, based on formulas that Dale supplied.

Savings in bank	Savings per month	Total in 12 mo.	Total in 24 mo.
$2,000	$100	$3,200	$4,400
$2,000	$200	$4,400	$6,800
$3,000	$100	$4,200	$5,400
$3,000	$200	$5,400	$7,800

This example is so trivial that it probably could be completed with a pencil in a shorter time than it would take to submit the spreadsheet to the computer. Nevertheless, it shows that you can use a spreadsheet to show the results of changes and to make the computer do most of the work. This chapter provides some information on how that happens.

► THE NATURE OF SPREADSHEETS

For hundreds, even thousands, of years businesses have used numbers to keep track of performance. For all but the last 20 or so years, manipulating all those numbers has been a tedious, error-prone process. Businesses used manual, paper-based **spreadsheets** to organize data in a grid of rows and columns (Figure 12-1a).

Unfortunately, creating a large spreadsheet manually is time-consuming and tedious, even when you use a calculator or copy results from a computer printout. Another problem with manual spreadsheets is that making a mistake is too easy. If you do not discover the mistake, the consequences can be serious. If you discover the mistake after the spreadsheet is finished, you must manually redo all the calculations that used the wrong number.

Electronic Spreadsheets

In 1979, Bob Frankston and Dan Bricklin introduced VisiCalc, the first electronic spreadsheet program, for the Apple II microcomputer. VisiCalc single-handedly changed the business world's perception of the personal computer from being an interesting toy to being an indispensable tool for financial analysis. An **electronic spreadsheet,** or **worksheet,** is a computerized version of a paper spreadsheet (Figure 12-1b). Working with a spreadsheet on a computer eliminates much of the toil of setting up a manual spreadsheet. In general, an electronic spreadsheet works like this: You enter the data you want on your spreadsheet, then key in the types of calculations you need. The electronic spreadsheet program automatically does all the calculations for you, completely error free, and produces the results in your spreadsheet. You can print a copy of the spreadsheet and store the data on your disk so that the spreadsheet can be used again. By the way, although this chapter examines spreadsheets in a general way, it illustrates spreadsheets using software called Microsoft Excel 2002, as shown in Figure 12-1b. Thus, although the screen is realistic, our area of concern is merely the spreadsheet, not the various menus and buttons that come with this specific software.

By far the greatest labor-saving aspect of the electronic spreadsheet is **automatic recalculation:** when you change one value or calculation on your spreadsheet, all dependent values on the spreadsheet are automatically recalculated to reflect the change. Suppose that one entry on a spreadsheet is rate, another is hours, and another is salary, which is the product of rate and hours. Values for rate and

	JAN.	FEB.	MAR.	APR.	TOTAL
SALES	1750	1501	1519	1430	6200
COST OF GOODS SOLD	964	980	932	943	3819
GROSS MARGIN	786	521	587	487	2381
NET EXPENSE	98	93	82	110	383
ADM EXPENSE	77	79	69	88	313
MISC EXPENSE	28	45	31	31	135
TOTAL EXPENSES	203	217	182	229	831
AVERAGE EXPENSE	68	72	61	76	277
NET BEFORE TAXES	583	304	405	258	1550
FEDERAL TAXES	303	158	211	134	806
NET AFTER TAX	280	146	194	124	744

(a)

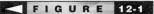

FIGURE 12-1

Manual versus electronic spreadsheets. (a) This manual spreadsheet is a typical spreadsheet consisting of rows and columns. (b) The same spreadsheet created with a spreadsheet program.

Microsoft Excel - Net after tax.xls

	A	B	C	D	E	F	G
1		Jan	Feb	Mar	Apr	Total	
2							
3	Sales	$1,750	$1,501	$1,519	$1,430	$6,200	
4	Cost of goods sold	964	980	932	943	3819	
5	Gross margin	786	521	587	487	2381	
6							
7	Net expenses	98	93	82	110	383	
8	Adm. expenses	77	79	69	88	313	
9	Misc. expenses	28	45	31	31	135	
10	Total expenses	203	217	182	229	831	
11	Average expenses	68	72	61	76	277	
12							
13	Net before tax	583	304	405	258	1550	
14	Federal tax	303	158	211	134	806	
15	Net after tax	$280	$146	$194	$124	$744	
16							
17							
18							
19							
20							

(b)

hours will be entered, but salary will be calculated by the spreadsheet software. But what if the rate changes or was entered incorrectly? Rate can be entered anew, but the person entering the data need not worry about salary because the spreadsheet will recalculate salary using the new value for rate. Although this example might seem trivial, the automatic recalculation principle has significant consequences for large, complex spreadsheets. A change in a single value could affect dozens or even hundreds of calculations, which, happily, the spreadsheet performs automatically.

"What-If" Analysis

Automatic recalculation is valuable for more than fixing mistakes. If a number is changed—not because it is incorrect but because a user wants to see different results—related calculations are also changed at the same time. This ability to change a number and have the change automatically reflected throughout the spreadsheet is the foundation of **"what-if" analysis**—the process of changing one or more spreadsheet values and observing the resulting calculated effect. Consider these examples:

- What if a soap manufacturer were to reduce the price of a certain brand by 5 percent? How would the net profit be affected? What if the price were reduced by 10 percent? By 15 percent?

- What if a general contractor were to subcontract with several workers but one of them reneged and the contractor had to hire someone more expensive? How would that affect the total cost?

- What if the prime lending rate were raised or lowered? How would this affect interest for the bank or the cost of a loan for bank customers?

Once the initial spreadsheet is set up, any of these "what-if" scenarios can be answered by changing one value and examining the new, recalculated results.

▶ **SPREADSHEET FUNDAMENTALS**

Before you can learn how to use a spreadsheet, you must understand some basic spreadsheet features. The characteristics and definitions that follow are common to all spreadsheet programs.

Cells and Cell Addresses

Figure 12-2 shows one type of spreadsheet—a teacher's grade sheet. Notice that the spreadsheet is divided into rows (horizontal) and columns (vertical). The rows have numeric labels, and the columns have alphabetic labels. There are actually more rows and columns than you can see on the screen. Some spreadsheets have thousands of rows and hundreds of columns—probably more than you will ever need to use.

The intersection of a row and column forms a cell. A **cell** is a storage area on a spreadsheet. When referring to a cell, you use the letter and number of the intersecting column and row. For example, in Figure 12-2, cell B9 is the intersection of column B and row 9—the grade of 25 for Vedder on Quiz 1. This reference name is known as the **cell address,** or **cell reference.** Notice that the alphabetic column designation always precedes the row number: B9, not 9B. After column Z, the column labels are AA, AB, and so on. Most spreadsheet programs go to at least column IV, 256 columns in all.

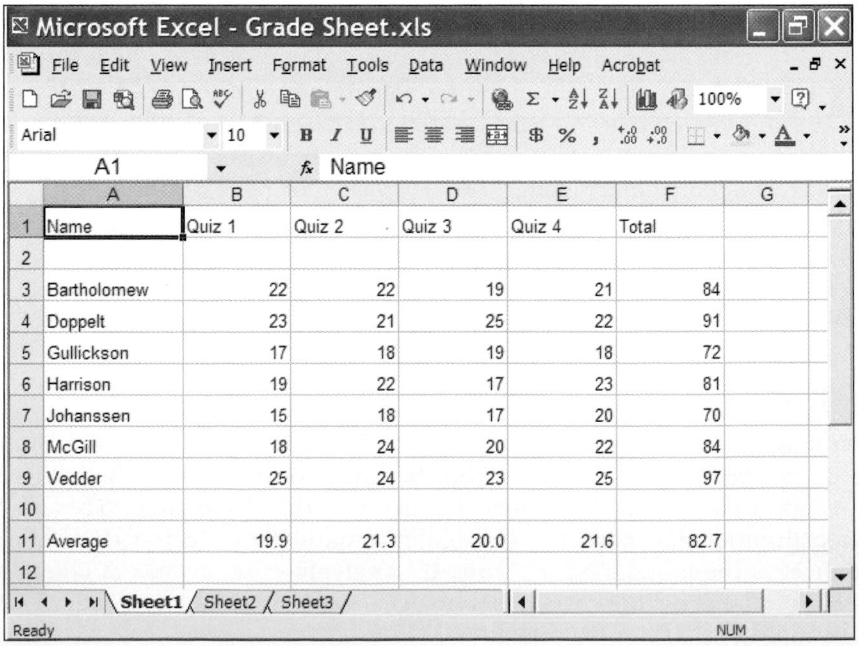

▶ **FIGURE 12-2**

Anatomy of a spreadsheet screen. This screen shows a typical spreadsheet— a teacher's grade sheet. It shows space for 12 rows numbered down the side and 7 columns labeled A through G. The intersection of a row and column forms a cell. Here, cell A1 is the active cell—the cell into which a user may key data. Only one cell may be active at a given time.

Microsoft Excel - Grade Sheet.xls

File Edit View Insert Format Tools Data Window Help Acrobat

	A	B	C	D	E	F	G
1	Name	Quiz 1	Quiz 2	Quiz 3	Quiz 4	Total	
2							
3	Bartholomew	22	22	19	21	84	
4	Doppelt	23	21	25	22	91	
5	Gullickson	17	18	19	18	72	
6	Harrison	19	22	17	23	81	
7	Johanssen	15	18	17	20	70	
8	McGill	18	24	20	22	84	
9	Vedder	25	24	23	25	97	
10							
11	Average	19.9	21.3	20.0	21.6	82.7	
12							

Sheet1 / Sheet2 / Sheet3 /

Ready   NUM

On a spreadsheet, one cell is always known as the **active cell,** or **current cell.** When a cell is active, you can enter data or edit that cell's contents. Typically, the active cell is marked by highlighting in reverse video or with a heavy border drawn around it. The active cell in Figure 12-2 is cell A1.

You can use a mouse or the cursor movement (arrow) keys to scroll through a spreadsheet vertically and horizontally.

Contents of Cells: Labels, Values, and Formulas

Each cell can contain one of three types of information: a label, a value, or a formula. A **label** provides descriptive text information about entries in the spreadsheet, such as a person's name. A cell that contains a label is not generally used to perform mathematical calculations. For example, in Figure 12-2, cells A1, A9, and F1, among others, contain labels. A **value** is an actual number that is entered into a cell to be used in calculations. In Figure 12-2, for example, cell B3 contains a value.

A **formula** is an instruction to the program to calculate a number. A formula generally contains cell addresses and one or more arithmetic operators: a plus sign (+) to add, a minus sign (–) to subtract, an asterisk (*) to multiply, and a slash (/) to divide. When you use a formula rather than entering the calculated result, the software can automatically recalculate the result if you need to change any of the values on which the formula is based.

In addition to the types of calculations just mentioned, a formula can include one or more functions. A **function** is like a preprogrammed formula. Two common functions are the SUM function, which adds numbers together, and the AVERAGE function, which calculates the average of a group of numbers. Most spreadsheet programs contain many functions for a variety of uses, from mathematics to statistics to financial applications. A formula or function does not appear in the cell; instead, the cell shows the result of the formula or function. The result is called the **displayed value** of the cell. The formula or function is the **content** of the cell.

Ranges

Sometimes it is necessary to specify a range of cells in order to build a formula or perform a function. A **range** is a group of one or more adjacent cells occurring in a rectangular shape; the program treats the range as a unit during an operation. Figure 12-3 shows some ranges. To define a range, you must indicate the upper-left and lower-right cells of the block. Depending on the particular spreadsheet software you are using, the cell addresses are separated by a colon or by two periods. For example, in Figure 12-2, the Quiz 1 range is B3:B9 (or B3..B9), and the Batholomew quiz range is B3:E3 (or B3..E3).

► SPREADSHEET FEATURES

After spreadsheet users master the basics, they are usually eager to learn the extra features, especially formatting and graphics, that make their work more useful or attractive. Formatting features take a worksheet beyond the historically plain page full of numbers. Here is a partial list of features you will probably find included with spreadsheet software:

- **Column width.** Columns containing labels—words—usually need to be wider than columns for numbers. Note, for example, that the leftmost column in Figure 12-1b is wider than the other columns to accommodate the data. Columns can also be made narrower. You can also alter the height of a row.

- **Headings.** If a heading is desired, you can create it as a wide column and even center it.

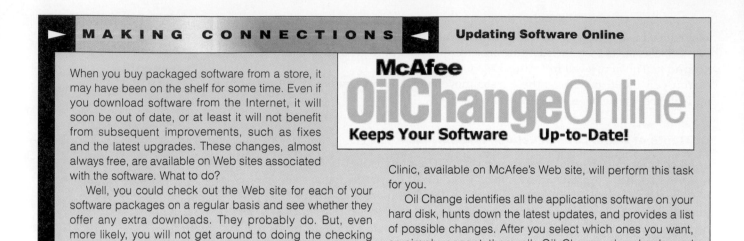

- **Number symbols.** If appropriate, a number value can be shown with a dollar sign ($), a percent sign (%), and/or commas and decimal places, as desired.

- **Appearance of data.** Spreadsheet data can be presented in one of many available fonts and in boldface or italic. Furthermore, data can be centered within the cell or can be justified right or left within the cell. Often an entire column of cells is justified right or left. In Figure 12-2, for example, all data in column A is left-justified; whereas data in columns B through F is right-justified.

- **Printing.** When a user is developing and experimenting with a spreadsheet, he or she is looking at the spreadsheet on the screen. But the finished product, or even a series of variations of the product, will probably be printed for distribution and examination. Spreadsheet software offers several printing options. For example, a

► **F I G U R E   12-3**

Ranges. A range is a group of one or more cells arranged in a rectangle. You can name a range or refer to it by using the addresses of the upper-left and lower-right cells in the group.

spreadsheet may be centered on the printed page. Margins may be altered. The entire page may be printed sideways, that is, horizontally instead of vertically. Vertical and horizontal grid lines may be hidden on the printed spreadsheet.

- **Security.** In a business environment, experts develop many spreadsheets for novice users, who simply enter numeric data in the proper cells and view the results. If the user mistakenly enters a number in a cell that contains a formula, the formula is destroyed. That formula no longer provides an automatic update when the data it relied on is changed, producing incorrect results. The spreadsheet developer can use security options to prevent the user from accidentally entering data into the wrong cells. Password protection can also be used to prevent unauthorized alteration of formulas or data.

- **Decoration.** Most spreadsheet packages include decorative features, such as borders, color options, and clip art.

The change from numbers to pictures—graphics—is a refreshing variation. Most spreadsheet software makes it easy to switch from numbers to pictures. That is, after you prepare a spreadsheet, you can show your results in graphic form. The value of business graphics will be discussed in detail later in the chapter.

▶ A PROBLEM FOR A SPREADSHEET

Gina Hagen, at age eight, was an entrepreneur. One hot summer day she borrowed some sugar and lemons from the kitchen and stirred up a pitcher of lemonade, which she proceeded to sell from a stand in front of her house. By the end of the day, she had gone through three pitchers and had taken in $12.75. Her joy subsided, however, when her mother explained that a business person has to pay for supplies—in this case, the sugar and lemons. But Gina was not deterred for long. In her growing-up years, she sold birdhouses, a neighborhood newsletter, and sequined hair barrettes. In the process, she learned that it was important to keep good business records.

A New Business

When Gina attended Ballard Community College, she noticed that the only beverages available were milk, coffee, and canned soft drinks. Thinking back to her early days, Gina got permission to set up a lemonade stand on campus. In addition to fresh lemonade, she sold bagels and homemade cookies. The stand was soon successful, and Gina eventually hired other students to manage stands on nearby campuses: Aurora, Eastlake, and Phinney.

Using Spreadsheets for the Business

When Gina took a computer applications course at the college, she decided that spreadsheets were appropriate for keeping track of her business. She began by comparing sales for the four campuses for the fourth quarter of the year. She sketched her spreadsheet on paper (Figure 12-4). As she started the spreadsheet software, Gina decided that she would also add some headings. In her first draft of the spreadsheet, Gina keyed in the campus names in column A and the campus sales for each of the three months in columns B, C, and D.

Gina does not, of course, have to compute totals—the spreadsheet software does that. In fact, the obvious solution is to key formulas using the SUM function to compute column and row totals. In cell E6, for example, Gina keys =SUM(B6:D6). This instructs the software to sum the values in cells B6, C6, and D6 and place the resulting sum in cell E6. Even though she typed a formula in the cell, the result is a value, in this case 4671 (Figure 12-5). Keep in mind that the resulting value in any cell

---

Spreadsheets in the Home

Family budgeting is the most common home use for spreadsheets. However, some people are more interested in "what-if" scenarios, for which a spreadsheet is the perfect tool. Here are some examples that users have dreamed up:

- What if I go back to work? Is it really worth it? You can factor in all the expenses of employment—travel, wardrobe, child care, taxes, and other disbursements—and compare the total against the income received.

- What if I start my own business? Can I make a go of it? Although estimates may be sketchy at best, a budding entrepreneur can approximate expenses (for materials, tools, equipment, office rental, and so forth) and compare them with anticipated revenues from clients over different periods of time.

- What if I jump into the stock market, or stick to a more conservative investment approach? A popular sport among investors is running dollar amounts and anticipated growth rates of various investment opportunities through spreadsheets. The results may give them a glimpse of their future financial picture.

- What if I save $50 per month for my child's education? How much money would be saved (with accumulated interest) by the time the child is 18? What if I were to save $75 or $100 per month?

► **F I G U R E** **12-4**

Spreadsheet planning.
A sketch of a spreadsheet is useful before invoking the software. This plan includes one row per campus and the monthly totals, and one column for the campus names, each month's sales, and the campus totals.

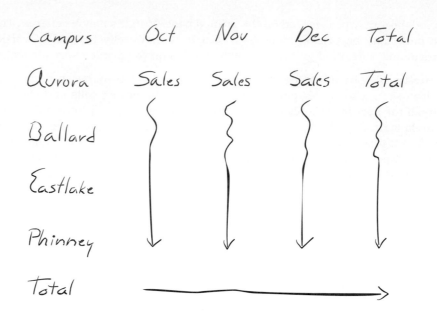

containing a formula changes if any of the values in the cells referenced in that formula change. For cell E6, the resulting value would change if there were a change to the values in cell B6, C6, or D6. The other cells containing totals (E5, E7, E8, B10, C10, D10, and E10) also contain formulas that calculate values. Cell E10, by the way, could sum up either column E (=SUM(E5:E8)) or row 10 (=SUM(B10:D10)). The result is the same either way.

Gina has been saving her spreadsheet on disk as she goes along. Now that the basic spreadsheet is complete, Gina saves it one more time and then prints it.

Changing the Spreadsheet: Automatic Recalculation

Gina has discovered an error in her spreadsheet: Cell D6, rather than containing 1430, should contain 1502. Again using her spreadsheet software, she needs merely to retrieve the spreadsheet from disk and make the single change to cell D6

► **F I G U R E** **12-5**

First draft of sales spreadsheet. This initial look at Gina's spreadsheet shows the headings and data keyed into the spreadsheet. Gina keyed formulas that include the SUM function in cells E5, E6, E7, E8, B10, C10, D10, and E10. Later, Gina will change a data item. She will also format the spreadsheet to improve its appearance; for example, the month headings (OCT, NOV, DEC) need to be centered over their appropriate columns.

Microsoft Excel - 4th Qtr Sales.xls

File Edit View Insert Format Tools Data Window Help Acrobat

Arial 12 B I U

H13

	A	B	C	D	E	F
1	GINA'S LEMONADE					
2	4TH Quarter Sales Report					
3	CAMPUS	OCT	NOV	DEC	TOTAL	
4						
5	Aurora	1006	978	956	2940	
6	Ballard	1675	1566	1430	4671	
7	Eastlake	1378	1340	1198	3916	
8	Phinney	1312	1390	1150	3852	
9						
10	TOTAL	5371	5274	4734	15379	
11						
12						

start E... M... C... 2 6:27 PM

F O C U S   O N   E T H I C S   **Lies and Spreadsheets**

Although electronic spreadsheets have made the actual computation of business and financial reports largely automatic, they have done little, if anything, to prevent fraud and misrepresentation. In fact, spreadsheets may have made misrepresentation more common by luring readers into a false sense of security based on the high accuracy of the calculations but ignoring mistaken underlying assumptions. Consider the ethical implications of these situations and indicate what you think the companies should do to correct them:

● A company shows graphs of increased revenue but omits graphs showing significantly increased expenses.

● The productivity column for last year was calculated on the basis of 200 employees working average 42-hour weeks, but the productivity column for this year is based on 150 employees working average 50-hour weeks.

● Your ISP reports adding 1000 new subscribers this quarter. It does not mention how many previous subscribers dropped out during the same period.

● An Internet startup company claims over 1 million Web page hits and goes on to project that 95 percent of these are potential customers.

(Figure 12-6). Note, however, that cell D6 is used for the totals calculations in cells E6 and D10. Furthermore, because either column E or row 10 is used to compute the final total in E10, changing either cell causes a change in the value calculated in cell E10. The spreadsheet software automatically made all these changes. Indeed, note the changed values in cells E6, D10, and E10, shown in Figure 12-6—all the result of a single change to cell D6.

Formatting and Printing

Now that Gina is satisfied with her spreadsheet calculations, she decides to make some formatting changes and then print the spreadsheet. She uses the spreadsheet software to make the changes (to see the changes, you can look ahead to Figure 12-7a). Here is a list of the changes she wants to make:

● Center the two major headings

● Use a different font on the two major headings and change them to boldface

◄ **F I G U R E   12-6**

The altered spreadsheet, reflecting automatic recalculations. Gina changed the value in cell D6, causing an automatic change to calculated values in cells E6, D10, and E10.

	A	B	C	D	E	F
1	GINA'S LEMONADE					
2	4TH Quarter Sales Report					
3	CAMPUS	OCT	NOV	DEC	TOTAL	
4						
5	Aurora	1006	978	956	2940	
6	Ballard	1675	1566	1502	4743	
7	Eastlake	1378	1340	1198	3916	
8	Phinney	1312	1390	1150	3852	
9						
10	TOTAL	5371	5274	4806	15451	
11						
12						

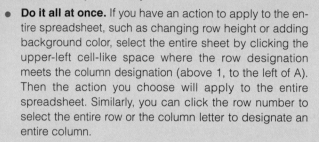

GETTING PRACTICAL   Spreadsheet Tips

Serious users of spreadsheets employ many, or even most, of the hundreds of options that are available with spreadsheet software. More ordinary mortals probably use only the basic features. But even minimalists like to use an extra gimmick now and again. Here are a few that are easy and handy:

● **Do it all at once.** If you have an action to apply to the entire spreadsheet, such as changing row height or adding background color, select the entire sheet by clicking the upper-left cell-like space where the row designation meets the column designation (above 1, to the left of A). Then the action you choose will apply to the entire spreadsheet. Similarly, you can click the row number to select the entire row or the column letter to designate an entire column.

● **Taller and wider.** Spreadsheets look better if they are not crowded. So find the Format menu and change the row height and perhaps the column width. This is especially helpful if you selected the entire spreadsheet first. A common scenario, however, is to improve the row height for the entire spreadsheet but to set the column width according to the width of the data content. You can, of course, make everything smaller instead if you must fit a lot of data on a page.

● **Go the max.** Use the MAX function to find the highest, the longest, the most expensive, and so forth—the maximum. Suppose, for example, that an expense spreadsheet lists the cost of meals by day along row 15, with a different column, B through F, for Monday through Friday. To determine the most expensive meal, use = MAX(B15:F15).

● **Drag data.** Highlight any cell. In its lower-right corner you can see a tiny square called the fill handle. If you want to duplicate data from one cell to any adjacent cell, drag its fill handle to the cell you want to fill with duplicate data. Suppose, for example, that you are making calculations on each row that always include 40 in one cell. Place 40 in the cell at the top of the appropriate column. Drag it down the column to the other rows. Then all cells in that column have the value 40 in them.

● **Add a new row or column.** Sometimes people get partway through a spreadsheet and realize that they forgot, or want to add, a new row or column in the middle. Click the number of the row that you want to be below the new blank row. Find the Insert menu and click Row; a new blank row appears above the row you designated. A new column is added to the left of the selected column. With each row or column addition, all rows or columns, and all calculations based on cells, are renumbered automatically.

● **Map it.** Spreadsheet software offers a variety of maps, such as the one of the countries of the world shown here. You can add extras, such as marking regions by name and color and adding "pins" for points of interest.

● Center CAMPUS, OCT, NOV, DEC, and both TOTAL labels, each within its own cell, and boldface each label

● Put each campus name in italic

● Present the sales figures as currency by adding dollar signs ($) and decimal points

● Use a vertical double border to separate the campus names from the sales figures, a horizontal double border to separate the headings from the sales figures, and a single horizontal border to separate the top two heading rows from the rest of the spreadsheet

● Remove the spreadsheet grid lines.

Note that the printed result need not include the alphabetic column labels or the numeric row labels (Figure 12-7a).

A Graph from Spreadsheet Data

Gina decides to make a chart to contrast the sales totals among the four campuses. These figures already exist in the last column of the spreadsheet, cells E5 through E8. Using the software's charting capability, Gina can select those cells and then request a three-dimensional pie chart to display them. She decides to specify that the sales figures be shown as percentages of total sales and that each pie wedge be

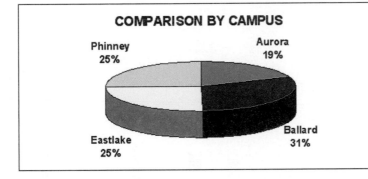

GINA'S LEMONADE

4th Quarter Sales Report

CAMPUS	OCT	NOV	DEC	TOTAL
Aurora	$ 1,006.00	$ 978.00	$ 956.00	$ 2,940.00
Ballard	$ 1,675.00	$ 1,566.00	$ 1,502.00	$ 4,743.00
Eastlake	$ 1,378.00	$ 1,340.00	$ 1,198.00	$ 3,916.00
Phinney	$ 1,312.00	$ 1,390.00	$ 1,150.00	$ 3,852.00
TOTAL	$ 5,371.00	$ 5,274.00	$ 4,806.00	$ 15,451.00

COMPARISON BY CAMPUS

Phinney 25%
Aurora 19%
Eastlake 25%
Ballard 31%

◄ **FIGURE** 12-7

The finished spreadsheet and a matching graph.
(a) On the final version of her spreadsheet, printed here, Gina has boldfaced and centered the headings and changed their fonts, added vertical and horizontal borders, used italics and boldface on certain cells, and expressed the sales figures as currency. (b) This simple pie chart shows the figures from the rightmost column of the spreadsheet, the campus totals, as percentages of total sales.

further labeled with the campus name, supplied from column A on the spreadsheet. After adding a title, "Comparison by Campus," Gina saves and prints the finished chart (Figure 12-7b).

► BUSINESS GRAPHICS

Graphics can show words and numbers and data in ways that are meaningful and easy to understand. This is the key reason they are valuable. Personal computers give people the capability to store and use data about their businesses. These same users, however, sometimes find it difficult to convey this information to others—managers or clients—in a meaningful way. **Business graphics**—graphics that represent data in a visual, easily understood format—provide an answer to this problem.

Why Use Graphics?

Graphics generate and sustain the interest of an audience by brightening up any lesson, report, or business document. In addition, graphics can help to get a point across by presenting numeric data (Figure 12-8a) in one simple, clear graph (Figure 12-8b). What is more, that simple graph can reveal a trend that could be lost if it were buried in long columns of numbers. In addition, a presenter who uses graphics often appears more prepared and organized than one who does not. To sum up, most people use business graphics software for two reasons: to view and analyze data, and to make a positive impression during a presentation. To satisfy these different needs, two types of business graphics programs have been developed: analytical graphics and presentation graphics.

Analytical Graphics

Analytical graphics programs are designed to help users analyze and understand specific data. Sometimes called analysis-oriented graphics programs, these programs

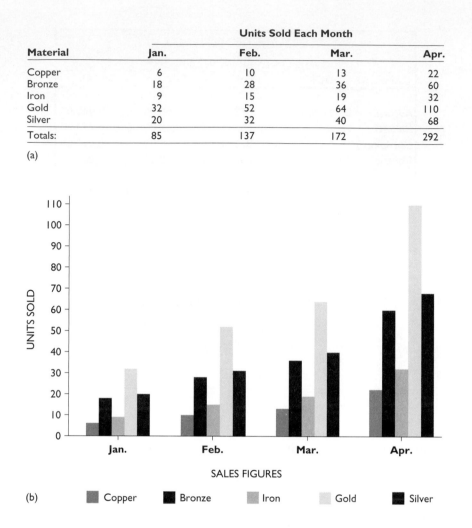

► **FIGURE 12-8**

Business graphics. (a) A large amount of data can be translated into (b) one simple, clear bar graph.

	Units Sold Each Month			
Material	Jan.	Feb.	Mar.	Apr.
Copper	6	10	13	22
Bronze	18	28	36	60
Iron	9	15	19	32
Gold	32	52	64	110
Silver	20	32	40	68
Totals:	85	137	172	292

(a)

(b) ■ Copper   ■ Bronze   ■ Iron   ■ Gold   ■ Silver

use already-entered spreadsheet or database data to construct and display line, bar, and pie chart graphs (Figures 12-9a through 12-9c). Spreadsheet software usually provides this option.

Although analytical graphics programs do a good job of producing simple graphs, these programs are too limited and inflexible for a user who needs to prepare elaborate presentations. For example, analytical graphics programs let you choose from only a small number of graph types, and the formatting features—graph size, color, and lettering—are limited. These restrictions may be of little concern to some users, but those who require sophisticated graphics will want to consider presentation graphics.

Presentation Graphics

Presentation graphics programs are also called **business-quality graphics.** These programs let you produce charts, graphs, and other visual aids that look as if they were prepared by a professional graphic artist (Figure 12-9d through 12-9f). However, you can control the appearance of the product when you create it yourself, and you can produce graphics faster and make last-minute changes if necessary.

Most presentation graphics programs help you do several kinds of tasks:

● Edit and enhance charts, such as analytical graphs, created by other programs

● Create charts, diagrams, drawings, and text slides from scratch

● Use a library of symbols, drawings, and pictures called **clip art** that comes with the graphics program

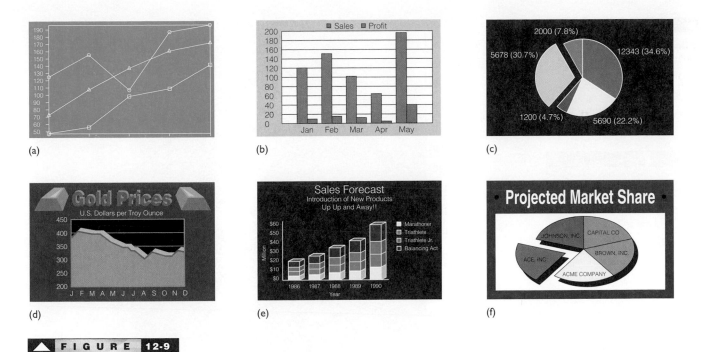

(a)

(b)

(c)

(d)

(e)

(f)

▲ **FIGURE 12-9**

Analytical graphics compared with presentation graphics. Analytical graphics (a, b, and c) are certainly serviceable, but they lack the clarity and appeal of presentation graphics (d, e, and f). Compare the line graphs (a and d), bar graphs (b and e), and pie charts (c and f).

- Permit an animated presentation so that, for example, letters of a title can swoop in one by one to create a dynamic effect

- Use small files that come with the program to add sounds—chimes, applause, swoosh, and even thunk—to your presentation

Although graphics hardware requirements vary, be aware that to use presentation graphics you need a high-resolution color monitor, possibly a color printer, and perhaps some method of transferring your computer-produced results to slides or transparencies or to a projector that can show computer monitor output on a wall screen.

► SOME GRAPHICS TERMINOLOGY

To use a graphics program successfully, you should know some basic concepts and design principles. Let us begin by exploring the types of graphs you can create.

Line Graphs

One of the most useful ways of showing trends or cycles over a period of time is to use a **line graph.** For example, the graph in Figure 12-10 shows company costs for utilities, supplies, and travel during a five-month period. Line graphs are appropriate when there are many values or complex data. In the business section of a newspaper, line graphs are used to show complex trends in gross national product, stock prices, or employment changes over a period of time. Also, corporate profits and losses are often illustrated by line graphs.

Notice, in Figure 12-10, the line that runs vertically on the left and the one that runs horizontally across the bottom; each line is called an **axis** (plural: axes). The horizontal line, called the **x-axis,** often represents units of time, such as days, months, or years; it can also represent characteristics, such as model number, brand name, or country. The vertical line, called the **y-axis,** usually shows measured values

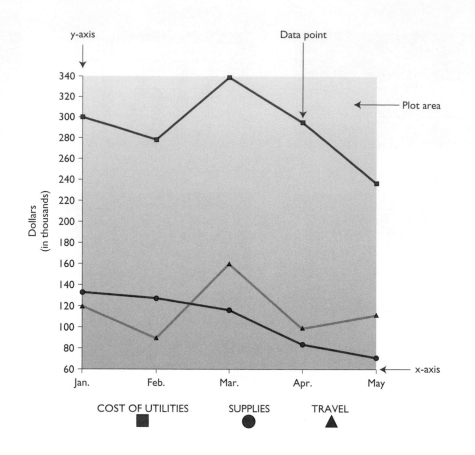

or amounts, such as dollars, staffing levels, or units sold. The area above the x-axis and to the right of the x-axis is called the **plot area**—the space in which the graph is plotted, or drawn.

Graphics programs automatically scale (arrange the units or numbers on) the x-axis and y-axis so that the graph of your data is nicely proportioned and easy to read. When you become proficient in using a graphics program, you can select your own scaling for the axes. Each dot or symbol on a line graph represents a single numeric quantity called a **data point.** You must specify the data to be plotted on the graph; many graphs are produced from the data stored in the rows and columns of spreadsheet files. This data is usually referred to as the set of **values.** The items that the data points describe are called **variables.** For example, in Figure 12-10 the variable Utilities includes the values 300, 280, 340, 300, and 240; the top line in the plot area shows how these values are graphed.

To make the graph easier to read and understand, **labels** are used to identify the categories along the x-axis and the units along the y-axis. **Titles** summarize the information in the graph and are used to increase comprehension. Every graph should have a title. It is surprisingly difficult to recall the exact meaning of an untitled chart that was produced just a few weeks before. For this reason most programs support not only titling the entire graph but adding separate titles to the individual axes as well.

Bar Graphs

Bar graphs are used for graphing the same kinds of data that line graphs represent. They are often used to illustrate multiple comparisons, such as sales, expenses, and production activities. Notice in Figure 12-9b that **bar graphs** shade a rectangular area up to the height of the point being plotted, creating a bar. These graphs can be striking and informative when they are simple. Bar graphs are useful for presentations because the comparisons are easy to absorb.

Neville Smythe,
Programmer (VBA Macros)

Neville likes to improvise. He gets bored easily, and can't stand a job where the daily grind is identical day after day after day after day. You get the picture. Fortunately, Neville works for a fast-paced financial consulting firm. He specializes in programming macros using Visual Basic for Applications (VBA), and while that is what he has to do day in and day out, every project is different, which suits Neville just fine.

Neville works along with the company's consultants, helping them create the tools they need for putting together their specialized reports, each unique to the contract underway. Using VBA, Neville assembles macros for Microsoft Office XP programs, such Excel or Access, as well as some more specialized software, like Microsoft Project or Crystal Reports.

Often working with two or three consultants during the day, Neville rarely has time to get bored at all, and juggling so many projects at one time often has him improvising to make sure he gets everything done.

Pie Charts

Representing a single value for each variable, a **pie chart** shows how various values make up a whole. These charts really look like pies; the whole amount is represented by a circle, and each wedge of the pie—a portion of the whole—represents a value. Figure 12-9c shows a pie chart.

Pie charts can show only the data for one time period, such as a single month. However, of all the graphics, the pic chart does the best job of showing the proportions for different variables. If a pie chart for expenses, for example, showed that more than half went for rent, that half-pie is easy to spot. Figure 12-9f shows one of the wedges pulled slightly away from the pie for emphasis. This type of pie chart is called an **exploded pie chart.**

▲

The most common applications software, word processing, deals with communicating with words. This chapter has addressed a subject that tends to be of more interest to businesses than to individuals: analyzing and communicating with numbers.

CHAPTER REVIEW

► Summary and Key Terms

- Forms that are used to organize business data into rows and columns are called **spreadsheets.** An **electronic spreadsheet,** or **worksheet,** is a computerized version of a manual spreadsheet.

- The greatest labor-saving aspect of the electronic spreadsheet is **automatic recalculation:** When one value or calculation in a spreadsheet is changed, all dependent values on the spreadsheet are automatically recalculated to reflect the change.

- **"What-if" analysis** is the process of changing one or more spreadsheet values and observing the resulting calculated effect.

- The intersection of a row and column forms a **cell.** The letter and number of the intersecting column and row is the **cell address,** or **cell reference.**

- The **active cell,** or **current cell,** is the cell in which you can type data.

- Each cell can contain one of three types of information: A **label** provides descriptive information about entries in the spreadsheet; a **value** is an actual number entered into a cell; and a **formula** is an instruction to the program to perform a calculation. A **function** is like a preprogrammed formula. Sometimes you must specify a **range** of cells, a group of adjacent cells in a rectangular area, to build a formula or perform a function.

- To create a spreadsheet, you enter labels, values, formulas, and functions into the cells. Formulas and functions do not appear in the cells; instead, the cell shows the result of the formula or function. The result is called the **displayed value** of the cell. The formula or function is the **content** of the cell, or the **cell content.**

- **Business graphics** represent business data in a visual, easily understood format.

- **Analytical graphics** programs help users to analyze and understand specific data by presenting data in visual form. **Presentation graphics** programs, also known as **business-quality graphics** programs, produce sophisticated graphics. Presentation graphics programs contain a library of symbols and drawings called **clip art** and also offer animation and sounds.

- A **line graph,** which uses a line to represent data, is useful for showing trends over time. A reference line on a line graph is an **axis.** The horizontal line is called the **x-axis,** and the vertical line is called the **y-axis.** The area above the x-axis and to the right of the y-axis is the **plot area.** Each dot or symbol on a line graph is a **data point.** Each data point represents a **value.** The items that the data points describe are called **variables. Labels** identify the categories along the x-axis and the units along the y-axis. **Titles** summarize the information in the graph.

- **Bar graphs** show data comparisons by the lengths or heights of bars.

- A **pie chart** represents a single value for each variable. A wedge of an **exploded pie chart** is pulled slightly away from the pie to emphasize that share of the whole.

▶ Critical Thinking Questions

1. Consider more "what-if" scenarios. What if I saved $100 a month? How soon could I buy a car? What if I saved $125 or $150 per month? If you have a price in mind for a car, what information could such a spreadsheet give you? What information could you get by varying interest rates and the price of the car? What if I bought the house by the lake instead of the house near work? The houses have different price tags and different expenses. These factors and others can be built into a spreadsheet and used to calculate monthly payments and other factors that might affect your budget. What factors might you include in your spreadsheet? (Hint: One factor might be reduced transportation costs for the house near work.)

2. How might you use a spreadsheet in your career? What use might these workers have for a spreadsheet: a video store manager, a dietitian, a civil engineer who designs bridges, a day care supervisor?

3. Business people who only occasionally give presentations say that one reason they prefer using graphics is that graphics focus the audience on the screen and thus reduce the nervousness of the speaker. What other advantages do graphics offer to the speaker?

4. In addition to standing on their own, spreadsheets are often used to back up a discussion or illuminate a point in a text report. With this is mind, word-processing programs let users import spreadsheets into text documents, such as reports or memos. This is just the sort of thing that give software suites value; the word-processing and spreadsheet programs are compatible and can exchange data easily. What scenarios can you imagine for a report with an embedded spreadsheet, even a small one, for these types of workers: a roofing subcontractor, a visiting nurse, an office project manager.

▶ STUDENT STUDY GUIDE

Multiple Choice

1 The active cell is the
   a. current cell
   b. range
   c. formula
   d. cell address

2. A preprogrammed formula is called a
   a. function
   b. graph
   c. range
   d. cell

3. A chart that shows how various values make up a whole is known as a
   a. function
   b. line graph
   c. pie chart
   d. bar graph

4. Business-quality graphics is another name for
   a. a recalculation
   b. a range
   c. analytical graphics
   d. presentation graphics

5. The intersection of a row and column creates a(n)
   a. active address
   b. formula
   c. cursor
   d. cell

6. The result of a formula in a cell is known as the
   a. label
   b. value
   c. range
   d. displayed value

7. Text information in a cell is called a
   a. label
   b. value
   c. formula
   d. cell address

8. A dot or symbol on a line graph is called a(n)
   a. label
   b. data point
   c. variable
   d. axis

9. The element that summarizes information contained in a graph is called the
   a. plot area
   b. title
   c. label
   d. axis

10. Art that is supplied with a graphics program is called
    a. a cell
    b. analytical
    c. clip art
    d. a range

11. In contrast to analytical graphics, presentation graphics are
    a. more sophisticated
    b. larger
    c. more accurate
    d. not used in business

12. When a wedge is made separate, the pie chart is referred to as
    a. exploded
    b. active
    c. referenced
    d. displayed

13. A cell entry that provides descriptive information is called a
    a. value
    b. data point
    c. label
    d. title

14. Automatic recalculation refers to the changes to values that are dependent on
    a. what if
    b. the axis
    c. a function
    d. a changed value

15 SUM is an example of a
    a. displayed value
    b. range
    c. label
    d. function

16 Each data point on a line graph represents a
    a. function
    b. pie wedge
    c. cell
    d. value

17. A reference line on a line graph is called a(n)
    a. axis
    b. label
    c. title
    d. data point

18. F2:G6 is an example of a
    a. function
    b. range
    c. value
    d. cell address

19. Which of these is a correct cell address?
    a. DD
    b. B6
    c. 2C
    d. F0

20. A set of adjacent cells that form a rectangle is called a
    a. data point
    b. function
    c. range
    d. cell reference

True/False

T   F   1. Another name for the content of a cell is the displayed value.

T   F   2. A rectangular group of cells is called a range.

T   F   3. Another name for the active cell is the cell reference.

T   F   4. A manual spreadsheet is capable of automatically recalculating totals when changes are made to figures in the spreadsheet.

T   F   5. A disadvantage of business graphics is that they depict data in a manner that is hard to grasp.

T   F   6. The displayed value of a cell is called its formula or function.

T   F   7. The shape of the set-apart portion of an exploded pie chart is a wedge.

T   F   8. A function is like a preprogrammed formula.

T   F   9. Another name for the current cell is a labeled cell.

T   F 10. In a spreadsheet, column widths and row heights can be altered.

T   F 11. Analytical graphics let you construct line, bar, and pie chart graphs.

T   F 12. Many presentation graphics programs can edit and enhance charts created by other programs.

T   F 13. Presentation graphics appear professionally produced.

T   F 14. Column widths in spreadsheets are fixed.

T   F 15. Analytical graphics use a library of symbols to enhance output.

T   F 16. The active spreadsheet cell is marked by the pointer.

T   F 17. Labels identify categories along graph axes.

T   F 18. On an exploded pie chart, one wedge is slightly removed from the pie for emphasis.

T   F 19. The greatest labor-saving aspect of an electronic spreadsheet is its ability to recalculate dependent values when the value it depends on is changed.

T   F 20. In a spreadsheet a label cannot be used for calculations.

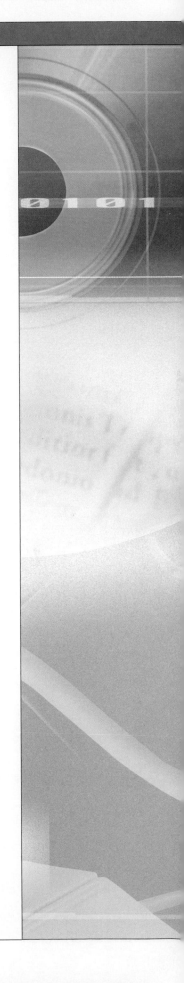

Fill-In

1. An actual number that is entered into a cell is a(n) _____.

2. The kind of analysis that lets a user change spreadsheet values and then observe the resulting effect is called _____.

3. Enhanced graphics are called _____.

4. In a spreadsheet a formula or function is called the cell content; the calculated result is called the _____.

5. The intersection of a row and column on a spreadsheet is called a(n) _____.

6. Plain line graphs are an example of _____ graphics.

7. Another name for a cell address is the _____.

8. Another name for the active cell is the _____.

9. In a line graph the horizontal axis is called the _____.

10. A preprogrammed formula is called a(n) _____.

11. A group of cells in a rectangular form is called a(n) _____.

12. The type of chart that has a single wedge separate from the rest of the chart is called a(n) _____.

13. When one value or calculation on a spreadsheet is changed, all dependent calculations are also changed by the software. This is called _____.

14. The combination of the letter and number of the intersecting column and row of a cell is called the _____.

15. Another name for an electronic spreadsheet is _____.

16. The type of cell that contains descriptive information is called a(n) _____.

17. A library of usable symbols and drawings is called _____.

18. In a line graph the vertical axis is called the _____.

19. How many values can a pie chart represent for each slice? _____.

20. The type of graph that is used to show a trend over time is called a(n) _____.

► ANSWERS

Multiple Choice

1. a	6. d	11. a	16. d
2. a	7. a	12. a	17. a
3. c	8. b	13. c	18. b
4. d	9. b	14. d	19. b
5. d	10. c	15. d	20. c

True/False

1. F	6. F	11. T	16. F
2. T	7. T	12. T	17. T
3. F	8. T	13. T	18. T
4. F	9. F	14. F	19. T
5. F	10. T	15. F	20. T

Fill-In

1. value
2. what-if analysis
3. presentation graphics
4. displayed value
5. cell
6. analytical
7. cell reference
8. current cell
9. x-axis
10. function
11. range
12. exploded pie chart
13. automatic recalculation
14. cell address
15. worksheet
16. label
17. clip art
18. y-axis
19. one
20. line graph

Planet Internet

Numerical Data on the Web

Each year, billions of images of numerical data—statistics, charts, graphs, maps, and interpretive graphics—are developed and printed. Increasingly, these graphics are finding their way onto the Web. In fact, the Web is also a prolific generator of numerical information. Web servers count the number of page views; network routers count data packets; e-commerce sites count sales, and business and scientific enterprises track and report their progress with charts, graphs, and tables.

Navigating this sea of information requires good charts, yet for all the ease with which spreadsheets and graphical presentation software can create and spread graphs on the Web, these tools provide no guarantee that the results are correct, informative, or even interpretable. Here are some general guidelines, adapted from Edward Tufte's work, *The Visual Display of Quantitative Information*.

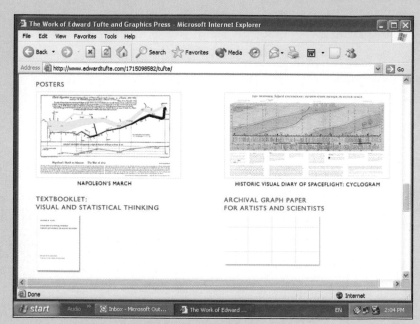

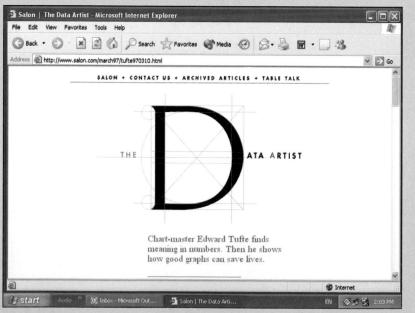

Maximize the Data-to-Ink Ratio

There's no real ink on the Web. But if you translate ink to pixels, this concept applies just as much to charts on the Web as it does to printed ones. Space on your Web page and your visitors' time are limited, so the worth of each bit of page that doesn't convey information should be ruthlessly examined.

Examples that violate this principle include bar charts constructed of stacked pictures and a particular artifact of the spreadsheet, the 3D graph.

Sure, those 3D bars might make your graphic of Web site hits resemble a small cityscape. However, the visual appeal is diminished when viewers find that the shadows, shading, rotations, and varied colors don't really add clarity and make printing the page an ink-draining chore.

Decorative elements that look good on your printer at 1,200 dpi might blur into graphical noise when rendered on a browser screen at 72 dpi.

Make sure each of those 72 dots per inch is conveying something important.

Erase Nondata Ink

It's really easy to add a lot of pixels to a graphic that don't convey any additional information or provide information that a reader could get from the surrounding page text or a caption.

Gridlines, colored backgrounds, labels for each data point, and excessive boxes all detract from the ease of understanding you really want for your graphs. Many spreadsheets produce some or all of these by default, so be careful.

Gridlines might make your results look more scientific, but few graphics require that viewers be able to scan exact values off the chart. If your readers need lots of numbers, use an HTML table. If they need to get the big picture quickly, use a simple graph with a plain background and a minimum of extraneous lines.

Revise and Edit

Review your graphs as critically as you would the text of your page, and revise and recreate as required. Is the graphic accurate, or could it be misleading? Examples include a group of charts intended for comparison in which every graph has a different scale. Because automatic scaling is the default behavior for most spreadsheets and presentation software, this is an easy way to accidentally mislead viewers. It's also easy to catch and fix with a few edits.

Look critically at your charts. Did you use the best kind of chart for your information? Pie charts, for instance, get really confusing if they have more than a handful of slices. Ask yourself which works better with your page layout: horizontal or vertical bars? Can these two graphics be combined into one, or would that be too cluttered?

Finally, don't forget the little things. Does the chart have a legend explaining what the various elements mean? Did you give it an informative title? How many charts have you seen that still have the default title Chart 1? Are your scaling and spelling accurate?

Good charts and graphs contribute positively to the usefulness and the attractiveness of your page. Poor ones mislead and alienate viewers.

Internet Exercises

1. **Structured exercise.** Starting from http://www.prenhall.com/capron, browse to Web sites describing good data display principles. Write a short essay, or give a brief presentation describing two design principles described on these pages.

2. **Free-form exercise.** Find examples of good and poor charts and graphics on the Web. Good places to look for sites with lots of charts include government and scientific sites, company annual reports, and Web server and network statistics. (Some starting places are linked on http://www.prenhall.com/capron.) If appropriate, you might want to work on this activity in teams, with each team reporting on different Web examples.

3. **Advanced exercise.** Using spreadsheet or presentation software and a small set of data, see which team can produce the worst chart. Good ideas for bad charts include misleading scaling, poor labeling, excessive use of color and lines, and poor editing. Analyze the charts each team produces in light of the suggestions given in your text for improved output.

Database Management Systems:
Getting Data Together

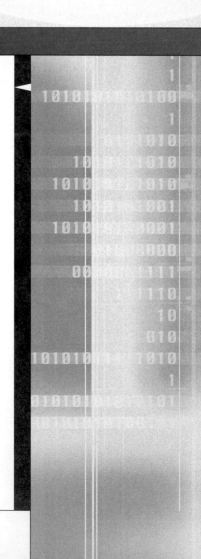

CHAPTER 13

LEARNING OBJECTIVES

Describe the hierarchy of data

Explain the differences between files and databases

List the four database models

Describe the concept of data integrity

Describe the functions of a database management system

Describe the process of creating a database in general terms

Compare and contrast relational and object-oriented databases

Explain what a data warehouse is and how it differs from a database

Suppose you have a really terrific recipe for chocolate chip cookies. In fact, your friends and family rave about your oatmeal-raisin cookies too, not to mention your snickerdoodles and macadamia nut specials. Thus encouraged, you open a small cookie shop. Just one. It is not too difficult to keep track of supplies—just multiply the ingredients of a few recipes.

But that simplicity has changed for Debbi Fields, whose Mrs. Fields Cookies has blossomed from a single store in Palo Alto, California, to a chain of more than 600 stores in almost every state and several foreign countries. Fortunately, her husband, Randy Fields, a computer programmer, put together a team of technicians to provide databases with every kind of information a store might need.

Recipes and ingredients are just the beginning. The databases specialize in planning and marketing strategies. For example, from data gathered and stored over a period of time, the database knows how meteorological conditions affect sales at each store. In Seattle, rain means more cookie sales; in Los Angeles, rain means fewer cookie sales. Stores in either city can plan the amount of cookies to bake accordingly. But the weather is only one factor. Cookies sold and dollars generated are updated at each store hourly. These records can be accessed in the future to predict sales. If, for example, a store sees that its sales are below predictions, workers are authorized to offer specials—say, a free soft drink or buy 5, get 2 free.

Employees at Mrs. Fields Cookies found it easy to learn to use the database software. The databases have many advantages—in particular, keeping consistent standards at each store. But the bottom line is that the computer databases increase productivity.

▶ GETTING IT TOGETHER: DATA MANAGEMENT

Suppose you have a collection of names and addresses, each on a separate index card, stored in an index card file (Figure 13-1). If you have only 25 cards, sorting the cards into alphabetical order or even finding all the people who have the same ZIP code is fairly easy. But what if you had 100, or 1,000, or 10,000 cards? What if you had several different boxes, one organized by names, one by cities, and one by ZIP codes? What if different file clerks added more cards each day, not knowing whether they were duplicating cards that were already in the file? And what if another set of clerks were trying to update the data on the same cards? As you can see, things might get out of hand. Enter computers and data management software.

The Hierarchy of Data

Before we can discuss the software used to manage data, you need to see how data is organized. Figure 13-2a shows the name and address data in list form. Figure 13-2b shows the same data arranged in field and record format. The **field** is the smallest meaningful unit of data and consists of a group of one or more characters that has a specific meaning. In Figure 13-2b, there are six fields: Last Name, First Name, Street, City, State, and Zip Code. The set of fields containing data about a single person makes up that person's **record.** In Figure 13-2b each row is a record. Note that although the data value in a field can vary from record to record, each record has the same fields in the same sequence. A collection of related records makes up a **file,** here the Name and Address file. The number of records in a given file can vary; Figure 13-2b shows five records—one for each person.

A-C

AKERS, TED
4302 LEMON AVE.
OAKLAND, CA
94709

Akers, Ted
4302 Lemon Ave.
Oakland, CA 94709

Brown, Ann
345 Willow Rd.
Palo Alto, CA 94025

Chandler, Joy
4572 College Ave.
Berkeley, CA 94705

James, Susan
822 York St.
San Francisco, CA 94103

Mead, Ken
8 Rocklyn Ave.
Tiburon, CA 94903

(a)

Field

LAST NAME	FIRST NAME	STREET	CITY	STATE	ZIP CODE
AKERS	TED	4302 LEMON AVE.	OAKLAND	CA	94709
BROWN	ANN	345 WILLOW RD.	PALO ALTO	CA	94025
CHANDLER	JOY	4572 COLLEGE AVE.	BERKELEY	CA	94705
JAMES	SUSAN	822 YORK ST.	SAN FRANCISCO	CA	94103
MEAD	KEN	8 ROCKLYN AVE.	TIBURON	CA	94903

Record

(b)

Data item

▲ **FIGURE 13-2**

Data hierarchy. In part (a) the name and address data is shown in list form. In part (b) the same data is organized into fields and records, with the columns representing the fields and the rows representing the records.

Files and Databases

Traditionally, information systems were developed by using a file-processing approach. Each application had its own files, and data was not shared among applications. This resulted in a great deal of **data redundancy**—the repetition of the same data values. Figure 13-3 illustrates a simplified version of a customer file. In this file, the Cust No (Customer Number) field is the primary key field. A **primary key field** (or just **primary key**) is a field whose value uniquely identifies a record. Here, each customer is assigned a unique customer number. Notice that the salesperson information (SlsLast, SlsFirst, Region, and Phone) is repeated for each customer serviced by that salesperson. This happens because each record contains data about two separate entities: the customer and the salesperson.

The database approach was developed to minimize this data redundancy by creating separate files for each entity. In database terminology, files are referred to as

► **MAKING CONNECTIONS** ◄ **TerraServer**

At the Microsoft TerraServer site you can find a collection of satellite images of just about any place on earth. The images are cataloged in a massive database and can be viewed online or purchased for a modest fee. The image shown on the left is a view of the Epcot theme park and surrounding resort areas at Disneyworld in Florida; the image on the right is of the shuttle launch pad at Kennedy Space Center. The TerraServer site is popular around the clock, receiving over 30 million hits per day.

CUST NO	CUST NAME	CITY	STATE	SLS LAST	SLS FIRST	REGION	PHONE
2934	Ballard Computer	Seattle	WA	Nguyen	Linh	NW	(206)634-1995
3007	Computer City	Miami	FL	Long	Teresa	SE	(305)734-2987
3107	Computer City	Orlando	FL	Long	Teresa	SE	(305)734-2987
3752	Upland computers	Phoenix	AZ	Abele	Lori	SW	(602)624-9384
3812	PSC Systems	San Francisco	CA	Nguyen	Linh	NW	(206)634-1955
4211	Computing Solutions	Tuscon	AZ	Abele	Lori	SW	(602)624-9384
4354	Digital Solutions	Chicago	IL	Egbert	Edwin	MW	(605)348-9217
6118	CyberMart	Atlanta	GA	Rodriquez	Frank	SE	(404)524-9384
6715	Enterprise Computing	Jacksonville	FL	Rodriquez	Frank	SE	(404)524-9384

▲ **FIGURE 13-3**

The Customer file. In this file, fields containing data about salespeople are repeated in several records. Note that Linh Nguyen's telephone number is different in the two records in which it appears. Which is correct?

tables. A **database** is a collection of related tables. Figure 13-4 shows the same data reorganized into a database containing two tables, one for customer data and one for salesperson data. A new field, Sales ID, has been created to serve as the primary key for the Salesperson table. The Sales ID field also appears in the Customer table, where it is used to link to the salesperson for each customer. Although each record in the Salesperson table must contain a unique value in the Sales ID field, many Customer table records may have the same value in that field, because one salesperson can service many customers. A field, such as Sales ID, that is used to link from one table (Customer) to the primary key of another table (Salesperson) is referred to as a **foreign key** in the table (Customer) where the link begins. Tables that are linked through foreign and primary keys are said to be **related.** Note that primary keys must contain unique values; whereas foreign keys may have duplicate values.

The reduction in data redundancy has several advantages. First, it saves a lot of data storage space. In our example the data for each salesperson appears only once in the Salesperson table, rather than in the record of every customer serviced by that salesperson. Other less obvious advantages arise when data is updated. If a salesperson's telephone number changes, the traditional file approach would require that it be updated in the record for each customer serviced by that salesperson. Using the database method, only one update in the Salesperson table would be needed. In addition to taking longer, the file method introduces a greater chance of error, because multiple entries increase the possibility of a data entry mistake.

► DATABASE CONCEPTS

Many database-management programs are available in today's market. Covering all the operations, features, and functions of each package would be impossible. Instead, this chapter examines database management in a generic way. The features discussed are common to most database software packages.

Database Models

The way in which a database organizes data depends on the type, or **model,** of the database. There are four main database models: hierarchical, network, relational, and object-oriented. Each type structures, organizes, and uses data differently. Although the hierarchical and network models have some advantages in efficiency, limitations in the area of flexibility and complexity have led to the relational model being the model of choice for current database development. Also, relational databases are available for personal computers as well as mainframes. A **relational database** organizes data in a table format consisting of rows and columns. Figure 13-4 illustrates the relational database model. The object-oriented model is a more recent development and will be discussed in more detail in a later section.

Cust No	Cust Name	City	State	Sales ID
2934	Ballard Computer	Seattle	WA	389
3007	Computer City	Miami	FL	230
3107	Computer City	Orlando	FL	230
3752	Upland Computers	Phoenix	AZ	114
3812	PSC Systems	San Francisco	CA	389
4211	Computing Solutions	Tucson	AZ	114
4354	Digital Solutions	Chicago	IL	386
6118	CyberMart	Atlanta	GA	159
6715	Enterprise Computing	Jacksonville	FL	159

(a)

Sales ID	Last Name	First Name	Region	Phone
114	Abele	Lori	SW	(602) 624-9384
159	Rodriguez	Frank	SE	(404) 524-8472
230	Long	Teresa	SE	(305) 734-2987
386	Egbert	Edwin	MW	(605) 348-9217
389	Nguyen	Linh	NW	(206) 634-1955

(b)

◄ **F I G U R E 13-4**

The database approach.
Here the data has been split into the Customer table and the Salesperson table. The salesperson data appears only once for each salesperson, and Linh Nguyen has only one telephone number.

Data Integrity

The term **data integrity** refers to the degree to which data is accurate and reliable. **Integrity constraints** are rules that all data must follow. One type of constraint applies to the acceptable values for a field. For example, a month number greater than 12 would be invalid. Also, a company's highest hourly pay rate might be $20.00, so any value greater than that would be invalid. The database designer determines appropriate value constraints for each field. Another constraint involves primary key values: Each record's primary key must be unique. You can't have two customers with the same customer number. A third constraint applies to foreign keys. To be valid, a foreign key field value must either match the value of a primary key in the related table or be blank. In the tables shown in Figure 13-4, this means that the Sales ID field in a Customer record must contain one of the Sales ID values in the Salesperson table or be blank, indicating that no salesperson has yet been assigned to that customer. If integrity constraints are not enforced when data is entered, the data is unreliable.

► DATABASE MANAGEMENT

A **Database Management System (DBMS)** is a software package that enables you to create a database, enter data into the database, modify the data as required, and retrieve information from the database. DBMS features that provide this functionality are described in the following sections.

DBMSs are available at all levels. Sophisticated database systems, particularly those designed for a mainframe computer environment, cost tens of thousands of dollars, and their complexity requires that they be planned and managed by computer professionals. On the other hand, database software that costs a few hundred dollars and can be used by a novice for simple or moderately complex problems is available for personal computers. That is, in contrast to complex databases that must be set up by professionals, a user could set up and use a database on a personal computer.

Data Dictionary

Each database has a **data dictionary** (also called a catalog) that stores data about the tables and fields within the database. For each table, the data dictionary contains the table name and any relationships with other tables. For each field, the data dictionary records the field name, data type (numeric, text, date), field size, and validation rules. The validation rules allow the DBMS to enforce the integrity constraints. Any attempt to enter invalid data results in an error message to the user.

Data Maintenance

Data maintenance consists of three basic operations: adding new data, modifying existing data, and deleting data. DBMS software generally provides two methods to perform these operations. In the first, the user interacts directly with the DBMS to perform the maintenance tasks. This method is most common for PC-based databases. The second method allows programs written by professional programmers to access the data using special commands built into the DBMS and is most commonly used in complex systems in larger businesses.

Data Retrieval

Data retrieval involves extracting the desired data from the database. The two primary forms of data retrieval are queries and reports. With a **query,** you present a set of criteria that the DBMS uses to select data from the database. For instance, you might ask for the name and address of all customers from New Jersey who have an account balance over $200. The selected data may be viewed on the screen, printed, or stored in a file. A **query language** enables you to prepare your query using English-like statements. Each DBMS may have its own query language, but most relational DBMSs also support **Structured Query Language (SQL)**, a standardized language that was developed specifically to write database queries. Figure 13-5a shows an SQL query. SQL commands may be entered directly by the user or included in programs written in many different programming languages.

Query-by-example (QBE) is another method for developing queries. QBE uses a graphical interface to enable you to specify your criteria for selecting records. As with query languages, each DBMS has its own QBE format; however, unlike query languages, there is no standard QBE format. Figure 13-5b shows a QBE query using Microsoft Access, a popular PC-oriented DBMS. Figure 13-5c shows the results of running this query on the data shown in Figure 13-4.

A **report** provides a formatted presentation of data from the database. Although there is some overlap between queries and reports, queries generally select a relatively small portion of the database and present the data in a standard format. Reports show larger amounts of data and allow you to format the output however you like. Also, query results are generally displayed on your monitor; whereas reports are normally printed. In our query example in Figure 13-5, there may only be a few customers from New Jersey with a balance above $200. A report might list all the customer data (not just name and address) for all customers in the database, with totals for each state. Reports are designed using a **report generator** built into the DBMS. Figure 13-6 shows a report created with Microsoft Access.

Concurrency Control

Most large-system databases allow concurrent access by many users. If several users attempt to update the same record at the same time, the updates might not be processed correctly. Figure 13-7 shows what could happen. To prevent this, DBMSs employ a **record locking** scheme. When the first user accesses a record for update, the DBMS locks out any further attempt at updating that record until the first update

◄ **F I G U R E** 13-5

```
SELECT Customer.[Cust Name], Salesperson.Region, Customer.City,
Salesperson.[First Name], Salesperson.[LastName]
FROM Customer INNER JOIN Salesperson ON Customer.[SalesID] =
Salesperson.[Sales ID]
WHERE (((Salesperson.Region)="SE"));
```

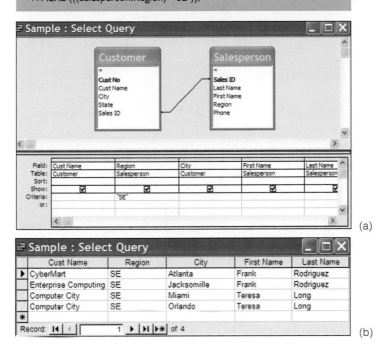

(a)

(b)

A database query. "Show me the customer name, region, city, and salesperson's first and last name for each customer in the Southeast region." This query requires extracting data from each of the two tables in Figure 13-4: customer name and city from the customer table and region and salesperson's first and last name from the Salesperson table. (a) shows the query as it is written in SQL. (b) shows the QBE screen from Microsoft Access, a popular PC-based DBMS. (c) shows the query results using the data from Figure 13-4.

is complete. Actually, in large database systems involving many related tables, concurrency control becomes much more complex but is handled correctly by the DBMS.

Security

Although data security has always been a concern, when that data is stored in a centralized database, rather than being spread among many separate application files, security becomes critical. Should anyone gain unauthorized access to the database, they have access to all the organization's data. On the other hand, having all the data in one location makes it easier to apply security measures. DBMS software provides a number of security features. Users may be required to enter a user ID and password to access the database. Specific privileges can be assigned to each user, defining that user's access to the data. **Read-only privilege** permits that user only to look at the data; no changes are allowed. **Update privilege** allows the user to make

Summary of Sales by Quarter
24-Jul-2000

Quarter: 1		
Year:	Orders Shipped:	Sales:
1997	92	$143,703
1998	178	$276,330

Quarter: 2		
Year:	Orders Shipped:	Sales:
1997	92	$145,655
1998	90	$191,362

◄ **F I G U R E** 13-6

A database report. This report generated from a database of sales data summarizes sales totals by year for each quarter (only two quarters are shown here).

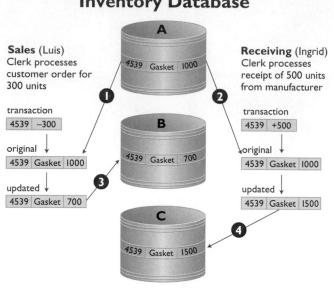

► **FIGURE 13-7**

Concurrent update problem. This illustrates what can go wrong when two users attempt to update a database record at the same time. Here Luis, the sales clerk, (1) reads the record for product 4539 to process a sale of 300 units. While the record is being processed, Ingrid, the receiving clerk, (2) reads the same record to process the receipt of 500 units from the manufacturer. Both see the original quantity of 1,000 units. Luis finishes processing first, (3) writing his updated record showing a new quantity of 700 units. Ingrid then finishes processing, (4) writing her updated record showing a new quantity of 1,500 units. The quantity should be 1,200 (the original 1,000 plus the received 500, less the 300 sold), but the record shows 1,500, because the result of Luis' transaction was overwritten by Ingrid's.

changes to the data; while a user with no privilege would not even be able to see the data. Many DBMSs apply these privileges at the field level; a user may be able to change some fields, just look at others, and not even see some fields.

Backup and Recovery

Occasionally, despite all precautions, the data in a database is damaged or destroyed. Hardware can fail, fire or floods can cause physical damage, and software or human errors can corrupt data. A DBMS provides backup and recovery features for recovering from these problems.

GETTING PRACTICAL — Databases on the Internet

Your college or university library provides many online databases for you to use in researching class assignments. These might include Academic Search Elite, which provides full-text articles on a wide range of academic subjects; the Literature Resource Center, which contains biographies, bibliographies, and critical analyses of current and past authors; and the Grove Dictionary of Art Online, covering all aspects of the visual arts. Some of these are available only from the library's computers, but most can be accessed from home with an ID and password provided by the library staff.

After your work is done, there are many other Internet databases available for your enjoyment. The Internet Movie Database provides information on just about any movie ever made in the

United States and many television shows and foreign films. You can even build your own personal movie database and receive an e-mail notice whenever one of your films is scheduled to be televised. If your interests run more to music, the Ultimate Band List might be just what you're looking for. Even if your favorite recording artists get very little airplay or press coverage, you'll be able to get information on their appearance schedule, new releases, and availability of prior releases.

For parents, the Database of Award-Winning Children's Literature allows you to tailor a reading list to your child's specific interests. You can choose on the basis of age, specific topics (for example, Christmas, or pirates), geographical setting, genre (history, biography, adventure, and so on), and other criteria.

A **backup,** or copy, of the database should be made periodically. Most DBMSs include backup routines; others rely on system utilities. If problems occur, **recovery** starts by replacing the damaged database with the good backup. Of course, all the maintenance activity that occurred between the making of the backup and its restoration has to be redone. Mainframe DBMSs generally include a feature that logs all maintenance transactions and then automatically reprocesses them when a backup is restored. PC-based DBMSs normally don't include this feature, leaving it to the users to reenter the lost transactions manually.

► AN EXAMPLE: CREATING AND USING A DATABASE

This section focuses on one database file and shows, generally, how data can be planned and entered. Lannes Murphy is a convention planner. She lives in Seattle and contracts with organizations that plan to hold conventions in that city. Lannes and her staff of five coordinate every physical aspect of the convention, including transportation, housing, catering, meeting rooms, services, tours, and entertainment.

Lannes began moving her files to a computer three years ago. She has found database software useful because of its ability to cross-reference several files and, in particular, to answer inquiries about the data. Lannes thinks the time is ripe to set up a database file for the tours she offers. She has noticed that clients ask many questions about the tours that are available in the area, including times, costs, and whether or not food is included. Also, clients want to know if much walking is included on the tour and whether there are stairs.

To answer these kinds of questions, Lannes or one of her staff has to shuffle through a thick folder of brochures and price lists. Lannes knows that she will be able to respond more quickly to client inquiries if this information is in her database file.

Creating the Database

After you have considered your needs, such as what reports you will need and inquiries you will want to make, there are two steps to creating a database table: (1) designing the structure of the table, and (2) entering the data into the table. Look ahead at Figure 13-10 to see what Lannes's final database will look like.

Determining the Table Structure

Lannes begins creating what will be called the TOUR database by sketching on paper the **table structure**—what kind of data she wants in each column (Figure 13-8). To

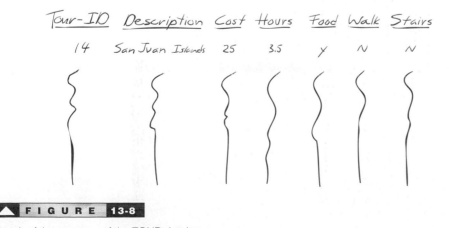

▲ FIGURE 13-8

Sketch of the structure of the TOUR database.

Cargo Containers

Massive ships crisscross the oceans, carrying goods from one port to another. Those goods are loaded into cargo containers that fit snugly together for maximum capacity.

Suppose that a ship carried 40 containers of goods from Hong Kong to Seattle. After the ship reaches its destination and the containers are unloaded at the dock, what happens to the containers? They belong, after all, to a Hong Kong firm. Should they be returned, empty, to their owners? Until recently, the answer to that question was an inefficient yes.

Now an Internet-based system is in place to let clients rent out their empty containers to a firm that needs to use them to ship goods in the direction opposite the one from which they came. A representative from Greybox Logistics Services, Inc. can use a database to search for an appropriate match. Greybox charges a fee for each box that changes hands, and the shipping companies save between $250 and $400 per container by having another company move it for them. This effective utilization plan is a winning strategy for all involved.

create the table structure, she must choose meaningful fields. The fields she chooses should be based on the information that she will want to retrieve from the database. Let us take a look at each type.

● **Field name.** Each field must be assigned a unique field name. Lannes plans to use these field names for her TOUR database: Tour-ID (identifying number for the tour, the primary key field), Description (description of the tour), Cost (cost of the tour), Hours (number of hours the tour takes), Food (yes or no on whether food is included in the tour), Walk (yes or no regarding whether there is much walking on the tour), and Stairs (yes or no on whether there are stairs on the tour).

● **Field type.** Although different software packages offer different field types, there are four commonly used types of fields: character fields, numeric fields, date fields, and logical fields. **Character fields** contain descriptive data, such as names, addresses, and telephone numbers. **Numeric fields** contain numbers used for calculations, such as rate of pay. When you enter a numeric field, you must specify the number of decimal places you want to use. Lannes will use two decimal places for Cost and one decimal place for Hours. **Date fields** are usually limited to eight characters, including the slashes used to separate the month, day, and year. **Logical fields** are used to keep track of true/false, yes/no conditions. For example, Lannes can keep track of which tours include food by making Food a logical field; when entering data for that field, she indicates Yes or No. Note that in Microsoft Access 2002, the software used here, this is indicated by checking (Yes) or not checking (No) a box.

● **Field widths.** The field width determines the maximum number of characters or digits to be contained in the field, including decimal points.

Setting Up the File Structure

We have used Microsoft Access to demonstrate how database software can accept a database table structure (Figure 13-9). Access presents the **Design view** to accept the file structure. Lannes will type one line for each field in her table. At a glance, the line consists of the field name (Tour-ID for the first field), Data Type (Text), and an

► **FIGURE 13-9**

Table structure. In the Microsoft Access Design view, one line is entered for each field. These field entries establish the structure of the Tour table. The upper portion shows the field list. The cursor has been placed in the Data Type column of the Food field, the drop-down arrow has been clicked to get a list of data types, and the Yes/No type has been selected. The lower portion shows various properties of the current (Food) field.

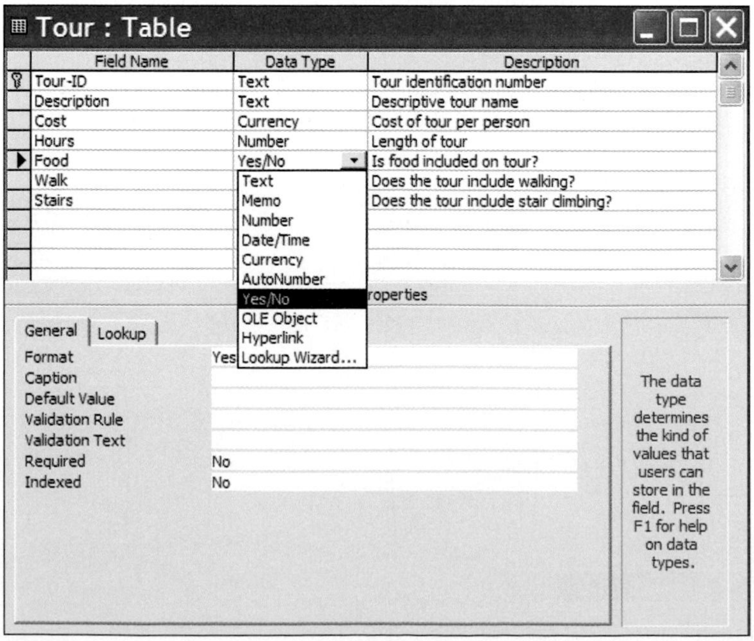

optional Description. Lannes designates the Tour-ID field as the primary key by clicking the key icon on the toolbar while entering that field. Access responds by showing a key symbol in the gray box to the left of the field name.

In the example shown in Figure 13-9, working on the line for the field Food (as indicated by the arrowhead on the left), she has selected the Yes/No choice for the Data Type, indicating that Food is a logical field requiring Yes/No data. Lannes proceeds to enter one line for each field in her table on the design view screen.

Entering the Data

When it is time to enter the data into the table, Access presents the table in **Datasheet view.** The fields that Lannes defined in the table structure—the Design view—are presented as headings across the datasheet (Figure 13-10). Lannes keys the appropriate data under each name—13 for Tour-ID, San Juan Islands for Description, and so on.

After Lannes has filled in all the data for the first record, the database program automatically displays another blank input line so that she can enter the data items for the fields in the second record. She will continue this pattern for each record. Eventually, she will signal the database software that she has entered all the records.

Using the Database

After she has entered the data, Lannes can perform operations to view and modify it. The following describe some of those operations:

- **List the records.** Lannes could ask for a list of all existing records, either displayed on the screen or printed out on paper. If she is displaying the records onscreen, the software displays only the number of records that fit on the screen. Scrolling up or down displays additional records. If there are a large number of fields in a record, Lannes could pan—scroll horizontally across the screen—to the left or right. Panning is a horizontal version of scrolling.

- **List specific fields.** In addition to listing all records, Lannes has the option of listing just certain fields of each record. Perhaps, to satisfy a customer request,

◄ **F I G U R E** **13-10**

The TOUR data. This is the Microsoft Access Datasheet view, in which all the data has been entered in each field. Notice that the Yes/No fields contain boxes that are either checked, indicating a Yes value, or unchecked, indicating a No value.

Tour-ID	Description	Cost	Hours	Food	Walk	Stairs
▶ 14	San Juan Islands	$25.00	3.5	☑	☐	☐
16	Local ferry ride	$2.50	1	☐	☐	☐
23	Boeing plant	$0.00	2.4	☐	☑	☑
26	Museum tour	$15.50	0	☐	☑	☐
34	Cityscape bus tour	$24.00	2.5	☑	☐	☐
35	Chinatown at night	$30.00	3	☑	☑	☐
36	Namedroppers tour	$25.00	3	☐	☑	☐
47	Northwest Trek	$12.50	4	☑	☐	☑
58	Mount Ranier	$22.00	5	☑	☑	☐
79	Seattle Locks	$0.00	2	☐	☑	☐
81	Underground tour	$5.50	1.5	☐	☑	☐
84	Puget Sound boat	$42.00	4.5	☑	☐	☐
∗		$0.00	0			

Record: ◄◄ ◄ 1 ▶ ▶◄ ▶∗ of 12

Tour identification number   NUM

Listing Records. This list shows only the Description and Cost fields from the Tour table.

Description	Cost
San Juan Islands	$25.00
Local ferry ride	$2.50
Boeing plant	$0.00
Museum tour	$15.50
Cityscape bus tour	$24.00
Chinatown at night	$30.00
Namedroppers tour	$25.00
Northwest Trek	$12.50
Mount Ranier	$22.00
Seattle Locks	$0.00
Underground tour	$5.50
Puget Sound boat	$42.00
	$0.00

she could list only the Description and Cost fields for each record (Figure 13-11). The software also offers the option of listing the fields in any order requested, not just the order in which they appear in the record. For example, Lannes could request a list of these fields in this order: Description, Tour-ID, Walk, and Hours.

● **Query.** Lannes can make a query—ask a question—about the records in the file. She will need to use a **relational operator** when entering instructions that involve making comparisons. Table 13-1 shows the relational operators that are commonly used. These operators are particularly useful when you want to locate specific data items. Suppose, for example, that on the basis of a client request, Lannes wants to find all the tours that cost less than $15. She could issue a query to the database software to find records that meet this requirement by using a command that includes the stipulation Cost < 15 (Figure 13-12a). The software would respond with a list of all records that meet the requirement, in this case a local ferry ride, the Boeing plant, Northwest Trek, the Seattle Locks, and the underground tour (Figure 13-12b).

● **Add new records.** Lannes can add records for new tours at any time.

● **Modify existing records.** Lannes may need to change an existing record. For example, in the TOUR file, it would not be uncommon for the price of a tour to change.

● **Delete records.** Sometimes a record must be removed, or deleted, from a database file. Perhaps a tour no longer exists or Lannes, for whatever reason, no longer

TABLE 14.1	Relational Operators
Command	**Explanation**
<	Less than
>	Greater than
=	Equal to
<=	Less than or equal to
>=	Greater than or equal to
< >	Not equal to

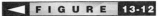

Query. (a) The query design to display records with a cost less than $15. (b) The query results.

(a)

Tour-ID	Description	Cost	Hours	Food	Walk	Stairs
► 16	Local ferry ride	$2.50	1	☐	☐	☐
23	Boeing plant	$0.00	2.4	☐	☑	☑
47	Northwest Trek	$12.50	4	☑	☐	☑
79	Seattle Locks	$0.00	2	☐	☑	☐
81	Underground tour	$5.50	1.5	☐	☑	☐
*		$0.00	0	▣	▣	▣

Record: ◄ ◄ 1 ► ►I ►* of 5

(b)

wants to promote the tour; she would then want to delete that tour from the TOUR file. Database-management software provides this option.

► OBJECT-ORIENTED DATABASE-MANAGEMENT SYSTEMS

The three traditional database models—hierarchical, network, and relational—were developed to store text and numeric data. Today, applications require many types of data: graphics, video, audio, and other complex data types. For instance, medical systems store X-rays, MRI scans, ultrasound images, and electrocardiograms. Geographical Information Systems (GIS) work with maps, and an educational instruction system manipulates audio and video segments as well as text and images. The **object-oriented database model** was developed to manipulate these complex

---

FOCUS ON ETHICS   **Who Gets to Know All About You?**

Ethical use of databases is a recurring matter requiring careful examination. Consider a medical database containing the following information for each individual: blood type, allergies, medical history, date of birth, marital status, next of kin, home address, employer, financial responsibility figures, DNA data, and a set of fingerprint images. Many people would agree that it is ethical and appropriate for emergency room personnel to have access to such information. The premise, of course, is that the information is used for medical purposes.

- Would it be ethical to let insurance companies have access to that database?

- Should an attorney be able to subpoena the database information in relation to a civil suit?

- One of the ethical themes in current discussions of database ethics is "opt-in" versus "opt-out." With opt-in, you must give your consent before information is shared, but with opt-out, you must explicitly withdraw your consent; otherwise, information you give can be freely shared. What are the costs and benefits of each? Which option do you find more defensible ethically?

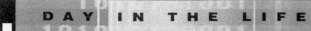

Gillian DeVries,
Database Administrator

The database administrator has a huge responsibility. First, and foremost, the database has to be kept running as long as possible, with an absolute minimum of downtime. For that reason, Gillian carries a pager everywhere. That would not be so unusual, except that the only "person" who has the pager number is the database server! Programmed to send the pager a message at the slightest error, the database server often has Gillian at the office at all hours of the day.

However, keeping the database server happy is the least of her worries. Gillian is also responsible for regular database backups, and for carefully scheduling

any server downtime for periods when it will affect the least number of users.

Gillian is also the programmer for the database. She is the person to whom the other employees in the company turn when they need her to program new functions or features into the database. This can be anything from specialized reports and queries, to e-mail templates that make use of database components.

Last, but not least, Gillian takes care of database security, ensuring that employees have access to only the parts of the database they need access to, and that they change their passwords on a regular basis (at least once a month).

data types. In this model, the object is the focus. An object represents a real-world entity, such as a patient, and includes data about the entity and operations (for example change address) that work with the data. The data can be any of the simple or complex types mentioned previously. Object-oriented concepts are discussed in more detail in the object-oriented programming section of the next chapter.

Object-oriented database management systems (OODBMS) have been developed to create and manipulate object-oriented databases. They are designed to incorporate object-oriented concepts along with the DBMS features discussed in the previous section. OODBMSs are most useful in systems with very large amounts of complex data. In most other situations, relational DBMSs (RDBMS) remain the standard for several reasons. First, OODBMSs are complex and have a steep learning curve. Only a limited number of people are qualified to work with OODBMSs, and these people command high salaries. Also, the larger RDBMSs, such as Oracle's Oracle9i and IBM's DB2, have incorporated some of the features of OODBMSs, particularly the ability to represent complex data types, such as audio and video. These enhanced RDBMSs are sometimes referred to as **object/relational database management systems (O/RDBMS)**.

► DATA WAREHOUSES

Databases are designed to provide support for the ongoing operations of an enterprise. They store data reflecting the current status of business operations and are kept up to date by **online transaction processing (OLTP)** software that processes the day-to-day transactions, such as sales and customer payments. But databases are not very well organized for data analysis involving past, present, and future directions for a business.

The data warehouse has been designed to fill this need. A **data warehouse** contains data that has been captured from the database in summary form, on a scheduled basis, over a period of time. Thus, while a database would contain data on all a business's currently unfilled customer orders, a data warehouse would store weekly (or even daily) sales totals for each customer for as long as the business has been keeping records. A data warehouse can also contain data gathered from external sources, such as local, regional, and national economic statistics. **Online analyt-**

ical processing (OLAP) software analyzes this data to produce information required by managers.

A more advanced method of analyzing the historical data in a data warehouse involves a concept called data mining. **Data mining** is the use of sophisticated statistical and artificial intelligence techniques to discover previously unrecognized patterns, relationships, correlations, and trends among the data in the data warehouse. Managers can then use this information to make strategic business decisions. John Deere, an agricultural tractor manufacturer, uses data mining to help it forecast tractor sales. So many factors influence tractor sales that traditional data analysis tools were producing poor results. The data mining approach not only uses John Deere's past sales data in the forecast, but also includes factors such as current and future farm-economic trends, crop prices and production levels, commodity futures, used equipment inventory levels, competitor incentives, and consumer confidence levels to produce much more accurate forecasts.

▲

In this chapter you looked at how data is organized and managed to meet user requirements. In the next chapter you step back and take a wider view of the process of analyzing user needs and developing entire systems to meet these needs.

Database of the Future

Before long, it is going to seem old-fashioned to call it "data." Traditional data is making room for audio, video, text, and images. The idea is simple in theory: Anything that can be conceived can be defined and captured. Once captured, it then can be converted to the basic 0s and 1s required for computer processing.

Working with a database will change too. The vehicle of choice will likely be an Internet site connected to a database in a way that is transparent—not obvious—to the user. For example, the screen could show a shiny car, say a red Corvette. By clicking the car, a General Motors marketer could bring up a profile of Corvette buyers.

Future thinkers wonder whether the term "database" is too mundane to convey the source of all this information. Perhaps. But the concepts of data storage and retrieval are still the same. Only the kinds of data and the elaborate retrieval methods will change.

CHAPTER REVIEW

▶ **Summary and Key Terms**

- The **field** is the smallest meaningful unit of data and consists of a group of one or more characters. The group of fields containing data about a single entity makes up a **record,** and the collection of related records is a **file.**

- The traditional file processing approach to information systems results in a great deal of **data redundancy**—duplication of data. Records in a file are identified by their **primary key field** (or just **primary key**), which contains a unique value for each record.

- A **database** is a collection of related files (**tables** in database terminology) in which each table contains data concerning only a single entity. Tables are linked, or **related,** when a field, called a **foreign key,** in one table contains the value of a primary key in another table.

- The four main database **models** (methods of organizing data within a database) are hierarchical, network, relational, and object-oriented. Most databases today use the **relational database** model, which organizes data in a table format using rows and columns.

- **Data integrity** refers to the degree in which data is accurate and reliable. **Integrity constraints** are rules that data must follow to maintain integrity.

- A **Database Management System (DBMS)** is a software package that enables the user to create a database, enter data into the database, modify the data as required, and retrieve information from the database.

- A database contains a **data dictionary** that stores data about the tables and fields within the database.

- **Data maintenance** consists of three basic operations: adding new data, modifying existing data, and deleting data; it is performed either directly through DBMS routines or by programs containing special commands.

- Data retrieval involves extracting the desired data from the database. **Queries** retrieve data from a database by presenting criteria that the DBMS uses to select the desired data. Queries are written using a **query language. Structured Query Language (SQL)** is a standard query language supported by most DBMSs.

- Queries can also be prepared by using a graphical interface to set criteria. This method is called **query-by-example (QBE)**.

- A **report** provides a formatted presentation of data from the database. Whereas query results are normally displayed on the screen, reports are generally printed. Reports are designed using a **report generator** built into the DBMS.

- The DBMS employs a **record locking** scheme to prevent problems that can occur when two users attempt to update the same record concurrently.

- One way to provide database security is for the DBMS to assign specific privileges to each user. **Read-only privilege** permits record viewing only, **update privilege** enables the user to make changes, and a user with no privilege is prevented from even seeing the data.

- Backup and recovery features of a DBMS assist the user in creating a **backup,** or duplicate copy, of the database at periodic intervals, and allow for **recovery** by restoring the database from the backup copy. Some DBMSs assist recovery by automatically reprocessing transactions processed after the backup was made.

- Creating a database starts with specifying the **table structure**—a list of fields including the field name, type of data stored in the field, and the size, or width, of the field. Data types supported by most DBMSs include **character fields,** which contain descriptions; **numeric fields,** which contain numbers for calculations; **date fields,** which contain dates; and **logical fields,** which keep track of true/false, yes/no conditions. In Microsoft Access, table structure is specified in the table's **Design view.**

- Data is entered into the table in **Datasheet view,** which lists all the records stored in the table.

- **Relational operators** are symbols that are used to make comparisons when formulating queries.

- The **object-oriented database model** was developed to manipulate complex data types, such as audio and video. It focuses on the object, which represents a real-world entity and contains both data and operations on the data. **Object-oriented database management systems (OODBMS)** create and manipulate object-oriented databases. **Object/relational database management systems (O/RDBMS)** are relational DBMSs enhanced with object-oriented capabilities.

- **Online transaction processing (OLTP)** software processes the day-to-day transactions of an organization by updating data stored in databases. Because databases are not organized to provide the data that management needs to make decisions, data warehouses were developed. A **data warehouse** contains data that has been captured from the database in summary form, on a scheduled basis, over a period of time. Data in a data warehouse is analyzed by **online analytical processing (OLAP)** software to provide information to management.

- **Data mining** uses sophisticated statistical and artificial intelligence techniques to discover previously unrecognized patterns, relationships, correlations, and trends among the data in the data warehouse.

▶ Critical Thinking Questions

1. Consider these workers as possible users of a database: a crime lab technician handling evidence, a tulip bulb grower who produces 47 varieties for more than 200 customers, a runners' club that tracks meets and member data. What data might such users want to look up? What data would they need to store? What fields might be key fields?

2. An environmental organization concerned about preserving undeveloped land keeps a database of its donors with these fields: last name, first name, street address, city, state, zip code, phone number, amount of last donation, date of last donation, amount of highest donation, date of highest donation, amount of average donation, code for special interests (M for moun-

   tains, R for rivers, and so forth). The organization regularly sends out form letters soliciting donations. The form letters are keyed to a particular donor population, for example, those who have not sent a donation in six months or those who might want to give to a special shorebirds preserve. Among the fields listed, which might be key fields?

3. For the data mentioned in Question 2, list some relational operators and appropriate fields that might be used for making a query to the database. Examples: Use the "equal to" operator to find donors in a certain zip code: ZIP = 22314; use "greater than" to find donors whose average donation is over $100: AVGDON > 100.

► DATABASE QUESTIONS AND EXERCISES

1. Effective use of a database depends partly on how much effort was devoted to its planning and design. Two considerations are as follows:

   • What fields of information are needed

   • What potential questions (queries) will be used to extract information from the database

   Too often people rush to create a database and begin to enter data without proper forethought. We will not make this mistake. Although we will only design a database, your instructor may have you implement it using appropriate database software.

   Suppose that you want to create a database of the movies that you own. Although the majority of your collection is on videotape, you have recently purchased a DVD player and are beginning to purchase movies on DVD. List at least six fields (for example the title of the movie) that you feel are appropriate for this database. Look at a newspaper or magazine movie review or at a book that describes movies to get some ideas for appropriate fields.

Field Name	Field Type	Field Width	Validation Rules
Title	text	30	

   Now list six types of queries that you would use to extract information from this database. Because the way in which queries are stated depends on the database application, state your queries in simple English (for example, how many movies are rated PG).

   Sometimes, you will discover that a query requires information (fields) that was not in the initial database design. For example, what is the total cost of your movie collection? Based on the fields that you chose, could this question be determined from the database? To answer this query, what field is required?

2. Design a database of your own following the format of question 1. Using your word processing skills, write a narrative that:

- Describes the purpose of your database. Why you would keep such a database, and what types of information you would extract from it?

- Identifies at least five fields that are needed, what their type, size, and possible validation rules should be, and why you chose these specific fields. Do not use text for all fields; include at least one date, numerical, or logical field. Create a table similar to the one shown here in your narrative (adding or deleting rows as needed), and enter your responses directly into the table:

Field Name	Field Type	Field Width	Validation Rules

- Contains five sample records that could appear in your database. List the records in table form like Figure 13-10.

- Lists, in simple English, five queries or processes (such as sorting of a field) that you would use to extract information from your database. Explain why these would be meaningful queries or processes for your database. (Note: your instructor may require you to implement your database using appropriate database software.)

3. Even a simple PC-based database such as Microsoft Access can be used as an object-oriented database by using the OLE Object data type.

   Reexamine question 1. In addition to traditional data types, such as text, numeric, date, logical, and so on, what type of object-oriented field could you use for the movie database?

   Likewise, reexamine the data fields that you selected in question 2. Are there any object-oriented fields that could be used in your self-designed database? If so, what would they be?

   If you cannot think of an object-oriented field for questions 1 or 2, briefly describe a database that could use an object-oriented field.

4. Access also allows Hyperlink fields.

   Reexamine question 1. What type of hyperlink fields could you use for the movie database?

   Likewise, reexamine the data fields that you selected in question 2. Are there any hyperlink fields that could be used in your self-designed database? If so, what would they be?

   If you cannot think of a hyperlink field for questions 1 or 2, briefly describe a database that could use a hyperlink field.

5. When referring to large-scale database-management systems, the terms data warehouse and data mining are sometimes used. Describe the differences between these two terms.

6. Contact your institution's computing services and find the name(s) of the database application(s) that they are using for administrative and academic activities. Ask which model they follow—hierarchical, network, relational, or object-oriented. (Note: these models are not mutually exclusive. For example, Microsoft Access is both a relational and an object-oriented database.)

7. Can faculty, staff, and students access your school's databases? Should certain user classifications be given limited access or even denied access? Should students be given access to their own records? If you answered yes, what type of access should students be granted and why? Is access to institutional databases limited to LANs, or can these databases be accessed from the Internet? Why would an institution choose not to make databases accessible from the Internet?

8. How does your institution's library provide access to its database of reference materials? Can patrons access the materials from both on-campus and off-campus? Can you use browser-based software to access information? In addition to standard "card catalog" information—author, title, publication date, and so on—can patrons access full-text versions of materials? Can anyone access these full-text materials or is access limited to faculty, staff, and students? If access to some materials is limited, how do faculty, staff, and students identify themselves as legitimate users?

9. Explain the differences between a primary key and a foreign key, and describe how each would be used in a relational database. Does every database require a primary key? Why or why not? Does every database require a foreign key? Why or why not? Can a primary key contain duplicate values? Why or why not? Can a foreign key contain duplicate values? Why or why not?

10. When using Microsoft Access, what are the differences between viewing a database in Design view and Datasheet view? Explain where and when you would use each of these views in the design, entry, and maintenance of a database. In which of these views are you able to enter or change validation rules?

11. Have you used the QBE feature in Microsoft Access? If you have used this database, comment on the ease or difficulty of forming queries or performing processes, such as sorting and counting. If you have not used Access, comment on the ease or difficulty of forming queries or processes with the database application that you have used.

12. Although databases originally stored date fields using eight characters— 09/09/68 (mm/dd/yy), why is this technique no longer satisfactory for storing dates? What new format should be used? What name was given to this problem?

13. Explain what is meant by the concurrent update problem. How is this potential problem resolved?

► STUDENT STUDY GUIDE

Multiple Choice

1. A _____ is the smallest meaningful unit of data.
   a. field
   b. record
   c. file
   d. database

2. A(n) _____ database organizes data in rows and columns.
   a. hierarchical
   b. network
   c. relational
   d. object-oriented

3. Which of the following is not a basic data maintenance operation?
   a. adding new data
   b. creating a report from existing data
   c. deleting existing data
   d. changing existing data

4. Which of the following privileges would allow a user to make changes to database data?
   a. update privilege
   b. read-only privilege
   c. write-only privilege
   d. no privileges

5. Which of the following is not true of object-oriented databases?
   a. They are the most common type of database in use today.
   b. They support complex data types such as audio and video.
   c. They work well with very large amounts of data.
   d. Some of their features have been incorporated into relational databases.

6. Which of the following would be most suitable for providing the information that top management would need to decide whether to build a new plant?
   a. data file
   b. database
   c. data table
   d. data warehouse

7. Which of the following is an acceptable-value integrity constraint?
   a. Each primary key value must be unique.
   b. The weekly hours worked cannot be greater than 60.
   c. The foreign key value must match a primary key value or be blank.
   d. Two users cannot update a record at the same time.

8. A data dictionary contains _____.
   a. table name and relationships with other tables
   b. field data types
   c. data validation rules
   d. All of the above are contained in a data dictionary.

9. Which of the following statements about primary and foreign key values is true?
   a. Only primary key values must be unique.
   b. Only foreign key values must be unique.
   c. Both primary and foreign key values must be unique.
   d. Neither primary nor foreign key values must be unique.

10. DBMSs can use _____ to implement concurrency control.
    a. integrity constraints
    b. relational operators
    c. SQL
    d. record locking

11. A well-designed database with all the students in your class would place the last name of each student in a
    a. table
    b. record
    c. field
    d. cell

12. A well-designed database with all the students in your class would place the information on an individual student in a
    a. table
    b. record
    c. field
    d. cell

13. A well-designed database with all the students in your class would place all of the basic data for all of the students into a
    a. table
    b. record
    c. field
    d. cell

14. Which of the following is a database model?
    a. relational
    b. hypothetical
    c. linkable
    d. none of the above

15. What does data maintenance consist of?
    a. adding new data
    b. modifying existing data
    c. deleting data
    d. all of the above

16. QBE stands for
    a. Query By Example
    b. Questionable Basic Entries
    c. Question By Entry
    d. none of the above

17. SQL stands for
    a. Search Quantity Lists
    b. Seek Questions Logically
    c. Structured Query Language
    d. none of the above

18. Microsoft's database application is called
    a. Excel
    b. Success
    c. Access
    d. Progress

19. Which of the following is not a relational operator
    a. =
    b. <
    c. >
    d. ?

20. Which of the following is used in the Access design view to specify logical field types?
    a. yes/no
    b. true/false
    c. neither a nor b
    d. both a and b

True/False

T F 1. A record is made up of files.

T F 2. The primary key field value must be unique for each record in a table.

T F 3. One advantage of eliminating data redundancy is a reduction in the space required to store a table.

T F 4. Data integrity refers to the accuracy and reliability of data.

T F 5. Databases are too complex for the average user and should be designed only by professionals.

T F 6. One disadvantage of databases is that they can be used by only a single user.

T F 7. A report provides a formatted presentation of data from the database and is normally printed.

T F 8. Almost all DBMSs provide automatic reprocessing of transactions when a backup copy of a database is restored.

T F 9. The two steps to creating a table are designing its structure and entering the data.

T F 10. The power of a relational database comes from connections among tables.

T F 11. Database records may be entered and modified but not deleted.

T F 12. The database model that is most commonly used on personal computers is the object-oriented model.

T F 13. OLTP software is used to keep databases up to date.

T F 14. Data warehouses contain external as well as internal data.

T F 15. OLAP software uses sophisticated statistical and artificial intelligence techniques to discover trends and patterns in data stored in a data warehouse.

T F 16. The data thesaurus stores data about the tables and fields of a database.

T F 17. Oracle9i is an example of an O/RDBMS.

T F 18. File locking prevents unauthorized users from changing data.

T F 19. In addition to formatted reports, most databases can be used to produce graphical output, such as bar graphs, line graphs, pie charts, and scatter diagrams.

T F 20. Many databases apply the read-only privilege and the update privilege at the field level.

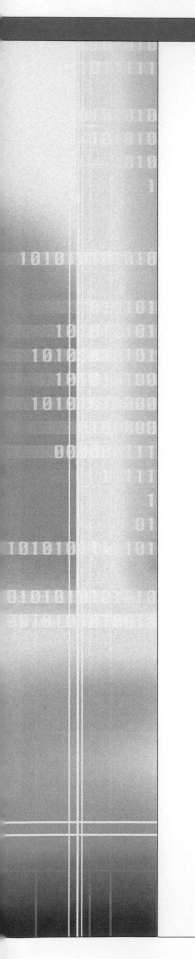

Fill-In

1. Data _____ results when data is repeated throughout a file.

2. The _____ key field uniquely identifies a record.

3. A(n) _____ key field links to a primary key in a related table.

4. A(n) _____ stores data about the tables and fields within a database.

5. Integrity _____ are rules that data must follow to be accurate and reliable.

6. A(n) _____ is a software package that is used to create and manage a database.

7. _____ is a technique used by DBMSs to prevent two users from updating the same record at the same time.

8. _____ is a standard query language that is supported by most DBMSs.

9. Fields of the _____ data type keep track of Yes/No conditions.

10. Symbols such as =, >, and < are called _____.

11. Network, hierarchical, and relational are three types of database _____.

12. In a relational database a file is referred to as a(n) _____.

13. In a relational database, a row represents a(n) _____.

14. The acronym _____ refers to an RDBMS that includes features of an OODBMS.

15. _____ software analyzes the data in a data warehouse to provide management with information.

16. Most databases today use the _____ database model.

17. A(n) _____ is a collection of related files (or tables).

18. A collection of related records makes up a(n) _____.

19. In Access, the _____ view is used to define a table's structure.

20. The _____ model was developed to manipulate audio and video data as well as text and images.

► ANSWERS

Multiple Choice

1. a	6. d	11. c	16. a
2. c	7. b	12. b	17. c
3. b	8. d	13. a	18. c
4. a	9. a	14. a	19. d
5. a	10. d	15. d	20. a

True/False

1. F	6. F	11. F	16. F
2. T	7. T	12. F	17. T
3. T	8. F	13. T	18. F
4. T	9. T	14. T	19. F
5. F	10. T	15. F	20. T

Fill-In

1. redundancy
2. primary
3. foreign
4. data dictionary
5. constraints
6. DBMS
7. record locking
8. structured query language (SQL)
9. logical
10. relational operators
11. models
12. table
13. record
14. O/RDBMS
15. OLAP (online analytical processing)
16. relational
17. database
18. file or table
19. design
20. object-oriented database

Planet Internet

E-commerce and the Borderless World

It may be a World Wide Web, but e-commerce neophytes will want to consider the opportunities and the potential problems before doing e-business across national borders.

Starting and operating a successful e-business is tricky enough, but things get even more complicated when you're interested in doing business internationally. Let's say you have an e-business, you've built a great Web site, and now it's time to make money all over the world! It's so easy to share information globally; surely you can make money globally, right?

Although many people would agree that you should aspire to an international market, there's a lot more involved than setting up a nice Web site, even one that addresses multiple languages and can handle different types of currency. According to industry research, 85 percent of e-commerce companies weren't selling to customers seeking delivery abroad at the beginning of the millennium. Those who do ship internationally were often ignoring compliance with the regulations of other countries and assuming that the customer would deal with such details as customs regulations.

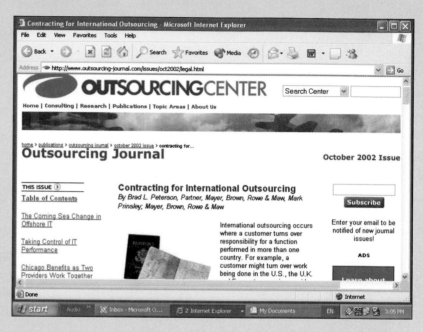

What is involved with handling this part of international business? For starters you need to calculate the total price your customer must pay. This is known as the "landed" cost, and it can vary greatly from country to country. It includes the cost of the products, shipping, taxes, duties, and insurance as well as import and export fees. Countries differ in content limitations as well; for example, Germany doesn't accept materials that it considers "pro-Nazi," and Singapore prohibits importing play money.

Then you have to deal with compliance laws. Did you know that U.S. export laws have restrictions addressing embargoed countries, sanctioned countries, denied persons, and debarred parties? Then it's time to do the proper paperwork and pay the necessary fees, taxes, and other charges to the countries. Finally, the customer receives the product.

Help is available. Even many large companies don't have the resources to deal with the customs regulations of dozens of countries and this service is available from companies, such as myCustoms and World Tariff.

Fledgling e-commerce sites shouldn't be completely turned off by the rigors of international business. If there is significant demand for your product across national borders, as a businessperson you should carefully investigate both the costs and the benefits of World Wide Web commerce.

Internet Exercises

1. **Structured exercise.** Begin with the URL http://www.prenhall.com/capron and go to the World Tariff site. What services does it offer?

2. **Free-form exercise.** Pick an e-business with which you are familiar that does not do international e-commerce as yet. What features does the company need to add to its Web site to support international e-commerce, according to the information provided in the previous exercise? What would you recommend the company do to prepare to successfully do business internationally?

3. **Advanced exercise.** Do a search to find a company that has been fined or reprimanded for improper international e-business dealings. What problem(s) did the company have? Could better use of technology or better use of business practices prevent the problem? What should another e-business learn from the mistakes of this other company?

Planet Internet

Computer
Graphics

Pictures Do Lie

The works on this page show how photographs can be manipulated by the computer. Begin with **1.** a photo of a building interior. then consider **2.**, photos of strolling tourists, a statue, and a painting. These four photos have been scanned into the computer and manipulated to become **3.**, a museum with artworks and tourists to view them. Note in particular the adjusted shape of the painting and the computer artist's addition of clouds in the skylight. **4.** Here is the intriguing result of computer imaging of four photos. The original photos were of trees, a sunset, a swan, and a red world logo. **5.** Here the artist has produced various computer-manipulated versions of an original photo of a child.

1.

2.

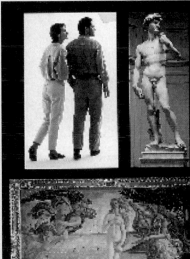

3.

5.

4.

Computer Graphics as Art

The computer artwork on the title page of this gallery, by Dave Martland, won best of the month in the abstract category in the annual contest sponsored by CorelDraw software.

6. Bill Frymire produced this work, which is something of a classic in graphic circles. The artist scanned his own thumb print to be used as the background. But all eyes are on Rex, his pet iguana.

7. This cathedral ceiling artwork , which Italian artist Antonio de Leo calls Duomo, won best of show in the CorelDraw contest.

8. Karin Kuhlman won best of the month in the landscape category in the CorelDraw contest.

9. Joseph Maas calls this work Chess Mystery.

10. This image, by Huan Le Tran, won best of the month in the abstract category in the CorelDraw contest.

6.

7.

8.

9.

10.

Computer Artists and Their Tools

We mentioned CorelDraw on the two prior pages; it is one of many software tools that graphic artists may use. Other popular software graphics packages are Studio Max, Ray Dream, Lightwave, POV Ray, and Bryce. Artists may use tools from different software on the same artwork. The artists whose work is shown on these two pages all use three-dimensional versions of the software. **11.** Marcus Benko calls this work Intruder; **12.** this is called simply Head Test, according to Jeremy Birn; **13.** David Brickley names his work Eagle. **14.** Kyle Nau, with this work called Country Store, won the grand prize in a contest sponsored by Marlin Studios, which encouraged entrants to use as many of the Marlin textures as possible. Marlin offers a CD-ROM with photorealistic real-world textures such as peeling paint, rust, corrosion, aged wooden planks, rusted metals, metal grates, concrete, windows, and doors.

More images from the artists' imagination: **15.** Fountain Pens by Kris Lazoore; **16.** Bug and Dolphin by Alberto Giorgi; and **17.** Pocketwatch by Kevin Odhner.

11.

12.

13.

14.

15.

16.

17.

Ray Tracing

An important aspect of realistic perspective is the use of light and shadow. Rather than adding these elements individually, graphic artists can use software to enhance their works. The "ray" in ray tracing refers to light rays, whose direction can be "traced" by the software. For example, a user can specify the location–point of view–of a light element, such as light from the sun or a nearby window or a lamp, and the software will add appropriate shadows. The light source need not actually be included in the image; it could be "off screen" but still cause shadows.

The works shown here were all entries in the Internet Ray Tracing Competition, which has a new contest every few months on a different theme. Examine them carefully to see how the artists made use of light and shadow.

18. Steve Gowers won first prize in the Summer theme contest with this rendition of a bucket of seashells.

19. Nathan O'Brien took second place in the contest with the theme Elements.

20. Gautam Lad submitted this entry, called Grade One, to the contest with the theme School.

21. Ian Armstrong won the honorable mention in the Flight category.

22. In the competition with a Time theme, Adrian Baumann won second place with this Admiral watch.

23. Nathan O'Brien won second place with this image, called Ode to Prianesi, in the imaginary Worlds contest.

18.

19.

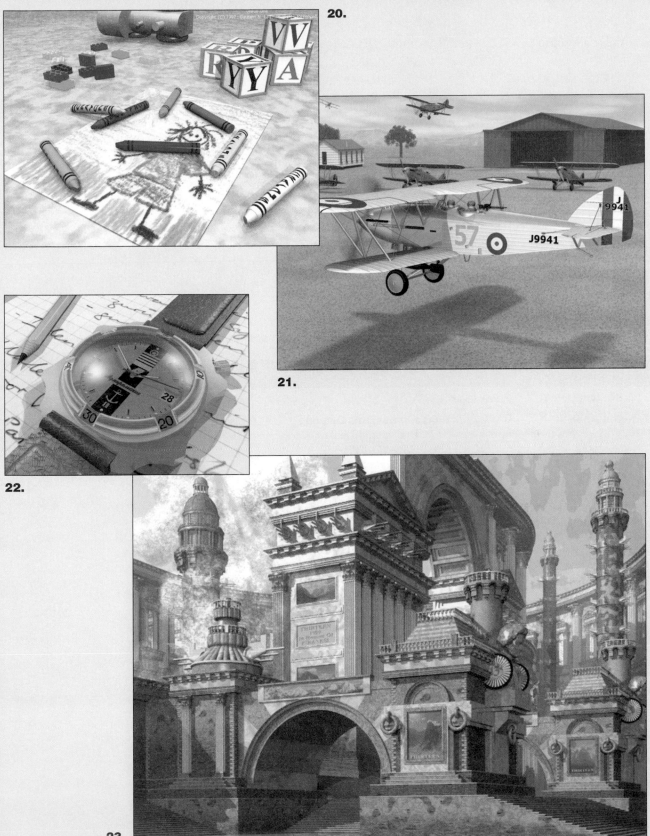

20.

21.

22.

23.

Systems Analysis and Design:
The Big Picture

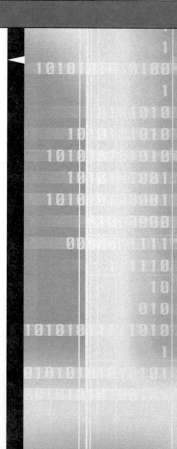

C H A P T E R 14

Tomima Edmark was enjoying a successful career as large-systems salesperson at IBM. One evening, as she was standing in line waiting to get into a movie, a curious question popped into her mind: Was it possible to turn a ponytail inside out? To greatly compress this success story, Tomima went on to invent the now-famous TopsyTail, a kind of hair barrette.

TopsyTail was widely imitated, forcing Ms. Edmark into litigation to defend her product rights. It is understandable that she would want to keep her new company's information—product designs, financial data, client list—under wraps. It helps, of course, that Ms. Edmark is computer-savvy.

Even so, Ms. Edmark shines as a hallmark of outsourcing, the practice of contracting out almost all company functions—forecasting, manufacturing, packaging, shipping, advertising, and customer service. Despite the fact that her company rings up millions of dollars of sales annually, the TopsyTail company has only a handful of employees. As Ms. Edmark notes, outsourcing lets her focus on researching and developing new products.

This true story is notable in that it is almost the reverse of what happens in many organizations, which mostly do their own product manufacturing and other related tasks but outsource the computing functions. As this chapter shows, the planning and maintenance required for computer systems are detailed and complex.

►◄ THE SYSTEMS ANALYST

People are often nervous when they are about to be visited by a systems analyst. A systems analyst with any experience, however, knows that people are uneasy about having a stranger pry into their job situations and that they may be equally nervous about computers. Before discussing how the systems analyst helps people address change, let us begin with a few basic definitions.

The Analyst and the System

Although a systems project will be described more formally later in the chapter, let us start by defining the words *system, analysis,* and *design.* A **system** is an organized set of related components established to accomplish a certain task. There are natural systems, such as the body's cardiovascular system, but many systems have been planned and deliberately put into place by people. For example, a fast-food franchise has a system for serving a customer, including taking an order, assembling the food, and collecting the amount due. A **computer system** is a system that has a computer as one of its components.

Systems analysis is the process of studying an existing system to determine how it works and how it meets users' needs. Systems analysis lays the groundwork for improvements to the system. The analysis involves an investigation, which in turn usually involves establishing a relationship with the client for whom the analysis is being done and with the users of the system. The **client** is the person or organization contracting to have the work done. The **users** are the people who will have contact with the system, usually employees and customers. For instance, in a fast-food system the client is probably the franchise owner or manager, and the users are the franchise employees and the customers.

Systems design is the process of developing a plan for an improved system, based on the results of the systems analysis. For instance, an analysis of a fast-food franchise might reveal that customers stand in unacceptably long lines waiting to order. A new system design might involve plans to have employees press buttons that match ordered items, causing a display on an overhead screen that can be seen by other employees, who can quickly assemble the order.

The **systems analyst** normally performs both analysis and design. (The term **systems designer** is used in some organizations.) In some computer installations a person who is mostly a programmer may also do some systems analysis and thus have the title **programmer/analyst.** Traditionally, most people who have become systems analysts started out as programmers.

A systems analysis and design project does not spring out of thin air. There must be an *impetus*—motivation—for change and related *authority* for the change. The impetus for change may be the result of an internal force, such as the organization's management deciding that a computer could be useful in warehousing and inventory, or an external force, such as government reporting requirements or customer complaints about billing (Figure 14-1). Authority for the change, of course, comes from higher management.

The Systems Analyst as Change Agent

The systems analyst fills the role of **change agent,** the catalyst or persuader who overcomes the natural reluctance to change within an organization. The key to success is to involve the people of the client organization in the development of the new system. The common industry phrase is **user involvement,** and nothing could be more important to the success of the system. Some analysts like to think in terms of who "owns" the system. If efforts toward getting user involvement are successful, the user begins to think of the system as *my* system, rather than *their* system. Once that happens, the analyst's job becomes much easier.

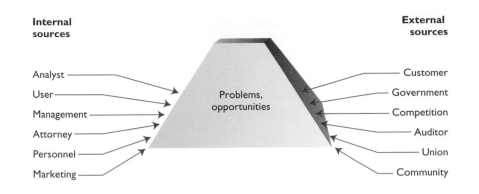

Internal sources

Analyst
User
Management
Attorney
Personnel
Marketing

Problems, opportunities

External sources

Customer
Government
Competition
Auditor
Union
Community

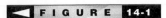

◀ FIGURE 14-1

Impetus for change.
Internal or external sources can initiate a system change.

What It Takes to Be a Systems Analyst

Before you can understand what kind of person might make a good systems analyst, it is necessary to look at the kinds of things an analyst does. The systems analyst has three principal functions:

- **Coordination.** An analyst must coordinate schedules and system-related tasks with a number of people: the analyst's own manager; the programmers working with the system; the system's users, from clerks to top management; the vendors selling the computer equipment; and a host of others, such as mail-room employees handling mailings and carpenters doing installation.

- **Communication, both oral and written.** The analyst may be called upon to make oral presentations to clients, users, and others involved with the system. The analyst provides written reports—documentation—on the results of the analysis and the goals and means of the design. These documents may range from a few pages long to a few inches thick.

- **Planning and design.** The systems analyst, with the participation of members of the client organization, plans and designs the new system. This function involves all the activities from the beginning of the project until the final implementation of the system.

In light of these principal functions, the kinds of personal qualities that are desirable in a systems analyst become apparent: an *analytical mind* and good *communication skills*. Perhaps not so obvious, however, are qualities such as *self-discipline* and *self-direction*, because a systems analyst often works without close supervision. An analyst must have good *organizational skills* to be able to keep track of all the facts about the system. An analyst also needs *creativity* to envision the new system. Finally, an analyst needs the *ability to work without tangible results*. There can be

---

FOCUS ON ETHICS   **The Systems Analyst as Change Agent**

A primary responsibility of the systems analyst is to interview users and help them to determine and elucidate their requirements for the system. However, this activity is never carried out in a vacuum, and in reality, the systems analyst must grapple with a number of social and political problems. Consider the following scenarios, identify the underlying ethical issues, and explain how you would deal with them if you were the systems analyst.

- You know that your boss is leaning heavily toward purchasing software from a particular vendor, but you

become convinced from your analysis that the boss's favorite solution won't meet the users' needs.

- Some managers are uncomfortable with your interviewing their subordinates, but you know that these are the people who best understand what the new system must do.

- The software development manager is so anxious to keep the work on the new system in house that you believe she will commit to schedules that can't be achieved.

► FIGURE 14-2

Phases of the SDLC.

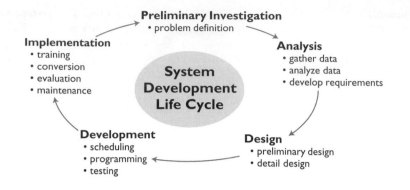

Preliminary Investigation
• problem definition

Implementation
• training
• conversion
• evaluation
• maintenance

System Development Life Cycle

Analysis
• gather data
• analyze data
• develop requirements

Development
• scheduling
• programming
• testing

Design
• preliminary design
• detail design

long dry spells when the analyst moves numbly from meeting to meeting, and it can seem that little is being accomplished.

► HOW A SYSTEMS ANALYST WORKS: OVERVIEW OF THE SYSTEMS DEVELOPMENT LIFE CYCLE

Whether you are investigating how to improve a bank's customer relations, how to track inventory for a jeans warehouse, how to manage egg production on a chicken ranch, or any other task, you will proceed by using the **systems development life cycle (SDLC)**. The systems development life cycle can be described in five phases (Figure 14-2):

● Preliminary investigation: Determining the problem

● Analysis: Understanding the existing system

● Design: Planning the new system

GETTING PRACTICAL | **Cranking Up Your Skill List**

When Althea Burgess was an adolescent, she wanted to be a doctor. However, she gradually realized that the ever-changing medical field meant that she would have to spend her entire career trying to keep up with the latest developments. So she went into the computer field instead.

This true little story is still amusing to Althea's family. Today everyone knows that the computer field is also ever-changing. Indeed, computer professionals soon discover that their original training is just the beginning. Many employers actually put a monetary premium on certain skills. No individual can have every skill. But a look at the most-wanted skills, by category, might give you an idea of a direction in which to go: For the Internet, learn XML and Java; in programming languages,

C++; in development tools, Microsoft Visual Basic, Visual C++, and PowerBuilder; for networking, TCP/IP and IPX; as a database, Oracle, DB2, and Microsoft SQL; in operating systems, Windows and Linux; for internetworking, Ethernet and ATM; for LAN administration, Windows NT Server and Novell Netware; and in client/server applications, Oracle and SAP.

Some of the names mentioned might be unfamiliar, because some of them are brand names. But you can find them on the Internet. SAP AG, for example, makes software to manage accounting, human resources, materials management, and manufacturing.

To give you an idea of the potency of training in SAP applications, both IBM and Microsoft use software from SAP to run their companies.

- Development: Doing the work to bring the new system into being

- Implementation: Converting to the new system

These simple explanations for each phase will be expanded to full-blown discussions in subsequent sections. It is important to note at this point that moving through these five phases is not necessarily a straightforward, linear process; that is, there will doubtless be adjustments to previous phases as you move along.

As you read about the phases of a systems project, follow the Swift Sport Shoes inventory case study, which is presented in accompanying boxes.

▶ PHASE 1: PRELIMINARY INVESTIGATION

The **preliminary investigation,** also called the **feasibility study** or **system survey,** is the initial investigation, a brief study of the problem to determine whether the systems project should be pursued. You, as the systems analyst, need to determine what the problem is and what to do about it. The net result will be a rough plan for how—and whether—to proceed with the project.

Before you can decide whether to proceed, you must be able to describe the problem. To do this, you will work with the users. One of your tools will be an **organization chart,** which is a hierarchical drawing showing the organization's management by name and title. Figure 14-3 shows an example of an organization chart. Many organizations already have such a chart and can give you a copy. If the chart does not

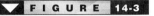

▼ FIGURE 14-3

An organization chart. The chart shows the lines of authority and formal communication channels. This example shows the organizational setup for Swift Sport Shoes, a chain of stores.

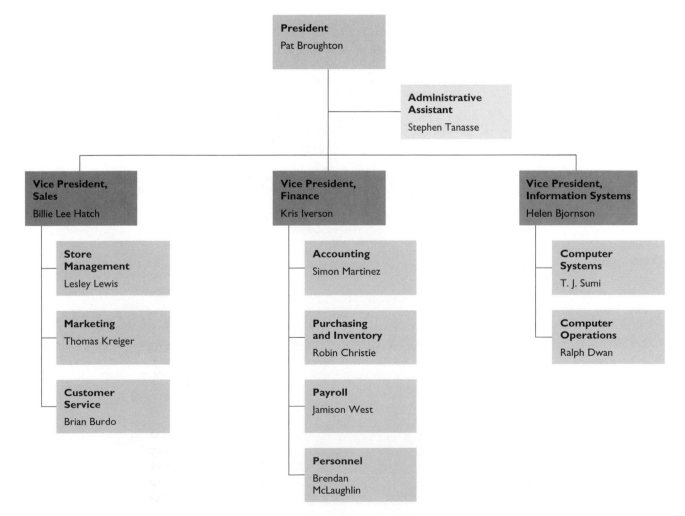

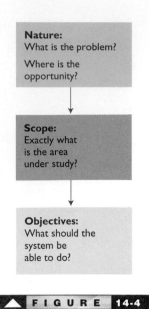

Nature:
What is the problem?

Where is the opportunity?

Scope:
Exactly what is the area under study?

Objectives:
What should the system be able to do?

▲ F I G U R E 14-4

Problem definition overview.

exist, you must ask some questions and then make it yourself. Constructing such a chart is not an idle task. If you are to work effectively within the organization, you need to understand the lines of authority through the formal communication channels. It is also important to discover any informal communication channels that exist across the organization chart. Failure to accommodate these informal channels in the design phase can cause problems with user acceptance of the system.

Problem Definition: Nature, Scope, Objectives

Your initial aim is to define the problem. You and the users must come to an agreement on these points: You must agree on the nature of the problem and then designate a limited scope. In the process you will also determine what the objectives of the project are. Figure 14-4 shows an overview of the problem definition process, and Figure 14-5 gives an example related to the Swift Sport Shoes project.

NATURE OF THE PROBLEM   Begin by determining the true **nature of the problem.** Sometimes what appears to be the problem turns out to be, on a closer look, only a symptom. For example, suppose that you are examining customer complaints of late deliveries. Your brief study may reveal that the problem is not in the shipping department, as you first thought, but in the original ordering process.

SCOPE   Establishing the **scope of the problem** is critical because problems tend to expand if no firm boundaries are established. Limitations are also necessary to stay within the eventual budget and schedule. So in the beginning, the analyst and user must agree on the scope of the project: what the new or revised system is supposed to do—and not do.

OBJECTIVES   You will soon come to understand what the user needs—that is, what the user thinks the system should be able to do. You will want to express these needs as **objectives.** Examine the objectives for the Swift inventory process. The people who run the existing inventory system already know what such a system must do. It remains for you and them to work out how this can be achieved on a computer system. In the next phase, the systems analysis phase, you will produce a more specific list of system requirements based on these objectives.

▶ F I G U R E 14-4

Problem definition. The nature and scope of the problem along with system objectives are shown for the Swift Sport Shoes system.

SWIFT SPORT SHOES: PROBLEM DEFINITION

True Nature of the Problem

The nature of the problem is the existing manual inventory system. In particular:

■ Products are frequently out of stock
■ There is little interstore communication about stock items
■ Store managers have no information about stock levels on a day-to-day basis
■ Ordering is done haphazardly

Scope

The scope of the project will be limited to the development of an inventory system using appropriate computer technology.

Objectives

The new automated inventory system should provide the following:

■ Adequate stock maintained in stores
■ Automatic stock reordering
■ Stock distribution among stores
■ Management access to current inventory information
■ Ease of use
■ Reduced operating costs of the inventory function

CASE STUDY

Preliminary Investigation

You are employed as a systems analyst by Software Systems, Inc., a company offering packaged software as well as consulting and outsourcing services. Software Systems has received a request for a consultant; the client is Swift Sport Shoes, a chain of stores carrying a huge selection of footwear for every kind of sport. Your boss hands you, a systems analyst, this assignment, telling you to contact company officer Kris Iverson.

In your initial meeting with Mr. Iverson, who is vice president of finance, you learn that the first Swift store opened in San Francisco in 1984. The store has been profitable since the second year. Nine new stores have been added in the metropolitan area and outlying shopping malls. These stores also show a net profit; Swift has been riding the crest of the fitness boom. But even though sales have been gratifying, Mr. Iverson is convinced that costs are higher than they should be and that

customer service has never been adequate.

In particular, Mr. Iverson is disturbed about inventory problems, which are causing frequent stock shortages and increasing customer dissatisfaction. The company has a low-end mainframe computer at headquarters, where management offices are located. Although there is a small information systems staff, their experience is mainly in batch processing for financial systems. Mr. Iverson envisions more sophisticated technology for an inventory system and figures that outside expertise is needed to design it. He introduces you to Robin Christie, who is in charge of purchasing and inventory. Mr. Iverson also tells you that he has sent a memo to all company officers and store managers indicating the purpose of your presence and his support of a study of the current system. Before the end of your visit with Mr. Iverson, the two of you construct the organization chart shown in Figure 14-3.

In subsequent interviews with Ms. Christie and other Swift personnel, you find that deteriorating customer service seems to be due to a lack of information about inventory supplies. Together, you and Ms. Christie determine the problem definition, as shown in Figure 14-5. Mr. Iverson accepts your report, in which you outline the problem definition and suggest a full analysis.

Wrapping Up the Preliminary Investigation

The preliminary investigation, which is necessarily brief, should result in some sort of report, perhaps only a few pages long, telling management what you have found and listing your recommendations. Furthermore, money is always a factor in go/no-go decisions: Is the project financially feasible? At this point management has three choices: They can (1) drop the matter, (2) fix the problem immediately if it is simple, or (3) authorize you to go on to the next phase for a closer look.

► PHASE 2: SYSTEMS ANALYSIS

Let us suppose that management has decided to continue. Remember that the purpose of systems analysis is to understand the existing system. A related goal is to establish the system requirements. The best way to understand a system is to gather all the data you can about it; this data must then be organized and analyzed. During the systems analysis phase you will be concerned with (1) data gathering and (2) data analysis. Keep in mind that the system being analyzed may or may not already be a computerized system.

Data Gathering

Data gathering is expensive and requires a lot of legwork and time. There is no standard procedure for gathering data because each system is unique. But there are certain sources that are commonly used: written documents, interviews, questionnaires, observation, and sampling. Sometimes you use all of these sources, but in most cases it is appropriate to use some and not others:

WRITTEN DOCUMENTS **Written documents** include procedures manuals, reports, forms, and any other kind of material bearing on the problem that you find in the organization. Take time to get a copy of each form an organization uses.

INTERVIEWS A key advantage of **interviews** is their flexibility; as the interviewer, you can change the direction of your questions if you discover a productive area of investigation. Another bonus is that you can probe with open-ended questions that people would balk at answering on paper. You can also observe the respondent's voice inflection and body language, which may tell you more than words alone. Finally, of course, there is the bonus of getting to know clients better and establishing a rapport with them, an important factor in promoting user involvement in the system from the beginning. Interviews have certain drawbacks: They are time-consuming and therefore expensive. If you need to find out about procedures from 40 mail clerks, you are better off using a questionnaire.

There are two types of interviews, structured and unstructured. A **structured interview** includes only questions that have been planned and written in advance. A structured interview is useful when it is desirable—or required by law—to ask identical questions of several people. In an **unstructured interview,** the interviewer (analyst) begins with a general goal but with few, if any, specific questions prepared. This type of interview can be useful in discovering unexpected information but requires effort on the analyst's part to keep it on track. Generally, the best approach involves a combination of structured and unstructured techniques, in which the analyst begins with a set of planned questions but is prepared to deviate from the plan based on user responses.

QUESTIONNAIRES Unlike interviews, **questionnaires** can be used to get information from large groups. Also, because of the large number of respondents, sometimes a trend or problem pattern emerges that would not be evident from a small number of interviews. Questionnaires allow people to respond anonymously and, presumably, more truthfully. Questionnaires do have disadvantages, however, including the problem of getting them returned and the possibility of biased answers.

Good questionnaires are difficult to prepare. The questions must be clear and straightforward and phrased in a way that does not lead the user to specific answers. If possible, try the questionnaire out on a small group before finalizing it.

OBSERVATION As an analyst and observer, you go into the organization and watch who interrelates with whom. In particular, you observe how data flows: from desk to desk, fax to fax, or computer to computer. Note how data comes into and leaves the organization. Initially, you make arrangements with a group supervisor and make everyone aware of the purpose of your visit. Be sure to return on more than one occasion so that the people under observation become used to your presence. One form of observation is **participant observation;** in this form, the analyst temporarily joins the activities of the group.

CASE STUDY

Systems Analysis

With the assistance of Ms. Christie, you learn more about the current inventory system. She helps to set up interviews with store managers and arranges to have you observe procedures in the stores and at the warehouse. As the number of stores has increased, significant expansion has taken place in all inventory-related areas: sales, scope of merchandise, and number of vendors.

Out-of-stock situations are common. The stock shortages are not uniform across all ten stores, how-

ever; frequently, one store will be out of an item that the central warehouse or another store has on hand. The present system is not able to recognize this situation and transfer merchandise on a timely basis. There is a tendency for stock to be reordered only when the shelf is empty or nearly so. Inventory-related costs are significant, especially those for special orders of some stock items. Reports to management are minimal and often too late to be useful. Finally, there is no way to correlate order quantities

with past sales records, future projections, or inventory situations.

During this period you also analyze the data as it is gathered. You prepare data flow diagrams of the various activities relating to inventory. Figure 14-7 shows the general flow of data to handle purchasing in the existing system. You prepare various decision tables, such as the one shown in Figure 14-8b.

Your written report to Mr. Iverson includes the list of system requirements in Figure 14-9.

SAMPLING   You might need to collect data about quantities, costs, time periods, and other factors relevant to the system. For example, how many phone orders can an order entry clerk take in an hour? If you are dealing with a major mail-order organization, such as L.L. Bean in Maine, this type of question might be best answered through a procedure called **sampling.** Instead of observing all 125 clerks filling orders for an hour, you pick a sample of three or four clerks. Or, in a case involving a high volume of paper output, such as customer bills, you could collect a random sample of a few dozen bills.

Data Analysis

It is now time to turn your attention to the second activity of this phase: data analysis. A variety of tools—charts and diagrams—are used to analyze data, not all of them appropriate for every system. You should become familiar with the techniques that your organization favors and then use the tools that suit you at the time. Two typical tools are data flow diagrams and decision tables. Data analysis shows how the current system works and helps to determine the system requirements. In addition, data analysis materials serve as the basis for documentation of the system.

Data Flow Diagrams

A **data flow diagram** (**DFD**) is a road map that graphically shows the flow of data through a system. It is a valuable tool for depicting present procedures and data flow. Although data flow diagrams can be used in the design process, they are particularly useful for facilitating communication between you and the users during the analysis phase.

There are a variety of notations for data flow diagrams. The notation used here has been chosen because it is informal and easy to draw and read. The elements of a data flow diagram are processes, files, sources and sinks, and vectors, as shown in Figure 14-6. Note also the DFD for Swift Sport Shoes (Figure 14-7) as you follow this discussion.

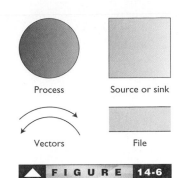

▲ **F I G U R E 14-6**

Symbols used in data flow diagrams. Circles represent processes, the actions taken on the data—comparing, checking, stamping, authorizing, filing, and so forth. Parallel lines represent a data store, a repository of data; this can be a disk file, a set of papers in a file cabinet, or even mail in an in-basket. Sources and sinks are represented by a square. A source is a data origin outside the system under study. An example is a payment sent to a department store by a charge customer; the customer is a source of data. A sink is a destination for data going outside the system; an example is the bank that receives money deposits from the accounts receivable department. The flow of data is shown using vectors or arrows.

◄ **F I G U R E 14-7**

A data flow diagram. This "map" shows the current flow of data in the purchasing department at Swift Sport Shoes. The diagram (greatly simplified) includes authorization for purchases of goods, purchase order preparation, and verification of the vendor's invoice against the purchase order. Note that the stores, vendors, and accounts payable are in square boxes because they are outside the purchasing department.

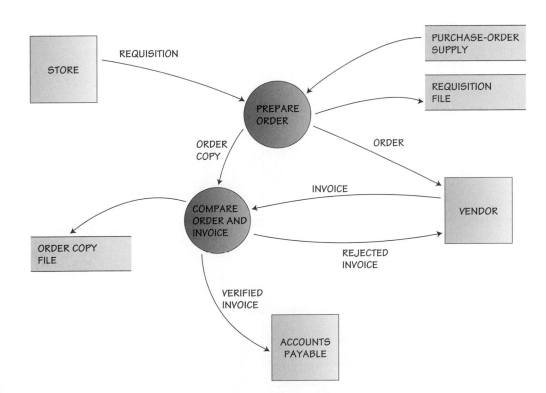

Decision Tables

A **decision table** is a standard table of the logical decisions that must be made regarding potential conditions in a given system. Decision tables are useful in cases that involve a series of interrelated decisions; their use helps to ensure that no alternatives are overlooked. Programmers can code portions of a program right from a decision table. Figure 14-8a shows the format of a decision table; Figure 14-8b gives an example of a decision table that applies to the Swift Sport Shoes system.

System Requirements

As we noted earlier, the purpose of gathering and analyzing data is twofold: to understand the system and, as a by-product of that understanding, to establish the **system requirements,** a detailed list of the things the system must be able to do. You need to determine and document specific user needs. A system that a bank teller uses, for example, needs to be able to retrieve a customer record and display it on a screen within 5 seconds.

The importance of accurate requirements cannot be overemphasized, because the design of the new system will be based on the system requirements. Furthermore,

▶ **F I G U R E 14-8**

Decision tables. (a) The format of a decision table. The table is organized according to the logic that "if this condition exists or is met, then do this." (b) A decision table example. This decision table, which describes the current ordering procedure at Swift Sport Shoes, takes into consideration whether a requisition for goods from a store is valid, the availability of the wanted goods in the warehouse or some other Swift store, whether the quantity ordered warrants an inventory order, and whether the order is a special order for a customer. Examine rule 4. The requisition is valid, so proceed. The desired goods are not available in either the warehouse or another store, so they must be ordered. However, there is not the required volume of customer demand to place a standard inventory order now, so the requisition is put on hold until there is. (In other words, this order will be joined with others.) Finally, because this is a special customer order and the order is on hold, a back order notice is sent.

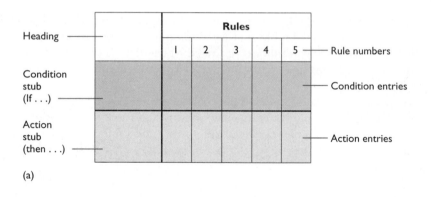

(a)

Order procedure	Rules					
	1	2	3	4	5	6
Valid requisition	Y	Y	Y	Y	Y	N
Available warehouse	Y	N	N	N	N	—
Available another store	—	Y	N	N	N	—
Required order volume	—	—	Y	N	N	—
Special customer order	—	—	—	Y	N	—
Transfer goods from warehouse	X					
Transfer goods from store		X				
Determine vendor			X			
Send purchase order			X			
Hold requisition				X	X	
Send back order notice				X		
Reject requisition						X

(b)

SWIFT SPORT SHOES: REQUIREMENTS

The requirements for the Swift Sport Shoes inventory system are as follows:

■ Capture inventory data from sales transactions
■ Implement automatic inventory reordering
■ Implement a standardized interstore transfer system
■ Provide both on-demand and scheduled management reports
■ Provide security and accounting controls throughout the system
■ Provide a user-oriented system whose online usage can be learned by a new user in one training class
■ Reduce operating costs of the inventory function by 20%

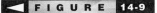

◀ **F I G U R E** 14-9

System requirements.
These are the requirements for an inventory system for Swift Sport Shoes.

the analyst and management must come to clear agreement on the system requirements, because a misunderstanding can result in a poor evaluation of the new system and even cause a delay in project completion. Note the requirements for the Swift system shown in Figure 14-9.

Report to Management

When you have finished the systems analysis phase, you present a report to management. This report summarizes the problems you found in the current system, describes the requirements for the new system, includes a cost analysis, and makes recommendations on what course to take next. If the project is significant, you might also make a formal presentation, including visual displays. If management decides to pursue the project, you move on to Phase 3.

▶ PHASE 3: SYSTEMS DESIGN

The systems design phase is the phase in which you actually plan the new system. This phase is divided into two subphases: **preliminary design,** in which the analyst establishes the new system concept, followed by **detail design,** in which the analyst determines exact design specifications. This phase is divided into two parts because an analyst wants to make sure management approves the overall plan before spending time and money on the details of the new system.

Preliminary Design

The first task of preliminary design is to review the system requirements and then consider some of the major aspects of a system. Should the system be centralized or distributed? Should the system be online? Can the system be run on the users' personal computers? How will input data be captured? What kind of reports will be needed? The questions can go on and on.

A key question that should be answered early on is whether packaged software should be purchased, as opposed to having programmers write custom software. This is referred to as the **make or buy decision.** This may be tricky because clients often think that their problems are unique. However, if the new system falls into one of several major categories, such as accounting or inventory control, you will find that many software vendors offer packaged solutions. A packaged solution should meet at least 75 percent of client requirements. For the remaining 25 percent, the client can adjust ways of doing business to match the package software or, more expensively, the packaged software can be **customized,** or altered, to meet the client's special needs.

CASE STUDY

Systems Design

The store managers, who were uneasy at the beginning of the study, are by now enthusiastic participants in the design of the new system they are counting on for better control over their inventory. As part of the preliminary design phase, you offer three alternative system candidates for consideration.

The first is a centralized system, with all processing done on the headquarters computer and batch reports generated daily and delivered by messenger to the stores. This system would provide little control in the stores, so it is not considered seriously, being mentioned only because of its relatively low cost. The third candidate takes the opposite approach, placing all processing in the stores on their own computers. This approach proves attractive to the store managers but does not give the headquarters staff as much control or vision as they need.

The second candidate, the one eventually selected, is a client/server network system that uses point-of-sale (POS) terminals and a server in each store, with a larger server at the headquarters office. The POS terminals will be connected to the in-store server, which supplies prices and also captures sales transaction data. The captured sales data will be sent to the main server at the end of the day, where it will be used to update the inventory file. In addition, it will produce inventory transfer reports that will be sent to the warehouse and reorder reports that will be sent to purchasing. A key ingredient of the proposed solution is an automatic reorder procedure. The computer generates orders for any product that is shown to be below the preset reorder mark. A further enhancement is that each store will have a terminal devoted to inquiries, via a server program, about product availability, with the capability of ordering product transfers from another store. This fairly simple system is appropriate for the present size of the organization, with only ten stores but will continue to be workable for growth to 20 stores. Figure 14-10 shows the overall design from a user's viewpoint.

You make a formal presentation to Mr. Iverson and other members of company management. Slides that you prepared on a personal computer (with special presentation software) accent your points visually. After a brief statement of the problem, you list anticipated benefits to the company; these are listed in Figure 14-11. You explain the design in general terms and describe the expected costs and schedules. With the money saved from the reduced inventory expenses, you project that the system development costs will be repaid in four years. Swift Sport Shoes management accepts your recommendations, and you proceed with the detail design phase. You then design printed reports and screen displays for managers; samples are shown in Figures 14-12 and 14-13.

There are many other exacting and time-consuming activities associated with detail design. Although space prohibits discussing them, here is a list of some of these tasks, to give you the flavor of the complexity: You must plan the use of wand readers to read stock codes from merchandise tags, plan to download the price file daily to be available to the store server and thus the POS terminals, plan all files on disk with regular backups on tape, design the records in each file and the methods to be used to access the files, design the data communications system, draw diagrams to show the flow of the data in the system, and prepare structure charts of program modules. (Figure 14-15 shows a skeleton version of a systems flowchart that represents part of the inventory processing.) Some of these activities, such as design of a data communications system, require certain expertise, so you may be coordinating with specialists. Several systems controls are planned, among them a unique numbering system for stock items and validation of all data input at the terminal.

You make another presentation to managers and more technical people, including representatives from information systems. You are given the go-ahead.

Another possibility is **outsourcing,** which means turning the system over to an outside agency to develop. Large organizations that employ their own computer professionals may outsource certain projects, especially if the subject matter is one in which a reputable outsourcing firm specializes. The outsourcing company then turns the completed system over to the client. Some organizations outsource most or all of their computer projects, preferring to avoid bearing the costs of keeping their own staff.

If you proceed with an in-house design, then, together with key personnel from the client organization, you determine an overall plan. In fact, it is common to offer alternative plans, called **candidates.** Each candidate meets the client's requirements but with variations in features and costs. The chosen candidate is usually the one that best meets the client's current needs and is flexible enough to meet future needs.

At this stage it is wise to make a formal presentation of the selected plan, or possibly of all the alternatives. The point is that you do not want to commit time and energy to—nor does the client want to pay for—a detailed design until you and the client agree on the basic design. Such presentations often include a drawing of the system from a user's perspective, such as the one in Figure 14-10 for the Swift Sport Shoes system. This is the time to emphasize system benefits; see the list in Figure 14-11.

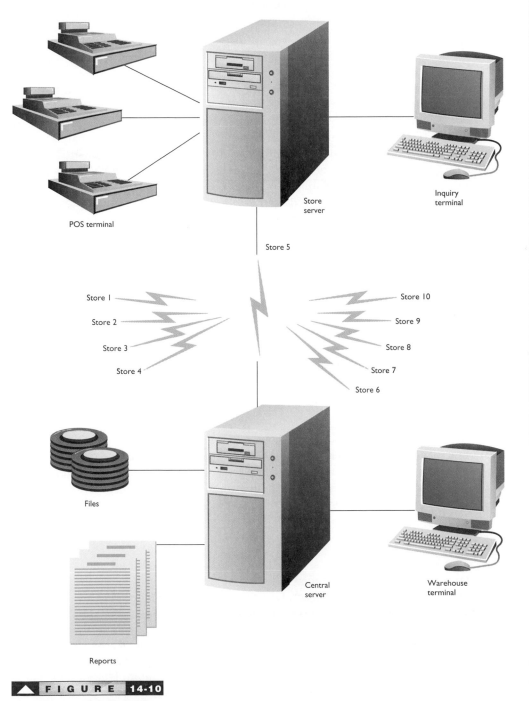

POS terminal

Store server

Inquiry terminal

Store 5

Store 1
Store 2
Store 3
Store 4

Store 10
Store 9
Store 8
Store 7
Store 6

Files

Reports

Central server

Warehouse terminal

▲ **FIGURE 14-10**

Overview of the system. This overview shows the Swift Sport Shoes inventory system from a user's point of view. Sales transactions begin at the point-of-sale terminals in the store, which get pricing data from the store's local server. Once a day, the sales data is uploaded over communication lines to the central server, which, among other things, updates the inventory files and produces reports. Also, store employees can use a local terminal to pose stock availability queries, via its own server, to the central server, which can send appropriate routing information to the warehouse.

Successful Systems Presentations

The following guidelines will pave the way to a successful systems project presentation:

● **State the problem.** Although you do not want to belabor the problem statement, you do want to show that you understand it.

● **State the benefits.** These are a new system's whole reason for being, so your argument here should be carefully planned. Will the system improve accuracy, speed up turnaround, save processing time, save money? The more specific you can be, the better. Use terminology appropriate to your audience.

● **Explain the analysis/ design.** Here you should give a general presentation and then be prepared to take questions about specifics. Remember that higher management will not be interested in hearing all the details.

● **Present a schedule.** How long will it take to carry out the plan? Give your audience the time frame.

● **Estimate the costs.** The costs include development costs (those required to construct the system) and operating costs (the ongoing costs of running the system). You will also need to tell your audience how long it is going to be before they get a return on their original investment.

● **Answer questions.** A good rule of thumb is to save half the allotted time for questions from your audience.

▶ FIGURE 14-11

Benefits. Benefits are usually closely tied to the system objectives. These are the anticipated benefits of the new Swift Sport Shoes inventory system.

SWIFT SPORT SHOES: ANTICIPATED BENEFITS

- Better inventory control
- Improved customer service
- Improved management information
- Reduced inventory costs
- Improved employee morale

Prototyping

Building a prototype—a sort of guinea-pig model of the system—has become a standard approach in many organizations. Considered from a systems viewpoint, a **prototype** is a limited working system or a subset of a system that is developed quickly, sometimes in just a few days. Many organizations use prototyping very loosely so that it has no true functionality but can produce output that looks like output of the finished system, enabling users to see and evaluate it. The idea is that users can get an idea of what the system might be like before it is fully developed. Used in this fashion, prototypes allow the analyst to verify that the system design meets the users' requirements.

Some organizations develop a prototype as a working model, one that can be modified and fine-tuned until it becomes the working system. No one expects users to be completely satisfied with a prototype, so requirements can be revised before a lot of resources have been invested in developing the new system. Could you adopt this approach to systems development? It seems at odds with this chapter's systems development life cycle, which promotes doing steps in the proper order. Yet many analysts in the computer industry are making good use of prototypes. The prototype approach exploits advances in computer technology and uses powerful, high-level software tools. These software packages enable analysts to build systems quickly in response to user needs. The systems that are produced can then be refined as they are used until the fit between user and system is acceptable. This approach works best with small-scale systems.

CASE: Computer-Aided Software Engineering

Computer-aided software engineering (**CASE**) involves the use of computer software to automate many of the tasks of the SDLC. Some CASE tools focus on a specific analysis or design task, such as creating data flow diagrams; others provide an integrated environment that supports the entire systems development process.

Detail Design

Let us say that the users have accepted your design proposal and you are on your way. You must now develop detailed design specifications, or a detail design. This is a time-consuming part of the project, but it is relatively straightforward.

In this phase, every facet of the system is considered in detail. Here is a list of some detail design activities: designing output forms and screens, planning input data forms and procedures, drawing system flowcharts, planning file access methods and record formats, planning database interfaces, planning data communications interfaces, designing system security controls, and considering human factors. This list is not comprehensive, nor will all activities listed be used for all systems. Some analysts choose to plan the overall logic at this stage, preparing program structure charts, pseudocode (a programming planning tool described in Chapter 15), and the like.

Normally, in the detail design phase, parts of the system are considered in this order: output requirements, input requirements, files and databases, systems processing, and systems controls and backup.

OUTPUT REQUIREMENTS   Before you can do anything, you must know exactly what the client wants the system to produce—the **output requirements.** As an analyst you must also consider the medium of the output—paper, computer screen, and so on. In addition, you must determine the type of reports needed (summary, exception, and so on) and the contents of the output—what data is needed for the reports. The forms that the output will be printed on are also a consideration; they may need to be custom printed if they go outside the organization to customers or stockholders. You might wish to determine the report format by using a **printer spacing chart,** which shows the position of headings, the spacing between columns, and the location of date and page numbers (Figure 14-12). You may also use screen reports, mock-ups on paper of how the screen will respond to user queries. A sample screen report is shown in Figure 14-13.

▼ F I G U R E   14-12

Example of a printer spacing chart. This chart shows how a systems analyst wants the report format to look—headings, columns, and so on—when displayed on a printer. This example shows discontinued items, a report that is part of the new Swift Sport Shoes system. Xs represent alphabetic data, and 9s represent numeric data.

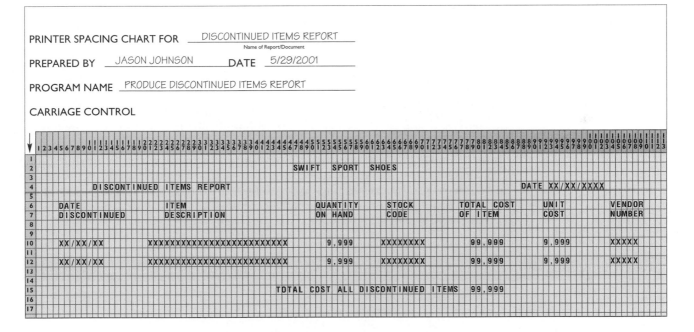

◄ F I G U R E   14-13

Example of a screen report. This screen report layout has been designed as part of the Swift Sport Shoes system. The purpose of the screen is to give information about how much of a given stock item is in each store. The report shows an approximation of what the user will see on the screen after entering a stock code.

INPUT REQUIREMENTS   After your desired output has been determined, you must consider the **input requirements** to produce it. First you must consider the input medium: Will you try to capture data at the source via POS terminals? Must the input be keyed from a source document? Next you must consider content again—what fields are needed, the order in which they appear, and the like. This in turn may involve designing forms that organize data before it is entered. You need to plan some kind of input validation process, a check that data is reasonable as well as accurate; you would not expect a six-figure salary, for example, for someone who works in the mailroom. Finally, you need to consider input volume, particularly the volume at peak periods. Can the system handle it? A mail-order house, for instance, might have to be ready for higher sales of expensive toys during the December holiday season than at other times of the year.

FILES AND DATABASES   You need to consider how the files in your computer system will be organized: sequentially, directly, or by some other method. You also need to decide how the files should be accessed, as well as the format of records making up the data files. If the system has one or more databases or accesses databases used in other systems, you have to coordinate your design efforts with the database administrator, the person responsible for controlling and updating databases.

SYSTEM PROCESSING   Just as you drew a data flow diagram to describe the old system, now you need to show the flow of data in the new system. One method is to use standard American National Standards Institute (ANSI) flowchart symbols (Figure 14-14) to illustrate what will be done and what files will be used. Figure 14-15 shows a resulting **system flowchart.** Note that a system flowchart is not the same as the logic flowchart used in programming. The system flowchart describes the flow of data through the system; a logic flowchart represents the flow of logic within a single program and is described in detail in Chapter 15.

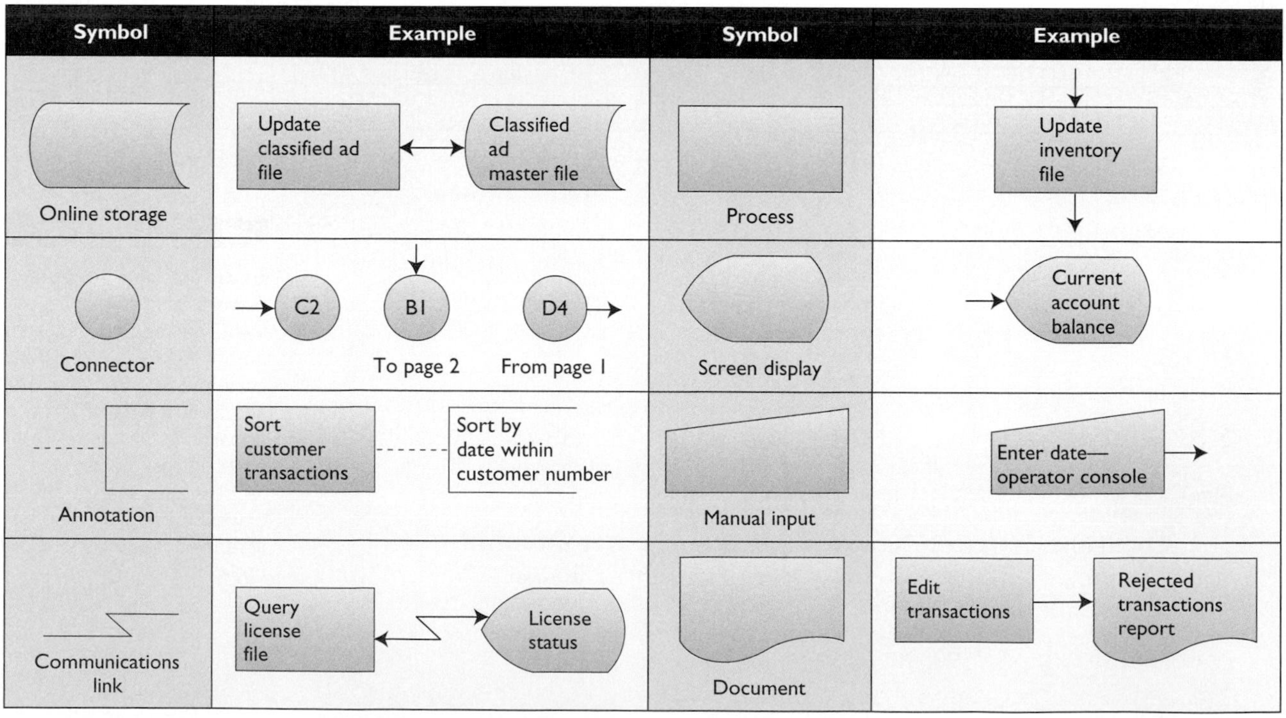

Symbol	Example	Symbol	Example
Online storage	Update classified ad file ⟷ Classified ad master file	Process	Update inventory file
Connector	→ C2 → B1 → D4 → / To page 2 / From page 1	Screen display	Current account balance
Annotation	Sort customer transactions ┄ Sort by date within customer number	Manual input	Enter date— operator console
Communications link	Query license file ← License status	Document	Edit transactions → Rejected transactions report

▲ F I G U R E 14-14

ANSI systems flowchart symbols. These are some of the symbols recommended by the American National Standards Institute for systems flowcharts, which show the movement of data through a system.

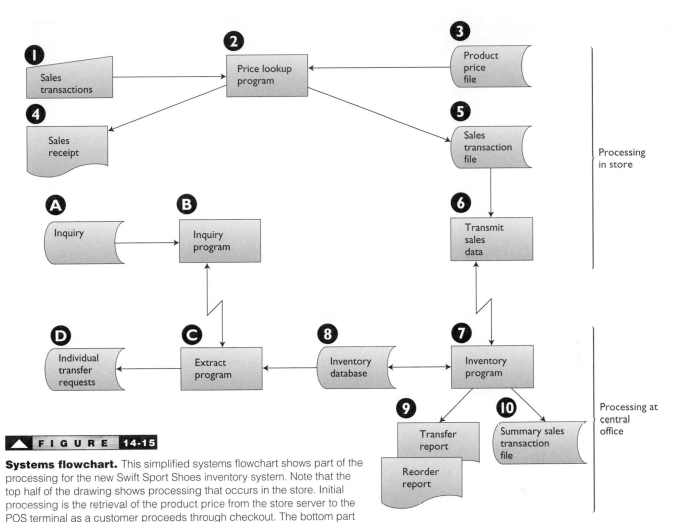

▲ **FIGURE 14-15**

Systems flowchart. This simplified systems flowchart shows part of the processing for the new Swift Sport Shoes inventory system. Note that the top half of the drawing shows processing that occurs in the store. Initial processing is the retrieval of the product price from the store server to the POS terminal as a customer proceeds through checkout. The bottom part of the drawing shows aggregate processing of all sales transactions from all stores, done on the computer at the central headquarters site. Also shown, on the left side of the chart, is an inquiry from a store to the central server. Step by step: The sales clerk (1) inputs sales transaction data, prompting (2) the POS terminal to look up the item price via an in-store server program, which gets the information from (3) the product price file and then (4) prints a sales receipt for the customer and also stores (5) the sales transaction data on a file. At the end of the sales day, (6) the store server runs a program to transmit the stored sales transactions over data communications lines to the central server, which (7) processes it for inventory purposes by updating the (8) inventory database, producing (9) transfer and reorder reports, and placing the sales transaction in (10) a file for subsequent auditing. In a separate process, in any store, an employee can use (A) a terminal to invoke (B) the store server program to send a product availability inquiry to (C) a program on the central server, which checks the inventory database and sends a response and possibly also sends (D) a message for action to the warehouse.

SYSTEM CONTROLS AND BACKUP   To make sure that data is input and processed correctly and to prevent fraud and tampering with the computer system, you will need to institute appropriate controls. In a batch system, in which data for the system is processed in groups, begin with the source documents, such as time cards or sales orders. Each document should be serially numbered so that the system can keep track of it. Documents are time-stamped when received and then grouped in batches. Each batch is labeled with the number of documents per batch; these counts are balanced against totals of the processed data. The input is controlled ensure that the data is accurately converted from source documents to machine-processable form. Data input to online systems is backed up by **system journals,** files that record every transaction processed at each terminal, such as an account withdrawal through a bank teller. Processing controls include the data validation procedures mentioned in the section on input requirements.

It is also important to plan for the backup of system files; copies of transaction and master files should be made on a regular basis. These file copies should then be

CASE STUDY

Systems Development

Working with Dennis Harrington of the Information Systems department at Swift, you prepare a Gantt chart, as shown in Figure 14-16. This chart shows the schedule for the inventory project.

Program design specifications are prepared using pseudocode, the design tool Mr. Harrington thinks will be most useful to programmers. The programs will be written in C++, because that is the primary language of the installation and it is suitable for this application. Three programmers are assigned to the project.

You work with the programmers to develop a test plan. Some inventory data, both typical and atypical, is prepared to test the new system. You and the programmers continue to build on the documentation base by implementing the pseudocode and by preparing detailed data descriptions, logic narratives, program listings, test data results, and related material.

stored temporarily in case the originals are inadvertently lost or damaged. Often the backup copies are stored off site for added security.

As before, the results of this phase are documented. The resulting report, usually referred to as the detail design specifications, is an outgrowth of the preliminary design document. The report is probably large and detailed. A presentation often accompanies the completion of this stage.

► **PHASE 4: SYSTEM DEVELOPMENT**

Finally, the system is actually going to be developed. As a systems analyst you prepare a schedule to monitor the principal activities in **system development**—programming and testing.

Scheduling

Many project-scheduling tools are available. Figure 14-16 shows a **Gantt chart,** a bar chart commonly used to depict schedule deadlines and milestones. In our example, the chart shows the work to be accomplished over a given period. It does not, however, show the number of work hours required. If you were the supervisor, it would be common practice for you to ask others on the development team to produce individual Gantt charts of their own activities. Organizations that want additional control may use **project management software,** which offers additional features, such as allocating people and resources to each task, monitoring schedules, and producing status reports.

► **FIGURE 14-16**

Gantt chart. This bar chart shows the scheduled tasks and milestones of the Swift Sport Shoes project. Notice that some phases overlap.

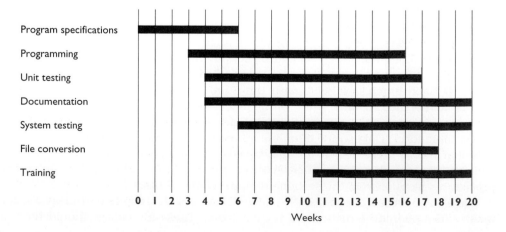

Programming

Until this point there has been no programming, unless, that is, some prototyping was done. So usually, before programming begins, you need to prepare program design specifications. Program development tools must be considered. Some of this work may already have been done as part of the design phase, but usually programmers participate in refining the design at this point. Program design specifications can be developed through detailed logic flowcharts and pseudocode, among other tools. The programming process is covered in more detail in the next chapter.

Testing

Would you write a program and then simply turn it over to the client without checking it over first? Of course not. Thus programmers perform **unit testing,** meaning that they individually test their own program pieces (units), using test data. Programmers even try inputting bad data so that they can be confident that their program can handle it appropriately. This is followed by **system testing,** which determines whether all the program units work together satisfactorily. During this process, the development team uses test data to test every part of the programs. Finally, **volume testing** uses real data in large amounts. Volume testing sometimes reveals errors that do not show up with test data, especially errors in storage or memory usage. In particular, volume testing of online systems reveals problems that are likely to occur only under heavy use.

As in every phase of the project, documentation is required. In this phase documentation describes the program logic and detailed data formats.

► PHASE 5: IMPLEMENTATION

You might think that implementation simply means stopping the old system and starting the new system. You are not alone. Many companies believe that also, but they find out that there is much more to it. Even though implementation is the final phase, a good deal of effort is still required, including the following activities: training, equipment conversion, file conversion, system conversion, auditing, evaluation, and maintenance.

Training

Often systems analysts do not give **training** the attention it deserves, because they are so concerned about the computer system itself. But a system can be no better than the people using it. A good time to start training—for at least a few of the users—is at some point during the testing so that people can begin to learn how to use the system even as the development team is checking it out. Do not be concerned that these users will see a not-yet-perfect system; users actually gain confidence in a developing system as errors get fixed and the system improves every day.

The **user's manual,** a document prepared to aid users who are not familiar with the computer system, is an important training tool. Some organizations employ technical writers to create the user's manual while the system is being developed. But documentation for the user is only the beginning. Any teacher knows that students learn best by doing. Besides, users are as likely to read a thick manual as they are to read a dictionary. The message is clear: Users must receive hands-on training to learn to use the system. The trainer must prepare exercises that simulate the tasks users will be required to do. For example, a hotel clerk learning a new online reservation system is given typical requests to fulfill—a family of four for three nights—and uses a terminal to practice. The user's manual is used as a reference guide. Setting all this up is not a trivial task. The trainer must consider class space, equipment, data, and the users' schedules.

Where Can I Hide?

On November 2, 1998, ABC News published election results on its Web site. The complete results of Senate and governors' races were on the Web for anyone to see. There was just one problem: No one had voted yet. The election was to be on Tuesday, November 3.

It is certainly true that we all make mistakes, but some mistakes are more public than others. This particular story is so chilling that it is still being discussed in systems circles. The phony numbers on the Web site had been for testing purposes only. Testing is, of course, an essential function of the system development process, but test results should not be seen by people who might mistake them for the real thing.

CASE STUDY

Implementation

While the system is being developed, you take advantage of the time to write the user's manuals. This is done in conjunction with training store personnel and managers in the use of the system. The training is not a trivial task, but you do not have to do all of it yourself. Training on the new POS cash registers, for instance, will be done by the vendor, while you plan training classes for the people who will use the local computers to run programs and send data to the computer at headquarters.

You will have separate classes to teach managers to retrieve data from the system via terminal commands. In both cases, training will be hands-on. Company personnel should find the training enjoyable if the onscreen dialog is user-friendly—that is, the user is instructed clearly every step of the way.

File conversion is painful. One evening after closing time, the staff works into the night to take inventory in the stores. Temporary personnel are hired to key an inventory master file from this data. Transactions for the master file are accumulated as more purchases are made, up until the time the system is ready for use; then the master will be updated from these transactions. After discussing the relative merits of the various system conversion methods, you and Ms. Christie agree that a pilot conversion would be ideal. Together you decide to bring up the original store first, then add other stores to the system one or two at a time.

To evaluate the new system, Mr. Iverson puts together a local team consisting of Ms. Christie, a programmer, and an accountant. Because your documentation is comprehensive, it is relatively easy for the team to check the system completely to see if it is functioning according to specifications. The evaluation report notes several positive results: Out-of-stock conditions have almost disappeared (only two instances in one store in one month), inventory transfer among stores is a smooth operation, and store managers feel an increased sense of control. Negative outcomes are relatively minor and can be fixed in a system maintenance operation.

Equipment Conversion

Equipment conversion can vary from almost none to installing a mainframe computer and all its peripheral equipment. If you are implementing a small- or medium-size system on established equipment in a major information systems department, your equipment considerations may simply involve negotiating scheduled run time and disk space. If you are purchasing a moderate amount of equipment, such as terminals or personal computers, you will be concerned primarily with delivery schedules, networking, and compatibility.

A major equipment purchase demands a large amount of time and attention. The planning for such a purchase, of course, must begin long before the implementation phase. For a major equipment purchase, you need site preparation advice from vendors and other equipment experts.

Personal computer systems are less demanding, but they too require site planning in terms of the availability of space, accessibility, and cleanliness. And as the analyst, you might be the one who does the actual installation.

File Conversion

File conversion may be very tricky if the existing files are being handled manually. The data must be prepared in such a way that it is accessible to computer systems. All the contents of the file drawers in the personnel department, for instance, must be keyed, or possibly scanned, to be stored on disk. Some scheme must be used to input the data files and keep them updated. You may need to employ temporary help. The big headache during this process is keeping all file records up to date when some are still processed manually and some have been keyed in preparation for the new system.

If you are modifying an existing computer system and thus have files already in computer-accessible form, you might need to have a program written to convert the old files to the format needed for the new system. This is a much speedier process than having to key in data from scratch. Nevertheless, it is not unusual for file conversion to take a long time.

System Conversion

During the **system conversion** stage, you actually "pull the plug" on the old system and begin using the new one. There are four ways of handling the conversion.

Direct conversion means that the user simply stops using the old system and starts using the new one—a somewhat risky method, since there is no other system to fall back on if anything goes wrong. This procedure is best followed only if the old system is very small or in unusable condition. A **phased conversion** is one in which the organization eases into the new system one step at a time so that all the users are working with some of the system. In contrast, in a **pilot conversion** the entire system is used by a designated set of users and is extended to all users once it has proved successful. This works best when a company has several branch offices or separate divisions. In a **parallel conversion,** the most prolonged and expensive method, the old and new systems are operated concurrently for some time, until users are satisfied that the new system performs to their standards.

System conversion is often a time of stress and confusion for all concerned. As the analyst, your credibility is on the line. During this time, users are often doing double duty, trying to perform their regular jobs and simultaneously cope with a new computer system. Problems seem to appear in all areas, from input to output. Clearly, this is a period when your patience is needed.

Auditing

Security violations, whether deliberate or unintentional, can be difficult to detect. Data begins from some source, perhaps a written source document or a transaction, for which there must be a record log. Eventually, the data is part of the system on some medium, probably disk. After the data is on disk, it is possible for an unauthorized person to alter it in some illicit way. How would anyone know that the disk files had been changed and, in fact, no longer matched the original source documents from which the data came? To guard against this situation, the systems analyst designs an **audit trail** to trace output back to the source data. In real-time systems, security violations can be particularly elusive unless all transactions are recorded on disk for later reference by auditors. Modern auditors no longer shuffle mountains of paper; instead, they have computer programs of their own to monitor applications programs and data.

DAY IN THE LIFE   **Jerry Park,**
EDI Systems Analyst

Jerry is a systems analyst/programmer working for a large furniture manufacturing company. Such a large company can't afford to lose any money on inefficient systems, especially in the Electronic Data Interchange network that connects the manufacturing locations to the sales network. Furniture retailers need to be able to place orders to the warehouse, which in turn needs to be able to indicate the needed products to the manufacturing plants, which then have to connect with their suppliers for the materials. Many separate companies form this long supply chain, and the only way to bridge it efficiently is by using an EDI-standardized network.

Enter Jerry Park. His job is to examine each link in the EDI network to evaluate its efficiency. What programs is a link us-ing to send and receive EDI data? Which programming languages are used to generate that data, and what standards do they employ? How often is that data translated from one language to another?

And with what degree of accuracy? Jerry must look for ways to improve the system's efficiency, and draft a plan to implement every change he proposes. In fact, in many cases Jerry will also be the project manager seeing that the improvements are implemented, which can often include rolling up his sleeves and digging into the coding just like the other members of his team.

"It takes an enormous amount of organization," observes Jerry. "But being a perfectionist, organization is something I've never lacked. This work suits me perfectly."

Evaluation

Is the system working? How well is it meeting the original requirements, benefits, and budgets? Out of such **evaluation** will come adjustments that will improve the system. Approaches to evaluation vary. Sometimes the systems analyst and someone from the client organization evaluate the system according to preset criteria that are directly related to the requirements that were determined during the systems analysis phase. Some organizations prefer to bring in an independent evaluating team, on the assumption that independent members will be free from bias and expectations.

Maintenance

Many consider maintenance to be a separate phase, one that begins only when the initial system effort is implemented and complete. In any case, **maintenance** is an ongoing activity, one that lasts the lifetime of the system. Monitoring must take place and necessary adjustments must be made if the system is to continue to produce the expected results. Maintenance tasks also include making revisions and additions to the computer system.

The maintenance task poses interesting problems for programmers. New programmers, fresh from school, may have written only new programs to submit for academic credit. Others have also written programs for their own purposes. But on the first job, they are likely to discover that their task is to make changes to programs written by others: maintenance. Some programmers like maintenance; in fact, sometimes a key programmer on development stays on the project to do maintenance, for both familiarity and job security reasons. Programmers who do not like maintenance must extricate themselves from each project as it nears completion and find a way to get on to the next new project. The systems analyst, by the way, has long since moved on to new projects.

▲

The proceeding discussion might leave the impression that by simply following a formula, you can develop a system. In fact, novice analysts often believe this to be true. Each system is unique, however, so no one formula can fit every project. It would be more correct to say that there are merely guidelines.

CHAPTER REVIEW

▶ Summary and Key Terms

- A **system** is an organized set of related components established to accomplish a certain task. A **computer system** has a computer as one of its components. A **client** requests a **systems analysis,** a study of an existing system, to determine how it works and how well it meets the needs of its **users,** who are usually employees and customers. Systems analysis can lead to **systems design,** the development of a plan for an improved system. A **systems analyst** normally does both the analysis and design. Some people do both programming and analysis and have the title **programmer/analyst.** The success of the project requires both impetus and authority within the client organization to change the current system.

- The systems analyst must be a **change agent** who encourages **user involvement** in the development of a new system.

- The systems analyst has three main functions: (1) **coordinating** schedules and task assignments, (2) **communicating** analysis and design information to those involved with the system, and (3) **planning and designing** the system with the help of the client organization. A systems analyst should have an analytical mind, good communication skills, self-discipline and self-direction, good organizational skills, creativity, and the ability to work without tangible results.

- The **systems development life cycle** (**SDLC**) can be described in five phases: (1) preliminary investigation, (2) analysis, (3) design, (4) development, and (5) implementation.

- Phase 1, the **preliminary investigation,** also known as the **feasibility study** or **system survey,** is the initial consideration of the problem to determine how—and whether—an analysis and design project should proceed. Aware of the importance of establishing a smooth working relationship, the analyst refers to an **organization chart** showing the lines of authority within the client organization. After determining the **nature of the problem** and its **scope,** the analyst expresses the users' needs as **objectives.**

- In phase 2, **systems analysis,** the analyst gathers and analyzes data from common sources such as written documents, interviews, questionnaires, observation, and sampling.

- The analyst must evaluate the relevance of **written documents,** such as procedure manuals and reports. **Interview** options include the **structured interview,** in which all questions are planned and written in advance, and the **unstructured interview,** in which the questions can vary from the plan. **Questionnaires** can save time and expense and allow anonymous answers, but response rates are often low. Another method is simply observing how the organization functions, sometimes through **participant observation,** which is temporary participation in the organization's activities. Statistical **sampling** is also useful, especially when there is a large volume of data.

- The systems analyst may use a variety of charts and diagrams to analyze the data. A **data flow diagram** (**DFD**) provides an easy-to-follow picture of the flow of data through the system. Another common tool for data analysis is the **decision table,** a standard table indicating alternative actions under particular conditions.

- The analysis phase also includes preparation of **system requirements,** a detailed list of the things the system must be able to do.

- Upon completion of the systems analysis phase, the analyst submits to the client a report that includes the current system's problems and requirements, a cost analysis, and recommendations about what course to take next.

- In phase 3, **systems design,** the analyst submits a general **preliminary design** for the client's approval before proceeding to the specific **detail design.**

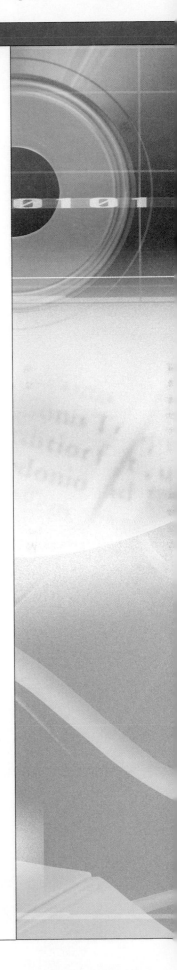

- Preliminary design begins with reviewing the system requirements, followed by the **make or buy decision** (perhaps with purchased software to be **customized** for the client), **outsourcing** to an outside firm, or in-house development with, perhaps, alternative **candidates.** The analyst presents the plan in a form the users can understand.

- The analyst may also develop a **prototype,** a limited working system or part of a system that gives users a preview of how the new system will work.

- **Computer-aided software engineering** (**CASE**) software tools can be used to automate some or all of the system development tasks.

- Detail design normally involves considering the parts of the system in the following order: output requirements, input requirements, files and databases, systems processing, and systems controls and backup.

- **Output requirements** include the medium of the output, the type of reports needed, the contents of the output, and the forms on which the output will be printed. The analyst might determine the report format by using a **printer spacing chart,** which shows the position of headings, columns, dates, and page numbers.

- **Input requirements** include the input medium, the content of the input, and the design of data entry forms. The analyst also plans an input validation process for checking whether the data is reasonable, and the analyst makes sure that the system can handle variations in input volume.

- The organization of files and databases must be specified. Systems processing must also be described, perhaps by using a **systems flowchart** that uses ANSI flowchart symbols to illustrate the flow of data or by using the hierarchical organization of a structure chart.

- The analyst must also spell out systems controls and backup. Data input to online systems must be backed up by **system journals,** files that record transactions made at the terminal. Processing controls involve data validation procedures. Finally, copies of transaction and master files should be made regularly.

- Phase 4, systems development, consists of scheduling, programming, and testing. Schedule deadlines and milestones are often shown on a **Gantt chart. Project management software** allocates people and resources, monitors schedules, and produces status reports.

- The programming effort involves selecting the program language and developing the program design specifications. Programmers then do **unit testing** (individual testing of their own programs), which is followed by **system testing** (assessing how the programs work together). **Volume testing** tests the entire system with real data. Documentation of phase 4 describes the program logic and the detailed data formats.

- Phase 5, **implementation,** includes **training** to prepare users of the new system; **equipment conversion,** which involves ensuring compatibility and providing enough space and electrical capacity; **file conversion** to make old files accessible to the new system; system conversion; the design of an **audit trail** to trace data from output back to the source documents; **evaluation,** the assessment of system performance; and **maintenance,** the monitoring and adjustment of the system.

- **System conversion** may be done in one of four ways: **direct conversion,** immediately replacing the old system with the new system; **phased conversion,** easing in the new system a step at a time; **pilot conversion,** testing the entire system with a few users and extending it to the rest when it proves successful; and **parallel conversion,** operating the old and new systems concurrently until the new system is proved successful.

▶ Critical Thinking Questions

1. Which qualities of a systems analyst do you consider to be the most important?

2. Would the following most likely be good projects for acquisition by purchase, for outsourcing, or for in-house development?
   a. An inventory control system for a pizza franchise
   b. A payroll system for a small retailer
   c. A system to network and provide basic software offerings for 13 office personal computers
   d. A system to draw airplane galley installation diagrams for an airline manufacturer
   e. A system to process market research data gathered for new toys to be produced by the country's largest toy manufacturer
   f. A system to permit networked artists to collaborate by computer on artistic ventures
   g. A system to manage patient appointments, dental records, and billing for a clinic with four dentists
   h. A system to track traffic tickets issued by the state highway patrol and convey this information to the state drivers' licensing agency
   i. A system to perform automated check writing and expense tracking for a funeral home
   j. A system to install a terminal in the field office of each franchisee, to be connected to the central headquarters of a truck rental company for the purpose of tracking truck locations

3. System evaluation can be done by the analyst and client organization or by an independent evaluating team. Discuss the strengths and weaknesses of each approach.

▶ STUDENT STUDY GUIDE

Multiple Choice

1. Testing of each individual program or module is called
   a. program testing
   b. system testing
   c. volume testing
   d. unit testing

2. The preliminary investigation of a systems project is also called a(n)
   a. analysis survey
   b. feasibility study
   c. systems design
   d. evaluation

3. The people who will have contact with the system, such as employees and customers, are referred to as
   a. programmers
   b. users
   c. systems analysts
   d. clients

4. The SDLC consists of
   a. two phases
   b. three phases
   c. four phases
   d. five phases

5. Phase 1 of a systems project involves
   a. a system survey
   b. a systems analysis
   c. data gathering
   d. questionnaires

6. The person who fills the role of change agent is the
   a. systems user
   b. administrator
   c. systems analyst
   d. client

7. The scope and true nature of the problem are determined during
   a. systems design
   b. systems development
   c. preliminary investigation
   d. systems analysis

8. A chart of positions and departments within an organization is a(n)
   a. data flow diagram
   b. organization chart
   c. project management report
   d. Gantt chart

9. Testing the system with large quantities of real data is called
   a. unit testing
   b. system testing
   c. parallel testing
   d. volume testing

10. In the course of a systems project, systems design
    a. follows systems analysis
    b. precedes systems analysis
    c. follows development
    d. is the fourth phase

True/False

T   F   1. Systems analysis is the process of developing a plan for an approved system.

T   F   2. Users are people who will have contact with the new system.

T   F   3. A systems analyst normally performs analysis and design.

T   F   4. Documentation is the least important aspect of a systems project.

T   F   5. A feasibility study needs to be conducted after data gathering.

T   F   6. Questionnaires are usually a more expensive form of data gathering than are interviews.

T   F   7. An organization chart shows the flow of data through an organization.

T   F   8. A decision table can help to ensure that no alternative is overlooked.

T   F   9. In some cases it is possible to acquire a new system by purchasing it.

T   F   10. Input requirements should be considered before considering output requirements.

Fill-In

1. The process that evaluates a currently existing system to determine how it works and how it meets user needs is called _____.

2. List the three principal functions of a systems analyst:
   a. _____
   b. _____
   c. _____

3. The data analysis tool used to illustrate information flow within a system is the _____.

4. As related to data, the two major steps of the systems analysis phase are
   a. _____
   b. _____

5. The overall name for the five phases involved in developing a new project is the _____.

6. The person or organization that contracts to have a system analysis done is called the _____.

7. _____ tools can be used to automate one or more of the tasks in the systems development process.

8. The type of interview that permits variation from planned questions is the _____ interview.

9. Because a systems analyst brings change to an organization, the analyst is often referred to as a(n) _____.

10. The by-product of understanding the system in the systems analysis phase is _____.

► ANSWERS

Multiple Choice

1. d	4. d	7. c	10. a
2. b	5. a	8. b	
3. b	6. c	9. d	

True/False

1. F	4. F	7. F	10. F
2. T	5. F	8. T	
3. T	6. F	9. T	

Fill-In

1. systems analysis
2. a. coordination
   b. communication
   c. planning and design
3. data flow diagram
4. a. data gathering
   b. data analysis
5. systems development life cycle (SDLC)
6. client
7. computer-aided software engineering (CASE)
8. unstructured
9. change agent
10. system requirements

Planet Internet

Career So Near

Many people, whether college students or experienced employees, dread the prospect of facing the world and begging for a job. Resources for this onerous task used to be limited to classified ads and perhaps a placement center. In recent years the Internet has expanded the job options available to include the world. A number of services specialize in matching employers with job seekers. Although assistance is available for first-time job seekers, and some sites even specialize in helping college students, it would be fair to say that many jobs posted on the Internet lean toward experienced people in the computer field.

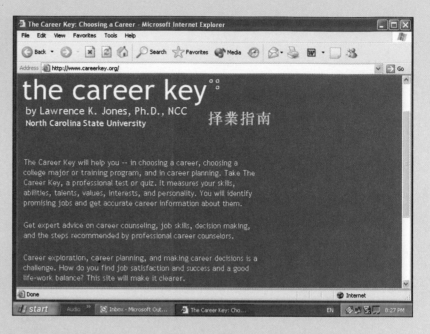

I'm a Student. What Can I Do?

You could start with Ask the Head-hunter, which provides interesting job-search tips. Job Trak and Monster.com are among the largest online job listing services in the United States and offer a wide variety of services. Earthlink's Dice.com focuses on computer-related jobs. These sites and others like them have one thing in common: They all promote their list of job seekers to employers. This is their profit center. For a fee an employer can search the site's database of job candidates.

The database search can be narrowed by using keywords that represent job titles or particular skills required. This connection between employer and job seeker is much speedier and more efficient than the traditional shuffling of piles of resumes.

Should I Put My Résumé on My Web Page?

Some job seekers have taken advantage of Web exposure by developing their own home page résumés. This goes so far beyond the traditional résumé that a new name should be invented for it. Typically, the candidate includes a nice photo and then offers perhaps a 10-to-15 line résumé. Why so short? Each résumé line has links!

For example, one line might refer to classes taken, with classes being a link. A potential employer merely clicks on the word "classes" to pop up a list of classes the job seeker has taken. Similarly, links can be made to intern work, laboratory assignments, extracurricular activities, work experience, special skills, and so forth. A person developing such a home page from scratch can make the résumé as varied as desired. Some schools permit students to post résumés on the school site for a limited time. Most career advice sites recommend having a file of the "traditional" paper version of your résumé available for easy printing from your page as well.

There are a few dozen sites devoted exclusively to résumés. They usually offer, among other things, tips on résumé writing. Other sites feature a résumé service as one of many options, allowing you to post your résumé on their sites. In fact, why not search the Web for résumés by other people in your chosen field to examine how theirs are constructed? It might help to see the way others put information into their résumé.

Many companies and government agencies now allow you to apply for positions by submitting your résumé to their site or by completing a web-based application form.

Where Else Can I Look for Jobs on the Web?

You can browse the Web pages of professional organizations in your field of study. Many of these sites will list current job openings and may help to give you some idea of the qualifications sought.

Don't forget to check out the Web pages of potential employers. Many companies have listings of current openings, and if you do get an interview, you may be able to use the information you gleaned from the company's page to impress the interviewer with your interest in and knowledge of their business. Be prepared for the question "Have you seen our Web page?"

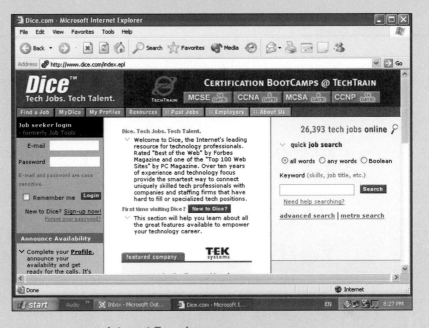

Internet Exercises

1. **Structured exercise.** Go to http://prenhall.com/capron and check out the Career Guidance Center Web site. What features are available on this Web site? What information does it have about employment trends in your field of interest?

2. **Free-form exercise.** Go to a portal such as Yahoo! or Netscape. What career-related services are available? Write a review for your classmates.

3. **Advanced exercise.** Using information provided on one or more résumé writing Web sites, write and post your résumé to the Web. If you have already done so, help a classmate, friend, or family member to write an Internet résumé, post it, and/or apply for a job online.

Programming and Languages:
Telling the Computer What to Do

CHAPTER 15

LEARNING OBJECTIVES

Describe what programmers do and do not do

Explain how programmers define a problem, plan the solution, and then code, test, and document the program

List and describe the levels of programming languages: machine, assembly, high level, very high level, and natural

Describe the major programming languages that are in use today

Explain the concepts of object-oriented programming

Roberta Matnick and Sean O'Connor met as freshmen at Oregon State University in an introductory business class. They became fast friends when they discovered that they were both majoring in accounting. The next semester, they signed up for an introductory computer course to get a good foundation in computer technology and, in particular, to become proficient in the use of spreadsheets.

After studying what programmers do, however, Roberta recalled her rusty BASIC programming from high school and decided to take a closer look. She signed up for a learn-at-your-own-pace lab course in BASIC programming. From there she gravitated to the computer science department, where she studied more programming languages and took a variety of theoretical courses. Roberta eventually decided on a computer science major but minored in accounting. Sean was not as taken with computers, particularly with the details of programming, and he remained an accounting major.

After graduation they found jobs in their respective fields. Their paths crossed again by chance seven years later when they began attending an evening M.B.A. program at a private university. Both accounting skills and computer skills were needed for various projects in the program. Roberta and Sean were able to help each other by contributing specific expertise. In particular, Sean came to appreciate the care and precision needed to write a computer program.

► WHY PROGRAMMING?

You have probably already used software, perhaps for word processing to create reports, or spreadsheets to solve problems. Software also enables you to surf the Web, download and listen to music, and play computer games. A **program** (another name for software) is a set of detailed, step-by-step instructions that directs the computer to do what you want it to do. Programs are written in a **programming language**—a set of rules that provides a way of telling the computer what operations to perform. A programmer can choose from many programming languages. The major languages are described on the following pages.

In this chapter, you learn about controlling the computer through the process of programming. Creating a program is a complex process. You will not be a programmer when you finish studying this chapter or even when you complete the final chapter. Programming proficiency requires practice and training that are beyond the scope of this book. However, you will learn about the processes that programmers follow to develop solutions to a variety of problems.

► WHAT PROGRAMMERS DO

In general, the programmer's job is to convert problem solutions into instructions for the computer. That is, the programmer prepares the instructions that make up a program, runs the instructions on the computer to see whether they produce the correct results, makes any necessary corrections, and then writes a report on the program. These activities are all done to help a user fill a need, such as paying employees, tracking customer orders, or registering students in classes.

Programmers are typically required to interact with a variety of people. Because many programs are one of several that make up a system, a programmer must coordinate with other programmers to make sure that all the programs in the system work together seamlessly. As a programmer, you might also coordinate with users, managers, and systems analysts as you all work together to complete a project.

► THE PROGRAMMING PROCESS

The process of developing a program is similar to any problem-solving task. There are five main steps in the programming process: (1) defining the problem, (2) planning the solution, (3) coding the program, (4) testing the program, and (5) documenting the program. We will discuss each of these in turn.

Defining the Problem

In some organizations, programmers receive a set of specifications from a systems analyst. In others, the programmers meet directly with users to analyze the problem and determine the users' needs. In either case, the task of problem definition involves determining what it is you know (input—the data given) and what it is you want to obtain (output—the results). Eventually, you produce a written agreement that specifies, in detail, the input data, the required output, and the processing required to convert the input into the output. This is not a simple process.

Planning the Solution

The next step is to design an **algorithm**, a detailed, step-by-step solution to the problem. There are a number of design tools that a programmer can use to develop the algorithm. Flowcharting and pseudocode are two of the most common. A **flowchart** is a pictorial representation of the solution algorithm. Symbols are used to represent actions, and arrows indicate the sequence in which the actions take place. Differently shaped symbols indicate different types of actions. The American National Standards Institute (ANSI) has developed a standard set of flowchart symbols. Figure 15-1 shows the symbols and how they might be used to represent a simple flowchart of a common everyday act, such as preparing a letter for mailing. Flowcharts can be awkward to create and modify. Few programmers use them for planning purposes, but they are useful as a visual representation of the problem-solving process.

Pseudocode, sometimes called structured English, is a nonstandard English-like language that lets you specify your algorithm with more precision than you can in

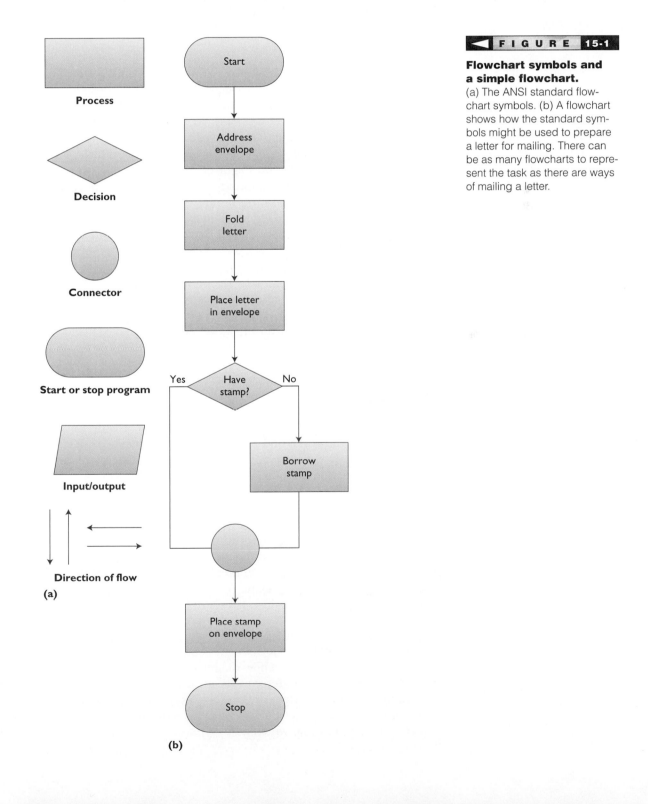

(a)

(b)

◄ **F I G U R E** **15-1**

Flowchart symbols and a simple flowchart.
(a) The ANSI standard flowchart symbols. (b) A flowchart shows how the standard symbols might be used to prepare a letter for mailing. There can be as many flowcharts to represent the task as there are ways of mailing a letter.

Easter Eggs

In the context of software—never mind the chocolate bunny stuff—an Easter Egg is a hidden feature or novelty that a programmer has added to software. This can be anything from a hidden list of the developers, to hidden commands, to jokes, to funny animations.

An amazing number of software packages have Easter Eggs; it would be safe to say that almost all have contained Eggs at one time or another. A true Egg must satisfy these criteria:

● It is undocumented and not a legitimate feature of the software.

● Given the instructions, anyone can reproduce the Egg.

● It must have been put there by programmers.

● It must be nondestructive.

Many Eggs are mildly entertaining. You may be able to produce Yogi Bear as follows: In America Online, type "box" as a keyword. Now, also as a keyword, type a cartoon character's name backwards, in this case "igoy." Will this Egg still work when you read this? Maybe, maybe not. Software manufacturers get word of Eggs and often remove them. Check the Easter Egg Archive site (www.eeggs.com) for new additions.

plain English but with less precision than is required with a formal programming language. Pseudocode allows you to focus on the program logic without worrying about the detailed rules of a particular programming language. However, pseudocode must eventually be converted to a programming language; it cannot be executed on the computer.

After completing the algorithm design, the programmer should perform a process called **desk-checking.** This involves sitting down with pencil and paper and "playing computer" by carrying out each step of the algorithm in the indicated sequence to verify that it produces the desired results. Some organizations formalize this process as a structured walkthrough, in which a programmer's peers review the algorithm design to verify its correctness.

Coding the Program

This step involves translating the algorithm from pseudocode, flowchart, or other planning tool into a formal programming language. Many programming languages are available: Visual Basic, C, C++, and Java are some examples. The different types of languages are discussed in detail later in this chapter.

Just as in human languages, programming languages have grammatical rules, or **syntax.** However, although you might be able to use poor grammar in English and still be understood by others, a program with even a minor syntax error will be rejected by the computer. The programmer must, therefore, have a detailed understanding of the syntax of the language used. Of course, using the language correctly is no guarantee that your program will work, any more than speaking grammatically correct English means that you know what you are talking about. The point is that correct use of the language is just the required first step.

The program is then keyed into the computer by using a text editor, a program that is similar to a word processor. In most current computer languages the text editor is part of a comprehensive package called an **integrated development environment (IDE)** that also includes translation and debugging software. Experienced programmers usually type their code directly into the editor, but as a beginner, you will probably want to write your code on paper first.

Testing the Program

In theory, a well-designed program can be written correctly the first time. However, this is an imperfect world, and programmers get used to the idea that newly written programs are likely to contain at least a few errors. Therefore, after coding the program, you must prepare to test it on the computer. This step involves these two phases:

TRANSLATION   The purpose of the translation phase is to convert the program from the programming language you used into the actual binary instructions that the CPU understands. Most commonly, this is done by a **compiler,** a system program that translates your program, called the **source module,** into a machine language version called an **object module.** If the compiler detects any **syntax errors** (violation of the language rules), it produces diagnostic messages describing those errors. For instance, if in C you forget to enter a semicolon at the end of a statement, the compiler responds, "Missing semicolon." Whereas older languages, such as COBOL and FORTRAN, produce a separate printed diagnostic report, current programming environments show diagnostic messages in an area of the screen below your program code. After you fix all the syntax errors, your object module is submitted to another system program called a **linkage editor** (or just **linker**). The linker combines the object module with prewritten modules from a system library to create a **load module,** which can be executed by the computer. This process is shown in Figure 15-2.

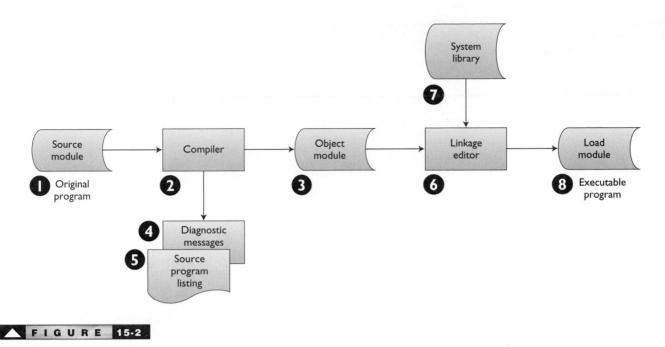

▲ **FIGURE** **15-2**

Preparing a program for execution. An original program, (1) the source module, is translated by (2) the compiler into (3) an object module, which represents the program in a form the machine can understand. The compiler may produce (4) diagnostic messages, indicating syntax errors. (5) A listing of the source program may also be output from the compiler. After the program successfully compiles, the (6) linkage editor links the object module with (7) system library modules as needed, and the result is (8) a load module, or executable program.

DEBUGGING   Next, you must run your program using carefully selected test data to determine whether it produces the correct results. Incorrect results indicate the presence of one or more **logic errors.** Programmers call these errors "bugs," and the process of locating and correcting them is referred to as **debugging** the program. A logic error could be as simple as typing a minus sign instead of a plus sign in a calculation or as complex as failing to provide an exit from a repeating group of instructions.

Documenting the Program

Although documenting the program appears as the last step in the programming process, it is actually performed throughout the entire process. Documentation consists of material generated during each step. The detailed problem definition, the program plan (flowchart or pseudocode), comments within the source program, and testing procedures are all part of the documentation package that is developed at this point. Other items in the package include a narrative description of the program, detailed layouts of input and output records, and a program listing.

► LEVELS OF LANGUAGES

Before looking at specific programming languages, we need to discuss the levels of languages. Languages are said to be "lower" or "higher," depending on how close they are to the language the computer itself uses (0s and 1s—low) or to the language people use (more English-like—high). Languages are generally divided into five levels, or generations, each containing improvements in ease of use and capabilities over the previous generation. The five generations are (1) machine language, (2) assembly languages, (3) high-level languages, (4) very high-level languages, and (5) natural languages.

There is a shortage of qualified personnel in the computer field, but paradoxically, there are many people at the front end trying to get entry-level programming jobs. Before you join their ranks, consider the advantages of the computer field and what it takes to succeed in it.

- **The joys of the field.** Although many people make career changes that take them into the computer field, few choose to leave it. In fact, surveys of computer professionals, especially programmers, consistently report a high level of job satisfaction. There are several reasons for this contentment. One is the challenge; most jobs in the computer industry are not routine. Another is security: Established computer professionals can usually find work, as long as they keep their skills up to date. And that work pays well—you should certainly be comfortable and, if you should happen to be part of an organization that offers stock options to all employees, possibly very comfortable. The computer industry has historically been a rewarding place for women and minorities. And finally, the industry holds endless fascination, since it is always changing.

- **What it takes.** Although some people buy a book and teach themselves a programming language, this is unlikely to lead to a job. You need some credentials, most often a two- or four-year degree in computer information systems or computer science. (Note that this degree will require math and science courses.) The requirements and salaries vary by the organization and the region, so we will not dwell on these here. Beyond that, the person

who is most likely to land a job and move up the career ladder is one with excellent communication skills, both oral and written. These are also the qualities that potential employers can observe in an interview. Promotions are sometimes tied to advanced degrees (for example, an M.B.A. or an M.S. in computer science).

- **Open doors.** The overall outlook for the computer field is promising. According to the Bureau of Labor Statistics, computer-related occupations occupy eight of the top ten positions in the list of high-growth jobs through 2010. The number of application software developers is expected to increase by more than 95 percent, while the number of systems analysts required will grow by 60 percent. The reasons for the continued job increase in the computer field are more computers, more applications of computers, and more computer users.

Traditionally, career progression in the computer field was along a path from programmer to systems analyst to project manager. This is still a typical direction, but it is complicated by the many options open to computer professionals. Computer professionals sometimes specialize in some aspect of the industry, such as communications, database management, personal computers, graphics, or, most especially, the Internet. Others may specialize in the computer-related aspects of a particular industry, such as banking or insurance. Still others strike out on their own, becoming consultants or entrepreneurs.

Machine Language

Ultimately, the computer understands only binary numbers—strings of 0s and 1s. Programs that are written in these 0s and 1s, representing the on and off electrical states of the computer, are in the actual **machine language.** All other languages must be translated into machine language before execution (Figure 15-3). Each type of computer has its own unique machine language. Primitive by today's standards, machine language programs are difficult for people to read and use. Although machine language was the only option for early programmers, the industry moved quickly to develop the next generation: assembly languages.

Assembly Languages

Today, **assembly languages** are considered very low level—that is, they are not as convenient for people to use as more recent languages. At the time they were developed, however, they were considered a great leap forward. To replace the 0s and 1s of machine language, assembly languages use mnemonic codes, abbreviations that are easy to remember: A for add, C for compare, MP for multiply, STO for storing information in memory, and so on. Furthermore, assembly languages permit the use of names—perhaps RATE or TOTAL—for memory locations, instead of the actual binary memory addresses. As with machine language, each type of computer has its own unique assembly language.

Because machine language is the only language the computer can actually execute, a translation program, called an **assembler,** is required to convert the assembly language program into machine language. Although assembly language is much easier than machine language, it still requires a detailed knowledge of the computer hardware and is tedious to use.

High-Level Languages

The first widespread use of **high-level languages** in the early 1960s transformed programming into something quite different from what it had been. Programmers no longer had to have detailed knowledge of the computer hardware; they could focus their efforts on solving problems. Languages were designed for specific types of problems and used syntax that was familiar to people working with those problems. For example, statements in FORTRAN, a language designed to solve mathematical problems, look very much like the formulas that mathematicians and engineers work with all the time. COBOL, by contrast, was designed to solve business problems and used commands and operations that were familiar to business people. As a result, programmers became much more productive, and programs could now direct much more complex tasks.

Of course, a translator is needed to translate the symbolic statements of a high-level language into executable machine language; this translator is usually a compiler. For any given high-level language, there are usually a number of compilers available, each of which translates a program in that language to the machine language for a specific type of computer.

Very High-Level Languages

Languages called **very high-level languages** are often known by their generation number; that is, they are called **fourth-generation languages** or, more simply, **4GLs.** Languages belonging to the first three generations are **procedural languages,** consisting of instructions that describe the step-by-step procedure to solve the problem. 4GLs are **nonprocedural languages.** In a 4GL program, the programmer specifies the desired results, and the language develops the solution. There are many different 4GLs; in contrast to high-level languages, most are available only from a single vendor.

Most experts say that the average productivity improvement factor is about 10; that is, you can be 10 times more productive using a 4GL than a third-generation language. Consider this request: Produce a report showing the total units sold for each product, by customer, in each month and year, with a subtotal for each customer. In addition, the output for each customer must start on a new page. A 4GL request looks something like this:

        TABLE FILE SALES

        SUM UNITS BY MONTH BY CUSTOMER BY PRODUCT

        ON CUSTOMER SUBTOTAL PAGE BREAK

        END

Even though some training is required to do even this much, you can see that it is pretty simple. The third-generation language COBOL typically requires more than 500 statements to fulfill the same request. It would be naive, however, to assume that all programs should be written using 4GLs; a third-generation language makes more sense for commercial applications that require a high degree of precision.

FD	71	431F	4153
F3	63	4267	4321
96	F0	426D	
F9	10	41F3	438A
47	40	40DA	
47	F0	4050	

▲ **FIGURE** **15-3**

Machine language. True machine language is all binary—only 0s and 1s—but because an example would take too much space here, we are showing an example of machine language in the hexadecimal (base 16) numbering system. (The letters A through F in hexadecimal represent the numbers 10 through 15 in the decimal system.) The computer commands shown, taken from machine language for an IBM mainframe computer, are operation codes instructing the computer to divide two numbers, compare the quotient, move the result into the output area of the system, and set up the result so that it can be printed.

Query languages are variations on 4GLs and are used to retrieve information from databases. Data is usually added to databases according to a plan, and planned reports may also be produced. But what about a user who needs an unscheduled report or a report that differs somehow from the standard reports? A user can learn a query language fairly easily and then request and receive the resulting report on his or her own terminal or personal computer.

Natural Languages

The fifth generation of languages is even more ill-defined than fourth-generation languages. They are most often called **natural languages** because of their resemblance to the "natural" spoken or written English language: That is, they resemble the way most people speak and write. A user of one of these languages can phrase a request for information in any number of ways. For example, "Get me tennis racquet sales for January" works just as well as "I want January tennis racquet revenue." The natural language translates human instructions into code the computer can execute. If it does not understand the user's request, it politely asks for further explanation. Natural languages are most commonly used by nonprogrammers to access data stored in databases. Natural language development is discussed in more detail in the section on artificial intelligence in the appendix.

▶ CHOOSING A LANGUAGE

How do you choose the language with which to write your program? In the business environment, the choice is often made for you. Most information systems organizations support a limited number of languages and determine which language will be used on each project. The choice of language might be based on the requirement to allow project programs to interface with existing applications in that language or on the necessity to execute the programs on various types of computers. Many companies hire programmers on the basis of their proficiency in the language(s) that company uses.

If you are planning on developing the next killer application on your own, or just want to write a few simple programs for personal use, you will probably choose the language you are most familiar with or that fits the program's requirements best.

▶ MAJOR PROGRAMMING LANGUAGES

The following sections on individual languages give you an overview of some third-generation languages that are in use today: FORTRAN, COBOL, BASIC, RPG, Visual Basic, C, C++, and Java. You will see a program written in each of these languages, as well as the output produced by each program. Each program is designed to accept a series of numbers entered by the operator, then compute and display the average of

The First Bug Was Real

It is a bit of a surprise to find that the software you are using does not always work quite right. Or perhaps the programmer who is doing some work for you cannot seem to get the program to work correctly. Both problems are "bugs," errors that were introduced unintentionally into a program when it was written.

The term *bug* comes from an experience in the early days of computing. One summer day in 1945, according to computer pioneer Grace M. Hopper, the Mark I computer came to a halt. Working to find the problem, computer personnel found a moth inside the machine. They removed the offending bug, and the computer was fine. The photo shows the actual logbook entry with the moth taped to the page. From that day forward, any mysterious problem or glitch was said to be a bug.

---

these numbers. Because all the programs perform the same task, you will see some of the similarities and differences among the languages. You are not expected to understand these programs; they are here just to give you a glimpse of each language. Figure 15-4 illustrates the program's logic using both a flowchart and pseudocode.

FORTRAN: The First High-Level Language

Developed by IBM and introduced in 1954, **FORTRAN**—which stands for FORmula TRANslator—was the first high-level language. FORTRAN is a scientifically oriented language; in the early days, the computer was used primarily for engineering, mathematical, and scientific tasks. As its name indicates, FORTRAN is very good at representing complex mathematical formulas. Most experienced engineers and scientists learned FORTRAN in college, and over the years many scientific and engineering applications have been written in FORTRAN. However C, C++, or Java have replaced FORTRAN as the languages used in most universities, and very little, if any, new application development is being done in FORTRAN. Figure 15-5 shows a FORTRAN program and its sample output.

COBOL: The Language of Business

By the mid-1950s, FORTRAN was in common use, but there was still no widely accepted high-level language for business applications. The U.S. Department of Defense in particular was interested in creating such a standardized language and called together a committee that, in 1959, introduced **COBOL,** which stands for COmmon Business-Oriented Language.

In keeping with business programming requirements, COBOL is very good for processing large, complex data files and for producing well-formatted business reports. COBOL is English-like; even if you know nothing about programming, you may still be able to follow a COBOL program's logic. This English-like appearance and easy readability are both its greatest strength and its greatest weakness. COBOL is widely disliked for its verbosity, but given most programmers' aversion to documenting their code, its understandability is a great plus. See Figure 15-6 for the sample COBOL program.

BASIC: The Beginner's Language

BASIC, which stands for Beginners' All-purpose Symbolic Instruction Code, was originally developed by Dartmouth professors John Kemeny and Thomas Kurtz in 1965 to teach programming to their students. With the introduction of the microcomputer in the late 1970s, the popularity of BASIC increased dramatically, owing to its two main characteristics: First, it is easy to learn, which allowed those early microcomputer buyers to write their own software. Second, the translator program that converts BASIC code into machine language takes very little primary memory, allowing it to fit on those early machines, which often had no more than 16K of memory. As microcomputers have become more powerful and capable of supporting more advanced languages, BASIC has all but disappeared. An enhanced version, Visual Basic, is described later in this chapter. The BASIC version of our sample program is shown in Figure 15-7.

RPG: Report Generation and More

RPG, which stands for Report Program Generator, was developed by IBM in 1965 to allow rapid creation of reports from data stored in the computer files. A predecessor of 4GLs, it allowed the programmer to simply describe the source data and the desired report format; then it created a program to produce the report. A complex report could be created much more quickly with RPG than with COBOL, the most

▶ F I G U R E **15-4**

Flowchart and pseudocode for averaging numbers. (a) This flowchart, along with (b) matching pseudocode, shows the logic for a program to let a user enter numbers through the keyboard; the program then averages the numbers. The user can make any number of entries, one at a time. To show when he or she is finished making entries, the user enters 999. The logic to enter the numbers forms a loop: entering the number, adding it to the sum, and adding 1 to the counter. When 999 is keyed, the loop is exited. Then the machine computes the average and displays it on the screen. This logic is used for the programs, in various languages, shown in Figures 15-5 through 15-11.

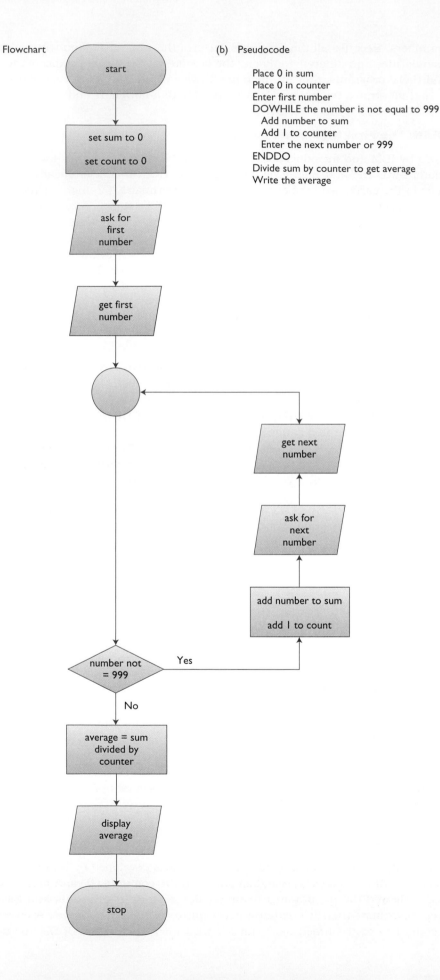

(a) Flowchart

start

set sum to 0

set count to 0

ask for
first
number

get first
number

get next
number

ask for
next
number

add number to sum

add 1 to count

number not
= 999   Yes

No

average = sum
divided by
counter

display
average

stop

(b) Pseudocode

```
Place 0 in sum
Place 0 in counter
Enter first number
DOWHILE the number is not equal to 999
   Add number to sum
   Add 1 to counter
   Enter the next number or 999
ENDDO
Divide sum by counter to get average
Write the average
```

```
C      FORTRAN PROGRAM
C      AVERAGING INTEGERS ENTERED THROUGH THE KEYBOARD
       WRITE (6,10)
       SUM = 0
       COUNTER = 0
       WRITE (6,60)
       READ (5,40) NUMBER
  1    IF (NUMBER .EQ. 999) GOTO 2
       SUM = SUM + NUMBER
       COUNTER = COUNTER + 1
       WRITE (6,70)
       READ (5,40) NUMBER
       GO TO 1
  2    AVERAGE = SUM / COUNTER
       WRITE (6,80) AVERAGE
 10    FORMAT (1X, 'THIS PROGRAM WILL FIND THE AVERAGE OF',
     * 'INTEGERS YOU ENTER ',/1X, 'THROUGH THE ',
     * 'KEYBOARD. TYPE 999 TO INDICATE END OF DATA.',/)
 40    FORMAT (13)
 60    FORMAT (1X, 'PLEASE ENTER A NUMBER ')
 70    FORMAT (1X, 'PLEASE ENTER THE NEXT NUMBER ')
 80    FORMAT (1X, 'THE AVERAGE OF THE NUMBERS IS ',F6.2)
       STOP
       END
```

(a)

```
THIS PROGRAM WILL FIND THE AVERAGE OF INTEGERS YOU ENTER
THROUGH THE KEYBOARD.  TYPE 999 TO INDICATE END OF DATA.
PLEASE ENTER A NUMBER    6
PLEASE ENTER THE NEXT NUMBER    4
PLEASE ENTER THE NEXT NUMBER    11
PLEASE ENTER THE NEXT NUMBER    999
THE AVERAGE OF THE NUMBERS IS    7.00
```

(b)

◀ **F I G U R E 15-5**

FORTRAN program and sample output. This program is interactive, prompting the user to supply data. (a) The first two lines are comments, as they are in the rest of the programs in this chapter. The WRITE statements send output to the screen in the format called for by the second numeral in the parentheses, which represents the line number containing the format. The READ statements accept data from the user and place it in location NUMBER, where it can be added to the accumulated total, SUM. The IF statement checks for 999 and, when 999 is received, diverts the program logic to statement 2, where the average is computed. The average is then displayed. (b) This screen display shows the interaction between program and user. The highlighted entries are the user's responses.

common business programming language of the day. Used in large installations as a supplement to COBOL, RPG became the primary language for IBM's midrange computers in following decades. IBM has been making continual improvements to RPG. The latest version, VisualAge RPG, includes the latest graphical user interface (GUI) development capabilities. Figure 15-8 shows the RPG version of our sample program.

Visual Basic

Microsoft introduced **Visual Basic** (often referred to as **VB**) in 1987 as its first visual development tool. It allows the programmer to easily create complex user interfaces containing standard Windows features, such as buttons, dialog boxes, scrollbars, and menus. Each of these features could take hundreds of lines of code to implement

▶ F I G U R E 15-6

COBOL program and sample output. The purpose of the program and its results are the same as those of the FORTRAN program, but (a) the look of the COBOL program is very different. Note the four divisions: Identification, Environment, Data, and Procedure. In particular, note that the logic in the Procedure Division uses a series of PERFORM statements, which divert action to other places in the program. After a prescribed action has been performed, the computer returns to the Procedure Division, to the statement after the one that was just completed. DISPLAY writes to the screen, and ACCEPT takes user input. (b) This screen display shows the interaction between program and user, with the user's responses highlighted.

```
***************************************************************
IDENTIFICATION DIVISION.
***************************************************************
PROGRAM-ID.  AVERAGE.
* COBOL PROGRAM
* AVERAGING INTEGERS ENTERED THROUGH THE KEYBOARD.
***************************************************************
ENVIRONMENT DIVISION.
***************************************************************
CONFIGURATION SECTION.
SOURCE-COMPUTER.            H-P 9000.
OBJECT-COMPUTER.            H-P 9000.
***************************************************************
DATA DIVISION.
***************************************************************
FILE SECTION.
WORKING-STORAGE SECTION.
01 AVERAGE        PIC ---9.99.
01 COUNTER        PIC 9(02)         VALUE ZERO.
01 NUMBER-ITEM    PIC S9(03).
01 SUM-ITEM       PIC S9(06)        VALUE ZERO.
01 BLANK-LINE     PIC X(80)         VALUE SPACES.
***************************************************************
PROCEDURE DIVISION.
***************************************************************
100-CONTROL-ROUTINE.
    PERFORM 200-DISPLAY-INSTRUCTIONS.
    PERFORM 300-INITIALIZATION-ROUTINE.
    PERFORM 400-ENTER-AND-ADD
            UNTIL NUMBER-ITEM = 999.
    PERFORM 500-CALCULATE-AVERAGE.
    PERFORM 600-DISPLAY-RESULTS.
    STOP RUN.
200-DISPLAY-INSTRUCTIONS.
    DISPLAY
      "THIS PROGRAM WILL FIND THE AVERAGE OF INTEGERS YOU ENTER".
    DISPLAY
      "THROUGH THE KEYBOARD. TYPE 999 TO INDICATE END OF DATA.".
    DISPLAY BLANK-LINE.
300-INITIALIZATION-ROUTINE.
    DISPLAY "PLEASE ENTER A NUMBER".
    ACCEPT NUMBER-ITEM.
400-ENTER-AND-ADD.
    ADD NUMBER-ITEM TO SUM-ITEM.
    ADD 1 TO COUNTER.
    DISPLAY "PLEASE ENTER THE NEXT NUMBER".
    ACCEPT NUMBER-ITEM.
500-CALCULATE-AVERAGE.
    DIVIDE SUM-ITEM BY COUNTER GIVING AVERAGE.
600-DISPLAY-RESULTS.
    DISPLAY "THE AVERAGE OF THE NUMBERS IS ",AVERAGE.
```

(a)

```
          THIS PROGRAM WILL FIND THE AVERAGE OF
          INTEGERS YOU ENTER THROUGH THE KEYBOARD.
          TYPE 999 TO INDICATE END OF DATA.

          PLEASE ENTER A NUMBER
          6
          PLEASE ENTER THE NEXT NUMBER
          4
          PLEASE ENTER THE NEXT NUMBER
          11
          PLEASE ENTER THE NEXT NUMBER
          999
          THE AVERAGE OF THE NUMBERS IS   7.00
```

(b)

```
'BASIC PROGRAM
'AVERAGING INTEGERS ENTERED THROUGH THE KEYBOARD
CLS
PRINT "THIS PROGRAM WILL FIND THE AVERAGE OF INTEGERS YOU ENTER"
PRINT "THROUGH THE KEYBOARD. TYPE 999 TO INDICATE END OF DATA."
PRINT
SUM=0
COUNTER=0
PRINT "PLEASE ENTER A NUMBER"
INPUT NUMBER
DO WHILE NUMBER <> 999
     SUM=SUM+NUMBER
     COUNTER=COUNTER+1
     PRINT "PLEASE ENTER THE NEXT NUMBER"
     INPUT NUMBER
LOOP
AVERAGE=SUM/COUNTER
PRINT "THE AVERAGE OF THE NUMBERS IS"; AVERAGE
END
```

(a)

▲ **F I G U R E   15-7**

BASIC program and sample output. (a) PRINT displays data right in the statement on the screen. INPUT accepts data from the user. (b) This screen display shows the interaction between program and user. The user's responses are highlighted.

```
THIS PROGRAM WILL FIND THE AVERAGE OF INTEGERS YOU ENTER
THROUGH THE KEYBOARD. TYPE 999 TO INDICATE END OF DATA.

PLEASE ENTER A NUMBER
?6
PLEASE ENTER THE NEXT NUMBER
?4
PLEASE ENTER THE NEXT NUMBER
?11
PLEASE ENTER THE NEXT NUMBER
?999
THE AVERAGE OF THE NUMBERS IS    7
```

(b)

in a language such as C, but they are included in a VB program by simply dragging an icon from a toolbar and dropping it in the desired screen location. VB automatically creates the code to respond to user manipulation—clicking a button or using the scrollbar, for example.

A major difference between Visual Basic and other popular programming languages is the way in which a user interacts with a program. With most programming languages, the program controls the user. The user can make an entry only when the program requests it. Visual Basic, by contrast, enables the user to control program execution. This type of program is referred to as being event-driven and is illustrated in the Visual Basic version of our averaging program (Figure 15-9). The programmer has only to write the code that Visual Basic activates when the user clicks the Compute Average button. All the code that creates the screen display and responds to the button click by activating the user's code is provided by Visual Basic. The ability to create user-friendly event-driven programs with attractive Windows-like interfaces quickly has resulted in Visual Basic becoming one of the most popular programming languages.

► **FIGURE** 15-8

RPG program and sample output. (a) The top portion of this program (lines beginning with A) describes the appearance of the input and output screens. The lower portion (lines beginning with D or C) contains the procedural code to accept the numbers and calculate the average. RPG is a positional language; the column in which an entry is made is critical. The RPG environment provides a text editor that assists the programmer in getting everything in the right columns. (b) This is the input screen. After entering a number where the dashes appear, the user would press the Enter key. An entry of 999 would produce (c) the screen showing the result. This program was written for the IBM AS400 midrange computer.

(a)
```
 * FILE:          QDDSSRC
 * MEMBER:        SCREEN
 * PURPOSE:       Prompt Screen for Three Numbers
 A                                         DSPSIZ(24 80 *DS3)
 A                                         PRINT
 A                                         INDARA
 A                                         HELP
 A           R SCREEN1
 A                                    1  2'IBM iSeries 400'
 A                                         COLOR(BLU)
 A                                    1 31'Three Number Prompt'
 A                                         DSPATR(HI)
 A                                    2  2'RPGLE'
 A                                         COLOR(BLU)
 A N99                                6 13'Enter a number from 1 to 998, or 9-
 A                                       99 to compute average:'
 A N99      NUMBER       3D 01 10 39DSPATR(HI)
 A N99                                     CHECK(RZ)
 A  99                               14 24'The average of numbers entered is:'
 A  99      AVERAGE      10 020 18 30EDTCDE(J)
 A  99                                     DSPATR(HI)
 A  99                               22 30'Press Enter to Exit'
 A  99                                     COLOR(BLU)


 * FILE:          QRPGLESRC
 * NUMBER:        NumPrompt
 * PURPOSE:       Prompt program for a three digit number
 * files
 FScreen    CF   E           WorkStn
 * declare standalones vaiables
 D Counter       S              5 0
 D Sum           S             10 0
 * Main Calcs - Start
 C              Exfmt     Screen1
 C              Dow       Number 999
 C              Eval      Sum = Sum + Number
 C              Eval      Counter = Counter + 1
 C              Exfmt     Screen1
 C              Enddo
 * Final Calcs - Start
 C              Eval      Average = Sum / Counter
 C              Eval      *In99 = *on
 C              Exfm      Screen1
 C              Eval      *InLR = *on
```

(b)
```
IBM iSeries 400                    Three Number Prompt
RPGLE



            Enter a number from 1 to 998, or 999 to compute average:
                                   --
```

(c)
```
IBM iSeries 400                    Three Number Prompt
RPGLE



                    The average of numbers entered is:

                                   7.00

                          Press Enter to Exit
```

```
'Visual Basic Program
'Averaging integers entered through the keyboard
Option Explicit
Dim intNumber As Integer
Dim intSum As Integer
Dim intCounter As Integer
Dim sngAverage As Single

Private Sub cmdAccept_Click()
    intNumber = Val(txtNum.Text)
    intSum = intSum + intNumber
    intCounter = intCounter + 1
    txtNum.Text = ""
    txtNum.SetFocus
End Sub

Private Sub cmdCompute_Click()
    sngAverage = intSum / intCounter
    lblResults.Caption = Format(sngAverage, "fixed")
    intSum = 0
    intCounter = 0
    txtNum.Text = ""
    txtNum.SetFocus
End Sub

Private Sub cmdExit_Click()
    End
End Sub
```

(a)

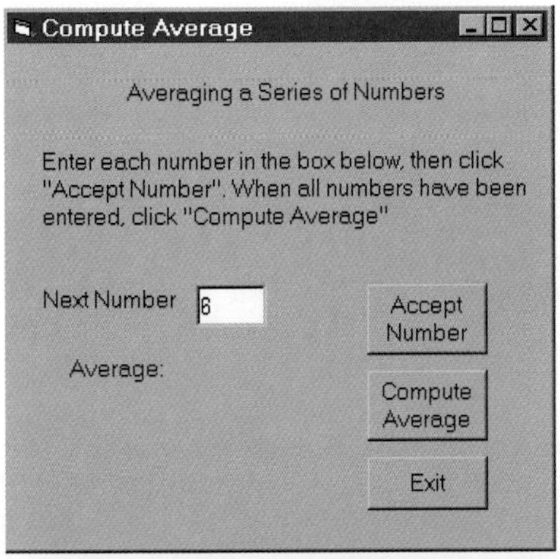

(b)

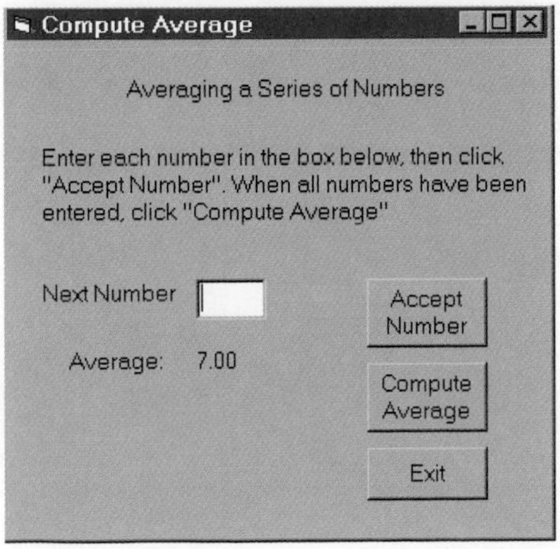

(c)

FIGURE 15-9

Visual Basic program and sample output. (a) Dim statements declare the variables used in this program. Visual Basic programs consist of a series of subroutines (Sub) that respond to user actions. This program has three; each is activated when the user clicks the corresponding button on the screen. The cmdAccept_Click subroutine converts the user's entry into a numeric value, adds it to the sum, and adds one to the counter. The cmdCompute_Click subroutine calculates the average, displays it, and resets the sum and counter to 0. The cmdExit_click subroutine ends the program. (b) This screen display shows the first value being entered. The user would then click the Accept Number button. Additional values would be entered, each followed by clicking the Accept Number button. (c) This screen display shows the result of clicking the Compute Average button after the three values (6, 4, and 11) have been entered.

C: A Portable Language

A language created by Dennis Ritchie at Bell Labs in 1972, **C** produces code that approaches assembly language in efficiency while still offering the features of a high-level language. C was originally designed to write systems software but is now considered a general-purpose language. One of C's primary advantages is its portability: There are C compilers for almost every combination of computer and operating system available today.

An interesting side note is that the availability of C on personal computers has greatly enhanced the value of personal computers for budding software entrepreneurs. Today C is fast being replaced by its enhanced cousin, C++, a language that will be discussed shortly. The C++ version of the averaging program is shown in Figure 15-10. The C equivalent would be very similar.

► **FIGURE 15-10**

C++ program and sample output. (a) The symbol // marks comment lines. All variable names, such as number, must be declared. The command cout sends output to the screen, and the command cin takes data from the user. (b) This screen display shows the interaction between program and user. The user's entries are highlighted.

```
// C++ PROGRAM
// AVERAGING INTEGERS ENTERED THROUGH THE KEYBOARD

#include <iostream.h>
main ()
{
  float average;
  int number, counter = 0; int sum = 0;
  cout << "THIS PROGRAM WILL FIND THE AVERAGE OF INTEGERS YOU ENTER \ n";
  cout << "THROUGH THE KEYBOARD.  TYPE 999 TO INDICATE END OF DATA. \ n";
  cout << "PLEASE ENTER A NUMBER";
  cin >> number;
  while (number !=999)
    {
      sum + = number;
      counter ++;
      cout << "\nPLEASE ENTER THE NEXT NUMBER";
      cin >> number;
    }
  average = sum / counter;
  cout << "\nTHE AVERAGE OF THE NUMBERS IS " << average
}
```

(a)

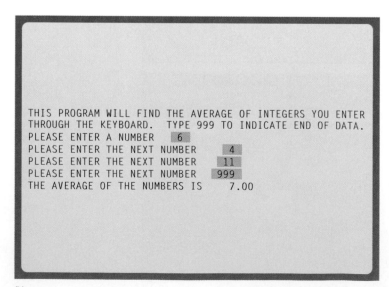

(b)

► JAVA

Programming languages rarely receive much media attention. But the language called **Java,** from developers at Sun Microsystems, has received continuous heavy coverage in the computer press, as well as frequent mention in the popular press. Java is a network-friendly programming language derived from C++ that permits a piece of software to run directly on many different platforms. A **platform** consists of a combination of hardware and operating system that provides the basic functionality of a computer. An example is the combination of some version of Microsoft's Windows operating system and Intel's processors, often referred to as the Wintel platform.

Programmers traditionally develop a program for a specific platform. They would have to recode the program completely for it to run on a different platform. But a programmer can write a program in Java, which operates across platforms, and have it run anywhere. So how does Java accomplish this cross-platform feat? Java programs are not compiled directly into machine language, but into an intermediate language called bytecode. This bytecode is then executed by a universal platform, called the Java Virtual Machine (JVM), which sits atop a computer's regular platform. Essentially, this universal platform is an extra layer of software that has been accepted as a standard by most of the computer industry—no small feat. The JVM translates compiled Java code into instructions that the platform underneath can understand. This extra layer of translation does result in some inefficiency, but the penalty is decreasing as the Java Virtual Machine matures. See Figure 15-11 for the Java version of our sample program.

When you consider that Java can run on many platforms, it is easy to see why it is relevant to Internet development; in fact, Java's earliest incarnations were in Web applications. Web pages can include Java miniprograms, called applets, which run on a Java platform included in the user's Web browser. These applets add all sorts of

(a)
```java
// Java Program
// Averaging integers entered through the keyboard
public class SumNumbers {
  public static void main(Stringt args[]) {
    int number, counter = 0, sum = 0;
    System.out.prntln("This program will find the average of integers you enter");
    System.out.println("through the keyboard. Type 999 to indicate end of data.");
    System.out.print("Please enter a number ");
    number = VCCinput.getInteger();
    while (entered !=999) {
      sum += number;
      counter++;
      System.out.print("Please enter the next number ");
      number = VCCinput.getInteger();
    }
    System.out.println("The average of the numbers is " + (double) sum / counter);
  } // end main method

} // end class SumNumbers
```

(b)
```
This program will find the average of integers you enter
through the keyboard. Type 999 to indicate end of data.
Please enter a number 6
Please enter the next number 4
Please enter the next number 11
Please enter the next number 999
The average of the numbers is 7.00
```

◄ **F I G U R E 15-11**

Java program and sample output. (a) System.out.print() and System.out.println() are Java's output methods that display data on the screen. The statement "sum += number" adds the value in the number variable to the value in the sum variable and the "counter++" statement increments the value in the counter variable by one. Accepting data from the keyboard is a complex process in Java; VCCinput.getinteger() is an installation-specific method that allows the operator to enter an integer value. (b) This screen display shows the interaction between program and user.

interesting enhancements to Web pages. Java has a good start on becoming the universal language of Internet computing.

▶ OBJECT-ORIENTED PROGRAMMING

The approach called **object-oriented programming** (**OOP**) is relatively new and distinctly different. An important emerging trend, this development deserves its own section. We can only introduce the concepts and terminology of object technology here. There is no expectation that you will understand exactly how OOP works; even professional programmers can take months of study and practice to gain that knowledge.

What Is an Object?

Consider items that, in everyday terms, might be called objects—for instance, a tire or a cat. Now affix known facts to these everyday objects. Without trying to be exhaustive, we might say that a tire is round and black and that a cat has four feet and fur. Taking this further, each object also has functions: A tire can roll or stop or go flat, and a cat can eat or purr or howl. In the world of object orientation, an object includes the item itself and also related facts and functions. More formally, in a programming environment an object is a self-contained unit that contains both data and related functions—the instructions to act on that data. This is in contrast to traditional programming, in which procedures are described in the program separate from the data.

The word used to describe an object's self-containment is **encapsulation:** An object encapsulates both data and its related instructions. In an object, the facts that describe the object are called **attributes,** and the instructions that tell the object to do something are called **methods** or **operations.** A specific occurrence of an object is called an instance; your pet kitty Tschugar is an instance of the object Cat.

Beginnings: Boats as Objects

Object orientation was first conceived in 1969 by Dr. Kirsten Nygaard, who was trying to develop a computer model of boats passing through Norwegian fjords. As Dr. Nygaard wrestled with the complex components of waves, tides, an irregular coastline, and moving boats, he hit on the idea of isolating each component into autonomous elements—objects—and then modeling the relationship between the elements. Consider the object Boat, shown in Figure 15-12. The object called Boat consists of the boat itself, its attributes, and its methods—descriptions of the things it does, such as move forward or change direction. It should be noted, however, that few objects have an inner life and can invoke their own methods spontaneously. Thus, methods in most cases are activated by an outside stimulus, called a **message,** that results in the change of the state of an object. For example, a *move* message would cause a boat object to activate its *move* method, which would change the value of its *location* attribute.

Using object-oriented programming, programmers define classes of objects. Each **class** contains the attributes that are unique to objects of that class. You can think of a class as a set of plans to create an object, just as house plans are used to build houses. In Figure 15-12, for example, a Boat object is an instance of the Boat class. In addition to classes, objects may be formed from subclasses. Objects are arranged hierarchically in classes and subclasses by their dominant characteristics. In Figure 15-12, some kinds of boats—sailboats, powerboats, and canoes—are subclasses of the class Boat.

An object in a subclass automatically possesses all the attributes of the class from which it was derived; this property is called **inheritance.** Only those attributes that are unique to the subclass need to be defined within the subclass. The Powerboat subclass would need to define the attribute *engine size*, because that is not an attribute of its parent class Boat, but it would automatically inherit the attributes

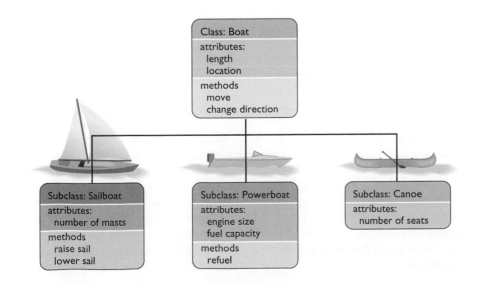

◄ **F I G U R E** 15-12

Object classes and subclasses. The subclasses Sailboat, Powerboat, and Canoe inherit the attributes *length* and *location* from the super-class object Boat, but each can define additional attributes. Under the property of polymorphism, each subclass can respond to the *move* message by using its own version of the *move* method.

length and *location* from the Boat class. The attributes of the class from which a subclass is derived need not be repeated in each subclass.

Even more savings accrue from the ability to reuse objects. As object technology is used by an organization, the organization gradually builds a library of classes. After a class has been created, tested, and found useful, it can be used again and again. Because each class is self-contained, it need not be altered for use in future applications. This reduces errors significantly, because new programs can be constructed largely from pretested error-free classes. Of course, organizations will not reap the benefits of reuse until they are a few projects down the line.

Activating the Object

You get an object to do something by sending it a command, called a message. The message tells the object what needs to be done, and the object's methods tell it how to do it. For example, the message *move* could be sent to objects belonging to any subclass of the Boat class—Sailboat, Powerboat, or Canoe. This brings up a fancy word that goes a long way toward revealing the value of object technology: *polymorphism*. When a message is sent, the property of **polymorphism** allows an individual object to know how, using its own methods, to process the message in the appropriate way for that particular object. For example, when the message *move* is received, an object of the class Sailboat knows that it is supposed to move under sail power, a Powerboat object knows that it moves by use of an engine, and a Canoe object knows that it moves by using paddle power. All the objects have a *move* method, but each subclass has its own implementation of that method.

Object-Oriented Languages: C++, Java, C#, and Visual Basic

The object-oriented language that currently dominates the market is C++, but that domination is being challenged by Java. As was described previously, **C++** is an enhancement of the C language. It includes everything in C and adds support for object-oriented programming. In addition, C++ also contains many improvements and new features that make it a "better C," independent of object-oriented programming. However, if you just use C++ as a better C, you will not be using all of its power. Like any quality tool, C++ must be used the way it was designed to be used to exploit its richness. Versions of C++ are available for almost all large system and personal computer platforms.

Java, the language threatening C++ dominance, is a "pure" object-oriented language; that is, it is impossible to write a non-object-oriented program. However, if you don't really understand object-oriented concepts, you can easily write a bad object-oriented program! Its main advantage, cross-platform compatibility, was described earlier.

A relatively new language, **C#** (pronounced "cee-sharp") is Microsoft's answer to Java. It has most of the same advantages over C++ as does Java, but it is designed to work within Microsoft's .NET environment. The .NET environment is designed for building, deploying, and running Web-based applications.

Many people referred to prior versions of Visual Basic as "object-oriented," because VB programs used "objects" such as command buttons, dialog boxes, scrollbars, and others. However, it wasn't until the current version, VB.NET, that Visual Basic supported the concepts of inheritance and polymorphism, thus meeting the criteria for a true object-oriented language.

Object Technology in Business

When businesses approach object technology, they are more likely to be interested in invoices and payroll checks than in cats or boats. Business items have their own attributes and methods, which can be coded into object classes. After the classes exist, they can inherit characteristics from higher classes. For example, subclasses relating to a customer account could inherit the customer address, which need not then be repeated in each subclass. In the fashion of object technology, business objects also respond to messages and, of course, can be reused.

▲

CHAPTER REVIEW

► Summary and Key Terms

- A **programming language** is a set of rules for telling the computer which operations to perform.

- A programmer converts solutions to the user's problems into instructions for the computer. These instructions are called a **program.** Writing a program involves defining the problem, planning the solution, coding the program, testing the program, and documenting the program.

- Defining the problem means discussing it with the users or a systems analyst to determine the necessary input, processing, and output.

- Planning involves designing an **algorithm,** a detailed, step-by-step solution to the problem. This can be done by using a **flowchart,** which is a pictorial representation of the step-by-step solution, or by using **pseudocode,** which is an English-like outline of the solution. Pseudocode is not executable on the computer. Before coding, the programmer should perform a process called **desk-checking,** carrying out each step of the algorithm in the indicated sequence to verify that it produces the desired results. A **structured walkthrough,** in which a programmer's peers review the algorithm design to verify its correctness, is often performed.

- Coding the program means expressing the solution in a programming language. The programmer must follow the language's **syntax,** or grammatical rules, precisely. Programmers usually use a **text editor,** which is somewhat like a word processing program, to create a file that contains the program. In most current computer languages the text editor is part of a comprehensive package called a **integrated development environment** (**IDE**) that also includes translation and debugging software.

- Testing the program consists of translating and debugging. In translating, a translator program converts the program into a form the computer can understand and, in the process, detects programming language errors, which are called **syntax errors.** A common translator is a **compiler,** which translates the entire program at one time and gives error messages called diagnostics. The original program, called a **source module,** is translated to an **object module,** to which the **linkage editor** (or **linker**) adds prewritten modules from a system library to create an executable **load module. Debugging** involves running the program to detect, locate, and correct mistakes known as **logic errors.**

- **Documentation** consists of material generated during each step and involves a detailed written description of the programming cycle and the program along with the test results and a printout of the program.

- Programming languages are described as being lower level or higher level, depending on how close they are to the language the computer itself uses (0s and 1s—low) or to the language people use (more English-like—high). There are five main levels, or generations, of languages: (1) machine language, (2) assembly languages, (3) high-level languages, (4) very high-level languages, and (5) natural languages.

- **Machine language,** the lowest level, represents data as 0s and 1s, binary digits corresponding to the on and off electrical states in the computer.

- **Assembly languages** use letters as mnemonic codes to replace the 0s and 1s of machine language. An **assembler** is a program that translates the assembly language into machine language.

- **High-level languages** are written in an English-like manner. Each high-level language requires a different compiler, or translator program, for each type of computer on which it is run.

- The first three generations of languages are **procedural languages,** in which the programmer describes the step-by-step solution to the problem. **Very high-level**

languages, also called **fourth-generation languages (4GLs),** are **nonprocedural languages** in which the programmer specifies the desired results and the language develops the solution. A variation on 4GLs are **query languages,** which can be used to retrieve data from databases.

- Fifth-generation languages are often called **natural languages** because they resemble "natural" spoken language.

- The first high-level language, **FORTRAN** (FORmula TRANslator), is a scientifically oriented language that was introduced by IBM in 1954. Its brevity makes it suitable for executing complex formulas.

- **COBOL** (COmmon Business-Oriented Language) was introduced in 1959 as a standard programming language for business.

- When **BASIC** (Beginners' All-purpose Symbolic Instruction Code) was developed at Dartmouth and introduced in 1965, it was intended for instruction in programming. Now its uses include business and personal computer applications.

- **RPG** (Report Program Generator) was developed by IBM in 1965 to allow rapid creation of reports from data stored in the computer files. It is currently used primarily on IBM midrange computers.

- Microsoft's **Visual Basic** enables the programmer to easily create programs with complex user interfaces containing standard Windows features, such as buttons, dialog boxes, scroll bars, and menus.

- Invented at Bell Labs, **C** offers high-level language features, such as structured programming. C code is almost as efficient as assembly language, and it is suitable for writing portable programs that can run on more than one type of computer.

- **Java** is a network-friendly programming language, derived from the C++ language, that permits a piece of software to run on many different **platforms,** the hardware and software combination that composes the basic functionality of a computer.

- The approach called **object-oriented programming (OOP)** uses objects, self-contained units that hold both data and related facts and functions—the instructions to act on that data. An object **encapsulates** both data and its related instructions. In an object, the facts that describe the object are called **attributes,** and the instructions that tell the object to do something are called **methods** or **operations.** A specific occurrence of an object is called an **instance.** An object's methods are activated by an outside stimulus, called a **message,** that results in the change of an object's state.

- An object **class** contains the characteristics that are unique to that class. Objects are arranged hierarchically in classes and subclasses by their dominant characteristics. An object in a subclass automatically possesses all the characteristics of the class to which it belongs; this property is called **inheritance.**

- After an object has been created, tested, and found useful, it can be used and reused in future program applications.

- A command called a message, telling what—not how—something is to be done, activates the object. **Polymorphism** means that an individual object receiving a message knows how, using its own methods, to process the message in the appropriate way for that particular object.

- The object-oriented language that currently dominates the market is **C++,** which is the object-oriented version of the programming language C. Versions of C++ are available for large systems and personal computers. **Java** is currently challenging C++ dominance. A relatively new language, **C#** (pronounced "cee-sharp") is Microsoft's answer to Java. It has most of the same advantages over C++ as does Java, but it is designed to work within Microsoft's .NET environment.

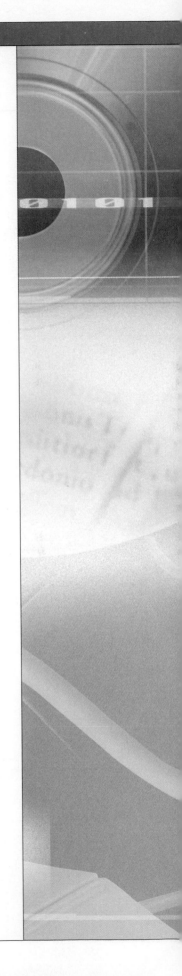

▶ Critical Thinking Questions

1. It has been noted that, among other qualities, good programmers are detail-oriented. Why might attention to detail be important in the programming process?

2. In addition to insisting on proper documentation, managers encourage programmers to write straightforward programs that another programmer can easily follow. Discuss occasions when a programmer might have to work with a program written by another programmer. Under what circumstances might a programmer completely take over the care of a program written by another? If you inherited someone else's program, about which you knew nothing, would you be dismayed to discover minimal documentation?

3. Should students taking a computer literacy course be required to learn some programming?

▶ STUDENT STUDY GUIDE

Multiple Choice

1. The presence of both data and its related instructions in an object is called
   a. C++
   b. orientation
   c. encapsulation
   d. inheritance

2. In preparing a program, one should first
   a. plan the solution
   b. document the program
   c. code the program
   d. define the problem

3. During the development of a program, drawing a flowchart is a means to
   a. plan the solution
   b. define the problem
   c. code the program
   d. analyze the problem

4. An English-like language that one can use as a program design tool is
   a. BASIC
   b. COBOL
   c. pseudocode
   d. Pascal

5. In preparing a program, debugging and translating are examples of
   a. coding
   b. testing
   c. planning
   d. documentation

6. The process of detecting, locating, and correcting logic errors is called
   a. desk-checking
   b. debugging
   c. translating
   d. documenting

7. Comments in the program itself are part of
   a. compiling
   b. linking
   c. translating
   d. documenting

8. The hardware/software combination that composes a computer's functionality is its
   a. platform
   b. pseudocode
   c. class
   d. syntax

9. The first high-level language to be introduced was
   a. COBOL
   b. Pascal
   c. FORTRAN
   d. BASIC

10. The ability of an object to interpret a message using its own methods is known as
    a. polymorphism
    b. inheritance
    c. encapsulation
    d. messaging

11. An English-like language that is used for business applications is
    a. C
    b. BASIC
    c. FORTRAN
    d. COBOL

12. Specifying the kind of input, processing, and output required for a program occurs in
    a. planning the solution
    b. coding the program
    c. flowcharting the problem
    d. defining the problem

13. Error messages provided by a compiler are called
    a. bugs
    b. translations
    c. diagnostics
    d. mistakes

14. After stating a solution in pseudocode, you would next
    a. test the program
    b. implement the program
    c. code the program
    d. translate the program

15. The highest-level languages are called
    a. 4GLs
    b. assembly languages
    c. high-level languages
    d. natural languages

16. To activate an object, send a(n)
    a. message
    b. method
    c. instance
    d. attribute

17. Popular object-oriented languages are
    a. C, COBOL
    b. C++, FORTRAN
    c. C++, Java
    d. COBOL, BASIC

18. Software that translates assembly language into machine language is a(n)
    a. binary translator
    b. assembler
    c. compiler
    d. link-loader

19. _____ is a language developed by IBM to allow rapid creation of reports from data stored in computer files.
    a. C
    b. COBOL
    c. BASIC
    d. RPG

20. In developing a program, documentation should be done
    a. as the last step
    b. only to explain errors
    c. throughout the process
    d. only during the design phase

21. A fourth-generation language that is used for database retrieval is a(n)
    a. high-level language
    b. query language
    c. assembly language
    d. machine language

22. The network-friendly language that is derived from C++ is
    a. Java
    b. RPG
    c. Visual Basic
    d. BASIC

23. The lowest level of programming language is
    a. natural language
    b. BASIC
    c. assembly language
    d. machine language

24. An assembly language uses
    a. English words
    b. 0s and 1s
    c. mnemonic codes
    d. binary digits

25. The Java language is
    a. machine-oriented
    b. problem-oriented
    c. document-oriented
    d. object-oriented

True/False

T F 1. The usual reason for choosing a programming language is simply that it is the one the programmer likes best.

T F 2. Developing a program requires only two steps: coding and testing.

T F 3. A flowchart is an example of pseudocode.

T F 4. Translating is the first phase of testing a program.

T F 5. A translator is a form of hardware that translates a program into language the computer can understand.

T F 6. Wintel is an example of a platform.

T F 7. Debugging is the process of locating program logic errors.

T F 8. The highest level of language is natural language.

T F 9. Pseudocode can be used to plan and execute a program.

T F 10. 4GLs increase clarity but reduce user productivity.

T F 11. An object encapsulates both data and its related instructions.

T F 12. C++ is particularly easy to use because it has fewer features than most languages.

T F 13. COBOL is very good for processing large, complex data files and for producing well-formatted business reports.

T F 14. BASIC is especially suited for large and complex programs.

T F 15. FORTRAN stands for FORms TRANsfer.

T F 16. Expressing a problem solution in Java is an example of coding a program.

T F 17. Diagnostic messages are concerned with improper use of the programming language.

T F 18. An assembly program translates high-level language into assembly language.

T F 19. An object subclass inherits characteristics from higher object classes.

T F 20. A specific occurrence of an object is called an instance.

T F 21. Polymorphism means that an object knows how, using its own methods, to act on an incoming message.

T F 22. Another name for a high-level language is 4GL.

T F 23. A query language is a type of assembly language.

T F 24. FORTRAN is used primarily in scientific environments.

T F 25. Low-level languages are tied more closely to the computer than are high-level languages.

Fill-In

1. The type of language that is used to access databases is called a(n) _____ language.

2. The type of language that replaced machine language by using mnemonic codes is called a(n) _____ language.

3. The object orientation property that permits a subclass to retain the characteristics of a higher class is called _____.

4. A query language is what level of language? _____.

5. A translator that translates high-level languages into machine language is called a _____.

6. The rules of a programming language are called its _____.

7. How many levels of language were described in the chapter? _____.

8. A source module is translated into a(n) _____.

9. The object orientation property that permits an object to use its own methods to act on a message is called _____.

10. Two commonly used OOP languages are

   a. _____

   b. _____

11. The hardware and software combination that composes the basic functionality of a computer is called a(n) _____.

12. A linkage editor transforms an object module into a(n) _____.

13. Languages that resemble spoken languages are called _____.

14. An early high-level language that is scientifically oriented is _____.

15. The command that activates an object is a(n) _____.

16. The programming process step that is best done throughout the process is

   _____

17. Two common methods of planning the solution to a problem are

   a. _____

   b. _____

18. List the two phases of testing a program:

   a. _____

   b. _____

19. The next step after a programmer has planned the solution is to

   _____

20. The term for the error messages that a translator provides is

   _____

▶ **ANSWERS**

Multiple Choice

1. c	6. b	11. d	16. a	21. b
2. d	7. d	12. d	17. c	22. a
3. a	8. a	13. c	18. b	23. d
4. c	9. c	14. c	19. d	24. c
5. b	10. a	15. d	20. c	25. d

True/False

1. F	6. T	11. T	16. T	21. T
2. F	7. T	12. F	17. T	22. F
3. F	8. T	13. T	18. F	23. F
4. T	9. F	14. F	19. T	24. T
5. F	10. F	15. F	20. T	25. T

Fill-In

1. query
2. assembly
3. inheritance
4. very high-level language, or 4GL
5. compiler
6. syntax
7. five
8. object module
9. polymorphism
10. a. C++
    b. Java
11. platform
12. load module
13. natural languages
14. FORTRAN
15. message
16. documentation
17. a. flowcharting
    b. writing pseudocode
18. a. translating
    b. debugging
19. code the program
20. diagnostics

Little Languages and the Web

Some programming languages are sufficiently popular, widespread, and long-lived that they rightly deserve to be characterized as "big" languages. COBOL, C, and C++ all fit this mold. They're big, powerful, and comparatively difficult to use and require the programmer to carefully tailor their use to the target computer.

Owing in part to the growth of the Internet, with its ability to instantly and widely disseminate information and innovation, there are now a host of other, special-purpose languages. These "little languages" are more limited in their aims than the big languages, such as C++, but they offer definite advantages for experienced and novice programmers.

Here are three examples of contemporary little languages. Some you have already encountered on the Web, even though you might not have realized that the Web servers you were browsing were programmed in languages with names such as Perl, TCL, or Python. Each of the languages now has a loyal following of programmers who take advantage of their open source to extend and improve them. Despite their current widespread support, each is very much the product of a single author who designed and developed the language initially.

The Practical Extraction Report Language (Perl) is largely the work of Larry Wall, who originally developed the language for system administrators in 1987. You have almost certainly used a Perl program without knowing it if you have filled in a Web form on an e-commerce site or browsed sites that extract information from databases or server files. Perl remains popular for Web programming because it is fairly easy to learn and lets Web developers extend their basic HTML pages with active content generated by running the Perl scripts they author. (One Perl Web site describes Perl as "the duct tape of the Internet.")

TCL (pronounced "Tickle" by those in the know) is the product of Dr. John Ousterhout, formerly a professor of computer science at the University of California at Berkeley. The Tool Command Language and its companion graphical user interface, Tk, are commonly used on Unix computers to produce reports and to analyze scientific data. Some Web servers are written entirely in TCL. TCL is the original "glue" language—one that allows a programmer to easily connect or glue existing programs together to make a larger system by reusing programs as building blocks.

PHP stands for Hypertext Preprocessor (get it?), and was originally conceived by Rasmus Lesdorf as a scripting tool for tracking and updating his online résumé. In 1997, it was completely rewritten by three programmers (Zeev Suraski, Andi Gutmans, and Rasmus), and it is those three (as well as the thousands and thousands of developers using the language) who still maintain PHP 4 today.

The main purpose of the PHP scripting language is to allow quick creation of dynamically generated Web pages, but it can be used for much more, such as search bars for Web browsers or to enable keyboard shortcuts for fast navigation of a Web site. Many major search engines and Web portals are now turning to PHP for their sites, such as Yahoo!

Although these little languages won't soon command the army of programmers currently coding in C and C++, you are increasingly likely to encounter them on the Web and in introductory programming courses. Perhaps in programming, as in so many other things, smaller really will turn out to be better.

Internet Exercises

1. **Structured exercise.** Starting with http://www.prenhall.com/capron, browse to one of the main sites supporting one of the languages above: Perl, PHP, or Python. Locate material on these Web pages that argues for the advantages of the chosen language over the "bigger" languages. Compare your results with those of other classmates who have investigated another language Web site.

2. **Free-form exercise.** Using a search engine or starting from some of the links provided at http://www.prenhall.com/capron, find one or more descriptions of programs actually written in Perl, TCL, or Python. Answer the following questions: What was the application supposed to do? Why did the authors choose this particular language? For what sort of business or industry was the application developed (e-commerce, scientific, general business, student project, etc.)? Compare your results to those obtained by classmates who have investigated other Web sites.

3. **Advanced exercise.** See whether you can write a short program in one of these little languages—maybe one that prints "hello world." Or try out a short sample program in Perl, TCL, or Python from one of the many Web sites supporting these languages. What problems did you encounter in getting your program to work? What do you like or dislike about the language you tried? Share your experiences with classmates who attempted other languages and with your instructor and more experienced programmers.

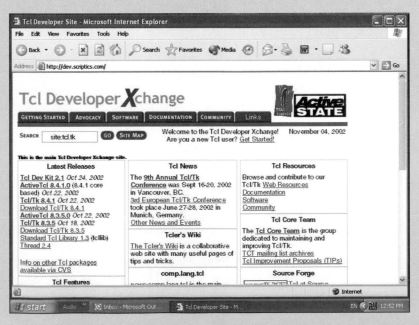

Planet Internet

Management Information Systems:
Classic Models and New Approaches

CHAPTER 16

Tom Freund pursued a business degree with the goal of a career in management. He was uncertain, however, about his career ambitions. He thought that someday he would like to be at the very top of an organization, perhaps with an office with a stunning view. He thought it was more likely, however, that he would end up somewhere in the middle, reporting to the top bosses but with responsibilities for major activities below him. He assumed that his entry into management would be at the lowest rung on the ladder, where he would be in direct contact with the workers, supervising their operations and making sure they had what they needed to do the job.

As it happened, Tom did all these things, but not in the way he expected. While he was in college, he began a computer word processing service, typing up his classmates' term papers and résumés. He used part of his profits to buy a laser printer and desktop publishing software. Thus he was able to produce professional-looking documents and was able to offer his services to local small businesses. Tom's business on the side grew beyond his expectations; he decided to go into business for himself full-time after graduation. Tom's company eventually specialized in the production end of publishing periodicals and paperback books. As the company grew, Tom managed at all levels and, eventually, did indeed have a corner office overlooking the cityscape.

Whether you manage your own company or someone else's—at the top, middle, or bottom level—the challenge is the same: to use available resources to get the job done on time, within budget, and to the satisfaction of all concerned. Let us begin with a discussion of how managers do this and then see how computer systems can help them.

▶ CLASSIC MANAGEMENT FUNCTIONS

Managers historically have had five main functions:

- **Planning,** or devising both short-range and long-range plans for the organization and setting goals to help achieve the plans

- **Organizing,** or deciding how to use resources, such as people and materials

- **Staffing,** or hiring and training workers

- **Directing,** or guiding employees to perform their work in a way that supports the organization's goals

- **Controlling,** or monitoring the organization's progress toward reaching its goals

All managers perform these functions as part of their jobs. The level of responsibility regarding these functions, however, varies with the level of the manager. The levels of management are traditionally represented as a pyramid, with the fewest managers at the top and the largest numbers at the lowest level (Figure 16-1). You will often hear the terms *strategic, tactical,* and *operational* associated with high-level managers, middle-level managers, and low-level managers, respectively.

Whether the head of General Electric or of an electrical appliance store, a high-level manager must be concerned with the long-range view—the *strategic* level of management. For this manager, usually called an executive, the main focus is planning. Consider a survey showing that Americans want family vacations and want the flexibility and economy of a motor vehicle; however, they also want more space than

▶ **FIGURE** 16-1

The management pyramid. (a) The classic view of management functions involves a pyramid featuring top managers handling strategic long-range planning, middle managers focusing on the tactical issues of organization and personnel, and low-level managers directing and controlling day-to-day operations. (b) The increasing use of networked personal computers in business is squeezing out middle- and low-level managers, thus flattening the pyramid.

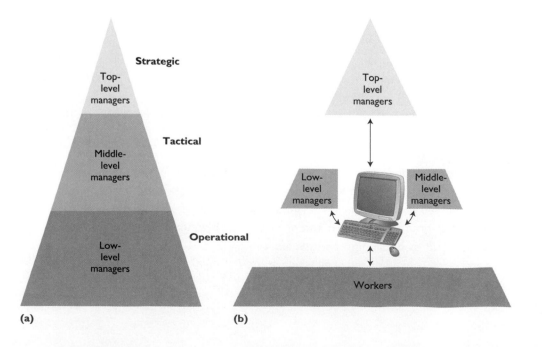

(a)

(b)

the family car provides. To the president of a major auto company, this information might suggest further opportunities for expansion of the recreational vehicle line.

The middle-level manager of that same company must be able to take a somewhat different view because his or her main concern is the *tactical* level of management. The middle manager will prepare to carry out the visions of the top-level managers, assembling the material and personnel resources to do the job. Note that these tasks focus on organizing and staffing. Suppose the public is inclined to buy more recreational vehicles. To a production vice president this might mean organizing production lines using people with the right skills at the right wage and perhaps farming out portions of the assembly that can be done by less expensive, less skilled labor.

The low-level manager, usually known as a supervisor, is primarily concerned with the *operational* level of management. For the supervisor the focus is on directing and controlling. Workers must be directed to perform the planned activities, and the supervisor must monitor progress closely. The supervisor—an assembly line supervisor in our recreational vehicle example—is involved in a number of issues: making sure that workers have the parts they need, checking employee attendance, maintaining quality control, handling complaints, keeping a close watch on the schedule, tracking costs, and much more.

To make decisions about planning, organizing, staffing, directing, and controlling, managers need data that is organized in a way that is useful for them. An effective management information system can provide it.

► MIS FOR MANAGERS

A **management information system (MIS)** can be defined as a set of formal business systems designed to provide information for an organization. (Incidentally, you may hear the term "MIS system," even though the "S" in the acronym stands for "system"; this is an accepted redundancy.) Whether or not such a system is called an MIS, every company has one. Even managers who make hunch-based decisions are operating with some sort of information system—one based on their experience. The kind of MIS we are concerned with here includes one or more computers as components. Information serves no purpose until it gets to its users. Timeliness is important, and the computer can act quickly to produce information.

The extent of a computerized MIS varies from company to company, but the most effective kinds are those that are integrated. An integrated MIS incorporates all five managerial functions—planning, organizing, staffing, directing, and controlling—throughout the company, from typing to top-executive forecasting. An integrated management computer system uses the computer to solve problems for an entire organization instead of attacking them piecemeal. Although in many companies the complete integrated system is still only an idea, the functional aspects of an MIS are expanding rapidly in many organizations.

The **MIS manager** runs the MIS department. This person's position has been variously called information resource manager, director of information services, chief information officer (CIO), and a variety of other titles. In any case, whoever serves in this capacity should be comfortable with both computer technology and the organization's business.

► THE NEW MANAGEMENT MODEL

The traditional management pyramid that we discussed earlier means a very specific kind of communication. An executive has time to communicate with perhaps a handful of people. Each of these people can convey information to another five or six people below him or her. Information trickles down, layer by layer, either in meetings or more informally.

A Flattened Pyramid

Enter the computer network. Networks connect people to people and people to data. Through e-mail, or perhaps groupware, information can be disseminated company wide as fast as fingers can fly over a computer keyboard. So much for passing along information through traditional hierarchical channels. The dispersion of information via the network has caused the traditional management pyramid to become flatter in structure and more physically distributed.

What are managers, so long the keepers of information, supposed to do now that, via the network, information is so freely available to so many workers? A good part of a manager's job, communicating above and below, has been replaced by the flow of information through the network. Many industries are finding that, to some extent, they can do without middle managers and have eliminated certain positions. Managers on all levels still have plenty to do, but they are doing it quite a bit differently from the ways of the past. Networks irrevocably alter the nature of managerial authority and work.

The Impact of Groupware

Consider the impact of groupware on worker interaction. Groupware permits information to be assembled in central databases. People working on a project contribute information to a database and can see and use information contributed by others.

The introduction of groupware can be a searing experience for some managers. Two reasons for this are changes in the way information is shared and changes in managerial authority. People acquire power in an organization by knowing things that others do not. Managers may feel threatened by groupware, because they are not accustomed to unstructured information sharing. Studies have shown that groupware works best in organizations in which there is already a fairly flexible corporate culture—that is, where an attitude of sharing and even egalitarianism already exists. Perhaps even more painful is the fact that managers might not enjoy being in the electronic spotlight when decisions that were once theirs alone are now fair game for

An executive has time to communicate with perhaps a handful of people. Each of these people can convey information to another five or six people. Information trickles down, layer by layer, either in meetings or more informally.

comment and change by everyone involved. Furthermore, in contrast to organizations whose focal point is the manager, groupware supports organizations that are team-based and information-driven.

Consider another change from the old ways. Say a particular aspect of a project requires collaboration between two people, Jack and Julie, from different operational units under different management. The traditional way of doing business is for Jack to go to his manager and then for Jack's manager to talk to Julie's manager, who talks to Julie. Then the information flows in reverse, back to Jack. Up, across, down, and then back again. Now it is possible to accomplish the same communication using groupware. Information moves laterally, from worker to worker, saving a round-about trip through the management maze.

As many managers have discovered, networks make leadership much harder. No longer able to look over their employees' shoulders, managers are learning to rely on other management techniques. They must first give careful attention to the selection and training of employees. Second, managers must set clear expectations for their employees. But most important, managers must use customer satisfaction as a measuring stick of employee performance in a networked environment.

GETTING PRACTICAL — Your Electronic Agent

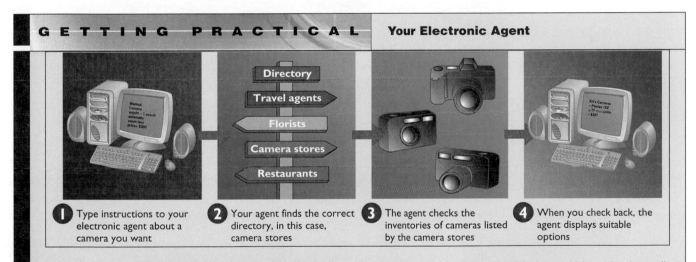

1. Type instructions to your electronic agent about a camera you want

2. Your agent finds the correct directory, in this case, camera stores

3. The agent checks the inventories of cameras listed by the camera stores

4. When you check back, the agent displays suitable options

You have an important job and an activity-packed life. You long ago stopped traipsing from store to store shopping for particular goods or services; instead, you use catalogs or the Yellow Pages and the telephone. You even do some shopping at Internet retail sites. A new camera? Flowers for a birthday? A Mexican restaurant? A vacation? The next logical step is to dispatch your own electronic agent to track down the best deal and, if you wish, purchase it for you.

An electronic agent, sometimes called a software agent, is a piece of software to which a person can delegate some degree of responsibility. The agent is given an order and goes shopping for you throughout the Internet. Suppose you have read some consumer articles and have decided that you want a camera weighing less than a pound with an automatic zoom lens for under $300. You type these instructions into your computer and let your software agent do the work.

While you go on with other tasks, the agent goes to a directory, finds camera stores, and then sifts through their camera inventories, looking for the required features and price. Eventually, the agent accumulates a list of acceptable choices, which is presented on your personal computer screen at your convenience. You can then choose which

one, if any, to purchase. A variation on this option is available: You can give your agent advance authority to purchase a suitable camera with the best price, probably charging it to a credit card.

Someone eavesdropping on a discussion of agents might think that a real person was being described. The agent, of course, is just sophisticated software. Agent software is available today. What are slow in coming, however, are businesses that are willing to pay to make their list of goods and services available to the network. It is a chicken-and-egg problem: Users will not flock to an online agency until many merchants and services are online, but the merchants and service providers will not sign up until there are many users.

Software agents are not limited to shopping. An agent is smarter than a standard search engine, partly because the agent indexes not the Web but the user. It knows its users' preferences and can, for example, find a list of appropriate restaurants in Phoenix for your next business trip. The list will include Mexican and Thai food (two of your favorites) but no fast-food joints or cafeterias (anathema).

Many companies organize their employees in teams, and eight people is usually considered an ideal team size. Each team is composed of people whose skills are needed for the task at hand.

Teamwork

The availability of networks and groupware coincides nicely with the concept of organizing employees into task-focused teams. Just as the manager is no longer the sole dispenser of wisdom and decisions, so the employee is no longer merely an individual in a static organization. Many companies are organizing their employees in teams. But a team has no permanence; work and people are organized around tasks. When a task is complete, the team is dispersed. When a new task is being tackled, a new team is assembled. Each team is composed of people whose skills are needed for the task at hand. In this kind of work environment, reorganization is a way of life.

Experts consider eight people to be an ideal team size. If a team gets much bigger than that, team members spend too much time communicating what is already inside their heads instead of applying that knowledge to their parts of the task. But what if the team is behind schedule? Imagine a status meeting in which it is revealed that a critical activity is behind schedule. The activity under scrutiny is to finalize product specifications for an electronic hoop, a toy that can be manipulated remotely and is expected to be a big hit for the upcoming holiday gift-buying season. This activity is critical because other activities down the line, including manufacturing and promotion, cannot begin until specifications are complete. The most common response to tardy projects is to add more people to the project, but this is exactly the wrong thing to do. If outsiders are belatedly added to an existing team, the project quickly comes to a halt while the new people are brought up to speed. And, of course, from that moment forward, there are more people with whom one must communicate.

What is the proper solution? There is no ideal answer, other than to plan better in the first place, but most organizations find that the better part of wisdom is to rely on the commitment of the original team members. The good news is that a properly composed team of an ideal size is less likely to get into trouble. Communication remains easy, and each member retains a strong sense of responsibility and participation while benefiting greatly from the contributions of teammates.

Top Managers and Computers

Since the early days of computing, managers at all levels have had computer support in the form of printed reports. In more recent times, most managers, even the most resistant executives, have succumbed to the personal computer. Managers have found personal computer software useful for every aspect of their jobs, from something as simple as sending an email message to complex chores, such as designing a compensation package for a thousand employees. For top managers, executives who must have the vision to guide the entire company, sophisticated software is needed.

Decision Support Systems

Imagine yourself as an executive trying to deal with a constantly changing environment, having to consider changes in competition, in technology, in consumer habits, in government regulations, in union demands, and so on. How are you going to make decisions about those matters for which there are no precedents? In fact, making one-of-a-kind decisions—decisions that no one has had to make before—is the real test of a manager's mettle. In such a situation you would probably wish you could turn to someone and ask a few what-if questions (Figure 16-2).

"What if . . . ?" That is the question business people want answered, especially when considering new situations. A **decision support system (DSS)** is a computer system that supports managers in nonroutine decision-making tasks. The key ingredient of a decision support system is a modeling process. A **model** is a mathematical representation of a real-life system. A mathematical model can be computerized. Like any computer program, the model can use inputs to produce outputs. The inputs to a model are called **independent variables** because they can change; the outputs are called **dependent variables** because they depend on the inputs.

Consider this example. Suppose that, as a manager, you have the task of deciding which property to purchase for one of your manufacturing plants. You have many factors to consider: the appraised value, asking price, interest rate, down payment required, and so on. These are all independent variables—the data that will be fed into the computer model of the purchase. The dependent variables, computed on the basis of the inputs, are the effect on your cash resources, long-term debt, and ability to make other investments. To increase complexity, we could add that the availability of workers and nearness to markets are also input factors. Increasing the complexity

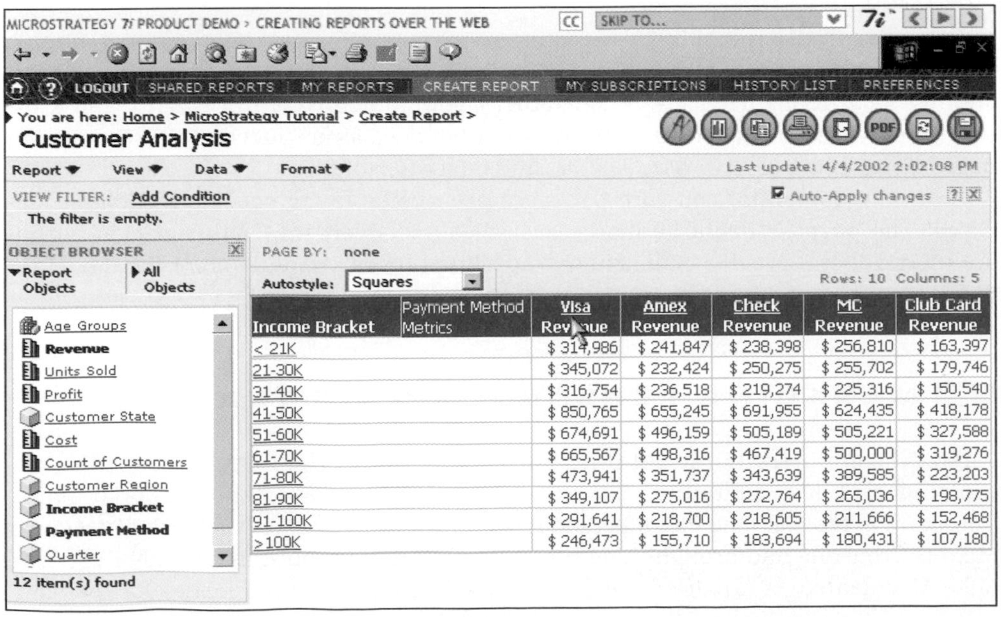

► FIGURE 16-2

Making decisions with the help of a computer.
Business people use computers to try different scenarios without investing a great deal of time and money.

is appropriate, in fact, because decision support systems often work with problems that are more complex than any one individual can handle.

Using a computer model to reach a decision about a real-life situation is called **simulation.** It is a game of "let's pretend." You plan the independent variables—the inputs—and you examine how the model behaves on the basis of the dependent variables—the outputs—it produces. If you want, you can change the inputs and continue experimenting. This is a relatively inexpensive way to simulate business situations, and it is considerably faster than the real thing. Of course, the results are meaningful only if the behavior of the model accurately reflects the real world.

The decision-making process must be fast, so the DSS is interactive: The user is in direct communication with the computer system and can affect its activities. In addition, most DSSs cross departmental lines so that information can be pulled from the databases of a variety of sources, such as marketing and sales, accounting and finance, production, and research and development. A manager who is trying to make a decision about developing a new product, for example, needs information from all of these sources.

A decision support system does not replace an MIS; instead, a DSS supplements an MIS. There are distinct differences between them. MIS emphasizes planned reports on a variety of subjects; DSS focuses on decision making. MIS is standard, scheduled, structured, and routine; DSS is quite unstructured and available on request. MIS is constrained by the organizational system; DSS is immediate and friendly.

Executive Information Systems

Top-level executives and decision makers face unique decision-making problems and pressures. An **executive information system (EIS)** is a decision support system especially made for senior-level executives. An executive information system is concerned with how decisions affect an entire organization. An EIS must take into consideration

- The overall vision or broad view of company goals

- Strategic long-term planning and objectives

- Organizational structure

- Staffing and labor relations

- Crisis management

- Strategic control and monitoring of overall operations

Executive decision-making also requires access to information originating outside the organization: from competitors, federal authorities, trade groups, consultants, and news-gathering agencies, among others. A high degree of uncertainty and a future orientation are involved in most executive decisions. Successful EIS software must therefore be easy to use, flexible, and customizable.

Several commercial software packages are available for specific modeling purposes. The purpose might be marketing, sales, or advertising. Other packages that are more general provide rudimentary modeling but let you customize the model for different purposes—budgeting, planning, or risk analysis.

▶ MANAGING PERSONAL COMPUTERS

Personal computers burst onto the business scene in the early 1980s with little warning and less planning. The experience of the Rayer International Paper Company is typical. One day a personal computer appeared on the desk of engineer Mike Burton—he had brought his in from home. Then accountants Sandy Dean and Mike Molyneaux got a pair of machines—they had squeezed the money for the com-

Top-level managers and decision makers, such as Bill Gates, face unique decision-making problems and pressures.

puters out of their overhead budget. Nobuko Locke, the personnel manager, got personal computers for herself and her three assistants in the company's far-flung branch offices. And so it went, with personal computers popping up all over the company. Managers realized that the reason for runaway purchases was that personal computers were so affordable. Most departments could pay for them out of existing budgets, so the purchasers did not have to ask anyone's permission.

Managers were tolerant at first. There were no provisions for managing the purchase or use of personal computers, and there certainly was no rule against them. And it was soon apparent that these machines were more than toys. Pioneer users had no trouble justifying their purchases; their increased productivity said it all. In addition to mastering software for word processing, spreadsheets, and database access, these users declared their independence from the MIS department (Figure 16-3).

However, managers were soon faced with several problems. The first was that no one person was in charge of the headlong plunge into personal computers. The second problem was incompatibility: The new computers came in an assortment of brands and models and did not mesh well. Software that worked on one machine did not necessarily work on another. Third, users were not as independent of the MIS department as they had thought; they needed assistance in a variety of ways. In particular, they needed data that was in the hands of the MIS department. In addition, companies were soon past the stage of the initial enthusiasts; they wanted all kinds of workers to have personal computers, and those workers needed training. Furthermore, in just a few years, most companies networked their computers together, bringing a whole new set of responsibilities and problems. Finally, many companies had so many personal computers that they did not know how many they had, where they were, or what software was on them. Many organizations solved these management problems in the following ways:

- They corrected the management problem by creating a new position called the personal computer manager, which often evolved into the network manager.

- They addressed the compatibility problem by establishing acquisition policies.

The personal computer manager must keep the network operational. The manager's basic task is to let network users share program and data files and resources such as printers.

- They solved the assistance problem by creating information centers and providing a variety of training opportunities.

- They used software to locate, count, and inventory their personal computers.

- They considered the total cost of ownership of personal computers.

Let us examine each of these solutions.

The Personal Computer Manager

The benefits of personal computers for the individual user have been clear almost from the beginning: increased productivity, worker enthusiasm, and easier access to information. But once personal computers move beyond entry status, standard corporate accountability becomes a factor. Large companies are spending millions of dollars on personal computers, and top-level managers want to know where all this money is going. Company auditors begin worrying about data security. The company legal department begins to worry about workers copying software illegally. Before long, everyone is involved, and it is clear that someone must be placed in charge of personal computer use. That person is the **personal computer manager.**

There are three prospective problem areas that need the attention of this manager:

- **Technology overload.** The personal computer manager must maintain a clear vision of company goals so that users are not overwhelmed by the massive and conflicting claims of aggressive vendors plying their wares. Users engulfed by phrases, such as "network topologies" and "file gateways," or a jumble of acronyms, can turn to the personal computer manager for guidance.

- **Data security and integrity.** Access to corporate data is a touchy issue. Many personal computer users find that they want to download (or access) data from the

Managers must monitor the use of personal computers in the workplace.

corporate mainframe to their own machines, and this presents an array of problems. Are they entitled to the data? Will they manipulate the data in new ways and then present it as the official version? Will they expect the MIS department to take the data back after they have done who knows what with it? The answers to these perplexing questions are not always clear-cut, but at least the personal computer manager will be tuned in to the issues.

● **Computer junkies.** What about employees who are feverish with the new power and freedom offered by the computer? When they are in school, these user-abusers are sometimes called hackers or crackers; on the job they are often called junkies because their fascination with the computer seems like an addiction. Unable to resist the allure of the machine, they overuse it and neglect their other work. Personal computer managers usually respond to this problem by setting guidelines for computer use.

The person who is selected to be the personal computer manager is usually from the MIS area. Ideally, this person has a broad technical background, understands both the potential and the limitations of personal computers, and is well known to a diverse group of users.

With the advent of networking, the personal computer manager is often the same person as the **network manager** or, if the network is a local area network, the **LAN**

manager. The network manager must keep the network operational. The manager's basic task is to let network users share program and data files and resources, such as printers. The network manager is responsible for installing all software on the network and making sure that existing software runs smoothly. The network manager must also make sure that backup copies are made of all files at regular intervals. In addition, the network must be kept free from viruses and other illegal software intrusions. The greatest challenge may be to make sure that the network has no unauthorized users.

Company managers often underestimate the amount of work it takes to keep even a small network going. In a large company, an individual or even an entire team of people may be dedicated to this task. In a small company, the network may be managed by someone who already has a full-time job at the company.

Personal Computer Acquisition

Workers initially purchased personal computers before any company-wide or even office-wide policies had been set. The resulting compatibility problems meant that they could not easily communicate or share data. Consider this example: A user's budgeting process calls for certain data that resides in the files of another worker's personal computer or perhaps involves figures output by the computer of a third person. If the software and machines these people use do not mesh, compatibility becomes a major problem.

In many companies, MIS departments have taken control of personal computer acquisition. The methods vary, but they often include establishing standards and restricting the number of vendors used. Most companies now have established standards for personal computers, for the software that will run on them, and for data communications. Commonly, users must stay within established standards, so that they can tie into corporate resources. Some companies limit the number of vendors—sellers of hardware and software—from whom they allow purchases. Managers have discovered that they can prevent most user complaints about incompatibility, not to mention getting a volume discount, by allowing products from just a handful of vendors.

The Information Center

The **information center** is the place where workers can get help with software problems. In large organizations, the information center, often called by other names, such as **support center,** offers help to users in several forms. The information center is devoted exclusively to giving users service. And best of all, user assistance is immediate, with little or no red tape.

Information center services often include the following:

- **Software and hardware selection.** The information center staff helps users to determine which company-approved software packages suit their needs.

- **Data access.** If appropriate, the staff helps users get data from the large corporate computer systems for use on the users' computers.

- **Network access.** A staff typically offers information about using the network system, tells how to obtain passwords and authorization, disseminates security information, and probably offers regular classes on the Internet.

- **Training.** Education is a principal reason for an information center's existence. Classes are usually small, frequent, and on a variety of topics (Figure 16-4). Some information centers offer miniclasses, or a series of miniclasses, during lunch breaks; brown bags are welcome. The information center is not the only form of training, however; we will discuss training in more detail shortly.

The information center.
Classes are held at the information center to teach managers and other employees how to use the company's computers.

- **Technical assistance.** Information center staff members stand ready to assist in any way possible, short of actually doing the users' work for them. That help includes advising on company standards for hardware purchases, aiding in the selection and use of software, finding errors, helping submit formal requests to the MIS department, and so forth.

To be successful, the information center must be placed in an easily accessible location. The center should be equipped with personal computers and terminals, a stockpile of software packages, and perhaps a library. It should be staffed with people who have a technical background but whose explanations feature plain English. Their mandate is "the user comes first."

Training: Pay Now or Pay Later

Any manager knows that simply dumping technology—hardware, software, networks, whatever—on workers in the hope of increased productivity would be a disaster. The first obvious approach is to provide training for the new technology, whatever it is.

Organizations tend to be remiss about training. Years ago, vendors typically included training as part of the hardware or software package. Once training became a separate item with a separate price tag, organizations were more apt to think they could get along without it. Furthermore, although training was once needed for just a few technical workers, now training is needed for entire populations of workers company wide.

The organizations that do offer training too often rely on the one-shot teacher-in-the-classroom model. This traditional approach, however, does not work well. To begin with, unless the classes are off-site or attendance is rigorously enforced, participation may be sporadic, because employees are more concerned about the real work that has to be abandoned on their desks. Furthermore, especially when new software is the topic, training lasting two days or two weeks, even hands-on in a computer-stocked classroom, yields minimal results.

Workers adopting new technology do need initial training, but they also need follow-up support. One approach that seems to work well is to cultivate home-grown gurus. When confronted with a computer problem, the first instinct of a baffled user is to consult a more knowledgeable friend or colleague. With this in mind, savvy companies, after the first round of training, ask for volunteers who would like to learn more. These users become the office gurus for that technology. Initially, they may not know a lot more than their colleagues, but they are usually a bit ahead and, by sheer numbers of consultations, accumulate more knowledge than other workers.

In-house support, such as an information center, can be a big factor in the success of new technology. The best guarantee that workers will absorb training, however, is proper motivation, achieved by getting them involved.

INVOLVING THE WORKERS   The catchphrase that is often used is "empowering the workers." It is a variation on the systems analyst's precept of user involvement. Rather than simply installing new technology and training the workers, begin with the workers—the people who will be using the technology. To put it another way, deal with the people at the same time you deal with the technology.

Paine Webber, a stock brokerage, offers a model approach. Paine Webber wanted to upgrade its brokers' 10-year-old computer system to a network that would offer far more information access and control. The systems analyst began by surveying the attitudes of the 5000-plus brokers. He discovered that approximately one third of the brokers thought that the current system met their needs, another third thought they would like some improvements, and the final third thought that the current system was hopelessly outmoded.

The company's response was to build a dazzling new system with the old system built into it. Paine Webber unfolded the new system branch by branch, emphasizing not the wonders of technology but what the system could do for brokers. The instructors were not technical types but specially trained Paine Webber employees who already knew the brokerage business. This worked well for everyone, even those who were initially reluctant. Workers whose comfort level was the old system could begin with that version, but most of them gradually picked up the features of the new system.

Another issue regarding worker involvement is the generation gap. Employees who grew up playing video games and using computers in school have a built-in advantage over their elders, who might show the foot-dragging signs of a precomputer upbringing. In fact, training experts recommend that big-time computerphobes loosen up by playing computer games. This way they will at least become comfortable with a mouse and with interactions that cause changes on the computer screen.

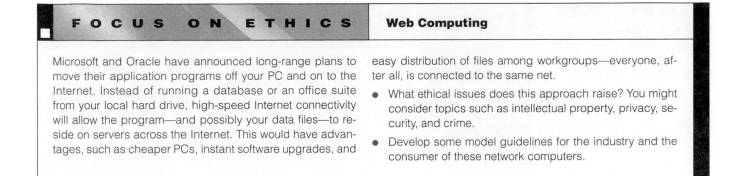

FOCUS ON ETHICS | **Web Computing**

Microsoft and Oracle have announced long-range plans to move their application programs off your PC and on to the Internet. Instead of running a database or an office suite from your local hard drive, high-speed Internet connectivity will allow the program—and possibly your data files—to reside on servers across the Internet. This would have advantages, such as cheaper PCs, instant software upgrades, and easy distribution of files among workgroups—everyone, after all, is connected to the same net.

- What ethical issues does this approach raise? You might consider topics such as intellectual property, privacy, security, and crime.
- Develop some model guidelines for the industry and the consumer of these network computers.

ENTER THE WEB   Can we be surprised that, along with seemingly everything else, training is also moving to the Web? Text-based training has been in decline for some time, in favor of instructor-led training, but now the trend is to use CD-ROMs and Web-based training (Figure 16-5). Because there is nothing to buy except the training software, computer-based training is an appealing option for small to medium-size businesses.

When convenience, interactivity, and affordability are high on the wish list for training, a Web-based approach may be the best answer. It promises training and collaboration that take place simultaneously at different locations, online mentoring and review, and customized lessons. A popular Web-based training site is SmartPlanet, which offers training in mainstream business and Internet applications (Figure 16-6).

Do You Even Know Where Your PCs Are?

Many corporate administrators, when put to the test, are embarrassed to admit that they do not know where corporate personal computers are in use in the company; in fact, they do not even know how many there are. One manager, for example, was quite certain that the company had 600 personal computers and an average of 12 users per printer. The reality turned out to be quite different; there were 1100 computers and one printer per computer. To make matters even worse, managers might have no idea what software is on the computers—Microsoft Excel or WordPerfect or perhaps the latest incarnation of the game Doom.

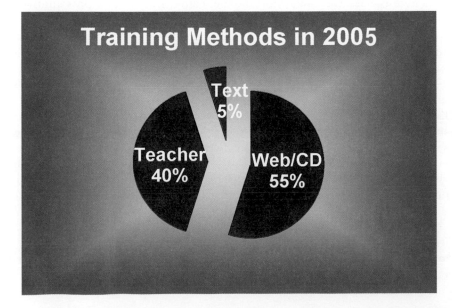

◄ **FIGURE 16-5**

Shift in training methods.
By the year 2005, more than half of all computer training will be computer-based.

▶ F I G U R E 16-6

Web-based training. The site for SmartPlanet, which offers training in computing and business topics.

SmartPlanet a service of CNET Networks ::::::::: POWERED BY ✳ element k

Gain the Skills You Need from SmartPlanet

Choose from over **600 high quality online IT courses** and put your career into high gear.

SmartPlanet allows you to focus on mastering the skills that you need to succeed. Learn with an *instructor* or *on your own*, on your schedule. We offer a variety of course libraries to choose from and a 14-day money-back guarantee.

Get started today by browsing our libraries below or sign up for a FREE TRIAL .

Experience SmartPlanet   *Why SmartPlanet?*

Returning Students
Enter your Username and Password below, and click LOGIN.

Username:

Password:

LOGIN
■ Remember me

New Students
Already purchased?
Enroll to establish a username and password.

Free Trial

MOST POPULAR COURSES

✓ Flash 5: Level 1
Part of the Basic Web Tools library

✓ Windows 2000: Designing a Secure Network
Part of the MCSE library

✓ Excel 2000:

Laptop Lane

Laptop Lane sounds more like a place to frolic in the park than what it really is: a private suite at the airport with access to computer connections. You can bring your own laptop computer and hook up to a high-speed line, or you can use one of the offices with fully equipped desktop computers. A concierge will lead you to an individual office where you can close the door and, in complete privacy, write, print, fax, e-mail, surf the Net, make conference calls, or do whatever job you need to do all in one place, right at the airport. Office rental is by the half hour.

This is a critical problem because administrators might have no idea how to budget for their personal computers. If the computers are hidden, then so are the costs of maintaining them. Clearly, administrators must confront the missing-computers problem.

Specialized computer services now offer a sort of lost-and-found for personal computers and related equipment. Corporate personal computers that are networked—and that means most of them—can be counted and interrogated by software set up on the network. The polling software not only counts computers but also determines their components and the software installed on them.

Remote Users

Many companies want their sales representatives out of the office, both to reduce office costs and to make the sales effort more effective. But these representatives must have adequate access to computer data. Offering remote users access to data residing in computers in the office frees them from having to carry around large amounts of data. Salespeople using laptop computers can connect to the home office to download pricing information from the mainframe to the laptop and to upload order entries from the field to the mainframe computer. The connection also manages electronic mail.

MIS managers have a variety of concerns about remote users and their access to information from the company's mainframe. The first concern is security. Remote users at the least should use a password when making connections. Training is a consistent problem because road warriors seldom come into the office for extended periods. Although it seems obvious, travelers need to be trained in preserving their expensive equipment; laptop computers are extremely vulnerable to loss and theft.

Total Cost of Ownership

The **total cost of ownership**—of personal computers—has become such a pervasive concern that magazine articles routinely refer to it by its acronym, **TCO,** without even bothering to explain what the initials represent. TCO methodology for calculat-

DAY IN THE LIFE

Victoria Beckingham,
IT Project Manager

Normally a very organized person at the best of times, Victoria would be lost without her Microsoft project software. As an IT project manager for a network consulting firm, she often has to manage two or three projects that are all underway at the same time. Without her software to keep track of all the little details, she would be swamped.

Each individual is accounted for in the software, as well as the tasks assigned him/her. What makes Victoria's job challenging is that sometimes the people on a project team are working in other states, or occasionally in another country. It's not always easy to keep in close touch with remote employees by phone, but the Internet makes things a lot easier.

Email is the main form of communication, naturally, but instant messaging and Internet chat also play a useful role, as they allow several team members to brainstorm together at the same time. Victoria has set a server for the project management software, so that a team member who is working remotely can log on via the Internet, and update his/her status on the project. With all this information readily available to her, Victoria can simply call up a report of everyone's task status, and then re-assign tasks as needed.

ing costs of computer ownership in business was first developed in the early 1990s by a consulting company called the Gartner Group. Since then, dozens of consulting firms have helped clients to apply TCO analysis to their operations. TCO was developed in response to perceived costs that missed the mark.

Early users thought that the costs of personal computers were paid back rapidly by increased productivity. If only the initial costs of hardware and perhaps some software are considered, that observation might be true. But the real costs—the total cost—entail training, support, upgrading, maintenance, hardware and software extras, and communications networks. That is, the total cost goes far beyond the computer itself. Some professionals have estimated that the annual total cost of ownership of a personal computer is approximately four times the original cost of the hardware.

Many companies are eager to discover the total cost of ownership and, in particular, to reduce those costs. The task is not a simple one. The main obstacle is the complex and nitty-gritty nature of the process itself. There is no simple answer or one-shot approach. Here are a few areas of concern.

LIMITED OPTIONS   A key factor was described previously: Standardize the process of ordering hardware and create a short list of standard options. Carrying this further, managers must define and enforce not only hardware standards, but also software and configuration standards. In essence, the less variation there is, the easier the system is to support—less training, fewer calls for help, and more fixes that help everyone. Defining standards takes an initial investment of time and then regular reviews to evaluate and update.

HELPFUL SOFTWARE   A software category that has proven effective is desktop management software, which can perform a variety of functions. From the manager's point of view, the most valuable function is collecting inventory data—who has what version of what software, how often it is used, and so forth. This data can be collected automatically over the network. Other useful products provide automatic electronic distribution of software and software updates. Most such products also check for viruses on a regular basis.

UNHELPFUL SOFTWARE   As one manager put it, "We have to limit users' abilities to get themselves in trouble." In effect, this manager was calling for standardized software. In addition to having official purchasing limitations, users must be pro-hibited from downloading shareware or installing games or other applications they bring from home. The added software can create complications that require extra troubleshooting. Minimizing those risks can reduce the total cost of ownership.

HARDWARE AND SOFTWARE UPGRADES   This is a tricky one. It seems that as soon as the deployment of one upgrade wraps up, plans are already starting to be made for the next. Many a manager has wondered whether the benefits of an upgrade outweigh the costs. Do the workers really need faster computers when their comput-erized tasks are limited to sending and receiving email and the occasional memo? Will the new software enhancements really be used or even noticed, by most work-ers? Increasingly, managers are minimizing hardware and software upgrades unless there is significant justification.

Tracking down TCO numbers can be hard work. Even worse, it may have political complications. For example, a staffer might not want to include the travel costs of a trip to a computer trade show. The TCO efforts, in the end, should pay off by giving managers a realistic picture of real computing costs. The net result should be better buying decisions and more efficient use of computer resources.

◪ LEADING BUSINESS INTO THE FUTURE

Who will manage businesses in the future? Someone once remarked, somewhat face-tiously, that all top management—presidents, chief executive officers (CEOs), and so forth—should be drawn from the MIS ranks. After all, the argument goes, computers pervade the entire company, and people who work with computer systems can bring broad experience to the job. Today, most presidents and CEOs still come from legal, financial, or marketing backgrounds. But as the computer industry and its profes-sionals mature, that pattern could change.

▲

There are challenges for managers at every level. In addition to the ordinary tech-nological changes for which they can be somewhat prepared, they face technology on the cutting edge, the subject of the appendix.

CHAPTER REVIEW

► Summary and Key Terms

- All managers have five main functions: **planning, organizing, staffing, directing,** and **controlling.** A management pyramid shows that top-level managers focus primarily on strategic functions, especially long-range planning; middle-level managers focus on the tactical, especially the organizing and staffing required to implement plans; and low-level managers are concerned mainly with operational functions—controlling schedules, costs, and quality—as well as with directing personnel.

- A **management information system** (**MIS**) is a set of business systems designed to provide information for decision-making. A computerized MIS is most effective if it is integrated throughout the entire organization.

- The **MIS manager,** a person who is familiar with both computer technology and the organization's business, runs the MIS department.

- The traditional management pyramid has been flattened by the dissemination and sharing of information over computer networks. The impact of groupware has removed exclusive manager access to information and has forced managers to share decision-making. Some companies are organizing workers into teams around tasks.

- A **decision support system** (**DSS**) is a computer system that supports managers in nonroutine decision-making tasks. A DSS involves a **model,** a mathematical representation of a real-life situation. A computerized model allows a manager to try various what-if options by varying the inputs, or **independent variables,** to see how they affect the outputs, or **dependent variables.** The use of a computer model to reach a decision about a real-life situation is called **simulation.** Because the decision-making process must be fast, the DSS is interactive, allowing the user to communicate directly with the computer system and affect its activities.

- An **executive information system** (**EIS**) is a decision support system for senior-level executives, who make decisions that affect an entire company.

- When personal computers first became popular in the business world, most businesses did not have general policies regarding them, which led to several problems. Many businesses created the position of **personal computer manager** (later called the **network manager** or **LAN manager**) to ensure coordination of personal computers, established acquisition policies to solve the compatibility problem, established **information centers** or **support centers** to provide assistance to users, provided formal and informal training for users, and used software to monitor their existing personal computers.

- Many organizations rely on the one-shot, teacher-in-the-classroom model for training if they offer training at all. Follow-up support is necessary, and can be provided through in house gurus or information centers. CD-ROM and Web-based training have also proved to be effective, both for initial and follow up training.

- Managers often have little idea of how many computers are in use within a department or company or what software is being used on them. Software is available to keep track of all hardware and software installed on company networks.

- **Total Cost of Ownership** (**TCO**) refers to a methodology originally developed by the Gartner Group to determine all the costs involved in owning personal computers. These costs involve not only the original purchase price of the hardware and software, but also less obvious costs such as training, support, upgrades, and maintenance.

► **Critical Thinking Questions**

1. Suppose a team of eight people in a construction firm is designing a new hospital. The team members, drawn from several departments, include two engineers, two architects, an electrician, a plumber, a graphic designer, and a planner. How and by whom might the classic management functions be carried out?

2. Describe a problem situation that could be simulated through a decision support system. Specify the input factors and the types of output.

3. What special pressures might there be on a network manager?

4. Explain the differences among strategic, tactical, and operational levels of management. Which managers are responsible for each level of management? Give specific examples of strategic, tactical, and operational decisions.

5. When referring to mathematical modeling, what is meant by the terms independent variables and dependent variables? Give an example of a mathematical model, and its independent and dependent variables. What is the role of simulation in mathematical modeling?

6. Do you agree with Microsoft and Oracle's announced long-range plans to move their programs from local PCs on to the Internet? What are the advantages and disadvantages to doing this? Explain why you do or do not support their initiatives.

7. Call or visit the nearest major airport and find out if they have a Laptop Lane or other method of allowing travelers to connect to the Internet. If they do, determine the following:
   - If a Laptop Lane, how many laptops can be docked at their facility (that is, maximum number of ports)?
   - Is the connection wireless or does it require a modem or a NIC (network interface card)?
   - How fast are their network or Internet connections?
   - What are the rates for using their services?

8. High-speed computer connections could lead to telecommuting. Define this term. What are the advantages and disadvantages of telecommuting? If you have decided on a specific career, explain why you personally would or would not want to telecommute.

9. Call or go to your institution's computing services and find the titles and responsibilities of the top-level manager(s), middle-level manager(s), and the low-level manager(s). Do these managers use any decision support systems in making judgments? If they do not, how do they make their strategic, tactical, and operational decisions?

10. What is meant by the term electronic agent? Have you used one? Give a specific example of where you could possibly use an agent, and explain what you would like the agent to do for you.

► STUDENT STUDY GUIDE

Multiple Choice

1. Which of the following is not one of the main functions of managers:
   a. controlling
   b. pyramiding
   c. organizing
   d. directing

2. A decision support system for senior-level executives is called a(n)
   a. model
   b. MIS
   c. EIS
   d. DSS

3. The inputs to a model are called
   a. dependent variables
   b. spreadsheets
   c. simulators
   d. independent variables

4. A mathematical representation of a real-world situation is called a(n)
   a. MIS
   b. task
   c. network
   d. model

5. A computer system that supports managers in nonroutine decision-making tasks is called a(n)
   a. information center
   b. variable
   c. DSS
   d. model

6. Low-level managers are usually most concerned with
   a. long-range planning
   b. scheduling and costs
   c. organizing and staffing
   d. planning and organizing

7. Widespread sharing of information via networks has caused traditional management pyramids to become
   a. suspended
   b. flattened
   c. expanded
   d. eliminated

8. Internal company training is likely to be provided by the
   a. simulator
   b. MIS
   c. information center
   d. LAN manager

9. The MIS manager needs to be familiar with both
   a. technology and the business
   b. models and simulators
   c. technology and information center
   d. EIS and DSS

10. MIS stands for
    a. Management information system
    b. Management internal simulation
    c. Multiple integrated system
    d. Model independent simulation

11. An MIS manager may also be known as a(n)
    a. information resource manager
    b. chief information officer (CIO)
    c. director of information services
    d. all of the above

12. The ideal team size consists of how many members?
    a. 4
    b. 8
    c. 12
    d. 14

13. DSS stands for
    a. Decision Support System
    b. Dependable Selection System
    c. Database Selective System
    d. none of the above

14. EIS stands for
    a. Electronic Information System
    b. Essential Integrated Software
    c. Established Interpretive Service
    d. Executive Information System

15. The information center or support center does not offer help with which of the following?
    a. software and hardware selection
    b. network access
    c. user training
    d. travel arrangements

16. Which of the following is not a problem area for a personal computer manager?
    a. technology overload
    b. information overload
    c. data security and integrity
    d. computer junkies

17. A shop foreman is an example of which of the following?
    a. top-level manager
    b. middle-level manager
    c. low-level manager
    d. none of the above

18. A DSS is used by
    a. top-level managers only
    b. middle-level managers only
    c. low-level managers only
    d. all levels of management

19. The traditional management pyramid is being flattened by a reduction in the number of which of the following?
    a. top-level managers
    b. middle-level managers
    c. low-level managers
    d. workers

20. Which of the following is a technique designed to determine the overall cost payback of personal computers?
    a. EIS
    b. CIO
    c. TCO
    d. MIS

True/False

T F   1. The information center typically offers users training and assistance.

T F   2. The function of the network manager is to help executives with decision support systems.

T F   3. Communication of information is most efficient through the traditional management pyramid.

T F   4. Decision support systems help managers in nonroutine decision-making tasks.

T F   5. A model is a mathematical representation of an artificial situation.

T F   6. Middle-level managers focus on planning.

T F   7. Inputs to a model are called independent variables.

T F   8. Groupware is usually focused on groups of executives.

T F   9. The use of personal computers by managers is declining.

T F 10. Simulation is using a model to predict real-life situations.

T F 11. Part of the reason for changes in the classic management model is the increased use of networked computers.

T F 12. A personal computer manager is concerned only with technical issues.

T F 13. The use of groupware encourages workers in different organizations to communicate laterally, as opposed to going through the traditional management hierarchy.

T F 14. The use of networked computers in the organization has made information more unavailable than ever to workers.

T F 15. The flattened management pyramid has significantly increased the need for middle-level managers.

T F 16. Executive decision-making also requires access to information originating outside the organization.

T F 17. The personal computer manager is often the same person as the network manager or LAN manager.

T F 18. Remote users accessing company databases are a minor security concern of MIS managers.

T F 19. Training experts often suggest that computerphobes loosen up by playing computer games.

T F 20. The Internet cannot provide interactive customized training lessons.

Fill-In

1. A(n) _____ is a set of formal business systems designed to provide information for an organization.

2. _____ refers to a methodology originally developed by the Gartner Group to determine all costs involved in owning personal computers.

3. The _____ is the place where workers can get help with software problems.

4. _____ facilitates teamwork by allowing project information to be assembled in centralized databases.

5. The availability of networks and groupware promotes organizing employees into task-focused _____.

6. A(n) _____ does not replace a management of information system; instead it supplements a management of information system.

7. _____ managers focus primarily on strategic functions.

8. _____ managers focus primarily on tactical functions.

9. _____ managers focus primarily on operational functions.

10. Some of the duties of the _____ are to ensure coordination of personal computers and establish acquisition policies to solve compatibility problems.

11. _____ is the managerial function that involves the hiring and training of workers.

12. _____ is the managerial function that involves decisions about using resources, such as people and materials.

13. _____ is the managerial function that monitors the organization's progress toward reaching its goals.

14. A(n) _____ is a piece of software to which a person can delegate some degree of responsibility.

15. The use of a computer model to reach a decision about a real-life situation is called a(n) _____.

► ANSWERS

Multiple Choice

1. b	6. b	11. d	16. b
2. c	7. b	12. b	17. c
3. d	8. c	13. a	18. d
4. d	9. a	14. d	19. b
5. c	10. a	15. d	20. c

True/False

1. T	6. F	11. T	16. T
2. F	7. T	12. F	17. T
3. F	8. F	13. T	18. F
4. T	9. F	14. F	19. T
5. F	10. T	15. F	20. F

Fill-In

1. Management Information System (MIS)
2. Total Cost of Ownership (TCO)
3. information center or support center
4. Groupware
5. teams
6. decision support system (DSS)
7. Top-level
8. Middle-level
9. Low-level
10. Personal Computer Manager (PCM)
11. staffing
12. organizing
13. controlling
14. electronic agent or software agent
15. simulation

Planet Internet

Research and Resources

Need information? Need it fast? Whether commonplace or rare, any information you need is probably somewhere on the Internet.

Government Resources

The federal government had a head start and has made excellent use of the Internet. You can use the resources of the Library of Congress, contact the House of Representatives, or even get information from the CIA. You may peruse recent Supreme Court decisions by topic or by case name.

Although you might have little inclination to do so, you can access the Internal Revenue Service site to get forms or advice. The U.S. Census Bureau has an enormous amount of information that is useful to businesses and organizations, large and small. The Smithsonian has searchable historic information and a significant online photo collection. The National Archives houses the Declaration of Independence, the Constitution, and a wonderful set of historic posters.

Information You Can Use

Consider bits of information you might need in any given week, for instance a weather forecast for your travel destination. Every sort of weather information is available, for regions and individual cities.

The Old Farmer's Almanac supplies crop information and even weather information. There are helpful Web sites devoted to education in general or to specific subjects. ScienceNet is a British Web site providing information about a wide range of science and math topics, including Not Just A Lab Coat, where information about science-related careers is provided from people who work in those areas. You can search their database for answers to questions or pose your own question for a later response.

A Vast Amount of Consumer Information Is Available on the Internet

Buying a new or used car? You can obtain pricing information, get reviews of specific car models, and even order the car itself over the Internet. Almost

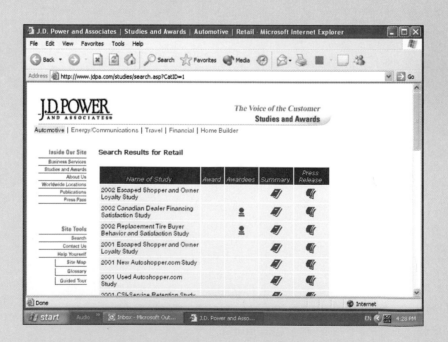

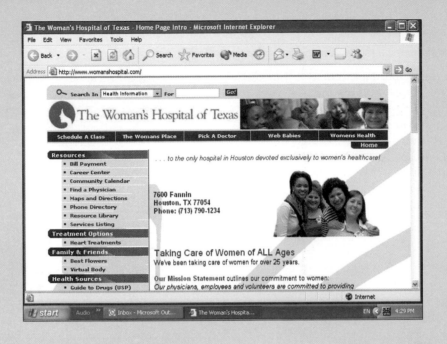

half (43 percent) of used vehicle buyers log onto the Internet to help them during the shopping process, according to the J.D. Power and Associates 2001 Used Autoshopper.com Study. This is a 27 percent increase over the 2000 study results, when only 34 percent of used vehicle buyers turned to the Internet. New vehicle shoppers continue to lead used vehicle shoppers in Internet usage, 62 percent versus 43 percent, respectively. The J.D. Power study is based on responses from more than 5300 consumers who recently purchased a 1996 to 2001 model-year used vehicle.

Concerned about Your Health or That of Family or Friends?

Many sites are devoted to providing medical information, including alternative medical information for those who want to consider a wide range of options. The Woman's Hospital of Texas, for example, provides a variety of information about women's health, with short articles about different topics weekly, an archive of past articles, and pictures of cute babies delivered at the hospital. The Black Health Network is a site aimed at African Americans that addresses a wide range of medical issues that are of particular interest to African Americans as well as medical topics relevant to all people. Their site includes articles, an FAQ, and information on how to find a Black Health Network doctor in your area.

Internet Exercises

1. **Structured exercise.** Begin with the URL http://www.prenhall.com/capron and check out the Exhibit Hall at the National Archives. You could look at World War II "powers of persuasion" posters or see the Apollo 11 flight plan.

2. **Free form exercise.** Assume that you will be going on a week-long vacation to visit friends and relatives in two different cities. On the basis of weather predictions, which city should you visit first to ensure the best weather at both cities? What type of clothing will you need for your vacation?

3. **Advanced exercise.** Pick a medical, historical, or art topic that is of interest to you. Many things that people think are facts are often merely frequently or loudly announced opinions. Write down three things that you think are facts about your topic. Then, beginning with the sites available from your text's Web site, determine whether your facts are truly facts. What research or data did you find to support your facts? Did you find out anything surprising?

The Continuing Story of
the Computer Age:
Past, Present, and Future

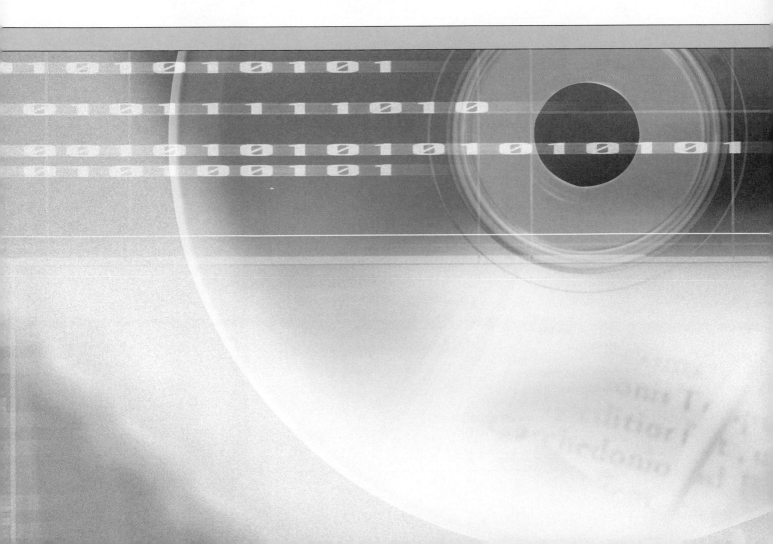

The Continuing Story of the Computer Age:
Past, Present, and Future

A P P E N D I X

LEARNING OBJECTIVES

► Describe the generations of computer design leading up to the present

► Describe the story of personal computer development

► Explain the underlying concepts and terms of artificial intelligence

► Explain the fundamentals of expert systems, robotics, and virtual reality

► Give examples of the impact these fields have on business and everyday life

Lisa Macon taught computer classes at Jackson Community College and worked on her Ph.D. in computer science on the side. She became quite interested in the artificial intelligence (AI) classes she was taking and thought her own students would be interested too. She did not want to teach a full-blown AI class but calculated that she could assemble an interesting introductory class that, for two Saturday sessions, would count as one credit.

Lisa got the class approved. She then encouraged enrollment by posting flyers noting that there were no prerequisites and that the class included a demonstration of a home-built robot. She anticipated a good deal of interest and arranged for a large classroom but was amazed when 247 students enrolled. One of them was Alex Martinez, who was majoring in computer information systems. He figured it could not hurt to have a class called Introduction to Artificial Intelligence on his résumé. Rather to his surprise, he enjoyed the class and came away with some idea of what artificial intelligence was all about.

Eighteen months later, as he was interviewing for his first job, Alex was startled to hear the interviewer say, "I see that you took an artificial intelligence class. Do you know what an expert system is?" Alex's first impulse was to protest that he really knew nothing at all about artificial intelligence, that it was just a little nothing class, but then—all this was in less than 10 seconds—he remembered what an expert system is. So he said, as calmly as possible, "An expert system is a computer system that lets the computer be an expert on some topic." The interviewer responded, "Well, you probably know more than I do."

As it happened, one of the groups managed by this interviewer had just been tagged to develop an expert system for an insurance waiver process. The AI professionals were already in place, but some other technical folks were needed as a supporting cast. To his stunned delight, Alex was hired and added to the team. He was no more than a gopher for a while, but it became an interesting experience. By the end of a year he had moved within the company to a more traditional programming environment. But Alex remained bemused that artificial intelligence had been his ticket in the door.

▶ THE COMPUTER AGE BEGINS

The remarkable thing about the computer age is that so much has happened in so short a time. We have leapfrogged through four generations of technology in about 55 years—a span of time whose events are within the memory of many people today. The first three computer "generations" are pinned to three technological developments: the vacuum tube, the transistor, and the integrated circuit. Each has drastically changed the nature of computers. We define the timing of each generation according to the beginning of commercial delivery of the hardware technology. Defining subsequent generations has become more complicated because the entire industry has become more complicated.

The First Generation, 1951–1958: The Vacuum Tube

The beginning of the commercial computer age can be dated to June 14, 1951. This was the day the first **UNIVAC—Universal Automatic Computer**—was delivered to a client, the U.S. Bureau of the Census, for use in tabulating the previous year's census. The date also marked the first time that a computer had been built for a business application rather than for military, scientific, or engineering use. The UNIVAC was really the ENIAC in disguise and was, in fact, built by Mauchly and Eckert, who in 1947 had formed their own corporation.

In the first generation, **vacuum tubes**—electronic tubes about the size of light bulbs—were used as the internal computer components (Figure A-1). However, because thousands of such tubes were required, they generated a great deal of heat, causing many problems in temperature regulation and climate control. In addition, although all the tubes had to be working simultaneously, they were subject to frequent burnout, and the people operating the computer often did not know whether the problem was in the programming or in the machine.

▶ FIGURE A-1

Vacuum tubes. Vacuum tubes were used in the first generation of computers.

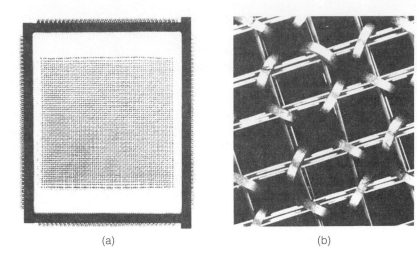

(a)   (b)

◄ **FIGURE** **A-2**

Magnetic cores. (a) A 6- by 11-inch magnetic core memory. (b) Close-up of magnetic core memory. A few hundredths of an inch in diameter, each magnetic core was mounted on wires. When electricity passed through a wire on which a core was strung, the core could be magnetized as either on or off.

The Computer Museum

The Computer Museum in downtown Boston, Massachusetts, is the world's first museum devoted solely to computers and computing. The museum shows how computers have affected all aspects of life: science, business, education, art, and entertainment. Over half an acre of hands-on and historical exhibits, the museum chronicles the enormous changes in the size, capability, applications, and cost of computers over the past 40 years. Two mini-theaters show computer classics as well as award-winning computer-animated films.

The Computer Museum Store offers a large selection of such unique items as state-of-the-art silicon chip jewelry and chocolate "chips," as well as books, posters, and cassettes.

Another drawback was that the language used in programming was machine language, which uses numbers. (Present-day higher-level languages are more like English.) Using numbers alone made programming the computer difficult and time-consuming. The UNIVAC used **magnetic cores** to provide memory. These consisted of small, doughnut-shaped rings about the size of pinheads, which were strung like beads on intersecting thin wires (Figure A-2). To supplement primary storage, first-generation computers stored data on punched cards. In 1957 magnetic tape was introduced as a faster, more compact method of storing data.

The Second Generation, 1959–1964: The Transistor

In 1947 three Bell Lab scientists—John Bardeen, Walter H. Brattain, and William Shockley—developed the **transistor,** a small device that transfers electronic signals across a resistor. (The name "transistor" began as a trademark concocted from "transfer" plus "resistor.") The scientists later received the Nobel Prize in Physics for their invention. The transistor revolutionized electronics in general and computers in particular. Transistors were much smaller than vacuum tubes, and they had numerous other advantages: They needed no warm-up time, consumed less energy, generated much less heat, and were faster and more reliable. In the late 1950s transistors were incorporated into computers.

During this generation another important development was the move from machine language to **assembly languages,** also called **symbolic languages.** Assembly languages use abbreviations for instructions (for example, L for LOAD) rather than numbers. This made programming less cumbersome.

After the development of symbolic languages came **high-level languages,** such as FORTRAN (1954) and COBOL (1959). Also, in 1962 the first removable disk pack was marketed. Disk storage supplemented magnetic tape systems and enabled users to have fast access to desired data.

Throughout this period computers were being used principally by business, university, and government organizations. They had not filtered down to the general public. The real part of the revolution was about to begin.

The Third Generation, 1965–1970: The Integrated Circuit

One of the most abundant elements in the earth's crust is silicon, a nonmetallic substance that is found in common beach sand as well as in practically all rocks and clay. The importance of this element to Santa Clara County, which is about 30 miles south of San Francisco, is responsible for the county's nickname: Silicon Valley. In 1965 Silicon Valley became the principal site for the manufacture of the so-called silicon chip: the integrated circuit.

An **integrated circuit (IC)** is a complete electronic circuit on a small chip of silicon. In 1965 integrated circuits began to replace transistors in computers. The resulting machines were called third-generation computers. Integrated circuits are made of silicon because it is a **semiconductor.** That is, silicon is a crystalline substance that conducts an electric current when it has been "doped" with chemical impurities implanted in its lattice-like structure.

The chips were hailed as a generational breakthrough because they had desirable characteristics: reliability, compactness, and low cost. Mass production techniques have made the manufacture of inexpensive integrated circuits possible.

The beginning of the third generation was heralded by the IBM 360 series (named for a full circle of service—360 degrees) in 1964. The System/360 family of computers, designed for both business and scientific use, came in several models and sizes. The "family of computers" concept made it possible for users to move to a more powerful machine without having to replace the software that already worked on the current computer. The equipment housing was blue, leading to IBM's nickname, Big Blue.

The 360 series was launched with an all-out, massive marketing effort to make computers business tools and get them into medium-size and smaller business and government operations where they had not been used before. Perhaps the most far-reaching contribution of the 360 series was IBM's decision to **unbundle** the software, that is, to sell the software separately from the hardware. This approach led to the creation of today's software industry.

Software became more sophisticated during this third generation. Several programs could run in the same time frame, sharing computer resources. This approach improved the efficiency of computer systems. Software systems were developed to support interactive processing, which used a terminal to put the user in direct contact with the computer. This kind of access caused the customer service industry to flourish, especially in areas such as reservations and credit checks.

The Fourth Generation, 1971–Present: The Microprocessor

Through the 1970s computers gained dramatically in speed, reliability, and storage capacity, but entry into the fourth generation was evolutionary rather than revolutionary. The fourth generation was, in fact, an extension of third-generation technology. That is, in the early part of the third generation, specialized chips were developed for computer memory and logic. Thus all the ingredients were in place for the next technological development: the general-purpose processor-on-a-chip, otherwise known as the **microprocessor,** which became commercially available in 1971.

Nowhere is the pervasiveness of computer power more apparent than in the explosive growth in the use of the microprocessor. In addition to the common applications of the microprocessor in digital watches, pocket calculators, and personal computers, you can expect to find one in virtually every machine in the home or business: cars, copy machines, television sets, bread-making machines, and so on. Computers today are 100 times smaller than those of the first generation, and a single chip is far more powerful than ENIAC.

▶ THE STORY OF PERSONAL COMPUTERS

Personal computers are the machines you can "get closest to," whether you are an amateur or a professional. There is nothing quite like having your very own personal computer. Its history is personal too, full of stories of success and failure and of individuals with whom we can readily identify.

Apple Leads the Way

The first generally available personal computer was the MITS Altair, produced in 1975. It was a gee-whiz machine, loaded with switches and dials but with no keyboard or screen. It took two teenagers, Steve Jobs and Steve Wozniak, to capture the public's imagination with the first Apple computer. They built it in that time-honored place of inventors, a garage, using the $1,300 proceeds from the sale of an old Volkswagen. Designed for home use, the Apple was the first to offer an easy-to-use keyboard and screen. Founded in 1977, Apple Computer was immediately and wildly successful. (Figure A-3 shows the cover page of the user's manual for the first commercial Apple computer.)

The first Apple computer, the Apple I, was not a commercial success. It was the Apple II that anchored the early years of the company. In fact, it was the combination of the Apple II and the spreadsheet software called VisiCalc that caught the attention of the business community and propelled personal computers into the workplace.

The IBM PC Standard

Announcing its first personal computer in the summer of 1981, IBM proceeded to capture the top market share in just 18 months. Even more importantly, its machine became the industry standard (Figure A-4). The IBM machine included innovations, such as an 80-character screen line, a full uppercase and lowercase keyboard, and the possibility of adding memory. IBM also provided internal expansion slots, so that peripheral equipment manufacturers could build accessories for the IBM PC. In addition, IBM provided hardware schematics and software listings to companies that wanted to build products in conjunction with the new PC. Many of the new products accelerated demand for the IBM machine. Many new companies sprang up just to support the IBM PC.

IBM made its computer from nonproprietary parts, opening the door for other manufacturers to do the same. Thus other personal computer manufacturers emulated the IBM standard, producing IBM **clones,** copycat computers that functioned identically to the IBM PC. The clones were able to run the large selection of software that had been designed for IBM computers. Almost all the major personal computer manufacturers today—HP, Dell, Gateway, and many others—continue to produce computers that have evolved from the original IBM standard. In fact, IBM-compatible computers now dominate the personal computer market, leaving IBM with a market share that is small when compared with its original success.

The Microsoft/Intel Standard

In the history of the computer industry, the spotlight has been on the fast-changing hardware. However, personal computer users now focus more on the tremendous variety of software. The dominant force in personal computer software is the Microsoft Corporation.

Microsoft supplied the operating system—the underlying software—for the original IBM personal computer. This software, called MS-DOS, was used by IBM and by the IBM clones, permitting tiny Microsoft to grow quickly. Microsoft eventually presented more sophisticated operating systems, notably Windows. The Windows operating system is used on computers powered by a microprocessor from the Intel Corporation; this potent combination, nicknamed Wintel, has become the dominant force in personal computer sales.

Nevertheless, the Wintel standard is ever open to challenge. Efforts to offer computers that simply bypass Windows have not made significant inroads. It is noteworthy, however, that handheld models, such as the Palm, which use neither Microsoft nor Intel products, are being used, to some degree, in lieu of personal computers. Furthermore, Linux, developed by Linus Torvalds at the University of Helsinki in Finland, offers personal computer users a graphical user interface operating system. Although copyrights are held by various creators of Linux's components, its distribution stipulations require that any copy be free. Despite its lack of a commercial marketing mechanism, Linux is making some inroads.

APPLE-1 OPERATION MANUAL

APPLE COMPUTER COMPANY
770 Welch Road
Palo Alto, Calif. 94304

▲ **FIGURE** A-3

Apple manual. Shown here is a collector's item: the very first manual for operation of an Apple computer. Unfortunately, the early manuals were a hodgepodge of circuit diagrams, software listings, and handwritten notes. They were hard to read and understand, enough to frighten away all but the hardiest souls.

▲ **FIGURE** A-3

The IBM PC. Launched in 1981, this early IBM PC rose to the top of the best-seller list in just 18 months.

THE ENTREPRENEURS

Ever thought you'd like to run your own show? Make your own product? Be in business for yourself? Entrepreneurs are a special breed. They are achievement-oriented, like to take responsibility for decisions, and dislike routine work. They also have high levels of energy and a great deal of imagination. But perhaps the key is that they are willing to take risks.

Steve Jobs

Of the two Steves who formed Apple Computer, Steve Jobs was the true entrepreneur. Although both were interested in electronics, Steve Wozniak was the technical genius, and he would have been happy to have been left alone to tinker. But Steve Jobs would not let him alone for a minute; he was always pushing and crusading. In fact, Wozniak had hooked up with an evangelist, and they made quite a pair.

When Apple was getting off the ground, Jobs wanted Wozniak to quit his job so that he could work full-time on the new venture. Wozniak refused. His partner begged and cried. Wozniak gave in. While Wozniak built Apple computers, Jobs was out hustling, finding the best marketing person, the best venture capitalist, and the best company president. This entrepreneurial spirit paid off in a spectacular way as Apple rose to the top of the list of personal computer companies.

Bill Gates

When Bill Gates was a teenager, he swore off computers for a year and, in his words, "tried to act normal." His parents, who wanted him to be a lawyer, must have been relieved when Bill gave up on the computer foolishness and went off to Harvard in 1974. But Bill started spending weekends with his friend Paul Allen, dreaming about personal computers, which did not exist yet. When the MITS Altair, the first personal computer for sale, splashed on the market in January 1975, both Bill and Paul moved to Albuquerque to be near the action at MITS. But they showed a desire even then to chart their own course. Although they wrote software for MITS, they kept the rights to their work and formed their own company. It was called Microsoft.

When MITS failed, Gates and Allen moved their software company to their native Bellevue, Washington. They had 32 people in their employ in 1980 when IBM came to call. Gates recognized the big league when he saw it and put on a suit for the occasion. He was offered a plum: the chance to develop the operating system (a crucial set of software) for IBM's soon-to-be personal computer. Although he knew that he was betting the whole company, Gates never hesitated to take the risk. He purchased an existing operating system, which he and his crew reworked to produce MS-DOS, which stands for Microsoft disk operating system. It was this product that sent Microsoft on its meteoric rise.

Michael Dell

The rise of the Dell Computer Corporation, founded by Michael Dell, is astonishing by any standard. It would be hard to say who is more pleased—customers, stockholders, or Mr. Dell himself. Customers, large and small, have learned that Dell personal computers are excellent and that company service is even better. Stockholders have enjoyed owning the fastest-rising stock of the 1990s. And Michael Dell? In addition to untold billions, he has the satisfaction of inventing a business model that is now copied worldwide.

The business began not in a fabled garage, but in a place just about as noteworthy for a good story line: Michael Dell's dorm room at the University of Texas. It was 1983, and he was 19 years old. He began with the premise of delivering high-performance computer systems directly to the end user. By not using resellers, Dell reduces both the cost of the computer and the time of delivery. Along the way, Dell adopted the Internet as a key sales tool. Dell generates millions in revenue every day from its Web site.

► THE INTERNET REVOLUTION

The word "revolution" is never far away when the discussion is about computers. But nothing in computer history has captured the attention of computer users as the Internet has. Even the acceptance of the personal computer pales in comparison. "Revolution" is truly an appropriate word. Chapter 8 contains a more detailed discussion of the influence of the Internet on business and society in general.

There are two critical points to understand, regarding the history of the Internet. The first is that the Internet was started as ARPANET, a network of equal computers that was designed as a Defense Department research project. Second, the Internet was made attractive to the average user by Dr. Tim Berners-Lee, who came up with the notion of hyperlinks, and Marc Andreesen, who produced the first graphical browser.

Unlike other parts of computer history, the Internet is well documented online. It makes sense to go to the source, rather than read an abbreviated version here. If you want to know more, submit words such as "Internet," "history," and "ARPANet" to a search engine, and numerous appropriate sites will be offered.

▶ THE FIFTH GENERATION: ONWARD

The term **fifth generation** was coined by the Japanese to describe the powerful, "intelligent" computers they wanted to build by the mid-1990s. Later the term evolved to encompass elements in several research fields related to computer intelligence: artificial intelligence, expert systems, and natural language.

But the true focus of this ongoing fifth generation is connectivity, the massive industry effort to permit users to connect their computers to other computers. The concept of the information superhighway has captured the imaginations of both computer professionals and everyday computer users.

▶ THE ARTIFICIAL INTELLIGENCE FIELD

Artificial intelligence (AI) is a field of study that explores how computers can be used for tasks that require the human characteristics of intelligence, imagination, and intuition. Computer scientists sometimes prefer a looser definition, calling AI the study of how to make computers do things that, at present, people can do better. The current definition is significant because artificial intelligence is an evolving science: As soon as a problem is solved, it is moved off the artificial intelligence agenda. A good example is the game of chess, once considered a mighty AI challenge. Now that most computer chess programs can beat most human competitors, chess is no longer an object of study by scientists and therefore no longer on the artificial intelligence agenda.

Today the term "artificial intelligence" encompasses several subsets of interests (Figure A-5):

- **Problem solving.** This area of AI includes a spectrum of activities, from playing games to planning military strategy.

- **Natural languages.** This facet involves the study of the person/computer interface in unconstrained native language.

- **Expert systems.** These AI systems present the computer as an expert on some particular topic.

- **Robotics.** This field involves endowing computer-controlled machines with electronic capabilities for vision, speech, and touch.

Although considerable progress has been made in these sophisticated fields of study, early successes did not come easily. Before examining current advances in these areas, consider some moments in the development of artificial intelligence.

Early Mishaps

In the first days of artificial intelligence, scientists thought that the computer would experience something like an electronic childhood, in which it would gobble up the world's libraries and then begin generating new wisdom. Few people talk like this today because the problem of simulating intelligence is far more complex than just stuffing facts into the computer. Facts are useless without the ability to interpret and learn from them.

An artificial intelligence failure on a grand scale was the attempt to translate human languages via the computer. Although scientists were able to pour vocabulary

▶ F I G U R E **A-5**

The artificial intelligence family tree.

Robotics:
Machines that can move and relate to objects as humans can.

Expert systems:
Programs that mimic the decision-making and problem-solving thought processes of human experts.

Natural languages:
Systems that translate ordinary human commands into language computers can understand and act on.

Problem solving:
Programs that cover a broad spectrum of problems, from games to military strategy.

Artificial intelligence

and rules of grammar into the computer, the literal word-for-word translations often resulted in ludicrous output. In one infamous example, the computer was supposed to demonstrate its prowess by translating a phrase from English to Russian and then back to English. Despite the computer's best efforts, the saying "The spirit is willing, but the flesh is weak" came back "The vodka is good, but the meat is spoiled."

An unfortunate result of this widely published experiment was the ridicule of artificial intelligence scientists, who were considered dreamers who could not accept the limitations of a machine. Funding for AI research disappeared, plunging the artificial intelligence community into a slump from which it did not recover until expert systems emerged in the 1980s. Nevertheless, a hardy band of scientists continued to explore artificial intelligence, focusing on how computers learn.

How Computers Learn

The study of artificial intelligence is predicated on the computer's ability to learn and to improve performance on the basis of past errors. The two key elements of this process are the knowledge base and the inference engine. A **knowledge base** is a set of facts and rules about those facts. An inference engine accesses, selects, and interprets a set of rules. The **inference engine** applies the rules to the facts to make up new facts; thus the computer has learned something new. Consider this simple example:

FACT: Amy is Ken's wife.

RULE: If X is Y's wife, then Y is X's husband.

The computer—the inference engine—can apply the rule to the fact and come up with a new fact: Ken is Amy's husband. Although the result of this simplistic example may seem of little value, it is indeed true that the computer now knows two facts instead of just one. Rules, of course, can be much more complex and facts more plentiful, yielding more sophisticated results. In fact, artificial intelligence software is capable of searching through long chains of related facts to reach a conclusion—a new fact.

Further explanation of the precise way in which computers learn is beyond the scope of this book. However, the learning discussion can be used as a springboard to the question that most people ask about artificial intelligence: Can a computer really think?

The Artificial Intelligence Debate

To imitate the functioning of the human mind, a machine with artificial intelligence would have to be able to examine a variety of facts, address multiple subjects, and devise a solution to a problem by comparing new facts to its existing storehouse of data from many fields. So far, artificial intelligence systems cannot match a person's ability to solve problems through original thought but must use familiar patterns as guides.

There are many arguments for and against crediting computers with the ability to think. Some say, for example, that computers cannot be considered intelligent because they do not compose like Beethoven or write like Shakespeare. The response is that neither do most ordinary human musicians or writers. You do not have to be a genius to be considered intelligent.

Look at it another way. Suppose you rack your brain over a problem, and then— aha!—the solution comes to you all at once. Now, how did you do that? You do not know, and nobody else knows either. A big part of human problem solving seems to be that jolt of recognition, that ability to see things suddenly as a whole. Experiments have shown that people rarely solve problems by using step-by-step logic, the very thing that computers do best. Most modern computers still plod through problems one step at a time. The human brain beats computers at "aha!" problem solving because it has millions of neurons working simultaneously.

Back to the basic question: Can a computer think or not? One possible answer: Who cares? If a machine can perform a task really well, does it matter whether it actually thinks? Still another answer is, yes, machines can really think, but not as humans do. They lack the sensitivity, appreciation, and passion that are intrinsic to human thought.

Data Mining

Computer brainpower can also be brought to bear on stores of data through **data mining,** the process of extracting previously unknown information from existing data. You might think that once data has been gathered and made available, you could know everything about it, but this is not necessarily so.

The information stored in hundreds of thousands of records on disk can be tallied, summarized, and perhaps even cross-referenced in some useful way by conventional computer programs. It is these traditional processes that produce the standard reports of business: bills, tax records, and annual reports. But conventional processes are unlikely to discover the hidden information that might give a competitive edge. The possible hidden information is just the sort of thing that a thinking person might uncover if the amount of data were of a manageable size. But no human can find nuances in massive data stores. Data mining, however, in a somewhat humanlike manner, might uncover data relationships and trends that are not readily apparent.

Companies are indeed using data-mining techniques to sift through their databases, looking for unnoticed relationships. Wal-Mart, for example, does this every day to optimize inventories. At the end of the day, all the sales data from every store comes into a single computer, which then interprets the data. The computer might notice, for example, that a lot of green sweaters have been selling in Boston and that,

Yes, We Have Bananas

You probably did not know that bananas are the most popular item in American shopping carts, more popular than bread or milk. But Wal-Mart knows. In fact, Wal-Mart, whose database is second in size only to that of the U.S. government's, knows all sorts of things about customers' buying habits.

Wal-Mart has found a new way to use the data it collects at cash registers. Using data-mining techniques, it can peruse the data to discover popular items and, more important, find useful combinations. One key fact they discovered was that people who bought bananas often bought cold cereal. Since bananas are so well liked and some folks buy cereal too, it makes sense to encourage all buyers to buy both products. The answer: Place bananas, in addition to their usual produce location, in the cereal aisle. Sales of cereal jumped.

As a result of data mining, other items that are now side by side on the shelf are bug spray and camping gear, tissues and cold medicine, measuring spoons and baking oil, and flashlights and Halloween costumes.

in fact, the supplies were depleted. The same green sweater is hardly selling at all in Phoenix. A human can figure out the reason: It is St. Patrick's Day, and there are many more people of Irish descent in Boston than in Phoenix. For next St. Patrick's Day the computer will order a larger supply of green sweaters for the Boston stores.

The Natural Language Factor

The language that people use on a daily basis to write and speak is called a **natural language**. Natural languages are associated with artificial intelligence because humans can make the best use of artificial intelligence if they can communicate with computers in natural language. Furthermore, understanding natural language is a skill thought to require intelligence.

Some natural language words are easy to understand because they represent a definable item: horse, chair, and mountain, for example. Other words, however, are much too abstract to lend themselves to straightforward definitions: justice, virtue, and beauty, for example. But this kind of abstraction is just the beginning of the difficulty. Consider the word *hand* in the following statements:

- Morgan had a hand in the robbery.
- Morgan had a hand in the cookie jar.
- Morgan is an old hand at chess.
- Morgan gave Sean a hand with his luggage.
- Morgan asked Marcia for her hand in marriage.
- All hands on deck!

As you can see, natural language abounds with ambiguities; the word *hand* has a different meaning in each statement. In contrast, sometimes statements that appear to be different really mean the same thing: "Alan sold Jim a book for five dollars" is equivalent to "Jim gave Alan five dollars in exchange for a book." It takes sophisticated software to unravel such statements and see them as equivalent.

Feeding computers the vocabulary and grammatical rules they need to know is a step in the right direction. However, as you saw earlier in the account of the language translation fiasco, true understanding requires more: Words must be taken in context. Humans start acquiring a context for words from the day they are born. Consider this statement: Jack cried when Alice said she loved Bill. From our own context, several possible conclusions can be drawn: Jack is sad. Jack probably loves Alice. Jack probably thinks Alice doesn't love him, and so on. These conclusions might not be correct, but they are reasonable interpretations based on the context the reader supplies. On the other hand, it would not be reasonable to conclude from the statement that Jack is a carpenter or that Alice has a new refrigerator.

One of the most frustrating tasks for AI scientists is providing the computer with the sense of context that humans have. Scientists have attempted to do this in regard to specific subjects and found the task daunting. For example, a scientist who wrote software so that the computer could have a dialog about restaurants had to feed the computer hundreds of facts that any small child would know, such as the fact that restaurants have food and that people are expected to pay for it.

▶ EXPERT SYSTEMS

An **expert system** is a software package that is used with an extensive set of organized data that presents the computer as an expert on a particular topic. For example, a computer could be an expert on where to drill oil wells, on what stock purchase looks promising, or on how to cook soufflés. The user is the knowledge seeker, usually asking questions in a natural, English-like format. An expert system can respond to an inquiry about a problem with both an answer and an explanation of the answer. For example, an expert system specializing in stock purchases could be asked whether stocks of the Milton Corporation are currently a good buy. A possible answer is no with backup reasons such as a very high price/earnings ratio or a recent change in top management. The expert system works by figuring out what the question means and then matching it against the facts and rules that it "knows" (Figure A-6). These facts and rules, which reside on disk, originally come from human experts.

But why go to all this trouble and expense? Why not just stick with human experts? Well, there are problems with human experts. They are typically expensive, they are subject to biases and emotions, and they may even be inconsistent. Finally, experts can resign or retire, leaving the company in a state of crisis. If there is just one expert, or even just a few experts, there might not be enough to satisfy the needs of the system. The computer, however, is ever present and just as available as the telephone.

Few organizations are capable of building an expert system from scratch. The sensible alternative is to buy an **expert system shell,** a software package that consists of the basic structure used to find answers to questions. It is up to the buyer to fill in the actual knowledge on the chosen subject. You could think of the expert system shell as an empty cup that becomes a new entity once it is filled: a cup of coffee, for instance, or a cup of sugar.

The most challenging task of building an expert system often is deciding who the appropriate expert is and then trying to pin down his or her knowledge. Experts often believe that much of their expertise is instinctive and therefore find it difficult to articulate just why they do what they do. However, the expert is usually following a set of rules, even if the rules are only in his or her head. The person ferreting out the information, sometimes called a **knowledge engineer,** must have a keen eye and the skills of a diplomat.

After the knowledge engineer uncovers them, the rules are formed into a set of IF-THEN rules. For example, IF the customer has exceeded a credit limit by no more than 20 percent and has paid the monthly bill on time for six months, THEN extend further credit. After the system is translated into a computerized version, it is reviewed, changed, tested, and changed some more. This repetitive process can take months or even years. Finally, it is put into the same situations that the human expert would face, where it should give equal or better service but much more quickly.

Aldo the Expert
The Campbell Soup Company has an expert system nicknamed Aldo, for Aldo Cimino, the human expert who knows how to fix the company's cooking machines. The human Aldo was getting on in years and was being run ragged, flying from plant to plant whenever a cooker went on the blink. Besides, how would the company manage when he retired? Now Aldo's knowledge has been distilled into an expert system that can be used by workers in any location.

◄ **F I G U R E A-6**

An expert system on the job. This expert system helps Ford mechanics track down and fix engine problems.

▶ ROBOTICS

Many people smile at the thought of robots, perhaps remembering the endearing C-3PO of Star Wars fame and its "personal" relationship with humans. But vendors have not made even a small dent in the personal robot market. The much-heralded domestic robots who wash windows have not yet become household staples. So where are the robots today? Mainly in factories.

Robots in the Factory

Most robots are in factories, spray-painting and welding, and taking away jobs. The Census Bureau, after two centuries of counting people, has now branched out and today is counting robots as well. About 15,000 robots existed in 1985, a number that jumped to 50,000 just 10 years later. What do robots do that merits all this attention?

A **robot** is a computer-controlled device that can physically manipulate its surroundings. There are a wide variety of sizes and shapes of robots, each designed for a particular use. Often these uses are functions that would be tedious or even dangerous for a human to perform. The most common industrial robots sold today are mechanical devices with five or six directions of motion so that they can rotate into proper position to perform their tasks (Figure A-7).

Recently, **vision robots,** with the help of a TV camera eye, have been taught to see in living color—that is, to recognize multicolored objects solely from their colors. This is a departure from the traditional approach, whereby robots recognize objects by their shapes, and from vision machines that "see" only a dominant color. For example, a robot in an experiment at the University of Rochester was able to pick out a box of Kellogg's Sugar Frosted Flakes from 70 other boxes. Among the anticipated benefits of such visual recognition skills is supermarket checkout. You cannot easily bar code a squash, but a robot might be trained to recognize it by its size, shape, and color.

Field Robots

Think of some of the places you would rather not be: inside a nuclear power plant, next to a suspected bomb, at the bottom of the sea, on the floor of a volcano, or in the middle of a chemical spill. But robots readily go to all those places. Furthermore, they go there to do some dangerous and dirty jobs. These days, **field robots**—robots "in the field"—inspect and repair nuclear power plants, dispose of bombs, inspect oil rigs used for undersea exploration, explore steaming volcanoes, clean up chemical accidents, and even explore a battlefield in advance of soldiers. Field robots are also used to check underground storage tanks and pipelines for leaks and to clean up hazardous waste dumps. An undersea robot ventured into the icy waters off Finland

▶ **FIGURE A-7**

Industrial robots. (a) These standard robots are used in the auto industry to weld new cars. (b) This robot is not making breakfast. Hitachi uses the delicate egg to demonstrate that its visual-tactile robot can handle fragile objects. The robot's sensors detect size, shape, and required pressure, attaining sensitivity almost equal to that of a human hand.

(a)

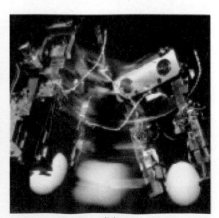
(b)

(a)　(b)　(c)

FIGURE A-8

Field robots. (a) Nicknamed Robotuna, this undersea robot under development at MIT will, scientists hope, be able to map the ocean floor, track schools of real fish, or detect pollution, and then swim home with the data. (b) Can a robot really fly? Yes. Flying robots have both military and civilian uses. This Sentinel robot can soar up to 10,000 feet to spy on an enemy, to inspect high-voltage wires, or to spot forest fires. (c) The robot called Spider checks gas tanks for cracks and sends computer images back to the ground, saving engineers from making a dangerous climb.

and scanned the sunken ferry Estonia, sending back pictures of its weakened bow, which was thought to be a cause of the disaster. Newer undersea robots are being designed to swim like fish (Figure A-8a). Going in another direction, space researchers look forward to the day when "astrobots" can be stationed in orbit, ready to repair faulty satellites. Field robots may be equipped with wheels, tracks, legs, fins, or even wings (Figure A-8b). As a future goal, scientists hope to use robots to construct a space station and base on the moon.

Field robots have largely been overshadowed by factory robots, mainly because until recently, field robots have lacked the independence of their manufacturing counterparts, needing to be controlled remotely by human operators. Now, however, enough computer power can be packed into a field robot to enable it to make most decisions independently. Field robots need all the power they can get. Unlike factory robots, which are bolted to the ground and blindly do the same tasks over and over again, field robots must often contend with a highly unstructured environment, which may include features, such as changing terrain and weather.

► VIRTUAL REALITY

The concept of **virtual reality,** sometimes called just **VR,** is to engage a user in a computer-created environment so that the user physically interacts with that environment. In fact, the user becomes so absorbed with the virtual reality interaction that the process is called **immersion.** Virtual reality alters perceptions partly by appealing to several senses at once—sight, hearing, and touch—and by presenting images that respond immediately to one's movements.

The visual part is made possible by sophisticated computers and optics that deliver to a user's eyes a three-dimensional scene in living color. The source of the scene is a database used by a powerful computer to display graphic images. The virtual reality system can sense a user's head and body movements through cables linked to the headset and glove worn by the user. That is, sensors on the user's body send signals to the computer, which then adjusts the scene viewed by the user. Thus the user's

GETTING PRACTICAL — Robots in Our Lives

If you think robots are not practical in your own life, think again. Like computers before them, robots will soon be everywhere. Here are some examples.

- **Fill it up.** If filling your car's gas tank is not a favorite chore, you will be pleased to know that robots are taking over. Drivers pull up to a specially equipped station, swipe a plastic "tank card," and enter an identification number. The unit identifies the make and model of the auto, then guides the robotic arm to the car's fuel filler door. After it is open, the robot then places the right grade and amount of gas in the tank and even replaces the cap.

- **My doctor the robot.** If you have orthopedic surgery, you might find that a key player alongside the surgeon is a robot. For example, to make room for a hip implant, a robotic arm drills a long hole in a thigh bone. Robotic precision improves the implant, reduces pain after surgery, and speeds healing.

- **Lending a hand.** Robots might soon be of significant use to the disabled. Researchers have already developed a robot for quadriplegics. The machine can respond to dozens of voice commands by answering the door, getting the mail, and even serving soup.

- **Road maintenance.** In California, road signs might soon say, "Robots at Work." Robots use lasers to spot cracks in the pavement and dispense the right amount of patch material. Soon robots will also be painting the road stripes.

- **One cool clerk.** The very latest in modern technology and artificial intelligence has been used to create the Super RoboShop, the world's most convenient convenience store. Human store clerks have been replaced by the cheery little Robo, a computer-controlled bucket that does your shopping for you. Can't find batteries? Robo can, sparing the weary shopper from wandering the aisles or interacting with another human being. RoboShop is basically a gigantic vending machine delivering an eclectic mix of products, everything from cookies to comic books to cologne. Customers enter code numbers for desired products using an ATM-like keypad, pay the machine, and Robo whizzes into action, picking each item from the display cases without smashing so much as a single egg. This shop might not be in your life just yet: The first dozen RoboShops were in Japan and they are just now being developed in New York City.

- **Going bump in the night.** Chip, the chunky errand boy on the night shift at Baltimore's Franklin Square Hospital, fetches medicine, late meals, medical records, and supplies. A robot, Chip finds his way using sensitive whiskers and touch pads. Nurses love him because he saves them from having to run all over the hospital.

body movements can cause interaction with the virtual (artificial) world the user sees, and the computer-generated world responds to those actions (see Figure A-9).

Travel Anywhere, but Stay Where You Are

At the University of North Carolina, computer scientists have developed a virtual reality program that lets a user walk through an art gallery. The user puts on a head-mounted display, which focuses the eyes on a screen and shuts out the rest of the world. If the user swivels his or her head to the right, pictures on the right wall come into view; similarly, the user can view any part of the gallery just by making head movements. This action/reaction combination presents realistic continuing changes to the user. Although actually standing in one place, the user feels as though he or she is moving and wants to stop short as a pedestal appears in the path ahead. It is as if the user is actually walking around inside the gallery.

In another example scientists have taken data about Mars, sent back by space probes, and converted it to a virtual reality program. Information about hills, rocks, and ridges of the planet are used to create a Mars landscape that is projected on the user's head screen.

► **FIGURE** A-9

Virtual reality. The virtual reality gear worn by this user allows him to immerse himself in an imaginary world created by the computer.

The Promise of Virtual Reality

An embryonic technology, such as virtual reality, is filled with hype and promises. It is the practical commercial applications for real-world users that show where this technology might lead. Here are some applications that are under development:

- Wearing head mounts, consumers can browse for products in a "virtual show-room." From a remote location a consumer will be able to maneuver and view products along aisles in a warehouse.

- Similarly, from a convenient office perch, a security guard can patrol corridors and offices in remote locations.

- Using virtual reality headsets and gloves, doctors and medical students will be able to experiment with new procedures on simulated patients rather than real ones.

Any new technology has its drawbacks. Some users experience "simulator sickness," even though they know the experience is not real. The developers of virtual reality are faced with daunting costs. Many hurdles remain in the areas of software, hardware, and even human behavior before virtual reality can reach its full potential.

▲

The immediate prospects for expert systems, robots, and virtual reality systems are growth and more growth. You can anticipate both increased sophistication and more diverse applications.

CHAPTER REVIEW

▶ **Summary and Key Terms**

- The first commercial computer generation dates to June 14, 1951, with the delivery of the **UNIVAC (Universal Automatic Computer)** to the U.S. Bureau of the Census. First-generation computers required thousands of **vacuum tubes,** electronic tubes about the size of light bulbs. The main form of memory was **magnetic core,** small, doughnut-shaped rings about the size of pinheads, which were strung like beads on intersecting thin wires.

- Second-generation computers used **transistors,** which were small, needed no warm-up, consumed less energy, and were faster and more reliable. During the second generation, **assembly languages,** or **symbolic languages,** were developed. Later, **high-level languages,** such as FORTRAN and COBOL, were also developed.

- The third generation featured the **integrated circuit** (**IC**)—a complete electronic circuit on a small chip of silicon. Silicon is a **semiconductor,** a substance that conducts electric current when it has been "doped" with chemical impurities.

- With the third generation, IBM announced the System/360 family of computers, which made it possible for users to move up to a more powerful machine without replacing the software that already worked on the current computer. IBM also **unbundled** the software, that is, sold it separately from the hardware.

- The feature of the fourth generation—the **microprocessor,** a general-purpose processor-on-a-chip—grew out of the specialized memory and logic chips of the third generation.

- The first personal computer, the MITS Altair, was produced in 1975. However, the first successful computer to include an easy-to-use keyboard and screen was offered by Apple Computer, founded by Steve Jobs and Steve Wozniak in 1977.

- IBM entered the personal computer market in 1981 and captured the top market share in just 18 months. Other manufacturers began to produce IBM **clones,** copycat computers that could run software designed for IBM computers.

- The leading software company worldwide is the Microsoft Corporation, which supplied the operating system for the original IBM personal computer and then went on to develop a variety of successful applications software.

- The term **fifth generation,** coined by the Japanese, evolved to encompass developments in artificial intelligence, expert systems, and natural languages. But the true focus of the fifth generation is connectivity, permitting users to connect their computers to other computers.

- **Artificial intelligence** (**AI**) is a field of study that explores how computers can be used for tasks that require the human characteristics of intelligence, imagination, and intuition. AI has also been described as the study of how to make computers do things that, at present, people can do better.

- Artificial intelligence is considered an umbrella term to encompass several subsets of interests, including **problem solving, natural languages, expert systems,** and **robotics.**

- In the early days of AI, scientists thought that it would be useful just to stuff facts into the computer; however, facts are useless without the ability to interpret and learn from them.

- An early attempt to translate human languages by providing a computer with vocabulary and rules of grammar was a failure because the computer could not distinguish the context of statements. This failure impeded the progress of artificial intelligence.

- The study of artificial intelligence is predicated on the computer's ability to learn and to improve performance on the basis of past errors.

- A **knowledge base** is a set of facts and rules about those facts. An **inference engine** accesses, selects, and interprets a set of rules. The inference engine applies rules to the facts to make up new facts.

- People rarely solve problems using the step-by-step logic that most computers use. The brain beats the computer at solving problems because it has millions of neurons working simultaneously.

- **Data mining** is the process of extracting previously unknown information from existing data.

- **Natural languages** are associated with artificial intelligence because humans can make the best use of artificial intelligence if they can communicate with the computer in human language. Furthermore, understanding natural language is a skill that is thought to require intelligence. A key function of the AI study of natural languages is to develop a computer system that can resolve ambiguities.

- An **expert system** is a software package that is used with an extensive set of organized data that presents the computer as an expert on a specific topic. The expert system works by figuring out what the question means and then matching it against the facts and rules that it "knows."

- For years, expert systems were the exclusive property of the medical and scientific communities, but in the early 1980s they began to make their way into commercial environments.

- Some organizations choose to build their own expert systems to perform well-focused tasks that can easily be crystallized into rules, but few organizations are capable of building an expert system from scratch.

- Some users buy an **expert system shell,** a software package that consists of the basic structure used to find answers to questions. It is up to the buyer to fill in the actual knowledge on the chosen subject.

- The person who works to extract information from the human expert is sometimes called a **knowledge engineer.**

- A **robot** is a computer-controlled device that can physically manipulate its surroundings. Most robots are in factories.

- **Vision robots** traditionally recognize objects by their shapes or "see" a dominant color. But some robots can recognize multicolored objects solely from their colors.

- **Field robots** inspect and repair nuclear power plants, dispose of bombs, inspect oil rigs for undersea exploration, put out oil well fires, clean up chemical accidents, and much more.

- **Virtual reality,** sometimes called **VR,** engages a user in a computer-created environment, so that the user physically interacts with the computer-produced three-dimensional scene. Because the user is so absorbed with the interaction, the process is called **immersion.**

Buyer's Guide:
How to Buy a
Personal Computer

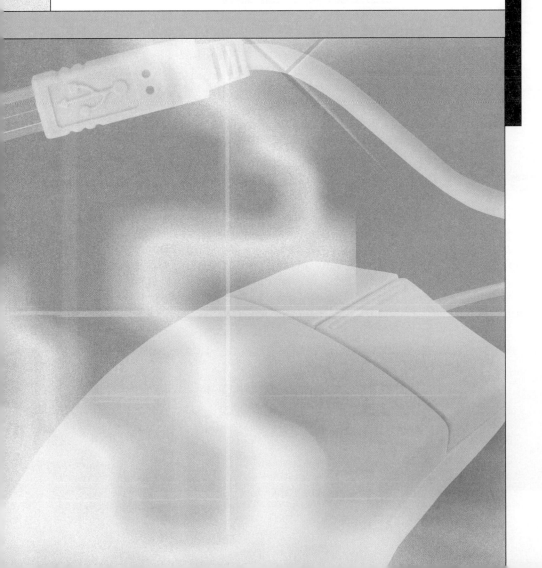

▶ WHERE DO YOU START?

We cannot select a new computer system for you any more than we can choose a new car for you. But we can advise you on which features to look for and which features to avoid. We won't suggest a particular brand or model—so many new products are introduced every month that doing so would be impossible. If you are just beginning, however, we can help you to define your needs and ask the right questions.

Maybe you have already done some thinking and have decided that owning your own personal computer offers advantages. Now what? You can start by talking to other personal computer owners about how they got started and what pitfalls to avoid. You can also read some computer magazines, especially those with evaluations and ratings, to get a feel for what is available. Next, locate several dealers. Most dealers are listed in the Yellow Pages, and many advertise in your local newspaper. Visit several. Don't be afraid to ask questions. You are considering a major purchase, so plan to take your time and shop around.

Finally, you might consider buying a computer system over the Internet or by direct mail. You can find advertisements in any computer magazine. Access the site (presumably, using someone else's computer) or call the listed toll-free number and ask them to send you a free brochure.

▶ ANTICIPATE YOUR SOFTWARE NEEDS FIRST

Before you buy a computer, it's important to know how you want to use it. This involves determining your software needs first and then buying the computer that runs the software you'll be using. What's the best way to determine your software needs? Research! Find out which software students in your area of study are using and which programs people working in your chosen career use. It's a good idea to interview friends, family, or people who work in your chosen field to find out what combination of software and hardware they prefer.

CHECK THE WEB SITE OR PHONE IT IN

These direct-mail dealers sell high-quality hardware at good prices. Check their Web sites or call these toll-free numbers to get free catalogs. You can also place an order via the Internet or by phone.

Dell Computer	IBM	Compaq Computer	Gateway
www.dell.com	www.ibm.com	www.athome.compaq.com	www.gateway.com
1-800-999-3355	1-888-746-7426	1-800- 888-0220	1-800-846-4316

THE MAJOR CHOICES

The PC Standard?

Although computers are sold under many brand names, most offer the "PC standard," also referred to as the business standard. The PC standard is usually a computer that uses the Microsoft Windows operating system and an Intel microprocessor, a combination sometimes called "Wintel." If you will be using your computer for business applications and, in particular, if you need to exchange files with others in a business environment, consider sticking with the standard. However, the Apple iMac, noted for its ease of use, is an attractive alternative, especially for beginners.

Family Computer or Business Computer?

Although the basic machine is probably the same, many dealers offer a "family computer" and a "business computer." The family computer typically comes with a good modem and sound system, a joystick, and plenty of educational, financial, and entertainment software. The business computer will typically have a modest sound system and, most likely, one good suite of business software for such tasks as word processing and spreadsheets.

Desktop or Notebook?

Do you plan to use your computer in one place, or will you be moving it around? Notebook computers, also called laptop computers, have found a significant niche in the market, mainly because they are packaged to travel easily. A notebook computer is lightweight (most about seven pounds and some as little as two and a half pounds) and small enough to fit in a briefcase or backpack. Today's notebook computers offer power and functionality equivalent to those of a desktop computer, but at a significantly higher cost.

Internet or In-Store?

Several reputable manufacturers sell reliable hardware via their Internet sites at good prices. However, they tend to be patronized by experienced users—businesses that order in bulk or individuals who are on their second or third computer and who know what they want. These buyers peruse the site and pick and choose the computer and options they want. They place an order via the site (or possibly over the phone) and have the new machine(s) delivered to the door. Because there is no retail middleman, they save money and also get the latest technology fast.

A first-time buyer, however, usually wants to kick the tires. You will probably be more comfortable looking over the machines, tapping the keyboard, and clicking the mouse. An in-store visit also gives you the opportunity to ask questions.

► WHAT TO LOOK FOR IN HARDWARE

The basic personal computer system consists of a central processing unit (CPU) and memory, a monitor (screen), a keyboard and a mouse, a modem, and assorted storage devices—probably a 3.5-inch diskette drive, a CD-ROM or DVD-ROM drive, and a hard disk drive. Most people also want a printer, and many merchants offer package deals that include a printer. Unless you know someone who can help you out with technical expertise, the best advice is to look for a packaged system—that is, one in which the previously mentioned components (with the exception of the printer) are assembled and packaged by the same manufacturer. This gives you some assurance that the various components will work together. Perhaps even more important, if something should go wrong, you will not have to deal with multiple manufacturers pointing fingers at one another.

Computer Housing

Sometimes called the computer case or simply "the box," the housing holds the electronic circuitry and has external receptors called ports to which the monitor, printer, and other devices are connected. It also contains the bays that hold the various disk drives. The monitor traditionally was placed on top of the computer case; there are still systems offered in that configuration. More common, however, is the minitower, in which the case stands on end and the monitor sits directly on the desk. The minitower was originally designed to be placed on the floor, conveniently out of the way. But the floor location turned out to be somewhat inconvenient, so many users keep their minitowers on the desk next to the monitor. The Apple iMac encloses all its internal equipment in a hemispherical base; the LCD monitor floats above the base on an adjustable arm.

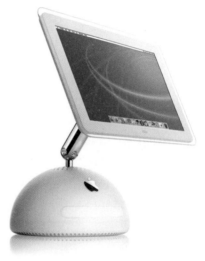

Central Processing Unit

If you plan to purchase a PC-standard machine, you will find that most software packages run most efficiently on computers using at least a 2.4GHz Pentium 4 microprocessor. Any earlier version of the Pentium should carry a bargain-basement price. A microprocessor's speed is expressed in gigahertz (GHz), and it is usually 2.4GHz and up: the higher the number, the faster, and more expensive, the microprocessor is. If you enjoy 3-D computer games, you'll want the fastest processor you can afford. Faster processors produce smoother, more realistic graphic animations.

Monitor

The monitor is an important part of your computer system; you spend all your computer time looking at it. Except in the case of the very cheapest personal computers, you can expect a color monitor as standard equipment.

SCREEN SIZE   Monitors for home use usually have a screen display of between 15 and 19 inches, measured diagonally. Generally, a larger screen provides a display that is easier to read, so most monitors sold today have at least 15-inch screens. However, the 17-inch screen reduces eyestrain and is well-suited for displaying Internet Web pages, graphics, and large photos and illustrations.

SCREEN READABILITY   You might want to compare the readability of different monitors. First, make certain that the screen is bright and has minimum flicker. Glare is another major consideration. Harsh lighting nearby can cause glare to bounce off the

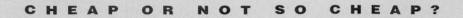

CHEAP OR NOT SO CHEAP?

A personal computer for under $1000? How about under $500? These bargain systems can handle what most home users want from a computer: word processing, games, e-mail, and Web surfing. However, the minimal system has limitations: The hard disk is small, there is marginal memory for games and other graphics-heavy programs, it has minimal expandability, and sound quality from the built-in speakers is only adequate. Worse, given its razor-thin margins, the vendor's customer service may be minimal too.

Sophisticated users know that they cannot get by with such a system; for example, they are likely to need several programs open at the same time, a strain on memory. But an inexpensive computer might be ideal for first-time buyers, especially those who are watching their budgets.

screen, and some screens seem more susceptible to glare than others. A key factor affecting screen quality is resolution, a measure of the number of dots, or pixels, that can appear on the screen. The higher the resolution—that is, the more dots there are—the more solid the text characters appear. For graphics, having more pixels means sharper images. The most commonly available color monitors are Super VGA (SVGA) and Extended Graphics Array (XGA): XGA is best for graphic animations.

ERGONOMIC CONSIDERATIONS Can the monitor swivel and tilt? If so, this will eliminate your need to sit in one position for a long period. The ability to adjust the position of the monitor becomes an important consideration when several users share the same computer, particularly people of different sizes, such as parents and children.

CRT VERSUS LCD Although CRT monitors are still less expensive than flat-panel LCD monitors, the price differential has decreased dramatically in the last year. If desk space is at a premium, flat-panel displays are definitely worth considering.

Input Devices

There are many input devices. We will mention only the two critical ones here: a keyboard and a mouse.

KEYBOARD Keyboards vary in quality. To find what suits you best, sit down in the store and type. You might be surprised by the real differences in the feel of keyboards. Make sure the keys are not cramped together; you will find that your typing is error prone if your fingers are constantly overlapping more than one key. Assess the color and layout of the keyboard. Ideally, keys should be gray with a matte finish. The dull finish reduces glare.

Should you consider a wireless keyboard? A wireless keyboard uses infrared or radio technology rather than wires to communicate with the computer. Thus you could use the keyboard at the far end of a conference table or on the kitchen table—any place within 30 feet of the computer. Furthermore, a touchpad, a mouse substitute, that can be used to drag the cursor or click screen objects is built into the keyboard.

MOUSE   A mouse is a device that you slide around on a tabletop or other surface to move the pointer on the screen. Because most software is designed to be used with a mouse, it is a necessary purchase and will likely come with any new desktop computer. An optical mouse is shown here. Optical technology eliminates the ball in the bottom of the mouse, allowing smoother pointer movement and eliminating the need for cleaning.

Secondary Storage

You need disk drives to read software into your computer and to store software and data that you wish to keep.

DISKS AND ZIP DRIVES   Some personal computer software today comes on diskettes, so you need a diskette drive to accept the software. Diskettes are also a common

medium for exchange of data among computer users. Most computer systems today come with a 3.5-inch diskette drive. A Zip drive is also an option for users who will be transporting large or numerous files.

CD-ROM AND DVD DRIVES   Most personal computer software comes on CD-ROM disks, which are far handier than multiple diskettes. But the main attraction is the use of high-capacity CD-ROMs for holding byte-rich images, sounds, and videos—the stuff of multimedia. The smoothness of a CD-ROM video presentation is indicated by its X factor, such as 16X, 24X, 40X. The higher the number, the better. CD-RW (rewritable) drives enable you to create your own CDs, storing large volumes of your own songs, photographs, or videos. Many systems now come with DVD drives, adding the capability of playing full-length movies on your PC.

HARD DISK DRIVE   A hard disk drive is a standard requirement. A hard disk is fast and reliable and holds lots of data. Software comes on a set of several diskettes or on optical disk; it would be unwieldy to load these each time the software is used. Instead, the software is stored on the hard drive, where it is conveniently accessed from that point forward.

All computer systems offer a built-in hard disk drive, with variable storage capacity; the more storage, the higher the price. Storage capacity is measured in terms of bytes—characters—of data. Keep in mind that software, as well as your data files, will be stored on the hard disk; just one program can take many millions of bytes. Hard disk capacity is measured in gigabytes—billions of bytes. The more the better, especially if you plan to save a lot of audio or video files.

Printers

A printer is probably the most expensive peripheral equipment you will buy. Some inexpensive models are available, but those who have a great concern for quality output might pay a hefty price. When choosing a printer, consider speed, quality, and cost, not necessarily in that order.

Ink-jet printers, in which ink is propelled onto the paper by a battery of tiny nozzles, can produce excellent text and graphics. In fact, the quality of ink-jet printers approaches that of laser printers. The additional attractions of low cost and quiet operation have made the ink-jet printer a current favorite among buyers, especially those who want color output.

Laser printers, which use technology similar to that of copying machines, are the top-of-the-line printers for quality and speed. The price of a low-end laser printer is within the budget of most users. Desktop publishers who produce text and graphics on the same page in particular favor laser printers. Affordable laser printers can produce output at 600 dots per inch (dpi), giving graphic images a sharpness that rivals that of photographs. At the high end, more expensive laser printers offer 1,200 dpi. However, this rich resolution may be of little value to a buyer who plans to produce primarily text.

Affordable color printers are available for a few hundred dollars, although some are priced much higher. Even at a high price, color printers are not perfect. The rich color seen on the computer screen is not necessarily the color that will appear on the printed output. Furthermore, note that color printers often have fairly high operating costs for staples such as special coated paper and color ink cartridges. Still, color printers, once prohibitively expensive, are both attractive and affordable.

All-in-Ones

An all-in-one machine combines the capabilities of a full range of office equipment into one device: Printing, faxing, scanning, and copying abilities are all available on the same machine. Some even include a telephone and answering machine. There

---

SYSTEM REQUIREMENTS

Make sure your hardware is compatible with the requirements of the software you are buying. You can find the requirements by reading the fine print on the software package. Here is a typical requirements blurb from a software package: Requires a personal computer with a Pentium or higher processor (Pentium III or higher recommended) running Microsoft Windows 98 or later operating system, 32MB of memory (RAM) minimum, 128MB recommended. Hard disk minimum installation 70MB, typical installation 120MB.

are certain advantages, such as installing and learning just one software package. Furthermore, the all-in-one reduces the number of cables cluttering the floor and, perhaps most importantly, takes up less space than that required by multiple machines. The major disadvantage is that an equipment problem will disable all capabilities. You can purchase an adequate, but somewhat limited all-in-one, for a few hundred dollars. Businesses that want color capabilities, speedy printing, and all-day fax capabilities will pay a steeper price.

Portability: What to Look for in a Notebook

Generally, you should look for the same hardware components in a notebook computer as you would in a desktop computer: a fast microprocessor, plenty of memory, a clear screen, and diskette and hard drives. A CD-ROM or DVD-ROM drive is an option in most models.

Most models include an internal modem. Another option is a PC Card modem that fits in a slot on the notebook. In either case you merely run a cord from the modem jack to the phone jack in the wall. Thus from your hotel room or from any place else that has a phone jack, you can be connected to online services, e-mail, and the Internet. Special wireless adapter cards are available for those who need access to wireless network access points.

You will have to make some compromises on input devices. The keyboard will be attached, and the keys may be more cramped than those on a standard keyboard. Also, traveling users often do not have a handy surface for rolling a mouse, so the notebook will probably come with a built-in pointing stick or a touchpad. If you prefer a mouse, you can purchase one separately.

Other Hardware Options

There are a great many hardware variations; we will mention a few here. Note that, although we are describing the hardware, these devices may come with accompanying software, which must be installed according to directions before the hardware can be used.

COMMUNICATIONS CONNECTIONS If you want to connect your computer via communications lines to the office computer, to an online service, such as America Online, or to the Internet or if you want to send and receive e-mail, you need a communications device. Although the choices are many and depend upon the type of connection you require, the most common device, by far, is the modem. This device converts outgoing computer data into signals that can be transmitted over telephone lines and does the reverse for incoming data.

Most computers come with an internal modem, out of sight inside the computer housing. Furthermore, most people choose a fax modem, which serves the dual purpose of modem and fax. Using a fax modem, you can receive a fax and then print it out or send a fax if it originated in your computer (using, for example, word processing software) or was scanned into your computer. Most new computers come equipped with a fax modem.

Many systems, especially notebook computers, now have built-in wireless communications capability using the IEEE 802.11b standard, commonly known as WiFi, or the even faster IEEE 802.11a standard, WiFi5.

OTHER INPUT DEVICES   If you are interested in action games, you might want a joystick, which looks similar to the stick shift on a car. A joystick enables you to manipulate a cursor on the screen. A scanner is useful if you need to store pictures and typed documents in your computer. Scanners are often purchased by people who want to put their photographs on the computer or to use their computers for desktop publishing. Finally, you can purchase voice input hardware, which is basically a microphone.

SURGE PROTECTORS   Surge protectors protect against the electrical ups and downs that can affect the operation of your computer. In addition, a surge protector provides a receptacle for all power plugs and a handy switch to turn everything on or off at once. Some of the more expensive models, really uninterruptible power supply systems, provide up to 10 minutes of full power to your computer if the electric power in your home or office is knocked out. This gives you time to save your work on disk (so that the work will not be lost if the power fails) or to print out a report you need immediately.

◢► WHAT TO LOOK FOR IN SOFTWARE

You will use software that was written for the operating system software of that machine. Microsoft Windows is the most popular operating system, and almost all new PC-standard computers come with Microsoft Windows XP preinstalled. Windows users will want applications software written for the Windows environment. If you're using a Macintosh, you will be running the Macintosh operating system (Mac OS). In this case, you will need application software written specifically for the Mac OS.

Hardware Requirements for Software

Identify the type of hardware required before you buy software. Under the heading System Requirements (sometimes called specifications) right on the software package, a list will typically include a particular kind of computer and operating system and the required amount of memory and hard disk space.

Brand Names

In general, publishers of well-known software offer better customer support than lesser-known companies do. Support might be in the form of tutorials, classes by the vendor or others, and the all-important hotline assistance. In addition, makers of brand-name software usually offer superior documentation and upgrades to new and better versions of the product.

Where to Buy Software

If you purchase your system as a complete package, it will most likely have some application software preinstalled on the hard drive. Less expensive systems might include an all-in-one personal productivity program, such as Microsoft Works, which has word-processing, spreadsheet, and database capabilities. More expensive systems will probably be accompanied by a suite of application software, separate programs for each of those areas. Microsoft Office is the best-known productivity suite. If your system is lacking application software, or if you have needs not met by the included software, you have several sources from which to choose.

COMPUTER SUPERSTORES   The computer superstores, such as CompUSA, sell a wide variety of computer hardware and software. Although their primary advantage is a vast inventory, they also offer on-site training and technical support.

WAREHOUSE STORES   Often billed as buyers' clubs, such as Sam's Club, the giant warehouse stores sell all manner of merchandise, including computer software.

MASS MERCHANDISERS   Stores, such as Sears, sell software along with their other various merchandise.

COMPUTER DEALERS   Some small retail stores sell hardware systems and the software that runs on them. Such a store usually has a well-informed staff and might be your best bet for in-depth consulting.

MAIL ORDER   Users who know what they want can get it conveniently and reasonably through the mail. Once you make initial contact, probably from a magazine advertisement, the mail-order house sends software catalogs regularly.

OVER THE INTERNET   Users who connect to the Internet often find it convenient to purchase software online. Each major software vendor has its own Web site and, among other things, offers its wares for sale. A buyer is usually given the choice of receiving the typical package—disks and documentation—through the mail or of downloading the software directly from the vendor's site to the buyer's computer.

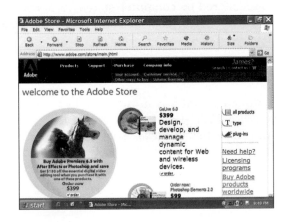

COLLEGE BOOKSTORE   College students can often purchase popular software packages at large discounts through their bookstore. It's in the publishers' best interests to have students familiar with their products when they graduate, so that the students will recommend the software to their new employers.

► NOW THAT YOU HAVE IT, CAN YOU USE IT?

Once the proud moment has come and your computer system is at home or in the office with you, what do you do with it?

Documentation

Computer systems today come with extensive documentation, the written manuals and disk files that accompany the hardware. Usually, a simple brochure with detailed drawings will help you plug everything together. The installation procedure, however, is often largely (and conveniently) on disk. The same brochure that helps you assemble the hardware will guide you to the software on the diskette or CD-ROM. Using the software, the computer configures itself, mostly without any assistance from you.

Software documentation usually includes a user's guide, which is a reference manual for the various commands available with the software. Software tutorials are also common and are useful for the novice and experienced user alike. Software tutorials often come on a separate diskette or CD-ROM, and they guide you as you work through sample problems using the software.

> ### QUESTIONS TO ASK THE SALESPERSON AT THE STORE
>
> - Can I expand the capabilities of the computer later?
> - Whom do I call if I have a problem putting the machine together at home?
> - Does the store offer classes on how to use the computer and software?
> - What kind of warranty comes with the computer?
> - Does the store or manufacturer offer a maintenance contract with the computer?

Training

Can you teach yourself? In addition to the documentation supplied with your computer, numerous books and magazines offer help and answer readers' questions. Other sources are classes offered by computer stores, local colleges, and the adult-education program at the local high school. These hands-on sessions may be the most effective learning method of all.

Maintenance Contract

Finally, when purchasing a computer, you might want to consider a maintenance contract, which should cover labor, parts, and possibly advice on a telephone hotline. Such contracts vary in comprehensiveness. Some cover on-site repairs; others require you to pack up the computer and mail it back to the vendor. Another option is that the replacement part—say, a new monitor—is sent to you, and you then return the old monitor in the same packaging.

A

Accelerated Graphics Port (AGP) A bus that is designed to provide a dedicated connection between memory and an AGP graphics card.

Access arm A mechanical device that can access all the tracks of one cylinder in a disk storage unit.

Access time The time needed to access data directly on disk, consisting of seek time, head switching, and rotational delay.

Accumulator A register that collects the results of computations.

Acquisition by purchase Buying an entire system for use by the organization, as opposed to designing a new system.

Active badge A badge that, embedded with a computer chip, signals the wearer's location by sending out infrared signals, which are read by computers distributed throughout a building.

Active cell The cell currently available for use in a spreadsheet. Also called the *current cell*.

Active-matrix LCD displays that produce a better image but use more power and are more expensive than passive-matrix displays.

ActiveX controls Similar to Java applets.

Adapter cards See *expansion board*.

Address A number used to designate a location in memory.

Addressable A computer display screen that can be used for graphics and is divided into dots.

Affiliate A Web site whose owner has contracted with the owner of a Web site that agrees to carry its banner ad.

Algorithm A detailed, step-by-step solution to a problem.

Alpha A processor used in high-end workstations and servers.

Alphanumeric data Letters, digits, and special characters such as punctuation marks.

ALU See *Arithmetic/logic unit.*

America Online (AOL) A major online service that offers a variety of services.

Amplitude modulation A change of the amplitude of the carrier wave in analog data transmission to represent either the 0 bit or the 1 bit.

Amplitude The height of the carrier wave in analog transmission. Amplitude indicates the strength of the signal.

Analog transmission The transmission of data as a continuous electrical signal in the form of a wave.

Analytical graphics programs A program which helps users to analyze and understand specific data by presenting data in visual form.

Anonymous FTP Meaning that a user can be named Anonymous and the password for downloading files on an FTP sever can simply be the user's e-mail address.

ANSI American National Standards Institute.

Anti-Cybersquatting Consumer Protection Act Provides penalties up to $100,000 for anyone registering a domain name using someone else's trademark.

Antivirus A computer program that stops the spread of a virus. Also called a *vaccine.*

AOL See *America Online.*

Applet A small program that can provide multimedia effects and other capabilities on Web pages.

Application service provider (ASP) A company that sets up and maintains applications software on its own systems and makes the software available for its customers to use over the Internet.

Applications software Programs designed to perform specific tasks and functions, such as word processing.

Arithmetic operations Mathematical calculations that the ALU performs on data.

Arithmetic/logic unit (ALU) Part of the central processing unit, the electronic circuitry of the ALU executes all arithmetic and logical operations.

ARPANet A network, established in 1969 by the Department of Defense, that eventually became the Internet.

Artificial intelligence The field of study that explores computer involvement in tasks requiring intelligence, imagination, and intuition.

ASCII (American Standard Code for Information Interchange) A coding scheme using seven-bit characters to represent data characters. A variation of the code, called ASCII-8, uses eight bits per character.

Assembler program A translator program used to convert assembly language programs to machine language.

Assembly language A second-generation language that uses abbreviations for instructions, as opposed to numbers. Also called *symbolic language.*

Asynchronous transmission Data transmission in which data is sent one byte at a time, with each byte preceded by a start signal and ended with a stop signal. Also called *start/stop transmission.*

ATM See *automated teller machine.*

Attribute In object-oriented programming, a fact related to an object.

Audio-response unit See *voice synthesizer.*

Audit trail A method of tracing data from the output back to the source documents.

Automated teller machine (ATM) An input/output device connected to a computer used by bank customers for financial transactions.

Automatic recalculation In a spreadsheet, when one value or calculation is changed, all values dependent on the changed item are automatically recalculated to reflect the change.

Automatic reformatting In word processing, automatic adjustment of text to accommodate changes such as margin width.

Auxiliary storage See *secondary storage.*

Axis A reference line of a graph. The horizontal axis is the x-axis. The vertical axis is the y-axis.

B

B2B Internet exchanges Electronic marketplaces that connect buyers and sellers in many industries.

Backbone The major communication links that tie Internet servers across wide geographical areas.

Background (1) In large computers, the memory area for running programs with low priorities. Contrast with *foreground.* (2) On a Web site, the screen appearance behind the text and images.

Backspace key In word processing and other applications, deletes the character to the left of the cursor.

Backup and restore Utility programs that facilitate making file backups and restoring damaged files.

Backup system A method of storing data in more than one place to protect it from damage or loss.

Backup A duplicate copy of a file made to protect against loss or destruction of the original.

Bandwidth The range of frequencies that can fit on one communications line or link at the same time, or the capacity of the link.

Banner ad On a Web site, a clickable ad, often in the shape of a rectangle, that can take a user to the site of the advertiser.

Bar code A standardized pattern of vertical marks that represents the Universal Product Code (UPC) that identifies a product.

Bar code reader A stationary photoelectric scanner that inputs bar codes by means of reflected light.

Bar graph A graph made up of filled-in columns or rows that represent the change of data over time.

Base station See *wireless access point.*

BASIC (Beginner's All-purpose Symbolic Instruction Code) A high-level programming language that is easy to learn and use.

Batch processing A data processing technique in which transactions are collected into groups, or batches, for processing.

Binary Regarding number systems, the binary number system uses exactly two symbols, the digits 0 and 1.

Binary system A system in which data is represented by combinations of 0s and 1s, which correspond to the two states: off and on.

Biometrics The science of measuring individual body characteristics; used in some security systems.

Bit A binary digit.

Blocking software Software that attempts to prevent children from accessing objectionable sites.

Bluetooth Wireless transmission that uses radio waves to connect mobile devices over distances less than 30 feet.

Boldface text A font style in which the text appears darker than normal.

Bomb An application that sabotages a computer by triggering damage—usually at a later date. Also called a *logic bomb.*

Boolean logic Regarding search engines on the Internet, a mathematical system that can be used to narrow the search through the use of operators, such as AND, OR, and NOT.

Booting Loading the operating system into memory.

Bpi See *Bytes per inch.*

bps Bits per second.

Bricks-and-clicks retailers Traditional retailers who have established Internet sites.

Bridge A device that recognizes and transmits messages to be sent to other similar networks.

Browser Software used to access the Internet.

Bus network A network that has a single line to which each device is attached.

Bus (or bus line) An electronic pathway for data travel among the parts of a computer. Also called a *data bus.*

Business graphics Represent business data in a visual, easily understood format.

Business-to-business (B2B) E-commerce that involves one business providing another business with the materials and supplies that it needs to conduct its operations.

Business-to-consumer (B2C) Retail transactions between an online business and an individual.

Button Clickable icon that represents a menu choice or option.

Byte Strings of bits (usually eight) used to represent one data character—a letter, digit, or special character.

Bytes per inch (bpi) An expression of the amount (density) of data stored on magnetic tape.

C

C A sophisticated programming language invented by Bell Labs in 1974.

C++ An object-oriented programming language; an enhancement of C.

Cable modem A fast communications link that uses coaxial television cables already in place without interrupting normal cable TV reception.

Cache A relatively small amount of very fast memory that stores data and instructions that are used frequently, resulting in improved processing speeds. See also *disk cache.*

CAD/CAM See *computer-aided design/computer-aided manufacturing.*

Candidates In systems analysis and design, alternative plans offered in the preliminary design phase of a project.

Carrier sense multiple access with collision detection (CSMA/CD) The line control method used by Ethernet. Each node has access to the communications line and can transmit if it hears no communication on the line. If two stations transmit simultaneously, they wait and retry their transmissions.

Carrier wave An analog signal used in the transmission of electric signals.

Cathode ray tube (CRT) The most common type of computer screen.

CD-R A technology that permits writing on optical disks.

CD-ROM See *compact disk read-only memory.*

CD-RW (compact disk-rewritable) A technology that enables you to erase and record over data multiple times.

Cell The intersection of a row and a column in a spreadsheet. Entries in a spreadsheet are stored in individual cells.

Cell address In a spreadsheet, the column and row coordinates of a cell. Also called the *cell reference.*

Cell contents The label, value, formula, or function contained in a spreadsheet cell.

Cell reference In a spreadsheet, the column and row coordinates of a cell. Also called the *cell address.*

Cellular modems Modems that can be used to transmit data over the cellular telephone system.

Central processing unit (CPU) Electronic circuitry that executes stored program instructions. It consists of two parts: the control unit and the arithmetic/logic unit. The CPU processes raw data into meaningful, useful information.

Centralized data processing Description of a computer system in which hardware, software, storage, and computer access is in one location. Contrast with *decentralized.*

CERN The name of the site of the particle physics lab where Dr. Tim Berners-Lee worked when he invented the World Wide Web; sometimes called the birthplace of the Web.

Change agent The role of the systems analyst in overcoming resistance to change within an organization.

Character A letter, number, or special character such as $.

Characters per inch (cpi) An expression of the amount (density) of data stored on magnetic tape.

Chief Information Officer (CIO) Top information systems in a company.

Children's Internet Protection Act (CIPA) An act requiring libraries receiving any type of federal funding to implement technology which blocks or filters certain objectionable material on the Internet.

Children's Online Privacy Protection Act (COPPA) An act requiring Web sites that target children under age 13 to post a privacy policy that clearly states what information they collect and set up parental notification and consent systems before gathering information from the children.

Circuit One or more conductors through which electricity flows.

CISC See *complex instruction set computer.*

Class In object-oriented programming, an object class contains the characteristics that are unique to that class.

Click stream The set of a series of mouse clicks that link from site to site.

Click through Leaving the current Web site for an advertised site.

Client (1) An individual or organization contracting for systems analysis. (2) In a client/server network, a program on the personal computer that allows that node to communicate with the server.

Client/server A network setup that involves a server computer, which controls the network, and clients, other computers that access the network and its services. In particular, the server does some processing, sending the client only the portion of the file it needs or possibly only the processed results. Contrast with *file server.*

Clip art Illustrations already produced by professional artists for public use. Computerized clip art is stored on disk and can be used to enhance any kind of graph or document.

Clock A component of the CPU that produces pulses at a fixed rate to synchronize all computer operations.

Clone A personal computer that can run software designed for IBM personal computers.

Cluster A fixed number of adjacent sectors that are treated as a unit of storage by the operating system; it consists of two to eight sectors, depending on the operating system.

CMOS See *complementary metal oxide semiconductor.*

Coaxial cable Bundles of insulated wires within a shielded enclosure. Coaxial cable can be laid underground or undersea.

COBOL (Common Business-Oriented Language) An English-like programming language used primarily for business applications.

Coding scheme (or code) Assigns each possible combination of 1s and 0s in a byte to a specific character.

Cold site An environmentally suitable empty shell in which a company can install its own computer system.

Collaborative software See *groupware.*

Collision The problem that occurs when two records have the same disk address.

Command A name that invokes the correct program or program segment. In an Ethernet network, when two workstations attempt to transmit a message at the same time.

Commercial software Software that is packaged and sold in stores. Also called *packaged software.*

Common carriers Providers of communications services, such as switched (dial up) and dedicated.

Communications Decency Act An act which attempted to prevent people from preying on children on the Internet, but was struck down by the Supreme Court.

Communications medium The physical means of data transmission.

Communications software Software that allows computers to communicate with each other via phone lines or other means.

Compact disc-recordable (CD-R) A technology that permits writing on optical disks.

Compact disk read-only memory (CD-ROM) Optical data storage technology using disk formats identical to audio compact disks.

Compact disk-rewritable (CD-RW) A technology that allows you to erase and record over data multiple times.

Compare operation An operation in which the computer compares two data items and performs alternative operations based on the results of the comparison.

Compiler A translator that converts the symbolic statements of a high-level language into computer-executable machine language.

Complementary metal oxide semiconductor (CMOS) A semiconductor device that does not require a large amount of power to operate. CMOS is often found in devices that require low power consumption, such as portable computers.

Complex instruction set computer (CISC) A CPU design that contains many instructions of varying kinds, some of which are rarely used. Contrast with *reduced instruction set computer.*

Computer A machine that accepts data (input) and processes it into useful information (output). A computer system requires four main aspects of data handling: input, processing, output, and storage.

Computer-aided design/computer-aided manufacturing (CAD/CAM) The use of computers to create two- and three-dimensional pictures of products to be manufactured.

Computer-aided software engineering (CASE) The use of software tools to automate some or all of the system development tasks.

Computer forensics Uncovering computer-stored information suitable for use as evidence in courts of law.

Computer Fraud and Abuse Act A law passed by Congress in 1984 to fight computer crime.

Computer Information Systems (CIS) The department responsible for managing a company's computer resources. Also called *Management Information Systems (MIS), Computing Services (CS),* or *Information Services.*

Computer-integrated manufacturing (CIM) The integration of CAD/CAM with the entire manufacturing process.

Computer literacy The awareness and knowledge of, and the capacity to interact with, computers.

Computer Matching and Privacy Protection Act Legislation that prevents the government from comparing certain records in an attempt to find a match.

Computer operator A person who monitors and runs the computer equipment in a large system.

Computer professionals People whose work focuses on the computer systems themselves, people with titles such as programmer, systems analyst, network administrator, and computer operator.

Computer programmer A person who designs, writes, tests, and implements programs.

Computing Services The department responsible for managing a company's computer resources. Also called *Management Information Systems (MIS), Computer Information Systems (CIS),* or *Information Services.*

Concurrently With reference to the execution of computer instructions, in the same time frame but not simultaneously. See also *multiprogramming.*

Conditional replace A word processing function that asks the user whether to replace text each time the program finds a particular item.

Consortium A joint venture to support a complete computer facility to be used as back up in an emergency.

Consumer-to-consumer (C2C) E-commerce that takes place between consumers over the many online auction sites.

Context sensitive In reference to an ad on a Web site, one that is related to the subject matter on the screen.

Continuous word system A speech recognition system that can understand sustained speech so that users can speak normally.

Control unit The circuitry that directs and coordinates the entire computer system in executing stored program instructions. Part of the central processing unit.

Cookie A small file stored on the user's hard drive that reflects activity on the Internet.

Coordinating In systems analysis, orchestrating the process of analyzing and planning a new system by pulling together the various individuals, schedules, and tasks that contribute to the analysis.

Copyleft An alternative means of controlling software rights in which everyone has permission to run, copy, or modify the program, and to distribute modified versions—but not permission to add restrictions of their own.

Copyright protection Provides the creator of a literary or artistic work control over the use and distribution of that work.

Cordless keyboards Keyboards that communicate with the system unit via infrared or radio waves.

Cordless mouse A mouse that uses infrared or radio waves rather than a cord to send signals to the computer.

CPU See *central processing unit*.

CRT See *cathode ray tube*.

CSMA/CD See *carrier sense multiple access with collision detection*.

Current cell The cell currently available for use in a spreadsheet. Also the *active cell*.

Cursor An indicator on the screen; it shows where the next user-computer interaction will be. Also called a *pointer*.

Cursor movement keys Keys on the computer keyboard that enable the user to move the cursor on the screen.

Custom software Software that is tailored to a specific user's needs.

Cut and paste In word processing and some other applications, moving a block of text by deleting it in one place (cut) and adding it in another (paste).

Cybersquatting Involves registering common words and phrases as domain names, with the intention of selling the domain name at a profit to a company that wanted a catchy, easily-remembered URL.

Cylinder A set of tracks on a magnetic disk, one from each platter, vertically aligned. These tracks can be accessed without repositioning the access arm.

Cylinder method A method of organizing data on a magnetic disk. This method organizes data vertically, which minimizes seek time.

D

DASD See *direct-access storage device*.

DAT See *digital audio tape*.

Data Raw input to be processed by a computer.

Data communications The process of exchanging data over communications facilities.

Data communications systems Computer systems that transmit data over communications lines, such as public telephone lines or private network cables.

Data compression Making a large data file smaller by temporarily removing nonessential but space-hogging items, such as tab marks and double-spacing.

Data dictionary In a database, a function that stores data about the tables and fields within the database.

Data diddling A method of computer crime in which data is altered before or as it enters the system.

Data Encryption Standard (DES) The standardized public key system by which senders and receivers can scramble and unscramble messages sent over data communications equipment.

Data entry operator A person who keys data for computer processing.

Data flow diagram (DFD) A diagram that shows the flow of data through an organization.

Data integrity Refers to the degree to which data is accurate and reliable.

Data item Data in a relational database table.

Data maintenance Consists of three basic operations: adding new data, modifying existing data, and deleting data; it is performed either directly through DBMS routines or by programs containing special commands.

Data mining The process of extracting previously unknown information from existing data.

Data mirroring In RAID storage, a technique of duplicating data on a separate disk drive.

Data point Each dot or symbol on a line graph. Each data point represents a value.

Data redundancy Duplication of data.

Data retrieval Involves extracting the desired data from the database.

Data striping In RAID storage, a technique of spreading data across several disks in the array.

Data transfer The transfer of data between memory and a secondary storage device.

Data transfer rate The speed with which data can be transferred between memory and a secondary storage device.

Data warehouse Contains data that has been captured from the database in summary form, on a scheduled basis, over a period of time.

Database An organized collection of related files stored together with minimum redundancy. Specific data items can be retrieved for various applications.

Database management software Programs that manage a collection of interrelated facts. The software can store data, update it, manipulate it, retrieve it, report it in a variety of views, and print it in as many forms.

Database management system (DBMS) A set of programs that creates, manages, protects, and provides access to a database.

Datasheet view In Microsoft Access, the table view in which the data records are shown on the screen.

DBMS See *database management system.*

Debugging The process of detecting, locating, and correcting logic errors in a program.

Decentralized Description of a computer system in which the computer and its storage devices are in one place, but devices that access the computer are in other locations. Contrast with *centralized.*

Decision support system (DSS) A computer system that supports managers in nonroutine decision-making tasks. A DSS involves a model, a mathematical representation of a real-life situation.

Decision table A standard table of the logical decisions that must be made regarding potential conditions in a given system. Also called a *decision logic table.*

Default settings The settings automatically used by a program unless the user specifies otherwise, thus overriding them.

Delete key The key used to delete the text character at the cursor location or a text block that has been selected or marked.

Demodulation The process a modem uses to convert an analog signal back into digital form.

Denial of service (DoS) An attack, in which a site is bombarded with so many requests that legitimate users cannot access it.

Density The amount of data stored on magnetic tape; expressed in number of characters per inch (cpi) or bytes per inch (bpi).

Dependent variable Output of a computerized model, particularly a decision support system. Called dependent because it depends on the inputs.

DES See *Data Encryption Standard.*

Design view In Microsoft Access, the table view used to create or modify a table's structure.

Desk-checking A programming phase in which a programmer manually steps through the logic of a program to ensure that it is error-free and workable.

Desktop publishing packages Software that meets high-level publishing needs to produce professional-looking newsletters, reports, and brochures.

Detail design A systems design subphase in which the system is planned in detail, including the details of output, input, files

and databases, processing, and controls and backup.

Device drivers Utilities that allow the operating system to communicate with peripherals.

DFD See *data flow diagram*.

Diagnostics Error messages provided by the compiler as it translates a program. Diagnostics inform the user of programming language syntax errors.

Differential backup Copies all files that have been changed since the last full backup.

Digital camera A camera that takes photos that are stored internally on a chip or card and then sent directly to your computer, where they can be edited and printed.

Digital divide A term that refers to the gap between those who have access to computer technology and those who don't.

Digital Millennium Copyright Act (DMCA) makes it illegal to use, develop or publish methods of breaking anti-piracy protections added to copyrighted works and bans devices designed for that purpose.

Digital subscriber line (DSL) A screen and keyboard that uses advanced electronics to send data at very high speed over conventional copper telephone wires.

Digital transmission The transmission of data as distinct on or off pulses.

Digital versatile disk (DVD) A form of optical disk storage that has a double-layered surface and can be written on both sides, providing significant capacity. Also called *DVD-ROM*.

Digitizing tablet See *graphics tablet*.

DIMMs Dual in-line memory modules.

Direct access The ability to go directly to the desired record by using a record key. Also referred to as random access.

Direct-access storage device (DASD) A storage device, usually disk, in which a record can be accessed directly.

Direct-connect modem A modem that is connected directly to the telephone line by means of a telephone jack.

Direct conversion A system conversion in which the user simply stops using the old system and starts using the new one.

Direct file organization An arrangement of records so that each is individually accessible by key field value.

Direct file processing Processing that enables the user to access a record directly by using a record key.

Disaster recovery plan Guidelines for restoring computer processing operations if they are halted by major damage or destruction.

Discrete word system A speech recognition system limited to understanding isolated words.

Disk cache An area of memory that temporarily stores data from disk that a program might need.

Disk defragmenters Utilities that relocate disk files into contiguous locations.

Disk drive A machine that allows data to be read from a disk or written on a disk.

Disk mirroring A concept associated with RAID that duplicates data on separate disk drives.

Disk pack A stack of magnetic disks assembled as a single unit.

Diskette A single disk, made of flexible Mylar, on which data is recorded as magnetic spots. A disk is usually 3.5 inches in diameter, with a hard plastic jacket.

Displayed value The calculated result of a formula or function in a spreadsheet cell.

Distributed data processing A computer system in which processing is decentralized, with the computers and storage devices and access devices in dispersed locations.

Document imaging A process in which a scanner converts papers to an electronic version, which can then be stored on disk and retrieved when needed.

Documentation The instructions accompanying packaged software. Documentation may be provided in a printed manual or in digital form on the distribution CD.

Domain name The unique name of a host computer on the Internet. Used in the Uniform Resource Locater (URL) of a Web page.

Dot-matrix printers Printers with print heads containing one or more columns of pins to produce images as a pattern of dots.

Dot pitch The amount of space between pixels on a computer display.

Downlink Strong outgoing signals sent by a communications satellite transponder to an earth station.

Download In a networking environment, to receive data files from another computer, probably a larger computer or a host computer. Contrast with *upload*.

DRAM See *dynamic random-access memory*.

DSL See *digital subscriber line*.

DSS See *decision support system*.

Dual-boot system A configuration that enables users to choose between two operating systems.

Dumb terminal A device that consists of a screen and keyboard, with no processing capability. Used to access a central computer.

DVD See *digital versatile disk*.

DVD+R Standard for writeable DVD.

DVD+RW Standard for rewriteable DVD.

DVD-R Standard for writeable DVD.

DVD-RAM A digital video disk format that enables users to record up to 2.6 GB of data.

DVD-ROM A digital video disk format capable of storing up to 4.7 GB of data, transferring data at higher speeds, and reading digital video disk and existing CD-ROM discs.

DVD-RW Standard for rewriteable DVD.

Dynamic random-access memory (DRAM) Memory chips that are periodically regenerated, allowing the chips to retain the stored data. Contrast with *static random-access memory*.

E

Earth stations Used in satellite transmission to send and receive signals.

EBCDIC Extended Binary Coded Decimal Interchange Code.

EDI See *electronic data interchange*.

EFT See *electronic fund transfer*.

Electronic commerce or e-commerce Buying and selling over the Internet.

Electronic data interchange (EDI) A set of standards by which companies can electronically exchange common business forms such as invoices and purchase orders.

Electronic fund transfer (EFT) Paying for goods and services by transferring funds electronically. May also refer to the transfer of funds between financial institutions.

Electronic mail See *e-mail*.

Electronic mail client software See *e-mail client software*.

Electronic software distribution Downloading software from the originator's site to a user's site, often for a fee.

Electronic spreadsheet A computerized worksheet used to organize data into rows and columns for analysis.

E-mail Sending messages from one terminal or computer to another.

E-mail address An address that a network or ISP provides a user.

E-mail client software Software on your PC that enables you to retrieve, create, send, store, print, and delete your e-mail messages.

Embedded systems Computer systems built into other products.

Encapsulation (1) In object-oriented programming, the containment of data and its related instructions in the object. (2) A way to transfer data between two similar networks over an intermediate network by enclosing one type of data packet protocol into the packet of another. Also called *tunneling*.

Encryption The process of encoding data to be transmitted via communications links, so that its contents are protected from unauthorized people.

Encryption key A code that converts the message into an unreadable form.

Energy management features Features that reduce the power requirements of computer systems.

Energy Star EPA standards for limiting power requirements.

Equal-to condition (=) A logical operation in which the computer compares two numbers to determine equality.

Equipment conversion The portion of the implementation phase of the SDLC that involves ensuring compatibility and providing enough space and electrical capacity for the new hardware.

Erase head The head in a magnetic tape unit that erases any data previously recorded on the tape before recording new data.

E-Rate program The federal government program that adds a little to everyone's telephone bill to provide rate subsidies for Internet access for schools and libraries.

Ergonomics The study of human factors related to computers.

Ergonomic keyboards Keyboards designed to provide users with more natural, comfortable hand, wrist, and arm positions.

ESS See *executive support system.*

Ethernet A popular type of local area network that uses a bus topology.

Ethics Refers to standards of moral conduct. Although unethical acts may be immoral, they are not always illegal, although illegal acts are almost always unethical.

E-time The execution portion of the machine cycle; e-time includes the execute and store operations.

Evaluation The portion of the implementation phase of the SDLC that involves the assessment of the new system's performance.

Event-driven When one program is allowed to use a particular resource, such as the central processing unit, to complete a certain activity (event) before relinquishing the resource to another program.

Executive information system (EIS) A decision support system for senior-level executives, who make decisions that affect an entire company.

Expansion boards Devices that enable you to connect various peripheral devices to the computer.

Expansion slots The slots inside a computer that allow a user to insert additional circuit boards.

Expert shell Software having the basic structure to find answers to questions that are part of an expert system; the decision rules and supporting data must be added by the user.

Expert system Software that presents the computer as an expert on some topic.

Exploded pie chart A pie chart in which one slice is pulled slightly away from the pie to emphasize that share of the whole.

External cache Cache (very fast memory for frequently used data and instructions) on chips separate from the microprocessor.

External modem A modem that is not built into the computer and can therefore be used with a variety of computers.

Extranet An intranet to which outsiders have been granted access privileges.

F

Facsimile technology (fax) The use of computer technology to send digitized graphics, charts, and text from one facsimile machine to another.

Fair Credit Reporting Act Legislation that allows individuals access to their own credit records and gives them the right to challenge them.

FAQ Frequently asked questions.

Fax See *facsimile technology.*

Fax modem A modem that enables the user to transmit and receive faxes; the modem also performs the usual modem functions.

Feasibility study The first phase of the SDLC, in which planners determine if and how a project should proceed. Also called a *system survey* or a *preliminary investigation.*

Federal Privacy Act Legislation stipulating that government agencies cannot keep secret personnel files and that individuals can have access to all government files, as well as to those of private firms contracting with the government, that contain information about them.

Fiber optics Technology that uses glass fibers that can transmit light as a communications link to send data.

Field The smallest logical unit of data, consisting of a group of one or more characters.

Field name In a database, the unique name describing the data in a field.

Field robot A robot that is used on location for such tasks as inspecting nuclear plants, disposing of bombs, cleaning up chemical spills, and other chores that are undesirable for human intervention.

Field type In a database, a category describing a field and determined by the kind of data the field will accept. Common field types are character, numeric, date, and logical.

Field width In a database or spreadsheet, the maximum number of characters that can be contained in a field.

File (1) A named location on disk containing data or executable code. (2) A collection of related records.

File compression utilities Programs that reduce the amount of space required by files.

File conversion The portion of the implementation phase of the SDLC that converts data files into the format required by the new system.

File manager utilities Programs that organize and manage disk files in a directory structure.

File server A network relationship in which an entire file is sent to a node, which then does its own processing. Also, the network computer exclusively dedicated to making files available on a network. Contrast with *client/server.*

File transfer protocol (FTP) Regarding the Internet, a set of rules for transferring files from one computer to another.

File transfer software In a network, software used to transfer files from one computer to another. See also *Download* and *Upload.*

Filter E-mail client software feature that can direct incoming e-mail and Web site information to specific folders and even reject certain types of information.

Filter software Offers some control over what e-mail messages will be accepted.

Find command Feature of many application programs that displays on the screen the exact page and place where a word or phrase is located. See *search command* also.

Find-and-replace feature Finds each instance of a certain word or phrase and replaces it with another word or phrase.

Firewall A combination of hardware and software that prevents unauthorized traffic between a company's network and the Internet.

Flame An insulting or abusive e-mail or newsgroup message.

Flame war An exchange of flames.

Flaming Sending insulting e-mail messages, often by large numbers of people in response to spamming.

Flash memory Nonvolatile memory chips.

Flatbed scanner A desktop scanner that scans a sheet of paper, thus using optical recognition to convert text or drawings into computer-recognizable form.

Flat-panel screen See *liquid crystal display.*

Flips-and-clicks retailers Mail-order retailers who have embraced the Internet.

Flowchart The pictorial representation of an orderly step-by-step solution to a problem.

Font A complete set of characters in a particular size, typeface, weight, and style.

Font library A variety of type fonts stored on disk. Also called *soft fonts.*

Footer In word processing, the ability to place the same line, with possible variations, such as page number, on the bottom of each page.

Footnote In word processing, the ability to make a reference in a text document to a note at the bottom of the page.

Foreground In large computers, an area in memory for programs that have a high priority. Contrast with *background.*

Foreign key In a database table, a field that is used to link to a primary key in a related table.

Format (1) The process of preparing a disk to accept data. (2) The specifications that determine how a document or worksheet appears on the screen or when printed.

Formula In a spreadsheet, an instruction placed in a cell to calculate a value.

FORTRAN (FORmula TRANslator) The first high-level programming language, introduced in 1954 by IBM; it is scientifically oriented.

Fourth-generation language A very high-level language. Also called a *4GL.*

Freedom of Information Act Legislation that allows citizens access to personal data gathered by federal agencies.

Freeware Software for which there is no fee.

Frequency The number of times an analog signal repeats during a specific time interval.

Frequency modulation The alteration of the carrier wave frequency to represent 0s and 1s.

Front-end processor A communications control unit designed to relieve the central computer of some communications tasks.

FTP See *file transfer protocol.*

FTP servers Servers that maintain collections of downloadable files.

Full backup The type of backup that copies everything from the hard drive to the backup medium.

Full-duplex transmission Data transmission in both directions at the same time.

Full justification In word processing, making the left and right margins even.

Function A built-in spreadsheet formula.

Function keys Special keys programmed to execute commonly used commands; the commands vary according to the software being used.

G

Gantt chart A bar chart commonly used to depict schedule deadlines and milestones, especially in systems analysis and design.

Gas plasma technology Technology that produces a brighter image and comes in larger sizes than LCD displays.

Gateway A collection of hardware and software resources to connect two dissimilar networks, allowing computers in one network to communicate with those in the other.

GB See *gigabyte*.

General-purpose register A register used for several functions, such as arithmetic and addressing purposes.

Gigabyte (GB) Approximately one billion bytes.

Gigahertz Billions of cycles per second.

Graphic artists People who use graphics software to express their ideas visually.

Graphical user interface (GUI) An image-based computer interface in which the user sends directions to the operating system by selecting items from a menu or manipulating icons on the screen by using a pointing device such as a mouse.

Graphics Images such as pictures or graphs.

Graphics adapter board A circuit board that enables a computer to display text and images on a monitor. Also called a *graphics card*.

Graphics card See *graphics adapter board*.

Graphics tablet An input device consisting of a rectangular board that contains an invisible grid of electronic dots.

Greater-than condition (>) A comparison operation that determines whether one value is greater than another.

Green computing Refers to addressing the environmental impact of computer use in an environmentally responsible manner.

Groupware Software that lets a group of people develop or track a project together, usually including e-mail, networking, and database technology. Also called *collaborative software*.

GUI See *graphical user interface*.

H

Hacker (1) An enthusiastic, largely self-taught computer user. (2) Currently, a person who gains access to computer systems illegally, usually from a personal computer.

Half-duplex transmission Data transmission in either direction, but only one way at a time.

Halftone In desktop publishing, a reproduction of a black-and-white photograph; it is made up of tiny dots.

Handheld scanner A small scanner that can be passed over a sheet of paper, thus using optical recognition to convert text or drawings into computer-recognizable form.

Hard copy Printed paper output.

Hard disk A rigid platter coated with magnetic oxide that can be magnetized to represent data. Hard disks are usually in a pack and are generally in a sealed module.

Hardware The computer and its associated equipment.

Hashing algorithm In random file organization, a mathematical operation that is applied to a key to yield a number that represents the disk address of a record.

Head crash The result of a read/write head touching a disk surface and causing all data to be destroyed.

Head switching The activation of a particular read/write head over a particular track on a particular surface.

Header In word processing, the ability to place the same line, with possible variations, such as page number, on the top of each page.

Health Insurance Portability and Accountability Act (HIPAA) An act which contains provisions requiring employers, health care providers, and insurance companies to take appropriate steps to protect the privacy of individuals' medical records.

Help Desk Devoted to giving users help with software selection, software training, problem resolution and, if appropriate, access to corporate computer systems.

Hierarchy chart See *structure chart.*

HiFD High-capacity disks whose drives can handle the new disks and the traditional 3.5-inch disk.

High-level language A procedural, problem-oriented programming language not tied directly to specific computer hardware.

Home page The main page of a Web site.

Host computer The central computer in a network, to which other computers, and perhaps terminals, are attached.

Hot list Regarding the Internet, a list of names and URLs of favorite sites maintained by a browser.

Hot site For use in an emergency, a fully equipped computer center with hardware, communications facilities, environmental controls, and security.

HTTP See *HyperText Transfer Protocol.*

Hyperregion On a Web page, an icon or image that can be clicked to cause a link to another Web site; furthermore, the cursor image changes when it rests on the hyperregion.

HyperText Transfer Protocol (HTTP) A set of rules that provide the means of communicating on the World Wide Web by using links. Note the http at the beginning of Web page URLs.

Hypertext On a Web page, text that can be clicked to cause a link to another Web site; hypertext is usually distinguished by a different color and perhaps underlining; furthermore, the cursor image changes when it rests on the hypertext.

I

IC See *integrated circuit.*

Icon A small picture on a computer screen; it represents a computer activity.

IEEE 1394 bus Also known as FireWire, a high-speed bus that is normally used to connect video equipment to a computer.

Imaging Using a scanner to convert a drawing, photo, or document to an electronic version that can be stored and reproduced when needed. Once scanned, text documents may be processed by optical recognition software so that the text can be manipulated.

Immersion Related to virtual reality. When a user is absorbed by virtual reality interaction, the process is said to be immersion.

Impact printer A printer that forms characters by physically striking the paper.

Implementation The phase of a systems analysis and design project that includes training, equipment conversion, file conversion, system conversion, auditing, evaluation, and maintenance.

Incremental backup A type of backup which copies only those files that have been changed since either the last full or incremental backup.

Independent variable Input to a computerized model, particularly a decision support system. Called independent because it can be changed by the user.

Indexed file organization A method of file organization in which the records are stored in sequential order, but the file also contains an index of record keys. Data can be accessed directly and sequentially.

Indexed processing See *Indexed file processing.*

Industry Standard Architecture (ISA) bus The oldest expansion bus still in common use. It is used for slow-speed devices such as the mouse and modem.

Inference engine Related to the field of artificial intelligence, particularly how computers learn; a process that accesses, selects, and interprets a set of rules.

Information Input data that has been processed by the computer; data that is organized, meaningful, and useful.

Information center A company unit that offers employees computer and software training, help in getting data from other computer systems, and technical assistance.

Information Services The department responsible for managing a company's computer resources. Also called *Management Information Systems (MIS), Computer Information Systems (CIS),* or *Computing Services.*

Information Technology (IT) department A department made up of the people who are responsible for the organization's computer resources.

Information utility A commercial consumer-oriented communications system, such as America Online, that offers a variety of services, usually including access to the Internet.

Inheritance In object-oriented programming, the property meaning that an object in a subclass automatically possesses all the characteristics of the class to which it belongs.

Ink-jet printer A non-impact printer that forms output text or images by spraying ink from jet nozzles onto the paper.

Input Raw data that is put into the computer system for processing.

Input device A device that puts data in computer-understandable form and sends it to the processing unit.

Input requirements In systems design, the plan for input medium and content and forms design.

Insertion point See *cursor*.

Instance In object-oriented programming, a specific occurrence of an object.

Instruction set The commands that a CPU understands and is capable of executing. Each type of CPU has a fixed group of these instructions, and each set usually differs from that understood by other CPUs.

Integrated application combines basic word processing, spreadsheet, and graphics capabilities in a single program.

Integrated circuit (IC) A complete electronic circuit on a small chip of silicon.

Integrated Services Digital Network (ISDN) A service that provides a digital connection over standard telephone lines. Although faster than using an analog modem, ISDN is much slower than DSL service.

Integrity constraints Rules established by database designers that prevent unreliable and inaccurate data from being entered into a database.

Intellectual property (IP) Refers to results of intellectual activity in the industrial, scientific, literary or artistic fields. IP is legally protected in several ways.

intelligent terminal A terminal that combines a keyboard and monitor with memory and a processor, giving it the ability to perform limited processing functions.

Interface card See *expansion board*.

Interlaced A screen whose lines are scanned alternatively, first the odd-numbered lines, and then the even-numbered lines. Although inexpensive, interlaced monitors are subject to flicker.

Internal cache Cache (very fast memory for frequently used data and instructions) built into the design of the microprocessor. Contrast with *external cache*.

Internal font A font built into the read-only memory (a ROM chip) of a printer.

Internal modem A modem on a circuit board. An internal modem can be installed in a computer by the user.

Internal storage The electronic circuitry that temporarily holds data and program instructions needed by the CPU.

Internet A worldwide public communications network once used primarily by businesses, governments, and academic institutions but now also used by individuals via various private access methods.

Internet directory A service that employs human researchers to organize and categorize Internet sites.

The Internet Non-Discrimination Act An act that extended the Internet tax moratorium until 2005.

Internet service provider (ISP) An entity that offers, for a fee, a server computer and the software needed to access the Internet.

Internet Tax Freedom Act A federal law that imposes a moratorium on taxes imposed on the Internet, and calls for a committee to study the matter.

Interrupt In multiprogramming, a condition that temporarily suspends the execution of an individual program.

Intranet A private Internet-like network internal to a company.

IP switches Internet protocol switches used to direct communications traffic among connected networks that have adopted the Internet protocol.

IrDA A wireless transmission that uses infrared to transmit data a few feet.

ISDN See *Integrated Services Digital Network*.

ISP See *Internet service provider.*

I-time The instruction portion of the machine cycle; I-time includes the fetch and decode operations.

J

Java A network-friendly programming language that allows software to run on many different platforms.

JavaScript and VBScript Scripting languages that are used to produce a series of instructions included with a Web page that are interpreted and executed by your browser.

Joystick A graphics input device that allows fingertip control of figures on a monitor.

Justification In word processing, aligning text along the left or right margins, or both.

K

K or KB See *kilobyte.*

Kernel The memory-resident portion of the operating system that controls operations and loads into memory nonresident operating system programs from disk storage as needed.

Kerning In word processing or desktop publishing, adjusting the space between characters to create a more attractive or readable appearance.

Key field See *primary key, foreign key.*

Keyboard A common computer input device similar to the keyboard of a typewriter.

Kilobyte (K or KB) 1024 bytes.

Knowledge base Related to the field of artificial intelligence, particularly how computers learn; a set of facts and rules about those facts.

Knowledge engineer Related to building an expert system, the person working to extract information from the human expert.

L

Label In a spreadsheet, data consisting of a string of text characters.

LAN See *local area network.*

LAN manager A person designated to manage and run a local area network (LAN).

Landscape mode Orientation setting in which output is printed across the wider dimension of the paper.

Laptop computer A small portable computer, usually somewhat larger than a notebook computer.

Laser printer A non-impact printer that uses a light beam to transfer images to paper.

LCD See *liquid crystal display.*

Leading In word processing or desktop publishing, the vertical spacing between lines of type.

Leased lines Communication lines obtained from a common carrier to provide dedicated service.

Less-than condition (<) A logical operation in which the computer compares values to determine whether the first value is less than the second value.

Level 1 (L1) cache See *internal cache.*

Level 2 (L2) cache Memory cache that can be either internal or external, depending on processor design.

Level 3 (L3) cache An additional layer of cache on an external chip.

Librarian A person who catalogs processed computer disks and tapes and keeps them secure.

Light pen A graphics input device that enables the user to interact directly with the computer screen.

line graph A graph in which a line connects the points in a data series, useful for showing trends over time.

Line printers Impact printers used on mainframe systems that print an entire line at a time.

Link (1) A physical data communications medium. (2) On the World Wide Web, clickable text or image that can cause a change to a different Web site.

Link/load phase A phase that takes the machine language object module and adds necessary prewritten programs to produce output called the load module; the load module is executable.

Linkage editor A system program that combines an object module with prewritten

modules from the system library to create an executable load module.

Linux   A Unix-like operating system that is freely available and not under control of any one company.

Liquid crystal display (LCD)   A flat-panel monitor used on laptops and some desktop systems.

Live banner   A type of Web site banner ad that lets a user get more information about a product without leaving the current site.

Load module   An executable version of a program.

Local area network (LAN)   A network designed to share data and resources among several computers, usually personal computers, in a limited geographical area, such as an office or a building. Contrast with *wide area network*.

Logic chip   A central processing unit on a chip, generally known as a microprocessor but called a logic chip when used for some special purpose, such as controlling some under-the-hood action in a car.

Logic error   A flaw in the logic of a program.

Logic flowchart   A flowchart that represents the flow of logic in a program.

Logical field   In a database, a field used to keep track of true and false conditions.

Logical operations   Comparing operations. The ALU is able to compare numbers, letters, or special characters and take alternative courses of action depending on the result of the comparison.

Lurking   Reading messages in newsgroups without writing any.

M

Mac OS   Introduced with Apple's Macintosh computer in 1984, this operating system had the first generally available GUI. Its latest version, Mac OS X, is still considered easiest to use for beginners.

Machine cycle   The combination of I-time and E-time, the steps used by the central processing unit to execute instructions.

Machine language   The lowest level of computer language; it represents data and instructions as 1s and 0s.

Magnetic core   A small, flat doughnut-shaped piece of metal used as an early memory device.

Magnetic disk   An oxide-coated disk on which data is recorded as magnetic spots.

Magnetic tape   A magnetic medium with an iron-oxide coating that can be magnetized. Data is stored on the tape as extremely small magnetized spots.

Magnetic tape unit   A data storage unit used to record data on and retrieve data from magnetic tape.

Magnetic-ink character recognition (MICR)   A method of machine-reading characters made of magnetized particles. A common application is checks.

Magneto-optical (MO)   A hybrid disk that has the high-volume capacity of an optical disk but can be written over like a magnetic disk. It uses a laser beam and a magnet to align magnetically sensitive metallic crystals.

Mail merge   Adding names and addresses, probably from a database, to a prepared document, such as a letter prepared using word processing.

Mail server   A server maintained by your network or ISP that provides you with an e-mail address, consisting of your user name and the mail server's domain name, and a mailbox to store your messages.

Mailbox   Program component that stores e-mail messages.

Main memory   See *memory*.

Main storage   See *memory*.

Mainframe   A large computer that has access to billions of characters of data and is capable of processing large amounts of data very quickly. Notably, mainframes are used by such data-heavy organizations as banks, airlines, and large manufacturers.

Maintenance   The portion of the implementation phase of the SDLC that involves the monitoring and adjustment of the system.

Make or buy decision   In the system design phase of the SDLC, the decision to either purchase an existing software package or to develop custom software.

Management Information Systems (MIS)   A department that manages computer resources for an organization. Also called *Computing Services* or *Information Services*.

Marc Andreessen Led a team that invented Mosaic, the first graphical browser, in 1993.

Mark In word processing, the user marks a certain section of text, called a block, by using some sort of highlighting, usually reverse video; the marked text can then be copied, moved, or deleted.

Mark sensing See *optical mark recognition.*

Master file A file containing semi-permanent data that must be updated to reflect business activity.

MB See *megabyte.*

Mechanical mouse A mouse that has a ball on its underside that rolls as the mouse is moved.

Megabyte (MB) Approximately one million bytes. The unit often used to measure memory or storage capacity.

Megaflop One million floating-point operations per second. One measure of a computer's speed.

Megahertz (MHz) One million cycles per second. Used to express microprocessor speeds.

Megapixels Millions of pixels.

Memory The electronic circuitry that temporarily holds data and program instructions needed by the CPU. Also called *main memory, main storage,* or *primary memory.*

Memory management The process of allocating memory to programs and keeping the programs in memory separate from one another.

Memory protection In a multiprogramming system, the process of keeping a program from straying into other programs in memory.

Menu An onscreen list that encourages pointing and clicking with a mouse.

Message In object-oriented programming, a command telling what—not how—something is to be done, which activates a method of the object.

Metasearch A search method that uses software to run queries on several search engines.

Method In object-oriented programming, instructions that tell the data what to do. Also called an *operation.*

Metropolitan area network (MAN) A network limited to a single metropolitan area.

MHz See *megahertz.*

MICR See *magnetic-ink character recognition.*

MICR inscriber A device that adds magnetic characters to a document, in particular, the amount of a check.

Microcomputer A relatively inexpensive type of computer, usually used by an individual in a home or office setting. Also called a *personal computer.*

Microprocessor A general-purpose central processing unit on a chip.

Microsecond One-millionth of a second.

Micro-to-mainframe link A connection between microcomputers and mainframe computers.

Microwave transmission Line-of-sight transmission of data signals through the atmosphere from relay station to relay station.

MIDI (Musical Instrument Digital Interface) A set of rules designed for recording and playing back music on digital synthesizers.

Millisecond One-thousandth of a second.

MIPS Millions of instructions per second. A measure of how fast a central processing unit can process information.

MIS See *Management Information Systems.*

MIS manager A person, familiar with both computer technology and the organization's business, who runs the MIS department.

MITS Altair Generally considered the first personal computer, offered as a kit to computer hobbyists in 1975.

Model (1) A type of database, each type representing a particular way of organizing data. The three database models are hierarchical, network, and relational. (2) In a DSS, an image of something that actually exists or a mathematical representation of a real-life system.

Modem Short for modulate/demodulate. A device that converts a digital signal to an analog signal and vice versa. Used to transfer data between computers over analog communications lines.

Moderated newsgroups Newsgroups controlled by a moderator.

Moderator A person who determines which messages are posted on a moderated newsgroup.

Modulation Using a modem, the process of converting a signal from digital to analog.

Monitor Hardware that features the computer's screen, includes housing for the screen's electronic components, and probably sits on a stand that tilts and swivels.

Monochrome A computer screen that displays information in one color, on a contrasting background.

Monolithic Refers to the inseparable nature of memory chip circuitry.

Mosaic The first Web browser, invented in 1993 by Marc Andreessen, co-founder of Netscape, Inc.

Motherboard Inside the personal computer housing, a board that holds the main chips and circuitry of the computer hardware, including the CPU chip.

Motion Picture Experts Group (MPEG) A widely accepted video compression standard.

Mouse A handheld computer input device whose movement on a flat surface causes corresponding movement of the cursor on the screen. Also, a mouse button can be clicked to make selections from choices on the screen.

Multimedia Software that typically presents information with text, illustrations, photos, narration, music, animation, and film clips—possible because the high-volume capacity of optical disks can accommodate photographs, film clips, and music. To use multimedia software, you must have the proper hardware: a CD-ROM drive, a sound card, and speakers. Multimedia also is offered on several Internet sites.

Multiplexer Combines the data streams from a number of slow-speed devices into a single data stream for transmission over a high-speed circuit.

Multiprocessing Using more than one central processing unit, a computer can run multiple programs simultaneously, each using its own processor.

Multiprogramming A feature of large computer operating systems under which different programs from different users compete for the use of the central process-

ing unit; these programs are said to run concurrently.

N

Nanosecond One-billionth of a second.

Natural language A programming language that resembles human language.

Natural languages Fifth-generation languages because the resemble natural spoken language.

Nature of the problem Discovered in the preliminary investigation of the systems development life cycle.

Navigation bar A set of links on a Web page.

NC See *net computer.*

Neighborhood Children's Internet Protection Act (NCIPA) A law that requires libraries receiving the E-Rate discount to establish an Internet safety policy to protect children.

Net box See *net computer.*

Net computer A computer used in conjunction with a television set to access the Internet. Also called a *net box,* or *Web TV.*

.NET Platform A Microsoft standard designed to allow easy development and deployment of Web-based software services accessible by any Web-enabled device.

Netiquette Appropriate behavior in network communications.

Network A computer system that uses communications equipment to connect two or more computers and their resources.

Network interface card (NIC) A circuit board that can be inserted into a slot inside a personal computer to allow it to send and receive messages on a local area network (LAN).

Network manager A person designated to manage and run a computer network.

Network operating system An operating system that runs on a network server and controls the operation of the network.

Newsgroup An informal network of computers that allows the posting and reading of messages in groups that focus on specific topics. More formally called *Usenet.*

Newsreader software Software that's used to participate in newsgroups.

NIC See *network interface card.*

No Electronic Theft (NET) Act Prohibits reproducing or distributing copyrighted material by electronic means, regardless of the purpose or motive.

Node A device, usually a personal computer, that is connected to a network.

Noise Electrical interference that causes distortion when a signal is being transmitted over communication lines.

Non-impact printer A printer that prints without striking the paper.

Non-interlaced (NI) A description of screens that scan all lines in order, a procedure that is best for animated graphics. See *interlaced.*

Nonprocedural languages Programming languages in which the programmer specifies the desired results and the language develops the solution.

NOS See *network operating system.*

Notebook computer A small portable computer.

Novell's Netware A popular network operating system designed for the client/server environment.

NSFnet The National Science Foundation network. A predecessor of the Internet.

numeric fields In database tables, fields which contain numbers for calculations.

O

Object In object-oriented programming, a self-contained unit that contains data and related facts and functions—the instructions to act on that data.

Object linking and embedding (OLE) A Windows technology that lets you embed or link one document with another.

Object module A machine language version of a program; it is produced by a compiler or assembler.

Object/relational database management systems (O/RDBMS) Relational DBMSs enhanced with object-oriented capabilities.

Object-oriented database management systems (OODBMS) DBMSs that are used to create and manipulate object-oriented databases.

Object-oriented database model Developed to meet the need of manipulating complex data types such as audio and video.

Object-oriented programming (OOP) A programming approach that uses objects, self-contained units that contain data and related facts and functions—the instructions to act on that data.

OCR See *optical character recognition.*

OCR-A The standard typeface for characters to be input by optical character recognition.

OCR software Software that converts a scanned image of a text document into text characters that can be manipulated by word processing software.

Office automation The use of technology to help achieve goals in an office. Often associated with data communications.

OMR See *optical mark recognition.*

Online In a data communications environment, a direct connection from a terminal to a computer or from one computer to another.

Online analytical processing (OLAP) software Software that analyzes data stored in a data warehouse to provide information to management.

Online service A commercial consumer-oriented communications system, such as America Online or the Microsoft Network, that offers a variety of services, usually including access to the Internet. Also called an *information utility.*

Online transaction processing (OLTP) software Processes the day-to-day transactions of an organization by updating data stored in databases.

OOP See *object-oriented programming.*

Open source concept Something that is freely available and not under control of any one company.

Open source software Software that is freely distributed in a format that allows programmers to make changes to it.

Operating environment Software designed as a shell, an extra layer, for an operating system, so that the user does not have to memorize or look up commands.

Operating system A set of programs that lies between applications software and the computer hardware, through which a computer manages its own resources.

Operation In object-oriented programming, instructions that tell the data what to do. Also called a *method.*

Optical character recognition (OCR) A computer input method that uses a light source to read special characters and convert them to electrical signals to be sent to the computer.

Optical disk drive Storage technology that uses a laser beam to store large amounts of data at relatively low cost.

Optical mark recognition (OMR) A computer input method that uses a light source to recognize marks on paper and convert them to electrical signals to be sent to the computer.

Optical mouse A mouse that uses a light beam to monitor mouse movement.

Optical recognition system A category of computer input that uses a light source to read optical marks, optical characters, handwritten characters, and bar codes and convert them to electrical signals to be sent to the computer.

Optical Scanner See *scanner.*

Opt-in policy Consists of businesses that notify customers of their privacy policy and the customers must specifically agree before the business can release their data to third parties.

Opt-out policy Consists of customers that are assumed to have agreed to the release of their data unless they specifically request the business to have it kept private.

Organization chart A hierarchical diagram depicting lines of authority within an organization, usually mentioning people by name and title.

Output Raw data that has been processed by the computer into usable information.

Output device A device, such as a printer, that makes processed information available to the user.

Output requirements In systems de-sign, the plan for output medium and content, types of reports needed, and forms design.

Outsourcing Assigning the design and management of a new or revised system to an outside firm, as opposed to developing such a system in-house.

P

Packaged software Software that is packaged and sold in stores. Also called *commercial software.*

Packet A portion of a message to be sent to another computer via data communications. Each packet is individually addressed, and the packets are reassembled into the original message after they reach their destination.

Page composition Adding type to a layout. In desktop publishing, the software may be called a page composition program.

Page frames Equal size portions of memory into which program pages are placed as needed for execution.

Page layout In publishing, the process of arranging text and graphics on a page.

Page table The index-like table with which the operating system keeps track of page locations.

Page template In word processing, a predesigned page that can contain page settings, formatting, and page elements.

Pages Equal-size blocks into which a program is divided to be placed into corresponding noncontiguous memory spaces called page frames. See also *page frames.*

Pagination In word processing, options for placing the page number in various locations on the document page.

Paging The process of dividing a program into equal-size pages, keeping program pages on disk, and calling them into memory as needed.

Pan To move the cursor across a spreadsheet or a database to force into view fields that do not fit on the initial screen.

Parallel conversion A method of systems conversion in which the old and new systems are operated simultaneously until the users are satisfied that the new system performs to their standards; then the old system is dropped.

Parallel port External connector that transmits groups of bits together and is used for faster devices, such as printers and scanners.

Parallel processing Using multiple processors, each with its own memory unit, that work at the same time to process data much more quickly than with the traditional single processor. Contrast with *serial processing.*

Participant observation A form of observation in which the systems analyst temporarily joins the activities of the group.

Partition A separate memory area that can hold a program, used as part of a memory management technique that divides memory into separate areas. Also called a *region.*

Pascal A structured, high-level programming language named for Blaise Pascal, a seventeenth-century French mathematician.

Passive matrix Flat-panel monitor technology that is cheaper than active-matrix and uses less power, but isn't as bright. See *active-matrix.*

Patents Protect inventions by granting the patent holder exclusive rights to the invention for 20 years. Business methods implemented in software may be patented.

PC card A credit-card-sized card, such as a modem or network interface card that slides into a slot in a notebook or laptop computer to provide additional functionality. Originally known as PCMCIA cards, named for the Personal Computer Memory Card International Association.

PC card bus A bus that accepts credit card-sized PC card devices and is normally found on laptops.

PDA See *personal digital assistant.*

Peer-to-peer network A network setup in which there is no controlling server computer; all computers on the network share programs and resources.

Pen-based computer A small, portable computer that accepts handwritten input on a screen with a pen-like stylus. Also called *personal digital assistant.*

Pentium 4 A processor made by Intel that is used in IBM-compatible PCs.

Peripheral Component Interconnect (PCI) bus A high-speed bus used to connect devices, such as hard disks and network cards, to a computer system.

Peripheral equipment All the input, output, and secondary storage devices attached to a computer.

Personal computer A relatively inexpensive type of computer, usually used by an individual in a home or office setting.

Personal computer manager A person responsible for coordination of personal computer use within a company.

Personal digital assistant (PDA) A small, portable computer that is most often used to track appointments and other business information and that can accept handwritten input on a screen. Also called a *pen-based computer.*

Personal Information Managers (PIMs) Programs that typically include an appointment calendar, address book, task manager, notepad, and calculator.

Petabyte (PB) About one quadrillion bytes.

Phase (1) In data transmission, the relative position in time of one complete cycle of a carrier wave. (2) In systems analysis and design, a portion of the systems development life cycle (SDLC).

Phased conversion A systems conversion method in which the new system is phased in gradually.

Picosecond One-trillionth of a second.

Pie chart A pie-shaped graph used to compare values that represent parts of a whole.

Piggybacking A technique in which an illicit user accesses a system via a legitimate user when the legitimate user fails to sign off properly.

Pilot conversion A systems conversion method in which a designated group of users try the system first.

Pipelining A microprocessor design in which one instruction's actions—fetch, decode, execute, store—need not be complete before another instruction begins.

Pixel A picture element on a computer display screen; a pixel is merely one dot in the display.

Plagiarism The representation of someone else's words or ideas as your own. Fair use allows you to include a portion of another's work within your own, but only if you properly cite, or identify, the source.

Platform for Privacy Preferences Project (P3P) A proposed set of standards that allows a Web site server to transmit its privacy policies electronically to the user.

Platform The hardware and operating system combination that comprises the basic functionality of a particular computer.

Plot area In Excel, the area in which a chart is drawn, that is, the area above the x-axis and to the right of the y-axis.

Plug and play A technology that lets the computer configure itself when a new component is added.

Plug-in Software that can be added to a browser to enhance its functionality.

PNG See *Portable Network Graphic.*

Pocket PC A PDA that can run stripped-down versions of some desktop software.

Point A typographic measurement equaling approximately 1/72 inch.

Pointer An indicator on a screen; it shows where the next user-computer interaction will be. Also called a *cursor.*

Pointing device Used to position the pointer on the screen.

Pointing stick A small pressure-sensitive post mounted in the center of the keyboard that uses pressure to indicate the direction of pointer movement.

Point-of-sale (POS) terminal A terminal used as a cash register in a retail setting. It may be programmable or connected to a central computer.

Point-to-Point tunneling protocol (PPTP) A standard tunneling protocol.

Polymorphism In object-oriented programming, polymorphism means that when an individual object receives a message it knows how, using its own methods, to process the message in the appropriate way for that particular object.

Pop-over ads Web advertisements that open in a new window on top of your current window.

Pop-under ads Web advertisements that open in a new window underneath your current window and only become visible when you close the window you are viewing.

Pop-up menu A menu of choices that appears, popping upward, when an initial menu choice is made.

Portable Network Graphic (PNG) A file format commonly used on Internet sites; PNG is nonproprietary and is replacing the GIF format.

Portal A Web site that is used as a gateway or guide to the Internet.

Portrait mode Paper output that is printed with the longest dimension up and down.

Ports External connectors that enable you to plug in peripherals, such as a printer, a mouse, and a keyboard.

POS terminal See *Point-of-sale (POS) terminal.*

POTS (plain old telephone service) The most common dial-up system.

POTS Plain old telephone service.

PowerPC A microprocessor used in the Apple Macintosh.

Preliminary design The subphase of systems design in which the new system concept is developed.

Preliminary investigation See *feasibility study.*

Presentation graphics software Software that can produce graphs, maps, and charts and can help people compare data, spot trends more easily, and make decisions more quickly.

Primary key In a database table, the field that uniquely identifies a record in the table.

Primary memory See *memory.*

Primary storage See *memory.*

Print preview command Allows a user to see in reduced size an entire page or two facing pages or even several consecutive pages.

Printer A device for generating computer-produced output on paper.

Printer spacing chart Shows the position of headings, columns, dates, and page numbers on printed reports.

Procedural languages Consist of the first three generation of languages in which the programmer describes the step-by-step solution to the problem.

Process (1) The computer action required to convert input to output. (2)An element in a data flow diagram that represents actions taken on data: comparing, checking, stamping, authorizing, filing, and so forth.

Processor The central processing unit (CPU) of a computer, a microprocessor.

Program A set of step-by-step instructions that directs a computer to perform specific tasks and produce certain results. More generically called *software.*

Programmable read-only memory (PROM) Chips that can be programmed with specialized tools called ROM burners.

Programmer/analyst A person who performs systems analysis functions in addition to programming.

Programming language A set of rules that can be used to tell a computer what operations to perform. There are many different programming languages.

Project management software Software that allocates people and resources, monitors schedules, and produces status reports.

PROM See *programmable read-only memory.*

Prompt A signal that the system is waiting for you to give an a command to the computer.

Protocol A set of rules for the exchange of data between a terminal and a computer or between two computers.

Prototype A limited working system or subset of a system that is developed to test design concepts.

Pseudocode An English-like way of representing the solution to a problem.

Public domain software Software that is uncopyrighted, and thus may be altered.

Public key encryption system An encryption system that uses a pair of keys: one to encrypt a message and the other to decrypt it.

Puck See *stylus.*

Pull-down menu A menu of choices that appears, as a window shade is pulled down, when an initial menu choice is made.

Pure-play Retailers who do business exclusively over the Internet.

Q

Query Retrieve data from a database by presenting criteria that the DBMS uses to select the desired data.

Query languages A variation on fourth-generation languages that can be used to retrieve data from databases.

Query-by-example (QBE) A method where queries can also be prepared by using a graphical interface to set criteria.

Questionnaires A technique used for gathering data in the analysis phase of the SDLC that can save time and expense and allow anonymous answers, but response rates are often low.

Queue A list of programs waiting to be selected for execution by the operating system.

R

Ragged-right text Occurs in a word-processed document when the left margin is aligned, resulting in an uneven right margin.

RAID See *redundant array of inexpensive disks.*

RAM See *random-access memory.*

Random-access memory (RAM) Memory that provides temporary storage for data and program instructions.

Random file organization See *direct file organization.*

Randomizing algorithm See *hashing algorithm.*

Range A retangular group of cells treated as a unit by a spreadsheet program.

Raster-scan technology A video display technology. The back of the screen display has a phosphorous coating, which glows whenever it is hit by a beam of electrons.

RDRAM Faster and more expensive type of DRAM.

Read/write head An electromagnet that reads the magnetized areas on magnetic media and converts them into the electrical pulses that are sent to the processor.

Read-only media Media, such as CDs, recorded on by the manufacturer that the user can read from but not write to.

Read-only memory (ROM) Memory containing data and programs that can be read but not altered. Data remains in ROM after the power is turned off.

Real storage That part of memory that temporarily holds part of a program pulled from virtual storage.

Real-time processing Processing in which the results are available in time to affect the activity at hand.

Record (1) A set of related fields. (2) In a database table, one row.

Reduced instruction set computer (RISC) A computer that offers only frequently used instructions. Because fewer instructions are offered, this is a factor in improving the computer's speed. Contrast with *complex instruction set computer.*

Redundant array of inexpensive disks (RAID) Secondary storage that uses several connected hard disks that act as a unit. Using multiple disks enables manufacturers

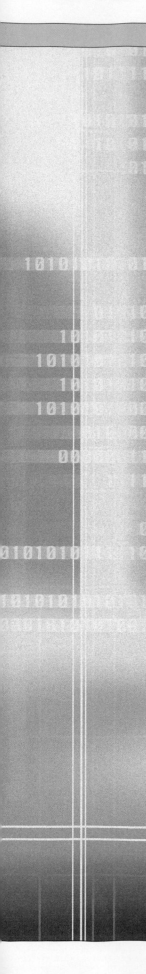

to improve data security, access time, and data transfer rates.

Refresh To maintain an image on a CRT screen by reforming the screen image at frequent intervals to avoid flicker. The frequency is called the scan rate; 60 times per second is usually adequate to retain a clear image.

Region A separate memory area that can hold a program, used as part of a memory management technique that simply divides memory into separate areas. Also called a *partition*.

Register A temporary storage area within the CPU for instructions or data.

Relation In the relational database model, a link between tables established by a common field. See *primary key, foreign key*.

Relational database A database in which the data is organized in a table format consisting of rows and columns, where the rows are the records and the columns are the fields.

Relational model A database model that organizes data logically in tables.

Relational operator An operator, such as = or >, that enables a user to make comparisons and selections.

Removable hard disk cartridge A supplemental hard disk that, once filled, can be replaced with a fresh one.

Report generator A DBMS feature that allows the user to easily design printed reports.

Resolution The clarity of a video display screen or printer output.

Resource allocation The operating system process by which system resources, such as CPU cycles and memory, are assigned to executing programs.

Response time The time between a typed computer request and the response of the computer.

Retrovirus A virus that is powerful enough to defeat or even delete antivirus software.

Reverse video The feature that highlights onscreen text by switching the usual text and background colors.

Ring network A "circle" of point-to-point connections between computers at local sites. A ring network does not contain a central host computer.

RISC See *reduced instruction set computer*.

Robot A computer-controlled device that can physically manipulate its surroundings.

ROM See *read-only memory*.

ROM burner A specialized device used to program progammable read-only memory (PROM) chips.

Rotational delay For disk units, the time it takes for a record on a track to revolve under the read/write head.

Router A special computer that directs communications traffic when several networks are connected.

RPG (Report Program Generator) A programming language developed by IBM in 1965 to allow rapid creation of reports from data stored in the computer files, it is currently used primarily on IBM midrange computers.

RSA A common public key encryption system named after its developers, Rivest, Shamir, and Adleman.

S

Salami A method of computer crime in which the criminal embezzles small "slices" of money from many transactions.

Sampling In systems analysis, collecting a subset of data relevant to the system under study.

Sans serif A typeface that is clean, with no serif marks.

Satellite transmission Data transmission from earth station to earth station via communications satellites.

Scalable fonts Type fonts which can be set to almost any size.

Scan rate The number of times a CRT screen is refreshed in a given time period. A scan rate of 60 times per second is usually adequate to retain a clear screen image.

Scanner A device that uses a light source to read text and images directly into the computer. Scanners can be of several varieties, notably handheld, sheetfed, and desktop.

Scavenging A type of computer-based crime in which the criminal searches company trash cans for proprietary information.

Screen A television-like output device that can display information.

Screen tip A small explanatory text message that appears when the screen pointer is positioned over a GUI element, such as a button or icon.

Scrolling A feature that enables the user to move to and view any part of a document on the screen.

SDLC See *systems development life cycle.*

Sealed module A disk drive containing the disks, access arms, and read/write heads sealed together.

Search command Displays on the screen the exact page and place where a word or phrase is located. Also called *find command.*

Search engine Regarding the Internet, software that lets a user specify search terms that can be used to find Web sites that include those terms.

Secondary storage Additional storage, often on disk, for data and programs. Secondary storage is separate from the CPU and memory. Also called *auxiliary storage.*

Sector On disk, a segment of a track that holds a fixed number of bytes.

Secure Sockets Layer (SSL) A protocol that provides for secure transmission of data between a user's computer and a Web host. Used to transmit sensitive data such as credit card numbers.

Security A system of safeguards designed to protect a computer system and data from deliberate or accidental damage or access by unauthorized persons.

Seek time The time required for an access arm to move into position over a particular track on a disk.

Select In word processing, to mark a certain section of text, called a block, by some sort of highlighting, usually reverse video. The text is usually selected in advance of some other command upon the text, such as Move.

Semiconductor A crystalline substance that conducts electricity when it is "doped" with chemical impurities.

Semiconductor memory Thousands of very small circuits on a silicon chip.

Semiconductor storage Data storage on a silicon chip.

Sequential file organization The arrangement of records in ascending or descending order by a certain field called the key.

Sequential file processing Processing in which transaction records are sorted into primary key sequence and processed in order to create a new master file.

Serial port External connector that transmits data one bit at a time and is typically used for slow-speed devices, such as the mouse and keyboard.

Serial processing Processing in which a single processor can handle only one instruction at a time. Contrast with *parallel processing.*

Serif Small marks added to the letters of a typeface; the marks are intended to increase readability of the typeface. Contrast with *Sans serif.*

Server (1) In a client/server network arrangement, the computer that controls and manages the network and its services; the server usually has hard disks that hold files needed by users on the network. (2) A computer used to access the Internet; it has special software that uses the Internet protocol.

Shareware Copyrighted software which is freely distributed under a "try before you buy" policy, in which the user is expected to send in a registration fee if the software is kept.

Sheetfed scanner Usually designed to fit neatly between the keyboard and the monitor, uses motorized rollers to feed the sheet across the scanning head.

Shell An early version of Windows that was merely a layer of software over the operating system.

SIMM See *single in-line memory module.*

Simplex transmission Transmission of data in only one direction.

Simulation The use of a computer model, particularly a decision support system, to reach decisions about real-life situations.

Single in-line memory module (SIMM) A board containing memory chips that can be plugged into a computer expansion slot.

Sink In a data flow diagram, a destination for data going outside the system.

Site license A software license that permits a customer to use the software on all computers at the specified location.

Smalltalk An object-oriented language that supports a particularly visual system.

Smart terminal A terminal that has some processing ability.

Social engineering A tongue-in-cheek term for con artist actions, specifically, hackers persuading people to give away their passwords over the phone.

Soft copy Computer-produced output displayed on a screen.

Soft font A font that can be downloaded from the font library on disk to a printer.

Software Instructions that tell a computer what to do. Also called *programs.*

Software piracy The unauthorized copying of computer software.

SOHO Abbreviation for small office, home office, a designated group for which software is designed.

Source In a data flow diagram, a producer of data outside the system.

Source data automation The use of special equipment to collect input data as it is generated and send it directly to the computer.

Source document An instrument, usually paper, containing data to be prepared as input to a computer.

Source module A program as originally coded, before being translated into machine language.

Source program listing The printed version of a program as the programmer wrote it, usually produced as a byproduct of compilation.

Spamming Mass advertising on the Internet, usually done with software especially designed to send solicitations to users via e-mail.

Speech recognition The process by which the spoken word is converted into computer text.

Speech synthesis The process of enabling machines to talk to people.

Spelling checker Program that includes a built-in dictionary.

Spider A program that follows links throughout the Web. Used to build a database of Web page contents for use by search engines.

Spooling A process in which files to be printed are placed temporarily on disk.

Spreadsheet A computer version of a paper worksheet, in which numeric data is organized into rows and columns. Calculations are performed based on user-written formulas.

SQL See *structured query language.*

SRAM See *static random-access memory.*

Star network A network consisting of one or more computers connected to a central host computer.

Start/stop transmission Asynchronous data transmission.

Static random-access memory (SRAM) A type of RAM that requires a continuous current to hold data. SRAM is usually faster but larger and more expensive than dynamic RAM. Contrast with *Dynamic random-access memory (DRAM).*

Storage register A register that temporarily holds data taken from or about to be sent to memory.

Streaming The downloading of live audio, video, and animation content.

Structured interview In systems analysis, an interview in which only planned questions are used.

Structured programming A set of programming techniques that includes a limited number of control structures and certain programming standards.

Structured Query Language (SQL) A standard query language supported by most DBMSs.

Structured walkthrough A process by which a programmer's peers review the algorithm design and/or program code to verify correctness and offer suggestions for improvement.

Style In word processing, the way a typeface is printed—for example, in italic.

Stylus A device moved around on a graphics tablet by the user.

Suite A group of basic software applications designed to work together. A typical suite application is mail merge, in which certain names and addresses from a database are applied to letters prepared using word processing.

Supercomputer The largest and most powerful category of computers.

SuperDisk See *HiFD.*

Supervisor program An operating system program that controls the entire operating system and calls in other operating system programs from disk storage as needed.

Support center An organizational unit that provides assistance to users, as well as formal and informal user training. See also *information center.*

Surge protector A device that prevents electrical problems from affecting data files.

SVGA (Super VGA) A superior screen standard with 800×600, 1024×768, 1280×1024, or 1600×1200 pixels. All SVGA standards support a palette of 16 million colors, but the number of colors that can be displayed simultaneously is limited by the amount of video memory installed in a system.

Symbolic address The meaningful name used in a computer program for a memory location. Instead of a number, for example, a symbolic address should be something meaningful, such as NAME or SALARY.

Symbolic language A second-generation language that uses abbreviations for instructions. Also called *assembly language.*

Synchronous transmission Data transmission in which characters are transmitted together in a continuous stream.

Synonym The name for a record's disk address, produced by a hashing scheme, that is the same as a pre-existing address for a different record.

Syntax The rules of a programming language.

Syntax errors Errors in the use of a programming language.

Synthesis by analysis Speech synthesis in which a device analyzes the input of an actual human voice, stores and processes the spoken sounds, and reproduces them as needed.

Synthesis by rule Speech synthesis in which a device applies linguistic rules to create an artificial spoken language.

System An organized set of related components established to perform a certain task.

System bus A device that transfers data between the CPU and memory. Bus width and speed affect system performance.

System clock The part of the central processing unit that produces pulses at a fixed rate to synchronize computer operations.

System conversion The step in the implementation phase of the SDLC in which the new system is installed and the old system removed. It may be done in one of four ways: direct conversion, immediately replacing the old system with the new system; phased conversion, easing in the new system a step at a time; pilot conversion, testing the entire system with a few users and extending it to the rest when it proves successful; and parallel conversion, operating the old and new systems concurrently until the new system is proved successful.

System journal A file whose records represent real-time transactions. Used to provide an audit trail and recovery capabilities for online transaction-processing systems.

System requirements A detailed list of the things a particular system must be able to do, based on the results of the systems analysis.

System survey The first phase of systems analysis, in which planners determine if and how a project should proceed. Also called a *feasibility study* or a *preliminary investigation.*

System testing The process in the development phase of the SDLC in which all the programs in a system are tested together using test data to ensure that they interact properly.

System unit The case that contains the motherboard and may also house various storage devices.

Systems analysis A phase of the systems development life cycle, involving studying an existing system to determine how it works and with an eye to improving the system.

Systems analyst The person responsible for analyzing an existing system, developing a new system design, and coordinating the development and installation of the new system.

Systems design A phase of the systems development life cycle, involving developing a plan for a new or revised system based on the results of the systems analysis phase.

Systems development life cycle (SDLC) The multiphase process required for creating or revising a computer system.

Systems development The phase of the SDLC in which the system design is used to

produce a functioning system. Activities include programming and testing.

Systems flowchart A drawing that depicts the flow of data through some part of a business system.

Systems software All programs related to coordinating computer operations, including the operating system, programming language translators, and service programs.

T

Table (1) In data organization, a collection of similar records. (2) In word processing, a set of data organized in rows and columns that can be inserted into a document.

Table structure A list of fields including the field name, type of data stored in the field, and the size, or width, of the field.

Tag In HTML, a command that performs a specific function.

Tape drive The device that reads data from and writes data on magnetic tape.

TCP/IP See *Transmission Control Protocol/Internet Protocol*.

Telecommuting Using telecommunications and computers at home as a substitute for working at an office outside the home.

Teleconferencing A system of holding conferences by linking geographically dispersed people together through computer terminals or personal computers.

Telnet A protocol that enables remote users to use their PCs to log onto a host computer system over the Internet and use it as if they were sitting at a local terminal of that system.

Template (1) In desktop publishing, a predetermined page design that lets a user fill in text and art. (2) In a spreadsheet program, a worksheet that has already been designed for the solution of a specific type of problem, so that a user need only fill in the data.

Terabyte (TB) About one trillion bytes.

Teraflop One trillion floating-point operations per second. One measure of a computer's speed, especially as related to parallel processors.

Terminal A device that consists of an input device (usually a keyboard), an output device (usually a screen), and a communications link to the computer.

Terminal emulation software Data communications software that makes a personal computer act like a terminal, so that it can communicate with a larger computer.

Text block A continuous section of text in a document that has been marked or selected.

Text editor Software that is somewhat like a word processing program, used by programmers to create a program file.

TFT See *active matrix display*.

Thesaurus program With a word processing program, this program provides a list of synonyms and antonyms for a selected word in a document.

Thin client A computer connected to a network that has no disk storage capability and is used basically for input/output.

Thrashing Occurs when the CPU spends all its time swapping pages in and out of real memory.

Time slice In time-sharing, a period of time—a fraction of a second—during which the computer works on a user's tasks.

Time-sharing A special case of multiprogramming in which several people use one computer at the same time.

Title The caption on a chart that summarizes the information in the chart.

Token passing The protocol for controlling access to a Token Ring network. A special signal, or token, circulates from node to node, allowing the node that "captures" the token to transmit data.

Token Ring network A network protocol that uses token passing to send data over the shared network cable. A computer that wants to send a message must capture the token before sending.

Toolbar A portion of the screen containing a series of buttons that can be clicked to activate program functions.

Top-level domain Regarding the Internet, in a Uniform Resource Locator (URL), the last part of the domain name, representing the type of entity, such as organization or education, or country.

Topology The physical layout of a local area network.

Total Cost of Ownership (TCO) A methodology originally developed by the Gartner Group to determine all the costs involved in owning personal computers.

Touch screen A computer screen that accepts input data by letting the user point at the screen to select a choice.

Touchpad An input device that uses finger movement on its surface to control the pointer.

Track On a magnetic disk, one of many data-holding concentric circles.

Trackball A ball used as an input device; it can be hand-manipulated to cause a corresponding movement of the cursor on the screen. Trackballs are often built in on portable computers.

Trademark A word, name, symbol or device used to distinguish one company and its products from another.

Training A step in the implementation phase of the SDLC in which users are instructed in how to use the new system.

Transaction A business event that requires a business's records to be updated.

Transaction file A file that contains all changes to be made to the master file: additions, deletions, and revisions.

Transaction processing The technique of processing transactions one at a time, in the order in which they occur.

Transistor A small device that transfers electrical signals across a resistor.

Translator Software, typically a compiler, that converts a program into the machine language the computer can understand.

Transmission Control Protocol/ Internet Protocol (TCP/IP) A standardized protocol permitting different computers to communicate via the Internet.

Transparent Computer activities of which a user is unaware even as they are taking place.

Transponder A device in a communications satellite that receives a transmission from earth, amplifies the signal, changes the frequency, and retransmits the data to a receiving earth station. The transponder makes sure that the stronger outgoing signals do not interfere with the weaker incoming signals.

Trapdoor A feature that allows system developers to bypass normal security procedures when working on the system. If not removed when the system is put into production, it can allow hackers to break into the system.

Trojan horse An application that covertly places destructive instructions in the middle of a legitimate program but appears to do something useful.

Tunneling A way to transfer data between two similar networks over an intermediate network by enclosing one type of data packet protocol into the packet of another. Also called *encapsulation.*

Twisted pairs Wires twisted together in an insulated cable. Twisted pairs are frequently used to transmit data over short distances. Also called *wire pairs.*

Type size The size, in points, of a typeface.

U

U.S. Copyright Act The law that provides for copyright protection of literary and artistic works.

Unbundle To sell software separately from the hardware on which it will run.

Undo command Reverses the effect of the previous action.

Unicode A coding scheme that uses two bytes (16 bits) to represent a character and can represent 65,536 different characters.

Uniform Resource Locator (URL) The unique address of a Web page or other file on the Internet.

Uninterruptible power supply (UPS) A device that includes both surge protection and battery backup, which allow you to continue operating your PC during power loss or brownouts.

Unit testing The process in the development phase of the SDLC in which individual programs are tested using test data to ensure that they meet the design specifications.

UNIVAC I (Universal Automatic Computer I) The first computer built for business purposes.

Universal Product Code (UPC) A code number unique to a product. The UPC code is the bar code on the product's label.

Universal serial bus (USB) An external bus architecture that connects peripherals,

such as keyboards, mice, and digital cameras.

Universal Service Fund Administered by the FCC, helps service providers with the higher costs of providing communication services to rural areas.

Unix A multiuser, time-sharing operating system that runs on all types of computers.

Unstructured interview In systems analysis, an interview in which questions are planned in advance, but the questionnaire can deviate from the plan.

UPC See *universal product code.*

Update To keep files current by changing data as appropriate.

Update privilege Allows the user to change existing data in a database. Specified in the user profile maintained by the DBMS.

Updating in place The ability to read, change, and return a record to its same place on the disk.

Uplink The transmission of a signal from an earth station to a communications satellite. See *downlink.*

Upload In a networking environment, to send a file from one computer to another, usually to a larger computer or a host computer. Contrast with *download.*

URL See *Uniform Resource Locator.*

Usenet An informal network of computers that allows the posting and reading of messages in newsgroups that focus on specific topics. Also called *newsgroups.*

User-friendly A term to refer to software that is easy for a novice to use.

User interface The method by which the user communicates with the operating system.

User involvement The involvement of users in the systems development life cycle.

Users Usually employees and customers that use a computer system. User-friendly.

Utility programs (utilities) Programs that perform many common system tasks for users.

V

Vaccine A computer program that stops the spread of a virus. Also called an *antivirus.*

Vacuum tube An electronic tube used as a basic component in the first generation of computers.

Value In a spreadsheet, a number or formula entered into a cell.

Variable (1) On a chart, the items that the data points describe. (2) In a program, a name assigned to a memory location, whose contents can vary.

VBScript See *JavaScript.*

Vector An arrow—a line with directional notation—used in a data flow diagram.

Vertical centering Adjusts the top and bottom margins so that the text is centered vertically on the printed page.

Vertical market A market consisting of a group of similar customers, such as dentists, who are likely to need similar software.

Very high-level language A fourth-programming generation language.

Video capture card A card that accepts an analog signal from a video source such as a TV or video camera and converts it into a digital signal for processing by a computer.

Video graphics Computer-produced animated pictures.

Video memory A high-speed form of RAM installed on the graphics card.

Video Privacy Protection Act Legislation that prohibits video vendors from revealing what videos their customers rent.

Videoconferencing Computer teleconferencing combined with cameras and wall-size screens.

Viewable image size (vis) The diagonal measurement of the portion of the screen that is usable for display. On CRT monitors, this is usually about one inch less that the rated size.

Virtual memory See *virtual storage.*

Virtual private network (VPN) Technology that uses the public Internet backbone as a channel for private data communication. See *tunneling.*

Virtual reality (VR) A system in which a user is immersed in a computer-created environment, so that the user physically interacts with the computer-produced three-dimensional scene.

Virtual storage A technique of memory management in which part of the application program is stored on disk and is brought into memory only as needed. The secondary storage holding the rest of the program is considered virtual storage.

Virus A set of illicit instructions that passes itself on to other programs with which it comes into contact.

Virus signatures Unique strings of bits that identify each virus. Users must frequently download the latest virus signature files from the publisher's Web site to maintain the proper level of protection.

Vision robot A robot that can recognize an object by its shape or color.

Visual Basic A programming language developed by Microsoft that allows the programmer to easily create programs with complex user interfaces containing standard Windows features such as buttons, dialog boxes, scroll bars, and menus.

Voice input Using the spoken word as a means of entering data into a computer.

Voice output device See *voice synthesizer.*

Voice synthesizer A device that converts data in main storage to vocalized sounds understandable to humans. Also called an *audio-response unit* and *voice output device.*

Volatile Subject to loss when electricity is interrupted or turned off. Data in semiconductor storage is volatile.

Volume testing The process in the development phase of the SDLC in which the programs in a system are tested with large volumes of real data to ensure that they function properly under heavy loads.

VPN See *Virtual private network.*

VR See *Virtual reality.*

W

WAN See *wide area network.*

Wand reader An input device that scans the special letters and numbers on price tags in retail stores and sends that input data to the computer. Often connected to a point-of-sale terminal in a retail store.

Web See *World Wide Web.*

Web cams Inexpensive video cameras that capture images that are then transmitted on the Internet.

Web site An individual location on the World Wide Web.

Web TV See *Network computer.*

Weight In word processing or desktop publishing, the variation in the visual heaviness of a typeface; for example, words look much heavier when in boldface type.

"What-if" analysis The process of changing one or more spreadsheet values and observing the resulting calculated effect.

White-hat hackers Also known as tiger teams or sometimes "intrusion testers" or "hackers for hire," highly trained technical people who are paid to try to break into a computer system in order to expose its vulnerabilities.

Wide area network (WAN) A network of geographically distant computers and terminals. Contrast with *local area network.*

Windows 2000 The last generation in the NT series.

Windows 95 An operating system developed for IBM-compatible PCs developed by Microsoft. Windows 95 is a true operating system that introduced numerous improvements over its predecessors.

Windows 98 A 32-bit operating system developed for IBM-compatible PCs by Microsoft as the successor to Windows 95.

Windows CE An operating system for palmtop and personal digital assistant computers developed by Microsoft.

Windows Me The last in the Win9x series of operating systems.

Windows NT A 32-bit operating system developed by Microsoft for use in corporate client/server networks.

Windows XP The latest generation of Windows that incorporates and extends the consumer-oriented features of Windows Me into the stable, dependable Windows 2000 environment.

Wire pairs Wires twisted together in an insulated cable. Wire pairs are frequently used to transmit data over short distances. Also called *twisted pairs.*

Wireless Transmitting data over networks using infrared or radio wave transmissions instead of cables.

Wireless access point Also called a *base station,* it connects to a wired network and provides wireless transmit/receive capabilities over a radius of several hundred feet.

Wireless Application Protocol (WAP) A protocol used by wireless access providers

to format Web pages for viewing on mobile handheld devices.

Wireless mouse A mouse that uses an infrared beam or radio waves rather than a cord to send signals to the computer.

Wireless transmission Techniques that are used to transmit data over short distances via infrared or radio waves.

Word The number of bits that the CPU processes as a unit.

Word processing Computer-based creating, editing, formatting, storing, retrieving, and printing of a text document.

Word wrap A word processing feature that automatically starts a word at the left margin of the next line if there is not enough room for it on the current line.

Worksheet Another name for an electronic spreadsheet, a computerized version of a manual spreadsheet.

Workstation (1) A computer that combines the compactness of a desktop computer with power that almost equals that of a mainframe. (2) A client computer on a LAN.

World Wide Web (the Web) An Internet subset of sites with text, images, and sounds; most Web sites provide links to related topics.

WORM See *write-once, read-many media.*

Worm A program that spreads and replicates over a network.

Write-once, read-many media (WORM) Media that can be written on only once; then they become read-only media.

Written documents One of the data sources used in the data gathering portion of the analysis phase of the SDLC, these can be forms, reports, or procedure manuals.

WYSIWYG An acronym meaning what you see is what you get; in word processing, the document appears on the screen just the way it will look when printed.

X

XGA (extended graphics array) A high-resolution graphics standard that provides high resolutions, supports more simultaneous colors than SVGA, and can be non-interlaced. Contrast with *SVGA.*

Z

Zapping The use of illicit software to gain entry to computer systems by bypassing security provisions.

Zip drive A device manufactured by Iomega Corp. that uses special high-capacity removable disks that are Incompatible with standard 3.5-inch diskettes.

Zone recording Involves dividing a disk into zones to take advantage of the storage available on all tracks, by assigning more sectors to tracks in outer zones than to those in inner zones.

of ChemNet.com, Hangzhou China ; 08.11:Reprinted with permission from www.eBay.com Courtesy of eBay, Inc., San Jose, CA.; 08.12:Reprinted with permission from www.Yahoo.com Courtesy of Yahoo, Sunnyvale, CA.; 08.13a:Reprinted with permission from www.expedia.com Courtesy of Expedia, Inc, Bellevue, WA.; ADL-08:Eyewire Collection Getty Images/ EyeWire, Inc.

Chapter Nine
09-06:SW Productions/Getty Images; 09-02: ©2003 Kensington Technology Group

Chapter Ten
10-02:ActivCard, Inc. 2003 All rights reserved; 10-03:Courtesy of Technology Recognition Systems; 10-05a:Photo of SurgeArrest courtesy of American Power Conversion; 10-05b: Photo of Back-UPS Pro 650 courtesy of American Power Conversion; 10-10b:Courtesy of Net Nanny Software International, Inc.

Chapter Eleven
11-01:Courtesy of Microsoft Corporation. All rights reserved; 11-02:Courtesy of Micrososft Corporation. All rights reserved; MRC11-01:©Herbert Simms; 11-04:Courtesy of Microsoft Corporation. All rights reserved; 11-07:Courtesy of Microsoft Corporation. All rights reserved; 11-08a:Used with permission of Western Governors University; 11-08b:Used with permission of Western Governors University; 11-09a:Courtesy of Microsoft Corporation. All rights reserved; 11-09b:Courtesy of Microsoft Corporation. All rights reserved; 11-10a:Courtesy of Microsoft Corporation. All rights reserved; 11-10b:Courtesy of Microsoft Corporation. All rights reserved; 11-11:Courtesy of Microsoft Corporation. All rights reserved; 11-12:Courtesy of Microsoft Corporation. All rights reserved; 11-13a:Courtesy of Microsoft Corporation. All rights reserved; 11-13b:Courtesy of Microsoft Corporation. All rights reserved; PI111-01:Used with permission; PI11-02:Used with permission; PI11-03:Courtesy of Imagine Media, Inc. ©2001 Imagine Media, Inc.

Chapter Twelve
12-01:Courtesy of Microsoft Corporation. All rights reserved; 12-02:Courtesy of Microsoft Corporation. All rights reserved; MRC12-01:Reprinted with permission from www.internet.com. ©2001 internet.com Corp. All rights reserved. Internet.com is the exclusive Trademark of internet.com

Corporation; 12-03:Courtesy of Microsoft Corporation. All rights reserved; 12-04: Courtesy of Microsoft Corporation. All rights reserved; 12-05:Courtesy of Microsoft Corporation. All rights reserved; 12-06: Courtesy of Microsoft Corporation. All rights reserved; PI12-02:This article first appeared in Salon.com, at http://www.Salon.com. An online version remains in the Salon archives. Reprinted with permission; CG12-01:Courtesy of Corel. Art by Dave Martland; CG12-06: Courtesy of Corel. Art by Bill Frymire; CG12-07:Courtesy of Corel. Art by Antonio De Leo; CG12-08:Courtesy of Corel. Art by Karin Kuhlmann.

Chapter Thirteen
13-05b:Courtesy of Microsoft Corporation. All rights reserved; 13-05c:Courtesy of Microsoft Corporation. All rights reserved; 13-09:Courtesy of Microsoft Corporation. All rights reserved; 13-12a:Courtesy of Microsoft Corporation. All rights reserved; 13-12b:Courtesy of Microsoft Corporation. All rights reserved; PI13-02:Courtesy of WorldTariff, A FedEx Trade Networks Company.

Chapter Fourteen
PI14-01:©2001 by BrassRing, Inc. Reprinted by permission only. All rights reserved; PI14-02:Courtesy of monster.com; PI14-03: Used with permission of Dice.com, High-Tech Jobs Online.

Chapter Fifteen
PI15-02:Used with permission.

Chapter Sixteen
16-06:Courtesy of SmartPlanet.com.

Appendix
A-07a:Dennis Budd Gray Stock Boston; A-09:James King-Holmes/W Industries/ Science Photo Library Photo Researchers, Inc.; SBA-03:SuperStock, Inc.; EAA:AP/Wide World Photos; EAB:Silver Burdett Ginn; EAC:B. Daemmrich Corbis/Sygma

Buyers Guide
BG-03:Apple Computer, Inc.; BG-06:Logitech Inc.; BG-08 Michael Newman PhotoEdit; BG-04:View Sonic Corporation; BG-05:View Sonic Corporation; BG-07a:Logitech Inc.; BG-07B:Logitech Inc.; BG-10:Hewlett-Packard Co.; BG-11:Brother International Corporation; BG-12.02:Apple Computer, Inc.; BG-13:Epson America, Inc.; BG-14:American Power Conversion Corporation

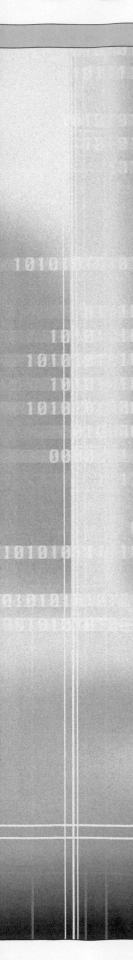

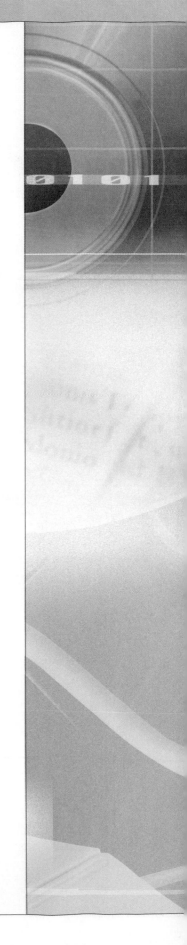

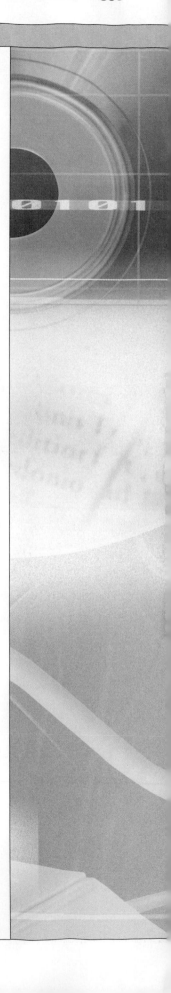

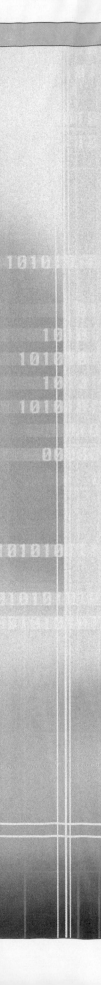